Settlers of the American West

ALSO BY MARY ELLEN SNODGRASS AND FROM MCFARLAND

Isabel Allende: A Literary Companion (2013)

Leslie Marmon Silko: A Literary Companion (2011)

Peter Carey: A Literary Companion (2010)

Jamaica Kincaid: A Literary Companion (2008)

Kaye Gibbons: A Literary Companion (2007)

Walter Dean Myers: A Literary Companion (2006)

World Shores and Beaches: A Descriptive and Historical Guide to 50 Coastal Treasures (2005)

Amy Tan: A Literary Companion (2004)

August Wilson: A Literary Companion (2004)

Barbara Kingsolver: A Literary Companion (2004)

Coins and Currency: An Historical Encyclopedia (2003; paperback 2007)

World Epidemics: A Cultural Chronology of Disease from Prehistory to the Era of SARS (2003; paperback 2011)

Encyclopedia of World Scriptures (2001; paperback 2011)

Who's Who in the Middle Ages (2001; paperback 2013)

Settlers of the American West

The Lives of 231 Notable Pioneers

Mary Ellen Snodgrass

McFarland & Company, Inc., Publishers
Jefferson, North Carolina

LIBRARY OF CONGRESS CATALOGUING-IN-PUBLICATION DATA

Snodgrass, Mary Ellen.
Settlers of the American west : the lives of 231 notable pioneers / Mary Ellen Snodgrass.
    p.   cm.
Includes bibliographical references and index.

ISBN 978-0-7864-9735-5 (softcover : acid free paper) ∞
ISBN 978-1-4766-1904-0 (ebook)

1. Pioneers—West (U.S.)—Biography.   2. Frontier and pioneer life—West (U.S.)
3. West (U.S.)—Biography.   4. West (U.S.)—Discovery and exploration.
5. West (U.S.)—History.   I. Title.

F590.5.S66 2015   978—dc23   2015003002

BRITISH LIBRARY CATALOGUING DATA ARE AVAILABLE

© 2015 Mary Ellen Snodgrass. All rights reserved

*No part of this book may be reproduced or transmitted in any form
or by any means, electronic or mechanical, including photocopying
or recording, or by any information storage and retrieval system,
without permission in writing from the publisher.*

On the cover: Swift's Station, Carson and Lake Bigler Road—
eastern summit of Sierra Nevada Mountains (Library of Congress)

Printed in the United States of America

*McFarland & Company, Inc., Publishers
Box 611, Jefferson, North Carolina 28640
www.mcfarlandpub.com*

For Mark Lyerly,
a faithful friend

Acknowledgments

Thanks to these individuals:
Karen Adams, reference, Hastings Public Library, Hastings, Nebraska
Susan Antipa, reference, Carson City Library, Carson City, Nevada
Bruce Beacock, archivist, Simcoe County Archives, Minesing, Ontario
Cheryl Cosart, branch manager, San Diego County Library, Santee, California
Elizabeth Hayden, reference, North Carolina State Library, Raleigh, North Carolina
Michelle Hudson and Richard Younce, reference, Eudora Welty Library, Jackson, Mississippi
Rowena Mangohaig, reference, Snoqualmie County Library, Washington
Clark McAbee, curator; Karen Meng, administrator, Orcas Island Historical Museum, Orcas Island, Washington
Cheryl Ogasawara, state reference librarian, Hawaii Public Library System, Honolulu, Hawaii
Martin Otts, reference, Patrick Beaver Library, Hickory, North Carolina
Sheri Perkins, reference, Tulsa Library, Tulsa, Oklahoma
Randal Pope, genealogist, Klamath Falls, Oregon
Dot Smith, city historian, Lisbon, Maine
Rodney Soares, reference, Tulare County Library, Visalia, California
Louise Svehla, e-reference, Hawaii Public Library System, Honolulu, Hawaii
Carol Whitten, reference, Kennebunk Free Library, Kennebunk, Maine
Earl Williams, Lisbon Historical Society, Lisbon, Maine

Also, thanks to the these institutions:
Laurance S. Rockefeller Library, California Institute of Integral Studies, San Francisco, California
North Carolina State Library, Raleigh, North Carolina
Oklahoma State University Library, Stillwater, Oklahoma
White Library at Emporia State University, Emporia, Kansas.

Contents

Acknowledgments vi
Preface 1
Introduction 5

The Westerners 7

Chronology of Pioneer Achievements 169

APPENDICES
A. Ethnicity 172
B. Departure 181
C. Destination 191
D. Religion 201
E. Occupation 207

Bibliography 225
Index 229

"We each have our turn at this earth."
—*The Good Earth,* Pearl Buck

Preface

Settlers of the American West investigates a broad swath of frontier America. The 89 entries cover 231 lives of multiple races, languages, and ethnicities. The text clusters families, clans, and associates integral to crossings of the Great Plains and the initiation of Western commerce and religious evangelism. Featured essays reiterate startling moments in social history, notably, the Donner party's vying for scraps of dog meat in the snow-blocked Sierra, Mormon prophet Joseph Smith's sharing of Henry Bailey Jacobs's wife, feminist Eliza Wood Farnham's recruitment of female pioneers, and Scout Jim Baker's concurrence with General John Milton Chivington on the need for genocide to rid the plains of Indians. Commentary supplies details of growing communities and the shaping of landmasses into roads, canals, territories, and states.

Text elucidates the aptitudes that newcomers brought to the frontier—sodding barns, breeding hybrid cattle and horses, growing hops for breweries, mining quartz, building corduroy roads, and stitching scraps into bed and couch covers. Essential to Western Americana, folk singers composed songs about cattle drives to Fort Laramie, Mormon hymns honoring hand-carters, and ballads mocking the saloon and brothel traffic in trail towns of Deadwood, Laredo, and Dodge City. Amateur authors wrote poems and editorials on the labor problems of Nebraska farmers, testified to the mayhem of coolie lynchings and Oklahoma land runs, and chronicled the dynamiting of right-of-way for the transcontinental railroad and the fortifying of haciendas against Sioux, Comanche, and Apache raids.

The pre-literacy and assimilation of non–English-speaking immigrants transformed data with respellings (McBeath/McBeth; Smeathers/Smithers; Richens/Richins) and new place names (Yerba Buena/San Francisco, California; New Amsterdam/Holland, Wisconsin; Westport/St. Louis, Missouri; Burlington/Longmont, Colorado). Essential to the history of frontier settlement, diaries and letters, such as the daybook of George Belshaw, Jr., filled in prices for soap and hay as well as the fate of wagoneers delayed by broken axles, changes of command, and quicksand. Analyses account for the formation of militias and major shifts in land ownership, particularly the loss of Alta California by Hispanics to Anglos and peace treaties with the Nez Percé that offered government-issue food and supplies in exchange for territory.

A chronology of major events sequences the post–Columbian advance of Francisco de Coronado into Texas along with the contributions of *coureurs de bois*, mountain men, freighters, and missionaries to multi-ethnic communities along the Great Lakes and in Wyoming and the Hawaiian Islands. Entries label benchmarks of Western Americana, especially the layout of Salt Lake City, shortcuts along the Oregon Trail, cholera epidemics, Comstock Lode, National Farmers' Alliance, Scandinavian colonies, Presbyterian Chinese Mission Home, and the golden spike joining the Central Pacific and Union Pacific rail lines into the transcontinental railroad.

Informative appendices align pioneer names by ethnicity, origin, and destination, pinpointing Norwegian Johanna Lahti colonizing Minnesota, South African storekeeper Eliza Mitchell setting up shop in Nebraska, Canadian carpenter James Thomson Kellie building Iowa homes, Chinese interpreter An Yane Chin

Preface

conferring with San Francisco police, and Swiss housewife Luisa Bonnema from Altnau raising a family in Wisconsin. Where established by history, identification of religious creeds details the moral forces undergirding establishment of such cities as Zeandale, Kansas; Nauvoo, Illinois; Box Elder Creek, Wyoming; Theresa, Wisconsin; and Tuscarora, Nevada. Additional facts in the fifth appendix outline occupations. The data enhance the purpose of the compendium by revealing the variety of aim and aptitude for settling the frontier, from orchardist, knife maker, and welder to federal court judge, chaplain, and bounty hunter.

Indexing opens additional avenues of research. Primary entries stipulate places (Death Valley, Willamette Valley, ghost towns), people (Quanah Parker, Kit Carson, Sitting Bull), groups (Lost Forty-Niners, Society of California Pioneers, Jayhawkers' Party), historical themes (Indian relocation, slavery, open range), transportation (Alaska Central Railway, Yellowstone Trail, Butterfield Overland Stage), communication (*Folsom Telegraph*, storytelling, *A Winter with the Mormons*), events (Old Crossing Treaty, Yom Kippur, Second Seminole War), education (homeschooling, Francophone community, singing schools), inventions (photography, concrete pipe, Colt five-shooter), and movements (Farmers Alliance, Underground Railroad, temperance) that influenced the period. Secondary elements expound on aspects of main topics, as with Civil War and the Grand Review of the Armies, mining and placer gold, and homesteading and the Homestead Act.

Introduction

Unfortunately for accurate reportage, Western history as depicted in literature, music, art, and film perpetuates stereotypes of the pioneer. Rereadings of period journals, legends, and media accounts refute the dominance of the gold-crazed '49er panning California streams for placer nuggets and the simple Eastern sodbuster and his wife and children traversing the Oregon Trail in a Conestoga wagon to build a log cabin on the fearsome plains and wrestle crops from virgin soil. While ennobling the woodsman's axe, the farmwife's churn, and the constable's badge, chronicles have shortchanged the whaler's harpoon and assayer's scales, minimized the labors of the innkeeper and inventor, and passed over the butcher's cleaver and the cane cutter's machete. The tunnel vision of American history continues to cheat the specialist—the interpreter, recruiter, sawyer, midwife, photographer, printer, and storyteller—of renown for professions requisite to a thriving, multi-faceted society.

In truth, from 1540 into the 1900s, a span of humankind civilized the frontier from the Mississippi River Valley as far west as Alaska and Hawaii. Worthy deeds ranged from stage ballerina Josephine Omohundro's stage productions for Colorado miners and Chuck Goodnight's herding in New Mexico to Arthur Wysinger's desegregation of a California high school, Zina Huntington Young's suffragism in Salt Lake City, and Texas priest Leopold Moczygemba's Polish-American parish building at Panna Maria. Frontier adventurers commingled languages, lifestyles, ethnicities, and actions as diverse as Kachina dancing at Isleta Pueblo, Alexander Toponce delivering mail in Chesterfield, Idaho, James Mitchell's real estate sales in Florence, Nebraska, and Friesian Dutch woodcutters operating lumber mills at Prairie La Crosse, Wisconsin. It is important to note that, in the legends of macho feats, too many ignore the boldness of Franciscan nuns upgrading a Molokai leper colony, Sue McBeth training Idaho Indians for the ministry, Phoebe Judson fostering orphans at Puget Sound, and Margaret Culbertson and Donaldina Cameron retrieving girls from sexual bondage in San Francisco's Chinatown. A thorough chronicle owes future generations the inclusion of both male and female pioneers committed to civilizing the frontier.

Essential to comprehension of the westering spirit, human idiosyncrasies account for the motivations of trailblazers. Varied aims tempted Asian, European, Pacific, Caribbean, and American pathfinders from urban life to the stimulus of populating an untrammeled land; for example, Haitian farmer Jean Baptiste du Sable's commercial startup in present day Chicago and Maurice Franklin's departure from Jamaica to build a synagogue in coastal California. Into explosive confrontations with Amerindians, miners and land speculators followed an itch ranging in degree from ambition to greed. Their advance toward rich lodes increased demand for a gamut of community builders—explorers and surveyors, scouts and guides, stockbreeders and merchants, grocers and financiers, surgeons and midwives, and politicians and entertainers, including cowboy songwriter Frank Maynard, band performer Henry Bailey Jacobs, and tale spinner Seth Kinman.

Despite planning and provisioning for long treks, westerers incurred the unforeseen, from physical and mental breakdowns, ambush, and cholera to floods, plagues of grasshoppers, drought, and overturned stagecoaches, the fate of North Dakota driver Hank Monk. The ambiguity of sovereignty and jurisprudence demanded pragmatism and consensus among honest settlers, especially in the Pacific Northwest territory claimed by both Americans and Britons. During the chaos of Oklahoma's one-day land run and the emergence of boom towns in Colorado, Nevada, Kansas, and Dakota Territory, squabblers and frauds cheated honest prospectors, drovers, and farm buyers, increasing the demand for marshals, vigilantes, rangers, posses, bounty hunters, and sheriffs. For mariners in port at San Francisco, no constabulary shielded tavern tipplers from illicit impressment onto ships' crews. No coast guard halted the Asian abductor from forcing Chinese girls into enslavement in Oregon mining camps or California casinos. Youth brought up amid plains endangerment, such as the Kansas-born household of Henry C. and Rosie Haag, learned to shoot and ride horseback while keeping watch for bears and Indian raids, a constant threat to the children of Ethan Allen Stroud in Calvert, Texas, and Eliza and Ezra Meeker in Puyallup, Washington.

Despite caution, some westerers died in the struggle, notably, missionaries Marcus and Narcissa Whitman, riders with the Texas Rangers, and wayfarers of the Donner party frozen in blizzards. Less well known, William Brown Ide's death from smallpox in the Sierras, Texas Jack Omohundro's demise from pneumonia in Colorado, tuberculosis among stoop laborers in Sacramento, and Hudson's Bay agent Charles Leon Arcouet's drowning at the Dalles dramatized the common perils of traversing the Oregon Trail and homesteading on isolated tracts without access to physicians and safe transport. Others encountered infidelity in their mates that destroyed marriages and left children undefended, the destiny of cook and foster mother Sarah Bowman in Galveston, Texas, Colorado mine assayer Wesley Neal, Denver philanthropist Augusta Tabor, and battered Lummi wife Lizzie Patterson in Portland, Oregon.

A select few adventurers turned natural resources into riches, the bases of family fortunes, dynasties, and international prominence enjoyed by Minneapolis forefather Pierre Bottineau, herder Jesse Chisholm on the Oklahoma plains, California raisin grower George Cowles, Arizona and New Mexico bear hunter Ben Lilly, and Union Oil progenitor Alphonzo E. Bell. Women, too, found opportunity in the West unequaled by the advantages of living in Baltimore, Philadelphia, and New York City. For Irish immigrant Jean Heazle, the freedom of a wrangler's boots and chaps enabled her to breed livestock in DeLamar, Idaho, an outdoor career typically closed to females. A similar freedom awaited quilter Grace McCance Snyder in Cozad, Nebraska; Nellie Trosper, a former depot waitress turned musher and innkeeper in Seward, Alaska; Elizabeth Parke Stratton, founder of a school in Fort Collins, Colorado; and horse dealer Kitty Wilkins, who preserved the brio of wild mustangs in Bruneau, Idaho.

For idealists, the West held out utopian visions of orderly settlements grounded in education, religion, and altruism, the aim of Baptist missionary John Calvin McCoy in Kansas City, Sioux Falls colonist James Magnus Wahl in Dakota Territory, investor Charles Lahti in St. Peter, Minnesota, and home economics teacher Kate McBeth, an educator of Nez Percé women at the Lapwai reservation in Idaho. In the path of horse soldiers and wagon train provisioners came dreamers Joseph Smith, Jr., the Mormon prophet, and Danish colonizer Peter Lassen, who mapped out the potential mega-state of Deseret and a county of the newly formed California Republic. Social workers and nurses Eliza Roxcy Snow, Clara Brown, Marianne Cope, and Olive Mann Isbell obeyed inner drives to do good among their own kind as well as to Indians, Mexicans, Polynesians, rural Mormons, and freedmen. Newcomers like Isaac C. Isbell and George Washington Bush expressed thanks to native American hunters for guidance to wild foods, sources of pure water, and healing plants on unfamiliar terrain. The compulsion to elevate native life to the plane of Euro-centric Easterners generated mixed results in tribes unwilling to emulate the arrogance of proselytizer

Hiram Bingham, missionary to Honolulu, or the venality of Uncle Dick Wootton, purveyor of home brew in Taos, New Mexico.

Following the Civil War and President Abraham Lincoln's emancipation of slaves, discoveries, setbacks, and progress triggered a subsequent critical mass of races—the final face-off between the technologically advanced newcomers and aboriginal Cheyenne, Lipan Apache, Sioux, Paiute, Shoshone, and Comanche. While the U.S. Congress pondered genocide as a deterrent to Indian wars, the U.S. Cavalry dragooned Amerindians onto reservations. Do-gooders herded native children into assimilation academies, particularly the grimly ethnocentric Indian school in Carlisle, Pennsylvania. Both alternatives to racial annihilation failed while prolonging the deracination and misery of America's first nations.

Ironically, during protracted social conflict, urbanization in the West spawned nostalgia. As the pure communistic Indian life of the Great Plains collapsed in the advance of stage and rail lines, telegraph wires, borax and quartz mining, dams, and irrigation systems, vagabonds and soldiers of fortune the world over wrestled with yearning for adventures in territory still raw and unpredictable, the motivation of Pierson Reading's exploits in northern California, William Lewis Sublette's trapping in Wyoming, Billie Lawing's boat excursions in Seward, Alaska, and Elias Pennington's desert trek to Tucson, Arizona. The states that took shape in the hands of immigrants and nesters bore into the present unparalleled chronologies—histories pocked with coercion, secessionism, and chicanery as well as epic hero tales, ribaldry, journalism, and informative writings, including dime novels about the Dalton Gang and gunman John Wesley Hardin, dispatches in the Fisk brothers' *Helena* (Montana) *Herald,* and Sarah Pratt Carr's historical retrospect *The Iron Way: A Tale of the Builders of the West* (1907).

For this compendium, a case-by-case survey of settler motivation and achievement reveals the conundrum of national identity, a sturdy mix of elements as diverse as East Indian, Bavarian, Chinese, French-Canadian, Potowatomi, New Zealand, Mexican, and Hispanic. Genealogies pinpoint strains of rebellion and enterprise in the scions of French Huguenots, Polish Jews, liberal Japanese Buddhists, and the Scots-Irish combatants in the American Revolution and Civil War. Pride in early lawmen and risk takers—Gonzales Ranger Mathew Caldwell, California wagon maker John Goller, labor leader Yemyo Imamura on Hawaiian plantations, and midwife and herbalist Juana Briones among dwellers of San Francisco's Presidio—balances the shameful acts of Western lore, from the persecution of Chinese railroad workers to the derogation of indigenous tribes as savages. A pragmatic view of human drive and depravity accepts the blend of good and evil in nation builders, the ones who slaughtered bison herds, printed native American dictionaries, invented quake-proof adobe housing, bilked amateur poker players in saloons, and bolstered Utah Mormons, native Hawaiians, and Minnesota's Catholic educators. Such is the story of the American West, a cherished quilt pieced together from opportunism and tenacity.

The Westerners

Arcouet, Amable (1797–1880), Jason Lee (1803–1845)

A multilingual mason, wheat factor, and fur trapper and *voyageur* (trader), Amable Arcouet took risks to make his living from the far north of the Western Hemisphere to Oregon and California. A native of St. Laurent in Montreal, Quebec, he was born on September 1, 1797, the seventh of the nine sons and five daughters of Marie Louis Gaudry and Michel Arcouette of Trois-Rivières, Canada. Amable Arcouet bore the name of his grandfather, Amable Gaudry, and traced his French lineage to Jean Pinard, a sixteenth-century merchant in Cognac, Dominique Gareau, a master tunneler from Saintonge, and Pierre St.-Denis, who emigrated from Dieppe to Ontario in the 1650s.

A devout Catholic, Arcouet never learned to read and write, but observed religious ritual. At age 26, he worked for the Hudson's Bay Company as a purchasing agent of beaver and otter fur. He succeeded as a go-between with North Canadian Indians at a time when agents faced hostility from the Dogrib and Yellowknife. During the decline in muskrat population to the east, on June 1, 1825, he moved northwest to Manitoba and to work as a mason on the

After Amable Arcouet left the Hudson's Bay Company housing on September 1, 1833, he relocated to a multicultural settlement in the Columbia District of the Pacific Northwest.

Bay at the York trading headquarters, which maintained annual commerce with Fort Vancouver.

Arcouet aided Sir George Simpson, the Hudson's Bay Company governor, in erecting Fort Langley, an outpost erected in 1827 on the undesignated American-British boundary. The fort occupied the south side of the Fraser River east of the Fort Vancouver harbor complex, which superintended coastal traffic to Alaska, Hawaii, China, and Mexico. Securing the British presence in the Northwest, Fort Langley managed trade in salted salmon and in cedar barrels, lumber, and shingles exported to the Hawaiian Islands.

The U.S.–Canadian Border

Arcouet left the Hudson's Bay Company on September 1, 1833. He relocated to the Columbia District, a polyglot region inhabited by Iroquois/Mohawk, Nisqually, Cree, Okanaga, Nez Percé, Tillamook, Makah, Kootenay, Ketse, Nass, Cayuse, Carrier, Umpqua, Otoe, Haida, Sioux, Chinook, Ute, Bannock, Kwantlen, Miami, Chilcotin, Cowichan, Lemhi, Shoshone, Flathead, Tsimshian, and Pend d'Oreille. The arrival of Russians, Scots, British, French, French Canadian and American trappers, and some Creoles, Japanese, and Hawaiians contributed to a multicultural environment. Ironically, white newcomers exterminated Digger Indians, a peaceful nation.

Although the Pacific Northwest remained largely unmapped and unscouted, opportunities in farming, coal mining, shipping, lumbering, and whaling drew a stream of immigrants, seamen, and adventurers along with interpreters and Methodist Episcopal missionaries. For the next two years, Arcouet freelanced a masonry project—a 20' × 20' powder magazine—on the southwest wall of Fort Vancouver. For fire safety, he walled the structure two feet thick with standard British brick and rough-hewn native stone.

The powder shed attested to Arcouet's meticulous planning. Mortared with Hawaiian coral lime and buttressed at the corners with round Douglas fir posts, the building protected 27 kegs of canister powder holding 66.6 pounds each and some 72 barrels of cannon powder containing 7,200 pounds of explosives. To the exterior, he attached 20-gauge metal sheathing with handmade spikes and fitted brass-hinged copper doors under a double peaked roof made from stone and fir shingles. The project, completed in 1835, earned him £8 and remained in use for decades.

Home and Family

In 1835, Arcouet homesteaded among Oregon's Indians and the log homes, apple orchards, and wheat farms begun by French Canadians and métis at French Prairie in the Willamette River Valley. He chose acreage in the St. Paul district southwest of Portland, a frontier territory still jointly occupied by Americans and English. Twice he collaborated with 19 local French Canadians and chairman Jason Lee of Quebec, the region's first Protestant missionary, in petitioning Bishop Joseph Norbert Provencher of Red River, Manitoba, for a priest. Known as the Champoeg meetings, the first government of Pacific Northwest colonies, the move toward an organized judicial system and parish attempted to distance devout Catholics from the rampant alcoholism, violence, and bigamy among white men who abandoned their Eastern households and established families with Indian and métis women.

In spring 1836, Arcouet assisted other men in building a log church at St. Paul. The town, served by the Hudson's Bay Company sidewheeling steamer *Beaver,* became a business nexus, a Northwestern wheat phenomenon, and the valley's center of Catholicism. While still trading with the Hudson's Bay Company, Arcouet chafed at the monopoly's policy to lease cattle, but not sell them to métis families. To end dependence on the British firm, on January 22, 1837, he and ten other ranchers joined the Willamette Cattle Company in sailing aboard the surveying brig *Loriot* to California. On July 27, he helped drive 40 horses and 750 cattle north from Monterrey to stock Oregon's ranches.

By 1838, the Willamette Valley population numbered 23 Canadian males and 18 Americans. On January 28, 1838, at a Methodist mission where evangelist Jason Lee converted Flathead Indians in Vancouver, Washington, Arcouet married Kilkotah Chamowash Clacalam, a Waponte Chinook wife from the Cowlitz River area and mother of their seven-year-old son Amable. The couple wed a second time in a Catholic ritual at St. Paul's Stellamaris Mission.

In January 1839, the community received the services of two Eastern Canadian Jesuit priests, François Norbert Blanchet and Modeste Demers. Among 35 métis converts, Blanchet legitimized the Arcouet's three children and gave Kilkotah, then four months pregnant, the baptismal name of Marguerite Arcouet. Of her nine children, survivors included daughters Lisette and Marguerite Clacalam and sons Amable "Ar-Quit-Te" or "Abraham," Isaac, Jean "John," Leon, and Michel Arcouet, a veteran scout of the Oregon Indian wars.

By 1841, the Arcouets and eighty other families formed a community of 350 citizens that was 70 percent French-Canadian and served by Justice of the Peace Joseph Gervais. The ethnic background began changing dramatically in 1843, when 1,000 Easterners followed the Oregon Trail to the Pacific Northwest, leaving in their wake a broad grassless, treeless track. The shift in population caused settlers to establish a provisional government to protect claims, mediate lawsuits, exterminate predatory wolves, and support Father Antoine Langlois's St. Paul mission school, which educated the Arcouet children. The rise in American immigration placed men like Arcouet in a one-third voting minority. As a result of group demand for structure, in a 52–50 vote, the Champoeg Meeting of May 2, 1843, defeated Arcouet and other French-Canadian voices from halting the British majority in creating Oregon's provisional government.

Pioneer Struggles

Hard luck dogged the Arcouets. After two years' work for the Hudson's Bay Company, Amable's 37-year-old brother, Charles Leon Arcouet, drowned because his boat overturned in a whirlpool at The Dalles on October 3, 1843. In deep winter, Amable retrieved the body from Wasco County and buried it in St. Paul. By December 1845, the Arcouets resided among 6,000 residents of the Willamette Valley, 80 percent of whom were Americans. By 1846, the British lost control of the far Northwest to American cattle ranchers, who ousted sheep herders from their ranks.

Following the death of 11-year-old Lisette Arcouet and Marguerite's unnamed newborn in 1848 (perhaps to epidemic measles), Amable joined 49ers from St. Paul in prospecting sites in California. He remained only three months and returned, luckily without contracting epidemic cholera. In 1851, the year he achieved natural citizenship, steamer traffic on the Willamette River boosted prosperity in barns, hardware stores, lumber and brickyards, mills, and warehouses. Unfortunately for Amable, a botched job as powder man on a mill canal at the Oregon City falls left him blind.

Because of a fall from a mount during the Snake War of 1864, a hard-fought military campaign in the Blue Mountains against Northern Paiute guerrilla war chief Paulina, 25-year-old Michel Arcouet suffered a debilitating shoulder injury. At war's end, he retired from the seventy-man volunteer militia under Captain Joaquin Miller to a mountain farm at Bee Creek in Clackamas County and worked sporadically at tracking and hunting. Michel joined farmer Jean Arquette, Amable and Marguerite's widowed son, as a family breadwinner.

Following the Rogue River Wars from October 1855 to October 31, 1856, the forcible removal of the Kalapuya and Upper Chinook to the Grand Ronde Reservation augmented a cultural void for women like Marguerite who married French Canadians. After her death on October 5, 1870, Amable survived another eleven years and died on July 8, 1880, leaving behind a thriving dynasty of Arquettes. The couple and Amable's brother Leon lie buried in Old Saint Paul Roman Catholic Mission Cemetery.

SOURCES

McArthur, Scott. *The Enemy Never Came: The Civil War in the Pacific Northwest.* Lincoln: University of Nebraska Press, 2012.

Watson, Bruce McIntyre. *A Biographical Dictionary of Fur Traders Working West of the Rockies, 1793–1858*. Kelowna, B.C.: Center for Social, Spatial, and Economic Justice, 2010.

Baker, Jim (1818–1898), Jim Bridger (1803–1881)

Plainsman "Honest" Jim Baker, a vigorous model of trapper, interpreter, and guide, spent 34 years scouting from Kansas and Missouri to California and Oregon and a quarter century ranching in Savery, Wyoming. A native of Belleville in St. Clair County, Illinois, Jim was born on December 19, 1818, to William and Phoebe Neeley Baker, Scots-Irish farmers outside Nashville, Tennessee. Jim, his younger brother John, and sisters Adelia, Elizabeth, and Eliza received minimal education.

After coming west on foot at age thirteen, Baker chose marksmanship, roping, and tracking as his future. On an 18-month contract as scout and beaver trapper for the American Fur Company in St. Louis, Missouri, in 1838, he worked for Virginia-born mountain man Jim Bridger as a pack train leader to the annual mountaineers' rendezvous in the Wind River Mountains in west central Wyoming. After traveling in April upriver to Westport, Missouri, by the steamer *St. Peter*, on May 22, 1839, Baker joined 75 men traveling with missionaries through hostile Arikara territory in 24 wagons pulled by 150 horses and mules. The eight-day expedition journeyed by keelboat up the Platte River to the Laramie Plains and Fort Bonneville in west central Wyoming.

After a year off the frontier in St. Louis, Baker's forays into the West took him on one-man trapping expeditions. In spring 1841, he pressed on to Henry's Fork, Idaho, to warn Dutchman Henry Fraeb, Bridger's partner, of mounting hostilities among Plains Indians. On August 21, 1841, on the Yampa River on the Colorado-Wyoming border, some 500 Arapaho, Cheyenne, and Sioux attacked Fraeb's trappers and Baker's search party in a six-day battle. Following Fraeb's death in the conflict, Baker led the struggle from behind a breastwork of horses and stumps and suffered injury before escaping six days later to Bridger's camp on the Green River. The largest confrontation between Indians and fur trappers, the battle coincided with a decline in the beaver population and the dwindling of fur trading.

A Prairie Career

As Baker's reputation grew for skillful Indian fighting and trail guiding, he became friends

In 1879, Jim Baker scouted for Wyoming cavalry in pursuit of the Utes who inflicted the Meeker Massacre.

with explorer John Charles Frémont and scout Kit Carson, who led travelers along the Oregon Trail into the Sierra Nevada in California. In 1845, Baker joined frontiersmen in herding around 4,000 horses from Mexican lands in Southern California as far south as the Sonoma River and Los Angeles. Adopted in 1847 as the "Red-Haired Shoshone," he dressed in buckskins and moccasins. During six marriages, he chose as mates Bannock, Flathead, and Shoshone women and a pair of Snake sisters, one named Morook.

In August 1847, Baker aided Shoshone chief Washakie, Jim Bridger's father-in-law, in recovering Washakie's 16-year-old daughter, Marina, and a girl named Winona, both captured by Blackfoot and abducted over lava beds. The chief gave Marina, sister of Little Fawn Bridger, to Baker. The couple produced sons, William and Joseph, and daughter Jennieve Jane Baker. Another adventure in the 1850s concluded with the rescue of Sioux from starvation during a blizzard and Baker's reward, marriage to Flying Fawn.

At age 29, Baker served the government as guide and a scout for a railroad party at Salt Lake City, Utah. As chief scout of General William Selby Harney at Fort Laramie, Wyoming, Baker applied his skill at Arapaho sign language and a Shoshone dialect. In the early 1850s, he wed a Sioux woman whom he had rescued from starvation. In June 1854, he and Jim Bridger led Irishman St. George Gore through the Rocky Mountains on a lavish hunt.

Baker's wife Eliza Yanetse produced twins in 1856. The survivor of the two, James C. Baker, united at age 17 with Lucinda Upchurch and sired the frontiersman's grandson, George Washington "Wash" Baker. Subsequent assignments took Jim Baker along the Oregon Trail to Fort Bridger over the winter of 1857–1858 as army scout during surveillance of Danites, a Mormon militia led by Lot Smith, and as trail guide for Randolph Barnes Marcy on a supply train from Fort Bridger, Wyoming, to Fort Union, New Mexico. During the layover, Baker bought civilized clothing, which he denounced as uncomfortable and foolish looking. The fort manager traded fresh dray animals in exchange for up to $50 in flour and sugar.

Career Change

As a homesteader during the Colorado gold rush, on July 3, 1859, Baker first raised cattle at his adobe ranch on Vasquez Fork (now Clear Creek) west of Denver. In addition to building a toll bridge on the Denver Boulder Wagon Road, he operated a stone coal (anthracite) mine and a ferry at Baker's Crossing. He lost Marina to drowning and many of his children to smallpox. His two surviving wives operated a general store, trading with Indians and immigrants.

For a year, Baker assumed the post of captain under John Milton Chivington, head of the 700-man Colorado Militia that, on November 29, 1864, burned out Chief Black Kettle's Southern Cheyenne village at Sand Creek, killing 133. Baker concurred with Chivington on the need to put down hostile Amerindians. In 1865, Baker served as guide and interpreter for Daniel Chessman Oakes, an agent and treaty maker to the Grand River, Yumpak, and Uintah Ute, including Chief Colorow and Aucotash. On April 17, 1867, Baker and his trapping party raided Southern Arapaho leader Little Raven in retaliation for the theft of horses and mules.

After selling his first home on May 15, 1873, Baker moved farther from civilization north of the Colorado border to Savery, Wyoming. He and four of his children—Joseph Baker (Marina's son) and daughters, Jennie Reschke, Isabel "Belle" E. Kinnear, and Madeline Adams—notched cottonwood logs and built a two-story home featuring dovetailing at the corners and loopholes in the third-story lookout tower. Short-term service under General George Armstrong Custer at Rosebud, South Dakota, in 1875 placed Baker at battles with the Oglala Lakota chief Crazy Horse in the Black Hills against gold prospectors encroaching on the Badlands at French Creek. At age 63, Baker scouted for Major Thomas Tipton Thornburgh, commander of Fort Steele, Wyoming, in pursuit of the Utes who inflicted the Meeker Massacre on September 29, 1879, at Milk Creek, Colorado, killing fourteen cavalrymen.

The former trapper and scout resided in peace for the remaining 17 years of his life and participated in a local celebration of Wyoming's admission to the Union on July 10, 1890. He died at his second ranch in Carbon County on the Little Snake River on May 15, 1898. On July 23, 1917, state preservationists moved his cabin to Frontier Park in Cheyenne, Wyoming. Upon the reestablishment of the Baker home at the Little Snake River Museum in July 1976 by the frontiersman's great grandson, Paul McAllister, Wyoming history elevated the stature of the unassuming scout. Baker lies buried in a nearby cemetery. In 1996, the city of Westminster, Colorado, honored Baker's memory with a statue.

Sources

Ricker, Eli S. *Voices of the American West: The Settler and Soldier.* Lincoln: Board of Regents of the University of Nebraska, 2005.

Robinson, Charles M., ed. *The Diaries of John Gregory Bourke: June 1, 1878–June 22, 1880.* Denton: University of North Texas Press, 2007.

Bell, James George (1831–1911), Susan Abia Hollenbeck Bell (1831–1905), John Edward "Ed" Hollenbeck (1829–1885)

Pioneer dynast James George Bell and his extended family built a farming and ranching community that evolved into Bell, California. Born to Scots Presbyterian parents in Bowling Green, Kentucky, on December 14, 1831, Bell was a conservative religious man. Moving west through Paris, Illinois, to Sedalia, Missouri, he married Dorothea "Dolly" A. Reasons on July 17, 1856. The couple produced four children—George Eddy, Mary Elizabeth, and Otis Freeman Bell, Sr.

After Dolly's death on November 27, 1864, James courted a second wife, the sister of his friend John Edward "Ed" Hollenbeck, a financier and entrepreneur who made his fortune in Nicaragua. In June 1866, in Sedalia, Missouri, James Bell wed German-American widow Susan Abia Hollenbeck Wells, a seamstress and activist born in 1852 in Hudson, Ohio. The couple's family included Maude Elizabeth and Frank R. Bell and Susan's four, Emma, Irene, Oren, and Jennie.

The Bell-Hollenbeck Alliance

On the advice of brother-in-law Ed Hollenbeck, in 1875, Bell moved to California and settled near Los Angeles at the town of Obed, which residents renamed Bell in 1898. In June, Susan, then six months pregnant, and four-year-old Maude followed by box car with the family furniture to San Francisco. They offloaded their goods to a ship bound for the wharf-less landing at Los Angeles and from there traveled by mule and buggy to their destination.

While building their Victorian farmhouse, the Bell family lived with Hollenbeck and supported his recovery from ill health. Susan gave birth to Alphonzo Edward "Phonzie" on September 29, 1875. She co-founded a sewing circle and established a reputation for fine stitchery and charitable endeavors, a typical outreach of housewives.

Bell and Hollenbeck partnered in agricultural investment and the breeding of shorthorn cattle, a stocky line suited to prairie foraging. Hollenbeck acquired 6,737 acres of land in Los Angeles County. At a 360-acre vegetable farm, which was once part of the Rancho San Antonio Spanish land grant, Bell completed a house and Bell Station Ranch in 1876.

Bell's investments furthered the growth of Obed as well as nearby Bell Gardens. The grounds abutted Bell Station, the watering spot for the Southern Pacific Railroad. The area flourished from a series of wells, which watered the five-acre plots that Bell leased to other growers.

Community Building

After Hollenbeck's death in 1885, Bell contributed to frontier history as postmaster, an elder of the Presbyterian Church, and, in 1887, one of the eleven co-founders of Occidental College, a co-ed Christian institution in Boyle Heights. In 1893, Maude Bell became one of the first two graduates. Her brother Alphonzo ranked first in his class. James George Bell retired to Alphonzo's alfalfa farm in Santa Fe

Springs. Six years after Susan's death from heart attack in 1905, James Bell died on November 23, 1911.

Alphonzo Bell made a fortune from developing Bel-Air Estates and the Bell Petroleum Oil Company and continued his mother's gifts to charitable, religious, and civic projects. His son, Alphonzo E. Bell, Jr., completed eight terms in the California legislature. On April 6, 2000, the California State Historical Society named the Bell House a cultural resource.

Source
Bell, Alphonzo. *The Bel Air Kid: An Autobiography of a Life in California*. Victoria, B.C.: Trafford, 2002.

Bingham, Hiram (1789–1869), Sybil Moseley Bingham (1792–1848)

The founders of Protestant missions in Honolulu, evangelist and lexicographer Hiram Bingham and teacher and seamstress Sybil Moseley Bingham set an example of piety and Western superiority among native Hawaiians. A descendent of English Congregationalists, Hiram was born on a farm in Bennington, Vermont, on October 30, 1789, the seventh child of Lydia Denton and Deacon Calvin Bingham. Ambitious and self-directed, in 1811, he underwent a religious conversion that outweighed his commitment to home and family.

Influenced by his older brother Amos, an itinerant minister, Hiram completed ministerial training on scholarship at Middlebury College and Andover Theological Seminary. He expressed his zeal by attending the Philadelphian Society, a libertarian discussion group, and by forming New England's first Sunday school, a source of scriptural knowledge and spirituality. Rather than remain on the farm to care for his parents, he planned a mission voyage to the Polynesians of the Sandwich islands, then a monarchy ruled by King Kamehameha the Great. Upon proposing to Sarah Shepherd in spring 1819, Hiram received a parental rejection, an obstacle to American mission requirements that evangelists be married men.

STONE CHURCH AT HONOLULU.

Missionaries Hiram and Sybil Bingham built Kawaiahao Church, a stone edifice in Honolulu, which the Reverend Bingham sketched in 1846.

Hiram had a chance meeting in Goshen, Connecticut, with Sybil Moseley, born on September 14, 1792, in Westfield, Massachusetts, to Sophia Pomeroy, granddaughter of colonial military hero Daniel Pomeroy, and Pliny Moseley, a descendent of New England colonists from Lincolnshire, England. After her parents' deaths in 1810, Sybil had borne responsibility for young siblings Annie and Sophia Moseley and had taught school at Hartford and Canandaigua, New York. Out of a mutual interest in missions, Hiram proposed marriage on September 29 and, on October 11, 1819, at Hartford, Connecticut, wed Sybil.

Into the Mission Field

Aboard the two-masted brig *Thaddeus* for a 164-day voyage from Boston, the Binghams set sail around Cape Horn, Chile, on October 23 with the Pioneer Company, a collaboration of six missionary couples. During the six-month sojourn, Sybil attempted to learn Hawaiian. Arriving at Kailua, Oahu, on April 14, 1820, the couple invited the new king, Kamehameha II, his father's widow, Kalakua, and Prime Minister Kalanimoku to dine on the ship and sang for them. Kalakua requested that the wives make an American gown for her. Because Bingham brought his wife and showed no interest in trade or land, the king granted the family-friendly mission one year to prove its benefits.

Upon sailing to Honolulu on April 19, the Binghams occupied a one-room, doorless grass hut. Limited to an annual salary of $250, the couple received gifts of breadfruit, coconuts, bananas, sweet potatoes, melons, sugarcane, fish, and a pig. Hiram furnished his wife with a rocking chair he made from driftwood and acacia koa and made a duplicate for Queen Ka'ahumanu. Sybil set up an outdoor laundry, taught stitchery to native girls, and sewed shirts and suits from broadcloth and linen for the king.

The evangelists set themselves above Polynesians by applauding the collapse of island taboos and the destruction of idols. The Binghams viewed the Pioneer Company as apostles and ingratiated themselves with chiefs and royalty as an overture to widespread conversions of islanders to Christianity. In Honolulu's first school on May 1820, Sybil, then two months pregnant, started teaching English to a dozen Anglo-Hawaiian girls, the beginning of literacy classes for forty women. She raised a stone wall to sustain the island's first night-blooming cereus.

With four mission families, the Binghams shared a frame house built and dismantled in Boston for reassembly in Honolulu. In the cellar dining area, they alternated their diet between salt beef or pork and potatoes and Polynesian menus of fish and poi, a pudding steamed from the taro root. On November 9, 1820, Sybil gave birth to Sophia Moseley Bingham, Hawaii's first white female child. Within months, Sybil nursed Queen Ka'ahumanu through illness and formed a lasting friendship that furthered the spread of Protestantism among islanders.

Meeting Island Needs

The Binghams brought disparate skills to the Hawaiian mission field. In January 1822, Hiram imported a printing press along with slates and chalk for seventy students. He started transliterating the Hawaiian language from a seventeen-letter alphabet, a preface to the unglottalized alphabet still in use. For participants in his evening singing school, he composed 47 hymns collected in *Na Himeni Hawaii: He Me Ori Ia Iehova, Ke Akua Mau* (Hawaiian Hymns and Songs to Jehovah, the Eternal God, 1823), the basis of modern Hawaiian music.

After polling other missionaries on adopting uniform orthography, in 1825, Bingham compiled a beginning reader and begin work on grammar and vocabulary. Over the next decade, he translated parts of the Bible into Hawaiian, which islanders learned by chanting in traditional *mele* (plainsong) cadences. To combat the debauchery and lawlessness of foreign sailors, the sources of venereal disease, he irked profligate foreigners and sailing crews by meddling in island governance and harbor policing of grog shops and gambling halls.

While teaching islanders Western housekeeping and sharing midwifery duties with fellow missionaries, Sybil Bingham suffered from exhaustion and disappointment. In spring 1822, she accepted the Hawaiian greeting of touching nose to nose and negotiated with Kamamalu, wife of Kamehameha II, to sew fabric into shirts. Sybil instructed Kamamalu on how to wear dresses, but the king's wife preferred shirts rather than the confining outfits of American women. In addition to teaching and compiling Hawaii's first phrase book, Sybil tailored a dress for Queen Ka'ahumanu and began fashioning bonnets for noblewomen, who sporadically abandoned nudity for attire suited to New England standards of modesty.

Female Hawaiians responded more positively toward proselytizing than males, who preferred the flamboyance of island gods and dance ritual. Significant to the mission in 1823 were the baptisms of Ka'ahumanu and six chiefs. The queen regent became an advocate for churches, schools, and American morals and law. In the same year, the missionaries lost their two-week-old son, Levi Parsons Bingham, to fever. In June 1825, Jeremiah Evarts Bingham, a 16-month-old toddler, died in Honolulu.

Lawfulness took years to instill, beginning with obligatory literacy and bans on flower leis, kites, hula, boxing and wrestling, tobacco, and rum. On February 26, 1826, the Binghams survived a mob attack on their residence by one hundred fifty merchant seamen from the U.S.S. schooner *Dolphin,* the first U.S. Navy vessel to berth in Honolulu. Lieutenant John "Mad Jack" Percival quelled the riot and returned his crew to the ship, but demanded that the king make Hawaiian girls available to sailors.

Following the death of Kamehameha II in July 1824 from measles during an expedition to London, Queen Ka'ahumanu took charge of Oahu and repudiated French Catholicism. In place of French advisers, she employed the Binghams in codifying Hawaiian law according to Western Protestant ideals. Until nine-year-old Kamehameha III reached adulthood, Hiram mentored him and encouraged his elevation of Protestantism to the state religion.

In the seven months preceding October 1825, with the aid of printed Elisha Loomis, Hiram issued 16,000 spellers and thousands of catechisms. He began building a congregation in 1828 in a 196 × 63-foot thatched church floored with mats. Chiefs enforced mandatory Sunday observances by threatening to confiscate property from disobedient islanders who retained superstitions and secretly practiced hula rituals.

Rewards of Missions

In 1829, the royal family gave the Binghams land at Punahou Spring on which to live away from the crowded Honolulu village and to profit from coral flats, salt beds, and fishponds. The children enjoyed boating in a fresh pond amid banana trees and walked nine miles to Hawaii's first school. Rapid immigration of whalers, merchants, traders, and missionaries under Kamehameha III in 1833 defeated Hiram's efforts to stem drunkenness, gambling, nudity, and prostitution and replace it with strict Calvinism. A public dance on February 28 celebrated Hiram's banishment and the return of island customs of polygamy, singing, hula, and games.

After Hiram's reinstatement in 1835, he persecuted French Catholics and again advocated hardline New England Puritanism, which admitted few Hawaiians to the ministry or church membership. He answered Governor Kekuanaoa's request that he start a second congregation at Kaumakapili in Honolulu. On July 31, 1838, Hiram replaced the thatched grass Kawaiahao church with an edifice built in New England style from 14,000 coral slabs quarried with shark-tooth saws from under water, a symbol of unwavering Calvinism. The edifice eventually housed 1,075 worshippers. On August 29, 1839, he dedicated the Honolulu church, an adobe and thatch sanctuary and assembly hall accommodating 2,500.

Aboard the barque *Flora* on August 3, 1840, the Binghams and eleven-year-old Elizabeth Ka'ahumanu, ten-year-old Hiram II, and six-year-old Lydia returned to New England. The family left behind the graves of the two sons who died on Oahu. Because of Sybil's poor health from daily labors and the bearing of seven children, their sabbatical turned into permanent separation from the Oahu mission. Hiram spent his time lecturing and writing.

In 1846, Hiram resigned from the American Board of Commissioners for Foreign Missions and turned his energies to the compilation of *A Residence of Twenty-One Years in the Sandwich Islands* (1847). At her death on February 27, 1848, in Easthampton, Massachusetts, Sybil left inter-island correspondence from other missionary wives, letters from her family, and a journal of her pioneer days in Honolulu.

At the New Haven Palladium on August 24, 1852, at age 62, Hiram wed Naomi Emma Morse of Westfield, Massachusetts, head master of the Young Ladies Seminary, a boarding school in York Square. Together, they opened a girls' seminary, which flourished until 1864. Hiram delighted in the 1856 ordination of Hiram II, a Yale graduate and missionary to Honolulu. Hiram, Sr. died at New Haven, Connecticut, on November 11, 1869, from typhoid pneumonia. The James Michener novel *Hawaii* (1959) ridiculed Hiram's religious fanaticism in the character Abner Hale, but exalted Sybil in the loving, selfless devotion of fictional Jerusha Bromley Hale.

SOURCES

Lal, Brij V., and Kate Fortune. *The Pacific Islands: An Encyclopedia*. Honolulu: University of Hawaii Press, 2000.

Restarick, H.B. "Sybil Bingham, As Youthful Bride, Came to Islands in Brig Thaddeus." *Honolulu Star-Bulletin* (15 August 1931).

Bonnema, Oepke H. (1825–1895), Harmen H. Bonnema (1827–1892), Luisa Spengler Bonnema (1838–after 1910), Broer Baukes Haagsma (1831–1907)

An altruistic grain factor and recruiter of immigrants, Oepke Haitzes Bonnema directed struggling, homeless Friesians to a lumber capital in Wisconsin. Born in Kimswerd, Wonseradeel, West Friesland, on May 26, 1825, to Styntje Jelles Fopma and Haitze Eeltjes Bonnema, he was named for his Uncle Oepke Bonnema. The younger Oepke preceded by two years his younger brother, Harmen Bonnema, born on April 2, 1827.

Two and a half weeks after Harmen's birth, Styntje succumbed to postpartum complications, leaving the boy motherless through toddlerhood. More changes in the family structure occurred on May 6, 1830, when Heitze took a second wife, Stijntje van Assen. On May 18, 1836, Haitze died. For the next 15 years until Stijntje's death on March 23, 1851, the family relied on their stepmother for solidarity.

Impressed by optimistic reports of Dutch colonists who settled in Iowa, Indiana, and western Michigan in the 1840s, Bonnema began talking up a prairie expedition in late 1852 among interested Friesians. With the assistance of accountant and schoolmaster Broer Baukes Haagsma of Skraerd, Friesland, Bonnema set out with ninety-one Dutch Reformed immigrants on the *City of Norwich* from Harlingen on the Zuider Zee north of Ijesselmeer on February 26, 1853. Dressed in traditional caps, earrings, and wood clogs, the pioneers shared space with cattle destined for sale in London, England.

The Colonists' Voyage

Financed by the largesse of Oepke Bonnema, the voyagers—24 children and 68 adults—passed through Norfolk, England, by train and reached Liverpool Station on March 1. Because they reached the harbor too late to board the next ship to Philadelphia, they spent three weeks exploring the English coast. On March 21, they embarked on one of the thirty-four immigrant vessels bound for North America and Australia, a testimony to the enthusiasm of northwestern Europeans for opportunities to advance on the frontier.

The sturdy three-masted bark H.M.S. *William and Mary*, carrying railroad iron and 208 Dutch, Irish, English, and German passengers, passed the Azores on April 11, 1853. On May 3, the vessel foundered in the Bahamas in ten fathoms of water off the island of Abaco, where the Isaac Rocks hoisted the hull amidships. Captain Timothy Stinson, two mates, and six sailors deserted the 180 remaining passengers, leaving them wailing for deliverance.

Already bereft of fourteen passengers killed

by fever, the pioneers survived two days of terror, in part because of their stoic self-reliance in manning pumps to reduce 10 feet of water in the hold. A day before the *William and Mary* sank, the black crew of the *Oracle,* a Bahamian coast guard cutter, rescued all travelers. At Nassau, survivors received overwhelming generosity, gifts of clothes and shoes, and rebooking on another ship on May 13, 1853. Their treatment by African islanders instilled admiration for nonwhite people.

Crossing the Gulf of Mexico, the Friesians reached the Mississippi Delta on June 8 and admired the beauty and prosperity of New Orleans. Local German-Americans donated hams and potatoes and oversaw transport of the group to a river steamer. On June 11, the immigrants moved north toward St. Louis, Missouri. Ten days later, they sailed for Iowa, reaching Davenport on June 28, 1853, to a welcome from fellow Friesians.

Building a Town

Traveling through Galena, Illinois, on July 1, 1853, Bonnema's party landed at Prairie La Crosse, a part of southwestern Wisconsin formerly ceded to whites by the Ojibwa. Broer Haagsma summarized the company's experience in a leaflet published in Harlingen on September 15, 1853. A Dutch-American, Herman De Jager, published his own version of the trip in the Holland, Michigan, *De Hollander,* a bilingual weekly. De Jager initiated a collection of funds to replace possessions lost in the shipwreck. More versions of the passage from England derived from pioneer Jan Bijlsma and from a telegram that concerned friends sent from Savannah, Georgia, to families in Friesland.

At Prairie La Crosse, Bonnema anticipated investment opportunities from virgin prairie and stands of birch, elm, maple, and oak and from the natural 15 × 3-mile terracing of the Black River south of Onalaska. On July 9, 1853, he purchased 80 acres west of the Mississippi River for himself. With concurrence from settlers Johannes Steenstra and Sjoerd Tjalsma, Bonnema selected 8 acres for plotting the townships of Hamilton and Onalaska on the Black River, where a ferry had been in operation since 1850. The Dutch colony took the name of Frisia, later altered to New Amsterdam, Wisconsin.

In fall, carpenters, farmers, a blacksmith, and a wagon maker joined in building five houses with lumber imported from Onalaska. A matrix of eleven streets took names of historic figures—Oepke, Lulop, Jelle, Sterford, Harmen, and others. Bonnema engaged David Woodward to build his residence on Main Street. Meanwhile, Bonnema supplied colonists from his dry goods store and post office, and, in 1855, delivered mail twice weekly to La Crosse. In 1856, he gave the town a lot for building a school/town hall and supported moderate Republicanism, the party of Abraham Lincoln.

On December 21, 1856, Bonnema married 16-year-old Ytje Steenstra, who was twelve at the time her parents and two siblings migrated with the colony from Franekeradeel, Freisland. The childless couple later parted. After marrying 22-year-old Swiss immigrant Luisa Spengler of Altnau on November 29, 1860, Bonnema shared his home with Harmen Bonnema and with New Amsterdam assessor Adolph Spengler, Luisa's brother. Oepke developed New Amsterdam's commerce with a hotel and stage coach station, tavern, and dance hall, but failed at schemes to market wheat in Chicago.

While Broer Haagsma rose in importance to Dutch consul after appointment by Abraham Lincoln, Bonnema became the area's major employer. The Black River powered Bonnema's sawmill, which planed 10,000 feet per day. More milling operations opened in 1868 and 1877 and added picket manufacture for pasture fencing. Bonnema marketed wood from Saint Louis and purchased half interest in a Mississippi steamer, a losing investment. His brother Harmen worked in merchandising and farmed 35.5 acres at Onalaska.

Residents established a Dutch Reformed church and opened businesses supplying corn and wheat grinding, wagons, metal tools, groceries, meat, and beer. Twenty new families arrived from Friesland, including Frouke Stellingwerf, a servant indentured to Bonnema in

1869. Following the closure of Oepke Bonnema's sawmill in 1868, he served as town treasurer and tended bar until 1879. By 1880, villagers occupied 200 houses. Oepke died on March 20, 1895, five years before the depletion of pine stands and the silting of the main channel of the Black River. Haagsma lived until 1907, when he drowned in the Mississippi River.

Source
Klinkenberg, Dean. *Driftless Area Travel Guide: Mississippi Valley Traveler.* St. Louis: Travel Passages, 2010.

Booth, Albert Anson (1850–1914), Ellen Eliza Carter Booth (1854–1935)

A machinist, stockman, and postmaster, Albert Anson Booth co-founded Edna Township in east central North Dakota and contributed to its governance. A native of Waukau, Wisconsin, he was born of English lineage on October 17, 1850, to Phercelia Fitch, a New Yorker, and Elliot Lansing Booth of Illinois. His father, a '49er at the California Gold Rush and successful gold prospector at Pike's Peak, Colorado, made and lost two fortunes from mining.

Albert Booth grew up and attended public schools in Syracuse, New York. After a divorce in 1864, his father settled in San Joaquin, California. Phercelia Fitch Booth remarried. At age 19, Albert settled near his mother in the prairie town of Fond du Lac, Wisconsin, to log for three years for Hamilton, Finley & Company. Employing 65 woodcutters, the steam-powered lumber yard contributed to a state industry by reducing 67,000,000 feet of lumber into 88,000,000 shingles worth $230,000 and laths and pickets valued at $150,000.

In 1878, Booth set out with his younger brothers and collaborators William E. and Edward Bush by covered wagon for Dakota Territory, where whites had claimed the 7 million-acre Black Hills of the Great Sioux Reservation following the 1875–1878 gold rush. The Booth brothers reached Valley City on May 24, 1879, and found the Sheyenne River valley rife with bear, elk, moose, and deer. On virgin prairie south of Orner Slough, Booth sliced sod with a plow to heap into a shanty and barn.

Hands-On Training

To earn cash, Booth labored with 600 seasonal drifters on the territory's largest farm at Casselton, Cass County, in the Red River Valley. The crew manned gang and sulky plows, broadcast seed, and hand-bound oats and wheat into shocks. Dakota's first bonanza speculator, Scottish "Wheat King" Oliver P. Dalrymple worked 73,600 acres—115 square miles—of fertile black alluvial mold up to three feet deep to grow alfalfa, flax, barley, rye, millet, timothy, clover, corn, and potatoes. Booth assisted the crew in transporting some 600,000 bushels of grain a year to Duluth, Fargo, and southbound steamers on the Red River.

On December 17, 1879, Booth rode to Waupon, Wisconsin, to wed an Irish-American wife, 25-year-old Eliza Ellen Carter of Tully, New York. In spring 1880, the couple set out for Dakota Territory with enough livestock and equipment to farm and raise breeder stock. Booth framed in a wood homestead and separate kitchen with lumber he transported from Sanborn west of Valley City. He established an isolated ranch on a quarter section (160 acres) in Barnes County, North Dakota, and practiced progressive methods, including mechanized threshing he had practiced on the Dalrymple farm. With the aid of immigrant workers from Norway and Sweden, Booth invested some $400 each in thirty shorthorn cattle, which won prizes at fairs in Illinois and Indiana.

Giving Back to the Community

After the birth of Edna Celia Booth, the couple's first child, on July 7, 1881, the parents named the township after her. Following her came seven more Booths—Alice Alberta, Elizabeth Ellen "Bessie," Leila Maude, Albert Anson, twins Blanch Irene and Frank Sanford, and Roy Carter. The family expanded Edna Stock Farm to 480 acres. From 1882 to 1884, Albert Booth ran the Edna post office, subsequently renamed Booth at its organization on September 20, 1886.

In the years following North Dakota's admission to the Union in 1889, the Booth family's contributions to community life included service on the Barnes County Commission and chairing the town supervisors. Albert supported fraternal organizations by joining the Ancient Order of United Workmen, Independent Order of Odd Fellows, and Masons. A proponent of the Booth School for elementary students, taught by Mary Ann Woodcock, he favored ample wages for teachers and community involvement in religious education and social activities. By selling homemade ice cream at fund raisers, he raised cash to stock the school library with books. Eliza Booth amassed funds to erect a church three miles southeast at Rogers.

At age fifty-seven, Booth left his homestead to manage the Nestor farm north of Valley City, where his children completed high school. Leila Maude Booth completed one year at the Normal School, but lacked living expenses to finish college. Albert Booth died on June 7, 1914. Eliza Booth lived with daughter Edna and son-in-law Orville Munden Wilkinson in Tacoma, Washington, until her death on July 10, 1935.

Sources
Compendium of History and Biography of North Dakota. Chicago: Geo. A. Ogle, 1900.
"Murray Bros. & Ward Land Company." *Minneapolis Golden Jubilee, 1865–1917.* Minneapolis: Lakeland Press, 1917, 166.

Bottineau, Pierre (1817–1895)

A Métis interpreter, land speculator, trapper, and surveyor of Minnesota and Dakota Territory, Pierre "Buchino" Bottineau plotted sites of new towns in the Red River Valley, including St. Paul, Minneapolis, Osseo, and Red Lake Falls, Minnesota. Born on January 1, 1817, in Pembina, a hunter's camp on a buffalo trail north of Grand Forks, on the Minnesota-Dakota Territory boundary, he was the third son of French-Canadian frontiersman Charles Joseph Bottineau of Quebec and his second wife, Margaret Clear Sky Woman, the Assiniboine-Ojibwa sister of Pembina Ojibwa chief Red Bear. Of French Huguenot ancestry, he bore the name of his Breton grandfather from Nantes.

Bottineau grew up in St. Boniface in the Selkirk Settlement (Red River Colony, Winnipeg) and learned hunting, marksmanship, and riding from Joseph. He lost his father to exposure in 1832 and, at age 15, passed to the care of a new mentor, *voyageur* Antoine "Le Gros" LeCompte, at St. Anthony, Minnesota. Until LeCompte's murder in 1840, he introduced Pierre to woods lore and scouting.

Although readied for frontier life, Bottineau remained unschooled and illiterate. Traveling from the Upper Mississippi as far southeast as Prairie du Chien, Wisconsin, in fur hat and rawhide coat and moccasins or snowshoes, he established a reputation as a messenger, scout, and agent for the Red River trading colony, which competed with the Hudson's Bay Company from 1811 over the next half century. In the aftermath of the 1815 Treaty of Ghent, Bottineau and his companions, Joseph Potvin, Louis Pierre Gervais, and Peter Raiche served U.S. officials in ensuring American control of land formerly in the domain of Great Britain.

In addition to trapping beaver and hunting buffalo for pemmican to sell to the Hudson's Bay Company, Bottineau guided pioneers in ox carts from southern Manitoba onto rich prairie land at Red Lake Falls, Minnesota, and into Dakota Territory, Montana, and Idaho. At St. Boniface Cathedral in Manitoba on December 1, 1836, Bottineau united with Genevieve "Jennie" Larance, a Métis from Red River and the mother of sons Jean Baptiste (John B.), Pierre, Leon, and Daniel and daughters Mary Jane, Genevieve Louisa, Rosalie, and Elsie. In early 1837, Bottineau shifted his allegiance from the declining British trading system to the Americans at Fort Snelling (present-day St. Paul, Minnesota).

Under manager Henry Hastings Sibley of the American Fur Company at Mendota, Bottineau pursued land speculation to the northwest above St. Anthony Falls. In May 1838, he guided a 40-family party of French, Scots, and Swiss, who traveled by barge from Traverse des Sioux to Fort Sibley. While traversing the plains, he bribed hostile Sioux for free passage with flour and tobacco, a common ingredient in healing poultices and religious offerings. After transporting livestock from the Red River Valley to the frontier, he profited from the sale of butter, cows, and oxen.

Relocation to the Southeast

Evicted from the riverbank across from Fort Snelling in late summer 1840, Bottineau pitched a skin lodge on his 100-acre claim at St. Paul, Minnesota, which he purchased from Benjamin Gervais. He and his older brothers, Charles and Sévère Bottineau, founded St. Paul Catholic Church and maintained their property for six years as the basis of a commercial network. By summer 1841, the Bottineaus had planted 20 acres. The claim included maple groves on Nicollet Island, where workers collected sap for boiling down into sugar. As manager of a Mackinaw transport system from St. Anthony Falls to Little Rock, Minnesota, Pierre Bottineau superintended supply routes to Indian tribes and U.S. government installations. He profited enough to purchase 320 acres along the Mississippi River that became the northeastern waterfront of Minneapolis.

On the Red River Trail in east central Minnesota, in 1849, Bottineau bought David Faribault's fur trading post at the confluence of the Elk and Mississippi rivers and built an inn the next year at Orono. Bottineau held the post of Ramsey County road supervisor. In 1851, he supplied timber for a dam at Nicollet Island. Over the next decade, the non–Indian population on former Sioux lands rose from 4,000 to 175,000 immigrants.

After Genevieve's death on April 9, 1851, Bottineau married Martha Charlotte Gervais of Lake Champlain, the French-Canadian daughter of his fellow frontiersman Louis Pierre Gervais, at St. John Evangelist in Little Canada, Minnesota, on January 6, 1852. The union produced daughters Amilie, Louise Marie Laura, Genevieve "Jennie," Agnes Virginia, Josephine, and Martha Mathilde and sons Louis, Charles C., George, Henry, Sidney Leon, Emile, George Pierre, Guillaume (William), Bernard Norman, and Noah Emil. On his 160 acres, Bottineau built a hand-hewn pine house in Greek revival style. For his family, he raised horses, pigs, cows, and sheep and preserved a Francophone community of settlers from Pembina, Quebec, and Little Canada, Minnesota.

Community Builder

On three square miles of wild meadowland known as Bottineau Prairie, on July 1, 1852, the frontiersman surveyed the environs of Osseo, Minnesota, a preliminary study for the Northern Pacific Railway. He platted the Minnesota towns of Maple Grove, St. Anthony, and Orono and purchased 700 acres of prime land. In interracial mediation between Europeans and native tribes, he urged English, French, Ojibwa, Cree, Mandan, Sioux, Assiniboine, and Winnebago to establish peace and arranged the punishment of Ojibwa murderers of timber cutters building a dam. For his diplomacy between races, he earned the title of "Walking Peace Pipe." In 1855, George Keller, the first resident priest in the area, celebrated mass at the Bottineau home. Over the next year, Bottineau superintended the building of the Church of St. Louis and guided explorers seeking locations for forts at Devil's Lake and along the Sheyenne River.

In a severe winter, a heroic ox-cart journey from St. Anthony, Minnesota, in January 1857 pitted Bottineau and his brother Charles against a blizzard outside St. Cloud. Temperatures fell to -38 Fahrenheit. To save a party of ten pioneers from starvation, on the 50-mile trek, the leaders killed the dray oxen for meat. Bottineau shot two buffalo to supply the expedition until the end of the 27-day passage to a campsite.

The mapping of Breckenridge, Minnesota, and Wahpeton, Dakota Territory, preceded rapid settlement and the entry of Minnesota into the union on May 11, 1858. After assisting land speculators at mapping rail lines, Bottineau received a share of 200 lots located too far from the railroad for him to turn a profit. On September 25, he completed a mission for Governor Henry Sibley to locate nine salt springs on the Wild Rice River in Becker County, Minnesota, but the Panic of 1857 continued to suppress investment in such ventures. On the Cheyenne River in 1859, he served the town of Dakota, Minnesota, as treasurer.

On June 19, 1862, he and 15-year-old son Daniel led James Liberty Fisk's Northern Overland Expedition of 130 investors and 40 security guards from St. Paul west toward the Pacific coast. During the expedition, angry Sisseton Sioux under Little Crow fought back against loss of native lands from mid–August through the end of September 1862, when Bottineau summoned the military from Sauk Center to the siege at Fort Abercrombie. The expedition continued west to Walla Walla, Washington, where they arrived on November 1. The following year at Huot east of Grand Forks, he furthered negotiations with the Pembina and Red Lake Ojibwa to sell 11 million acres in the Red River Valley to the United States under the Old Crossing Treaty, which he witnessed with an X at the signing on October 2.

Homesteading

Amid the fever of the Civil War, the Homestead Act, which President Abraham Lincoln signed on May 20, 1862, revived westering, particularly among citizens avoiding the North-South clash. Some 75,000 pioneers pressed into Minnesota to build homes and farms on free plots of 160 acres. Investment in railroads increased Bottineau's contract business at establishing forts, rail lines, and agreements with displaced Indians. Within three weeks of the surrender ending the Civil War, his son, Corporal Peter Bottineau, died of yellow fever after fighting for the 5th Regiment of the Minnesota Infantry. Bottineau's mother, Margaret Bottineau, lived with the family until her death that same year.

Armed with a Spencer .44 sporting rifle, in 1869, Bottineau undertook his most crucial contract trip. He led financier Jay Cooke's party of 70 newspapermen, bureaucrats, and entrepreneurs from St. Cloud to Bismarck, North Dakota. The expeditioners pressed on west to the 2 million-acre Yellowstone, a proposed national park and route for the Northern Pacific Railway. The linkage of the Twin Cities with the Red River Valley in 1871 presaged rapid metropolitan growth and commerce. For his own family and farm, Bottineau disliked the urban area at Osseo.

In a 17-day trek in May 1876, Bottineau guided 119 French-Canadian colonists from St. Paul to fertile farmsteads in Hennepin and Ramsey counties. The newcomers established Gentilly, Crookston, and Red Lake Falls. As an investment, Bottineau and son Jean Baptiste bought 9,000 acres in Polk and Red Lake Counties. Relocated to Red Lake Falls, Bottineau and sons Henry and William built a two-story brick house and planted a garden in view of a bend of the Red River. In 1878, he set out for Canada to recruit another party of would-be Americans. At age sixty-five, he retired from his labors. For Bottineau's efforts as a mediator for the Ojibwa in Washington, D.C., the U.S. Congress extended a retirement pension of $50 per month.

From 1882 to 1887, Bottineau continued to promote settlement of the northern plains by supporting St. Joseph Church at Red Lake Falls and chairing the city council. He handled such problems as cattle roaming the town and the hiring of a street commissioner and marshal. In 1889, the year that Minnesota gained statehood, Bottineau, at age seventy-two, negotiated another land deal with the Ojibwa that relocated them to the White Earth Reservation. On July 26, 1895, he died from an illness contracted while he hunted moose at Thief River Falls.

At St. Joseph's Cemetery, Bottineau took to his grave the titles of "Daniel Boone of the West" and "Kit Carson of the Northwest." His surname survives in a street in Hennepin County, a park and library in Minneapolis, and in Bottineau, county seat of Bottineau County on the Manitoba border. Both his son John Baptiste and granddaughter Martha Bottineau earned law degrees from Georgetown College and protected the Turtle Mountain Ojibwa and Métis from government encroachment. A dance production, *Bottineau Jib: Untold Tales of Early Minnesota* (2011), preserved the frontiersman's legend.

See also Fisk, James Liberty.

Sources

Hallberg, Jane, Barbara Sexton, and Mary Jane Gustafson. *Pierre Bottineau: A Founder of Osseo, Minnesota*. Brooklyn Park, MN: Brooklyn Historical Society, 2000.

Snodgrass, Pat. *Brooklyn Park and Brooklyn Center*. Chicago: Arcadia, 2009.

Stone, Ted. *The Legend of Pierre Bottineau and the History of the Red River Trail*. Edmonton: Eschia Books, 2013.

Bowman, Sarah A. (1812–1866)

A cook, nurse, launderer, madame, and innkeeper, Sarah A. Knight Bowman developed opportunities for women into a profitable life. Born of Irish ancestry on June 5, 1812, in Clay County Missouri, she received no education, but gained a strong work ethic. In July 1845, while her husband served in the 7th infantry at the Jefferson Barracks recruitment center in Lemay, Missouri, she became the camp launderer, seamstress, first aid specialist, and preparer of meals and snacks. She earned for her tall, sturdy frame the nickname "The Great Western," a reference to a trans–Atlantic paddlewheel steamer. She claimed to have worked for General Zachary Taylor at Indian Key, Florida, in August 1840 during the Seminole War and married infantryman John Langwell.

When the army marched south to Corpus Christi Bay, Texas, in July 1845, Sarah purchased a wagon and span of mules to carry her stores and kitchen equipment and followed the soldiers to the Rio Grande. Near the Mexican border, while medical transport moved her injured husband toward Point Isabel west of the Padre Islands on March 21, 1846, she set an example of bravado for besieged soldiers to emulate. By May 1846, she had married Jack Borginnis and set up an officers' dining hall at Fort Brown (formerly Fort Texas), a stronghold during the Mexican-American War of 1846–1848.

Military Hero

Philadelphia and New York newspapers lauded Sarah for continuing to knead bread and ladle up bean soup from May 3–10, 1846, during General Marianio Arista's shelling of Fort Brown. Under fire from cannon and grenades, she suffered a bullet hole in her bonnet and the shattering of a bread tray from her hands. Unruffled, she continued delivering coffee in buckets to gunners and transporting the wounded to aid stations until Arista's retreat to Palo Alto, Texas.

With the aid of black and Mexican workers, Sarah opened the American House inn and saloon at Matamoros and operated a stable. As General Taylor advanced his largely Irish-American troops into Mexico in September 1846, she replicated American House at Monterrey and Saltillo. During the Battle of Buena Vista on February 22–23, 1847, she declined to join the noncombatants in a bunker and continued bandaging casualties, reloading rifles, and distributing coffee and meals.

A spirited patriot, Sarah requisitioned a musket and joined the fray against Mexican General Santa Anna. Her audacity cost her a saber slash to the cheek, which she avenged by killing her Mexican attacker. She recovered the remains of a friend, Captain George Lincoln, from the battlefield and superintended his burial before purchasing his horse and dispatching it to his family in Boston.

From El Paso to Yuma

To claim a place among military families moving northwest, in 1848, Sarah, then a widow, welcomed to her tent a third husband, a soldier named Davis. As the first white woman in El Paso, Texas, in 1849, she established an inn and bordello at the Ponce de Leon Ranch, where she raised vegetables and developed fluency in Spanish. She profited from the 4,000 speculators hurrying to the California Gold Rush.

A year later, Sarah wed German immigrant Alfred J. Bowman, an army horse soldier, and leased her hotel to the military. When Alfred mustered out of the army on November 30, 1850, he and Sarah headed to Fort Yuma, Arizona, to search for gold. Armed with six-shooters, in 1852, Sarah joined the hospital staff as a matron and operated Yuma's first business, a dining hall, brothel, and laundry for officers.

While sheltering Indian and Mexican or-

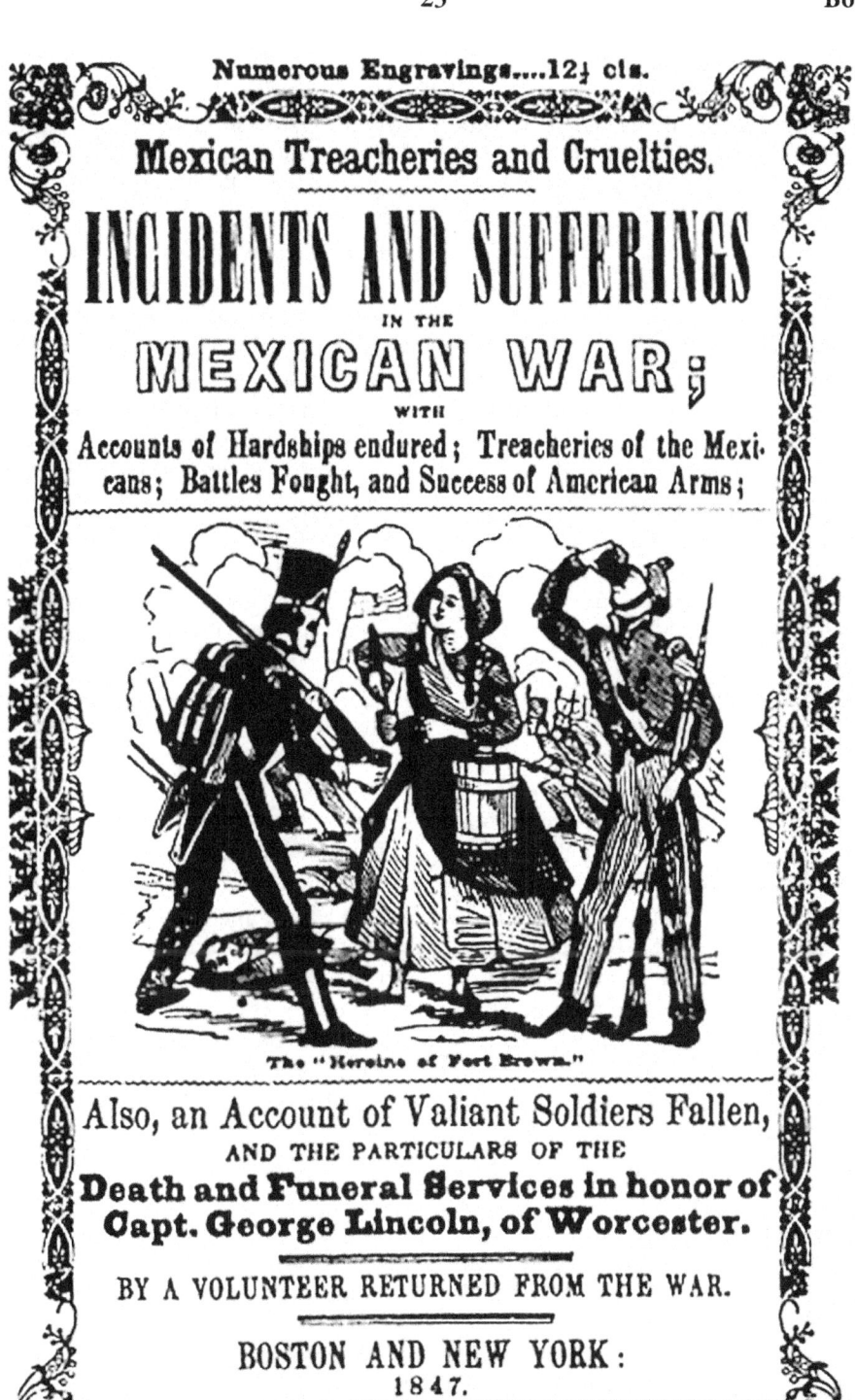

From May 3 to 10, 1846, during General Marianio Arista's shelling of Fort Brown, Texas, Sarah Bowman tended the wounded and served bread and coffee to artillerymen.

phans, to prevent their abduction, Sarah expanded her inn keeping with properties on the Mexican border at Fort Buchanan on Sonoita Creek and at Patagonia. When Sarah reputedly had an affair with Colonel Samuel Peter Heintzelman in 1854, Alfred Bowman took up with a younger woman and abandoned his wife and their adopted daughter, Nancy Skinner Bowman.

Sarah Bowman continued mothering orphaned Mexican and Indian children and training them in domestic work. A tarantula bite killed her on December 23, 1866. The military interred her remains at Yuma with honors.

Source
Cook, Bernard A., ed. *Women and War: A Historical Encyclopedia from Antiquity to the Present*. Santa Barbara: ABC-Clio, 2006.

Briones de Miranda, Juana (1802–1889)

An Afro-Latina-Indian businesswoman and scion of Mexican settlers of California, Juana Gertrudis Briones established medical care and midwifery in San Francisco. A first-generation Californio born in 1802 in Villa Branciforte at the Santa Cruz Mission, she was a granddaughter of explorer Vicente Briones and one of the seven children of Mexican parents, María Ygnacia Ysadora Tapia and Marcos José Briones, an infantryman stationed at Monterey. The family resided at El Polin Springs in the Presidio, where their mother died on May 14, 1812. Their grandparents, Mexican colonizers María Tapia and Ygnacio Briones, surveyed San Diego in 1770 with the Gaspar Bautista de Portolá Expedition.

Briones committed herself to family. In 1820, at age eighteen, she wed an indio herder, Apolinario Miranda of Pótam on the Gulf of California. He became a Presidio security guard and cavalryman like his father, Alejo Feliciano Miranda. While living in a compound with the families of Juana's sisters, Guadalupe and María de la Luz Briones, the couple had eleven children, three of whom died in infancy. One survived with mental retardation. Apolinario moved the family to a new residence at El Ojo de Agua de Figueroa.

At a farm at North Beach in Yerba Buena (present-day San Francisco), after 1835, Juana Briones reared seven surviving children. In 1838, she adopted an Indian orphan, Cecilia Chochuihuala. The family survived on the proceeds from sewing, hide trading, renting saddle horses and tack, and the sale of vegetables, fruit, beef, eggs, and milk to merchants. The provisioners of whaling vessels bought her foods with a long storage life—pumpkins, potatoes, cabbage, and onions.

Although illiterate, Briones served her neighbors as an herbalist and *curandera* (healer). She tended patients with home-grown herbs and learned from the Ohlone the curative value of native plants and their methods of making poultices and setting bones. She also hid runaways eluding enslavement on passing ships. During the Marin County smallpox epidemic of 1834, which decimated the Miwok, she traveled to homes of the sick, regardless of their ethnicity. The experience helped her train Gregorio's son, Pablo Briones, who became a physician.

Because of Apolinario's drunkenness, beatings, incestuous advances to his daughter María Presentación, and failure to support the household, in 1844, Juana sought an ecclesiastical separation. She abandoned him and reclaimed her maiden name. With her sisters' aid, she stocked a series of hideaways as refuges from Apolinario. To secure property rights in an androcentric society, she and her sisters formed legal alliances with Mexicans, native Californios, and Indians through adoption, intermarriage, tenancy, and godmother relationships.

In the Los Altos Hills in 1844, Briones negotiated a price of $300 with an Ohlone, José Gorgonio, for Rancho La Purísima Concepción, a 4,400-acre tract in Santa Clara County. Within the year at present-day Palo Alto, to house her sisters and children, she constructed a three-room quake-proof, erosion-proof residence from redwood framing, which she insulated with adobe. With the admission of California to the U.S., she fought efforts to seize her land and, by 1856, obtained the patrimony of her children after Apolinario's death.

Briones kept investing in land in 1885. After she died in Mayfield, California, on December 3, 1889, her family buried her at Holy Cross Cemetery. Her name is attached to a park and elementary school and to the Juana Briones Heritage Foundation. A century later, the 1989 Loma Prieta earthquake damaged the Briones house.

Sources

Coté, John, and Suzanne Herel. "160-year-old Home Can Be Demolished." *San Francisco Gate* (9 March 2007).

McDonnell, Jeanne Farr. *Juana Briones of 19th Century California*. Tucson: University of Arizona Press, 2008.

Brown, Clara (1800–1885)

Cook, launderer, and midwife Clara Brown contributed her earnings to Methodist church service and the rescue of Southern freedmen. Born into bondage in Spotsylvania County outside Fredericksburg, Virginia, on January 1, 1800, she claimed Cherokee blood through her maternal grandmother. Clara worked the 95-acre tobacco farm of white planter Ambrose X. Smith. At age nine, she traveled to Logan County, Kentucky, over a wilderness road to clear virgin land. While her mother aided her mistress, Myra Smith, Clara learned to cook, bake, make candles, and read and write.

In 1818, Brown wed an Afro-Cherokee slave named Richard. The couple occupied a log cabin and bore four children—Richard, Margaret, and twins Paulina Ann and Eliza Jane Brown. In the late 1820s, Paulina drowned while swimming, thrusting Eliza Jane into hysteria. During the settlement of her owner's estate in 1835 after he died of pneumonia at age 36, auctioneers at Russellville allotted the surviving five family members to different buyers. Brown and her mother passed to George Brown, a Kentucky planter and haymaker in Gallatin on the Indiana border. Margaret, who remained behind, died in her teens of disease.

After George Brown's death in 1856, Clara received manumission from his daughters, but she could not live free in Kentucky. She found consolation in segregated services at a German Methodist church. By cooking and cleaning for Jacob Brunner, a St. Louis merchant hit hard by the Panic of 1857, "Aunt Clara" traveled by flatboat and west by wagon train to Kansas Territory. Passing through Leavenworth among settlers, cavalry, prospectors, traders, and drovers, she profited from the demand for her laundry. For companionship, she joined a Baptist church.

Pioneer to Colorado

After the Brunners left for California, Brown found a new job in April 1859 cooking, churning butter, and baking bread for 26 members of Benjamin Franklin Wadsworth's convoy from Arvada, Colorado, to placer mines on Pike's Peak. Constant walking beside the wagons required nightly darning of hose and repair of shoes. Safely through Kiowa territory, she reached the Republican River in central Colorado in June, a summer when 40,000 immigrants turned back.

Clara arrived during the gold rush, becoming the first black female at an historic locale overrun by brawlers and opportunists. As the region's population rose to 34,277, at Auraria (present-day Denver), Brown worked at the City Bakery and attended a Methodist church. She traveled west 40 miles to Gregory Gulch (currently Central City) by stagecoach, disguising herself as a white man's slave to gain passage. At an abandoned miner's cabin in 1861, she operated the new territory's first commercial laundry and endured the insults of rowdies on the street.

With earnings from child care, cooking, laundry, catering, rehabilitating the sick, and midwifery, "Old Aunt Clara" amassed $10,000. One of the wealthiest females in the West, she invested wisely in mining and real estate at Boulder, Denver, Idaho Springs, Georgetown, and Central City. She paid letter writers to collaborate in the rescue of relatives from bondage. The scramble for rescue from slavery ended on January 1, 1863, after President Abraham Lincoln issued the Emancipation Proclamation freeing 4 million bondsmen.

When the gold rush ended in 1863, Brown aided impoverished miners. In spring 1864, a flood destroyed her cabin in Mountain City (east Denver), leaving untouched only her properties in Boulder and Central City. At the end of the Civil War in April 1865, she bankrolled newly freed Southern blacks intent on an unfettered life and chance for education and advancement on the frontier.

Searching for Eliza

Following a 12-day stagecoach journey to Kentucky, in October 1865, Brown traced rumors of her family's whereabouts to Gallatin, Tennessee. Her brother Richard had disappeared in the shifting of blacks after the Emancipation Proclamation of 1863. She learned that her husband labored in cotton somewhere in the plantation South and Margaret died of lung disease at the Abednigo Shelton plantation in Morgantown, Kentucky. Eliza Jane had passed to James Covington in Logan County.

Brown bought train tickets for sixteen former slaves and orphans to follow her back to Denver. For the new members of her foster family, she found jobs. To make them self-sufficient, she paid for education for the illiterate. For her philanthropy, local citizens dubbed her the "Angel of the Rockies."

To further Christianity, Brown donated her dwelling for home prayer services and a Methodist Sunday school for all races. She began raising funds to build a permanent church. In 1872, the congregation completed St. James United Methodist Church. She also donated to a Catholic building project. After a fire destroyed three of Brown's investment properties in 1873, friends donated free lodging at a cottage in Denver into the late 1870s.

Brown, at age 79, increased her labors during the Black Exodus from the plantation South. In the years following Colorado's admission to the Union on August 1, 1876, she traveled to an "Exoduster" community in Kansas to help with farming the prairie. As a representative of Governor Frederick Walker Pitkin, she recruited laborers for the mining industry. Within the year, she lapsed into poverty, in part from being defrauded of $4,000.

In declining health from heart disease and diminished vision, Brown spent her last five years living on Arapaho Street in Denver with a friend and advertised a $1,000 reward for information about Eliza Jane. With help from the *Denver Republican,* a telegram and train trip on the Union Pacific on March 3, 1882, reunited her with her widowed daughter, Eliza Jane Brown Brewer, a launderer living 600 miles away at Council Bluffs, Iowa. Brown resided with Eliza Jane and reared Eliza's daughter Cindy in Denver, where Clara died on October 23, 1885.

Distinguished citizens listed Clara Brown as the first black female member of the Society of Colorado Pioneers. A stained glass window in the Colorado capitol honors Brown. A biographical opera, composer Henry Mollicone and librettist William Luce's *Gabriel's Daughter* (2003), honors Brown's good works with the solos "Lullaby," "Somewhere You Are, Eliza," and "Glory Day."

SOURCE

Baker, Roger. *Clara: An Ex-Slave in Gold Rush Colorado.* Central City, CO: Black Hawk, 2003.

Bush, George Washington (ca. 1779–1863), Isabella James Bush (1801–1866)

The first black pioneer to settle in Washington State, George Washington Bush had a lengthy career as soldier, *voyageur*, guide, stockman, trapper, and community builder. An only child from Philadelphia, Pennsylvania, he was born in 1779 to an Irish domestic and East (or possibly West) Indian shipman Matthew Bush of indeterminate race. Bush grew up under Quaker philosophy and studied in Philadelphia.

Devoted service relieved Bush from dependence on white employers. He joined his parents in working as a domestic in the home of Stevenson, a British shipper. At his employer's death, he inherited the Stevenson fortune. A strategist at the Battle of New Orleans on January 8, 1815, and soldier at the Black Hawk War (1832), Bush left the military to become a *voyageur* (trader). His journeys west in early manhood lack dates and places, but suggest that he trapped for the Hudson's Bay Company and farmed in Tennessee.

In Clay County, Missouri, on July 4, 1831, Bush wed a white Tennessee-born nurse, Isabella James, daughter and sister of German-American Baptist ministers. The couple produced ten sons—William Owen, Thomas Jackson January, Joseph Talbot "Tall," Rial Bailey, and Henry Sanford, who accompanied them to the frontier. Subsequently, they added Lewis Nisqually to the family as well as four infants who died young.

Escaping Racism

George and Isabella Bush left Jackson, Missouri, to escape a drought and elude anti–Negro persecution, notably, the outlawing of miscegenation and integration of schools. In a large train of eighty families, on May 1, 1844, Bush's household, Kentucky merchant Michael Troutman Simmons and wife Elizabeth Kindred Simmons, Elizabeth's parents, Samuel Crockett, Reuben Crowder, Jesse Ferguson, John Minto, George Jones, and James McAllister followed the Oregon Trail west under the command of Captain Robert Wilson Morrison. For the trip, Bush invested in six Conestoga wagons, a year's supplies, seeds and fruit trees, and silver and gold ingots hidden under a false floor.

The crossing took eight months. To ward off hunger, Bush bought additional provisions of flour and sugar for the Kindred and Jones families. At Fort Bridger in southwestern Wyoming, he supplied a company of thirty-one wayfarers for the last leg of the trip. The party reached The Dalles in Wasco County, Oregon, in December 1844.

Because of racist laws preventing blacks from purchasing land, the wagon train passed over the Columbia River to Fort Vancouver, a Hudson's Bay Company trading post northeast of Portland. After separating from the elder Kindreds in Oregon, in winter 1845, the Bush and Simmons families traveled up the Columbia and Cowlitz rivers by boat. Living communally, they shared a 40' × 20' longhouse on the prairie lighted by fish oil lamps and slept on woven mats atop fragrant cedar boughs.

Cutting a road from Cowlitz Landing as they struggled on to Bush Prairie, in mid–June, the sojourners began the 100-mile trek through thick forest on foot with wagons and pack train bearing hand tools and seeds. In July 1845, Simmons used a hiatus to scout the land north to the Deschutes River, a powerful current suited to grist milling and lumbering.

In crude dirt-floored shanties shared with another family, the Simmons and Bush households camped at Washougal, worked at logging and shingle making, and secured their livestock until late summer 1845. For provisions, they imported potatoes, wheat, peas, and cattle from Fort Nisqually, a British outpost in present-day Washington. Once settled in the wilderness, the settlers traded with the Nisqually and Siwash and received gifts of furs. With native guidance, the pioneers hunted, scavenged fern root and camas, and hunted and fished the region for deer, elk, bear, wild fowl, oysters, clams, and salmon.

Settling the Land

The Bush-Simmons party built a community at Bush Prairie on the southern coast of Puget Sound at New Market (present-day Tumwater, Washington), and raised wheat, peas, potatoes, rye, oats, and hops. The settlement of land north of the river introduced an American claim of 640 acres in territory disputed by Great Britain at the same time that Bush set a precedent for other pioneers of color. Bush violated Oregon law by farming while plotting to venture south to California or New Mexico if racism became virulent on Puget Sound. In addition to agriculture, he and Simmons collaborated on a flour fanning mill, granary, and sawmill and set up Simmons's timber company at Budd Inlet.

Under the Oregon Treaty of June 15, 1846, the Bush-Simmons claims fell within U.S. territory, but the Donation Land Act of 1850 or "Lash Law" excluded blacks from claiming parcels under penalty of a public flogging of twenty to thirty-nine strokes. Isabella Bush's turkey flock and the sale of butter, eggs, and wool turned the Bush farm into a paying proposition. The Bush-Simmons party drew pioneers to western Washington State, ensuring its sovereignty. To welcome newcomers, the two families met wagoneers on the trail and offered flour, root vegetables, and huckleberry pie and pudding as well as a temporary stay in one of a dozen log cabins built as a way station.

By 1853, seventeen families began farming Bush Prairie. Because of the poor yield of 1852–1853, the Bush family shared their crops with new settlers. Bush fought off cougars and bears from his livestock and raised a double row of saplings set upright in a trench as a stockade during the Indian war of 1855–1856, which pitted Chief Leschi's Nisqually, Puyallup, and Duwamish against whites. The Bush family survived the war and outbreaks of measles and smallpox, but did not secure rights to their property until the U.S. Congress granted ownership to the black pioneer on February 10, 1855. During this era, the family maintained a tutor to educate their sons.

By 1860, Bush cultivated 800 acres, a model agrarian stronghold for the state of Oregon, and opened his estate for barbecues and house parties. He died of cerebral hemorrhage on April 5, 1863, at his home at Bush Place, Thurston County. The oldest son, William Owen Bush, co-founded St. Peter Hospital in Olympia in April 1889 and Washington State University in 1890 and served in the 1889 sessions of the Washington Territorial legislature. Joseph Talbot Bush was a veteran of the Indian Wars and the Civil War. Five paintings completed by artist Jacob Lawrence in 1973 featuring the Bush-Simmons party with their families and livestock survive in Tacoma at the Washington State History Museum.

See also Simmons, Michael Troutman.

Source
Millner, Darrell. "George Bush of Tumwater: Founder of the First American Colony on Puget Sound." Columbia Magazine 8:4 (Winter 1994–1995).

Caldwell, Mathew H. (1798–1842)

An Indian fighter, organizer of the Gonzales-Sequin Rangers, and signer of the Texas Declaration of Independence, Mathew H. "Old Paint" Caldwell helped to secure Texas under American sovereignty. A native of Warren, Kentucky, born on March 8, 1798, he was a brother to Curtis, Meron, and Solomon W. Caldwell, the children of Scots father Matthew Curtis Caldwell and his second wife, Nancy White of North Carolina. The grandson of a Scots immigrant, the frontiersman wed Martha A. Caldwell around 1825 and settled his family in Gasconade, Missouri, in 1818, where he traded with Indians.

On February 20, 1831, Caldwell moved his wife and children Martha Elizabeth, Lucy Ann, and Hugh Curtis, named for his Scots grandfather, to Green DeWitt Colony in southeast Texas as subscribers to the Tennessee-Texas Land Company. In DeWitt, Gonzales, Guadalupe, and Lavaca counties, some 166 families formed a farming community.

In territory unprotected by a standing army, Caldwell purchased the James Hinds residence southwest of Hallettsville on June 22, 1831. Because of the ferocity and persistence of Comanche and Kiowa raiders, Caldwell joined the security force of Gonzales rangers, a volunteer patrol mounted on fast horses. In a period fraught with fears for family as Sam Houston tried to make peace with the Comanche, Caldwell's wife died at Gonzales around 1833.

In April 1835, Caldwell joined a posse of twenty-seven men in tracking some fifty Comanches for murdering thirteen French and Mexican traders. The posse slew most of the Indians and recovered stolen goods. When Lieutenant Francisco Castaneda and 100 Mexicans attempted to seize the Gonzales cannon, on October 1, 1835, Caldwell rode from farm to farm between Gonzales and Mina in Bastrop County calling men to the battle of Gonzales. To outwit the enemy, the rangers adopted a practice of relay firing, which provided cover for rifleman during reloading. From fellow volunteers, Caldwell earned the nickname "Old Paint" for the white hairs that dotted his beard and chest.

Lawman and State Leader

Although only semi-literate, Caldwell reported on the basic expenditures for maintaining a state militia. On December 18, 1835, he served as sub-contractor of blankets, soap, grain, coffee sugar, salt, corn meal, five tons of pork, and forty cattle for the provisional army, which he helped recruit on February 4. He also requisitioned powder, lead, and two cannon, a 4-pounder and a 6-pounder.

Because of an assault on his person on December 22, 1835, Caldwell dispatched rangers to apprehend settler Joseph P. Lawler, for whom Caldwell posted a $100 reward. Still recovering a month later, Caldwell urged the provisional government of Texas to support the Gonzales rangers with enough cash to buy supplies. He received $300 on January 20, 1836, and duly reported dispersals, including the hiring of two black drovers to supply steers for meat. The day-to-day struggle by Caldwell and his fellow pioneers secured Texas liberty from Mexico.

On March 1, 1836, Caldwell represented Gonzales at the Independence Convention of 1836 at Washington-on-the-Brazos and negotiated the right of settlers to appoint men to offices in the Gonzales Rangers. On March 3, 1836, Caldwell and fifty-nine fellow delegates signed the Texas Declaration of Independence legitimizing the Republic of Texas. Subsequent signatures on the Texas Constitution on March 17 completed legalities for forming a republic. As a convention courier, Caldwell carried news of the alliance to the Texas volunteer army and surveyed enemy positions on the frontier.

During the Texas-Indian Wars, the crisis that pioneers faced from the Comanche-Kiowa alliance involved Caldwell as both home owner and military captain. The fall of the Alamo on March 6, 1836, to Mexican general Santa Anna cost Gonzales County all of its thirty-two rangers. Caldwell responded by a combined attack by Delaware, Comanche, Kiowa, and Wichita in May by scouring the region for more volunteer rangers. In Washington County in May 17, 1837, he wed his second wife, Hannah Morrison, who helped him reclaim their land in fall after devastating Comanche raids.

At the burned ruins of Gonzales, Caldwell accepted appointment as the first county sheriff. By 1838, he received deeds to land in Guadalupe County as payment for the Gonzales Rangers and began clearing scrub and brush to ready lots for homes. He confidently plotted the town of Walnut Branch (present-day Seguin), defended the right of ministers to preach, and recruited twenty-nine frontiersmen as lawmen to guard the county's log fort.

On January 15, 1839, Caldwell accepted President Mirabeau Buonaparte Lamar's appointment as infantry captain and the task of protecting land surveyors and shielding Goliad from Santa Anna's troops. On February 4, Caldwell recruited volunteers for the Gonzales Ranging Company of Mounted Volunteers to protect the region from San Antonio to the Rio Grande. On March 23, 1839, Caldwell's men mustered as the First Regiment of Infantry of Texas and rousted Alcalde (magistrate) Vicente Córdova from Mill Creek back to Mexico. Four times during the autumn and winter, the rangers fought Indian attackers.

Fighter of Texas Enemies

As a result of failed hostage negotiations at San Antonio on March 19, 1840, Caldwell recovered from a rifle bullet to the right leg incurred at the Council House Fight against Chief Mukwahruh and his Penateka Comanches, a band prominent in Texas history. White soldiers retaliated, killing twelve Comanche chiefs and twenty-three warriors. In August, Caldwell led a company against Buffalo Hump's war party of 500 mounted braves. The Indians, enraged at an attack on their peace ambassadors, tortured and executed the remaining white and Mexican hostages and burned homes in eastern Texas, killing twenty-five settlers and stealing horses. Pursuit took Caldwell's rangers southeast to Victoria on the Gulf of Mexico.

As a result of a running gun battle at Plum Creek on August 12, 1840, with the combination of cannon and coordinated rifle fire, Caldwell's rangers defeated Buffalo Hump's massed forces. The Texans forced the Indians west from present-day Lockhart and recovered stolen horses, mules, and gold bullion. Superb Texas marksmanship cost the Comanches eighty casualties.

While representing settlers on the Texas Santa Fe expedition to Comancheria (eastern

New Mexico) to trade hostages with the Comanches, Caldwell and his scouting party suffered from dwindling food and water. On October 5, 1841, Mexican authorities captured him and his son Curtis at Tucumcari, New Mexico. Along with some three hundred Texans, Mathew and Curtis Caldwell trudged south for months to the dungeon of Perote Castle in Mexico City. Both survived.

Paroled in April 1842 under an oath to stop fighting Mexicans, Caldwell harangued 225 rangers amassed on Cibolo Creek on September 18, 1842, and led them to open prairie, site of the battle of Salado Creek. Faced by 500 Mexican cavalry, from positions in pecan trees along the creek bottom, Caldwell's men created a ruse indicating great numbers. The Texans, newly armed with Colt revolvers, crushed Mexican general Adrián Woll, a French mercenary who retreated over the Hondo and Rio Grande rivers to Coahuila.

Revered as the "Paul Revere of the Texas Revolution," Matthew Caldwell died on December 28, 1842, at his home in Gonzales from complications of his Mexican imprisonment and combat wounds. His defense of DeWitt colony settlers won him respect and the naming of Caldwell County, courthouse, town of Caldwell, and Caldwell House Hotel in Burleson County in his honor. A monument marks his tomb in the Gonzales Memorial Cemetery. In 1868, his son, Hugh Curtis Caldwell, became the first Dallas planner of the channel linking North Texas with seagoing vessels.

See also Sowell, Andrew Jackson.

Sources
Moore, Stephen L. *Savage Frontier: 1842–1845*. Denton: University of North Texas Press, 2010.
Moore, Steve. "Matthew 'Old Paint' Caldwell." *Texas Ranger Dispatch* 11 (Summer 2003).

Campbell, Robert (1804–1879), Virginia Kyle Campbell (1822–1882), William Lewis Sublette (1798–1845)

An unschooled Scots-Irish fur trader, financier, mediator, and entrepreneur, Robert Campbell spent five years on moneymaking expeditions to Dakota, Utah, and Wyoming territories before becoming a freight mogul in St. Louis, Missouri. A native of Plumbridge, County Tyrone, in Northern Ireland, he was born at Aughalane House on February 12, 1804, to Hugh Campbell, a member of the Argyle Clan and the Scots Presbyterian Church, and second wife Sarah Elizabeth Buchanan Campbell, a cousin of President James Buchanan. In penury after widowhood in 1810, Elizabeth raised six children on the proceeds of turning flax into linen. Until age eighteen, Robert assisted her by apprenticing at the weaver's trade.

Having no hope of an inheritance, Robert decided to treat chronic respiratory infection and seek his fortune with his older brother Hugh in America. In August 1822, Robert took passage on the schooner *Climax,* traveling from Londonderry by way of Newfoundland to Philadelphia. At Milton, North Carolina, he learned merchandising from David Kyle. To ease consumption of the lungs, in January 1824, Robert Campbell dressed in fringed buckskins and fur coat and booked a Mississippi River transport to Missouri. By autumn 1824, he settled in St. Louis clerking for John O'Fallon, a wealthy sutler for the U.S. Army.

Because Campbell answered an ad in the *Missouri Gazette* to ally with the Rocky Mountain Fur Company, in 1825, Hugh and Ann Campbell scolded their brother for choosing a frontier life. In Shoshone territory, Campbell clerked for fur traders William H. Ashley and Jedediah Strong Smith. With seventy mules carrying $20,000 in supplies, on November 1, 1825, the trio traveled with sixty-seven frontiersmen to the first Rocky Mountain rendezvous at Burnt Fork, Wyoming, on the Green River. The company arrived on May 25, 1826, at Bear Lake. After selling their wares, they transported pelts over the Bighorn and Yellowstone rivers to St. Louis.

In 1826, Campbell attended the second rendezvous, held in Cache Valley at Cove, Utah, where he met Lincoln, Kentucky, frontiersman William Lewis "Bill" Sublette, a descendent of Huguenot refugees who fled Sedan, France, in 1700 for safety in Virginia. In 1822, Sublette had departed life with his siblings in St. Charles,

In 1870, Robert Campbell worked out of Fort Laramie, Wyoming, as a commissioner to the Sioux led by Chief Red Cloud.

Missouri, to join William H. Ashley's fur trading company. Over the next decade, Campbell partnered with Sublette in buying beaver and otter pelts. At five more rendezvous in Utah, Idaho, and Wyoming, Campbell traded buffalo hides and transported goods via keelboat and supply train to Missouri.

Campbell proved his mettle in winter 1827–1828, when he survived attack by Blackfeet and a six-weeks trek in snowshoes. He left on the next seasonal route with Jim Bridger and ten other mountain men to trap among the Crow in northeastern Wyoming. The haul in September 1829 included forty-five packs of beaver pelts worth $22,476. With Indians along the Missouri River, Campbell and Sublette traded whiskey, grain alcohol, rum, and supplies—hatchets, shovels, knives, guns, lead, gunpowder, tobacco, kettles, meat, calico, thread, ribbon, blankets, and soap—and the mirrors, bells, buttons, and beads that whites traded with Indians. In hostile territory, the two men anticipated lethal struggles and exchanged verbal wills.

The Campbell-Sublette Partnership

Following a one-year sojourn in Ireland, Campbell revived his role in the fur trade. At the battle of Pierre's Hole, Idaho, on July 17, 1832, he saved his partner's life after a Blackfoot warrior shot Sublette through his left shoulder blade. Through objective observations and civil exchanges with natives, Campbell became an amateur ethnographer. He accepted a commission from Iron Wristband, an Eastern Shoshone chief, to write letters of peace to the Crow.

Sublette and Campbell erected trading posts along the Missouri River and stocked them with furs cached in trapping country. They completed Fort Sublette in 1833 on Dakota Territory's northwestern border with Montana near the juncture of the upper Missouri and Yellowstone rivers. In mid–September 1833, the partners vied successfully for buffalo robes against the American Fur Company's agents at Fort Union at a time when beaver pelts earned $12 per pound. An overturned shallow-draft bullboat, a wood-frame circle covered in hides, dumped Campbell in the Yellowstone River on December 31 along with his weapons, saddlebags, and all but four packs of beaver pelts. A Crow party recovered the boat.

On the Oregon Trail on June 1, 1834, Campbell and Sublette began erecting the wood stockade of Fort William (later Fort Laramie), a trading center with the Assiniboin and Cree in southeastern Wyoming at the confluence of the Laramie and North Platte rivers. For travelers moving west, the partners conveyed mail and goods by bullboat. According to Campbell's diary, by September 22, he moved into a dirt-floored house and subsequently hosted amateur hunters from Holland and Germany for dinner. On December 6, 1836, a Philadelphia weekly, the *National Atlas and Tuesday Morning Mail,* turned Campbell's letters to his brother Hugh into a travelogue detailing encounters with Jim Bridger, Kit Carson, and Crow chief Rotten Belly.

Dosed on quinine, bitters, and morphine, Campbell recuperated from intermittent chills and fever in spring 1835 at Sulphur Springs, Sublette's resort and racetrack overlooking the Missouri River. After selling Fort William at a profit, on January 1, 1836, the partners renegotiated their business arrangement. They abandoned the dwindling beaver pelt business, which fell over 71 percent to $3.50 per pound, and opted for standard wholesaling of imported and domestic garments, shoes, and hats from a city warehouse.

In November, Campbell met a first-generation Irish American, Virginia Jane Kyle, the 13-year-old cousin of Hugh's wife and an alumna of Freeman's Finishing School. Virginia tended Campbell's sickbed at Hugh's home in Philadelphia. Robert recovered enough strength to found Sublette & Campbell, a dry goods emporium on North Main Street in St. Louis. Against the advice of brothers Hugh and William Robert courted Virginia.

Husband and Father

During economic hard times brought on the Panic of 1837, Robert Campbell invested in a rental farm, home lots, and sawmill in Fenton, Missouri, and freight hauling in St. Louis and Kansas City. He married Virginia on February 24, 1841, in her hometown of Raleigh, North Carolina. Residing at the Planters House Hotel in St. Louis and subsequently at Lucas Place, Virginia freed the three slaves she received as an inheritance from her father, Hazlett Kyle. She welcomed to the Campbell family home a sister, Eleanor Kyle Otey, wife of a slave trader, and their mother, Lucy Ann Winston Kyle.

On January 15, 1842, Campbell purchased Sublette's share of their business and renamed his retail firm R. Campbell & Company, merchandizer of dry goods and native wares. He assumed presidency of the First Bank of Missouri in 1843 and branched out to the St. Louis Hotel Company, St. Louis Insurance Company, and board chair of the Merchants National Bank of St. Louis. After the death of Sublette on July 23, 1845, at Pittsburg, Missouri, Campbell continued to expand trade. His steamboats—the packet *A. B. Chambers* and the sidewheeler *Robert Campbell Jr.*—carried passengers and freight up and down the Missouri as far as forts William and Union and returned with buffalo hides, which earned up to $50 per pelt.

Campbell developed a reputation for honesty, patriotism, and commitment to the Democratic Party. In the first year of the Mexican-American War of 1846–1848, he served as colonel in the Missouri Militia, recruited and drilled volunteers, and raised money and supplies throughout the Mississippi Valley. During the Irish famine of 1847, Campbell shipped seed to tenant farmers in Glenella Valley. By 1848, his business flourished with the help of junior partner William Campbell, selling pioneering supplies to frontiersmen setting out for the far west. R.&W. Campbell Company also stocked new locations along the frontier.

Campbell joined negotiations to stem Indian attacks on settlers and railed against corrupt politicians. On the Platte River plain, he joined Father Pierre Jean DeSmet at the 1851 Fort Laramie Council. At the largest warrior conference in North America, 10,000 Sioux, Crow, Cheyenne, Arapaho, Aricara, Shoshone, Mandan, and Minnetaree attended discussions and, on September 17, signed a peace treaty promising nonviolence toward pioneers traversing the Oregon Trail, which totaled 400,000 emigrants by 1869.

Robert and Virginia moved into Lucas Place in 1854 and contributed Irish shamrocks and Celtic embellishments to Missouri architecture. In 1859, Hugh and Mary Kyle Campbell left commercial ventures in Philadelphia and joined Robert and Virginia in operating the family's St. Louis emporium. The closing of the Mississippi River during the Civil War imposed hardships on their river trade. On September 17, 1863, the Union Army commandeered the 450-ton sidewheeler *Robert Campbell, Jr.*, which plied the waters between Memphis and Vicksburg until the vessel burned on September 28. Campbell invested in New Mexico gold mining and cattle markets and, in August 1866, purchased the Southern Hotel, the finest luxury quarters in St. Louis.

At the peak of his career in 1868, Campbell accepted President Ulysses S. Grant administration's offer of a place on the Indian Commission, for which he toured major reservations. Campbell joined Virginia in providing cash and transportation that June for the DeSmet peace council and food and clothing missions among the hard-pressed Sioux at Fort Rice and Fort Sully. In 1870, Campbell returned to Fort Laramie as a commissioner to the Sioux led by Chief Red Cloud. The Scotsman's investments advanced passenger travel between Missouri and the Gulf of Mississippi and amassed $8 million in stock, interest in two railroads, 5,000 acres of land, and cash reserves of $2 million, which he willed to his sons.

A backer of Campbell's visions for St. Louis, Virginia devoted herself to domestic needs. She survived 19 pregnancies, but reared only three sons to adulthood—Hugh, Hazlett Kyle, and James Alexander Campbell, all of whom she homeschooled and introduced to culture during European tours. The birth defects and illnesses that killed her other children involved poisoning from lead plumbing and cholera, pneumonia, and diphtheria polluting untreated water from the Mississippi River.

A philanthropist and progressive in her own right, Virginia Campbell applied considerable initiative and charm to St. Louis society. She served the Mount Vernon Ladies Association, a sisterhood that helped restore and preserve the Virginia home, furnishings, and deer park of George and Martha Custis Washington. In April 1873, Lucas House entertained prominent guests, including President Ulysses S. Grant, First Lady Julia Dent Grant, and General William T. Sherman.

At Robert Campbell's death in St. Louis on October 10, 1879, his family interred him at Bellefontaine Cemetery. At Virginia's death on January 30, 1882, her grave contributed to a Campbell enclave of both parents and 12 of their children. Family correspondence preserved eyewitness details of pivotal moments in U.S. history. In 1989, restorers moved Robert Campbell's stone manse in Plumbridge to a park outside Omagh, Ireland. The Campbell House Museum, noted on the National Register of Historic Places, retains its federalist appeal.

Sources

Bennemann, William. *Men in Eden: William Drummond Stewart and Same-Sex Desire in the Rocky Mountain Fur Trade.* Lincoln: University of Nebraska Press, 2012.

MacCulloch, Patrick C. *The Campbell Quest: A Saga of Family and Fortune.* St. Louis: Missouri History Museum, 2009.

Carr, Sarah Pratt (1850–1935), Robert Henry Pratt (1824–1920), Louisa Merrill Pratt (1827–1919), Byron Oscar Carr (1835–1913), Narcissa Whitman (1808–1847), Marcus Whitman (1802–1847)

Unitarian minister, missionary, writer, suffragist, and librettist Sarah Amelia Pratt Carr lived the trials of a Western American and memorialized one of the frontier's female martyrs. Born on July 17, 1850, in Freeport, Maine, to Louisa Prince Merrill and seaman and railroad construction manager Robert Henry Pratt, she claimed sixteenth-century forebears from Chesham and East Stafford, England. In 1849 before her birth, her father traveled by sea around Cape Horn to San Francisco and settled near the Napa Valley orchards and vineyards of his brothers, William Augustus and George Lincoln Pratt.

In the first years of the California Gold Rush, Robert Pratt began work in the mines at Trinity River on the California-Oregon border. In toddlerhood in 1852, Sarah traveled by mule back with her mother some 30 miles over the Isthmus of Panama to reach the Pacific coast and join her father. The family located in the southwest at Santa Rosa, California, in 1857 to farm and raise livestock.

The Transcontinental Railroad

Robert Pratt earned lasting fame as a facilitator of the Transcontinental Railroad. Beginning on October 30, 1863, in northeastern California, he supervised 350 laborers in completing a 60-mile toll road, which opened on June 15, 1864, averaging forty-six wagons per day. The job kept the Pratts on the move and frequently separated Robert from his wife and daughter. For travel, they relied on the Wells Fargo stagecoach company and the California & Oregon Stage Line. On October 31, 1864, they celebrated the entry of Nevada to the Union as the thirty-sixth state.

In a series of work camps along the Dutch Flat and Donner Lake Wagon Road northwest of Lake Tahoe on the California-Nevada boundary, Sarah observed Robert purchasing wagons and teams, clearing away snow, laying the roadbed, and hauling branches, shrubs, and roots for fuel. Progress coincided with the addition of Nebraska to the Union in 1865 and the displacement of Washoe, Paiute, and Shoshone natives, who found work with rail crews.

Louisa Pratt produced Alice, Eliza Talbot, and Henry Merrill Pratt, all of whom died in early childhood. Three more siblings—Harriet Emily, Bradley Newcomb, and Carlin Louise Pratt—lived to adulthood. Beginning in 1867, the family occupied a railroad car on a siding in Carlin, Nevada. By March 5, 1868, Robert oversaw completion of the Virginian & Truckee Railroad, which linked Virginia City to Carson City. As wagon master of materials from Reno, Nevada, to Promontory Summit, Utah, in 1869, Robert began grading roadbeds for the Central Pacific Railway at Dutch Flat and Downieville, the shortest, cheapest route to Washoe, Nevada, and the Humboldt and Reese Rivers.

Daily from the Missouri River to the Sierra Nevada, Sarah lived the progress of the 70-pound steel rails, which extended 560 miles from Reno, Nevada, to Utah. Guards deterred hostile Paiutes, who obstructed builders, seized two wagon trains, rustled stock in the Mormon Basin, and attacked pioneers in their false-front stores, cabins, tents, huts, and lean-tos. While residing on the Mojave Desert, Sarah profited from her cultured New England parents, who hired tutors and governesses to upgrade her education.

Sarah later wrote about the visionary builders Collis Potter Huntington and Leland Stanford and about William "Uncle Billy" Dodge driving the Butterfield Overland Mail, the world's longest cross-country route. As silver mining flourished and lured more speculators to the area, she regretted the racism that pitted frontiersmen against Paiutes. She also pitied blue-coated Chinese immigrants, whom overseers herded like cattle and disciplined like dogs with whips.

On May 10, 1869, Robert Pratt participated in the hammering of the golden spike at Promontory, Utah. As the rails inched along, he advanced to transportation master at Salt Lake City in 1872, over the snowy peaks at Sacramento, California, in 1879, and on to San Francisco. At the end of 30 years' service to the Central Pacific Railroad, he retired to a 160-acre ranch and vineyard near Napa Valley, one of the world's lushest grape-growing terroir.

A Unitarian Missionary

Sarah Pratt's wedding took place in the family rail car at Carlin. On February 15, 1872, she married banker Byron Oscar Carr of Concord, New York. The couple had met while Byron served the Central Pacific Railroad as rail division superintendent at Truckee, California. A Civil War veteran of the New York Cavalry and widower with two children, he sired Sarah's three—Mary Louise, Wray Torrey, and George Pratt Carr, who died at age two in Albany, New York, in 1877.

The Carr family migrated from Memphis, Tennessee, to Louisville, Kentucky, where Byron inspected steamboats on the Mississippi River. In Truckee, California, in 1883, he superintended the Southern Pacific Railroad. At San

In 1869, a golden spike joined the Central Pacific and Union Pacific rail lines at Promontory, Utah.

Francisco, Carr managed the People's Home Savings Bank in the late 1880s and early 1890s and weathered a run on the bank in January 1891. After the bank failed in March 1894, Carr advanced to the Bank of Lemoore, California, and built an estate, Valle Vista, at St. Helena north of Oakland, California.

Mentored by the Reverend Charles William Wendte of Oakland, a German-American Unitarian theologian, in the 1890s, Sarah Carr ministered to the girls and women of rural Unitarian congregations in Hanford, Lemoore, Visalia, and Fresno, California. At Lemoore in 1893, she initiated a women's club with 29 members who raised public health standards in the San Joaquin Valley. At her ordination in 1894, wellwishers accepted her into the ministry and valued her poem "Heritage" (1894), a reflection on the myriad experiences that form an individual's life.

Writing the Pioneer Story

After Byron Carr's illness forced the family to relocate to Seattle, Washington, in 1900, they lived with Sarah's stepson, Eugene Merwin Carr, and his wife, Alice Preston Carr. Byron and Sarah eked out a living from Byron's army pension and relied on the aid of a Norwegian servant. Sarah and her mother joined the National American Woman Suffrage Association and promoted full citizenship for females.

After Byron Carr's death on November 1, 1913, Sarah returned to Los Angeles and wrote verse and novels, including the children's book *Billy To-Morrow* (1909) and the historical retrospect *The Iron Way: A Tale of the Builders of the West* (1907). In 1908, the historical novel, which she dedicated to her father, appeared in five newspapers in Oklahoma and Ohio.

For *Narcissa*, or *The Cost of Empire* (1911), a four-act opera written by her daughter, Mary Carr Moore, Sarah composed the libretto. The text focused on the violence erupting from an ethnic clash in the Northwest Territory between the Cayuse and Nez Percé Indians and two Presbyterian medical missionaries to Oregon Territory (present-day Walla Walla, Washington), Marcus Whitman and Narcissa Prentiss Whitman, the first white woman to cross the Rocky Mountains. From their departure with seven covered wagons from Angelica, New York, in March 1836 until the massacre that killed them on November 29, 1847, the Whitmans supported the advance of Protestantism on the Pacific coast.

With a granddaughter and two great-grandsons, Sarah Pratt Carr spent her widowhood in Los Angeles at her daughter's home. At her death in San Diego in 1935, Sarah's name appeared among the pioneers of California and the Unitarian ministry.

Sources

Farquhar, Francis P. *History of the Sierra Nevada*. Berkeley: University of California Press, 2007.
Gullett, Gayle. *Becoming Citizens: The Emergence and Development of the California Women's Movement, 1880–1911*. Champaign: University of Illinois Press, 2000.
Wright, Cynthia J., and Judy Cox-Finney. *Lemoore*. Charleston, SC: Arcadia, 2010.

Chiles, Joseph Ballinger (1810–1885)

A guide for pioneer trains, Joseph Ballinger Chiles settled in Davis, California, and operated Rancho Laguna de Santos Calle and a grain mill and ferry. Born in Clark County, Kentucky, on July 16, 1810, to Sarah Ballinger and farmer Henry Chiles, a veteran of the War of 1812, Joseph grew up in a large household—brothers James C., John, Richard Ballinger, Christopher Lillard, Joel Franklin "Frank," William G., Henry T., and Alexander M.E. and sisters Susanna and Elizabeth J. Chiles. The family claimed English forebears from Jamestown Colony and ancestral heroes of the American Revolution.

In Jackson County, Missouri, at age 20, Joseph Chiles operated a farm and raised livestock, a training ground for his frontier cattle breeding. At Winchester on August 1, 1830, he wed Kentuckian Mary "Polly" Ann Stevenson. The couple produced James Ramsay "Joe Jim," Frances "Fanny," Elizabeth E. "Lizzie," and Mary E. "Lizzie," Chiles. In 1832, Joseph served the county as justice of the peace.

In 1837, Chiles's wife died. Along with his brothers Henry and James, he volunteered for a Missouri infantry regiment to fight under Colonel Zachary Taylor in the Seminole Wars, notably, the Battle of Lake Okeechobee, Florida, on December 25, 1837. Henry died in the fray, which killed 649 or more than 81 percent of an 800-man regiment. James refused field dressing of a wound to the side, which he survived.

Venturing West to California

In 1841, Chiles left his son "Joe Jim" and three daughters in Jackson County, Missouri, with his brother, Joel Franklin Chiles, wife Azubah, and the family's thirteen children. In May, Joseph led the thirty-three-member John Bartleson-John Bidwell Party and their oxen and farm wagons in a 5-month trek from Sapling Grove, Missouri, to Fort Hall, Idaho. Journeying over the Sierra Nevada with Belgian missionary-cartographer Pierre Jean DeSmet, Jesuit priests Nicholas Point and Gregory Mengarini, and three Catholic laymen, the party encountered Cheyenne and Shoshone, mapped Indian villages, and purchased for food balls of honey mixed Indian style with insects. On November 4, 1841, the Bartleson-Bidwell convoy became the first immigrant train to reach California.

In 1842, Chiles joined explorer and trapper Charles Hopper in an expedition to central California and earned a reputation for hunting grizzly bears and playing the fiddle. On return from Sutter's Fort to Missouri in April 1843 with a party of thirteen, Chiles came close to death outside Santa Fe on the Old Spanish Trail from an attack by Apaches, masters of guerrilla raiding tactics. The 4,000-mile expedition complete, Chiles pursued his pioneering career of recruiter for seven additional convoys, beginning with the sixty-member Chiles Party. Laden with supplies for trade, the company set out from Independence with eight wagons in late May 1843, the year that 1,000 settlers headed for Oregon Territory. Feeding on deer and wild turkeys along the way, they reached Fort Laramie on July 17, 1843.

The Chiles party hired mountain man Joseph Reddeford "Joe" Walker to guide them south over the Rocky Mountains. At Fort

Boise, Idaho, on the Malheur River, John Boardman and thirty mounted explorers from the group made their way into northern California. Upon reaching the Raft River, Idaho, on September 20, the pack train separated from the wagon train and turned south, blazing the California Trail from Fort Hall, Idaho, to the Humboldt River, a region notorious for patchy, stubby grass and drinking water priced at $2 per gallon. Finding buffalo depleted, they camped at Bear River, Utah, and bagged antelope, bear, deer, and elk for food. The company reached Sutter's Fort on November 10, 1843.

A California Settler

In 1844, Chiles learned from a Canadian trapper about Spanish land grants in what became Chiles Valley. With dual citizenship in the U.S. and Mexico, he purchased from the Mexican government Rancho Catacula. He completed transfer of 8,545.72 acres from Governor José Manuel Micheltorena on November 9, 1844. At his cabin and the subsequent adobe, he raised cattle, hogs, and mules and distilled whiskey. In 1848, he led the first wagon train through Carson Pass and pioneered the cut-off through the Forty-Mile Desert from Humboldt Sink to the Carson River.

Chiles improved his investment with a dam, blacksmith forge, and wagon shop. The 1848 Treaty of Guadalupe Hidalgo affirmed his property rights. During the California Gold Rush of 1849, he transported a millstone over the Sierra Nevada and ran a flour mill on the Sacramento River, where he sold his products

After Joseph Ballinger Chiles blazed the California Trail through the Sierra Nevada in 1843, wagon trains wound over rutted roads from settlement to settlement.

under the Catacula label into the 1880s. He and dairyman Jerome C. Davis, husband of Joseph's daughter Mary Amanda, and nephew Isaac Skinner "Ike" Chiles managed a rope ferry that earned some $2,500 per week.

On November 8, 1850, along the Arroyo de Napa (Chiles Creek) in Davis, California, land barons Marcos and Manuel Vaca sold Chiles 4,327 acres of Rancho Laguna de Santos Calle for $10,000. Chiles transported his children to their new home and served as vice president of the Society of California Pioneers, an organization dedicated to preserving the state's cultural history. His brother William followed the family to California, where he contracted cholera from contaminated water and died in 1851.

Chiles built a two-story ranch house for his family. On his last visit to Missouri on December 25, 1853, he wed Margaret Jane Garnhart, a 26-year-old Virginian, and returned with her to Napa County. The couple reared six children—William Garnhart, Amelia Jane, Susan Anna "Susie," Dixie Virginia, Joseph Ballinger, Jr., and Henry Lee Chiles.

Details of Joseph Chiles's later years remain fragmentary. By October 1858, the state and county was levying taxes of $1,259.08 on Chiles's immense holdings. Widowed a second time, on April 14, 1883, he married Californian Mary Elizabeth "Mollie" Owens. Joseph Chiles sickened the following year, transferring responsibility for his ranch to Henry Lee Chiles, and died in St. Helena, California, in June 25, 1885.

Source

McLynn, Frank. *Wagons West: The Epic Story of America's Overland Trails.* New York: Grove, 2002.

Coleman, William Tell (1824–1893)

A notable shipper, borax miner, and the "Lion of the Vigilantes," community builder William Tell Coleman helped to quell violence and build industry in San Francisco, California. A native Kentuckian, he was born of English-Irish-Scots-Welsh lineage at Cynthiana on February 29, 1824, to Baptist parents, Synthia Davis Chinn and Napoleon Bonaparte Coleman, an attorney and state legislator. William Tell descended from planters and academics dating back to the Norman-French De Cheyn line.

Orphaned by age nine, Coleman grew up on the tobacco farm of his grandfather Raleigh Chinn and learned to train racehorses. Coleman longed to attend West Point, but wisely accepted apprenticeships in surveying, insurance, and lumber concerns in Wisconsin Territory. After studying civil engineering at St. Louis University in 1840, he required treatment for consumption in Florida and Louisiana. While he superintended his uncle's plantation at Baton Rouge, readings in frontier literature turned his attention to opportunities on the Pacific Coast.

At age 25, Coleman and his younger brother, DeWitt Clinton Coleman, organized a westering expedition. In May 1849, they left St. Louis for San Francisco by the Mormon Trail, a 1,300-mile route from Nauvoo, Illinois, to Salt Lake City, Utah. On passing through Salt Lake City, he expressed pity for destitute Mormons by donating bacon, flour, sugar, coffee, and tea to their pioneer parties. He reached Sacramento on August 14, a profitable commercial center where horses sold for as much as $80 each, and opened William T. Coleman & Company, Contractors and Builders.

A California Home

By speculating on apple pies, flour, pickles, potatoes, barley, and patent medicine, Coleman exploited the residents of mining towns. He found panning for gold along the American River in Placerville, California, more dangerous and less lucrative than commerce. On January 1, 1850, he moved to San Francisco. At California and Corner Front streets in 1852, he managed a line of clipper ships loaded with mining and panning tools, weapons, tents, clothing, and canned fruit and salmon. His probity advanced the reputation of California merchants and financiers.

During the populist movement of 1851, Coleman directed civic leaders and merchant members of the San Francisco Society of Regulators, a law and order brotherhood that mustered a militia and suppressed criminals and pirates. Through illegal deportation, jailing, kangaroo courts, and more than one hundred hangings, over a five-year period, the vigilantes quelled arson, robbery, and murder. To uplift city integrity, Coleman superintended the disempowerment of corrupt city management.

On August 11, 1852, Coleman married 24-year-old Caroline M. Page "Carrie" Gay, widowed daughter of Daniel Dearborn Page, the second mayor of St. Louis. The Colemans occupied a house on Mission Avenue, where Carrie slowly recovered from bronchitis. The couple produced daughters Carrie Bird, Lillia Carrie, and Julia M. and sons William Tell, Jr., Robert Lewis, Clark Page, and Carlton Chinn Coleman.

Coleman promoted citizenship by presiding over the Chamber of Commerce and the California Pioneers and serving on the board of California State College. In 1853, he volunteered to tend the sick on the steamer *Tennessee* as it journeyed from Panama to San Francisco. To lower the mortality rate, he ordered fumigation with burning sulfur and deck cleaning. His crew soothed fever with the ship's supply of ice.

Investments

From an office in New York City, in 1857, Coleman operated the global shipping of mining supplies, ores, wool, hides, and salmon from Riverside and Los Angeles as far away as London. Before the Civil War, he advocated support for the Union. Afterward, he promoted the Freedmen's Bureau and boosted the town of San Rafael, California. He bought 8,000 acres in 1871, and built a courthouse and warehouse. To irrigate his parks, orchards, and vineyards, he developed the Marin County waterworks with supplies directed from Lagunitas Creek through a wood flume, a system pictured in May 1875 in *Harper's Weekly*.

In 1871, Coleman invested in borax strikes in Columbus Marsh, Nevada, and bought shares in the Sonoma and Marin Railroad. In San Rafael, he funded the Hotel Tamalpais and Hotel Rafael, which offered resort amenities of tennis courts, stables, and observation tower. Turmoil during rail strikes in July 1877 aroused anti–Asian prejudice, which Coleman battled through legal policing. The Committee of Public Safety, a community regiment of 6,500 men armed with pick handles, enforced an evening curfew. Employing a ward system, volunteers prevented arson by Chinese laborers and expelled criminals from the peninsula.

Following the discovery of a boron compound called ulexite in remote desert land in 1881, Coleman pioneered the borax industry, a source of enamel glaze, non-toxic detergent and deodorizers, cosmetics, and fire retardants. He and partner Francis Marion Smith invested $20,000 in the Greenland Salt and Borax Mining Company. In Inyo County, Coleman named a Colemanite mine and Furnace Creek Ranch "Lila C" after his daughter, who died at age six along with 8-year-old Julia from epidemic diphtheria, for which the only treatment was a throat swab of kerosene.

Two employees, a muleskinner (teamster) and a swamper (assistant driver), ran each twenty-mule team from the Harmony Borax Works in Death Valley at Furnace Creek Springs on the California-Nevada border. A pair of horses and eighteen mules pulled steel and oak double wagons loaded with 10 short tons (9 metric tons) 160 miles, a ten-day trip across the Mojave Desert to Wadsworth, Nevada. The 100-foot transportation system, a Western icon, suffered no losses or crashes.

Over a six-year period, the borate refinery evaporated and crystallized ore. The company shipped 10,000 tons (9 metric tons) of salt, soda, hand soap, and borax via the Death Valley Railroad to the Tonopah and Tidewater Railroad and south to the Atchison, Topeka and Santa Fe. In summer, when desert heat halted activity across the sand and gravel of the badlands and over the Panamint Mountains, Coleman shifted his industry to the Amargosa Borax Works at Resting Spring.

A borate strike in the Calico Mountains in 1883 initiated new investments for Coleman and research into borax refinement at his lab in Alameda, California. He placed his son-in-law, William Robertson, over the new addition. By 1885, Coleman's mining of $1 million in salt outpaced gold and silver mine production.

After Congress removed tariffs on imported

borax, Coleman's bankruptcy on May 7, 1888, and the loss of $2 million shocked Californians. In 1890, his mining venture passed to Smith, who consolidated refineries under the name Pacific Coast Borax Company, a producer of refined borax and boracic acid. After selling his San Rafael home and the Marin County waterworks to settle debts, Coleman died on November 22, 1893, leaving $580,000 to his family and $20,000 in legacies to the local Catholic and Protestant orphanages.

Sources

Fay, Ted. *The Twenty Mule Team of Death Valley.* Charleston, SC: Arcadia, 2012.

Gibson, Jack. *Mount Tamalpais and the Marin Municipal Water District.* Charleston, SC: Arcadia, 2012.

Cope, Sister Marianne (1838–1918)

A nurse administrator and medical missionary to Molokai, Hawaii, Marianne Cope achieved sainthood by devoting herself to the care of lepers. A Hessian from Heppenheim in West Germany, she was born Maria Anna Barbara Koob on January 23, 1838, to Barbara Witzenbacher and Peter Koob, a farmer and day laborer. After immigrating with four siblings to Utica, New York, in 1839, she attended the St. Joseph Parish School, facilitated by the St. Joseph Society, which aided German immigrants.

At age thirteen, Cope left school to work in a clothing factory and delayed her vocation to a nunnery by supporting her invalid father and his ten children. In summer 1862, a month after the death of Peter Koob, 24-year-old Cope entered St. Francis Convent, a Franciscan nunnery in Syracuse. On November 19, 1862, she adopted the name Sister Marianne and chose teaching as her calling.

A spiral of challenging assignments threatened Cope's tenacity and health. She taught German immigrant children at several New York institutions. In 1865, she advanced to principal at St. Peter's School, a newly opened German-American academy at Oswego, vicaria (assistant minister) of St. Anthony's Convent, and mother superior of the Convent of St. Teresa.

In 1866, Cope co-founded New York's first Catholic hospital, St. Elizabeth's Hospital in Utica, a four-story outreach begun in a tenement. She instituted high standards of cleanliness and shocked the public by admitting all patients, regardless of ethnicity or race. Her philosophy of care for the poor and for alcoholics modernized attitudes toward racial integration and addiction. As superintendent of St. Joseph's Hospital Health Center in 1869, she furthered the transfer of Geneva Medical College from Hobart College to the College of Physicians and Surgeons at Syracuse University and employed medical students in patient care.

A Pioneer in Hawaii

Upon receiving a request from King David Kalakaua to assist Hawaii's lepers, Cope embraced the challenge of ministering to victims of a contagious disease, a task rejected by fifty other congregations. The leprosy epidemic, which had raged in Hawaii from 1863, dated to the arrival of Chinese immigrants. The disease had spread so rapidly among native Hawaiians that, in 1865, King Kamehameha V feared for the survival of the race. He exiled 140 victims under permanent quarantine to Kalawao, a 4-square-mile colony on Molokai, without benefit of medical treatment. In addition to illness and certain death from leprosy, the sick had survived the volcanic eruption of Mauna Loa and a subsequent earthquake in late March 1868. Another mass confinement in 1874 by King Lunalilo had raised the colony's population by 500 lepers, who endured a three-day cyclone on November 20, 1874.

With Rosalia McLaughlin, Martha Kaiser, Leopoldina Burns, Mary Charles Huffmann, and Cresentia Eilers, Cope left eighty Sisters of St. Francis behind and sailed aboard the iron steamer S.S. *Mariposa*, reaching Honolulu on November 8, 1883. At Kakaako Hospital in Oahu, the women received and diagnosed lepers from the island cluster before assigning them to a Molokai colony, a 2,500-acre complex at Kalaupapa Peninsula. Without assistance, the sick resided in caves and prefabricated huts and survived on provisions tossed from an escarpment or floated in on the tide.

At Wailuku, Maui, in 1884, Cope established Malulani Hospital, a name chosen by Princess Liluokalani meaning "under heaven's protection." Government dismay at a deteriorating situation in the overcrowded Kakaako Hospital recalled Cope to Oahu, where the odor of decay from sores combined with maggots, lice, and bedbugs to horrify lay nurses and visitors. Cope demanded sanitation and more compassionate care for patients, who huddled on straw beds in filthy wards.

In recognition of Cope's cheerful consolation of lepers, the king named her a Companion of the Royal Order of Kapiolani. In November 1885, she promoted the rescue of the daughters of lepers at the Kapiolani Home, an orphanage operated by nuns. She impressed the sisters by supplying hair ribbons, scarves, and pretty dresses to the patients as well as tablecloths in the dining hall and bedspreads and paintings to brighten rooms.

A Permanent Assignment

The closure of Kakaako Hospital in 1887 and the banishment of 1,200 lepers resulted in Cope's opening of a home for female lepers at Kalaupapa. She and two sisters, Leopoldina Burns and Vincentia McCormick, accepted the assignment along with permanent social ostracism. In November 1888, Cope settled at the compound and tended Father Damien de Veuster, the leper's salvation, until his death on April 15, 1889. She assumed responsibility for young male lepers at the Boys' Home at Kalawao and directed a donation from sugar factor Henry Perrine Baldwin to the construction of Baldwin House, a girls' school.

At the commune, Cope gained renown for retrieving lepers from social degradation as untouchable outcasts. Her upgrading of lives ended residency in straw shelters and replaced rags with dignified clothing. In addition to supplying nutritious meals, she introduced gardens, music, needlework, and counseling and freed non–Catholics for pastoral visits.

In 1895, Cope divided the burgeoning leper colony into residential cottages at the Bishop Home for girls and women and a separate mission to sons of male lepers under the supervision of four Brothers of the Sacred Heart of Jesus and Mary. Wracked by lung hemorrhages, she retreated to a wheelchair in old age and died of heart and kidney failure on August 9, 1918. In her memory, the Sisters of Saint Francis expanded their mission to a nursing school, child development center for emotional problems, home health care service, and chronic care facility for the elderly. Honors to Mother Marianne include beatification in 2005, a shrine at the Syracuse motherhouse, and, in 2010, a portrait statue in Honolulu. She achieved canonization in 2012.

Sources
Kuhns, Elizabeth. *The Habit: A History of the Clothing of Catholic Nuns.* New York: Random House, 2007.
O'Malley, Vincent J. *Saints of North America.* Huntington, IN: Our Sunday Visitor, 2004.

Cowles, George A. (1836–1887), Jennie Frances Blodgett Cowles Santee (1838–1931)

The national raisin king, farmer and financier George Algernon Cowles developed two ranches in San Diego, California, with orchards, grain and potato fields, and vineyards. A native farmer in Hartford, Connecticut, he was born of English colonial ancestry at Bloomfield on April 5, 1836, the seventh of the twelve children of Susan Walker and Algernon Sidney Cowles, a broadcloth weaver. While attending night school and the Commercial College, at age fourteen, he apprenticed in selling dry goods and furniture for B.&W. Hudson.

On September 25, 1858, in Chicopee, Massachusetts, Cowles married Jane Frances "Jennie" Blodgett of English colonial ancestry, the daughter of education advocate Roswell Blodgett and treasurer of a Congregationalist Sunday school in Lowell. After service in the Connecticut infantry of the Union Army, in 1865, Cowles built a cotton mill that burned within the year. He moved to New York, where he established a cotton brokerage and, in 1866, presided over the New York Cotton Goods Exchange.

In retirement in 1869, Cowles and his wife toured Europe, California, and Florida, where malaria compromised his health. To repel water and control moth infestation and mildew, Cowles patented a processing solution for cotton canvas, flannel, and wool kersey, lightweight broadcloth. He sold his processed fabrics to quartermasters of the U.S. military until 1875.

The El Cajon Valley

Traveling by stage from San Francisco to southern California, Cowles scouted real estate in the El Cajon valley in San Diego County and bought the Miner House and two ranches, Magnolia and Woodside, a total of 4,000 acres. In spring 1878, he settled at Cowlestown and began developing a thoroughbred horse and cattle business as well as roses and ornamentals. He profited from planting cereal grains, olive slips, Alexandria variety muscat grapes, thirty-two types of vines, and apple, peach, pear, apricots, persimmon, plum, and nut trees.

On cropland valued as high as $150 per acre, Cowles dug a 20-foot well, accessed by a 16-foot windmill for residential use, but he farmed without irrigation. Of all his agrarian experiments, the third year after planting slips, he succeeded at olive growing at the rate of 2,000 gallons per acre. His vineyard staff shipped thousands of boxes of cured raisins across the U.S. and Europe, competing with fruit grown in Chile and Malaga, Spain.

Investing in the Future

Cowles facilitated the creation of a fire department in 1880 and the passage of 23.5 miles of the California Southern Railroad track through the El Cajon valley. The next year, he co-founded San Diego Gas Company. In 1884, he promoted the area with visionary investments in the El Cajon Land Company, which developed 6,600 acres along the San Diego River. The consortium recruited settlers by contributing the Lakeside Inn and public park at Lindo Lake, a draw to vacationers.

Although plans for a wine-growing bonanza failed, Cowles succeeded at finance and fruit. In 1885, he challenged other raisin growers to compare their harvests to his seasonal pick of 3,000 boxes. The output of 2 tons per acre increased Pacific farming wealth. He founded San Diego Marine Way & Drydock Company and directed the Commercial Bank, Consolidated National Bank, and, in May 1886, the San Diego County Savings Bank.

At the Florence Hotel on November 26, 1887, Cowles succumbed to an intestinal complaint, leaving to his memory the naming of Cowles Mountain, a popular hiking spot. His wife inherited some $500,000 and continued operating his ranch business. After remarriage to realtor Milton Santee in 1890, Jennie encouraged local schooling at her ranch house and gave land to the community for building the Santee School, which received twenty-nine students on May 25, 1891. In July 1891, the U.S. Postal Service renamed Cowlestown for Milton Santee.

Sources
McGinty, Brian. *A Toast to Eclipse: Arpad Harasthy and the Sparkling Wine of Old San Francisco.* Norman: University of Oklahoma Press, 2012.
Wu, Judy Tzu-Chun. *Doctor Mom Chung of the Fair-haired Bastards: The Life of a Wartime Celebrity.* Berkeley: University of California Press, 2005.

Culbertson, Margaret (1834–1897), Donaldina Mackenzie Cameron (1869–1968), Tien Fu Wu (1861–ca. 1940s), Ah Yane Chin (1869–?)

During the settlement of California, missionary and teacher Margaret Culbertson devoted her career to rescuing and rehabilitating enslaved Chinese women from San Francisco brothels and domestic enslavement. A native of East Groveland, New York, born in 1834, she was the third child and first daughter of the nine offspring of Nancy Johnson and Samuel C. Culbertson, a descendent of Scots Covenanters and immigrants from Londonderry, Ireland, who fought in the French and Indian War (1754–1763). Another branch of her family derived from Aberdeenshire, Scotland.

In 1876, Margaret Culbertson traveled to the Pacific coast as governess for the small boys of the Mills family. To carry out Presbyterian missions, two years later, she chose to remain unmarried and childless. While dedicating her labors to social reform, she countered an evil she dubbed "Mongolian vice," the recruitment of Asian girls to San Francisco, ostensibly for the marriage market matching immigrant wives with California's Asian bachelors.

Stolen Lives

The enlistment and kidnap of nubile females from southern China had gained strength from the terrors of the Taiping Rebellion (1850–1864). The unsavory reputation of San Francisco's bordellos arose between 1850 and 1870, when the Chinese population increased from seven to more than 4,000, with men outnumbering women by twenty-one to one. One consortium of importers, the ruthless Hip Yee Tong, began shanghaiing girls in 1852 and earned $10,000 a year from sex trafficking by a total of 6,000 abductees, whose life expectancy sank to five years. Tong highbinders (enslavers) cut losses by dumping damaged or infected girls on the street or selling them into arranged marriages.

Culbertson decided at age forty-four to represent the Woman's Occidental Board of Foreign Missions in San Francisco as a champion of female liberty. In 1874, she headquartered in a port city where 61 percent of Chinese women ages nine to twenty-five worked as *mui tsai* (servants) or in the sex trade. Auctions placed the most appealing in Chinatown's parlor houses and the rest in gambling and opium dens and sordid cribs in Spofford Alley, where misfortunate girls conducted commercial sex behind barred windows for 25 cents a customer. Culbertson's first rescues involved ten Chinese girls, but quickly grew to 400.

As director of the Presbyterian Chinese Mission Home on Sacramento Street in San Francisco, in 1878, Culbertson began sheltering girls and women immured by oppressors and brutalizers in Chinatown. Some of the victims sent messages begging for refuge. With the collaboration of the San Francisco police and the California Society for the Prevention of Cruelty to Children, formed on August 30, 1876, Culbertson raided brothels and retrieved incarcerated females.

At five brothels in slimy, smoky Spofford Alley, one of four principle slums permeated with filth and stench, Culbertson retrieved girls who survived pregnant and terrified of execution. In Sullivan's Alley, she investigated the sixteen establishments that offered sex for hire. Some inmates suffered scarring from beatings, scalding, branding, notched ears, lacerated eyes, syphilis, tuberculosis, and malnutrition. By 1880, the Workingmen's Party declared the back alleys a public nuisance.

Rescuing Women

Culbertson and a circle of supporters and volunteers armed themselves with axes and sledge hammers and sped by hired carriage to rendezvous. Gentle hands, such as those who snatched Liang May Seen from concubinage for hire on July 21, 1889, placed the runaways in a permanent town home on Sacramento Street, safe from slave auctions and sexual exploitation. Death threats from highbinders forced Culbertson to accept full-time police protection of the premises from such threats as assaults on their reputations, stalking, and a stick of dynamite left in the foyer. To elicit public sympathies, Culbertson published stories of female bondage in the California press.

From an initial residency of ten members of the Light House Mission Band, Culbertson increased the number of Chinese inmates to 392, including Ah Tsun, a preteen tricked and shanghaied, and Chun Fah, a child sold to a slave trafficker by her impoverished parents. In addition to converting the women to Presbyterianism, Culbertson protected them from organized crime and trained them in English and work skills, including sewing, knitting, child care, and household accounts. She made use of Ah Tsun and Chun Fah's bilingualism in English and Cantonese for court testimonials, casino and prison visits, medical and religious instruction, and betrothals to Christianized Chinese males across the West.

Complications from injuries received in a rescue ended Culbertson's community work in 1893. By 1895, she fostered her niece, Anna Culbertson, who attended art school. To extend the shelter's prevention of moral corruption of young Asian women, Culbertson relied on a 25-year-old Scots sewing teacher, Donaldina Mackenzie "Dolly" Cameron, who emigrated from New Zealand in 1871. Dolly maintained that a hateful patriarchy caused Chinese men to devalue women. She engaged two former slaves, Tien Fu Wu and Ah Yane Chin, a female mission interpreter born in Sze Yup, China, to defend vulnerable females in court. In gratitude for Cameron's support, the victimized Chinese girls decorated her bedroom Asian style.

Culbertson's sisters Elizabeth, Nancy, and Matilda Culbertson engaged an ambulance to return her to the Culbertson family's New York home. On the way at Avon Springs, New York, Margaret died on July 31, 1897. Donaldina Cameron continued Presbyterian rescue work in Montana during a vacation in 1902 and published an exposé of conditions for Chinese women in the West in the book *The Yellow Slave Traffic* (1912). Into the 1910s, Donaldina bore the derisive names of "white devil" and "Jesus Woman" and operated Cameron House, which continued to retrieve some 3,000 women from brutality.

SOURCES
Duncan, Patti. *Tell This Silence: Asian American Women Writers and the Politics of Speech.* Iowa City: University of Iowa Press, 2004.

Wu, Judy Tzu-Chun. *Doctor Mom Chung of the Fair-haired Bastards: The Life of a Wartime Celebrity.* Berkeley: University of California Press, 2005.

Dale, Frank (1849–1930), Martha Wood Dale (1859–1930)

A first-generation American patriot and pioneer of Kansas and Oklahoma, Judge Frank J. Dale II contributed to the district and territorial justice system as well as community development. The seventh of the eleven children of English immigrants–farmer, grain dealer, and Methodist minister Franklin Dale, Sr., and Martha Webster Dale, both of Hull, Yorkshire—he was born on November 26, 1849, at Somonauk on a 116-acre farm in DeKalb County, Illinois. He claimed as ancestors the immigrants who settled Daleville, Pennsylvania, in 1806 and ministered to the poor. At age twelve, he moved with his family to Leland, Illinois.

In 1863, Dale volunteered as a trainee at Camp Butler in Springfield until his father reported that the boy was only fourteen years old—four years too young for enlistment with the Union Army. In 1871, he left farming and school teaching to study law in Wichita, Kansas, with his younger brother, Judge David Mark Dale, a future candidate for governor. Frank also hunted buffalo during the three-year boom in hides purchased by the British military for boots, saddles, and belts. By 1874, of the 4.5 million buffalo slaughtered, two-thirds were killed for their pelts alone.

In 1874, Frank and another brother, banker John William "Will" Dale, homesteaded with pioneers at Greeley. Donors sent money and supplies to the agrarian region, which grasshoppers beset from July to September, destroying orchards and fields and forcing newcomers out of business. Frank's older sister, Mary Elvina Dale, settled at Mount Hope, Kansas, and their brother, stockman and hardware dealer Arthur H. Dale, a Civil War veteran, remained in Leland, Illinois, to raise cattle on a 460-acre spread. In a prosperous era that saw the addition of 2,100 miles of track to the Atchison, Topeka, and Santa Fe Railroad, Frank continued to involve himself in Leland and invested in its farmland.

Frank Dale served as Greeley town clerk before settling northwest of Wichita in Sedgwick County at Andale, former Osage territory area heavily homesteaded by German-American veterans of the Civil War and named for Frank's brother Will, a town founder. After Frank's brother David joined his corner office, in 1881, Frank received the job of assistant county attorney. By 1885, he was defending sodbusters against grifters by accepting appointment as registrar of the U.S. Land Office. On June 10, 1885, he married a New Yorker, Martha I. Wood of Fairfield, an advocate of women's clubs who taught public school in Wichita.

Justice in Oklahoma

Dale boarded a train for Guthrie in Logan County, Oklahoma, on April 22, 1889, when he opened a partnership with attorney W.W.

Thomas and acquired 80 acres at Oklahoma Station, a railroad watering stop and the location of the 1892 Dale family reunion. From May 26, 1893, to March 1, 1898, Judge Dale served as chief justice of the Kansas Territorial Supreme Court, an appointment made by President Grover Cleveland. Dale partnered with other investors to found the *Guthrie Daily Leader,* a Democratic publication that remained a leading territorial daily for 103 years.

In November of his first year on the bench hearing cases from Lincoln, Logan, Payne, and Wood counties, Judge Frank Dale handed down to a poisoner the district's first death sentence, carried out by hanging. Despite the high morality rate for territorial law officers during the 1893–1894 predations by the Doolin-Dalton Gang, known as the Wild Bunch, Judge Dale ignored anonymous death threats. During the murder trial of one gang member for the shooting death of Deputy Marshal Thomas Hueston at Ingalls, Roy "Arkansas Tom Jones" Daugherty, on May 21, 1894, the judge posted guards throughout Guthrie and had security forces search court attendees for concealed weapons. Judge Dale reduced the charge to manslaughter and sentenced Daugherty to 50 years at the McAlester state prison.

Judge Dale acknowledged the exigencies of frontier lawlessness, which preyed on Arkansas, Kansas, and Oklahoma. In a landmark decision for Western jurisprudence, previous to the Battle of Ingalls, a lawbreakers' haven, he urged U.S. Marshal Evett Dumas "E.D." Nix to value a live lawman over a dead felon. The order resulted in the formation of an elite cadre of one hundred marshals, including gunfighters Bill Tilghman and Chris Madsen and tracker Heck Thomas, a trio known as the "Three Guardsmen." From 1893 to 1894, they arrested three hundred defiant outlaws and recovered nine corpses of desperadoes who had robbed banks, stagecoaches, railroads and depots, stores, post offices, and express companies. Among the dead were Bill Dalton and Bill Doolin.

Town Builder

Upon leaving the bench with an illustrious reputation for fighting crime, Dale partnered with Judge Andrew Gregg Curtin Bierer, a pioneer during the 1889 Oklahoma Land Run. Upon retirement, Dale opened a practice in Guthrie, Oklahoma, and platted an 80-acre parcel received in payment for a case into a segment of Oklahoma City. As a businessman, Dale promoted the Guthrie Commercial Club, telephone company, National Bank, Farmers and Merchants Bank, Methodist University of Oklahoma, and the Choctaw, Oklahoma and Gulf Railroad, plotted over former Potowatomie territory between Hutchinson and Wichita.

Still promoting the frontier in his sixties, Frank Dale presided over the admission of Oklahoma to statehood in 1907, chaired the Oklahoma Humane Society, and joined the state bar association to facilitate a highway network. In land disputes over oilfields on the Oklahoma-Texas border, he represented his state's interests. Martha Dale facilitated the building of the Guthrie library.

Dale had no children, but reared nieces and nephews. One nephew, future surgeon Charles N. Johnson, attended Northwestern University medical school on a $10,000 loan from his uncle. Following a three-month illness, Dale died at home in Guthrie on February 10, 1930, and was eulogized at the First Presbyterian Church. His wife lived four months as a widow and died on June 24, 1930. Their joint will left bequests to forty-five relatives.

The family name survives in the towns of Andale, Kansas, and Dale, Oklahoma, a stop on the Rock Island Railroad. During World War II, the judge's name returned to prominence in the naming of the U.S. merchant vessel *SS Frank Dale,* a ship chartered in 1943 by the North Atlantic & Gulf Steamship Company. The neo-classic Dale home and terraced lawn on North Thirteenth Street received honors as a repository of history.

Source
Smith, Robert Barr. *Tough Towns: True Tales from the Gritty Streets of the Old West.* Guilford, CT: Globe Pequot, 2007.

DeVere, Pearl (1859–1897)

A successful madam in Denver, Pearl DeVere provided entertainment for the successful entrepreneurs of Cripple Creek, Colorado. She was born Eliza Martin in Evansville, Indiana, in October 1859 to Civil War veteran John Marshall Martin and Nancy Martin, the mother of three sons and two daughters. In the mid–1870s, Pearl arrived in Denver under the name "Mrs. Martin" and worked as a prostitute. To cover her trail, she reported to her sister that she ran a millinery and couturier, two of the few respectable jobs for single women.

In El Paso County, Colorado, in 1887, Pearl DeVere attracted admirers to her statuesque beauty. She married Albert Young but lived apart from him in her own house. Historians surmise that she surrendered an unnamed baby daughter for adoption. She dyed her hair red, dressed in kid shoes, diamonds and sapphires, and taffeta gowns, and lived under assumed names, including Isabelle Martin and Mrs. E.A. Martin, the name of her brother.

A Career Madam

During the Silver Panic of 1893, Pearl sought the prosperity beyond Ute Pass at Cripple Creek, which became Colorado's second largest town in 1891 after Bob Womack's big gold strike. The site of 150 digs and the state's last placer mining bonanza, Cripple Creek supplied gold to a dwindling stockpile at the federal reserve and sparked the 1894 strike of miners demanding a raise in their $3-a-day wages and reduced hours. Under the name Pearl DeVere, at age 31, she competed against other "variety dens"—Blanche Burton's parlor house, Nina Wetteruth's, Mother Jones's, Kittie Townley's, Lottie's Place, the Bon Ton, Ella Holden's "The Library," the Red Light, and Pearl Sevan's "Old Faithful." As an edge against the future, she bought 2,000 shares of Victor Gold Mining Company and 1,000 in Ela Helean Gold Mining.

In a class by herself, Pearl dressed in chic bustled outfits and offered lavish services to a population exceeding 15,000, including strikebreakers, hired guns, and the state militia. Unlike other prostitutes' shacks, tents, and skin dives, her bordello on Myers Avenue built a reputation for clean, healthy, well paid working girls dressed in stylish fashions. In exchange for 60 percent of the brothel's income, Pearl bought off Cripple Creek officials and supplied each sex worker with individualized bedroom suit, curling irons, corset chairs, and belladonna leaves to increase the gloss of their eyes.

In public, Pearl demonstrated her ideal of the well-groomed businesswoman in a sealskin coat and silk serge afternoon suits. On errands about Cripple Creek, she either rode sidesaddle in derby hat or drove a red-wheeled phaeton pulled by a brace of black horses. Under the protection of Sheriff Hiram "Hi" Wilson, she and her four employees reached a compromise with the disapproving middle class by shopping Bennett Avenue dress boutiques on Mondays while proper wives did laundry. In exchange for Pearl's compliance, Wilson taxed her $16 per month and $3 from each of her girls. The best of her stable—Nell McClusky, Laura Evens, and Lola Livingston—advanced to their own establishments.

In 1895, Pearl lived with a married factory operator and ore miller, C.B. Flynn, who borrowed $2,500 from her that he never repaid. During their union, Cripple Creek reached a population of 10,000, a boost to Pearl's business. On April 25, 1896, a fire erupted at Jennie LaRue's room above a dance hall. Flames destroyed Pearl and Flynn's property and his and wiped out the cribs of some 350 sex workers, leaving only ten buildings intact. Flynn moved to Monterrey, Mexico, to smelt iron and steel.

With $3,100 borrowed from widowed investor Orinda J. Straile, in December 1896, Pearl erected the Old Homestead, a two-story brick casino on Myers Avenue. After viewing bawdy houses in Paris, she outfitted her parlor house with maid service, chef, a viewing room, electricity, plumbing, and telephone. She graced a ballroom, winery, dining room, private suite, and three parlors with opulent brass fixtures, piano, chandeliers, velvet wallpaper, braided portieres, carpet, and oak tables. She wisely displayed high quality staff to clients and, for $250 per night, treated them to poker, feasting, and parties hosted by girls checked monthly for venereal disease.

Pearl's Legend

Pearl's death left much unexplained. On June 4, 1897, a rich patron from Denver brought her wine, caviar, wild turkey, and a costly sequined pink chiffon gown from Paris. While two orchestras played, Pearl and her admirer quarreled. After his departure, she died in her bed at 3:00 a.m. on June 5, 1897, despite the intervention of Dr. J.H. Hereford. The media speculated that she committed suicide from an apparent morphine overdose.

Pearl's sister arrived at the Fairley Brothers & Lampman Mortuary before the burial, learned Pearl's real profession, and returned home in disgust. To rescue Pearl's belongings from the auction block, an unnamed donor mailed $1,000 to pay her final expenses. Local admirers underwrote a lavish funeral and burial at Mt. Pisgah Cemetery, for which Pearl lay in a rose-topped lavender casket dressed in a signature pearl-encrusted gown amid the twenty-piece Elks Club Band and four mounted guards.

Pearl's business sold for $5,000 and remained profitable until 1917. It closed permanently during the Great Depression. In 1858, Coloradans turned the Old Homestead into a museum, detailed with lavender porch and bay window. Admirers replaced a wood grave marker with a granite heart and ringed the plot with stones and wild rose bushes.

Sources

MacKell, Jan. *Brothels, Bordellos, and Bad Girls: Prostitution in Colorado, 1860–1930.* Albuquerque: University of New Mexico Press, 2004.

Wommack, Linda. *Our Ladies of the Tenderloin: Colorado's Legends in Lace.* Caldwell, ID: Caxton, 2005.

Docher, Anton (1852–1928), Juan de Padilla (?–1544)

A French missionary, Anton Jean Baptiste Docher evangelized Southwestern Indians and considered himself an adoptee of pueblo peoples. Born of peasant stock in 1852, Docher was the last of the six children of Elizabeth Garce and vintner Antoine Docher. He grew up in the wine country of Auvergne at Le Crest near Puy de Dôme in south central France, a region known for Côtes d'Auvergne wine and a lava corona that dominated the Limagne Plain.

Docher and his two brothers learned vineyard culture in early boyhood. He attended the Petit Seminary of Saint Sauveur from ages eighteen to twenty-six. After a year of training in philosophy under Franciscans at the Grand Seminary of Clermont-Ferrand, in 1879, he entered the military and achieved the rank of sergeant. For combat wounds at Tunis, Tunisia, and medal for action in Indochina (Vietnam) during the French Colonial Wars, he earned the French Croix de Guerre. Outraged by French colonialism and in treatment for tuberculosis at Le Crest, at age thirty-three, he joined the staff of the Petit Seminary as prefect (disciplinarian).

Docher journeyed to north central New Mexico on October 21, 1887, to ready himself for ordination under Father Peter Eguillon, the rector at the Cathedral of Santa Fe. Three years later, he labored for a year at outposts in Bernalillo and Taos before succeeding seminarian Andres Antoine Echallier at the Tanoan pueblo of Isleta, home of the Southern Tiwa. On December 28, 1891, Docher arrived by pinto pony to Isleta's Catholic plaza, established in 1613 on agrarian land originally visited by Spanish conquistador Francisco de Coronado in 1540. As "The Padre of Isleta," he attended a reception of grilled rabbit and mutton that began a 34-year parish ministry headquartered at the San Agustín de la Isleta Mission church.

The Parish Priest

For the task, Docher learned the guttural Keresan dialects and studied pueblo ethnography. He also performed priestly duties at Acoma, Laguna, Los Lunas, and Peralta, where he crossed the river over a bridge with loose boards. Pueblo Indians valued Docher as "Tashide" (Little Priest or Helper) for planting shade trees in native communities, acquiring

At Isleta Pueblo in Bernalillo County, New Mexico, in 1891, Father Anton Docher learned Keresan dialects and studied pueblo ethnography and adobe architecture. Here, in a photograph from 1937, is an old adobe house with recessed portico.

an antique church bell for the mission, and contributing to the housing and education of orphans. To foster local foods and ornamentals, Docher maintained a garden. To reward his beneficence, women clustered in the plaza to light votive candles and presented cake, bread, meat pies, and fresh corn, onions, melons, grapes, and apples.

One boy, Tomás Chavez, became like an adopted son of Docher, who gave him land and a home at Los Lunas at his marriage to Lolita Delores. Like the padre in boyhood, Chavez raised wine grapes and supplied Docher with communion wine for mass. In return, Docher rewarded Chavez's girls, Margaret and Stella Chavez, with peacock feathers. At the vintner's death, Docher paid tuition for his fatherless children to enter the Sisters of Loretto Academy, opened to female students of all ethnicities in Santa Fé in the 1870s.

Because of Docher's progressivism toward ancient religions, he accepted indigenous spring rituals, drumming, and crop and rain dances as part of local culture and housed native crafts and artifacts, including a painting of Our Lady of Guadalupe, a syncretic Mexican saint. He agreed with author and Indian activist Charles Fletcher Lummis that strict white boarding academies such as the Carlisle Indian School in Pennsylvania endangered natives by destroying fragile memories of family, tribe, and language. Docher also "rescued" children from Protestant proselytizers by insisting that they attend mass and pray to the Great Father, the Virgin Purissima (most chaste virgin), and El Santo Nino, the Holy Boy, for guidance.

The priest's notable acts include investigation of a mystical tapping and rising of the casket of Father Francisco Juan de Padilla, a former military chaplain who crossed the Staked Plains of Texas with Coronado. As a missionary to Tarascan tribes, Padilla died of arrow wounds by sacrificing himself to attacking Quivira Indians on November 30, 1544. At present-day Hutchinson in the Texas Panhandle, citizens revere Padilla as its first Christian martyr.

In April 1895, Docher claimed that he prayed to Padilla to cure a gangrenous wound on his hand and escaped amputation when the arm suddenly healed. Docher remained vigorous into the twentieth century, when he provided the hybrid church architecture with two wood towers in Gothic mode. Other parishes in Valencia County sought his advice on spirituality and Christian ethics.

Defender of the Tiwa

Docher enlightened outsiders on the integrity of Tiwa communities. In June 1913, he published in *The Santa Fé Magazine* an ethnological survey of pueblo life and governance. His awards include a French-African War medal and the Order of Leopold, a knighthood conferred by King Albert of Belgium and Queen Elisabeth of Bavaria after World War I. In exchange, Docher presented the royal couple with a silver and turquoise cross cast by Tiwa artisans.

At the San Agustín de la Isleta Mission, one of the most impressive territorial mission churches, Docher upgraded the packed earth floor of the original sanctuary nave with boards, re-plastered the facade, and installed a stove for heat and interior preservation. In 1923, at age seventy-one, he acceded to parishioners' wishes and remodeled the church. He buttressed the towers with adobe blocks and rescued the altar from water damage to its deteriorating timber and earthen walls. He replaced a flat roof with peaked metal and added a front porch and steeples at the two front corners.

In old age, Docher suffered diminished vision from cataracts that forced his retirement. Pope Pius XI granted dispensation for him to celebrate Mass from memory. Docher left behind an archive of Tiwa artifacts, including pottery, baskets, hunting weapons, finger rings, turquoise beads, and kachina dolls. On a visit to Docher's church by lantern light at Christmas 1925, folklorist Elsie Clews Parson described the merger of Tiwa dance and processional into a hybridized Catholic mass.

In 1925, Docher entered St. Joseph Hospital at Albuquerque, where he remained until his death on December 18, 1928. Parishioners provided a blanketed Indian honor guard and buried their padre under the chapel's altar alongside Friar Padilla. Biography and fiction retain his service to Isleta, New Mexico, particularly Willa Cather's *Death Comes for the Archbishop* (1927), Julia Keleher and Ruth Chant's *The Padre of Isleta* (2009), and Samuel Gance's *Anton ou la trajectoire d'un père: L'histoire romancée du père Anton Docher* (2012).

Sources
Keleher, Julia, and Elsie Ruth Chant. *The Padre of Isleta*. Santa Fe: Sunstone, 2009.
Secord, Paul R. *Albuquerque Deco and Pueblo*. Charleston, SC: Arcadia, 2012.

Ebbetts, John A.N. (ca. 1815–1854), William Robinson Goulding (1805–1865), George Henry Goddard (1817–1906), Seymour Treadwell Moore (1827–1876)

Merchant adventurer and surveyor John Augustus Nicoll Ebbetts (also Ebbets) led one of the wealthiest trains of westerers by a lesser-known southern route to California to set up businesses and homes. The fourth of five children, he was born of Dutch-English lineage on July 1, 1815, in New York City to Sarah Woodward, a Baptist from New York, and John Ebbetts, an employee of John Jacob Astor's Pacific fur operation. He descended from English immigrants from Surrey.

In largely unexplored territory, the elder John Ebbetts set an example of pioneering capitalism by captaining Astor's flagship *Enterprise* and headquartering in Hawaii. On voyages to the Tlingit, Aleut, Kodiak, and the Spanish colonies on the North Pacific coast and maritime Russian fur trading posts at New Archangel (Sitka), Alaska, in 1809 and 1810, Ebbetts carried molasses, glass beads, rum, brandy, and canvas. Until the decline of the seal and otter population in the 1810s, the pelts he acquired found buyers at Guangzhou in Canton, China, in exchange for tea, silk, and porcelain. Before the War of 1812 ended trade in Asia for the Pacific Northwest, the return on Ebbetts's investment rose as high as 500 percent.

With the enthusiasm of his sea captain father for frontier profits, in 1836, a year after his father's death at sea, the younger Ebbetts took up East Coast commerce in imports and trading for the American Fur Company. In New York on December 30, 1839, he wed Amanda Malvina Heath, mother of George Augustus Ebbetts. During an economic downturn in the late 1840s, he left his family on Long Island to head the New York Knickerbocker Exploring Company. The explorers traversed trade routes of fifteen Indian tribes, including the Miwok and Washoe in northern California. Each of the sixty-four members invested between $200 and $500 in the seven-month transcontinental crossing.

In San Francisco in 1866, George Goddard, the founder of a new American school of painting, focused on watercolors and landscapes. This Goddard painting from 1853 is entitled *Sonora Jany*.

Route to California

Business opportunities, the purpose of the Knickerbocker mule train, led the urbanites to depart individual lives in Connecticut, Maine, New Jersey, and New York with confidence in their venture. One member, surgeon William Robinson Goulding of York, England, compiled *California Odyssey: An Overland Journey on the Southern Trails, 1849,* a journal of the group's exploits. Tuolumne County cartographer and naturalist George Henry Goddard of York, England, led the survey team and later mapped California and its goldfields. Along the route, the company increased in number to 100 members, who made the trip widely scattered to ensure firewood and water and forage for their animals.

Varied in ages from seventeen to fifty-three, the wealthy entrepreneurs set out in 1849 during the California Gold Rush. Amid herds of buffalo, on February 17, the party booked the steamer *Hudson* out of Pittsburgh, Pennsylvania, to Fort Smith, Arkansas. On March 20, the company took a southern route through Santa Fe, New Mexico, southern New Mexico, and Arizona Territory. On the way, they traded with Cherokee and Choctaw for food and horses. Guided by West Point graduate Seymour Treadwell Moore, an explorer and surveyor from Wooster, Ohio, the retinue crossed an alternative route to California over the Sierra Nevada in April, 1849. In Calaveras and Alpine counties, the entourage mapped the volcanic peaks and glacial valleys of the high Sierras. The Knickerbockers reached San Francisco aboard the steamer *Oregon,* a low point in the gold rush when disappointed opportunists and speculators returned in mass to the East.

Ebbetts chose the pass which carries his name as a possible route for a transcontinental railroad. In Utah Territory in 1853, he chaired the seventeen-man Atlantic & Pacific Railroad Committee that pledged to finance a study of one of the five routes selected by the U.S. Congress in 1850 for future development. Ebbetts relied on the advice of chief engineer Moore, a seasoned mountain man and Indian fighter, and George Henry Goddard, a civil engineer, landscape artist, surveyor, and creator of *Map of the State of California* (1857).

Lacking up-to-date charts, the party, with $2,500 advance money for their mule train, set out from Stockton, California, on October 7, 1853, over the Sonora Emigrant Road to locate a rail route east of the Virgin River. With little water, food, and forage, they traveled to the Wassuk Range south of Walker Lake and around the Columbus Salt Marsh in the central Nevada wilderness. On return, they scouted the Mormon counties of Millard, Washington, and Iron, a constituency superintended by Brigham Young, the president of the Church of Jesus Christ of Latter-day Saints.

Desert Trek

In November 1853, Ebbetts's company and its weary pack animals camped for four days at Fish Lake and hunted deer, ducks, and rabbits. As streams rose to the surface after dark, they watered their mules late at night and limited themselves to a meal of bread and raw bacon. On November 8, they sewed moccasins from mule sinew and skins to cover their battered feet.

The Ebbetts-Moore expedition crossed Death Valley before completing a recommendation for a rail route. Severely handicapped by dying mules and lack of water, at Eureka Valley in Trinity County, the men camped at Last Chance Spring. On November 11, 1853, they departed north through rocky environs of Last Chance Canyon west of the California-Nevada boundary and celebrated shore birds and drinkable water on return to Fish Lake Valley, a gathering place for Nevada tribes. During the night, Indians killed a mule and disabled three more. When the company arrived safely in mid–November in San Francisco, they recommended passage of the railway through central Nevada.

On December 19 and 20, 1853, Ebbetts's diary of the trans–Sierra expedition served the *San Francisco Daily Herald and Mirror* as a travelogue revealing unexplored parts of the Great Basin, the massive watershed extending from Oregon to the Gulf of California. On a Pacific crossing from San Francisco north to Petaluma, California, Ebbetts died from the boiler explosion that sank the steamboat *Secretary* on April 15, 1854, in San Pablo Bay. Passengers reported that the steamer, built of recycled parts, engaged in a race against the steamer *Nevada*.

At a time when gold prospectors took the Ebbetts route to mountain goldfields, in 1855, Goddard employed the aneroid barometer in his survey of California's eastern boundary for the Utah legislature. He also charted the Western Pacific line out of Sacramento, for which feat Mount Goddard carried his name. After settling his wife, Emily von Essen Goddard, and their two sons and daughter in San Francisco in 1866, he opened a studio and focused on watercolors and landscapes. Acclaimed as the founder of a new school of painting, Goddard exhibited four times between 1873 and 1888 and in Paris at the Louvre. Plans for a memorial gallery at Stanford University ended in 1906 after an earthquake and fire destroyed Goddard's collection, probably precipitating his death.

In 1864, Ebbetts Pass became the Big Trees toll road to the Carson Valley Road for thousands of prospectors and silver miners, who trekked through Paiute lands while heading for the Comstock Lode in Washoe County, Nevada. Political squabbling halted the plan to survey the Sierra Nevada route for a possible road, but the route found use in the 1880s with construction of the Carson and Colorado Railway from Carson City to Los Angeles.

Sources

Goulding, William R. *California Odyssey: An Overland Journey on the Southern Trails, 1849.* Norman, OK: Arthur H. Clark Company, 2009.

Steele, Edward Eugene. *Ebbets: The History and Genealogy of a New York Family.* St. Louis: E.E. Steele, 2005.

Farnham, Eliza Wood (1815–1864), Thomas Jefferson Farnham (1804–1848), Georgiana Bruce Kirby (1818–1887), Richard Cornelius Kirby (1817–1904)

Reformer, writer, teacher, and rancher Eliza Wood (or Woodson) Burhans Farnham survived a life of loss and provided the suffrage movement with bicoastal views of American women. Born of Dutch-English lineage at Potter Hollow near Rensselaerville, New York, on November 17, 1815, to Quaker Mary Wood and Cornelius Burhans II, a Methodist Episcopalian, she grew up motherless after age four and became a virtual servant to the Warrens, an atheistic aunt and drunken uncle on a farm in Maple Springs east of Lake Chautauqua.

Eliza was accustomed to overcoming obstacles through self-reliance. In 1831, she reunited with her brothers Kelly E. and Henry J. "Hal" and sisters Phoebe Margaret and Mary W. Burhans and briefly enrolled at the Albany Female Academy, the nation's oldest independent girls' school. Self-educated from reading French essayist Voltaire and colonial patriot Thomas Paine, she developed agnosticism in part because of orthodox religion's shaming of the body. At age 20, she recovered from exhaustion at the residence of Mary and her husband, John M. Roberts, near Pekin in Tazewell County, Illinois.

On July 12, 1836, while living on the prairie on the banks of the Illinois River, Eliza wed attorney and travel writer Thomas Jefferson Farnham, a Vernon native of English ancestry, and relocated to Tremont, then Peoria. Sickness and death occluded the joys of beginning a family. A month after Mary's death, the Farnhams' first son, Charles Farnham, died before his first birthday on August 14, 1838, from the Great Plains Smallpox Epidemic, which spread from an American Fur Company steamer among the Mandan, Blackfoot, Assiniboine, Arikara, Crow, and Pawnee.

Championing the West

The following May 30, in hopes of establishing American rights to the West and ridding the frontier of Indians, Thomas left Independence, Missouri, to explore Oregon. He traveled with the Peoria Company of nineteen men, seven of them from England. At the time, the town specialized in supplying dray animals and offered five hundred blacksmiths at forty-seven forges, three livery stables, three harness and saddlery shops, and two makers of ox yokes.

Led by Methodist missionary Jason Lee of Quebec, the wagon train, called the "Oregon Dragoons," followed the 2,000-mile Oregon Trail under the banner "OREGON or the GRAVE," stitched by Eliza Farnham. By July 5, 1839, group leadership disintegrated at Bent's Fort, Colorado, concluding with Thomas's expulsion from the bulk of the convoy. With a band of five pioneers, he reached the Walla Walla River on September 23, where trekkers sometimes left their animals to forage through the winter. They portaged along the Columbia River to Fort Vancouver in present-day Washington. Based on his assessment, he requested federal annexation of the West and military protection of pioneers.

Following five weeks in the Willamette Valley, on December 4, 1839, Thomas Jefferson Farnham departed via the barque *Vancouver* on a three-week voyage to Honolulu, where he remained for three months. During the sojourn, he supported independence of the island kingdom and promoted a joint stock company to cultivate Hawaiian soil. As royal envoy for Kamehameha III, he earned $1,800, but accomplished little on the king's behalf.

Farnham's return voyage to Alta California on the schooner *Don Quixote* ended in April 1840. In Monterey, he negotiated release of American and British prisoners whom Mexicans had accused of plotting a revolution. He purchased property in Santa Cruz from Californios, the Hispanic Catholics whose land claims dated to during Spanish rule. Ending a 16-month separation, in August 1840, the Farnhams reunited in Poughkeepsie, New York.

Motherhood and Widowhood

After Thomas issued *Travels in the Great Western Prairies* (1841), Eliza worked as matron of the women's sector of Sing Sing state prison, a target of her campaign for criminal rehabilitation. She abolished the obligatory silence rule and organized prison music and literacy programs and coursework in math, history, geography, health and physiology, and astronomy. After the birth of sons Charles Haight "Charlie" and Edward Hallock "Eddie" Farnham, Eliza struggled to care for Eddie, who suffered from to congenital spinal disease. In 1843, she suffered the death of brother Kelly Burhans and six-year-old nephew Edward from scarlet fever.

About the time that Thomas Farnham moved to San Francisco to farm, Eliza published *Life in Prairie Land* (1846), a popular survey of the independent frontier housewife. The book earned a second printing in part for its environmental concerns. Controversy over her liberal attitudes caused her to leave Sing Sing in 1848. After failed attempts at practicing law and operating a freight line in California, Thomas died of malaria in Santa Cruz on September 13, 1848, leaving his wife and sons a ranch.

Following collaboration with Samuel Gridley Howe at the New England Asylum for the Blind in Boston, Eliza Farnham returned to New York City and, on February 2, 1849, issued a handbill from her quarters on Barclay Street near the Battery calling for volunteer women to populate and civilize the West. She proposed that the Association of California Women provide wives for the 90 percent male population. Initially, she received 200 applications, but recruitment failed.

In widowhood on May 20, 1849, Eliza Farnham sailed on the *Angelique* around Cape Horn, where the ship's captain deliberately abandoned her at Valparaiso, Chile. Following two months later aboard the *Louis Philippe* to reunite with Charlie and Eddie, in February 1850, she settled at Santa Cruz, California, to nurse Eddie through illness. In search of liberation from Eastern aesthetes, nonetheless, she recoiled from the alcoholism, swearing, violence, and gambling among frontier males enraptured with greed from the 1849 California Gold Rush.

With a nanny—Lucy Sampson—and Unitarian partner Georgiana Bruce Kirby, a reformer and suffragist from Bristol, England, and wife of English whaler and tanner Richard Cornelius Kirby of Staffordshire, Farnham operated El Rancho La Libertad, a 200-acre ranch. Their endeavors consisted of building poultry pens, starting pear and olive orchards, and cultivating potato fields. Although she disdained traveling on horseback by sidesaddle, her riding American style in "Turkish pants" drew attention to her domestic feminist philosophy.

Departing from Eastern restraints on female behavior, Eliza and Georgiana camped out several days at Oatnook with male friends. Eliza's description of frontier bounty included beach shells, seals, the moods of Monterey Bay, and picnics on rich cream, turnips, radishes, and strawberries. Her writings visualized fields of lupines, *Arnebia euchroma*, clover, wild oats, and mallows. Essays included enlarged on locating whalebones and on Spanish styles of herding cattle and horses. Other commentary on mining techniques, vigilantism, Jesuit missions, and ecology indicated her promotion of the frontier lifestyle as opposed to the venality and urban decay of San Francisco.

In Soquel, California, on March 23, 1852, Farnham wed Irish engineer and street paver William Alexander Fitzpatrick, a drunkard and terrorizer of women during their four-year union. She bore daughter Mary Fitzpatrick, who died in 1854 at age two of hydrocephalus. The following year, her nine-year-old son Eddie succumbed to his birth defect. Fitzpatrick abandoned the family.

Androcentric laws stripped Eliza Farnham of the property she inherited from Thomas. She taught at Santa Cruz and issued essays for the monthly magazine *California Farmer* and the *Hesperian: A Western Quarterly* in support of suffrage, vigilantism, and female independence. In February and April 1856, she lectured in Sacramento on character building, spiritualism, and the redemptive power of the frontier. On June 30, 1856, she became the first citizen of Santa Cruz County to obtain a divorce and promptly sailed on the mail steamer *John L. Stephens* to the east coast with son Charlie.

Surviving on Two Coasts

On return to New York, Eliza Farnham studied homeopathic medicine and lectured and wrote on cultural regression in the West and the need for women of character to create families on the Pacific Coast. To support herself and pay her son's tuition at Eagleswood Military Academy in Perth Amboy, New Jersey, in October 1856, Eliza issued the first book about the West Coast written by a woman—*California, In-doors and Out, Or, How We Farm, Mine, and Live Generally in the Golden State,* a critique of lawlessness and male degeneracy, alcoholism, and indolence on the frontier. In November 1857, she founded the Women's Protective Emigration Society, which recruited forty jobless seamstresses from England, Ireland, and Scotland for domestic work in Illinois and Indiana.

At New York's Broadway Tabernacle, Eliza addressed the 1858 National Woman's Rights Convention on the subject of female superiority over men at endurance and moral rectitude. Her text encouraged women to embrace pioneering with fervor as a source of equal opportunity for females. After publishing *My Early Years* (1859), she settled in Stockton, California, to manage the state mental asylum, where her ex-husband dwelled among the insane. She harangued California legislators to upgrade crowded, inhumane conditions at San Quentin Prison, where Warden John F. McCauley ruled like a feudal lord.

On August 21, 1862, Eliza returned east from San Francisco to Panama aboard the steamer *SS Sonora.* Amid the fury of the American Civil War, she joined the Women's Loyal National League to press for a presidential decree ending slavery. She departed a speaking engagement in Philadelphia to nurse the casualties from the Battle of Gettysburg (July 3–4, 1863). Arriving to Chambersburg at the Christ Lutheran Church temporary hospital on July 6, she published a letter in the journal *Common Sense* the following month about the carnage. During her residence in a tent city, consumption infected her lungs.

Months before her death from tuberculosis at Milton-on-Hudson in New York City on December 15, 1864, Eliza Farnham clarified feminist philosophy in *Woman and Her Era* (1864), in which she described female goals as superior to those of males. In addition to denouncing men as ethically inferior, she depicted religion as arbitrary and hostile to women. Feminist historians honor her for lionizing female pioneers in the West.

SOURCES

Levy, JoAnn. *Unsettling the West: Eliza Farnham and Georgiana Bruce Kirby in Frontier California.* Santa Clara, CA: Heyday Books, 2004.

Roberts, Brian. *American Alchemy: The California Gold Rush and Middle-Class Culture.* Chapel Hill: University of North Carolina Press, 2000.

Fisk, James Liberty (1835–1902), Lydia Ann Burson Fisk (1835–1876), Robert Emmett Fisk (1837–1908), Elizabeth Chester Fisk (1846–1927), Van Hayden Fisk (1840–1890), Andrew Jackson Fisk (1849–1910), Stephen Edward Liberty (1843–1911), William Henry Illingworth (1844–1893)

A journalist and guide to some five hundred pioneers, scout James Liberty Fisk promoted westering by leading convoys of settlers to Montana and Idaho over a route later followed by the Great Northern Railroad. A New Yorker of Irish lineage, he was born in Royalton on September 12, 1835, to Jerusha Theresa Loveland and attorney James Byron Fisk, brother of Indian scout John Fisk. The Fisk clan dated its beginnings to Suffolk, England, in 1399, and took their surname from the Scandinavian word for "fish."

The Fisk family displayed the restlessness and adaptability common to frontiersmen. James Liberty and his five brothers and sister grew up in Warren, Pennsylvania, where their father practiced law. While living in Lafayette, Indiana, James Liberty Fisk proved his versatility by taking jobs in rafting, farming, building carriages, and writing for the *Daily Courier,* which published articles on frontier exploration. In his late teens, his family relocated northwest to a farm near White Bear Lake, Minnesota, an area he later surveyed and platted.

After marrying Lydia Ann "Goodie" Burson of Schoolcraft, Michigan, in 1857, Fisk aimed to increase the state's influence over commerce between the Mississippi Valley and the Pacific Northwest. In St. Paul, Minnesota, he joined civil engineer William Henry Nobles, builder of the Fort Ridgely and South

Pass wagon road across Minnesota to the Nebraska border. As the Dakota Land Company secretary in the late 1850s, James Fisk recruited pioneers, most of whom chose lots at the confluence of the Big Sioux and Missouri rivers. Waterpower aided them in transporting poles north for shoring up their sod huts.

At the onset of the American Civil War in April 1861, James Fisk, a skilled sharpshooter, joined the Third Minnesota Volunteers as an infantryman. He saw action outside Columbia, Tennessee, before his promotion to captain. On May 19, 1862, Secretary of War Edwin McMasters Stanton appointed Fisk to assistant quartermaster and entrusted him with $5,000 to superintend emigrants on a federally funded expedition to the West.

The Northern Overland Expedition for the Protection of Emigrants coordinated a group of pioneers traveling 1,375 miles from Fort Abercrombie, Dakota Territory, to Fort Walla Walla, Washington. For the convoy, Fisk borrowed a 12-pound howitzer and stocked food and medicine, guns, and ammunition. As gifts for trading with friendly Crow and Gros Ventres, he packed blankets, sugar, and tobacco.

The Fisk Expeditions

On June 4, 1862, Fisk posted a notice in a daily, the St. Paul, Minnesota, *Pioneer and Democrat,* seeking potential settlers. He hired experienced guides—mountain man Pierre Bottineau and his 15-year-old son Daniel—to lead 130 investors and 40 security guards. The convoy departed from St. Paul, on June 16 by the northern route. Traveling north of the Missouri River, the pioneers in eighty-eight wagons passed through the Dakota Territory in July. According to diarist Samuel Robert Bond, on August 8 at Valley City, North Dakota, the birth of a son to Mary Jane Abbott and Josephus Stark added the infant Julian Fisk Stark to the roster.

Fisk's company fought off angry Sisseton Sioux under Little Crow in August. To ensure safety, they engaged a cavalry escort before leaving Fort Union, Montana, on August 23, 1862. The company journeyed on to Fort Benton—the "birthplace of Montana"—the flatboat center on the Missouri River headwaters, arriving on September 5. Moving west toward the gold fields of Idaho Territory on the Salmon River west of Oregon, the convoy headed for the Beaverhead gold mines on Grasshopper Creek near Bannack in southwestern Montana. By November 1, the train arrived in Walla Walla, where Fisk liquidated his wagons and gear as ordered.

Upon return to Washington, D.C., on February 17, 1863, Fisk received Congressional appointment to another expedition, which left Fort Ripley, Minnesota, on June 25 with a budget of $7,000. Amid hostile natives, he arrived at Fort Benton with sixty-two pioneers. Despite his success, carelessness, deviations from official orders, and financial mismanagement beset his reputation.

Fisk's train continued to Virginia City and Bannack, Montana. He returned from Salt Lake City, Utah, via the Butterfield Overland Stage to its terminus in St. Louis, Missouri. After retracing his steps to retrieve lost luggage, he reached Washington, D.C., on December 13, 1863. In early 1864, he presented a gift of gold nuggets from Idaho to President Abraham Lincoln as well as a map of a proposed migrant and military road to the goldfields of Montana and eastern Idaho.

During the Washington furor over the Civil War, on February 23, 1864, Fisk lobbied to arrange a third frontier expedition. To display confidence in a future wagon road, mail route, or rail line guarded by army forts, he made speeches in Chicago and New York City and advertised in the *Milwaukee Sentinel* on March 14, 1864, recruiting gold prospectors. In part because of wartime inflation, on March 16, he faced charges of overdrafts on his military funds. The unpaid bills required written justification of expenses and letters of intent that dragged on until Fisk settled the matter on June 1 with his next government advance.

Shaping Western Travel

While James Fisk delayed in the nation's capital, he pressed Congress to pass wagon road legislation. Before trade boards, the media, and chambers of commerce in New York,

Chicago, and Milwaukee, he excelled at boosterism for investment opportunities in Montana and Idaho. Guided again by Pierre Bottineau, on July 15, 1864, he led a third party of pioneers from St. Cloud, Minnesota, to Fort Rice, North Dakota, a new addition to the U.S. fort system that shielded the upper Missouri River from attack by Lakota Sioux.

At 166 miles west of the fort in the Little Missouri Badlands, on September 2, 1864, Sitting Bull, Gall, and 100 Hunkpapa Sioux buffalo hunters besieged James Fisk's wagon train. Fierce fighting wounded Sitting Bull and cost lives on both sides. The Sioux negotiated for four wagons and forty cattle in exchange for captive Fanny Wiggins Kelly, whom they had abducted the previous month at the Battle of Killdeer Mountain. A petition to Fort Rice for army intervention on September 18 gained Fisk an escort of 900 cavalrymen. The soldiers ended the contretemps with the Sioux, but did not free Kelly from her kidnappers.

In late January 1865, James Fisk faced charges printed in the *New York Times* the previous November of poisoning Indians by leaving strychnine-laced hardtack in camp at Red Buttes on the Cannon Ball River for Hunkpapa Sioux raiders to find and eat. His influence sinking in Congress, Fisk failed to recruit another train and resigned from the army on June 12, 1865. He remained in Georgetown, D.C., at the Union Hotel with his wife and their infant daughter Dell while planning the transportation of a printing press, farming and mining equipment, and a sawmill to Yellowstone, a 2-million acre landmark in western Wyoming.

The fourth trek over the northern route departed Fort Ripley, Minnesota, on June 25, 1866, with 300 miners and settlers organized like soldiers and assigned to guard 160 wagons labeled "U.S." James Fisk took his family and youngest brother, Union cavalry veteran Andrew Jackson Fisk of Cattaraugus County, New York. Their brother, Union infantry veteran Robert Emmett Fisk of Ohio, joined James as second in command. Another Ohio-born brother, Van Hayden Fisk, applied his military training to the job of train master, assisted by French-Canadian scout and translator Stephen Edward Liberty of Quebec.

Along the way, photographers William Henry Illingworth and assistant George Bill made thirty stereoscopic views of a camp in St. Cloud, Indian villages, the wagon train, a Pawnee village, and forts Benton and William, and the only pictures ever taken of Fort Union, Montana. In late summer, the company explored the Bear Paw Mountains of north central Montana. On August 25, they encountered brightly dressed Gros Ventres. By September 7, 1866, they reached Fort Benton, Montana, and purchased goods from merchant George Steel. James Fisk auctioned his supplies, tents, and wagons before departing from the pioneers. For his successful leadership, the Sioux named him "Great Chief who knows no fear."

Frontier Journalism

The Fisk brothers provided skills for growing communities, including Van Hayden's publication in Broadwater, Montana, of the weekly *Townsend Tranchant*. In November

On the way to Montana in 1866, photographers William Henry Illingworth and assistant George Bill made stereoscopic views of Winnebago and other Indians.

1866, Robert Fisk began publishing the weekly *Helena Herald* while Andrew Fisk managed advertising. The paper's advocacy for freeing slaves incited word battles with the anti-abolitionist newspaper the *Rocky Mountain Gazette*.

After hostilities with Red Cloud and 2,000 Oglala Sioux warriors in June 1866 prevented convoys from traveling the Bozeman Trail, a passage from Dakota Territory to Bannack, Montana, in 1867, James Fisk served in the Montana militia, which drafted 800 volunteers. He advanced to recruiting officer with the rank of captain. For six months, he edited the *Helena Herald*, which was then a daily and a public bindery owned by the Fisk brothers.

As Montana Territory approached a population of 20,600, in 1869, James Fisk served as treasury auditor. In February 1875, he and Lydia Fisk bought land on the north shore of White Bear Lake, where Northwest Mountain Police patrols suppressed lawlessness and gambling. During a period of frontier arson, robbery, and murder in November 1879, Robert Fisk advocated vigilantism. Andrew worked in farming, soldiery, government printing, and mining and, in 1885, held the office of the Montana State Press Association treasurer. In the decade following North Dakota's admission to the Union in 1889, Andrew accepted appointment from President William McKinley as Helena's postmaster, a task he maintained for more than a decade.

In retirement in 1897 from declining health, James Fisk resided in Ramsey, Minnesota, and petitioned U.S. Army bureaucracy in vain for a military pension. On November 2, 1902, he died at the Minnesota Soldiers' Home in Minneapolis. Family diaries and letters from Robert's wife, Congregationalist teacher and writer Elizabeth "Lizzie" Chester Fisk of Haddam, Connecticut, preserved for posterity the role of the Fisk family in the settlement of Helena.

See also Bottineau, Pierre; Kelly, Fanny Wiggins.

Sources

Hanshew, Annie. *Border to Border: Historic Quilts and Quiltmakers of Montana*. Helena: Montana Historical Society, 2009.

White, Helen McCann. "Captain Fisk Goes to Washington." *Minnesota History* (15 February 2011): 216–230.

Folsom, Joseph Libbey (1817–1855)

A soldier and investor, Joseph Libbey Folsom shaped military and community development of San Francisco. Born of English lineage near Lake Winnipesaukee in Meredith, New Hampshire, on May 19, 1817, he was the fourth of the five children of farmers Mary Libbey and Abraham Folsom, a veteran of the War of 1812. The military claimed his grandfather, Abraham Folsom, during the American Revolution and his uncle, Nathaniel Folsom, in the Indian Wars.

Losses marked the history of the Folsom clan, beginning in 1819 with the death of 11-month-old Charles P. Folsom, Joseph little brother. The sale of family property after his father's death in 1824 forced the Folsoms to move to Northfield. While recovering from fever at Kimball Union Academy, a private boarding school, in May 1834, Joseph received nurse care from his 20-year-old brother, Abraham Decatur Folsom, who died of the same infection.

With the recommendation of U.S. Congressman Franklin Pierce, in June 1836, Joseph Folsom entered West Point, distinguished himself academically, and graduated in 1840. Until August 1842, he fought for the 5th Infantry in the Second Seminole War and relocated Creek Indians from northern Alabama to Indian Territory (present-day Oklahoma). After three years' service in the Pacific Northwest, in April 1844, Folsom returned to his alma mater to teach field tactics. At the outbreak of the Mexican-American War on April 25, 1846, he applied to rejoin his regiment.

On a six-month voyage begun in 1846, Captain Folsom sailed around Cape Horn to Yerba Buena, California, arriving in March 1847 with the 770-man First Regiment of New York Volunteers garrisoning the harbor. During the U.S. takeover of Mexican territory west of the Sierra Nevada, as quartermaster, he reconnoitered San Francisco Bay and rented its first wharf for the army in Yerba Buena Cove. At Portsmouth Square, to finance the militia, he served the port for two years as harbormaster and customs collector of several thousand dollars annually from foreign and domestic vessels. In June 1848, to billet troops and protect indigenous tribes, he reserved property for the Presidio and Black Point that enclosed land from Alcatraz Island to the summit of San Francisco.

Folsom recognized the future promise of Pacific Coast resources to the U.S. economy. He estimated the removal of gold from California by September 1848 at $500,000. For future historians, on August 23, 1848, he presented the National Institute (present-day Smithsonian Institution) the first gold flake discovered at Sutter's Mill.

Amid shore lawlessness, in late 1848, Folsom co-sponsored The Hounds, waterfront bounty hunters who arrested deserting sailors, street thugs, and ex-convicts. Punishment for thievery ranged from cropping of ears to lashing. In May 1849, he invested in the construction of a wharf between Clay and Sacramento streets, where Pacific Mail steamers from Chagres, Panama, docked in October 1850. Because of the upsurge in dock traffic as a result of the rush for gold, the port collected annual revenues of $1,200,000.

Timely Purchases

Folsom's initial purchase of lots in the sandy hills from U.S. vice-consul William Alexander Leidesdorff, an Afro-Carib-Polish native of the Danish West Indies, rose in value from $800 to $8,000. At Leidesdorff's sudden death, Folsom sailed to St. Croix to buy the entire 35,521-acre land grant from Anna Marie Sparks, Leidesdorff's mother, for $50,000. She demanded—and got—an additional $25,000. On November 13, 1849, by purchasing Rancho Rio de los Americanos from the Leidesdorff heirs for $75,000, Folsom acquired a debt of $40,000.

Despite the annoyance of squatters, Folsom made a good life. He settled his goods and office in the one-story adobe bungalow and viewed the bay from its piazza. After the land value spiraled to $1,500,000 in the wake of the 1849 Gold Rush, the investment established his fortune, but forced Folsom into a higher tax bracket and persistent court battles over U.S. government claims to his land. On Market Street in 1850, he co-formed the Society of California Pioneers, which developed culture, a museum, and library archiving artifacts dating before December 31, 1849.

Under the Treaty of Guadalupe Hidalgo, signed by representatives of the U.S. and Mexico on February 2, 1848, Folsom's land claim started through a Public Land Commission investigation in 1852. He moved a house to Folsom and Second streets and began surveying and selling lots and lobbying for rail connections to Sacramento. In 1853, he invested in the Sacramento Valley Railroad, California's first rail line, by which president William Tecumseh Sherman connected Sacramento and Folsom.

Folsom foresaw a genteel populace dominating San Francisco. To lure more developers, he built the Metropolitan Theatre, an opulent four-tiered hall opened at Montgomery Street on December 24, 1853. Under gaslight, it became a venue for opera and drama performed by such stars as singer Anna Bishop in *Der Freischutz* and actors Catherine Sinclair in *The School for Scandal* and Edwin Booth in *Richard III*. At California and Sansome streets, he managed the Jones House (later Tehama House), a three-story hotel housing ranchers and army officers. The property consisted of stables, conservatory, carriage house, and orchards and vineyards.

A Collapsing Fortune

Although Folsom was worth $11 million, he found himself land rich and cash strapped. Lacking funds, he failed to pay his 1855 street assessment. He developed his property along the American River and, in February 1855, chaired the board of the Sacramento Valley Railroad. He platted Granite City (present-day Folsom, California), which he had surveyed for a potential rail line. Adjacent land known as the Negro Bar mining camp attracted free blacks and provided a transportation hub to the goldfields.

At age 38, Folsom recuperated from facial neuralgia, insomnia, and pneumonia at Mission San José (present-day Fremont, California), a compound containing a hotel, saloon, and dry goods store. Sudden death from kidney failure on July 19, 1855, left his fiancée in mourning and plunged his mother, sister, and nephew into litigation in U.S., Mexican, Danish, and West Indian courts over the legal title to Rancho Rio. Executors quickly liquidated Tehama House furnishings and silver. Sparks realized the value of her deceased son's property and protested the original agreement.

Sale of the disputed property on January 10–11, 1856, brought $607,695 for 2,048 lots. The total estate netted Folsom's heirs more than $1.4 million. Later that year, as Granite City took the name Folsom to honor its founder, the area acquired a sizable population of Chinese laborers and a newspaper, the *Folsom Telegraph*. Workers hired by civil engineer Theodore Dehone Judah in February 1856 were laying rails for the Sacramento Valley Railroad, the first rail line built in the trans–Mississippi West. The rail became the western terminus of the Central Pacific Railroad.

A year later, the Natoma Water and Mining Company acquired 5,000 acres of Folsom's ranch for dredging operations, farming, quarrying and mining, and a water reservoir. In 1858, the Department of the Interior disputed Folsom's original survey. From July 1860 to July 1861, the Magnolia House Inn at Folsom quartered the western end of the Pony Express. In 1863, Folsom penitentiary provided convict labor for Horace Gates Livermore's damming of the American River for irrigation and hydroelectric power.

Sources
Palgon, Gary. *William Alexander Leidesdorff—First Black Millionaire, American Consul, and California Pioneer.* Atlanta: Lulu, 2005.
Richards, Rand. *Mud, Blood, and Gold: San Francisco in 1849.* San Francisco: Heritage House, 2009.

Franklin, Selim (1814–1884), Edward Franklin (1809–1873), Lumley Franklin (1808–1873), Lewis Abraham Franklin (1820–1879), Maurice Abraham Franklin (1817–1874), Victoria Jacobs Franklin (1838–1861), George Adolph Reich (1846–1896)

San Francisco pioneer, auctioneer, and realtor Selim Franklin, the head of a vigorous Jewish clan, gained a reputation for land speculation and commerce. Born in 1814 in Liverpool, England, to Miriam Abrahams of Arundel, Sussex, and Lazarus "Lewis" Franklin, an English-Polish financier and merchant, Selim claimed as an ancestor a Silesian grandfather, Rabbi Menachem Mendel Franckel of Wroclaw (present-day Breslau), Poland. Like others of the Franklin family, Selim apprenticed with a silversmith.

An eager '49er, Selim emigrated from London to San Francisco aboard the English bark *St. George* on March 1, 1849. On arrival from the 220-day voyage on October 12, he established a family enclave with older brothers Emanuel "Edward" Franklin, a land speculator; merchant Lumley Franklin; and younger cousins Lewis Abraham Franklin, an attorney and reformer, and miner and pharmacist Maurice Abraham Franklin. Lewis and Maurice arrived at Chagres, Panama, on January 39, 1849, from Kingston, Jamaica, aboard the schooner *Sovereign*. The pair traveled via Acapulco, Mexico, to California aboard the English bark *John Ritson,* arriving on May 18.

Commerce and Judaism

After reaching San Francisco, Lewis and Maurice opened a wood and canvas storefront on Jackson and Kearny streets. On September 16, 1850, they welcomed from thirty to fifty Jews to the first observances in the West of Rosh Hashanah and Yom Kippur. The celebrants formed the Kearny Street Hebrew Congregation, who observed Ashkenazic liturgy. Lewis delivered the first Jewish sermon in the trans–Mississippi frontier, published on November 15, 1850, in *The Asmonean,* a New York family newspaper devoted to business, politics, religion, and literature. He urged attendees to build a synagogue and form a unified Jewish community.

In 1850, Selim partnered with his brother Edward in operating a dry goods and mining gear store on Clay Street Wharf, a pier enlarged that year from 900' × 40' to 1,800' × 40'. The following year, the Folsoms continued bayfront commerce on Battery and Sacramento streets at Long Wharf with Franklin Real Estate and Auctioneers. They advertised their dwellings, ranches, and other properties in the *Daily Alta California* and held sales every Wednesday at noon.

In summer 1851, Lewis Folsom sailed south by coaster to Old Town San Diego. On the west side of the plaza, he and partner Thomas Whaley of New York City, a Christian, opened a mercantile, the Tienda California (California store). While living in a boarding house, Lewis initiated Jewish services and practiced law as Southern California's first Jewish attorney. Whaley and Lewis shared storekeeping on the Christian and Jewish sabbaths.

During an uprising on November 27, 1850, of the Cahuilla, Cupeño, Diegueño, Luiseño, and Yuma, Lewis joined the local militia as quartermaster. In retirement after April 1852, he railed against public filth, alcoholism, crime, and corruption in area law enforcement. To improve conditions, he accepted the post of justice of the peace and notary public. By August 1853, he advanced to county judge. His protest of the interruption of Yom Kippur prayers set a national precedent recognizing the right of American Jews to religious holy days.

In 1852, Lewis and Maurice Franklin purchased the Exchange Hotel, a three-story adobe inn they renamed Franklin House and used as a makeshift synagogue. The hostelry accommodated professional men as well as Lewis's office and Maurice's drugstore. The brothers replicated the successful inn with the second Franklin House in San Diego, completed in 1855 with stagecoach service to steamers in San Diego Bay.

In 1854, Maurice Franklin masterminded an effort to build a road to Temecula, halfway between Los Angeles and San Diego. In spring 1856, he co-directed the San Diego & Gila Pacific and Atlantic Railroad Company with the aim of extending it to Yuma, Arizona, and the Atlantic Coast. On March 31, 1857, Maurice wed Victoria Jacobs, a 19-year-old Polish-English diarist from Manchester, England. He presented her a journal as a nuptial gift and settled her at Franklin House.

Two years later, Maurice dissolved the partnership with Lewis and moved to San Bernardino to be near Victoria's sister Leah and parents, Hannah and Mark Jacobs, who operated a hotel, newsstand, and clothing emporium, La Tienda Barata (The Cheap Store). Maurice opened an upstairs studio, M.A. Franklin's Premium Photographic Gallery, which flourished into the 1870s. At his pharmacy, the San Bernardino Drug Store, he and associate, pharmacist George Adolph Reich of Sroclaw, Poland, specialized in patent medicine, chemicals, toiletries, perfume, brandy, and whiskey, the standard treatment for human or animal snakebite.

After Victoria Franklin's death in childbirth on November 12, 1861, Maurice published her journal, *Diary of a San Diego Girl, 1856*. On September 15, 1864, he wed his sister-in-law, 23-year-old Jane Jacobs, and joined Mark Jacobs in founding the Congregation Ohabai Shalome of San Francisco. In 1865, Franklin established the Hebrew Free School of San Bernardino and taught gratis, a service that earned him an inscribed silver pitcher in March 1866.

The Franklins in Victoria

After a fire destroyed the store of Selim and Lumley Franklin in 1858, they rebuilt their Pacific Coast business as the only British-born immigrants in colonial Victoria, British Columbia. During the Fraser River Gold Rush, which began in March 1858, the pair founded a realty and auction house on Yates Street and, in December, advertised in *The British Colonist* photos, books, carriages, livestock, wagons, furniture, and land. Crown colony governor James Douglas appointed Lumley and Selim Franklin as the area's official auctioneers, a profession organized at the Anchor Rooms on January 26, 1859. In the wake of an international dispute over the San Juan Islands between Vancouver and Seattle in 1859, Selim advised Queen Victoria on American claims to "manifest destiny."

Selim Franklin's influence in Victoria included becoming the first Jewish legislator in British North America. By 1863, Lumley Franklin chaired the board of the Eureka Copper Company. From June 7 to October 21,

1864, Selim headed the Vancouver Island Exploring Expedition, during which his surname attached to the Franklin River. In November 1865, after citizens of Victoria elected Lumley Franklin mayor, he pressed for the union of Victoria with Vancouver, which occurred in 1867. In June 1867, Lumley began a two-year term on the Vancouver Island Board of Education.

In 1866, Selim Franklin returned to San Francisco. His brother Edward died at his two-story home, the Franklin Canyon Adobe, in Martinez, California, in 1871. Edward's executor, Lumley Franklin, expired in San Francisco on August 3, 1873, from paralytic stroke. Cousin Maurice Franklin died in San Francisco on September 2, 1874; Lewis succumbed in London in 1879. After serving on the board of the Geographical Society of the Pacific and the Mineral Fork Mining and Silver Company in Utah, Selim died in 1884. His nephew, Selim Maurice Franklin, co-founded the University of Arizona.

Sources

Beasley, Edward. *Empire as the Triumph of Theory.* New York: Routledge, 2005.

Humphreys, Danda. *On the Street Where You Live: Sailors, Solicitors, and Stargazers of Early Victoria.* Surrey, B.C.: Heritage House, 2011.

Kahn, Ava Fran, ed. *Jewish Voices of the California Gold Rush: A Documentary History, 1849–1880.* Detroit: Wayne State University Press, 2002.

French, Erasmus Darwin (1822–1902)

Medical doctor Erasmus Darwin French moved west to explore and prospect for precious metals. A native of Middlesex, New York, and the third of eleven children, he was born on January 20, 1822, to Amanda Hazeltine and farmer Harvey French, a descendent of Anglo-Scots dating to late fifteenth-century Essex, England. At age thirteen, Erasmus entered Albion Seminary, newly established by Methodist Episcopal pioneers in Albion, Michigan, and studied medicine under an uncle, Dr. Joel W. French, the area's pioneer physician. Darwin practiced medicine with Dr. Frank French for two years in Hillsdale County.

In December 1845, Darwin French set out on his own and joined the army at Fort Leavenworth, Kansas, the oldest military post in the trans–Mississippi West. He reached Santa Fe, New Mexico, in 1846 with the First Dragoons, a 150-man regiment of mounted infantry led by Commander Stephen Watts Kearny. In company with Kit Carson, on December 6, French served during the Mexican-American War of 1846–1848. As an army physician, he treated the wounded at the battle of San Pasqual at present-day San Diego, California, where the Californios (Hispanic land owners) killed nineteen Americans and wounded fifteen.

French revived his ventures upon mustering out in early 1847 and took a job at Los Angeles Hospital as steward to military surgeon John Strother Griffin. French invested in seven lots on Coronado Beach, flatland used for pasturing cattle. On 160 acres outside Fort Tejon in the Tehachapi Mountains northeast of Los Angeles, French raised cattle until Agua Caliente Indian attacks forced him to abandon his adobe outside Grapevine Canyon in 1851.

Death Valley Ventures

In late January 1850, French outfitted guides to rescue the Arcan-Bennett party from Wisconsin. Known as the Lost Forty-niners, they had camped at Indian Wells during December in the driest part of the Mojave Basin and awaited death from starvation. French led survivors to Rancho Ex-Mission San Fernando, where they bought jerky, wheat flour, yellow beans, oranges, rope, saddles, and pack horses. Upon reaching civilization, the party named the area "Death Valley."

From talk of a rich lode that prospector Jim Martin located in 1849 at the Lost Gunsight lead-silver mine, in Autumn 1850, French organized Death Valley's first mining team. In company with three companions and an Indian guide named Ignacio, he began exploring Owens Valley, Panamint Springs, and Tucki Mountain. On January 12, 1858, in San Jose, California, he married 28-year-old Cornelia Seymour Cowles of St. Clair, Illinois, mother of twins Lulu Charlotte and Lila, who died in infancy, and sons Alfred Channing, John, and Addison Paine French. Returned to ranching in San Jose, French established a home at Chico and remained until 1860.

French returned to prospecting from March to July 1860 with a company of twelve prospectors, who mapped passable routes from Butte County and sources of pure water. Traveling southeast from Owens Lake from Visalia, Walker's Pass, Darwin Canyon, and Panamint Valley, the party located an abandoned Mormon- or Indian-built lead furnace at Furnace Creek in the Amargosa Range and, at Salt Creek Flat, remains of the Jayhawker Party, including the emigrants' wagons, ox yokes, guns, and cooksite. After finding ore-bearing strata at Silver Mountain, from 1860 to 1865, French operated the Darwin silver mines in the New Coso Mining District near Bodie. At age forty-eight, he farmed at Poway and chaired the county commission of San Diego County.

Farmer and Writer

The area outside Bodie, California, regained prominence from 1870 to 1877 after the discovery in the Coso Range of lead, gold, and silver. In 1874, the Old Coso Road connected Coso to the town of Darwin, from which two sixteen-mule teams of the Cerro Gordon Freight Company hauled silver bullion worth $700 per ton. Investment in livestock reached up to $80 per mule or $1,280 per team.

Provisions arrived from Lone Pine. Within a year, a pipeline carried water some 8 miles to supply the two smelters that purified silver-bearing lead ores. By 1879, the Darwin silver boom ended. A fire on April 30, 1879, halted the violent activities that characterized the Centennial Saloon and fourteen other dance halls and filled columns in the *Coso Mining News*.

French continued developing his property by planting San Diego County's only vineyard in 1881. In 1887, he dictated memories of his medical work during the battle of San Pasqual, a conflict that decided California's future. At age seventy-seven, he composed an epic poem, *The Power of Destiny Revealed in Our War with Spain and the Philippines* (1899), which honors American commanding officers.

Around 1894, the French family appears to have relocated to Ensenada, Baja California Norte, southeast of Tijuana, Mexico. Son Alfred Channing French followed his father's mining career by working in a copper mine in Gila, Arizona. Darwin French died in Ensenada in September 1902. Perpetuating his name between the Inyo Mountains and Argus Range after 1926 are tourist and hiking sites—the ghost town of Darwin, Darwin Wash, Darwin Bench, Darwin Creek, Darwin Falls, Darwin Canyon, and Darwin Falls Wilderness.

SOURCE
Palazzo, Robert P. *Death Valley*. Charleston, SC: Arcadia, 2008.

Goller, John (1825–1874), James Welch Brier (1814–1898), Juliet Wells Brier (1813–1913)

German prospector, blacksmith, and carriage maker John Goller established the first manufactory in Los Angeles, California. Born in Bavaria on July 7, 1825, he grew up among miners and learned the ironworking trade before emigrating to the German community in St. Louis, Missouri. On April 5, 1849, he departed from Galesburg, Illinois, with John Graff, arriving at Little Salt Lake, Utah. In August, Graff, Goller, and seven other independent emigrants joined one hundred and six prospectors of the Jayhawkers' Party.

With some shifting of wagons to other trains, the Jayhawkers departed for the Sierra crossing in October and made history by discovering Death Valley, California, at midnight on December 24, 1849. The company slaughtered and roasted an ox for Christmas dinner. The Americans ridiculed the non–English speakers as "Buzzard Dutch" for devouring their cattle down to the intestines, hooves, and hide. The passage lengthened from episodes with cattle stampedes and rustlers, cholera, quicksand, and threats by Timbisha Indians.

Over the uncharted Southern Emigrant Trail in southwestern Utah, the '49ers set out over the Mojave Desert to the Santa Clarita Valley, where the Reverend James Welch Brier, a Congregationalist minister, his wife, Juliet

Wells Brier, and their three sons—eight-year-old Christopher Columbus, six-year-old John Wells, and ten-year-old Kirke White Brier—shared water and crackers with Graff and Goller. As the party walked the Armagosa sector of the western Mojave, Goller and a collaborator, Wolfgang Tauber of Joliet, Illinois, collected gold nuggets at Nitre Spring.

Vaqueros rescued the party from starvation, including the entire Brier family. After the loss of three lives from exposure and fever, the emigrants reached José Salazar's San Francisquito Ranch north of Los Angeles on February 4, 1850. Wolfgang Tauber died at sea within months of the bonanza. In later years, Californians elevated the Jayhawkers to prominence among pioneers, but joked about the Lost Goller Mine.

Pioneer Manufacturer

Emaciated on arrival to the Pacific Coast, Goller worked for a gunsmith. In 1851, he purchased for $8,000 a major tract of the José Maximo Alanis estate, Rancho San José de Buenos Ayres. With the loan of $500 from vintner Louis Wilhardt, Goller built an awning and wagon business on Commercial and Los Angeles streets and rented out the one-story adobe residence attached to his shop. Because of the scarcity of iron, he charged $16 to shoe a horse.

While plotting routes back to the Lost Goller Mine, Goller retrieved from the desert discarded iron wheel rims and nails and recycled them into horseshoes and branding irons. He added to his stock of metal by purchasing junk. In addition to making and repairing singletrees, plows and harrows, axles, shutters, railings, and doors, in 1853, he began crafting the city's first conveyances—buggies, carts, covered spring wagons, Concord stagecoaches, hackneys, lighters, and velocipedes, which he advertised in the weekly Los Angeles *Star*. His staff grew to eight wheelwrights and twenty-six workers manning five forges, with James Baldwin as foreman.

Goller involved himself in the presidential campaign for Franklin Pierce and, in 1852, organized the city's first political procession. In 1854, he wed Paulena Neidt of San Francisco, mother of their two daughters, and drove his family in a dignified carriage. By 1855, he built a brick warehouse and employed East Prussian immigrant Frank Lecouvreur as one of three carriage painters.

In partnership with John J. Tomlinson, the Goller & Tomlinson firm ventured into transport to Sacramento, San Pedro, Shasta, and Eureka. Goller served as city councilman and city cavalry farrier in 1857 and arranged shipping from Sepulveda Landing, the pier of developer Augustus W. Timms at the port. After sparks inflamed Goller's factory roof on February 25, 1858, he co-formed the city's first volunteer fire department and demanded that the city supply the company with horses.

Goller's clients included the federal government, for whom he produced wide gauge freight wagons in 1859 suited to Mojave Desert trails from Fort Yuma, Arizona. In 1861, he made fifty lances for the volunteer rangers and repaired the locks, chains, and bars of the city jail, earning $789. Service to the city involved Goller in police, tax collection, and street repair committees. Slow repayment of debts to his forge forced him to post collection notices in the *Semi-Weekly Southern News*.

Goller continued manufacturing wagons for use over the state of California. Miners on the Colorado River purchased Goller's rolling stock to transport equipment from Los Angeles. By 1868, Benjamin Phelps, owner of the Vulture Mining Company in Maricopa County, Arizona, ordered thirty freight wagons from Goller to carry ore to refining mills.

Goller invested in realty and a city water company and, in 1867, co-formed the first Los Angeles gas company, which made fuel for burners and street lamps from two tons of asphalt per day. He displayed his model of the bridge to span the Los Angeles River in 1869. In June 1870, for a $5 commission, he forged a branding iron for the city composed of the letters LAC. Farmers in San Diego and San Francisco purchased his spring buggies, which featured his unique brace and C springs, patented in 1870.

Near the Goller home at the entrance to

Calle de Los Negros (Alley of the Blacks) during the riot of October 24, 1871, he could hear a barrage of gunfire from 6:00 to 9:00 p.m. when the altercation turned into slaughter. He witnessed from the family porch roof the shooting, hanging, and mutilation of seventeen Chinese, America's largest mass lynching. Among the victims were the Chinese doctor Chien Lee "Gene" Tong, an Asian woman, and a 14-year-old boy.

Goller's protest to the 500 mostly white male vigilantes about the endangerment of his wife, ten-year-old Louisa, and eight-year-old Christina resulted in a rifle and knife brandished at him. The following day, a boaster thrust into Goller's face a queue lopped from a Chinese victim hanged on a length of clothesline from the boarding house across from the wagon shop. For the first time, the media spread Los Angeles news worldwide, forcing solid citizens to suppress lynch mobs and reform the city's social structure.

Return to Prospecting

Goller branched out to the manufacture of expressman William George Fargo's wagon brakes and repair of steam boilers and train engines. After he joined F. Foster's wheelwright forge at Aliso Street, competition and business losses in the 1870s cost Goller much of his investment. By 1872, he declared bankruptcy, in part from unwise loans to friends. He lost Paulena to a severe illness in July 1873.

During the last years of his life, Goller returned to his original love, crafting wagons, and, in fall 1873, finished America's first barouche, a shallow carriage made fashionable in France. He partnered with Tehachapi stockman and orchardist Grant Price Cuddeback to search for Goller and Tauber's original mother lode. At a spring in the southern El Paso Mountains, Goller discovered more placer nuggets.

On retracing his steps, Goller struck a small vein in Red Rock Canyon near Ricardo, reducing skepticism about his earlier claims. Speculators combed 3,000 acres in search of the source. After his death from liver disease on July 7, 1874, a respelling of his name and legends of the region's only placer mine survived in Goler Gulch, Goler Wash, and Goler Canyon, a pass between Panamint Valley and Death Valley.

Sources
Johnson, John, Jr. "How Los Angeles Covered Up the Massacre of 17 Chinese." *LA Weekly* (10 March 2011): 1.
Zesch, Scott. *The Chinatown War: Chinese Los Angeles and the Massacre of 1871*. New York: Oxford University Press, 2012.

Goodnight, Charles (1836–1929), Elija Goodnight (1831–1929), Mary Ann Dyer Goodnight (1839–1926), Leigh Richmond Dyer (1849–1902), Oliver Loving (1812–1867), John Simpson Chisum (1824–1884), John George "Jack" Adair (1823–1885), Cornelia Wadsworth Ritchie Adair (1837–1921)

Rancher, surveyor, and Texas Ranger Charles Foxwing "Chuck" Goodnight, Jr., established longhorn breeding at Palo Duro in the Texas Panhandle, the start of the nation's first billion-dollar industry. The fourth of the five children of Mary Charlotte Sheek Collier and Charles Foxwing Goodnight, he was born on March 5, 1836, at Macoupin County, Illinois. His maternal relatives pioneered land in Spotsylvania, Virginia. Of Anglo-German ancestry on the paternal side, the family altered the spelling of Gutknecht to Goodnight after the immigration of Charles's great grandparents, Catherina and George Gerick Goodnight, from Mecklenburg, Germany, to Harlen Station, Kentucky.

By age four, Charles the younger was fatherless. With only six months of classroom education in a country school, he never learned to read or write, yet produced one of the pioneer achievements of the Old West. At age ten, he and his mother, four siblings, and stepfather Hiram Henry Daugherty traveled 800 miles southwest to Texas cow country and settled at Old Nashville at the confluence of the Brazos and Little rivers. He learned tracking from Caddo Jake and worked as a cotton freighter ferrying bales to Houston. At age 17, he joined his stepbrother, John Wesley Sheek, in raising 400 cattle at Black Springs.

At Fort Belknap in 1854, Goodnight met his life's love, 15-year-old Mary Ann "Molly"

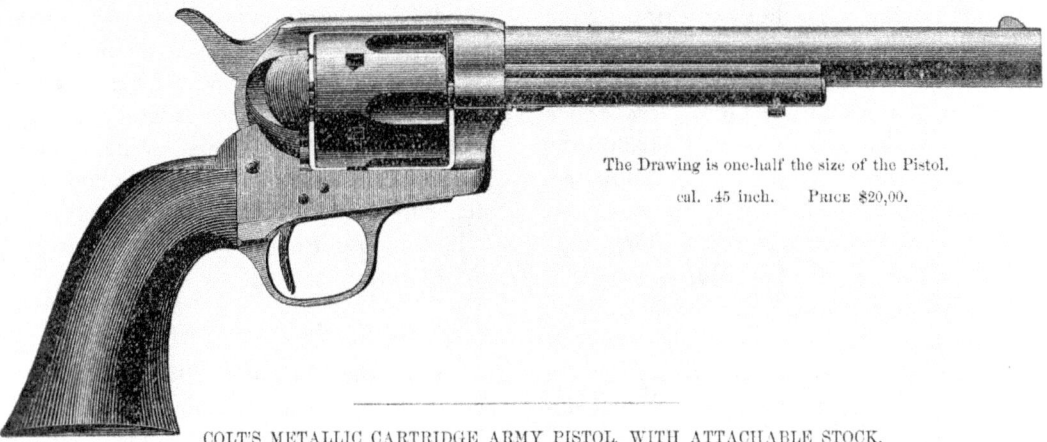

COLT'S NEW MODEL ARMY METALLIC CARTRIDGE REVOLVING PISTOL.

The Drawing is one-half the size of the Pistol.
cal. .45 inch.   PRICE $20.00.

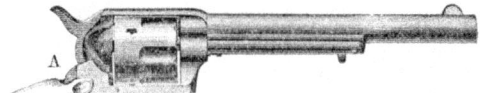

COLT'S METALLIC CARTRIDGE ARMY PISTOL, WITH ATTACHABLE STOCK.

Dyer of Madison County, Tennessee. By age twenty, he left herding at Palo Pinto in north central Texas to fight with the state militia against Comanche rustlers. In 1857, Goodnight rode with Captain Jack Cureton's Texas Rangers as a scout and trail guide. He led a foray by sixty rangers along Mule Creek to a Noconi Comanche camp and, on December 18, 1860, participated in the killing of Chief Peta Nocona, a fierce raider. The skirmish preceded the recovery of Cynthia Ann Parker, Nocona's captive wife for 24 years and the mother of Comanche leader Quanah Parker.

With Cureton's Rangers, in 1861, Goodnight served in the Confederate army as a scout. While fending off Comanche and Kiowa raids, he traveled northwest Texas, New Mexico, and Indian Territory (present-day Oklahoma) and ventured as far north as Canada. His older brother, Elija Goodnight of the Fourth Mounted Volunteers, supplied the rebel army with cattle. In an era of dwindling buffalo herds, the increase in demand for beef also boosted need for breeders of mounts suited to long rides and capable of withstanding the strain of trailing, roping, and herding cattle.

Career Cattleman

Upon return to Texas in 1864, Charles Goodnight rounded up feral cattle left untended dur-

Charles Goodnight's cowboys armed themselves with Colt revolvers and pursued rustlers.

ing the first three years of the Civil War. He pastured stock as far west as the extinct Capulin volcano in New Mexico. In September 1865, his cowboys armed themselves with Colt revolvers after Indians stole 2,000 of Goodnight's herd from Elm Creek in Lubbock Texas.

On June 6, 1866, Goodnight partnered with Oliver Loving, a rancher and shipper from Kentucky and descendent of a Revolutionary War veteran. Loving pioneered a 700-mile crossing of the Staked Plain of New Mexico to the Pecos River. For a profit of $12,000, the two participated in the herding of 2,000 free-range longhorns from Belknap, Texas, to Fort Sumner, New Mexico, a reservation where the U.S. government fed soldiers as well as 8,000 Mescalero Apache and Navajo. For trail drovers, the partners employed eighteen cowboys, many of them former infantrymen and troopers recently mustered out of the Confederate Army.

During the trek, Goodnight revamped an army-surplus Studebaker wagon and invented the chuckwagon for cooking on the trail, a source of enticement to the best employees. The path he and Loving blazed earned the name Goodnight-Loving Trail (or Pecos Trail), the route they traversed to supply the U.S. military with beef cattle. In autumn 1866, Goodnight collaborated with John Simpson "Cow John" Chisum, a Tennessee-born stockman and owner of the Jingle-Bob spread near Lincoln, New Mexico, whose Anglo-Scots ancestry traced back to a twelfth-century Scots named Chisholm from Roxburghshire. The two drove a herd to the 40-square mile Bosque Redondo Reservation. The meat provisioned the 9,000 Navajo and Mescalero Apache residents whom General James Henry Carleton attempted to turn into homesteaders, tradesmen, and farmers.

By 1867, when the U.S. Army opened forts Richardson, Concho, and Griffin to protect cattle herds and pioneers, the Goodnight-Loving Trail extended from Alamogordo Creek, New Mexico, to Belknap, Texas, and north through Granada, Colorado, to Cheyenne, Wyoming. Another route reached rail stockyards in Abilene, Dodge City, and Wichita, Kansas, which supplied beef to Chicago slaughterhouses and steakhouses along the Atlantic coast. For assistance on the drive, Goodnight hired his 18-year-old brother-in-law, Leigh Richmond Dyer.

Secured in part by cavalry patrols, in spring 1867, Chisum moved 600 cattle over the Goodnight-Loving Trail to army provisioners at Fort Sumner, New Mexico. Wounded from a Comanche attack during the third cattle drive, Oliver Loving died of gangrene on September 25, 1867, at Fort Sumner. When winter passed, Goodnight had his partner's body exhumed from the fort's cemetery and, on March 2, 1868, transported it home over 600 miles to Weatherford, Texas.

The Goodnights and JA Ranch

Chisum, the owner of 80,000 cattle, continued supplying animals to Goodnight at his Rock Canon Ranch in Pueblo, Colorado, for transport to the Union Pacific Railroad at Cheyenne, Wyoming. Goodnight married Mary Ann "Molly" Dyer on July 26, 1870, in Hickman, Kentucky. For six years during the silver boom, the couple lived in Pueblo at Old Home Ranch and planted an apple orchard. He co-formed the Stock Growers' Bank of Pueblo and speculated in realty, Goodnight's Opera House, and meatpacking. In partnership with Chisum, in 1871, Goodnight made $17,000.

Relocated to Texas, Mary Ann Goodnight, the only non–Indian woman in the area, taught pupils in a bunkhouse classroom. The couple supported nondenominational evangelism, the building of a Methodist church, and the Goodnight Academy, a school for ranch children. In 1873, a national financial panic depleted Goodnight's holdings. Left with 1,600 head of cattle in autumn 1875, he moved south to Rincón de las Piedras, New Mexico. The year brought news of future profits from Chicago's Union Stock Yard and Transit Company, established in 1875 by butcher Gustavus Franklin Swift.

On October 23, 1876, Goodnight and partner John George Adair of Queen's County, Ireland, amassed the million-acre JA Ranch in Palo Duro Canyon, where Goodnight built a temporary cottonwood and cedar dugout. The JA became the only working breeder ranch in the Texas Panhandle and the fount of the southwestern cattle industry. Maintaining 100,000 head of stock with ranch foreman Leigh Dyer, Goodnight pioneered the breeding of herefords with longhorns and cattle with bison for beefalo, which he called "cattalo." He pastured a bison herd at Caprock Canyon that provided stock for American and European animal parks and herds for Yellowstone, a 2-million acre landmark that Congress declared a national park on March 1, 1872. Adjacent to the ranch, Leigh Dyer bred shorthorn cattle on a 320-acre tract.

While pushing the first shorthorns to Dodge City, Kansas, the "Queen of Cow Towns," in summer 1878, Goodnight, armed with his faithful Winchester rifle, blazed the Palo Duro-Dodge City Trail. Because of the destitution of reservation Comanche, he negotiated with Quanah Parker to provide a beef a day if Indians promised not to steal JA cattle. With his co-formation of the Panhandle Stock Association at Mobeetie in March 1880, ranchers improved breeding techniques and banded against Billy the Kid's gang, which drove stolen Texas cattle into New Mexico until the leader's death on July 14, 1881.

By 1882, Goodnight's partnership with Adair earned them $512,000. As open-range grazing came to an end, Goodnight became the first Panhandle rancher to employ barbed wire. At Adair's death on May 14, 1885, Goodnight owned 1,325,000 acres. He continued his ranching partnership with Adair's widow, Cornelia Wadsworth Ritchie Adair of Pennsylvania, and domesticated beefalo hybridized from buffalo and polled Angus. A stomach ailment in 1887 forced Goodnight to sell the JA spread.

Old Age and Legacy

Goodnight owned Quitaque Ranch and sections outside Fort Worth, where, in December 1887, the family built a two-story home and operated the Goodnight-Thayer Cattle Company and a public menagerie of elk, antelope, and prairie fowl. They lost their investment in a Chihuahua silver mine nationalized by Mexico. In 1898, they bankrolled Goodnight College and supported Indian lobbying in Washington, D.C. In 1919, W.J. McAlister purchased the spread with the stipulation that Goodnight live out his days on the land.

A widower after April 11, 1926, Goodnight hired telegrapher and nurse Corinne Oletta Goodnight from Montana as a caretaker. On March 5, 1927, he married his nurse and began wintering in Phoenix, Arizona. At his death in Tucson, Arizona, on December 12, 1929, he was buried in the Goodnight plot in Amarillo.

The Goodnight name survives in a statue in Canyon, Texas, in street names, the town of Goodnight, and the annual Goodnight Chuckwagon Cookoff in Clarendon. The National Register of Historic Places lists the former JA Ranch, which anchors the Charles Goodnight Historical Center. In 1985, Larry McMurtry's novel *Lonesome Dove* dramatized the brotherhood of Goodnight and Loving.

SOURCES
Hagan, William T. *Charles Goodnight: Father of the Texas Panhandle.* Norman: University of Oklahoma Press, 2007.
Hedstrom-Page, Deborah. *From Ranch to Railhead with Charles Goodnight.* Nashville: B&H Publishing, 2007.

Gwydir, Rickard Daniel (1844–1925)

A pioneer, soldier, and Indian agent in the Pacific Northwest, Rickard Daniel O'Connell Gwydir incorporated cultural tolerance in his treatment of tribes deracinated from Spokane, Washington. He was born in Calcutta, India, on November 7, 1844, to Irish parents—Jane Prendible Farmer of Limerick and soldier Richard McKenna Gwydir. While serving in the British Army, his father died in 1846 at the onset of the 1846–1863 Asiatic Cholera Pandemic that spread from Lower Bengal along the Arabian coast to the Middle East as far as Siberia, Scandinavia, Ireland, Spain, the Balkans, and Texas.

Mother and son moved to England before immigrating to Covington, Kentucky, via Brooklyn, New York, where she married Daniel Ruttle. After the birth of two sons and a daughter to the Ruttles, Rickard sometimes adopted his stepfather's surname. At the outbreak of the American Civil War, Gwydir fought for the Confederacy as a scout and spy for Morgan's Raiders. From June 11 to July 26, 1863, the regiment of 2,460 expert cavalrymen burned bridges, boats, and depots and seized smoked hams, cash, horses, and loot from farms and homes in Indiana and northern Ohio.

In his twenties, Gwydir worked at a pork abattoir and learned distilling. He advanced to Covington's city auditor and public works supervisor and actuary for the U.S. Internal Revenue. From 1869 to 1877, he superintended construction of the Cincinnati Southern Railroad, the only major railway built by a city. After his marriage in Dearborn County, Indiana, on October 7, 1879, Gwydir and wife Mary Emma Dobell of Cincinnati, Ohio, reared four children—Nell M., Jane, Sue B. "Susie," and Rickard Davezac Gwydir. In 1885, Jane died at age two.

Settling Washington Territory

In May 1887, Gwydir accepted a presidential appointment from the Grover Cleveland administration as federal agent to twelve confederated tribes at Chewelah on the Colville Indian Reservation in Washington Territory. His assignment, to settle the Nez Percé and Sanpoil, took him to the Nespelem River valley, where whiskey smugglers and intrusive prospectors raised mistrust in the Indians. To function closer to Fort Spokane, Gwydir moved his office south to the banks of the Spokane River. At a tense parley on July 22, he employed delaying tactics as well as cavalry and infantry to stave off a lethal clash between squabbling tribes led by Chief Moses of the Sinkiuse-Columbia and Prophet-Chief Skolaskin of the Sanpoil.

Gwydir's suggestion of a native police force and court system incited anger and threats from Skolaskin, a vocal opponent of Gwydir and President Cleveland. Justifications of the evangelism by Catholic priest Etienne DeRouge failed to satisfy Moses, who refused to give up polygamy. The Spokane adapted well to agriculture and a court system, which enabled Gwydir to suppress gambling and whiskey peddling, the source of 90 percent of crime among Valley Indians. The Nez Percé, breeders of the famed Appaloosa hunting horses, depended on government allotments, but ignored Gwydir's directions about efficient operation of a sawmill and the need for permission before leaving the reservation to visit the Lapwai.

Through letters to Commissioner of Indian Affairs John D.C. Atkins and annual reports on Indian welfare, Gwydir lobbied for fair treatment of the Spokane, Sanpoil, Okanogan, Sinkiuse, Skolaskin, Coeur d'Alène, Calispel, and Nez Percé. On November 21, 1887, he informed Commissioner Atkins that opening the Colville Reservation to white pioneers had sparked anger in Chief Skolaskin. Unsympathetic Washington insiders suspected that Gwydir coddled chiefs Joseph and Moses by allowing them to flout regulations.

In April 1888, a measles outbreak pressed Gwydir to sooth the Nez Percé, who feared that white medicine was responsible for the death of Joseph's only child, Jean Louise. Gwydir proposed that officials invite to Washington, D.C., Chief Skolaskin, main agitant of discontent. To halt the trading of cows and horses for whiskey, Gwydir posted a border patrol. He furthered good will by treating chiefs Joseph and Moses to meals at his table. By his retirement in 1889, the year that Washington entered the Union, government shipments of clothing, food, and farm tools assisted the Sanpoil in adapting to changes in their lifestyle.

Miner and Administrator

At age forty-five, Gwydir altered his career simultaneous with the annexation of Washington to the United States and the 1889 gold rush north of the Pend-d'Oreille River on the Idaho-Washington border. He worked the goldfields of the Columbia River basin and northern Idaho, where prospectors found nuggets in river sand and gravel bars. By 1893, he moved on from placer mining to Chinese Inspector for the U.S. Treasury, a post overseeing customs, immigration, and anti-smuggling border patrols.

A resident of Spokane after 1901, Gwydir compiled in articles for the *Spokane Falls Review* his reflections on settlers and natives, including commentary on Chief Joseph, a daring fugitive from government control who had sought sanctuary with the Hunkpapa Sioux in

Canada. Until 1914, administrative work occupied Gwydir with sidewalk inspection, licensing, and employment as deputy sheriff and court bailiff. At age seventy-three, he ran for Spokane city council. After Gwydir died on November 7, 1925, veterans of the Union and Confederate armies served as pallbearers.

Sources
Gwydir, Rickard D. *Recollections from the Colville Agency, 1886–1889.* Spokane: Arthur H. Clark, 2001.
Ruby, Robert H., and John Arthur Brown. *The Spokane Indians: Children of the Sun.* Norman: University of Oklahoma Press, 2006.

Hamilton, Ezra (1833–1914)

Soldier, miner, inventor, and manufacturer Ezra M. Hamilton contributed to the propagation of alfalfa, orchards, and vineyards and to the commerce and development in Willow Springs, California. Born on February 22, 1833, at Mount Sterling in Brown County, Illinois, to William and Nancy Antle Hamilton of Anglo-Norman ancestry, he was the second of seven children. At age sixteen, Ezra fed an urge for pioneering while working as a cook and steward on Mississippi River steamers. Four years later, he abandoned his sweetheart and, with five yoke of oxen, journeyed to California with only one carpetbag and $15. At the time, horses cost up to $70 each while oxen brought as little as $13 per animal. In the goldfields, he panned ore to earn $8,000 to match Nancy's savings before proposing marriage.

Hamilton harbored naiveté about the dangers of the West fed by sensational media stories of savage Native Americans. Over the Oregon Trail, in anticipation of Indian attack, he armed himself for nightly patrols with a Colt revolver, rifle, and knife. On the approach to Fort Laramie, Wyoming, a region notorious for alkaline water, he thoughtlessly destroyed Sioux burial platforms, a crime that Indians punished by death. On a visit to his girl in Klamath County, Oregon, in late October 1855, he arrived during the Rogue River Indian Wars caused by white encroachment in Plains Indian land. On arrival in northern California in 1856, he established the Hamilton Mining Company in Shasta County, where he also farmed on the Canon ranch at Redding.

In 1861, Hamilton came east to Minnesota to marry Sarah Landson and settled in Minneapolis on Lake Calhoun. During the Civil War, he joined the First Minnesota Volunteers, who saw action at the battles of Bull Run, Wilderness, Cold Harbor, Petersburg, Richmond, and Antietam. He participated in the Confederate surrender at Appomattox on April 9, 1865, and, on May 23–24, marched in Washington, D.C., at the Grand Review of the Armies.

A Return to the West

At a low point in his life, Hamilton suffered the death of two children. After the demise of his wife Sarah and Charles, their third child, in 1867, Hamilton labored at carpentry and stone masonry and farmed with his parents in Maine. He invented a peat presser, which formed high density briquettes for domestic fuel.

On April 21, 1869, Hamilton wed 26-year-old Harriett Ann Moffett of Richfield, Minnesota. Their union produced Fred M., Truman Worthy, Eugene H., and Walter Lester Hamilton. In 1872, Ezra joined a mining expedition to southwestern Montana Territory. On September 20, 1875, he retired to California for health reasons. The family built a house on Avenue 23 in East Los Angeles.

As in his youth, Hamilton worked in construction, but directed his skills toward civic improvement. On October 23, 1877, he patented molds for concrete or cement sub-irrigation pipes, which won an award in 1880 from the State Agricultural Society. He co-formed the Workingmen's Party and, by defeating the city political machine, won election as an independent to the Los Angeles city council in 1878 and 1883. In his second term, he supported populist, anti-railroad politics and advocated streetlights. In 1880, he won election to the Chicago Convention as a delegate of the Greenback wing of the Workingmen. His gardening won $2 in awards for watermelons and cantaloupes.

In 1882, Hamilton invested in a clay pit at Tropico Hill and ordered a carload of silica from Rosamond to strengthen vitrification. At a wood-fueled kiln of the East Los Angeles Pottery and Sewer Pipe Works in Rosamond, California, he fired clay for firebrick, drain and roofing tile, water and sewer pipe, demijohns, terra cotta pottery, and rockinghamware and stoneware. To lessen the company overhead by two-thirds, in 1884, he converted his furnace to oil.

In 1886 and 1887, Hamilton won awards from the California State Agricultural Society for water filters and coolers, an extruder of continuous pipe, fireproof chimneys, and artistic pottery. Following the national depression of 1893, the demand for municipal clay pipe declined in the subsequent fiscal year. The following year, his son Eugene died.

Gold and Investments

When Hamilton's health declined, in March 1896, he and his son Fred spied gold in clay quarried from Antelope Valley at the ridge of Crandall Hill, later called Hamilton Hill. In collaboration with Truman and Lester Hamilton, he operated the Fay, Lida, and Home 1 and Home 2 mines with steam equipment, producing ore assayed at $35 per ton. Ezra Hamilton's philosophy varied from other prospectors' get-rich-quick schemes. Rather, he removed conservative amounts of gold from the ledge and considered the remaining vein a repository of future earnings.

With the profits of $46,000 on the first shipment, Hamilton built a five-stamp mill and opened the Fairview, Big Tree, and Gold King mines. In 1900, he liquidated most of his mining assets for $100,000 and invested $3,500 in 160 acres at Willow Springs. In 1908, he sold the Lida Mine to the Antelope Valley Milling Company.

In 1902, Hamilton's investments strayed from mining into the developing field of health tourism. He paid $3,500 for 160 acres in the Mojave Desert, where he developed the twenty-three springs at the former stage station of Willow Springs into a resort. He erected stone residences and a sanitarium treating respiratory ills. For convenience, he connected Rosamond to the compound with a nine-mile private telephone line.

Hamilton's curiosity led him to invent a pipe-laying device, cement storage reservoirs, and asbestine (magnesium silicate) irrigation system for alfalfa fields, vineyards, and orchards. To develop his investment, he built an ice plant, garage, electric power plant, school, bathhouse, swimming pool, and dance hall. He continued putting money to work by purchasing goldfish, mulberry-fed silkworms from Japan, and copper mines in Owens, Arizona.

Hamilton promoted California history by joining the Los Angeles County Pioneers. A widower in 1904, he married Elsie E. Galloway of Canada and built an Indian Lodge at Rosamond. While his son Fred managed the resort, Ezra served Willow Springs as postmaster. Son Truman owned and operated the two-story Hamilton House Hotel at Rosamond. In 1907, Hamilton won a lawsuit against big business for possession of overlapping mineral claims he made in Kern County in 1898. By 1910, he owned ten claims outside Willow Springs.

At age 79, Ezra Hamilton began inventing for the automobile industry by designing a tire and a wave motor. He also proposed a method of removing alcohol from wine. He died on July 4, 1914, leaving to his widow, three surviving sons, and five grandchildren a substantial estate. His diary preserved observations on pioneering covering Indian wars, mining, Indian and Chinese residents of California, and Los Angeles government. Overall, his gold strike produced some $3,500,000 in ore.

SOURCE
Lindsay, Brendan C. *Murder State: California's Native American Genocide, 1846–1873*. Lincoln: University of Nebraska Press, 2012.

Hayashi, Harvey Saburo (1867–1943), Matsu Kawarada Hayashi (1877–1972)

A learned physician and newspaper editor, Dr. Harvey Saburo Hayashi and his wife, educator Matsu Kawarada Hayashi, improved conditions for *issei* (first generation) Japanese laborers in Kona, Hawaii. Born on February 22, 1867, to a samurai in Aizu-Wakamatsu, Fukushima, Japan, Hayashi came of age at

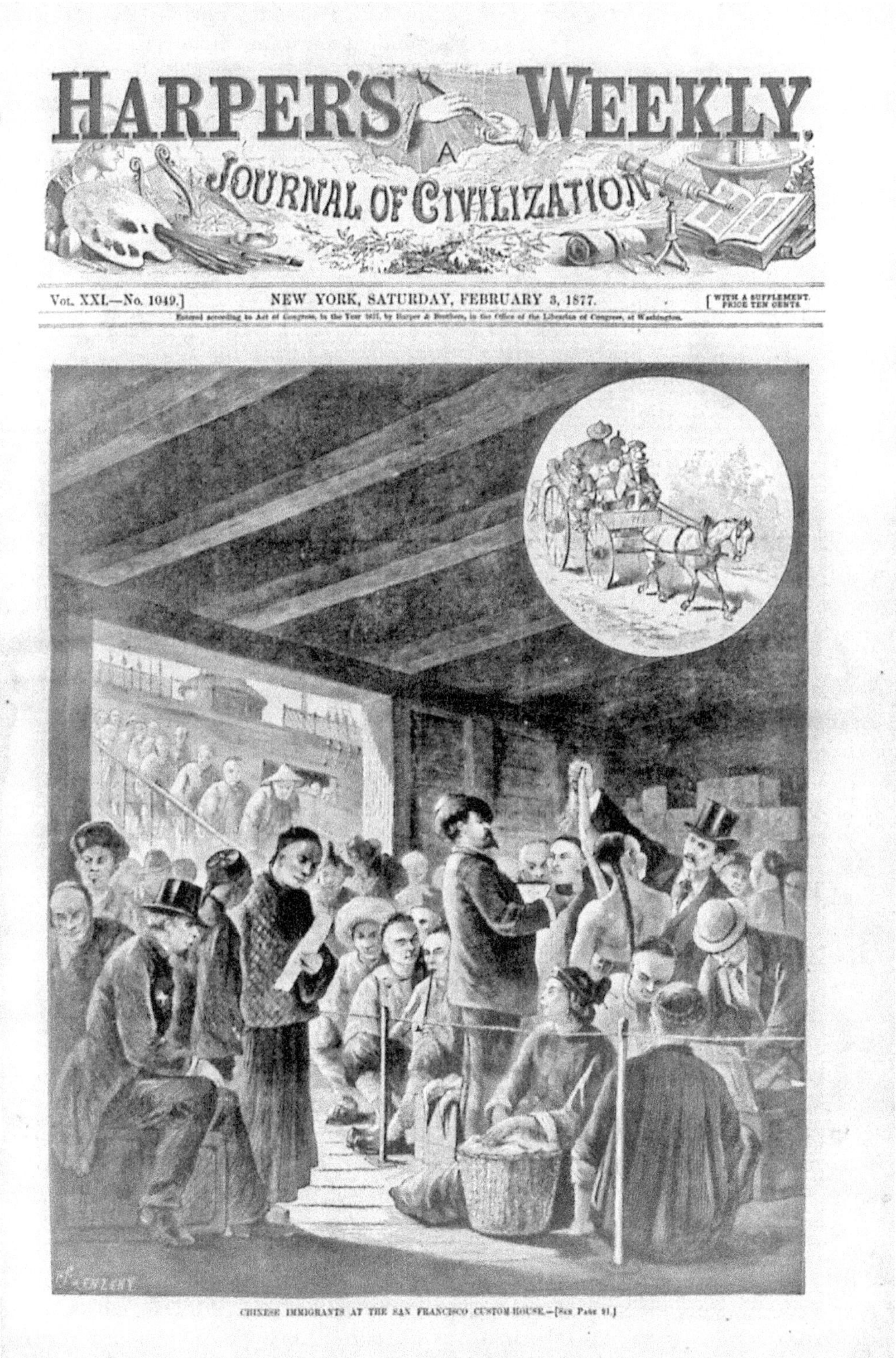

Above and following page: White and Japanese Americans charged immigrant Chinese with opium smoking, gambling, idol worship, illegal immigration and clannishness in Chinatowns.

Tonami in northern Honshu, where his father entered exile in punishment for rebelling against the Meiji emperor Mutsuhito. After high school, Hayashi earned honors at age eighteen from the Aomori Prefectural Medical School.

Against his father's wishes, Hayashi set out for the North American frontier. In April 1885, he sought further medical training by traveling from Tokyo to San Francisco, California. By working as cabin boy and conversing with the ship's captain, he earned cash and learned English. On arrival he entered night school and found a job as houseboy to rich whites. He harvested on fruit farms and studied pre-med courses.

With four years of homeopathy training with a class of eleven students at Hahnemann Hospital and College in Philadelphia, Hayashi graduated on December 10, 1891. Under the English name "Harvey," he opened an office in Sacramento, where he treated leprosy and tuberculosis among immigrant stoop laborers. To escape West Coast racism, in 1893, he planned to continue his education in Germany. To save money, he migrated to Hilo, Hawaii, with a Congregationalist missionary, Jiro Okabe, founder of the Hilo Japanese Christian Church.

Hayashi wrote "My Advice to the Japanese Immigrant Laborers by the Feared, 1893," an evaluation of white American laws restricting immigration from China. The essay blamed anti–Asian hostility on Chinese opium smoking, gambling, idol worship, illegal immigration, and clannishness in Chinatowns. He warned that mounting Japanese prostitution and acceptance of one-quarter the wages paid to Chinese workers could cause a serious backlash in Congress. To elevate the status of Japanese newcomers, he urged clean clothes and skin, nail, and oral hygiene.

At the Honomu Plantation near Hilo, Hayashi initiated medical care of issei workers, whom white doctors refused to treat. He founded a rural practice at Holualoa, Kona, where he brought his Japanese wife, Matsu Kawarada, in January 1896 aboard the *Tenyo Maru*. Born on January 28, 1877, to the samurai social class of her husband, she gave birth to Sansei Hayashi, followed by Chisato "Doc" Shigeki, Tsusake, Yuki, Mari, Michiko Horiuchi, Fusa Sakamoto, Suenichi, Yachiyo, Ensei, Juro, Matsusaburo, and Utako.

Rearing a large family on the earnings of a country doctor inspired Hayashi to connect with local people via a home-based clinic, Japanese cemetery, benevolent association, labor organization, and newspaper. In February 1897, he mimeographed Hawaii's second Japanese newspaper, the bilingual weekly *Kona Hankyo* (Kona Echo), a voice for community unity and progress for four decades. At the North Kona Japanese Language School in 1898, Matsu taught island children.

To encourage humanitarian teachings and moral behaviors, Harvey Hayashi advocated Christian evangelism and education in the scriptures. He lauded Christian interpreters as reliable mediators of immigrant problems. His essay "Reasons for the Necessity of Evangelists in Every Plantation" (October 1909) identified Christian churches as forces for literacy and sources of language classes and night schools.

Hayashi died on June 1, 1943, and was buried at Central Kona Union Church Cemetery. Matsu Hayashi lived to age 95 and shared his gravesite at her death on May 20, 1972. Chisato Hayashi followed his parents' example by graduating from the University of Hawaii and teaching high school math. After earning a medical degree at the University of Chicago in 1934, he practiced family medicine at Holualoa and, in 1939, at the Kona Hospital at Kealakekua.

Source
Kinro, Gerald. *A Cup of Aloha: The Kona Coffee Epic*. Honolulu: University of Hawaii Press, 2003.

Heazle, Jean Bruce (1879–1949), Samuel A. Bruce (1839–1900), George Whiteley Bruce (1851–1927), Mary Elizabeth Bruce Sothern (1856–1935), George Robert Heazle (1876–1924)

Scots-Irish immigrant Jean Bruce "Jeannie" Heazle cut timber, mined, and operated a dairy and cattle ranch on a par with her male relatives, Samuel A. and George Whiteley Bruce. Born in Bray, County Wicklow, near the Irish Sea on September 15, 1879, to Harriett Margaret Bruce and Benjamin Alfred Heazle (or Hazle) of Rathdown, Jean was the fourth of a Wesleyan Methodist family of eight. She and her siblings—Annie Bruce, John "Jack" Bruce, George Robert, Benjamin Alfred, Connie, Mary Violet, and Susie Heazle—were the great-grandchildren of weaver, dyer, and seed merchant Henry Heazle of County Cork and the grandchildren of gentleman farmer and trader John Bruce, a commissioner of Bray.

When Jean reached age five, her mother died. Jean's father later wed Sophia Woods. Her maternal uncles, Robert, Josiah W., and John Bruce, settled in Idaho in the 1860s to mine and breed horses. At the time, outlawry, mail and ore robbery of freight wagons and passenger stages, and revenge killings stirred vigilantism as the only recourse of law-abiding settlers. By 1864, the region supported the Halliday Overland Mail and Express, which headquartered in Bannock County.

A fourth uncle at War Eagle Mountain, Idaho, quartz-miner Samuel A. Bruce, a veteran of the U.S. Navy during the Civil War, partnered in the Cumberland Mine at Silver City. Another uncle, butcher George Whiteley Bruce, a veteran wounded during the Bannock Indian War of June–August 1878, raised beef and dairy cattle and fruit at his ranch at Castle Creek in southwestern Idaho. George Bruce also operated the Owyhee Meat Company and warehouse farther west at DeLamar, selling beef, mutton, pork, sausage, and veal.

To make his living by mining gold and silver in Silver City, Idaho, Jean's older brother, miner Jack Bruce, departed for Idaho on January 30, 1885, traveling through Liverpool, England, and sailing on the S.S. *Lord Gough* to Philadelphia. Two more siblings followed within the year. George Robert Heazle and a younger brother, rancher and postmaster Benjamin Alfred "Ben" Heazle, passed through Glasgow, Scotland, in 1894 and boarded the three-masted steamer S.S. *Anchoria*. On September, the brothers underwent U.S. immigrant processing at Ellis Island. Four years after Idaho joined the Union on July 3, 1890, George Heazle ran a grocery store at Murphy, Idaho, where he and Ben served as postmasters.

From Queenstown, Ireland, Jean Heazle, a passenger on the S.S. *Rhynland*, a four-masted steamer, immigrated to the United States in summer 1897 and reached Philadelphia on June 14. Wearing boy's clothing to protect her from male opportunists, she arrived at the Owyhee County home of her aunt, Margaret Elizabeth Bruce Sothern, where Jean hoped to recover from the tuberculosis that infected one lung. The fourth woman in the area, she worked as a teacher to the north in Silver City and kept books and delivered groceries by buckboard for her brother George's grocery store.

At her homestead in DeLamar on Louse Creek, Jean kept her hair cut short and dressed in men's Levis, denim shirts, and boots for the job of felling timbers to sell as mine supports. As the sole owner of the Jean Heazle Horse and Cattle Company on Diamond Creek outside Murphy, she matched strength with her male relatives and often beat them at cutting wood, branding animals, and driving nails. Her brothers John and George died in 1917 and 1924 respectively and Ben in 1936.

Jean Heazle continued to raise livestock, including 107 cattle and 20 horses, many of which she called by name. In 1944, she had no cash to pay her taxes. After Sheriff Claude Sullivan confiscated her livestock and locked her in jail, she convinced him to let her go free. She returned by night, held the guard at gunpoint, and let her animals out of the Murphy city lockup.

Jean's aunt, Margaret Elizabeth Bruce Sothern, the wife of DeLamar miner Alfred Richard Sothern and raised a pioneer family of seven. Two of the boys helped Jean on her ranch. The Sotherns retired to California in the 1880s after Alfred contracted brown lung. Jean, the last citizen of DeLamar, Idaho, leased her cattle to the Gusmans and became a recluse in a ghost town. At her death on November 1, 1949, she was residing alone on her property with chickens and cats. The Jean Heazle Spring bears her name.

Source
Gilbert, Nina Bachman. "The Jean Heazle Story." *Owyhee Outpost* 41 (2009): 37–52.

Holmes, Julia Archibald (1838–1887), James Henry Holmes (1833–1907)

Canadian reformer, egalitarian, teacher, and journalist Julia Annie Archibald Holmes set a record for frontierswomen by climbing Pike's Peak. Of Irish-Scots-Canadian extraction, she was born on February 15, 1838, in Noel, Nova Scotia, second of the eight children of carpenter and house builder John Christie Archibald and Jane O'Brien, a suffragist and friend of Susan B. Anthony. In the spirit of Archibald forebears who pioneered Truro, Massachusetts, she emigrated with her family at age ten to Worcester, where she worked in a woolen mill.

Dispatched with twenty-seven other pioneers by the New England Emigrant Aid Company to combat the advance of slavery into the West, the Archibalds settled on the Wakarusa River at Osawatomie, Kansas Territory, on July 17, 1854. At their 160-acre farm on the Neosho River, they opened the parlor to abolitionist meetings and operated an Underground Railroad depot. They supported the Free State Party and militant sectionalism of outlaw John Brown and co-founded Lawrence, Kansas, a landmark on the Oregon Trail.

At Lawrence on October 9, 1857, Julia married a divorced attorney and editor, James Henry Holmes, the pacifist son of a New York broker and a correspondent for the *National Era*. The couple lived at James's homestead in Emporia. She subscribed to *The Lily*, America's first national suffragist magazine. After she discovered editor Amelia Bloomer's proposal to replace petticoats, corsets, and skirts with Turkish pants, the "American costume," Julia became known as a "Bloomer Girl."

At age twenty, Julia fled Kansas with her husband, whom Missouri militia hunted for avenging the murder of John Brown's twenty-five-year-old son, Frederick Brown, shot and killed by Kansas legislator Martin White on August 30, 1856, for alleged horse thievery. Julia taught her eighteen-year-old brother Al-

In 1858, the Holmes family traveled over the Santa Fe Trail to Central City, Colorado, hunting buffalo for food along the way.

bert William Archibald to speak Spanish as part of his preparation to trade in the Southwest. During one of the nation's greatest migrations, in fall 1858, the couple and Albert joined butcher John Easter, security guard George W. Smith, and forty gold prospectors of the "Pike's Peak or Bust" era. In an ox cart, they traveled over the Santa Fe Trail from Lawrence 500 miles to Central City, Colorado, hunting buffalo for food along the way.

Walking the Santa Fe Trail

In her journal, Julia jotted observations on female equality to dispatch to the Whig press and *The Sybil,* a semi-monthly women's journal devoted to dress reform. She commented on the challenge of walking in calico pants and moccasins and extending her physical capacity from three miles to ten. Along the way, she nurtured a motherless buffalo calf. At night, she volunteered for a turn guarding the fifteen wagons and raged because her male companions refused her the opportunity. When a band of Cheyenne offered to trade two female Indians for her, James declined the deal.

At Bent's Fort on June 28, 1858, Julia stopped along the Arkansas River to view the Rockies, which were seventy miles away. The party followed the Fountain River and camped at Manitou Springs in July. On August 1, Julia put on calico dress and bloomers, moccasins, and hat to ready herself for scaling the 14,115-foot summit, which the party revered as a symbol of U.S. wealth and power. For herself, James Holmes, guide John D. Miller, and prospector George Peck, she packed a quilt and clothing, two quarts of water in a canteen, nineteen pounds of bread, one pound each of pork and sugar, twelve ounces of coffee, utensils, and tin cup and plates.

During "Mrs. Holmes's Ascension" two miles from the top, on August 4, the Lawrence party encountered snow squalls and discovered that they gripped rocks more easily with bare feet than with hands. To reach the top, they abandoned their gear on the fourth day and made a camp they called Snowdell. From the pinnacle, Julia wrote letters and read the musings of essayist Ralph Waldo Emerson on friendship. All climbers inscribed their names on a boulder.

On to New Mexico

Prospecting produced group dissension rather than riches. Separating from the convoy in fall 1858, Julia and James led the Holmes party south over the Santa Fe Trail and crossed the Arkansas River at the Cimarron Cutoff. On September 8, the couple reached Taos, New Mexico, a former Hispanic land purchased by the U.S. under provisions of the Treaty of Guadalupe Hidalgo in 1848. Julia learned Spanish and taught school at Fort Union. In her correspondence for the *New York Herald Tribune,* she detailed such facts as the cost of freight hauling over the Santa Fe Trail, the use of a portable cook stove on the trail, and expanses of wild roses on the prairie.

James and Julia Holmes produced two children, Ernest Julio and Phoebe, who were born in Santa Fe. After the couple launched a newspaper, the bilingual *Santa Fe Republican,* James Holmes recruited black soldiers for the Union Army. Amid pro-slavery elements, on August 1, 1861, he incurred a jail term for sedition, which plea-bargaining reduced to suspension and the silencing of Holmes's newspaper. He fought during the Civil War in James Lane's Frontier Guard. Following Chiricahua Apache chief Cochise and strategist Mangas Coloradas's brutal raids against miners, pioneers, and their livestock, James accepted a Lincoln appointment as Secretary of New Mexico Territory, then consisting of New Mexico, Arizona, and southern California.

The couple's abolitionist sentiments caused their ouster from the territory. On return to the east in 1863 to live with relatives in Tennessee and support Abraham Lincoln's presidency, Julia gave birth to June and Charles Sumner Holmes, both of whom died in childhood. Julia and her mother campaigned for women's rights at the National Woman Suffrage Association convention on January 19, 1869, in New York City and, in Washington, D.C., promoted an end to slavery. In 1870, Julia divorced James and clerked in the Bureau of Education as a statistician and head of the Division of Spanish Correspondence. From her research into child labor and factories in lower Manhattan, she published *Children Who Work* (1871).

Julia sorrowed over a coal oil explosion that killed her daughter, teacher Phoebe Holmes, who lived nearby. Julia died on January 19, 1887. On a federal pension, James returned to Sag Harbor, New York, and sired six children by Esther Maria Deavitt Holmes. After losing his property to squatters in Emporia, Kansas, he abandoned Esther in 1893. In 1897, he married and deserted a Portuguese bride, Grace Sylvieria of Lisbon, mother of a son, James Townley Holmes. One of the last survivors of John Brown's Kansas army, the elder James Holmes died in Red Bank, New Jersey, November 20, 1907.

Source
Shirley, Gayle C. *More Than Petticoats: Remarkable Colorado Women*. Guilford, CT: Globe Pequot, 2002.

Imamura, Yemyo (1867–1932)

A sixteenth-generation Buddhist priest and pioneer educator in Hawaii, Yemyo Imamura applied progressive methods to the racial and labor problems faced by Asian immigrants. Born in Togo near Fukui City, Japan, on May 27, 1867, he was the oldest son of Mitue and Yejitsu Imamura, both members of temple clans. At age three, he lost his mother and baby brother Yeun and passed to the care of a loving, enlightened stepmother, Misao Satomi.

In preparation for the priesthood, in 1876, Imamura sought ordination into the Buddhist priesthood. At age seventeen, he enrolled in literature at an ecumenical temple school in Kyoto that set the course of his liberal religious philosophy. During the enlightened Meiji era that moved Japan from cultural and political isolation, the staff incorporated studies of Western democracy, altruism, and religion. They refuted entrenched conservatism and the long-standing feudal practices among Japanese Buddhists that esteemed aristocrats above peasants.

Imamura served as principal of Kyoto Middle School before training in an all-embracing philosophy under his uncle, the Reverend Ama Tokumon, a liberal Kyoto priest. After preparation at Kyoto in English and reformed Buddhism at the Hongwanji Futsukyoko (Common Study School), the forerunner of Ryukoku University, Imamura joined the Association for Overseas Religious Propagation, a Buddhist mission campaign among Christians. In July 1888, he edited the monthly *Hanseikai Zasshi* (Reflective Pose), a progressive attempt to alleviate bias against Buddhism and to rid young priests of intemperance. His ideology boosted lay activism across Japan.

Spreading the Faith

In March 1891, a period of dramatic confrontation between Japanese envoys and representatives from Hawaii and Russia, Imamura received a scholarship to Keio University to study the enlightened education methods taught by Fukuzawa Yukichi, a proponent of utilitarianism. Perhaps because liberal Buddhism failed in Asia, in 1899, Imamura left Fukui aboard the *Shinyo Maru* for the Hawaiian islands to construct Honolulu's first Buddhist temple to serve immigrant pioneers. At age 33, he joined his scholarly uncle, Abbot Myonyo Ohtani, and cousins, Lady Takeko Kujo and Abbot Kozui Ohtani.

Over three years of mentoring, Imamura prepared himself for Americanizing Asian-Americans and easing their racial and cultural struggles. During rampant Sinophobia, he ministered to plantation workers and to 7,000 residents of Chinatown displaced by the bubonic plague of October 1899 and the 1900 Honolulu fire set to quell infection over thirty-eight acres. Upon his advance to bishop, Imamura promoted methods of adapting conservative Buddhism to American philosophy as a means of disseminating the faith among Caucasians.

Imamura offered spiritual sustenance to the "coolie" class in press gangs by teaching them that they were beloved by Buddha. With British Buddhist Ernest Hunt, Imamura compiled 138 responsive readings and 68 gathas (hymns) in an English hymnal, *The*

Ceremony for Use in Buddhist Temples. Imamura and Hunt co-authored catechism and opened a dharma (Sunday school) at the first temple at Fort Street near Kukui Plaza in Honolulu. Advocating education at temples and the Japanese high school, he guided *nisei* (second-generation) Japanese youth to negotiate a place for themselves in a multiethnic society.

By conducting services in English, publishing the Hawaii Buddhist Annual, forming a Boy Scout troop, and welcoming Caucasian members to the International Buddhist Institute, Imamura demonstrated the universality of the faith. At age fifty-one, he designed a temple headquarters combining a Japanese altar with Western pulpit, a dome, and pew seating rather than traditional tatami mats. As leader of Buddhist initiatives, he consulted with visiting theologians from Ceylon, China, and Japan. With the aid of Hunt, Imamura began a Japanese book collection that formed a reference core for the University of Hawaii.

Maintaining Japanese Principles

During 32 years as bishop, Imamura championed laborers on rural sugar plantations through a temple network that offered singing and spiritual readings. For the sake of social welfare, in response to the classification of 65,000 Japanese immigrants as permanent settlers in 1903, he urged the preservation of twenty-two after-school Japanese language schools, the acceptance of a Japanese-American press, and coexistence of religious faiths. By supporting broad-minded learning, he defended the place of nonsectarian Buddhism in science and democratic government.

On August 2, 1904, Yemyo Imamura and wife Kiyoko produced a son, Kanmo, the next in the family line of Buddhist clergy. In 1904 and 1920, Imamura intervened on behalf of 3,000 striking laborers at the Waipahu sugar plantation and urged the Hawaiian Sugar Planters' Association to raise wages from 77¢ more than 62 percent to $1.25 a day. Allied with the Reverend Albert Palmer of the Central Union Church and officials of the Young Men's Buddhist Association, Imamura helped to quell a riot and marched to Honolulu with Oahu strikers, who brandished a portrait of Abraham Lincoln, a symbol of racial emancipation.

As the first licensed American Buddhist, in 1908, Imamura began performing marriages and advocating social interaction for immigrants and their "picture brides." To integrate the Shin Buddhist doctrine of the pure heart with the American language, he dispatched English-speaking men and women to theology schools in Japan. During an influenza epidemic in summer 1918 that killed 1,088, Imamura consoled the suffering and opened temples and language schools to workers evicted from plantation barracks. He compiled a religious summary, *History of Missionary Work in Hawaii* (1918) and, the following year, opposed a crusade to limit hours of Japanese language instruction and to require teachers to pass certification exams in English grammar and American civics and history.

In 1927, the U.S. Supreme Court concurred with Imamura and others on the importance of language schools to immigrant acculturation. Nonetheless, at his death from heart attack on December 22, 1932, his conservative successor, Bishop Giyko Kuchiba, undermined liberal policies and reverted to the centrality of Japanese ethnicity and language. In 1967, Imamura's son and daughter-in-law, Kanmo and Jane Matsuura Imamura, restored the bishop's Hawaiian projects. The bishop's grandson, Ryo Imamura, became a psychology professor and Buddhist theologian and priest.

Sources
Asato, Noriko. *Teaching Mikadoism: The Attack on Japanese Language Schools in Hawaii.* Honolulu: University of Hawaii Press, 2006.
Burgan, Michael. *Buddhist Faith in America.* New York: Facts on File, 2003.

Isbell, Olive Mann (1824–1899), Isaac Chauncy Isbell (1800–1886), Antoine Robidoux (1794–1860)

The first Anglo teacher in California, Olive Mann Isbell carried East Coast educational methods to Pacific Indians. A descendent of colonists from Norfolk, England, Olive was born on August 8, 1824, in Plymouth, Massachusetts, to nurse Amanda Blakeslee and Warner Mann, a schoolmaster. As pioneers in Ohio, the couple co-founded Ashtabula, where Warner served as town justice of the peace and postmaster.

A relative of educator Horace Mann and scion of English colonists from Cornwall, Olive married Isaac Chauncy Isbell, a surgeon from Bloomfield, New York, on March 10, 1844, in Wadsworth, Ohio. Isaac, a native of Connecticut and descendent of English colonists from Surrey and Cornwall, trained at Western Reserve College in Cleveland, Ohio, and practiced medicine for two years in Kane County, Illinois. In the midst of turmoil over the Mormon pilgrimage to Nauvoo, Olive taught school.

Setting out with savings of $2,000 from Greenbush, Illinois, from mid–April to October 1, 1846, the Isbells and Isaac's older brother James joined wagon master Joseph Aram's convoy of 130 pioneers in thirty-two wagons over the Oregon Trail. On the way, James's five-year-old son Alexander died in a wagon accident. Taking the standard route, the immigrants passed through Fort Madison, Iowa, on their way to Santa Clara County. Under the guidance of French-Canadian scout, fur trapper, and interpreter Antoine Robidoux (or Rubidoux), the founder of St. Joseph, Missouri, they traded on the way with the Sioux. A decade later, Robidoux estimated that only three frontiersmen out of 200 survived the perils of the Rocky Mountains.

The Aram convoy passed the ill-fated Donner Party, thus escaping a frontier tragedy of slow starvation and death. Upon arrival at Fort

During the 1849 California Gold Rush, Isaac Isbell prospected for gold at Sutter's Mill and Stanislaus.

Laramie, Wyoming, the wayfarers treated the Arapaho and Sioux to a feast as a bribe ensuring safe passage to Fort Hall, Idaho. The Indians even assisted the travelers in recovering straying animals to spare them the going rate of $20 per hundredweight for fresh packhorses.

War at the Mission

From the Bear River, the train received an escort from the battalion of General John C. Fremont, popularly revered as "the Pathfinder." At the Santa Clara Mission de Asis, on October 16, Aram and the immigrants sheltered under a leaky roof in an adobe horse stable from the Mexican-American War of 1846–1848 and aided General Fremont in his fight against the army of Francisco Sanchez. In addition to cooking military rations for soldiers, Olive Isbell poured lead into molds for bullets, cleaned rifles, treated head and leg wounds, and fought an epidemic of typhoid fever with Isaac's stock of drugs. After the war, she rehabilitated Isaac from typhoid pneumonia, sitting by him for six weeks to nurse him through the fever.

To protect children from the turmoil, in mid–December 1846, "Aunt Olive" repurposed a room in the adobe stable into a school. On the dirt floor, she built a fire to dry out dampness and warm twenty pupils seated on boxes and benches. While she guarded the students with a rifle, the children shared a few McGuffey's readers, spellers, geography and math books, quill pens, and three slates. They practiced the alphabet by scratching the letters on the floor and writing them on their hands with charcoal.

After a two-month session, the Isbells and five pioneer families moved to Monterey in early March 1847, where newcomers built a fort. While Isaac operated Washington House, the area's first American hotel, Olive installed another classroom over the Colton Hall customhouse and jail. The first twenty-five students paid fifty cents per week for twelve-week terms for a total tuition of $150. Enrollment grew to fifty-six pupils, only two of whom spoke English. To understand them, Olive received tutoring in Spanish from the Abrego brothers.

Ranching and Its Aftermath

In October 1847, the Isbells sold the hotel, bought a ranch at French Camp (present-day Stockton), and purchased 600 cattle plus horses, dairy cows, and poultry. During the 1849 California Gold Rush, Olive remained behind in their one-room cabin while Isaac joined the Stockton Mining company and prospected for gold at Sutter's Mill and Stanislaus. Olive collected ribbon, lace, beads, buttons, and handkerchiefs to pay the mill's Indian laborers and sewed gowns, dresses, and petticoats to trade to the Indians for gold. She supplied French Camp with chickens, eggs, milk, cream, and butter and sold meals of steak and omelet with coffee.

May 1, 1850, the Isbells sold their ranch and returned east. In 1856, they bought a 10,000-acre ranch on the Frio River near present-day Cancon, Texas, and, until 1861, raised 7,000 cattle. The Civil War forced them to take refuge in Mexico, from which they sailed up the Pacific Coast to San Francisco. They returned to Santa Clara, where Isaac opened a medical practice. In 1867, a fall from a cliff crushed Isaac's legs, leaving him permanently disabled.

After Isaac's death in 1886 at Santa Paula, Olive obtained a pension of eight dollars per month from the Mexican government and moved south to remain near her husband's grave. She died on March 26, 1899. In 1926, a middle school in Ventura County bore her name in honor of her contributions to California education.

SOURCE

Pryor, Alton. *Fascinating Women in California History.* Roseville, CA: Stagecoach, 2003.

Ise, Rosena Haag (1855–1947), Henry C. Ise (1841–1900), Rosena Christina Freihoffer Haag (1826–1892), Johann Christoph Haag (1817–1890)

A Kansas homesteader born to immigrant pioneers, Rosena Christina "Rosie" Haag Ise attained the family dream after the death of her husband. Her parents, Rosena Christina Freihoffer and Johann Christoph Haag, a vineyard keeper, emigrated from Kleinbottwar, Württemberg, on July 6, 1852, and settled with sons Chris and Willie on a 30-acre farm near Racine, Wisconsin. A German-American born on October 7, 1855, at Theresa in Dodge County northwest of Milwaukee, Rosie was the fourth child and first daughter.

The Haag family lived in a dirt-floored log shanty chinked with mud. To anchor straw beds topped with feather ticks, they nailed boards to the wall. The children went barefoot year round while stacking firewood and carrying water one-quarter mile uphill from the creek. They sickened from malaria. Typhoid fever weakened Rosie's father and destroyed his career in corn, wheat, and rye farming and orchard cultivation. For additional cash to buy cloth, Rosie picked and sold gooseberries and wild strawberries and began hiring out as a domestic from age eight until her marriage.

In 1859, the Haags sold their dwindling assets for $300. Traveling southwest to be near Rosie's older brother, Christopher "Christ" Gottlieb Haag, they relocated on 30 acres at Holton in northeastern Kansas Territory, birthplace of the last five of their family of eleven. In a drought throughout the winter of 1860, the household faced near starvation. During a blizzard, they relied on relief supplies of corn meal and beans sent from Atchison. Mother Rosena Haag's poorly healed broken arm halted the kneading of dough for bread and limited her cooking to mush, which her children began to hate.

After the admission of Kansas to the Union in January 29, 1861, Rosena Haag mourned the deaths of her one-year-old son Willie and infant Albert from year-lond epidemic measles that swept the Union army. She regretted the paltry education that her daughter Rosie received from homeschooling, spelling bees, and "singing schools," Protestant gatherings in which participants learned to interpret shaped notes. As the children adapted to the prairie, Christoph Haag threatened to disinherit them if they spoke English. At age thirteen, Rosie nursed the whole family through epidemic typhoid.

The Haag fortunes improved, enabling them to purchase two more farms. As law officers suppressed frontier violence, in 1871, Christoph Haag homesteaded at nearby Ross north of Downs in north central Kansas. In autumn 1872, he introduced Rosie to German immigrant Henry Christopher Ise, who courted the black-haired beauty in the kitchen while she knitted. The fifth of the six children of Johanna Klumpf and Georg Christoph Eisenmanger, a roofing tile manufacturer, Ise was born Christoph Heinrich Eisenmanger in Sindringen on April 29, 1841.

To avoid conscription into the Germany army, on March 8, 1857, Ise had left Württemberg at age sixteen with his older brother and sister, Johann Georg and Luise Katherina "Kate" Eisenmanger. He arrived at Utica, New York, and found work on the first enlargement of the Erie Canal. With Kate, he moved west by train to Lake County, Ohio, and, in late 1859, settled in Somonauk, Illinois, where he learned to read and write English.

A Civil War private in the 10th Illinois Volunteer Infantry on August 28, 1861, Ise had served in Illinois, Kentucky, and Arkansas under his Anglicized name. At Bridgeport, Alabama, he survived wounding at the Battle of Chickamauga on September 19, 1863. He recovered without hospitalization and, in summer 1864, participated in the siege of Atlanta. Combat left him with a stomach ailment and arthritic shoulder. On May 23, 1865, he marched in the Grand Review of the Armies in Washington, D.C., before settling near Kate at State Center, Iowa, to work as a freelance plowman at the rate of $1.25 per acre.

The Ise Farm

Haag claimed 60 acres of free farmland at Ross, Kansas, benefits for veterans promised by the Homestead Act, which President Abraham Lincoln promoted on May 20, 1862. Beginning in June 1871, Henry's planting thrived on rich soil between Dry and Twelve Mile creeks in Osborne County, part of the Great Prairie where buffalo still migrated. Among other bachelor farmers in their soddies and dugouts, he built a 15' × 18' log cabin, chinked it with clay, sodded the roof, dug a cellar, and sank a well. With his farmstead ready for a wife, on October 20, 1872, he began a letter-writing campaign to win Rosie.

In an Evangelical Unitarian service at Holton on May 19, 1873, Rosie Haag, then age seventeen, married Henry Ise, then age thirty. To welcome his bride, he put a floor and cottonwood ceiling in his cabin and helped her dig up a yellow rose bush, bachelor buttons, marigolds, and asparagus crowns from her mother's yard to transplant to the new home. Rosie's father presented the newlyweds a family Bible and toasted their union with homemade wine from the cellar.

On the way west to Ross, the couple spent their wedding night in the straw-filled bed of their wagon. On the sixth day, following a ferry ride over the Republican River, they arrived at Henry's spread, where Rosie scanned the sod henhouse and thatched straw stable. Indoors, she found spartan furnishings made of nail kegs, cottonwood planks, and wood crates. To rid the ticking of bedbugs, she fumigated with kerosene and a feather. To ward off prairie winds, Henry sheltered their home in a row of cottonwoods.

The Ises raised livestock; planted corn, oats, and wheat; and sold hay and timber from their woodlands. As the postmaster and justice of the peace at New Arcadia, Henry earned cash for settling disputes and issuing marriage licenses. Rosie turned up a vegetable bed and planted cucumbers, peas, turnips, beans, tomatoes, and lettuce. She braided husk rugs and leached lye from ashes for softening and hulling dried corn into hominy. In town, she sold butter and eggs. Henry built a granary and a sleigh to take them on winter visits to neighbors.

The Ises produced five girls and seven boys—Albert Henry, Alma Laura, Edward William "Billy," Minnie Alice "Doll," Charles David "Daniel," Walter "Walt" John, Hulda Louise, John Christopher, Estelle May "Stella," Mary Rose, Herman Thomas "Hap," and Frank Harold "Dutch" Ise. In July 1874, Albert died at four months of age. After his burial in a homemade cottonwood coffin, Rosie framed a lock of his hair and mounted it on the wall. Because of sorrow, a drought, blizzard, and, plague of grasshoppers that devoured crops from July into September, Henry muttered threats to return to Iowa.

A Profitable Farm

With profits from 40 bushels of wheat per acre, by 1875, Henry proved his homestead claim and purchased a rake, drill, cultivator, mower, and corn planter and a sewing machine for Rosie. As the family grew, he quarried white limestone for a breezeway and addition to the cabin. Rosie served sugar with the breakfast milk and kept her toddlers warm by stuffing the parlor rag carpet with straw. Although she was frugal and burdened with washing, ironing, and mending for local bachelors to earn extra cash, she welcomed her ailing sister, Anna Maria "Mary" Haag, in May and nursed her during a decline from bone cancer.

The Ise children attended a German-English Sunday school at the Rose Valley Church and enrolled at the one-room Ise School, a sod-and-board structure later replaced by a dugout. Henry awakened his daughters by tapping on the kitchen ceiling with a broom to stir them from their loft bedroom and set Alma, the oldest, to husking corn in the field. With the efforts of the whole family, they earned 45¢ per bushel from the sale of apples.

John Christopher overcame paralytic polio by developing his intellectual and musical gifts. Memoirs record his whittling with a jackknife, mastering skill games with darts and bullwhip, and traveling to and from classes by a cart pulled by a black dog named Coalie. John's brother Charles earned tuition money each summer by running a steam thresher. The other children made their own dugout, whistles, stilts, bows and arrows, playhouses, and swings.

A prosperous, respected citizen, in 1880, Henry purchased 36 acres on the Kansas Central Railroad lines, which linked Leavenworth with northern Kansas the previous spring. Thieves and freeloaders in passing wagons provoked the couple's suspicion of strangers. Within a year, on 237 acres, the couple grew corn and raised cattle, horses, and pigs. When the family reached eight members, Henry laid out the perimeter of a six-room, two-story farm house featuring two porches, pantry, kitchen and parlor chimneys, and privy.

In 1884, the Ises enhanced the worth of the farm to $4,000 with harvests of corn, wheat, millet, and oats and orchard pickings of apples, peaches, cherries, pears, and plums. The family enjoyed small luxuries, for example, a parlor organ and the addition of small squares of colored glass admitting light through the front door. In 1888, the couple mortgaged their homestead for $350 to pay for a windmill. They retired their debt and, with a legacy from Rosie's deceased mother, in 1893, bought more land for $3,100.

By 1895, the Ises' 420 acres constituted the town's largest farm. A year later, farm profits paid for a water pump, summer kitchen, stereoscope, and horse and pony for the children. In failing health from stomach cancer, Henry surveyed his homestead from a buggy and, on August 27, 1900, dictated his Civil War memories to daughter Alma. He died on November 21, 1900, leaving Rosie to rear and educate five children ages fifteen to five. His parlor funeral drew a line of mourners three miles long.

Rosie's Farm

Henry's will left Rosie in control of the farm and provided $500 cash for John, their crippled son, if Rosie should die intestate. For the next decade, Rosie lived on her income from grain, fruit, and livestock while modernizing the house. From the U.S. government, she received a widow's pension of eight dollars, which rose to twelve dollars in 1909. She used Henry's life insurance to purchase another farm and sent nine of her children to college. Like his father, mother, and grandfather before him, Billy Ise moved west to Delta, Utah, to farm.

Rosie managed family matters, traveling to California and Washington with Alma, encouraging Daniel and Walt through law school, and directing Minnie's wedding at the farmhouse. Rosie nursed John through leg amputation and rehabilitation with an artificial limb in 1903 and attended his graduation from Kansas University in 1908. She cheered Hap during World War I and Walt through military service on Negros Islands in the Philippines, where he disproved a report of his death in action.

Before settling in Lawrence, Kansas, at age 54, Rosie sold the homestead and, in March 1909 advertised her belongings for auction. Items brought from 5¢ for wire to as much as $276 for horses. Her investment in the children's careers enriched the family with teachers, writers, lawyers, a college professor, principal and football coach, farmer, pharmacist, and optometrist.

Economist John Ise immortalized Rosie and Henry's pioneering farm in a biography, *Sod & Stubble* (1936), and submitted the manuscript for his mother's approval. He followed with *Sod-House Days: Letters from a Kansas Homesteader* (1937), which detailed emotional moments in the family's pioneering. After Rosie's death on August 2, 1947, at age 91, her children buried her beside Henry's remains.

SOURCES
Ise, John C. *Sod & Stubble*. New York: Wilson-Erickson, 1936.
Wright, Mary Lindley. *Prairie Legacy*. Self-published, 1981.

Judson, Phoebe Goodell (1831–1926), Jotham Weeks Goodell (1809–1859), Holden Allen Judson (1827–1899), Nathan Edward Goodell (1839–1886), Henry Martin Goodell (1843–1905), George Judson (1860–1891)

Memoirist, foster mother, and educator Phoebe Newton Goodell Judson, a matriarch of one of North America's foremost pioneer clans, secured the beginnings of Western Washington University. Native Canadians from Ancaster, Ontario, and scions of English immigrants named Goodale, she and twin Mary Weeks Goodell were born on October 24, 1831. They and their nine siblings were the children of Anna Glenning "Annie" Bachelor of Toronto and Jotham Weeks Goodell, a Presbyterian minister from Marlborough, Massachusetts. At age six, the twins lived in Vermilion, Ohio, strolled the shores of Lake Erie, and educated themselves through reading.

After marrying Holden Allen Judson of Vermilion, an abolitionist of English lineage, on June 20, 1849, Phoebe made her home with her in-laws and gave birth to Anna Louisa "Annie" Judson, the first of her five birth children, one adopted son, and four foster children. Influenced by the Oregon Donation Land Act of 1850, Jotham and Annie Goodell anticipated an easier life on free grants of 640 acres to married couples. Led by Holden, the Goodells migrated to Oregon Territory in 1851 with their eleven-year-old son, Nathan Edwards Goodell. Phoebe remained behind with Anna.

Detained by winter, Jotham Goodell settled his family in the Salt Lake Basin of Utah for the snowy months and wrote nine letters later published in the *Oregonian* and compiled into *A Winter with the Mormons* (1852). He charged prophet Brigham Young with profanity, militance, and despotism in wanting to turn the republic into the theocracy of Deseret. Goodell accused the Latter Day Saints of exploiting their creditors, refusing to sell supplies to outsiders, and engaging in "vile" concubinage.

The Goodells reached Portland, Oregon, on June 7, 1851, and chose a tract in Polk County west of Salem. Holden made a brief attempt at prospecting in California before retracing his steps to Vermilion in 1852.

The Judsons Emigrate

Though the Judsons lacked farming skills and owned no weapons, they mulled over the appeal of free government land in the west, an offer extended into 1855. On March 1, 1853, Holden and Phoebe with toddler Anna set out for Washington, a 70,000 square-mile territory that Congress established the previous February 8. Phoebe confided in a diary her hopes of finding an ideal home site by a stream overlooking snowy mountain tops.

The wagon train took the homesteaders by way of Cincinnati, Ohio, to Kansas City. The trek passed through St. Louis by steamboat and on by the steamer *Kansas* up the Missouri River. During a five-week stopover in West Port, Missouri, the Judsons had a wagon custom built. Accompanying twenty people in a carriage and five covered wagons, the family's

Jotham Goodell's *A Winter with the Mormons* (1852) charged prophet Brigham Young and other Mormon men with engaging in "vile" concubinage.

ox-drawn conveyance departed Missouri on May 1, 1853. The wayfarers carried with them the traditions, values, and prejudices of Easterners, including stereotypes about "uncivilized" Indians.

During a tense period in early June 1853 along the Snake River marked by fear of Pawnee attack, Phoebe Judson enjoyed the peace she found in nature. In a year when some 27,500 settlers took the Overland Trail west, she remarked on the continual passage of wagons. Upon arrival at La Bonta Creek, Wyoming, on June 26, she gave birth to son Charles La Bonta Judson. Without pausing for her recuperation from childbirth, the convoy took the trail through Wyoming to the Columbia River, where they floated their wagons across the narrows at Fort Dalles, Oregon.

By late summer 1853, the Judsons left the cheerless Columbia plains and, following the directions of Nez Percé chief Red Wolf, set out on their own for the green mountains of Willamette, Oregon. Befriended by Blackfeet, the couple paddled a dugout canoe to their 320-acre tract at Grand Mound in western Washington Territory, then populated by 4,000 whites. Traveling with their only books, a bible and a Webster's dictionary, they had to lighten the load by abandoning a trunk and rocking chair.

Washington Settlers

In the back country in a clutch of 25 log cabins at the southern tip of Puget Sound, Phoebe Judson was the only white female. Supplies transported by steamer and offloaded onto canoe arrived up the Nooksack River by hand delivery. The absence of news from the East heightened her isolation, forcing her to master shooting a rifle in case of attack. She began learning to speak Chinook and admired the industry of native women, who taught her how to collect and dry nourishing and healing plants, roots, and berries.

Living in a cedar and fir cabin alongside the Goodells and local Chehalis Indians, in winter 1853, the Judsons pastured two oxen, a dairy cow, and calf. They planted fruit and nut trees, raised poultry, and shared simple snacks of bread and syrup with native visitors. The family opened their home to Skoqualamooch, a ten-year-old abused Chehalis orphan whom they named Jack Judson. Because of his white upbringing, his tribe demeaned him as worthless.

Because of the gravelly soil at Grand Mound, in 1854, the Judsons migrated to more arable land at Claquato in the Nooksack Valley. On October 8, Phoebe's brother, William Bird Goodell, and his wife and son and Holden Judson's sister, Lucretia R. "Trecia" Judson, and parents—Charles and Louisa Judson—completed the crossing to join the clan. In October 1855, the Puget Sound War over the loss of Nisqually land rights forced the Goodells to move in with the Judsons.

While skirmishes raged at Tacoma, Seattle, and Walla Walla, the extended Goodell-Judson family sheltered in the Claquato Stockade Fort, but continued farming their land. Phoebe Judson became a charter member of her father's congregation, the Claquato Chehalis Presbyterian Church. She and her husband had their children baptized.

After Holden Judson's election to the Washington state legislature in 1858, Phoebe and the children lived in the capital at Olympia with Trecia Holden Corliss and her husband, George W. Corliss, a U.S. Marshal in Oregon and Washington territories from 1856 to 1858. Holden sold his Claquato property and purchased land in Whatcom and a grocery store in Olympia. The family's departure from Claquato, coupled with the death of the Reverend Goodell in 1859, stymied the growth of the Presbyterian community.

After Oregon's admission to the Union on February 14, 1859, as the thirty-third state, the population of Washington Territory reached 11,578 by 1860. The politics of the early 1860s thrust the Judsons into emotional turmoil. Some 15,000 pioneers fled Eastern dissension over abolitionism and located at the Grande Ronde and Powder river valleys, the Klamath Basin, east of the Cascade Mountains, and along the Crooked River into Ocho, further distancing Oregonites from national distress. At the outbreak of the American

Civil War, combat reports traveled slowly to the Pacific Northwesterners, carried in part by prospectors seeking gold at Auburn, Griffin Gulch, and Sparta. To protect pioneers like the Judsons from lawless opportunists, a volunteer infantry formed on October 18, 1861, and occupied forts Walla Walla, Colville, Vancouver, Steilacoom, and Hoskins. At the time, Steilacoom consisted of seventy residences, six mercantiles, three hotels, three sawmills, two forges, and a carpentry shop, flour mill, wharf, and tailoring store.

Because George and Trecia Corliss found contentment on a sheep farm in Las Cruces, California, the Judsons considered leaving Washington and joining them. In a violent era when Mexican outlaws burned the Corlisses alive in their home on January 16, 1864, predations by the CSS *Shenandoah* inflicted arson, terrorism, and plunder on lumber vessels in Puget Sound. A year after the Civil War, women orphaned and widowed by combat journeyed to western Washington in search of stable homes and jobs in schools, inns, cafes, and clothing shops. In April 1866, Phoebe and Holden chose to settle in Puget Sound on Whidbey Island, an area served by an expanded lighthouse system. At their isolated haven, Phoebe bore son George—named for George Corliss—and daughter Mary "Mollie" Judson.

More catastrophes marked the Judsons' years of pioneering, including the drowning of livestock in a flood, Holden's infection with typhoid fever, and the beheading of a friend by Haida Indians. On June 5, 1869, four-week-old Carrie, Phoebe's fifth child, died of whooping cough. Around 1870, Jack Judson married Mary and, at their government claim, displayed pictures of Jack's foster parents. The two produced a daughter, Elizabeth Judson, Phoebe and Holden's first grandchild and an addition to the state's twenty-four thousand citizens.

The Judsons acquired half–Lummi daughters, Dollie and Nellie Patterson, after their mother Lizzie escaped her captor-husband, James Alexander Patterson, and fled. Lizzie later died of tuberculosis. Patterson sealed the adoption by giving Holden twenty head of cattle, title to his squatter's cabin, and 160 acres in Nooksack Valley at the village of Squahalish five miles from the British Columbia border. Amid firs and cedars, the homestead that the family occupied in 1871 on Whatcom Bay fulfilled Phoebe's dream of ideal domestication. Cooking at the clay fireplace centered her daily chores.

Whatcom Bay Home

Phoebe Judson adapted immediately to Lynden, her new home in view of Mount Baker, Washington. In addition to becoming more assertive, she established a relationship with local Nooksack and Lummi as healer and Protestant evangelist. She observed the forced training of native youths at the Indian school in farming and sewing, a coercion that defeated the educators' purpose. While operating a large dairy farm, Holden Judson served as postmaster of Lynden and county commissioner.

In October 1871, Anna Judson, then a widow, joined her son and daughter-in-law. Phoebe's brother, merchant Nathan Edwards Goodell, opened a mining supply store in 1879 on the upper Skagit River, the first trading post outside Mount Vernon. Their younger brother, Henry Martin Goodell, operated the Hannegan ferry south of Lynden over the Nooksack River and served as the town's justice of the peace.

At the Judson house, Charles Montgomery Tate, a Methodist missionary and linguist, began instructing the Nooksack and Salish. Phoebe masterminded group projects, including clearing log jams and blazing a trail to the communal fish trap, an underwater rock lane that channeled fish into a shallow pool. In 1881, the dynamiting of logjams freed the Nooksack River for the arrival of the steamer *Willie*, which lessened some of the family's isolation.

In the mid–1880s, Phoebe supported women's rights and, following the passage of women's suffrage in 1888, served on juries and the election board. While Holden manufactured hoops and poles and built an opera house and community center, in 1886, Phoebe and her son, surveyor George Judson, fostered construction of the Northwest Normal School, a women's teacher's academy at Bellingham. The school preceded the founding of Western Washington University and, in 1889, Washington's admission to the Union.

With the incorporation of Lynden on March 16, 1891, Holden became the town's first mayor. Phoebe prospered at tending her foster children, including Nora McClanahan, who died on March 8, 1891, of tuberculosis at age twenty. In widowhood after Holden's death on October 26, 1899, Phoebe continued rearing mixed-race orphans as well as a niece and three nephews. After publication of her journal, *A Pioneer's Search for an Ideal Home: A Personal Memoir* (1925), she died on January 16, 1926. Friends of Aunt Phoebe gather annually to contribute data about the Goodell-Judson clan.

Sources
Peters, Harold J., ed. *Seven Months to Oregon Revisited: As Reflected in the Wyoming County Mirror*. Santa Clara: Harold J. Peters, 2012.

Welsh, Robert L. *The Presbytery of Seattle 1858–2005: The "Dream" of a Presbyterian Colony in the West*. Bloomington: Xlibris, 2006.

Kellie, Luna Sanford (1857–1940), James Thomson Kellie (1850–1918), J.M. Sanford (1836–1910), Fred Sanford (1861–?)

A populist Midwesterner and labor leader of English descent, Luna Elizabeth Sanford "Lou" Kellie promoted temperance and economic justice for farm families. She was born on June 9, 1857, in Pipestone, Minnesota, the eldest of the five children of Martha Lois Smith of Vermont and James Manley "J.M." Sanford, a worker on the Cairo & St. Louis and the Northern Pacific Railroad and labor lecturer for the Nebraska farmers' alliance. Three years after the death of Luna's year-old brother, James Francis Sanford, on May 18, 1863, J.M. suffered wounds from grape shot to the chest at the Battle of Vicksburg, Mississippi.

Luna spent part of the Civil War in Vermont with Grandfather Samuel Smith and her cousin Charlie Smith. The reunited Sanford family rented a house in Lansing, Minnesota, in 1869. After relocating to Madison, Wisconsin, the household migrated to Rockford, Illinois, where Luna attended the Methodist Episcopal church on Court Street. She enrolled at the Rockford Female Seminary on Rock River, the leading girls' academy in the Midwest, and dreamed of a university education.

In 1871, Land Commissioner George S. Harris's pamphlets for the Chicago Burlington and Missouri (B&M) Railroad enticed the Sanfords south with promises of homesteads west of Lincoln, Nebraska, at low prices and ten years' credit at 6 percent interest. J.M. Sanford chose to work a farm in Austin, Minnesota, but incurred bankruptcy by hard times over the winter of 1872–1873, losing his horse and wagon. While he labored in St. Louis, Missouri, on a bridge gang, in March 1873, Luna met his foreman, James Thomson "J.T." Kellie, a Scots-Canadian Presbyterian from Toronto.

Following the deaths of his wife Martha and infant daughter, Stella Smith Sanford, from malarial typhoid in November 1873, J.M. married Jennie Taylor, the 22-year-old stepmother to Frederick Manley "Fred" Sanford, age fourteen, John Samuel "Johnny" Sanford, age eleven, and four-year-old Susie Smith Sanford. Jennie bore a son, George Doolittle Sanford, the first of her three children. At Carondelet, Missouri, on December 31, 1874, Luna wed J.T., who worked for the Northern Pacific Railroad laying rail from Manly to Cedar Rapids before joining her in Nebraska.

Homesteading in Nebraska

While J.M. Sanford sought a homestead and timber claim in spring 1875, the Sanford family journeyed by wagon the next winter to Adams County in south central Nebraska. Settlers passing over the prairie observed the alignment of buffalo skulls into religious patterns, which the Pawnee revered as forms of respect for the Earth Mother. Sanford and his twenty-four-year-old brother, Joseph W. Sanford, broke 50 acres, dug a well, and built a barn and two-room dugout with log roof before planting strawberries, currants, and apple, cherry, plum, and peach trees. A cave served as an equipment shed. Fred, in his mid-teens, managed a team of ornery bulls.

In the same year, the Kellies began a family of eleven children with firstborn William Sanford "Willie" Kellie. J.T. remained in St. Louis to finish building the bridge. During a Sioux uprising in spring 1875 that resulted in nine deaths of pioneers and the rustling of 138 animals, Luna and five-month-old Willie traveled two days by Union Pacific Rail to Grand Island, Nebraska. They shared a car with soldiers going west to join General George Armstrong Custer's troops in suppressing the belligerent Sioux.

In the summer of 1875, Luna and Willie began a 20-month residence with her siblings, her father, and his new wife in a two-room sod hut. Homesteaders formed "claim clubs," local militia shielding farm families from outlawry and Sioux forays. Reunited in February 1877, J.T. and Luna farmed a 160-acre homestead until 1884 while residing in a straw-roofed, 8' × 10' sod hut. Over a fire of prairie grass and corn stalks, Luna prepared meager suppers of greens and pancakes.

Hungering for a windless day and the sight of trees and neighbors, Luna remained on the homestead for the next 18 months before venturing to Hastings, Nebraska. After she and J.T. purchased cattle, chickens, and a wagon, they both exulted in landed independence by working 18-hour days at cutting hay and broomcorn. During an early blizzard, they shared the small residence with their herd and sufficed on boiled oatmeal. In summer 1877, Luna harvested radishes, carrots, beets and beet greens, peas, tomatoes, melons, cucumbers, corn, and beans from her garden, but longed for bread. A neighbor's gift of flour saved the Kellies from starvation.

The deaths in infancy of James Alexander "Jimmie" Kellie and Susie Kellie, the collapse of the straw roof, and the sudden departure of the Sanford brothers grieved Luna, whose breast milk lapsed from exhaustion and malnutrition. Loss of strength forced her to sit to wash dishes and to dream of a vacation at Yellowstone, Wyoming, which Congress had declared a national park on March 1, 1872. Upon Johnny Sanford's return, she celebrated by reading aloud from Mark Twain's novels. The birth of Jessie Kellie on October 30, 1880, and Fred Sanford's return a month later restored her optimism.

While rearing a toddler, Luna sold hay, pork, butter, eggs, and Brahma hens to freighters traveling as far away as Denver. In a time of high farm yield and low prices, in 1882, the Kellies involved themselves in the Farmers' Alliance and protested corrupt grain elevator operators, who set arbitrary prices for grain. J.T. and Luna also advocated extending full citizenship to women, prohibiting liquor at the polls, and lengthening the school year.

Political Activism

Because of a cash-poor economy and the failure of the wheat crop in 1883, J.T. worked at house and barn construction to retire an $800 mortgage and pay for his purchases of a windmill, header, and plow. Luna nearly died in June giving birth to John Frederick "Fred" Kellie. Neuralgia and diphtheria threatened the survival of J.T. and Willie. At a time when the B&M Railroad cleared $2 million per month on bloated passenger and freight charges, Luna accused investors of profiting from farmers' misery.

By trading livestock and farm for Sanford's land, in March 1884, J.T. moved his family north to a sod hut in timber country at Hartwell, Nebraska. The Kellies planted 100 apple trees and harvested fruit from 40 acres. At Minden, they ran a grocery store and added sons Francis Manley "Frank" and Chester Williams Kellie to the household. As realism redefined family fortunes, Luna abandoned views of female activism as unwomanly and began supporting grassroots politics in Kearney County.

As co-civilizers of the Great Plains, the Kellies joined the Farmers' Alliance when it formed in January 1888 and championed agricultural cooperatives. Demanding a reckoning for the beleaguered farmer, the movement grew from 230 chapters to 2,000 in two years' time. By 1890, Luna, J.T., and fellow alliance recruiters had enrolled 250,000 women, most of whom advocated equal education and economic independence for females. On September 23, protesters in 1,600 farm wagons joined a parade at Hastings to sing Luna's diatribe "Dear Prairie Home" (1890), which compared East Coast financiers to Shylock. The bribery of politicians with free train passes became an issue among plains settlers, who sang Luna's song "The Independent Broom" (1890) about "sweeping the state" clean of dishonesty.

Luna stated an anti-capitalist, pro-suffrage stance in issues of a domestic monthly, the *Farmer's Wife*. In original protest ditties and broadsides, such as "The Donkey's Song" (September 1890); "Good-bye, Oh Tommy, Good-bye" (September 1890), a lampoon of a loan shark; "Senator Paddock's Sentiments," "Man the Pumps," and "Lament of the G.O.P." (1890), satires of unethical politics; and "Our John" (1890), a gibe at Union Pacific price gouging, lyrics identified the worst of oppressors of homesteaders. Her songs "Marching for Freedom" (August 1890), "Vote for Me" (1890), and "Who Has Managed" (September 1890) noted that slaves lived better before the Civil War than pioneers in Nebraska. In October 1890, she published "The Pauper's Cowhides," a denunciation of "schemers" William G. Comstock and Bartlett Richards, president of the Nebraska Land and Feeding Company, who illegally fenced in 212,000 acres of public land.

Support for Homesteaders

Luna's socialist concepts appealed to farm communities, particularly "Spread the News" (1890), a paean to unity, and "The Independent Man" (1890) and "Good-bye, My Party, Good-bye" (1890), calls to desert party politics. In July 1892, she boldly issued a feminist essay, "Toilers Unite, Organize and Educate Women." Her speech "Co-operation" (1892) stressed the nobility of dairying and the benefits of teamwork in an economic milieu exploited by bank and railroad capitalists.

In summer 1893, Luna championed the construction of the Gulf and Inter-State Railway, a north-south transcontinental line linking Canada to Galveston, Texas. After the panic of 1893, in spring 1894, she published "A Song of the Times," a rally of voters to support justice for homeowners, the purpose of the march on Washington, D.C., by Coxey's Army. At a state convention in January 1894, where J.T. served on the resolutions committee, Luna delivered a speech—"Stand Up for Nebraska"—to farmers. While simultaneously caring for baby Lois, Luna denounced mortgage rates and stressed the need for a populist party.

Journalists printed Luna's essay in papers at Hastings, Lincoln, and Omaha, Nebraska. Delegates almost unanimously proclaimed her secretary of the Nebraska Alliance. Because of her limited farm wardrobe, she declined to move to Lincoln. In a wing of the Kellie home, she turned a bedroom into an office for answering mail and keeping accounts. To meet the mail train twice daily, her boys made the trip by pony.

On June 14, 1894, the Dallas, Texas, *Southern Mercury* printed "Christ Was a Populist Too," in which Luna stressed the Christian concepts of neighborliness and charity to the poor. As state secretary of the Nebraska Farmers' Alliance, Luna—with the help of daughters Jessie, Edith May, Luna Elizabeth, and Martha Lois Kellie—published the weekly *Prairie Home* to a circulation of 300 paying an annual subscription of 50¢. In *The Farmers' Alliance in Nebraska: A History of Its Later Period from 1894 to 1901*, Luna raised public awareness of the railroad freight costs and bank lending rates that prevented farm families from profiting from their labors.

After a debilitating illness in 1899, Luna joined J.T. in attending a farmers' convention in Cincinnati, Ohio. While mothering her youngest, Helen Goff, Sophie Smith, and Elsie Kathryne Kellie, in 1900 Luna ran for superintendent of Nebraska public schools. Upon selling her printing press, Luna retreated from radical journalism and stopped voting in elections. J.T. set about enlarging the farmhouse. Luna's mistrust of lawyers and party politics soured her on William Jennings Bryan's 1900 and 1908 campaigns for the U.S. presidency.

Strokes diminished J.T. before his death on

April 29, 1918. In retirement in Phoenix, Arizona, Luna fought despair and disillusion over trying to maintain a consensus among populists. In 1925 at age sixty-eight, she wrote a memoir of drought, disease, and locust damage and of corporate monopolies and vote buying that disempowered homesteaders. She died in Phoenix on March 4, 1940.

Source
Hagenstein, Edwin C., Sara M. Gregg, and Brian Donahue, eds. *American Georgics: Writings on Farming, Culture, and the Land.* New Haven: Yale University Press, 2011.

Kelly, Fanny Wiggins (1845–1904), Josiah Shawhan Kelly (1824–1867), Sarah Luse Larimer (1836–1913) William Jackson Larimer (1828–1895)

The legendary captive of the Oglala Sioux, Fanny Wiggins Kelly lectured about her ordeal and published a kidnap novel, a feminist genre that focused on the hardships of both Sioux and pioneer women. A native of South Orillia in Simcoe County, Ontario, she was the child of farmer James and Margaret Wiggins. About the time of mounting "Western fever," the family lived on Lake Simcoe among Ojibwa amid prosperous lumbering and planted 18 acres of their 100-acre parcel.

To improve their lot, the Wiggins household made its way to Geneva, Kansas, with a New York abolitionist colony. En route along polluted streams in 1856, James died of cholera, leaving fatherless nine-year-old Fanny, her sister, and their two brothers. The family reached their destination, where Fanny acquired 159 acres in Anderson County, Kansas, on April 1, 1861.

In November 1863, Fanny wed Kansas native Josiah Shawhan Kelly, an Irish-American farmer and veteran of the Union army. Because of his declining health, on May 17, 1864, the couple set out for the western plains across Montana Territory to Bannock City over the Bozeman Trail, a route from Dakota Territory that had already directed 1,500 emigrants to the frontier. With dreams of traveling to the Idaho goldfields, the Kellies drove fifty milk cows and twenty-five calves and packed whiskey, coffee, flour, and dried fruit, as directed by recruiter pamphlets and by historian Francis Parkman's *The Oregon Trail* (1849). Around June 1, photographer Sarah Luse and farmer William Jackson Larimer and their seven-year-old son, Frank Eugene, joined the wayfarers.

At night on the westering trek, the Kelly family tented with seven-year-old Mary Hurley, the daughter they adopted from Fanny's sister, and black servants Andy and Franklin, former slaves of the Cherokee. Along the route, six male emigrants joined the convoy, bringing the total to eleven. After crossing the Kansas River, Fanny admired the hardihood of female emigrants, who gathered buffalo chips for cooking fuel. The company bound four wagons into a raft for rowing over the Platte River in eastern Nebraska.

Capture by Sioux

The traversing of the Overland Trail coincided with increased tensions among Plains Indians of Dakota, Montana, and Idaho. On July 12, 1864, Oglala Sioux chief Ottawa and a war party of 250 halted the train at Little Box Elder Creek Valley (present-day Douglas) in east central Wyoming and demanded a horse, clothing, sugar cookies, and flour. While the company prepared supper for the Sioux, with arrows, revolvers, knives, spears, and tomahawks, the attackers slew four men, wounded two, and plundered boxes and trunks. Josiah Kelly, who had been away from camp chopping wood, fled through rattlesnake-infested undergrowth with Andy following and reported the attack at Deer Creek Station, South Dakota.

Of the two women and two children kidnapped by Ottawa's band, Sarah Larimer and her son Frank fled; on July 14, 1864, Mary Hurley died of three arrow wounds. As the Sioux abductors forced Fanny Kelly north and west toward the Powder River in southeastern Montana, during the first week's ride, she hid letters, which she dropped to mark the trail. She passed to the control of Ottawa, then in his mid-seventies, and cohabited with his six wives.

On July 20, 1864, the kidnappers reached a Sioux village near the Tongue River in northern Wyoming, where Fanny observed polygamy and the women abandoned by white soldiers. Out of pity for the murder of Mary, Ottawa's six wives gave Fanny a foster child named Yellow Bird. On July 21, Fanny recalled seeing a buffalo hunt.

General Alfred Sully's forces belabored the Sioux east into the Dakota BadLands, yet failed to rescue her. On return to the devastated Wyoming camp, Fanny met Mary Boyeau, a 16-year-old American-French girl seized from Spirit Lake during the Minnesota massacre of 1862. Mary confided the atrocities the Santee Sioux committed against an infant and adult white females.

Negotiating a Release

Over five months of captivity, Fanny Kelly lost track of time. She bargained with $120 in cash, enduring beatings, burning with firebrands, and death threats from arrows. On September 5, 1864, the Sioux forced her to correspond with wagon train leader James Liberty Fisk, who failed to negotiate her release with the offer of three wagons of provisions. She dispatched a warning to him that the Sioux planned to murder him if he entered their village.

Heavy September rains worsened Fanny Kelly's arthritis. Around October 1, 1864, the Sioux captors shuttled Kelly from the Yellowstone River in east central Montana to a Hunkpapa Sioux village. She encountered 14-year-old Charles Sylvester of Quincy, Illinois, whom the Indians had seized at age seven. Josiah Kelly and his brothers bargained in vain for Fanny by giving clothing to Chief Young-Man-Afraid-of-His-Horses, a lieutenant of Red Cloud.

A reward of nineteen horses for Fanny's return muddled the issue of her liberation, which she discerned from a growing understanding of Sioux conversations. At the demand of General Sully, the Blackfeet Lakota sued for peace by parlaying with the Oglala. During extreme cold in November 1864, Blackfeet leader Kill Eagle seized Fanny from captivity. When white traders entered the negotiation to obtain a reward for Fanny's release, the Blackfeet murdered all but one.

Return to Freedom

Fanny facilitated her rescue by posting a letter to General Sully via Jumping Bear, a Sioux infatuated with the captive. The text alerted Sully that Blackfeet plotters intended to besiege Fort Sully, South Dakota, under the pretext of returning her. When eight Sioux chiefs completed a 200-mile journey to the fort on December 12, 1864, the army freed her and presented her clean Caucasian clothing. A New Year's day entertainment honored her presence. (An alternate ending of Kelly's liberation declared that Sitting Bull escorted her to the fort.)

Josiah and Fanny Kelly reunited at the fort and met crowds of well wishers at Sioux City and Council Bluffs, Iowa, and St. Joseph, Missouri. Passing through Leavenworth, Kansas, the couple journeyed back to Fanny's mother at Geneva and settled in central Kansas at Ellsworth, a new town under constant alarm of Indian attack. Fanny and Josiah operated a profitable rooming house.

Fanny was 35 weeks pregnant when a cholera epidemic swept Kansas towns and army posts, allegedly introduced by Buffalo Soldiers passing through on the way from Missouri to New Mexico Territory. Among the 1,500 victims, the disease killed Josiah on July 28, 1867. A week later, Fanny gave birth to Josiah Kelly, Jr., on August 4, at St. George, Kansas, and survived a bout of cholera that a doctor treated with sweating and mustard plasters. On her migration west to Sheridan, she encountered two familiar Sioux at Fort Hays, Kansas.

Because of rampant cholera and scurvy on the swampy tent grounds of Fort Hays, Fanny Kelly sold her property and determined to emigrate to Wyoming. William J. and Sarah Luse Larimer, survivors of the Battle of Killdeer Mountain, gave Fanny and her son a home at Sherman Station, Wyoming Territory, where the Larimers operated a photography studio and grocery store. While Fanny labored as the family's laundress, Sarah Larimer stole Fanny's memoir and had it published in Philadelphia under the title *The Capture and Escape; or, Life Among the Sioux* (1870). Because Fanny pressed a lawsuit against the Larimers, a Kansas judge settled the matter in Fanny's favor and ordered Sarah's spurious books destroyed.

A Famed Memoirist

After a year, Fanny Kelly traveled to Washington, D.C., to petition President Ulysses S. Grant for compensation by the Indian Bureau of $5,000. While working at the patent office, she attended councils at which the Sioux chief Red Cloud stated his grievances about possession of the Powder River Valley to Jacob Dolson Cox, the Secretary of the Interior. Brule Sioux chief Spotted Tail and three others attested to Fanny Kelly's right to an annuity in a document that they signed on June 9, 1870.

In 1871, Kelly published an original version of her abduction entitled *Narrative of My Captivity among the Sioux Indians.*. She dedicated the text to the cavalrymen who helped Josiah rescue his wife and to the soldiers who welcomed her to Fort Sully. In a foreword, she hoped that readers would not sink into speculation and false assumptions about her ordeal, a veiled attempt to end rumors of rape or sexual torment. In 1872, Congress appropriated $10,000 for restitution to Fanny, who invested it in real estate.

On May 5, 1880, in a Presbyterian ceremony, Fanny wed Virginia-born newspaperman William F. Gordon, a Union Army veteran and, in 1883, editor of the *Oklahoma War Chief* at Arkansas City, Kansas. She devoted herself to charities aiding war widows. She retired to Washington, D.C., where Gordon died on October 13, 1893. Fanny succumbed to cerebral hemorrhage on November 15, 1904.

See also Fisk, James Liberty.

SOURCES

Kelly, Fanny. *Narrative of My Captivity among the Sioux Indians.* Hartford, CT: Mutual Publishing, 1871.

Naparsteck, Martin. *Sex and Manifest Destiny: The Urge That Drove Americans Westward.* Jefferson, NC: McFarland, 2012.

Key, Ambrose W. (1829–1908), Mary Jones Garrett Key (1835–1927), George Key (1795–1864), Rebecca Mintun Key (1799–ca. 1860)

A son of pioneers and hardy settler of parts of Missouri, Texas, and Kansas, Ambrose W. Key diversified his commercial interests from trading and storekeeping to wood milling, tanning, freight, farming, and horticulture. A native of Crawfordsville, Indiana, of English lineage, he was born fourth of fifteen children on November 27, 1829, to New Jerseyite Rebecca Mintun Rardin, a descendent of a Revolutionary War veteran, and George Key, a Methodist Episcopal blacksmith from Franklin, Virginia. A frontiersman by nature, George farmed and traded with the Indians along the rivers of Iowa and Indiana.

Two years after the Black Hawk purchase of former Winnebago, Fox, and Sauk lands on September 21, 1832, for $640,000, George Key joined the first pioneers to settle in Marshall Township, Iowa. He built a rail pen around a covered wagon as temporary housing and sold pork. He engaged in transporting provisions by flatboat from the Wabash River up the Ohio River to Cairo, Illinois, then west along the Mississippi River to a warehouse at Burlington in southeastern Iowa. In an act of charity in 1836, he presented a nursing mother, Rachael Higbee, with a split bottom chair to ease her early motherhood.

George Key homesteaded a 240-acre claim in Louisa County in 1836 and 1837 and returned to Crawfordsville for the winter. In spring 1838, nine-year-old Ambrose aided his mother, nine siblings—Julia Ann, Eliza Jane, Lucinda, Solomon P., Harriet "Hettie," Mahetable, Darius, James Alvin, and infant John H. Key—and ten hired men in relocating the household from Indiana to Iowa by a carriage and three wagons to their new home, called Virginia Grove. Led by Rebecca Key, the 300-mile journey required 45 days over flooded roads to drive horses, cattle, and 100 sheep. The family left behind Ambrose's married sister Hannah.

At Virginia Grove, the Key household, including toddlers David K. and Joseph Stoner

Key, dressed in homemade linsey-woolsey, attended school in a log building fitted with a fireplace, puncheon floor, and slab seats. At home, in lieu of a grist mill, the Key children and George's two grandchildren operated four tin corn graters to make meal for mush and cornbread. By 1853, a year of epidemic typhoid, George Key raised award-winning corn at the rate of 120 bushels per acre. In 1859, he joined other settlers at the Wapello courthouse to form the Louisa County Iowa Pioneer Society and served in the territorial road commission, which eased transportation along the Skunk River to the center of the state.

Moving South

At age 26, Ambrose Key invested in an 80-acre government tract in Louisa County in southeastern Iowa, where his father expanded the family holdings to 2,000 acres. By 1856, Ambrose operated a mercantile in Wapello, where his brother, Darius Key, farmed 1,200 acres, raised angus cattle, and co-founded a wheat mill. In February 1857, Ambrose raised $20,000 in stock subscriptions to promote the passage of the Fort Wayne & Platte River Air Line Railroad through Burris City.

On July 24, 1857, Ambrose Key felt so sure of profits in Burris City and Louisa County that he invested in the Ellsworth Hotel, a two-story brick structure housing sick river travelers. Flooding of the Iowa and Mississippi rivers, the worst in American history, destroyed the hotel in mid–April 1858, drowning fourteen guests in the marble-floor billiard room. With the onset of typhoid, Burris City turned into a ghost town, ending plans for the building of the Air Line Railroad and quashing Key's investment.

On May 21, 1859, in Tipton, Missouri, Ambrose Key wed twenty-four-year-old Ohio native Mary Jones Garrett, a descendent of eighteen-century immigrants from Worchestershire, England, and daughter of the founder of Garrettsville, Ohio. As of 1860, the couple had established a dry goods store Navasota, Texas, where they produced sons Sidney D. and Joseph Francis M. Key. George Key, a recent widower, joined his son's family before the onset of the American Civil War. Both Ambrose and his father served in the Confederate "Rebel Texas" regiment and entered Union custody after their capture at Vicksburg, Mississippi.

The war altered the Key clan. Combat brought about the deaths of George Key and his son, David K. Key, a soldier in the 6th Iowa Infantry who fell in combat at Shiloh, Tennessee, on April 6, 1862, along with 65 comrades. Ambrose's brother, John H. Key, also in the 6th Iowa, suffered critical battle wounds at Missionary Ridge, Tennessee, on November 25, 1863, and Big Shanty during the battle of Kennesaw Mountain, Georgia, on June 27, 1864. Solomon P. Key incurred a thigh wound in Missouri and capture during service with the Iowa 1st Cavalry "Hawkeye Rangers" on September 29, 1863, when he entered a prisoner of war camp at Atchafalaya, Louisiana. Brothers James Alvin Key and bugler Joseph Stoner Key mustered out unhurt.

In Texas and Kansas

Like his father, near war's end, Ambrose Key looked to the West for opportunity. Into the mid–1860s, he ran a sawmill and lumber yard east of Houston, Texas, on the San Jacinto River before investing in a tannery and second sawmill producing doors, blinds, and window sashes. After George Key's death in August 1864, Ambrose liquidated the estate. Because of his ill health and animosity toward supporters of the Union, in 1865, the Key family lived in St. Louis, Missouri, where he traveled as a grain salesman. Heading a wagon convoy, in 1867, Ambrose Key joined the last of the Oregon Trail generation and moved to Westport, Missouri, to launch a trade and freight business through Indian Territory (Oklahoma) to Texas. The couple added two daughters to the family, Nellie G. Key and Gertrude S. P. Key.

Within months after the Treaty of Medicine Lodge of October 28, 1867, settled Arapaho, Cheyenne, Comanche, and Kiowa on reservations in Indian Territory (Oklahoma), Ambrose Key purchased a 65-acre fruit farm on Gibbs Road in Shawnee southwest of Argentine, Kansas. A proponent of small fruit, he raised three acres of grapes, ten of raspberries, blackberries, two of strawberries, 75 gooseberry and currant bushes, 350 cherry trees, 200 plum trees, and 600 peach trees as well as Ben Davis, winesap, early harvest, red June, red astrachan, and winter pippin apples. Ambrose served five terms on the school board and, in 1891, advanced to membership in the Missouri Valley Horticultural Society, which promoted propagation of currants, sweet and sour cherries, and black and red raspberries. He died of stomach cancer on August 17, 1908, in Wyandotte, Kansas. His widow survived him by nineteen years, died in 1927, and was buried beside him.

Source

Shortridge, James R. *Cities on the Plains: The Evolution of Urban Kansas*. Lawrence: University of Press of Kansas, 2004.

Kinman, Seth (1815–1888), Pearson Barton Reading (1816–1868)

An ebullient hunter, innkeeper, and prospector, Seth Kinman told pioneer stories and recorded frontier exploits in a scrapbook and memoir. A scion of an eighteenth-century immigrant from Rheinland-Pfalz, Germany, he was born on September 29, 1815, in Uniontown, Pennsylvania, the only child of Eleanor "Ellen" Bower and James Kinman, an innkeeper, millwright, and ferryman on the Susquehanna River. While the family lived near Springlake, Illinois, on the Mackinaw River, he received minimal literacy skills. The Kinmans moved east to Tazewell County, Illinois, in 1830, where he worked as a miller and sawyer while hunting and trapping with cousins for relaxation.

After his father's death in 1839, 25-year-old Kinman married Anna Maria Sharpless of Sunbury, Pennsylvania, and sired James "Cal" Carlin Sharpless, Austin, Ellen E., and Roderick Christopher Carson "Kit" Kinman. Seth farmed and ran the Eagle Hotel in Pekin, Illinois, before joining the 1849 California Gold Rush. For two years, he accompanied pioneer Pierson Barton Reading's convoy up the Pacific Coast to Vancouver on the bark *Josephine*. The expedition searched for placer gold along the Trinity River in Shasta County, where Reading became the first white settler in 1845. After a year exploring Humboldt Bay during the rainy winter of 1852–1853, Kinman settled at a cabin on the Eel River near present-day Ferndale with twelve men, including portraitist Stephen William Shaw.

California Mountain Man

The death of ten-year-old James and six-year-old Austin Kinman in early December 1852 during a cholera epidemic and of wife Anna Maria Kinman on April 20, 1853, caused Seth to traverse the West once more on foot. He retrieved his remaining family—eight-year-old Carlin, five-year-old Ellen, and three-

In 1855, Seth Kinman hunted southern Oregon and sold deer and elk meat to the army.

year-old Roderick—and his mother from Illinois in May 1854. The clan resettled at Table Bluff, California, in 1855 and operated a dairy at Bear River Ridge for five years. Seth hunted from Bear Valley north into Oregon and, on contract from Fort Humboldt, sold deer and elk meat to the army for 25 cents per pound.

Using his jackknife and animal parts collected over seven years of mountaineering, Kinman experimented with crafting chairs from grizzly bear skins and elk hooves and antlers. Taking passage on the *Golliah* to San Francisco and, on June 20, 1857, on the *Golden Age* through Panama, he carried a model of his craft to Washington, D.C. Before photographers and reporters from New York, he presented a chair to President James Buchanan, who reciprocated with gifts of a rifle and two pistols.

In October 1858, Kinman made the first land purchase in Humboldt County. He established a saloon and inn and began farming 80 acres east of Table Bluff, California, where he tinkered with inventions. On a government appointment during the Indian wars of Northern California, he guided the troops that forced the peaceful Wiyot, Karuk, Yurok, Chilula, Whilkut, Hupa, and Athapaskan of Humboldt County onto eight reservations. After the foundering of the Pacific Mail steamer *Northerner*, a 1,350-ton side-wheeler, off Centerville Beach at 5:00 p.m. on January 5, 1860, Kinman secured himself to a rock to try to save the 108 passengers on the San Francisco-to-Victoria run. With the aid of Centerville postmaster Arnold Berding, he rescued some of the 38 passengers and 32 crew and 45 bags of mail from the surf.

Kinman's life blended acts of generosity and selflessness with wholesale murder. In May 1860, he joined local whites in warding off local Wiyot Indians, who had dwindled from genocidal attacks to 10 percent of their former population of 2,000 and retaliated by slaughtering cattle herds. In May 1864 at the end of the Bald Hills War (1858–1864), Kinman participated in the mass carnage of natives by the California Volunteer Infantry. The Mattole, Nangatl, Lassik, and Sinkyone edged close to extinction.

Frontier Folklorist

A two-year tour took Kinman to Illinois and Pennsylvania performing as raconteur, docent for a museum of frontier exotica, and seller of postcards, which photographer Matthew Brady made of Kinman in fur hat and fringed buckskins adorned with bear claws. On November 26, 1864, Kinman took an elk horn chair to President Abraham Lincoln. The frontier musician serenaded Lincoln with "John Brown's Body" and "Essence of Old Virginia" played on a mule skull fiddle with a rib strung with mule tail hair for a bow.

Kinman filed for a patent on February 14, 1865, for a rifle support and brace. He returned in April 1865 to Washington to join Lincoln's funeral procession through New York as far west as Columbus, Ohio. Kinman crafted a bearskin chair for the library of President Andrew Johnson and, on September 8, 1865, demonstrated a bit of puppetry that caused the head to rise and the jaws to snap. In 1869, Kinman again filed a patent, this time for a mechanical potato digger.

In 1876, the year that Kinman dictated an autobiography to Henry H. Niebur, he gave an autographed elk horn chair to Rutherford B. Hayes, then governor of Ohio. In his late sixties, Kinman managed the two-story clapboard Table Bluff Hotel and Pioneer Saloon, where he adorned the bar with horns, antlers, Indian spears, boar-skin stools, bear foot chair, stuffed bear head, and photos of regional events. In 1883, he introduced the first cattle herd to Humboldt County. In 1885, he collaborated with his sons Carlin and Roderick Kinman in establishing a Los Angeles frontier museum and in touring Sacramento, Eureka, and San Francisco with his collection, which included a 1,635-pound bear carcass.

Kinman's accidental shot below the knee and subsequent leg amputation killed the famed hunter on February 12, 1888. He went to his grave in buckskins and fur hat. Display of his curiosities in the 1893 Chicago World's Fair extended his notoriety as a mountain man.

SOURCES

Ferndale Museum. *Ferndale*. Charleston, SC: Arcadia, 2004.

Seacrest, William B. *California Disasters, 1812–1899*. Sanger, CA: Quill Driver, 2005.

Lahti, Peter J. (1834–1911), Johanna Gustava Palovainio Lahti (1840–1919), Charles Lahti (1859–1932)

A hunter, trapper, and farmer and son of immigrant pioneers, Peter Johnson Lahti established a foothold in Minnesota for Finnish sodbusters. Born Petter (or Pere) Johansson Lahti on August 28, 1834, at Nikkala in south central Finland, he was the son of farmers Brita Lisa Henriksdotter and Johan Jakobsson Lahti. Johan Lahti's ambitions inspired him to migrate to Norway in 1858.

On January 13, 1861, Peter Lahti wed Johanna Gustava Palovainio in Vadsø, Norway, who was already mother of their fourteen-month-old son Karl (or Kaarlo) Johan and Solomon Lahti, who apparently died in infancy. Departing with other Finns from Hammerfest in March 1864, Peter joined his parents and younger sisters, Brita Karolina, Maria, and Susanna, and sailed aboard a Norwegian vessel on a seven-week journey from the port of Hammerfest, Norway, to Montreal and Quebec.

Across Lake Michigan to Chicago by steamer, Peter and Johanna Lahti extended the long trek by train northeast toward Red Wing, Minnesota, a region similar in climate, soil, and forests to their homeland. Males found steady work felling trees to fuel river steamers. To avoid cholera epidemics that killed some twenty-five immigrants annually, the Lahtis continued northwest to begin a Finnish colony southeast of Minneapolis at Franklin. The family arrived on April 4, 1864, with two children of relatives, Frans Oskar and Hilda Karolina Lahti.

In autumn 1864, Peter Lahti joined the 25,000 Minnesotans who entered the First Minnesota Heavy Artillery after its formation on August 14. Garrisoned under the command of Colonel William Colvill, a hero wounded at the Battle of Gettysburg on July 4, 1863, Lahti trained at Chattanooga, Tennessee. He and seventeen-year-old Matti Niemi-Johnston served ten months on Missionary Ridge south of Lookout Mountain in anticipation of Confederate General John Bell Hood's push north, which never came. Peter and Matti mustered out in September and returned to central Minnesota.

Settling Southern Minnesota

In October 1865, Peter searched Renville County for farmland under the Homestead Act, which allotted to Union Army veterans free 160-acre tracts on 270 million acres in public domain. He migrated due west to St. Peter, a settlement vying for state capital where Scandinavians introduced Americans to the sauna. In May 1866, he became Minnesota's first Finnish pioneer after he staked a claim on a tract in Birch Cooley northwest of Franklin's "Finntown," Minnesota's original Finnish settlement. With Matti Niemi's aid, Peter proved up his homestead with a sod-roofed log cabin and cattle shelter. His *pesäpaikka* (nesting place) preceded the establishment of 4,700 Finnish farms, the largest number in the U.S.

Lahti found trappers conspiring to ward off pioneers by fostering terror of a Dakota Sioux attack, which chiefs Little Crow and Grey Bird had previously led against isolated farmsteads at New Ulm on August 19, 1862. The U.S. Army reassured pioneers by staffing Fort Ridgely with infantry and cavalry as a buffer against Sioux predations. By April 2, 1867, the settlement of Birch Cooley had survived a two-year cholera epidemic and advanced to an official township governed by officials elected that same year.

In summer 1868, the Lahtis relocated among pioneers living in dugouts with hay roofs. To counter false impressions of danger to settlers, Lahti dug a well, cultivated 37 acres, planted an apple orchard, and erected a pigsty, chicken coop, and warehouse. He hired Finns to work his land and colonize the area, which offered permanent residences, a blacksmith shop, and general store. Contributing to the enclave were Mikko Heikko, a trapper and lumberman from the Tornio River Valley; Matti and Maria Korpi Niemi and their infant son Kalle from Kemi; and Antti and Maria Matlena Helppi Rovainen from Kittilä. Within a year, Antti Rovainen died, leaving Maria to rear their two children and to work as a reading and catechism teacher, midwife, and farmer.

At the village of Camp north of Bird Island Lake in south central Minnesota, Peter trapped and pursued a business in muskrat, fox, mink, and weasel furs. Assisting him in 1870 was his nine-year-old son Karl Johann, who took the name Charles Lahti. In a prosperous year, father and son sold 9,000 muskrat hides for $1,125, the smallest bringing in a dime each.

The Lahti Farm

From 1867 to 1881, the Lahti family increased with the births of Hilda Johanna, Oscar Bay, Frank Bay, Katherine Carrie Bay, August, Mary, Annie Hannah, and Mina Lahti and two infants who died at birth. The translation of "Lahti" to "Bay" added an American branch to the family tree. The children attended district schools as well as the Finnish Apostolic Lutheran Church, begun with home services in Finnish at Cokato in 1875 and formally organized five years later. The Lahtis and other members passed a collection basket to defray travel expenses for the pastor, the Reverend Jakob Wuollet, an immigrant evangelist from Kokkola, Finland.

At age eighteen, Charles Lahti migrated to Minneapolis to work on the Saint Paul and Pacific Railroad. In 1879, Peter Lahti became the first Finnish advertiser in the *Sankarin Maine* weekly after he offered a herd of dairy cows for sale in Hancock and Calumet, Michigan, perhaps transporting them by barge to the St. Paul depot and by boat from Duluth over Lake Superior. Charles returned home in 1880 and leased the family homestead before purchasing it in 1885. The sale occurred after Johanna and Peter Lahti fought over financial control. Johanna had had a court declare Peter insane and remand him to an asylum.

After Minnesota entered the Union in 1889, through additional land transactions, Charles increased the Lahti farm to 416 acres plus 160 acres in Aitkin Country and two farmsteads east of Tampa, Florida. Finnish settlers suffered a cholera epidemic in 1899, which struck stockmen and cost the lives of hundreds of hogs. Bird Island remained the rare place were farm animals escaped infection. In August 1895, August Lahti died from a mining accident under a deluge of ore. Peter died on July 17, 1911, in Franklin, Minnesota, and lies buried in the Finnish Cemetery.

Sources

Alanan, Arnold Robert. *Finns in Minnesota*. St. Paul: Minnesota Historical Press, 2012.

Holmio, Armas Kustaa Ensio. *History of the Finns in Michigan*. Hancock, MI: Finlandia University, 2001.

Lambert, Rebecca H. (1806–1886), Harriet J. Bunker (1800–1895)

The founder and life member of the Ladies' Seamen's Friend Society of San Francisco, Rebecca H. Gatchell Lambert devoted her reformism to protecting homeless sailors from dissolute lives, harbor thugs, shanghaiing, and illicit jailing. She was born in Lisbon, Maine, in 1806. She wed childhood sweetheart Thomas Lambert, captain of the brig U.S.S. *Lackawanna,* on December 16, 1827, in New York. In widowhood in 1842, when she worked as a dressmaker, she identified with other females wed to seagoing men who had "swallowed the anchor."

Despite sectarian squabbles between Methodist Episcopalian and Wesleyan Methodist coastal evangelism and the social approbation toward women fraternizing with sailors, Lambert persevered in raising funds to improve mariners' lives. She ennobled the task as "the Lord's work." Supervised by a board of seven men, in April 1849, she assisted in the incorporation of the Mariners' Family Industrial Society of the Port of New York, which she served as financial agent.

Members bought twelve sewing machines to employ seamen's wives as seamstresses and allotted clothing and bedding to women and children made destitute by the disablement or deaths of waterman husbands and fathers. At the Sailor's Home overlooking the East River on Cherry Street, workers distributed bibles and opened lending libraries stocked with the American Seamen's Friend Society's periodical *The Sailor's Magazine and Seamen's Friend, Naval Journal,* and *The Mariners' Magazine.* Volunteers held prayer meetings and served communion to Christian crewmen shipping out of Boston and New York City.

A Mission to Seamen

In 1854, Lambert applied her zeal to San Francisco's Barbary Coast, where foreign elements dominated the waterfront and transported a variety of immigrants and social ills to coastal California during the gold rush of 1849. Female efforts were slow in suppressing the harbor's rowdyism, prostitution, drunkenness, and lawlessness. In the early 1850s, local volunteers hosted a chaplain at a house of worship with an average attendance of 150. By 1850, the San Francisco Sailor's Home, a rented property on Battery and Vallejo streets, housed an average of 600 boarders paid for with annual receipts of $3,000. Volunteers welcomed homeless residents with clean linens, wholesome food, and surroundings beneficial to ailing and injured mariners.

From 1852 to 1886 at the home and aboard the ship *Panama*, Lambert issued alerts to vulnerable men about foreign "crimps" (agents) perpetrating the illegal conscription of ships' crews. The forcible impressment occurred in the port in sight of the toney neighborhood of Rincon Hill, which overlooks Yerba Buena Cove. In the mid–1850s, the Sailor's Home offered financial help and transportation for abductees back to family. To ensure a permanent refuge, the society took formal shape on March 26, 1856.

An Organized Outreach

In April 1858, members solicited donations and entrusted the fund to officers Lambert and Harriet J. Bunker of Massachusetts. Monetary gifts underwrote weekly visits to the U.S. Marine Hospital at Harrison and Spear streets and the Mariners' Church, a nondenominational institution promoting Christianity at Drumm and Sacramento streets. In February 1861, the society urged the state to appropriate funds to build a permanent residence extending "salutary benefits" for aged and disabled watermen. The petition nudged legislators toward eradicating the reputation of California for frontier violence and vice, but the proposal failed.

During Lambert's appointment as society financial agent in 1867, her campaign harnessed the energies of elite female canvassers, who raised $6,000 in two years. Meanwhile, the Sailor's Home occupied the Mercantile Hotel on Front Street before relocating to Hilloran House on Davis Street. When the property became uninhabitable in 1868, Lambert's staff had to abandon their sailors' lodgings.

Late in the 1860s, Lambert advocated appropriate burial for unidentified master mariners in San Francisco's City Cemetery on Telegraph Hill in view of the bay, a task supported by the Marine Hospital Mission. By 1874, the society amassed $10,000, raised in part at the city's Industrial Fair from meals served at the New England Kitchen. On August 11, 1876, Lambert successfully appealed to the U.S. Congress for use of the abandoned Marine Hospital.

In 1877, the society opened 200 quarters in the four-story Sailor's Home, an event depicted in the December 1 issue of *Frank Leslie's Illustrated Newspaper.* In one week, 106 sailors claimed residence. Lambert pressed authorities for standard maritime contracts and labor conditions for sailors. Her goals for more equitable treatment of seamen ranged from uniform pay to suppression of shipboard abuse.

A year after Lambert's death in 1886, the society honored her federal lobby for sailors in August 1887 with honorary membership. Harriet Bunker died on April 21, 1895. Henry Daniel Cogswell, a temperance crusader from Oakland, underwrote a memorial stele in Lincoln Park. In 1910, officials exhumed mariners' bodies and moved them to Colma in the original wood coffins provided by the U.S. Marine Hospital staff.

SOURCE
Cherny, Robert W., ed. *California Women and Politics: From the Gold Rush to the Great Depression.* Lincoln: University of Nebraska Press, 2011.

Lassen, Peter (1800–1859), William Brown Ide (1796–1852), Isadore Meyerowitz (ca. 1820–1856)

During the establishment of U.S. sovereignty over the Pacific Coast territories, Danish blacksmith and rancher Peter Lassen (or Lawson) pioneered a route from the Mississippi River Valley to the California goldfields, where he acquired a fortune. A native of Farum northeast of Copenhagen, he was born "Peter Larsen" in poverty on October 31, 1800. One of three children of itinerant farm laborer Peter Nielsen, he lived in Hilleroud at age nine and later changed his surname to Peter Larsen Farum.

Lassen completed elementary school and moved to Kalundborg in his early teens to study blacksmithing for six years with an uncle, Christen Nielsen. In 1823, he worked at a forge in Copenhagen, completed service in the city militia, and achieved the status of master ironsmith. He attempted to start an ironworking business in 1827, but failed. Upon emigration from Elsinore on September 25, 1830, he chose the current spelling of Lassen as his patronym. He passed through New York and, on January 1, 1830, reached Boston, Massachusetts.

After a lengthy period of farming and forge labor in Philadelphia, St. Louis, and Keytesville in north central Missouri, in spring 1839, Lassen and twelve other emigrants departed from Westport over the Oregon Trail to the Pacific Coast. They joined Congregational missionary and carpenter Asahel Munger of Litchfield, Massachusetts; preacher John Smith Griffin of Connecticut; and trappers and representatives of the American Fur Company attending the annual rendezvous on the Green River at Pinedale, Wyoming. The rapid depletion of emigrant stores forced the wayfarers to hunt buffalo and deer along the Platte River and fish for trout, salmon, catfish, and sucker.

The company found no guide available at Fort Hall, Idaho, and continued west. Arriving at Oregon City in autumn 1839, Lassen remained in the Willamette Valley through the winter. Aboard the three-masted barkentine *Lausanne* in May 1840, he paid $60 for the five-week passage south to Bodega, a harbor in northwestern California governed by Russian Commandant Alexander Rottscheff. At the time, Bodega's residents resented the intrusion of alien pioneers and, in July, tried to obstruct Lassen's emigration.

After traveling inland to Sutter's Fort, Lassen and companion William Wiggins took a sailboat to San Francisco. Lassen found work in gunsmithing and general repair at a forge at Branciforte Pueblo in San Jose County, California. In spring 1841 at Isaac Graham's Zayante Rancho and tannery outside Santa Cruz (present-day Mount Hermon), Lassen purchased land adjacent to the Sacramento River suitable for California's first water-powered sawmill.

In fall 1842, lacking staff for the sawmill, Lassen worked for John Sutter at his New Helvetia ranch in exchange for cattle, horses, and

In spring 1839, Peter Lassen set out for Oregon and fished for trout, salmon, catfish, and sucker to feed the wagon train.

mules. As a member of a posse searching for stolen horses in 1843, Lassen rode from Sutter's Fort in Sacramento northwest toward Red Bluff. After taking his pay in livestock, he chose virgin land he wanted to settle at the intersection of Deer Creek and the Sacramento River. In December 1843, Lassen set out for Tehama County to raise some 300 head of cattle. He arrived through floods in February 1844 that destroyed the crops at Sutter's Fort and stimulated mosquito populations, the source of malaria.

Exploring Northern California

When Lassen acquired Mexican citizenship on December 26, 1844, Governor Manuel Micheltorena issued a grant for the five-league (22,206-acre) Rancho Bosquejo on Deer Creek, also called Lassen's Rancho (present-day Benton City). Lassen hired Indian laborers to erect a farmhouse. He established wheat, cotton, vineyards, sheep, pigs, and chickens. In anticipation of expanded settlement, he built a forge and log store.

In 1845, Lassen quarried grindstones from Stony Creek into the summer, when he ferried them downriver by canoe. In October, he acquired a partner, widower William Brown Ide, a farmer and surveyor from Rutland, Massachusetts, who traversed the Oregon Trail from Independence, Missouri. Ide reached Sutter's Fort on October 25, 1845, with valuable tools—mill irons and a circular saw. At Lassen's direction, Ide erected a sawmill at present-day Vina in Tehama County before involving himself in the Bear Flag Revolt of June 14, 1846, the beginning of American annexation of Alta California from Mexico. Ide advanced to judge and became the first and only president of the California Republic.

To finance another colonization effort, Lassen sold a square league along the creek to trapper Daniel Sill, who started the rival settlement of Danville. In company with Kit Carson and John Frémont aboard the Robert Field Stockton train of forty-nine emigrants, on June 30, 1847, Lassen returned east to recruit more settlers and guide a dozen wagons to northern California. He reached Independence, Missouri, in November 1847 and secured a charter for the Benton City Masonic Lodge. After departing in May 1848, to avoid the Donner Pass, he experimented with a variation of the California Trail, which turned south at Fort Hall, Idaho. He traversed northwest Nevada over the Black Rock Desert between the Jackson Range and the Calico Mountains.

Via the Lassen Cutoff, the convoy proceeded over rough terrain through Devil's Garden on the Pit River and east of Lassen Peak to a tract in Alta California in the Sacramento River Basin. The route traversed territory occupied by hostile Pit River Indians. Because the disgruntled travelers lost their way over narrow mountain trails, they cut down ten wagons into carts to ease the passage. In September 1848, Lassen followed Oregon guide Peter Hardeman Burnett from Lassen Peak to Sacramento Valley, arriving at his ranch in late October and quickly amassing wealth from placer gold.

Over the next year, while some 8,000 emigrants followed Lassen's Cutoff, the Danish recruiter built an adobe house and ran a store that sold flour, provisions, and whiskey to travelers. In September 1849, he lured more settlers by advertising the advantages of his route in handbills and articles issued in the *New York Herald* on February 12, 1849, and in the *Milwaukee Sentinel and Gazette* on February 27, 1849. Because of near disasters from hunger, sickness, and snow, survivors of the arduous trip renamed the cutoff "Lassen's Death Route." By 1850, newcomers to California chose easier itineraries, streamlined at Red Bluff by William Ide's ferry.

Ambition proved Lassen's undoing. To transport provisions, in May 1850, he deeded half his land to Joel Palmer to finance purchase of the vessel *Lady Washington*, the first steamer to travel from Sacramento to Red Bluff. Furor over the California Gold Rush and Palmer's failure to pay for his property foiled Lassen's plan to control new settlements and enlarge Benton City. The theft of his cattle, sinking of the *Lady Washington,* and swindling by Palmer forced Lassen to liquidate the remainder of his property.

Prospecting for Gold and Silver

Lassen relocated southeast to Plumas County and searched the Sierras for gold at mythic Gold Lake, a geographical hoax perpetrated by Thomas Robert Stoddard, a British emigrant who convinced several thousand miners to follow his trail from Marysville. With the aid of Russian-Jewish '49er Isadore Meyerowitz, Lessen, affectionately known as "Uncle Pete," began building a log trading post at Indian Valley in summer 1850 and completed it in March 1851 with a brush roof. By 1852, cabbage, potatoes, turnips, and beets from the garden he planted with Meyerwitz brought 15¢ per pound from eager emigrants. One turnip brought $1.20. Smallpox killed William Ide on December 19, 1852, robbing Lassen of a collaborator.

Get-rich-quick schemes inflamed Lassen's ambitions. In October 1855, he and Meyerwitz squatted at a long log cabin to the northeast in Honey Lake Valley outside Susanville. To enrich himself, Lassen split rails and sawed planks for sluices for the gold strike he worked near the cabin. From bunchgrass along Lassen Creek, he reaped 20 tons of hay to feed his cattle, horses, and oxen. However, a mild winter foiled his plan to profit from livestock feed. In July 1856, drowning ended his reliance on trading partner Isadore Meyerwitz, who died at Honey Lake with his Maidu wife from the capsizing of a sailboat Meyerwitz had made from a box wagon.

To avoid county taxes, on April 26, 1856, Lassen promoted the creation of Nataqua Territory, an independent district east of the Sierra Nevada. In July 1856, he took the job of county surveyor. The rectangle he surveyed over northwestern California and much of western Nevada measured 220 miles by 150 miles. He petitioned the U.S. Congress to grant sovereignty to Nataqua Territory to protect residents from the Paiute and Shoshone. He also formulated plans for law enforcement, which languished during deep snows, isolating settlers from California. Until U.S. Congressmen refused the request, Lassen served as governor of Nataqua with Isaac Newton Roop as assistant.

In hopes of profiteering on newcomers, in 1857, Lassen led miners 124 miles northeast from Susanville to the Black Rock silver field in western Nevada. He guided more immigrants over the Pacific Wagon Road and claimed to have discovered Noble's Cutoff, named for merchant William Nobles. On October 25, 1858, Lassen bought milling apparatus and a threshing machine in preparation for more projects. Late in the winter of 1857–1858, to keep the peace, he negotiated treaties between Nataqua and the Paiute and Shoshone and summoned U.S. cavalry to shield pioneers from attack.

During an ambush allegedly by Northern Paiute, Lassen and Edward Clapper died of rifle fire at Clapper Canyon, Nevada, at dawn on April 26, 1859. Because no one stole the miners' packs, pioneer legend claimed that a fellow traveler, trader Americus (or Lemericus) Wyatt, murdered both prospectors. After a hasty burial, rescuers returned to exhume Lassen's remains and reinterred them at Susanville with Masonic honors.

On April 1, 1864, an official survey legitimized Lassen County, California. The name survives in Lassen Butte, Mount Lassen, Lassen Meadows, Lassen College, Lassen National Volcanic Forest, Fernley & Lassen Railroad, Lassen Lodge, and Lassen View. Lassen's monument in Farum, Denmark, preserves his influence on early Nordic settlers. The William B. Ide adobe survives as a California state historic park.

Sources

Johnston, Ken. *Legendary Truths: Peter Lassen & His Gold Rush Trail in Fact & Fable.* N.p.: Pronghorn Press, 2012.

Massey, Peter, and Jeanne Welburn Wilson. *Backcountry Adventures: Northern California.* Castle Rock, CO: Adler, 2002.

Lawing, Nellie Trosper (1873–1956), William "Billie" Lawing (1879–1936)

A legendary innkeeper and survivalist, Nellie Trosper Bates Neal Lawing endorsed Alaska as a land of adventure and natural wonders. Born in Buchanan, Missouri, on July 25, 1873, to Jennie Gibson and Robert Nathan Trosper, Southern farmers of Anglo-German ancestry, she was the eldest of twelve children. In girlhood, she learned farm work and woods lore and envisaged an unconventional life for a woman as an Alaskan musher and bear and moose hunter.

Poverty defined Nellie's teens. In 1885, she left school to work in Topeka, Kansas, as a waitress on the Fred Harvey restaurant chain at a depot of the Atchison, Topeka and Santa Fe Railway. In 1901, three years after her mother's death and her father's remarriage, she departed from the family to work her way west to Colorado and Wyoming with a string of inn and depot diner jobs. In 1903, she managed a boarding house at Cripple Creek, a substantial Colorado mining community, and may have married a man named Bates. To protect herself from robbers, she carried a Colt .45 and shot a would-be thief.

On February 21, 1906, at age 33, Nellie married 29-year-old mine assayer Wesley Neal of Moberly, Missouri, and made their home in a gold camp at Cripple Creek. Because of Neal's alcoholism, she left him and migrated to Washington State, a center of shipbuilding and the smelting of copper, lead, gold, and silver. News of a rail line built in 1914 from Fairbanks to Seward turned her thoughts once more toward Alaska, a territory still in the frontier stages of development.

Territorial Alaska

On July 3, 1915, Nellie arrived at Seward aboard the steamer *Alameda* to take a government job teaching school. She worked as a domestic and cooked and transported freight by wagon for the Kenai Alaska Gold Mine, a landmark strike that produced 428 ounces of silver and 1,852 ounces of gold from quartz veins at its Crown Point location. In December 1915, Nellie trekked on snowshoes to take possession of an abandoned cabin and earned her living by hunting and trapping for meat to feed miners and pelts of ermine, fox, mink, rabbit, and lynx for sale to traders. On foot and with a dog team, she rescued stranded settlers from snow banks and foul weather.

By spring 1916, Nellie became the first female contract provisioner for the Alaska Central Railway, which extended an all-weather line from Seward 470 miles to Fairbanks. She opened Grandview roadhouse at Curry on mile 45 and offered room and board to laborers. To shelter her dog team, she felled and sawed logs for buildings. With the aid of two cooks and two waiters, over a period of three months, she served 467 meals a day at the rate of 50¢ per meal and $1 per night for lodging. During the removal of snow to free a train stuck in a snowstorm on November 10, 1916, during the first month of service to Anchorage, Nellie made coffee, ham and egg sandwiches, and doughnuts for the laborers.

Because of rescuing a mail carrier at night in a blizzard with her dog team on January 20, 1917, Nellie earned a reputation for hardihood by stabilizing the postman at her warm cabin and completing his route 280 miles north to Hunter. Local settlers awarded her a diamond and gold necklace. As government agents extended the rail line in 1918 to Nenana on the Tanana River in east central Alaska, she managed the Kern Creek Roadhouse southeast of Anchorage on the Turnagain Arm, where she shot a predatory 9.5-foot brown bear six times before killing it.

At the end of World War I, Nellie worked at mining before securing another roadhouse contract at Dead Horse Hill. In 1921, at age forty-eight, she competed against three top dog racers and came in fourth, receiving applause and a box of candy. Upon the accidental death of Nellie's husband, shop foreman Kenneth Holden later that year, she transported his coffin to Seward for shipment to his mother in Seattle.

On July 15, 1923, President Warren G. Harding, First Lady Florence Kling Harding, and Secretary of Commerce Herbert Hoover visited the widow and admired her stuffed eagles, moose and caribou heads, and bear, wolverine, and musk ox hides. The next month, she bought the town of Roosevelt north of Seward. She married Holden's cousin, 44-year-old William "Billie" Lawing of Murfreesboro, Tennessee, on September 3, 1923. The ceremony took place on the stage of Seward's Liberty Moving Picture Theater, the former Seattle Bar at the corner of Fourth and Washington.

Kenai Lake Lodge

Twenty-five miles north of Seward, in 1925, the Lawings operated the two-story Kenai Lake Lodge at Roosevelt, which they renamed "Lawing," and opened a museum, trading post, and post office on 4.3 acres of land. Billie ran a 35-foot lake cruiser, which he named the *Nellie Neal*. Nellie expanded their holdings to include a kitchen built over the lake, barn, windmill and 1,000-gallon water tank, four cabins, boathouse and garage, cafe and bar, whelping shed for housing pups, and greenhouse, where she started seedlings each winter. The government installed a telephone for Nellie's communications with railroad personnel.

Guests and expeditioners traveling the Seward Highway ate well at the roadhouse, where Nellie served fresh fish, game, domesticated rabbit, garden vegetables, and sourdough pancakes. For ice cream, she froze canned milk with glacier ice. Visitors circulated Nellie's yarns about the Alaska wilds, such as her taming of bear cubs and the attachment of a fishing line directly to a bell on the kitchen range to ensure a fresh catch of trout. At her Kenai Lake home in 1933, she began compiling an autobiography.

Nellie became a widow once again in March 1936 after Bill died of heart attack while sawing lake ice. She planned a cross-country bus tour to display her furs and Alaskana memorabilia. On the 15,000-mile trip, she failed to find a publisher for her book, but did introduce listeners to the beauties of the Kenai Peninsula. In Washington, D.C., she presented four Alaska potatoes to president Franklin D. Roosevelt. In November 1938, she proposed establishment of a pioneer women's home at Fairbanks.

In her sixties, the Alaska pioneer starred in an MGM film, *In the Land of Alaska Nellie* (1936) and summarized her life in the biography *Alaska Nellie* (1940), published in Seattle. For Roosevelt's third inauguration on January 20, 1941, she received tickets to the Washington, D.C., event and presented him an autographed copy of her life story. At the Seward USO during World War II, she entertained troops.

In 1949, Nellie deeded her property to the Alaska Territory in exchange for a pension and medical insurance. In her final months, she incurred expensive hospital treatment and the theft of her diamond necklace. Within four months after a celebration of her exploits on "Alaska Nellie Day," Nellie Lawing died in poverty on May 10, 1956. The Resurrection Bay Historical Society at Seward archived her writings, photos, and scrapbook of clippings. The Lawing homestead survives on the National Register of Historic Places.

Sources
Johnson, Kaylene. "Next Stop, Pristine Wilderness." *Los Angeles Times* (20 February 2005).
Jones, Cherry Lyon. *Remarkable Alaska Women*. Guilford, CT: Globe Pequot, 2006.

Leavitt, Hiram Lewis (1824–1901), Eliza S. Reed Leavitt (1829–1910s)

A late '49er, innkeeper, and judge, Hiram Lewis Leavitt transported his family to a spot in California that became the town of Bridgeport. Born on April 2, 1824, in Grantham, New Hampshire, he was the first son and second of the six children of Elizabeth "Betty" Brown and Josiah Leavitt, grandson of a Harvard-educated physician, horologist, and inventor, Josiah Leavitt. The family claimed Puritan English descendants from Hingham, Norfolk, and from Bolton Percy, Beverly, and Harewood, Yorkshire, whose lineage dated to the early fifteenth century. The Leavitts migrated in the 1630s to Plymouth in Massachusetts Colony and supported Congregationalism.

In Boston, on September 16, 1849, Hiram wed 20-year-old Eliza S. Reed of Boothbay, Maine, a first-generation Anglo-American whose father, Charles Reed, relocated from Liverpool to upper New England. Hiram and Eliza Leavitt produced daughter Ida, born in Boston in 1851. Like Hiram's venturesome ancestors, he followed the rush of prospectors to San Francisco on the Pacific Coast.

The Post–'49ers

In November 1856, Hiram returned to Massachusetts and packed his wife and five-year-old Ida on a vessel bound around Cape Horn for California. According to frontier newspapers, Hiram Leavitt became a Tuolumne County pioneer in 1860. In a dynamic era, he observed the shift in the ethnic population as ranches displaced the indigenous Miwok, white men returned east to fight in the Civil War, and Chinese males arrived from East Asia to build the Transcontinental Railroad and found the area's Chinatown.

When the prospecting bonanza ended, the Leavitts settled at Indian Valley (present-day Leavitt Meadow) in Mono County. In the primitive beginnings of frontier transportation, they ran Leavitt Station, a stage depot for Adam & Company's California and Atlantic Express, and operated a hotel serving passengers traveling to and from the Bodie Gold Mine. At Sonora, Eliza Leavitt bore two sons, Alfred Lewis Leavitt in 1859 and Charles Almond Leavitt in 1861.

When the Sonora Pass wagon road opened high in the Sierras in the early 1860s, the family traveled to Leavitt Meadow. At the eastern extreme of the pass during the 1863 land rush, they built a two-story inn on the road along West Walker River, a thoroughfare for miners headed for Aurora, Nevada. Hiram served as a trustee of the school district. During heavy snows, he traveled house to house on snowshoes to deliver the mail.

Litigation and Innkeeping

In 1867, Leavitt moved the family to Sonora, California, where Ida married Samuel Hopkins, the builder of the family inn and residence. From 1870, Leavitt served as Mono County judge at the Bridgeport courthouse, where he settled patent lawsuits and heard a tense case involving miners and the Bodie Miners' Union. In September 1874, he hired laborers to improve the courthouse, an attractive two-story landmark on Main Street.

Hiram and Eliza Leavitt also operated a steep-gabled three-story hostelry, Leavitt House, erected in 1877 on Main Street. Patrons enjoyed upscale dining and rooms appointed with antiques and drank at a bar tended by the host. On February 23, 1879, Leavitt advertised the family inn in the *Chicago Tribune*. In the 1890s, he became heavily involved with the Republican Party.

Hiram Leavitt died on April 24, 1901, in Klamath Falls, Oregon, where his son Alfred practiced law and served as circuit court judge. The family hotel changed hands and became the Bridgeport Inn. The Leavitt surname survives in the eastern Sierra Nevada at Leavitt Lake, Leavitt Peak, Leavitt Meadow, Leavitt Falls, and Leavitt Creek.

SOURCE
Lawyer's Record and Official Record of the United States. New York: A.S. Barnes & Company, 1872.

Lilly, Ben (1856–1936)

Hunter and trapper Benjamin Vernon Lilly dedicated his career to reducing populations of black bears, cougars, wolves, alligators, razorback hogs, and coyotes. An Alabaman born of Anglo-Scots lineage in Wilcox County on December 31, 1856, he was the first of the seven children of an educated mother, astronomy teacher Margaret Anna McKay, and wheelwright and blacksmith Albert Lilly who shod horses for the Confederacy during the Civil War. A grandson of gunsmith Benjamin Franklin Lilly, young Ben honed his marksmanship on birds, bats, and buzzards and practiced the calls of wild beasts.

Reared a devout Christian in Mississippi, Lilly learned blacksmithing, his father's trade. He attended a boy's academy, Jackson Military High School, until 1868, when he fled from classes and parental control. In a series of jobs, he worked in cattle and logging and operated a forge in Memphis, Tennessee, and at Mer Rouge in Morehouse Parish in northeastern Louisiana, for an uncle and benefactor, cotton planter Vernon L. Lilly. For personal use, Ben carved hunting horns to muster his dogs.

The Free Life of a Hunter

Lilly's outdoor training in walking like a bear readied him for the life of a stalker protecting pioneer farmers and ranchers from predators. In his early twenties, he inherited his uncle's cotton farm, an expanse of swamp, woods, and 300 acres of cotton on the Bayou Bonne Idee. He married Amazon Lelia Bunckley in autumn 1880. Even with the birth of their son, Vernon "Dick" Lilly, Ben found no satisfaction in domesticity. After a divorce, Lelia went insane.

Lilly continued fashioning iron into traps and buckhorn-handled hunting and skinning knives, notably, the Lilly knife or "Arkansas toothpick," a dagger featuring an S-shaped blade tempered in panther oil. At his first wife's death, in Morehouse Parish on February 10, 1891, he wed twenty-four-year-old Mary Etta Sisson, mother of Hugh Kenneth Lilly, Ada May Lilly, and Verna B. Lilly. On his way from Mer Rouge to the Atchafalaya Swamp, in 1901, Ben Lilly abandoned his family. His steady animal slaughter wore out his knives within months.

In 1904, Lilly and Georgia-born hunter Ben Hooks settled in Big Thicket, a dense forest in southeast Texas, and maintained packs of hunting hounds trained to scent bears and mountain lions. To avoid hurting the dogs, Lilly preferred a blade kill to a bullet. At age fifty, he deeded his land to his spouse and rambled at will, sleeping on the ground and abstaining from the trail on the Sabbath. To earn money for the axe, ammunition, corn meal, salt, blanket and tarp, and dog supplies he cached in caves, he sold wild honey, alligator hides, and bear meat. For a campsite meal, he preferred duck and cougar steak.

Becoming a Legend

Lilly's hardihood and facile storytelling entertained Theodore Roosevelt in 1907 during a tramp through Tensas Bayou in northeastern Louisiana, where the president's humane treatment of a bear resulted in the media nickname "Teddy Bear." The following year, Lilly moved to Gila Wilderness in west central New Mexico and kept burros near his cave home at the confluence of the Gila River and Sapillo Creek. On daily hunts, he worked as a government bounty agent ridding the region of predators that endangered cattle. As wild game vanished, in July 1908, he directed his treks across the Rio Grande into the Santa Rosa Mountains in Southern California.

Armed with Bowie knife and Winchester rifle and a pack of seven dogs, in 1916, Lilly hunted for pay from Show-Low to Blue and Quemado, Arizona. The U.S. Biological Survey paid him a commission to collect rare birds and animals. His record year ended with a kill of 118 bears. With the aid of naturalist Ned Hollister, superintendent of the National Zoological Park, Lilly supplied the Smithsonian Institution with specimens of the Nelson grizzly bear, the rare ivory-billed woodpecker, otter, wild turkey, and Mexican gray wolf, a small rare subspecies.

From a two-year expedition into the Sierra Madre, along Camino Real in Chihuahua, Mexico, and as far north as Canada, the hunter's health foundered in 1928 in El Paso, Texas, from pneumonia. Retired in 1931, "Ol' Lilly" kept a diary at the Grant County farm on Big Dry Creek at Pleasanton, New Mexico. He died on December 17, 1936, at his headquarters on the G.O.S. Ranch near Buckhorn northwest of Silver City, New Mexico. A bronze plaque in a granite boulder outside Pinos Altos honors the Southwest's last mountain man.

SOURCES
Fowler, Ed. *Ed Fowler's Knife Talk II: The High Performance Blade.* Iola, WI: Krause, 2003.
Salmon, Maynard Hubbard. *Gila Libre: New Mexico's Last Wild River.* Albuquerque: University of New Mexico Press, 2008.

Macy, Obed (1801–1857), Lucinda Polk Macy (1807–1872), Oscar Macy (1829–1910), John Calvin McCoy (1811–1889), Urania K. Macy Cheesman (1828–1916), David Williams Cheesman (1822–1884)

Blazers of an experimental route to Los Angeles, California, physician and chronicler Obed Macy and his son, publisher Oscar Macy, brought their talents to the small mission town. Of English Massachusetts Quaker lineage, Obed was born to Mary Barnard and William Macy on December 14, 1801, in New Garden in Guilford County, North Carolina.

In Bruceville, Indiana, on October 17, 1824, at age 23, Obed wed seventeen-year-old Lucinda Polk, a Midwesterner born of Danish-Russo-Norman-Scots-Irish lineage dating to the seventh century and including Campbells, Stewarts, Montgomerys, and Bruces.

Obed Macy set up a medical practice in Indiana. Of the couple's thirteen children, two daughters—Amanda and Margaret—died in early childhood. In 1835, Obed maintained a Macy genealogy and compiled a history of Nantucket honoring its first settler, Thomas Macy, a Baptist weaver and sawyer from Chilmark, England, who arrived in North American in 1635 at Amesbury, Massachusetts. To avoid Puritan encroachments on civil liberties, Thomas moved to a new colony at Nantucket.

On March 1, 1850, Obed and Lucinda and their nine children joined the Macy-Cheesman party, some 300 pioneers in a 90-wagon convoy bound from Washington, Indiana, for San Francisco. On the way through Westport (present-day Kansas City), Missouri, they bought provisions for themselves and their oxen at the store of Lucinda's Indiana-born cousin, John Calvin McCoy. Known as the father of Kansas City, McCoy, a Baptist missionary, channeled goods through Westport Landing, his pier on the Missouri River.

Crossing the Plains

During the nine-month trek, the Macy children lived challenging frontier adventures. Five-year-old Lucinda Macy learned the alphabet from the Bible. Because of a widespread outbreak of contagion from contaminated water, her thirteen-year-old brother, Charles Macy, died of cholera on June 14, 1850, at Fort Kearney, Nebraska. The Macy-Cheesman train lost three weeks during the virulent epidemic, which steamboats carried up the Mississippi. After trading for scarce quantities of soap and hay, two essentials for treating and feeding dray animals, the company reached Salt Lake City on August 16, in part because of abundant firewood, pasturage, and spare wheels and axles from abandoned wagons along the way.

To ease the hardships of 22-year-old daughter Urania K. Macy Cheesman during late pregnancy with her first child, Dr. Macy relied on the ministrations of his son-in-law, attorney David Williams Cheesman of Illinois, who claimed English lineage dating to tenth-century Lancashire. The extended family settled among Mormons on North Temple Street. They remained through mid–September and the birth of Randolph Cheesman.

For cash to complete the journey, David harvested and sold grass hay. Extra draft animals and cattle chained together pulled each wagon up slopes from the confluence of the Santa Clara and Virgin rivers. Unfortunately for the emigrants, Ute Chief Wakara sold them horses stolen from local Californios, who pressed suit in court for the return of their mounts.

David Cheesman compiled events from the crossing in a journal, *By Ox Team from Salt Lake to Los Angeles, 1850,* which recorded the Sierra crossing from October 8, 1850, until the end of December. As the emigrants covered the last 400 miles on foot against stiff Santa Ana winds, Bright, Cheesman's wheeler ox, dropped dead in his traces outside Bitter Springs. Subsisting on mustard greens, convoy members hurried through Cajon Pass and halted at Palomares Rancho (present-day Pomona) on New Year's Day, 1851.

The lush green of California overwhelmed the Macy-Cheesman convoy. From Hispanic residents, the wayfarers purchased new supplies of raisins, beef, and popcorn. A few pioneers paused to prospect for gold at Salt Spring, one of the watering holes in the San Joaquin Valley. Along the most arduous stretch, Dr. Macy and daughter Nancy brought up the rear guard and treated weak dray animals with handfuls of flour until they could replenish their livestock at the Mojave River.

Choosing a Home

The Macy family camped at San Gabriel with the rest of the Cheesman party and reached San Francisco on February 7, 1851. Over the next ten months, the Macys pioneered the town of El Monte, which drew fifty more families in 1852 at a nexus of roads to

San Pedro, San Bernardino, and Los Angeles. Obed Macy grew and harvested onions, which he transported by sea to San Francisco for a profit of thousands of dollars.

Twelve miles west, the Macys resettled in Los Angeles in 1852 to rear their family and lost two more daughters, Alice and Christiana, to sudden death. In 1853, Lucinda Macy entered Mrs. Adam Bland's girls' academy. Obed treated patients and ran the Alameda bathhouse, fed by a water wheel. For more profit, he and Lucinda operated the Bella Union Hotel, a one-story adobe stage stop on Maine and Commercial streets along the Banning–San Pedro route of the Banning shipping line. The hotel quartered the county courthouse as well as social events. In 1855, Macy served a partial term on the Los Angeles city council.

Oscar Macy, born sixth of thirteen children in Knox County, Indiana, on July 7, 1829, studied at home with his father. After failing at gold mining in Yuba County, California, he worked at printing the *Alta California* at Sacramento and at his father's hotel. After Obed Macy's death on July 19, 1857, Oscar superintended the printing of the semi-weekly *Southern Vineyard*. In his forties, while managing 5,000 sheep on Catalina Island, he published the bilingual *Los Angeles Star* at the Bella Union.

In 1871, Oscar Macy served as member of the board of supervisors, during which he promoted the construction of a county jail. Further public record detailed his mother's death in 1872, D.W. Cheesman's term as assistant treasurer of the U.S. Mint in 1877, and Oscar's advancement to city treasurer in 1886 and jailer in 1892. Oscar retired at age 74 and died in 1910, leaving memoirs of his crossing of the Great Plains at age twenty-one. The family surname attached to Macy Street and Macy Bridge, the first viaduct over the Los Angeles River.

Sources

Lee, Portia, and Jeffrey Samudio. *Los Angeles, California*. Chicago: Arcadia, 2001.

Lyman, Edward Leo. *Overland Journey from Utah to California: Wagon Travel from the City of Angels*. Reno: University of Nevada Press, 2004.

Maynard, Frank H. (1853–1926)

Cowboy, carpenter, memoirist, and songwriter Francis Henry "Frank" Maynard typified the Hollywood cinema notion of the Western cowpuncher during the great trail drives over the plains. The third of the seven children of Georgiana Taylor Metcalfe and Horace Maynard, a Civil War veteran from Ohio, Frank, a native of Iowa City, Iowa, was born of Anglo-Norman origin on December 16, 1853. In 1869, he labored on a freighter plying the Platte River.

During the Kansas transportation boom, sixteen-year-old Maynard headquartered with an aunt in Towanda in east central Kansas, while he drove cattle from Missouri to Colorado. When his family joined him in Towanda, before the Kansas Pacific Railway simplified hauling, Frank and Horace Maynard extended a freight line from Emporia, Kansas, to Wichita carrying Eastern manufactured goods and foodstuffs to pioneers.

The emergence of the buffalo hide business in the early 1870s offered hunters near instant wealth at the rate of $50 per pelt. At age 17, Maynard stalked herds in fall in Kingman County, Kansas, and traded pelts and hides with the Osage in February 1872 outside Medicine Lodge on the Kansas border with Indian Territory (Oklahoma). By spring 1873, buffalo skinners had slaughtered so many beasts that few herds browsed the hunting grounds. Within a year, the total kill reached 4.5 million.

From Hunter to Wrangler

In company with rowdy ex–Confederates, Frank launched a career as a drover, herding horses south to Jacksboro in northern Texas and cattle to Granada, Colorado. In February 1875, he signed on with stockman Peter Moore to herd beefs from Hutchinson, Texas, to Gypsum Hills, Kansas. Because plainsmen encountered hostile Comanche and rustlers, Kansans supported the hiring of sheriffs and marshals, including Illinois-born sharpshooter James Butler "Wild Bill" Hickok, an expert with the .36-caliber Colt Navy revolver during his work as marshal of Abilene, Kansas.

During Maynard's time as a range rider for

wealthy Kansas stockman William Bradford Grimes in winter 1875–1876, Indians set fire to grassland of the coastal plains, forcing Grimes's 15,000 steers out of Indian Territory. By April, Maynard moved south to herd for Eugene Bartlet Millett and Seth Mabry at Ellsworth, Texas, and to tend pastured cattle at Kanopolis in central Kansas through the summer. He ended the year driving beefs from Wichita to Sun City, and wintered a herd at Cimarron in western Kansas for John Wylie "Bud" Driskill.

While actively wrangling in 1876, Maynard captured in writing the terms and place names of Western renown—draw poker, Boot Hill, Cimarron, Dodge City, the Brazos. He adapted an Irish ballad, "The Unfortunate Lad," into "The Dying Cowboy," also known as "The Streets of Laredo." The dirge regrets the plainsman's life of drinking, gambling, broken hearts, and random violence. He gathered trail stories of grasshopper swarms, rat infestations, German homesteaders, stampedes, Mexican bandits, lynchings, stalking by a gunman named Slusher, and friendships with showman Buffalo Bill Cody, Arapaho and Comanche braves, gunman Bat Masterson, and lawmen Wyatt Earp, Ed Masterson, and Bill Tilghman. Maynard's observations of Amerindian adaptation to the ways of whites recorded the pairing of plainsmen with Indian brides.

The Settled Life

On a drive to Sioux country at the Red Cloud Agency in 1877, Maynard recuperated from illness at Ogallala, Nebraska. He began a three-year courtship with his future wife, eighteen-year-old Flora V. Longstreth, who rejected cowboys as potential husbands. By April 1878, he joined a roundup outside Dodge City, a Kansas cow town known for gambling, prostitution, and violence. At Fort Reno, Kansas, in July, Maynard harvested hay and survived the threat of Northern Cheyenne who escaped the reservation.

After Maynard's marriage to Flora in Colorado Springs on April 24, 1881, he took a job as carpenter and joined Trinity Methodist Church. At Cripple Creek, Colorado, he invested in a tellurium vein of the Buckeye Gold Mining and Milling Company at Boulder and undertook a building project at Grand Junction in western Colorado. By the mid–1880s, blizzards, tick fever epidemics, railroad stockyards, and fencing with barbed wire ended the profitability of long cattle drives over the open range.

In 1887, Maynard settled permanently at Colorado Springs. At age 58, he began writing and, with the advice of novelist Jack London, published *Rhymes of the Range and Trail* (1911). To maintain ties with the past, he worked as a rodeo night watchman and composed an article about the 1874 attack of Comanche warrior Quanah Parker on local citizens of Adobe Walls, Texas. In 1923, feature writer Elmo Scott Watson popularized Maynard's cowboy years in a dime novel. After a lengthy battle with heart disease, Maynard died on March 28, 1926, at Colorado Springs. His memoir survives as *Cowboy's Lament: A Life on the Open Range* (2010).

Sources
Hoy, Jim, ed. *Cowboy's Lament: A Life on the Open Range.* Emporia, KS: Emporia State University, 2010.

_____. *Flint Hills Cowboys: Tales from the Tallgrass Prairie.* Lawrence: University Press of Kansas, 2006.

McBeth, Kate Christine (1832–1915), Susan Law McBeth (1830–1893), Charles Edgar Monteith (1847–1915)

Sister missionaries, home economist Kate Christine and lexicographer Susan Law McBeth introduced plains Indians to literacy, Presbyterianism and domestic skills. Born at Doune in south central Scotland, in 1830, Sue McBeth was the older sister of Kate, who was born in Knoxville, Ohio, on August 7, 1832. The daughters of Mary Henderson of Sterling and stonemason Alexander McBeath of Perth, the sisters gained liberal attitudes toward Indians and abolitionism while they grew up with three siblings near an uncle in Wellsville in eastern Ohio. The McBeth cellar served as a depot of the Underground Railroad at a dangerous crossing the Ohio River opposite Virginia.

Until the birth of brother Robert, the loss of two sons in infancy defeated the Scots family, which longed for a male to carry the McBeth surname and Scots Presbyterian traditions. The death of Alexander McBeth in 1847 ended the family's daily Bible readings and singing of traditional Scots hymns. The loss forced Sue to work in millinery to underwrite her tuition to Steubenville Female Seminary, a Presbyterian college 17 miles from Wellsville that gained a reputation for promoting ethics and intellectualism.

Following successful teaching posts at the Wellsville Institute and the Fairfield Female Seminary in Iowa, in 1858, Sue, at age twenty-eight, traveled by rail to St. Louis and by steamer along the Mississippi and Arkansas rivers to Indian Territory (Oklahoma) in spring 1860 to begin mission work teaching Choctaw girls. She advanced to a similar post in 1860 at Goodwater Mission, Oklahoma, where the assimilation movement was beginning to strip tribes of culture and replace nativism with Christianity and Atlantic Coast morality. Sue quailed at the sight of lizards and scorpions and needed help removing a tick from her arm. Bordered by Texas secessionists, the school closed at the onset of the Civil War at the insistence of slave-owning Choctaws.

Throughout the Civil War, Sue worked in administration of Fairfield University in Iowa. In 1863, she became one of the first women to join the medical relief effort outside St. Louis, Missouri, for the U.S. Christian Commission at Jefferson Barracks at Lemay, a recruiting post and hospital treating more than 18,000 combat victims. In addition to nursing, she issued leaflets for soldiers later compiled in *Seeds Scattered Broadcast: Or, Incidents in a Camp Hospital* (1869). From 1866 to 1873 at a St. Louis church, she directed the Home for Young Women, a Presbyterian refuge for seamstresses, and taught at Lindenwood College for Women in Saint Charles, Missouri. The decline of Sue's mother and the sudden death from typhoid of her fiancé, Eben Law, a former prisoner of war at Alton, Illinois, triggered a stroke that paralyzed Sue and impaired her gait. Although crippled and lacking theological training and ordination, Sue, one of the first female appointees of the Presbyterian Board of Foreign Missions, traveled by Central Pacific rail to Ogden, Utah. She arrived among the Nez Percés in October 1873 to teach at the Fort Lapwai reservation.

The following year, Sue took the role of Presbyterian educator at the Kamiah Valley day school in Idaho and evolved a practical ministry for Indian clergy. Within the year, she filled eight pages with 15,000 words of Sahaptin vocabulary to send to the Smithsonian Institution and compiled a grammar of Nez Percé vernacular. In June 1877, Sue retreated to Portland, Oregon, during the Nez Percé War, which pitted the warriors of Chief Joseph against 2,000 U.S. cavalry. In October 1877, she returned to her one-woman theological seminary to educate twelve young braves, who called her Pika (mother). In 1880, her charges rewarded her with a three-room frame home.

A Joint Effort

Through service to the Ladies' Foreign Mission Society, Kate McBeth arranged to reunite with her beloved sister. She left Ohio for Chicago in mid–September 1879 and journeyed by way of San Francisco and Portland, Oregon, to Lapwai. She reached the fort in October before traveling the 80 miles to the men's and women's mission schools at Kamiah. In contention with Catholic missions, in 1880, the sisters began inculcating Indians with Western culture with the intent of suppressing native "heathenism" evidenced in drumming, dance, gambling, medicine bundles, conjuring, polygamy, drinking, and horse-racing. Ironically, a male-dominated consistory dominated by envious men fired Sue ostensibly because she had neglected the classroom for proselytizing Indians with Protestantism.

Kate McBeth focused on shaping the younger women for literacy, Christianity, sewing, knitting, bread making, and marriage. Students reported her enthusiasm for cooking, cleaning homes, and neighborliness among residents of cabins and tepees. In addition to Bible, her classes covered hygiene, gardening, table manners, and politics and prepared natives for Christian work teaching Sunday school and leading evangelism. To the women's delight, Kate learned to ride astride a pony.

Living outside the locked campus of the Fort Lapwai Industrial School, the McBeths escaped the 1881 smallpox outbreak, as did their brother Robert, an Indian trader at Yankton, South Dakota, from 1871 to 1883. Throughout the 1880s, the sisters achieved exemplary reports on effective teaching. Sue compiled a history of her early mission to the Choctaw and influenced the spread of Presbyterianism to the nearby Shoshone, Umatilla, and Bannock. Eventually, the sisters differed in the purpose of the women's academy and Sunday school.

In 1885, the McBeths' ethnocentric methods annoyed Indian agent Charles Edgar Monteith, a New Yorker who had served the Nez Percé reservation since 1882. He exiled Sue over her suppression of violence at a July Fourth picnic and her worsening of conflict among tribe members. Reports of antipathies resulted in the agent's firing the following year. Sue settled at Mount Idaho, where Indians continued visiting her. Kate relocated to a new cottage at Lapwai and functioned as the only Protestant missionary. A church squabble in 1890 at Kamiah involved the sisters in the formation of the Second Indian Presbyterian Church.

In the months of Sue's invalidism from kidney disease, nine students sought ordination into the Presbyterian ministry; nonetheless, the theological seminary closed. Sue died of Bright's disease on May 26, 1893, and was buried at the Kamiah Mission Church cemetery. Kate destroyed criticism of Sue in her diary and mailed Sue's Sahaptin/English dictionary and Nez Percé grammar to the Smithsonian Institution.

In 1899, a niece, Mary M. "Mazie" Crawford, daughter of Kate and Sue's sister Mary, assisted Kate in the outreach to families and in home visits to the ill and bereaved. From segments of Kate McBeth's journal and legends told by student Mark Arthur, Mary Crawford published *The Nez Percés Since Lewis and Clark* (1908). After Charles Monteith's death at Lewiston on March 18, 1915, and Kate's death on October 29, 1915, Mazie continued the mission to Lapwai until its closure in 1932. Mazie Crawford reprised the history of the McBeth sisters' mission in *The Nez Percés Since Spalding* (1936).

Sources

Johnson, Yvonne, ed. *Feminist Frontiers: Women Who Shaped the Midwest*. Kirksville, MO: Truman State University Press, 2010.

Szasz, Ferenc Morton. *The Protestant Clergy in the Great Plains and Mountain West, 1865–1915*. Lincoln: University of Nebraska Press, 2004.

Tonkovich, Nicole. *The Allotment Plot: Alice C. Fletcher, E. Jane Gay, and Nez Percé Survivance*. Lincoln: University of Nebraska Press, 2012.

McCarty, Jonathan Warren (1833–1900), Candace McCarty Belshaw (1826–1892), George Belshaw, Jr. (1815–1893)

Farmer, storekeeper, and mail carrier Jonathan Warren McCarty contributed agricultural expertise to the settlement of Stuck River Valley, Washington. He was the last of eight children born of Anglo-Irish-Welsh Baptist lineage in La Porte, Indiana, on May 20, 1833, to Deida Young (or Walker) of North Carolina and Judge Benjamin Franklin McCarty, La Porte's postmaster, first sheriff, and state representative. The siblings traced their lineage to thirteenth-century England and claimed as their paternal great-grandparents Darby and Hannah Richardson McCarty of Tyrone, Ireland, original settlers of Browntown, Virginia.

Jonathan shared his family's fervor for pioneering. At age six, he moved with his family by ox-drawn wagon to Lake County, Indiana. The McCartys held Baptist services at their home and operated a hotel and a flourmill on Cedar Creek. On July 1, 1839, the family opened a general store selling molasses for $1 a gallon, tea at 50¢ a pound, raisins for 25¢ per pound, sugar for 17¢ per pound, and five bricks for 1¢.

The Way West

On March 23, 1853, Jonathan McCarty traversed the 2,000-mile Oregon Trail in company with older sister Candace and her husband, English wagon train master George Belshaw of Nottinghamshire. The convoy consisted of ten wagons and twenty-five emigrants bound for Washington Territory. In the last three years of the Great Migration begun in 1843, the train set out from West Creek, Indiana, by ox teams of eight to ten animals and traveled at a steady rate of 10 miles per day.

Oxen became a standard choice for dray animals because Indians could not steal or stampede them. However, supplies for tending the oxen ranged from rope, 20-inch wood pickets, shoes, and nails to extra packsaddles, hames, and singletrees to support the yokes. Livestock profited from strict observance of the Sabbath, when families baked a week's worth of bread, repaired wagons, and washed and dried laundry. Belshaw recovered his loss on an exhausted cow by swapping it for $6 worth of supplies as a trading post.

The Belshaw-McCarty company camped on the Illinois River, where men pulled wagons across an aqueduct by hand. En route to the Mississippi River in heavy rain on April 4, 1853, the train suffered a tornado, mired wheels, exposure to smallpox, and three wagon collisions. A cattle stampede threatened the replacements for exhausted oxen, wasted animal stamina, and quartered the resale value of dray animals in the Pacific Northwest, where cows brought four times the price of oxen.

Ferriage over the Mississippi cost $3 per wagon. After crossing the Missouri River by steamer on May 8, the wayfarers observed an historic migration of one hundred wagons bound for the West. At a sizable profit, use of a ferry cost $5 per wagon and 40¢ per herd animal. At Papea Creek, Indians slew six oxen.

On May 25, six more wagons and twenty-seven passengers joined the convoy. Traversing the Platte River in central Nebraska in June, the westerers killed and ate a bear and an 800-pound buffalo. By July 1, they reached the Rocky Mountains and traded with Snake Indians along the Green River, where drivers swam their animals across to avoid paying ferriage as high as $7 for a wagon and $1 each for livestock. In August, fever beset the immigrants as they faced ascending the Cascade Range. On October 6, 1853, Jonathan's sixteen-day-old niece, Gertrude Columbia Belshaw, died at Oregon City, Oregon, of a gastric infection.

The McCarty Farm

At Pierce County in October 1853, Jonathan McCarty labored at logging and lumbering to secure cash to buy a claim. His sister and brother-in-law and their children—Frank E., William M., Ann L., Marshal W., Mary H., John E., and Stephen R. Belshaw—grew wheat in Eugene, Oregon. On land shared with Muckleshoot Indians between Stuck Creek (present-day White River) and the Puyallup River, Jonathan found soil suited to establishing daffodil and tulip beds, vegetable gardens, berry and hops fields, rhubarb stands, and cherry orchards. At Puyallup Valley on January 7, 1855, he wed eighteen-year-old Missouri native Ruth Jane Kincaid, who reared their children—Charles C., Clara Antoinette, Laura Candace, Mary Estelle, William W., and Frank Truman McCarty—in the Presbyterian faith.

In 1857, the government removed the Muckleshoot nation to Muckleshoot Prairie (present-day Auburn, Washington) and sold former Indian land to whites. On fertile Pacific Coast grassland on the Puget Sound between Seattle and Tacoma, McCarty raised timothy hay at the rate of five tons per acre. He also delivered mail to Seattle. Chinook served his family as a language for communicating with local tribes, who protested the government policy of forcing natives onto reservations.

In fall 1855, the Nisqually, led by Chief Leschi, threatened the McCartys and Ruth's parents, Nancy Jane Woolery and William Moore Kincaid, during the Puget Sound Indian War. Until March 1856, the extended family sheltered with the 4th and 9th Infantry and 3rd Artillery Regiment at Fort Steilacoom, a military sanctuary and road network through the Naches Pass built by the U.S. Army for the protection of homesteaders. Fortunately for their comfort, wood frame buildings and a chapel replaced earlier log structures. Because the fort's regulars lacked manpower for patrols, Jonathan McCarthy rode with the volunteer rangers for three months to break up rebellious war parties.

During the residency of women and children in the fort, Ruth McCarty tended toddler Charles C. McCarty and gave birth to her third child and first daughter, Clara Antoinette. Upon return to the farm in 1858, the family found their house, barn, livestock, and crops destroyed. Only the home of Mary Ann Richardson and Willis Boatman and their three sons, pioneers from Sangamon, Illinois, survived the Puyallup Valley onslaught.

Starting Over

Jonathan McCarty began rebuilding and flourished at growing hay and hops, the foundation of Portland's brewing center. To provide schooling for their children, in 1870, Jonathan and Ruth urbanized the clan in Seattle, where they kept shop. In 1878, Ruth gave birth to her last child, Frank Truman McCarty, who, in adulthood, settled in Sumner and established a creamery.

With a major in science, in June 1876, Clara McCarty became the first degreed graduate of the Territorial University (present-day University of Washington). She doubled the size of the one-woman faculty of Seattle's South School in September 1876. With a master's degree from the University of California at Berkeley, in 1879, she ran successfully for Pierce County school superintendent. During major surgery on September 9, 1880, Ruth McCarty died at age forty-four in Sumner, leaving Clara as substitute matriarch.

Jonathan McCarty married Sara Ann "Sally" Westbrook of Tacoma on February 22, 1883. In 1889, the year that Washington became a state, he leased his farm and moved to Tacoma, where he managed rental property. He died in Sumner on May 14, 1900. His remains, along with those of Ruth McCarty, lie buried in the Sumner pioneer cemetery. The family name survives in McCarty Hall at the University of Washington.

SOURCE

Anderson, Ruth, and Lori Price. *Puyallup: A Pioneer Paradise*. Charleston, SC: Arcadia, 2002.

Mead, James R. (1836–1910), Agnes Barcome Mead (1841–1869), Jesse Chisholm (1806–1868)

Trader and memoirist James Richard Mead co-founded Wichita in south central Kansas and contributed frontier chronicles to the Kansas State Historical Society and *Scientific American*. The scion of a Revolutionary War hero, General Ebenezer Mead, and the son of Mary Emmes James and Presbyterian pastor Enoch Mead, he was born of English lineage in New Haven, Vermont, on May 3, 1836. While James was a preschooler, the Reverend Mead relocated his family to the Iowa Territory mission field in Rockingham to escape cold New England winters.

At the Mead farm outside Davenport, Iowa, in 1839, James and his younger sister Lizzie gained perspective on riding horseback, canoeing, pioneering, meeting the Sioux and Fox, trapping birds, and hunting deer. He completed home schooling under his mother's tutelage. At Iowa College at Grinnell, for two years, he developed clear composition of travelogues and plains natural history. In his late teens, he kept accounts for the Rock Island Flour Mill and transported corn by flatboat on the Kaw River.

From May to July 1859, Mead journeyed with two companions to Burlingame in Kansas Territory to hunt antelope and buffalo commercially along the Saline River and to barter with the Cheyenne, Kaw, and Sioux. During the expedition, he met his future wife, Agnes Barcome, born of French Canadian lineage in 1841 in Quebec. The following year, he erected a permanent camp and, on August 1, 1860, registered his homestead on Spillman Creek. He assigned the names Paradise, Wolf, Beaver, and Twelve-Mile to surrounding tributaries.

After entry into the Union settled bloody conflicts in Kansas, on December 1, 1861, Mead wed Agnes at Towanda. For a year on the banks of the Saline, they made a home. Threat of Indian attack and epidemics of cholera, measles, and smallpox forced the couple to move their residence to Salina, Kansas, from summer 1862 to 1863. Neighbors elected Mead county surveyor. Agnes journeyed to her in-laws at Davenport and, on January 13, 1863, gave birth to James Lucas "Bunnie" Mead. Contributing to fears, outriders, rustlers, and William Clarke Quantrill's paramilitary raiders, armed with long-barreled cap-and-ball Colt revolvers, encouraged vigilantism into late summer 1863.

Establishing a Town

On the Whitewater River in spring 1864, James Mead built Wichita's first permanent edifice, a trading post at Towanda on the west side of the Arkansas Valley, which Agnes helped to run. Participation in a three-week buffalo hunt earned him $500 for 350 hides and 1.75 tons of tallow. Mead's barter in wolf, beaver, coyote, and otter skins flourished with Indians as far south as Indian Territory (present-day Oklahoma).

Throughout the era, Mead chose local negotiation of racial animosities. In summer 1864, the family store housed a post office, inn, and the local Wichita Indian agent, Major Milo Gookins, an appointee of President Abraham Lincoln the previous year. With a partner, guide, and interpreter Jesse Chisholm, a Cherokee-Scots trader from Hiwassee, Tennessee, in spring 1865, Mead herded 3,000 steers to the Fox and Sauk Reservation. Mead spoke for the Wichita at government conferences preceding the Treaty of the Little Arkansas with the Arapaho and Cheyenne on October 14, 1865. He served in the Kansas House that year and three years later in the state senate.

In January 1866, Mead and Chisholm opened a trading post on the North Canadian River at Council Grove, Oklahoma, to barter tobacco, sugar, coffee, and blankets to the Osage for pelts. Three months later, Chisholm stocked wagons with hides and items to sell south at Camp Wichita, which the army developed into Fort Sill. To provision the store with goods transported from Emporia and Fort Leavenworth, in summer 1867, Chisholm initiated the Chisholm Trail through Abilene, an 800-mile herding and Overland Mail stage route from Red River, Texas, northeast to Kansas City on the Kansas-Missouri border.

In a period marked by reduced income during a malaria epidemic, tick fever, and bouts of grasshopper infestation, Mead returned to Council Grove in April with furs, buffalo robes, and 250 cattle worth $16 each. To spark business, he bribed drovers to route their herds through his trading post. For the next 17 years, the surge in traffic turned Abilene into a notorious haven for spendthrift cowboys and gunmen, including noted outlaw John Wesley Hardin.

The rise of Cheyenne forays against Kansas settlers in April 1867 and against herders passing through Abilene, Dodge City, and Wichita required collaboration among sheriffs, vigilantes, and the 9th and 10th Cavalry, black troopers better known as Buffalo Soldiers. On July 20, 1867, Mead joined local white men in another treaty council with Apache, Comanche, Arapaho, Wichita, and Kiowa. As a result, on October 21, Arapaho Chief Ravel, Southern Cheyenne Chief Black Kettle, Comanche Chief Ten Bears, and Kiowa Chief Satanta approved the Treaty of Medicine Lodge, which placed tribes on Oklahoma reservations for training in agriculture and trades. Across 500,000 acres of designated state land, Buffalo Soldier patrols from Fort Clark west of Corpus Christi on the coast and at Fort Davis and Fort Stockton north of the Rio Grande secured work crews building corduroy roads and the Kansas Pacific Railway, another boost to Mead's commercial venture.

Dreams of Wealth

By 1868, Wichita incorporated, taking the name of Caddoan speakers who had occupied the region for 2,000 years. Rapid growth generated a realty bonanza, which Mead and others exploited through the Wichita Town and Land Company. The consortium envisioned funneling profits from the Texas cattle trade into the urban development of the prairie featuring a livestock depot, five-acre lots, parks, schools, and churches. After a government inquiry discovered improprieties in plans for sale of land to the Union Pacific Railroad, Mead and his collaborators reduced their grandiose project.

More frightening obstacles stanched Mead's ambitions. A Pawnee raid in March 1868 forced him to dispatch his pregnant wife and children to his parents' home in Davenport. The death of Agnes Mead from puerperal fever on April 19, 1869, and the demise of their infant son, J. William "Willie" Mead, on August 10 precipitated James's sale of the Towanda trading post. Single parenthood ended Mead's freedom of travel for business. For the sake of seven-year-old James Lucas, six-year-old Elizabeth Agnes "Lizzie," and four-year-old Mary Eleanor "Mamie" Mead, the plainsman settled in Wichita and engaged Elizabeth Inman Mathewson as a nanny. He bought twenty lots on January 28, 1870.

In October 1872, Mead moved his children into a two-story brick and stone home place at the corner of Broadway and Central Avenue, for which he paid $10,000. He equipped the bathroom with Wichita's first bathtub. To enhance and shade an urban neighborhood, he offered free cottonwood saplings for residents to plant along Emporia, Lawrence, and Topeka avenues.

Investments and Agriculture

Mead weathered shifts in the economy from scarce buffalo and the resettlement of Indians farther west and sought new directions for investment. In June 1871, he raised $200,000 in local bonds to connect Wichita to Newton by a 30-mile spur line. He served the Wichita & Southwestern Railroad as president and the Topeka & Southwestern Railway as director. After the arrival of the first train on May 16, 1872, he focused his business on investments with the Savings Bank of Wichita, cattle, and hides, which tanners sold to the British army for leather boots and belts. Ruined by the Panic of 1873, he returned to trade with Indians and raised fruit, grain, and livestock on his acreage.

In January 1873, Mead married his eighteen-year-old housekeeper, Lucy A. Inman of St. Louis. As the price of hides and pelts dropped, he concentrated his investments on cattle, Kansas real estate, and, in 1879, the Alpine, Tin Cup, El Capitan, and Champion mines, branches of JRM mining in Gunnison County, Colorado. He continued buying stock in Western mining with a purchase in 1888 in the boomtown of Rimini, Montana (now a ghost town) and, the following year, in the Travis Placer Mining Company in Helena.

At his second wife's death, in 1896, Mead married Fern F. Hoover of Perry, Oklahoma, and sired daughters Ignace Fern and Loreta. He bought shares in the First National Bank of Wichita and, with son Bunnie Mead, in a Chicago bicycle company that tapped the second wave of the bicycling fad. In his late sixties, Mead fostered the Kansas Academy of Science and Sons of the American Revolution and stated his interest in the wooly mammoth skeleton unearthed in 1904 at Medicine River, Montana. On July 12, 1909, at the opening of Wichita's Douglas Avenue Bridge, he delivered a dedication address that memorialized pioneers fording the river at the same spot.

At his death on March 31, 1910, James Mead retained a reputation for honesty, enthusiasm, and intelligence. His correspondence and ledgers archived details of frontier commerce, Indians, petroglyphs, and native fruits. His memoirs recounted friendships with showman William F. "Buffalo Bill" Cody, army scout Kit Carson, Southern Cheyenne Chief Black Kettle, and Kiowa Chief Satanta. The family surname survives in Mead Avenue, Mead Street, Mead's Corner, and Mead Island.

See also Chisholm, Jesse.

SOURCES

Mason, James E. *Wichita's Riverside Parks*. Charleston, SC: Arcadia, 2011.

Mead, James R. *Hunting and Trading on the Great Plains, 1859–1875*, ed. Ignace Mead Jones. Wichita: Rowfant Press, 2008.

Shortridge, James R. *Cities on the Plains: The Evolution of Urban Kansas*. Lawrence: University of Press of Kansas, 2004.

Meeker, Ezra M. (1830–1928), Eliza Jane Sumner Meeker (1834–1909), Oliver Perry Meeker (1828–1861)

A renowned westerer, farmer, and author, Ezra Manning Meeker promoted the settlement of Puyallup, Washington. An Ohioan of English lineage, he was born in Huntsville on December 29, 1830, to Phoebe Shaw Baker of Maryland and Jacob Redding Meeker, a farmer and miller from Elizabeth, New Jersey. With four brothers and a younger sister, after 1841, he came of age outside Indianapolis, Indiana, during the initial rush of pioneering over the Oregon Trail. Sparsely educated, he assisted the printer of the *Indianapolis Journal* and carried papers to subscribers. In his mid-teens, he supervised the family farm.

On May 15, 1851, Ezra Meeker married Eliza Jane Sumner of Spring Valley, Indiana, a suffragist and partner in a cross-country trek to Oregon Territory that changed their lives. They rented acreage at Eddyville, Iowa, in October 1851. Ezra labored with a surveying team until his older brother, Oliver Perry Meeker, enticed him to risk a 2,000-mile journey west to obtain free homesteads and a more salubrious climate. For provisions, Eliza dried yeast cakes and pumpkins and garnered flour, cornmeal, eggs, butter, and beef jerky.

Previous to the six-month expedition with their seven-week-old son, Marion Jasper Meeker, the adults—Ezra, Eliza, and Oliver—set their sights on a residence near the Pacific Ocean. They and their livestock departed Iowa by ox team on April 14, 1852, and followed the Platte River toward Kearney in Nebraska Territory, where Oliver Meeker suffered a bout of cholera from septic drinking water. As the train turned northwest at Fort Boise, Idaho, along the Snake River, the company struggled with parched land and rugged mountains.

After taking a steamer from the Cascades along the Willamette River, Eliza and Ezra Meekers arrived at Portland on October 1, 1852, and reunited with Oliver, who had driven the livestock overland. During a stopover, Ezra worked on the docks unloading the bark *Mary Melville*. In St. Helens, Ezra and Oliver operated a boarding house for sixty laborers, a project that lapsed after workers lost their jobs.

Making a Home

On January 20, 1853, Ezra began building a cabin at Kalama and made $800 at Astoria from retrieving logs floating past by flood. Despite the cyclical flooding, Eliza dried potato eyes for a crop of 400 bushels that raised $400. In April, the Meeker brothers pressed on to Puget Sound and homesteaded on the Puyallup River at McNeil Island, where Indian women taught them to steam clams. Oliver built a cabin across the bay from Steilacoom. A year later on February 26, 1854, Eliza gave birth to Ella Antoinette Meeker.

Oliver returned east to bring Jacob and Phoebe Meeker and two of their seven children—17-year-old Usual Clark Meeker and eighteen-year-old Hannah Jane Meeker and her husband, Jesse Dunlap—to Washington Territory in 1854. Ezra met the train at the Naches Pass in August with supplies. Because of the deaths of Phoebe from cholera at Laramie, Wyoming, on June 18, 1854, and Clark, who drowned in the Sweetwater River near Independence Rock, Wyoming, on July 6, Jacob Meeker abandoned homesteading. He settled at Steilacoom to tend the J.R. Meeker & Sons store rather than risk life in the wilderness.

Ezra Meeker continued to search for acreage in unsettled land. Because of a Yakima Indian uprising in spring 1855 following a gold strike on the Yakima Reservation, Meeker joined his father and brother Oliver in constructing a blockhouse, a family-sized stronghold. On November 5, 1855, Meeker secured 325 acres at Swamp Place southeast of Tacoma, where he planted an orchard and vegetable beds.

In the aftermath of the Puget Sound Indian War of summer 1856 involving the Cayuse,

On the way to Oregon Territory in 1851, Ezra Meeker (shown here) and his wife Eliza left Iowa and crossed the Continental Divide.

Walla Walla, and Yakima, Ezra served on a jury at Steilacoom on November 16–17, 1856, hearing the case against the Nisqually chief Leschi. Meeker joined Father William Kincaid in voting to acquit Leschi of murdering Colonel Benton Moses during combat. A second trial condemned Leschi to the gallows.

Losses and Responsibilities

Although the birth of Thomas A. Meeker on December 22, 1857, and Caroline "Caddie" Meeker on January 16, 1859, increased the family to six, difficulties beset Ezra's farm, which proved unproductive. On January 5, 1861, Oliver drowned when his steamer *Northerner* foundered on a rock off Cape Mendocino during a coastal voyage to San Francisco. Deep in debt, Ezra labored at clearing land and ran unsuccessfully in 1861 for the territorial legislature and in 1869 for county surveyor. A fifth child, Fred Sumner Meeker, was born on December 13, 1861, followed on October 24, 1869, by Olive Grace Meeker.

Upon moving to Puyallup Valley in 1862, despite roving mountain lions, the Meekers flourished at growing hops for beer, earning $185 on the year's harvest. Ezra expanded his farmland to 500 acres and erected a hop kiln to supply the German-American brewery of Henry Weinhard at Portland. With less than one percent of Washington Territory under cultivation, Meeker recruited farmers by disseminating a monograph, "Washington Territory West of the Cascades" (1870). After traveling by transcontinental railway to New York City to meet with financier Jay Cooke, Mead promoted the expansion of rail travel into Washington State.

In 1877, Ezra Meeker formally platted Puyallup and worked as postmaster. His donation of cash and land for a hotel, theater, civic buildings, schools, a woodworking factory, roads, and parks set the town on the way to prosperity. Within three years, he amassed the largest fortune in Washington Territory. By 1882, hops brought a dollar per pound. Within months of Washington's admission to the Union in 1890, Meeker moved his family into a substantial two-story mansion. He accepted the job of the town's first mayor, invested in an electric company with older brother John Valentine Meeker, a teacher, and son Fred Meeker, and co-founded the Washington State Historical Society.

The aphid blight of 1891 and the panic of 1893 reduced Ezra Meeker once more to penury. In the mid–1890s, he and sons Fred and Marion tried to profit in Cook Inlet from the Alaska gold rush. In 1897, the trio attempted a similar revitalization by working two tunnels and three shafts in Kootenay, British Columbia. Eliza and Ezra Meeker dried 15 tons of fruit, potatoes, cabbage, parsnips, squash, turnips, onions, eggs, and buttermilk in winter 1897 and transported them to Skagway, Alaska, on March 20, 1898, and down the Yukon River to Dawson City, where he operated a log grocery store.

By 1901, Ezra lost his investment of $19,000 through speculation. On January 30, 1901, his 40-year-old son Fred died of alcoholism and pneumonia in Dawson City. Ezra's daughter, Caroline Meeker Osborne, rescued the Puyallup home from foreclosure by purchasing it for her own family. While caring for her invalid mother, she honored her family's heritage by supporting the Washington State Pioneer's Association and the Westminster Presbyterian Church.

Preserving the Trail

To retain the history of westering, Ezra Meeker surveyed the Lewis and Clark trail to Portland and reviewed the post-war hanging of Chief Leschi in a reflection, *The Tragedy of Leschi* (1905). In his mid-seventies, Meeker memorialized the Oregon Trail by reversing his wagon trip and plotting monuments along an 8,000-mile route in Boise, Idaho, and the Continental Divide in Wyoming. On November 29, 1907, he met President Theodore Roosevelt, a champion of the West.

After his wife's death on October 15, 1909, in Seattle at age eighty, Meeker replicated the Oregon Trail journey of the ox-drawn wagon. By 1912, he had raised 150 roadside markers along the "Pioneer Way." Four years later, he traversed the country again by car and pressed President Woodrow Wilson to support the building of a national highway. In 1922, Meeker established the Oregon Trail Memorial Association. Two years later, he made a new journey by plane and returned to the White House to meet President Calvin Coolidge.

Ezra Meeker died of pneumonia on December 3, 1928. In memory of his heroic preservation of Western history, his statue still stands in Puyallup at Pioneer Park. Eliza Sumner Meeker retains fame for organizing the first Puyallup library and for supporting full citizenship for women.

Sources
Hunsaker, Joyce Badgley. *Seeing the Elephant: The Many Voices of the Oregon Trail*. Lubbock: Texas Tech University Press, 2003.
Larsen, Dennis M. *Slick as a Mitten: Ezra Meeker's Klondike Enterprise*. Pullman: Washington State University Press, 2009.

Merritt, Josiah (1803–1882)

As a pioneer orchardist, musician, and farmer, Josiah Merritt shifted from family man to virtual hermit on the rim of Washington's Cascade Range. Born of English background in Burlington, New Jersey, in 1803, he was the fifth of the eight children of Quakers Mary Garwood and Caleb Merritt, a soldier in the Mount Holly, New Jersey, militia, and founder of Merrittstown, Pennsylvania. The couple had immigrated to Athens, Ohio, by flatboat and pirogue in June 1800 with five-year-old daughter Hepzibath and sons Caleb and Abraham Merritt, ages three and one. In addition, Josiah had three stepsiblings born in Burlington to Caleb's first wife, Mary Bennett.

Although Caleb held the offices of justice of the piece and county commissioner, Josiah and siblings Thomas Jefferson, Sidna, Susan, and Jonathan Merritt remained unschooled and footloose. On February 16, 1832, in Athens, Ohio, a month after Caleb Merritt's death, Josiah married 21-year-old Sarah Luckey, also of Burlington, New Jersey. The couple settled on 80 acres at South Brown in Vinton County, Ohio. They produced seven children: William Cummings, Miles Osgood, Huldah, Lucy Ann, Susan M., Josiah Lawson, and Rufus Clinton Merritt.

The Itch to Go West

In 1860, the Merritts resided in Knox, Ohio. Around that time, Josiah left his family to seek his fortune in Washington Territory. He focused on territory north of Snoqualmie Pass, which contained mineral deposits and offered a likely route for a toll road and railroad. As more prospectors migrated farther west to Cariboo, British Columbia, Josiah staked a silver claim on the Snoqualmie Prairie at the foot of Uncle Si's Mountain. In 1862, he homesteaded on a 400-acre claim on the forks of the Snoqualmie River at North Bend, Washington.

A genial neighbor, "Uncle Si" played the fiddle for barn dances in Snoqualmie County. He made his living selling vegetables and $400 worth of bacon from his hogs. Over King County to Everett and Seattle on Puget Sound, he delivered goods by sled, canoe, and backpack.

On January 17, 1866, Merritt acquired title to two more sections totaling 105.75 acres. An accidental slice with a scythe to the tendons of his left foot forced him to hobble and plow from the back of a pony. A fight with Indians about theft from Merritt resulted in hand-to-hand grappling. One Indian boy intervened by striking Merritt over the head. Two mysterious fires led him to believe that the Indians were retaliating for the charge of thievery.

A Family Reunion

In 1870, while Sarah Merritt remained in Ohio with son Rufus, then nineteen years old, Josiah cohabited with an Indian. He returned home to sell the family property and bring his wife and son to Snoqualmie. The third white female in the valley, Sarah earned the nickname "Aunt Sally." Bits of history suggest that she went insane from the isolation of the Merritt cabin from society. In 1876, his daughter, Lucy Ann Merritt Camp, and her husband, Jeremiah Camp, came to Sarah's aid by transporting her to the east of the Snoqualmie Pass, where she died around 1877.

Si Merritt died of pneumonia in February 1882 and was buried among pioneers at Fall City Cemetery in Fall City, Washington. The following year, Lucy, Jeremiah, and Josiah's three grandsons began their own homestead in Walla Walla, Washington. On the way west in Winfield, Kansas, on March 27, 1883, Lucy gave birth to Josiah's grandson, Ira Miles Camp, who extended the family reputation for hardihood.

Josiah Merritt's name survives in Merritt Avenue and Big Si and Little Si mountains, favorites with climbers. In November 1908, E.J. Siegrist photographed "Uncle Si's Cabin, a shot of a log cabin with two windows, plank door, and shingled roof and surrounding picket fence at the foot of the Cascades.

Source
Beckey, Fred. *Columbia River to Stevens Pass.* Seattle: Mountaineers Books, 2000.

Miller, Mary Foote (1842–1921), Lafayette Miller (1840–1878)

Coal miner, city planner, and financier Mary Elizabeth "Molly" Foote Miller, the "Mother of Lafayette," pioneered the development of north central Colorado's economy. A native of Geneseo, New York, she was born on August 3, 1842, to Episcopalian parents, Sarah "Sallie" Cole of New York and hotelier John B. Foote of Massachusetts, a successful miner in the California Gold Rush. Mary came of age in a pioneer family that settled first in Hastings, Michigan, then in Independence, Iowa, where she advocated Christian temperance from girlhood.

Mary's husband, Lafayette Miller, was a native of Toulon, Illinois. The son of Mary Ann Able and physician John Miller of New Jersey and relative of New England colonists from Kent and Hertfordshire, England, he was born on March 18, 1840, the third of eleven children. He grew up in Buchanan County, Iowa, where he met Mary, and graduated from Western College in Toledo, Iowa. On December 24, 1862, Mary and Lafayette married in Quasqueton, Iowa, and proposed taking advantage of the Homestead Act promising 160 acres of unoccupied public land.

In an ox-driven wagon, the Millers joined their three wagons and twelve yoke of oxen to a fifty-wagon caravan on June 1, 1863. Under sporadic attack by Arapaho and Cheyenne, the company traversed the 575-mile Smoky Hill River route west from Missouri through Kansas to Colorado. The couple carried with them the region's first threshing machine. Within two months, the Colorado War erupted along the Arkansas River between silver miners and the allied force of Arapaho and Cheyenne. In September, the Millers settled in a log cabin thatched with hay at Burlington (present-day Longmont) in north central Colorado on the St. Vrain Creek, a tributary of the South Platte River.

On the Denver-to-Cheyenne, Wyoming, segment of the Overland Trail, the Millers operated Rock Creek Station, a Wells Fargo Mail coach stop and roadhouse northwest of Denver, and sold butter and eggs in Black Hawk, Colorado. At the end of the Colorado War in 1865, Mary's older brother, twenty-year-old stockman James B. Foote, joined their business. With the set-up of Colorado Territory's first circus in 1869, the inn received 100 arrivals.

Homesteading

Under the 1871 Homestead Act, a revision of President Abraham Lincoln's land giveaway of 1862, Lafayette and Mary Miller paid $1.25 per acre for a 1,280-acre farm on Rock Creek. Their tract produced orchard fruit, berries, small grains, corn for their pigs, and hay for their cattle and horses. James Foote's property adjoined the Miller farm. To satisfy the stipulations of homesteading, the family constructed a double residence for the two households over the joint boundary.

After roadhouse business lessened with the completion of the Colorado & Southern Railroad, in February 1876, the Millers resettled in Boulder. Lafayette Miller and James Foote opened a butcher shop and became town trustees. Lafayette joined the Masons and Odd Fellows, served as a volunteer fireman, and ran for mayor. Mary held a seat on the school board.

Lafayette's demise from kidney disease on May 28, 1878, left Mary responsible for their ranch and children—two teenagers, Thomas

Jefferson and Charles L. Miller, George Ira, James Pierson, Frank Samuel, and Amelia Alfaretta, then age six months. Out of necessity, Mary sold the meat market and relocated her family south of Denver to Willow Glen.

Wealth from Coal

Mary Miller discovered a 14-foot coal vein and inaugurated Colorado coal mining in 1884 with the digging of the Simpson Mine, leased by British engineer John Simpson of Cumberland. On February 26, 1887, Mary lost eleven-year-old Frank, her fifth son, to disease. On 150 acres of donated land east of Boulder, in 1888, she laid out a town, naming it for her husband and decreeing it a temperance stronghold. In addition to selling commercial lots, promoting the planting of elms, and organizing Lafayette's Methodist church, she built a house in the city limits on East Cleveland Street and taught classes in her parlor until the construction of the first school.

Another loss, the death of twelve-year-old Amelia, left Mary Miller with four sons. George became a farmer and owner of the Lafayette Supply Company. With the aid of Thomas, Charles, and James, an attorney educated at the University of Colorado, in 1892, she co-founded and ran the town's first bank, becoming the world's first female banker. The Miller Bank, located on East Simpson Street, became the Lafayette Bank, with James as vice president and cashier, and acquired a western branch in Louisville, Colorado. On December 18, 1895, Mary lost her trusted brother, James Foote, who died in his sleep of a stroke.

In dedication to sobriety, in 1900, Mary ran for state treasurer and senator on the Prohibition slate. In 1902, her oldest son, thirty-seven-year-old Thomas Jefferson Miller, the town's former mayor, died in an accident at Strathmore Coal Mine, leaving Mary with three sons as collaborators on her projects. In 1914, shaky loans of $90,000 to the United Mine Workers bankrupted the Millers and their bank. Much loved for her business acumen and community activism, Mary Foote Miller died in Lafayette on November 14, 1921. The Simpson Mine is now a Lafayette city park.

SOURCE
Stull, James B. *Erie*. Charleston, SC: Arcadia, 2011.

Mitchell, James C. (1810–1860), Eliza Krosnick-Vandenberg Mitchell (1809–1881)

Ferryman, merchant, and realty speculator James Comly Mitchell developed an abandoned Mormon settlement called Winter Quarters into Florence, Nebraska. Born the eighth of the ten children of Hannah Comly and Walter Mitchell in Pangborn, Pennsylvania, in 1810, he claimed English heritage from Yorkshire and Somersetshire. Shortly after the death of his four-year-old brother Richard, in 1825, James went to sea. Within three years he captained the *Lyden* and the *Lady Washington* over the New York-to-Liverpool route.

In St. Martin in the Fields, Liverpool, on April 8, 1836, Mitchell married twenty-seven-year-old Eliza Krosnick-Vandenberg of Cape Hope, South Africa, the widow of Royal Navy chaplain John Vandenberg. The couple remained in England until 1838. Mitchell moved his wife and 16-year-old stepdaughter, Hannah Vandenberg, to Bellevue, Iowa, along the Mississippi River in 1840 to serve as Indian commissioner. The couple adopted a daughter, J. Ann Floyd. Hannah married Nathaniel Kilborn, a flour miller from Missouri.

Pioneering in Iowa

In 1850, Mitchell returned from a brief foray to the California Gold Rush with the intent of benefiting from Iowa settlers by selling them stores and equipment. Contributing to his plans, talk of routing a transcontinental railroad along the Platte River held promise of prosperity and growth. He shared his Bellevue home with the Kilborns.

The Mitchells managed a dry goods store in Council Bluffs, Iowa, where James purchased seventeen tracts in partnership with John C. Sublette. The Mitchells' daughter Ann died after falling from a horse. After securing two hundred seventy-seven tracts across the Missouri River near present-day Omaha, Nebraska, around 1852, Mitchell developed the planned community of Cutler's Park. The property had served as the former headquarters of 2,500 Mormons, who had vacated on September 11, 1846, after a lethal epidemic of scurvy. The location contained a stable riverbed named Rock Bottom, a possible location for a railroad bridge.

Mitchell operated Missouri River ferry crossings, beginning with Elk Horn and Loup Fork Ferry at Iron Bluffs on March 14, 1853. His holdings increased on May 10 with the launching of the Winter Quarter Ferry. In spring 1854, Mitchell platted the town of Florence, which his wife named for Hannah and Nathaniel's daughter, Florence Vandenberg Kilborn. Mitchell reserved a spot for a capitol once Nebraska became a state. His vision of a state nexus drew strength from the presence of missionaries, adventurers, fur traders, and the solders at forts Kearny, Mitchell, and McPherson, which suppressed uprisings of Sioux, Missouri, Omaha, Otoe, Fox, Iowa, Kansa, Ponca, Sac, and Pawnee.

Prosperity at Florence

In addition to owning a saloon, Mitchell completed Nebraska's first brick house suited to the town's foremost citizen and promoter. For his family's convenience, he installed an iron front gate, purchased a bathtub and fashionable furnishings, and hired a housekeeper. On December 20, 1854, he acquired the Council Bluffs and Nebraska Ferry, and, in 1856, the steamer ferry *Nebraska No. 2*, which carried passengers to St. Louis and Council Bluffs from the Florence crossing.

Mitchell co-formed the Florence Land Company on May 12, 1855, which promoted territorial growth as far away as Columbus, Indiana. He gained a place on the First Territorial Council and edited the Florence *Courier*. Within two years, the town acquired a post office, Florence House Hotel, and four stores as well as a pharmacist, physician, and lawyer to serve 100 residents. On January 27, 1857, he conferred with other directors of the Missouri Bridge Company on location of an abutment at the river, the basis for a future bridge across the Missouri River.

The Bank of Florence, the state's first financial institution, flourished for a year before collapsing in the Panic of 1857. A decade before March 1, 1867, when Nebraska entered the Union as the thirty-seventh state, Florence lost out to Omaha, which became the state capital and commercial hub of eastern Nebraska Territory. Mitchell lobbied in Washington, D.C., for a railroad crossing at Florence. His hopes deflated, he died at age forty-nine in summer 1860, a century before his idea for a bridge became reality. His wife remained with her son-in-law's family until her death in 1881.

Source
Wishart, David J., ed. *Encyclopedia of the Great Plains*. Lincoln: University of Nebraska Press, 2004.

Moczygemba, Leopold (1824–1891)

A Texas colonist and missionary to Karnes County, Texas, Leopold Bonaventure Maria Moczygemba aided Polish pioneers on the U.S. frontier, earning for himself the title of "Patriarch of American Polonia." Prussian by birth in Upper Silesia on October 18, 1824, in Pluznica Wielka, he was one of the ten children of Ewa Kravietz and Leopold Moczygemba, a miller and innkeeper. After attending school in Gliwice and Opole, he studied in Osimo, Italy, at the Conventual Franciscan Seminary, where he first wore a friar's habit.

Following ordination into the priesthood at Pesaro, Italy, on July 25, 1847, Moczygemba continued his education at the Franciscan friars' convent in Wurzburg, Bavaria. Although relatives and neighbors petitioned for Father Leo's assignment near home, at age 28, he decided to accept a Texas ministry at Bandera among German-speaking Catholics and embarked on a nine-week sea voyage to southern Texas.

A Colony in Texas

In 1854, Moczygemba welcomed an influx of 800 Polish relatives and neighbors, who had traveled through Berlin on September 26 to Bremen to board the bark *Weser* and the brig *Antoinette*. On the Atlantic crossing, Father Leo's sister-in-law died at sea. In mild winter weather, the company reached Galveston on December 3, 1854, and relied on German speakers to acclimate them to Texas. The Poles pressed northwest on foot 150 miles through mesquite, sagebrush, and cactus to the confluence of Cibolo Creek with the San Antonio River. On December 24, 1854, they celebrated mass under a live oak and begin recruiting Poles to join them in Texas.

Father Leo and his four assistant priests filled the social and religious needs of Eastern European colonists arriving from Opole, Strzelce, Toszek-Gliwice, Lubliniec, and Olesno, Prussia, to Castroville, Fredericksburg, and New Braunfels, Texas. From John Twohig, a San Antonio financier, Moczygemba purchased 213 acres for a colony and 25 acres for a religious campus, dedicated on September 29, 1856. Twohig cheated the priest by charging $6 per acre, four times the standard price.

In open land where population density averaged two residents per square mile, the recruits established a pioneer village south of Austin at Panna Maria, the nation's oldest Polish settlement. The village and Bandera, Texas, became the first Polish-American parish. In 1855, the pastor erected the Immaculate Conception Church dedicated to the Virgin Mary. Parents opened St. Joseph's School, a Polish elementary academy, in a barn. In October 1855, a group of 700 immigrants began the second wave from Bremen to Texas.

At first, colonists rejoiced in leaving poverty, military conscription, and high taxation in Prussia for a land offering open grazing, free hunting, ample garden space, religious freedom, and snowless winters. The newcomers built lean-tos and huts and thatched them at a steep angle until 1858, when they had the leisure to gather stones and mix adobe for permanent residences. Floods, drought, malaria, thieves, and a plague of grasshoppers created more hardships than the missionaries could manage. The absence of trading posts and peddlers raised the demand for sewing supplies, tools, and wagons. In October 1856, disgruntled settlers threatened Father Leo's life.

Leaving Texas

While Father Leo superintended the Franciscan mission to some 1,000 Poles, in summer 1858, he petitioned the Vatican in person for more field workers. To relieve the colonial contretemps at Panna Maria, Pope Pius IX appointed Moczygemba an envoy to the United States. In November 1858, Father Leo relocated to Syracuse and Utica, New York, to serve Polish parishes. In the meantime, the Panna Marians developed patriotic leanings and contributed soldiers to the Confederacy during the Civil War.

In autumn 1869, Moczygemba spent a year at St. Peter's Basilica in Rome. He left the Franciscan Order in September 1870 to support his widowed mother and four brothers in Texas. The change of vocation linked him with Poles struggling on the frontier to build parishes and schools. In 1874, he returned to Panna Maria to survey progress in language and cultural adaptation. Within months, lightning destroyed the original sanctuary.

After three years presiding over the Polish Roman Catholic Union Convention in Milwaukee, Wisconsin, in 1879, Moczygemba gained permission from Pope Leo XIII to build a university to educate Polish-Americans. That same year, he left the Franciscans to joint the Resurrectionist Congregation, a Polish religious institution. At age 60, he completed the Polish Seminary in Detroit, Michigan, which began training Polish and Slavic priests in 1886.

In October 1887, Moczygemba returned to the Franciscan order until failing health ended his service on May 15, 1888. In addition to serving parishes in Parisville and Hilliards, Michigan, he aided convents in Detroit and Dearborn. After his death in Dearborn on February 23, 1891, he remained buried in Detroit until 1974, when the pioneer village of Panna Maria, Texas, reclaimed his remains.

Sources
Anderson, Dale. *Polish Americans*. Milwaukee, WI: Gareth Stevens, 2007.
Radzilowski, John. *The Eagle & the Cross: A History of the Polish Roman Catholic Union of America, 1873–2000*. New York: Columbia University Press, 2003.

Monk, Hank (1826–1883)

A romantic figure in transportation history, Henry James "Hank" Monk earned the nickname "Knight of the Lash" for his reckless stage driving and salty dictates to horse teams. A New Yorker born of Anglo-German lineage in Waddington on March 24, 1826, he descended from Vermont settlers along the St. Lawrence River. The grandson of Chief Justice James Monk of Montreal, Hank was second of three sons and three daughters of Polly Poor and innkeeper George Wagner Monk, agents of the Underground Railroad in a three-generation collaboration involving Hank and his grandfather.

Monk began his career at age twelve as driver between Waddington and Massena southwest of Montreal. For the Clark House Hotel, he covered routes connecting stations at Fort Covington and Ogdensburg, New York. The 1849 California Gold Rush drew him west, but his mother persuaded him to stay in New York. At age twenty-five, he appears to have moved across the river to work as a stable groom in Williamsburg, Ontario.

Career in the Sierras

In 1852, Monk got his wish, arriving in north central California before the gold era of the stagecoach. He took a post with James E. Birch for the California Stage Company, the region's largest transporter and the first to cross the Sierra Nevada. Until Birch's death in August 1857, Monk hustled stages from Auburn to southwest Placerville and Sacramento, the hub of overland freight, milling machinery, payroll, and passenger transport. At an unknown time, he married an Irish bride, Anna Smith.

Working for Jared Burdick Crandall in summer 1857, Monk drove a tri-weekly Carson Valley Express route for the Pioneer Stage Company from Placerville to Genoa, Nevada, completing the round trip in 24 hours. Distinguished gentlemen opted to ride with the driver on top of the sturdy Concord coach pulled by six horses. Two years later, he manned transport between San Francisco and "Hangtown," an early name for Placerville. In June 1859, during the suppression of native Washoe, Monk's coach carried a nervous passenger, Horace Greeley, editor of the *New York Tribune*.

During winter in the early 1860s on the way from Lake Tahoe to Carson City, Nevada, Monk halted his wheelless stage on runners every twelve miles to change horses. He spent down time at the Warm Springs Hotel, built in 1860 to handle travelers to the Comstock Lode, the nation's first major silver strike. A mishap that severed the wagon tongue took a simple rope lashing for Monk to continue his route. Making light of the incident, he declared the makeshift connection useful for turning corners.

Following new silver strikes, in 1864, Monk drove daily runs for the James M. Benton Stage Line, where employees dubbed Monk "the Whip." Around 1865 the year that Nevada became the thirty-sixth state of the Union, Monk played tricks on the elite, once depositing one polished boot of a Comstock investor outside a hotel chamber and leaving the other one muddy. By the 1870s, his coaches departed the livery at Third and Carson streets to carry tourists from the Virginia and Truckee Railroad depot to the steamer *Niagara*, an excursion boat on Lake Tahoe.

Late Career

Hank was a widower after Anna's death on February 4, 1874. During a surge in robberies into the late 1870s, he rode the Sierra Nevada trails and delivered the Wells Fargo weekly express mail. He took the 17-mile run from Carson City to Silver City and served Gold Hill, Virginia City, and Glenbrook, the terminus of the Butterfield Overland Stage.

Completing the drive in "Hank Monk time," Monk stopped for a breather at the Ormsby House, a popular three-story hotel and casino. Other assignments sent him to Reno, Bodie, and Steamboat Springs. He drove former president Ulysses S. Grant in 1879 on a circuitous jaunt from Clear Creek Canyon through Spooner Summit to Carson City.

In 1880, Monk resided with the James M. Benton family in Carson City. In South Dakota, Monk hired on with the Spearfish-Deadwood line in 1881, when the company ran a three-hour route daily. His physique lost muscle to alcohol, causing him to overturn a coach for the first time. In 1882, he rejected an offer of $250 a month to drive the stage for a traveling Wild West show. On February 28, 1883, he died of pneumonia at Carson City.

Monk's name survives in Hank Monk Avenue in South Lake Tahoe, Nevada; in stories by humorists Mark Twain and Artemus Ward; and in "The Hank Monk Schottische" (1878), a lively dance tune composed by John P. Meder. In 1886, Western author Joaquin Miller collaborated with composer John Philip Sousa on the play *Tally-Ho,* which they named for Monk's favorite stagecoach.

SOURCES

Ballew, Susan J., and L. Trent Dolan. *Early Carson City.* Charleston, SC: Arcadia, 2010.
Southerland, Cindy. *Cemeteries of Carson City and Carson Valley.* Charleston, SC: Arcadia, 2010.

Morrison, John L. (1819–1899)

A Scots Presbyterian carpenter and builder, John L. Morrison co-founded the territory of Oregon on land claimed by both Great Britain and the U.S. An emigrant from Edinburgh to Connecticut in 1830, he apprenticed in woodworking in his pre-teens, learning wainscoting, molding, and beading for ceilings and mantels. Led by Indian agent and Methodist missionary Elijah White, Morrison left Independence, Missouri, on May 15, 1842, with three horses and two cows and crossed the prairie in company with Asa Lovejoy, Ronald C. Crawford, Medorem Crawford, and Hugh Burns, the territory's first mailman.

The convoy's sixteen wagons held 109 settlers who made the first journey by whites over an unknown route and the first to bring small children. At Fort Laramie, Wyoming, the company engaged guide Osborne Russell for $500 to lead the way to Fort Hall, Idaho. At Devil's Gate, Wyoming, immigrants had to bribe 200 Sioux to release two emigrant captives. Along Green River, Wyoming, the travelers dismantled their transport to simplify passage through the Snake River Canyon and Blue Mountains. The journey ended at Fort Vancouver, Washington, on September 20, 1842.

A Booming Community

After supplies arrived from Boston on the coastal trader *Chenamus* to Willamette Falls, Morrison and his partner, Jehu Scudder, a representative of the territorial government, made a living at a flour and lumber business in Oregon City on Morrison Street. In 1843, Morrison labored for the Methodist Episcopal Church at Mission Bottom, a training center for Indians 10 miles north of Salem. In an era when more than 1,000 newcomers reached Oregon Territory, he and his associate, freighter Ronald C. Crawford of Seattle, worked in the building trade and constructed the first frame house in Portland, a home for merchant Francis William Pettygrove, a pioneer from Maine.

Morrison joined a consortium of fifty-one men on May 2, 1843, at Champoeg settlement to finalize a provisional territorial government. Following an attack by Clackamas raider Cockstock at a private home on French Prairie, on March 9, 1844, Morrison co-formed the territory's first militia, the Oregon Rangers. As first lieutenant, nine days later, he began drilling volunteers at the three-story Oregon Institute, the first American school west of Missouri.

By April 29, Morrison had assisted in the recruitment of twenty-six horsemen. In an official letter, he questioned the sincerity and financial backing of the militia, which proved its efficacy to the Willamette Valley by capturing alleged Indian horse thieves in July 1846 and negotiating a truce. The Hudson's Bay Company disapproved of a regiment of mounted riflemen; nonetheless, fellow colonists supported a standing militia against the possibility of more Indian raids.

In 1846, the builder persevered at his profession, completing a house for Captain Nathaniel Crosby, founder of the town of Milton, with materials that Crosby shipped around Cape Horn in the bark *Toulon.* In 1849, Morrison constructed Barclay House overlooking the Willamette River for county coroner and surgeon Forbes Barclay. Because of a shortage of construction workers during the California Gold Rush, the house cost $17,000 to build. On August 22, 1850, Morrison ordered the nails to construct the first capitol of Oregon Territory, a three-story edifice at Main and Sixth streets. Legislators met there until the selection of Salem as capital.

Morrison's Travels

The Oregon projects finished, Morrison traveled to California with the '49ers and settled at Tuolumne County. He wrote to Medorem Crawford from San Andreas on March 23, 1859, asking for advice on property purchases from Joel Palmer at Dayton, Oregon. Morrison returned north with tales of mining experiences at Placerville, California, and Deer Creek, Nevada.

Later in 1859, Morrison resettled on the north end of Puget Sound in the San Juan Islands, a cluster depleted of fur-bearing animals by trappers for the Hudson's Bay Company. He sailed to Washington Territory in 1865 and assumed ownership of timberland and a shingle mill in Skagit County. In autumn 1873, he sold his woodlot. He profited on the sale, but lost money to unreliable attorneys on the transfer of his Portland property.

On Orcas Island, the largest of the San Juan cluster, Morrison moved to the home he built for J.W. Gray. For the Grays' furnishings, Morrison hand-planed kitchen cabinets and a maple dining table. In 1879, Morrison homesteaded on Shaw Island at a log cabin in rowing distance from the Gray homestead.

During the decade preceding Washington's admission to the Union in 1889, the carpenter engaged his talents in handcrafting a colonial home with a unique entrance. At age ninety, John L. Morrison died in the model residence of respiratory disease on December 22, 1899, willing his property to a sister in Pennsylvania. His name attached to Morrison Street and the Morrison Street bascule bridge, a drawbridge over the Willamette River in Portland listed on the National Register of Historic Places.

SOURCE

Fuller, Tom. *Oregon's Capitol Buildings*. Charleston, SC: Arcadia, 2013.

O'Farrell, John A. (1823–1900), Mary Ann O'Farrell (1840–1900)

Irish immigrants Mary Ann Chapman and John Andrew O'Farrell promoted Catholicism in frontier Idaho. Born in Country Tyrone, Ulster, Ireland, on February 12, 1823, John enrolled in Naval School at Cork at age thirteen. In 1838, he crewed on a voyage to Calcutta, India. At age twenty, he left New York City and rounded Cape Horn. At the time of the 1849 California Gold Rush, he settled at Monterey to mine under the influence of John Sutter, who launched a surge in prospecting after discovery of gold nuggets at his mill in Coloma, California, on January 24, 1848.

In 1853 during the Crimean War, O'Farrell fought for England and earned the Medal of Valor after being wounded by the French at the Siege of Sebastopol in September 1854. On return to the United States, in July 1858, he prospected for gold at Pike's Peak, Colorado, and accompanied men who found placer gold in a Kansas creek. In 1859, he married an Irish widow, Mary Ann Chapman Lambert. A native of County Cork, she was born in 1840 and migrated with her family to New Orleans, Louisiana, at the beginning of the Great Potato Famine. After fourth grade, she studied at the Ursuline Academy, a French convent school.

After the death of Mary Ann's father, her mother relocated to Louisville, Kentucky, where Mary Ann met her first husband. Following the birth of a daughter, Mary Ann Lambert, in 1856, the parents divorced. Mary Ann Chapman Lambert worked at her family's grocery store in Louisville, where she wed John O'Farrell on October 16, 1859.

The O'Farrell Household

With John's adoption of his stepdaughter, the O'Farrells formed a family. After the nationalization of Idaho Territory on March 4, 1863, the trio traveled four months in a convoy of fourteen wagons. They homesteaded in Boise Valley, Idaho, becoming substantial land holders of twenty lots. On a segment of the Oregon Trail in June 1863, the couple cleared land across from the Fort Boise main gate and constructed the first log cabin in Boise, a nexus blessed with water, grass, stone, and wood.

The one-room, dirt-floored residence, built

of roofing poles and cottonwood logs felled along the Boise River, required extensive trim work with the broad axe. At the steeple-notched corners, clay mortar and willow chinking warded off moisture to prevent rot. Fabric nailed to the interior smoothed the walls, which enclosed 200 square feet of space. Following a Bannock-Shoshone massacre at Soda Springs on the Oregon Trail, on July 4, 1863, the Union Army repositioned Fort Boise 50 miles east of land formerly held by the Hudson's Bay Company. To stem an era of revenge killings, stage robbery, rustling, and vigilantism, the military garrisoned the fort with a cavalry company and three of infantry.

As order replaced rampant lawlessness, in late summer 1863, Mary Ann O'Farrell organized Catholic mass at her home and extended benevolence to the sick and indigent. By the second year in Boise, John upgraded the residence with hand-split shingles on the roof, oak plank ceiling and flooring from a local sawmill, and board and batten siding on the gable ends. A brick chimney and fireplace, hinged door, painted casings with glass windows, and wallpaper reduced the rustic beginnings of the family home. In 1865, Boise supplanted Lewiston as Idaho's state capital.

In 1867, the O'Farrells fostered five children, including Rosa Winnemucca, the seven-year-old niece of a Paiute chief, and had her christened in January 1869. On January 17, 1869, the couple produced a daughter, Gertrude O'Farrell, followed on December 21, 1870, by daughter Isabella. During their eight years in Idaho, the O'Farrells moved to a brick dwelling and donated a site for Boise's first church, built in 1870 by two priest-missionaries, Father Toussaint Mesplié from France and Father Andrew Z. Poulin of Canada, and Colonel Arthur St. Clair, commander of Fort Boise.

The Growing Family

In 1871, the O'Farrells began seven years' residency in Salt Lake City, Utah, where he commuted to the Ontario Silver Mine in Park City. John served one term as a territorial legislator and invested in the New York Canal. Mary Ann O'Farrell gave birth to Evelyn in November 1874 and Teresa in December 1876, but lost seven-year-old Isabella to disease on November 24, 1877. The couple produced Angela in February 1882, and Regina Marie "Virginia" in August 1886. Within months of Idaho's admission as the forty-third state in 1890, Rosa died.

John O'Farrell built a brick colonial revival house in 1892 and painted the two-story exterior white. The following year, he and Patrick Lee patented an efficient, durable train car coupling. John survived five months after his wife's death on May 22, 1900, and succumbed on October 29 of the same year, leaving four survivors—Evelyn, Teresa, Angela, and Virginia O'Farrell.

SOURCE

Transactions. New York: American Institute of Mining, Metallurgical, and Petroleum Engineers, 1897.

Omohundro, Texas Jack (1846–1880), Josephine Antonia Omohundro (1836–1886)

Pioneer scout and cowboy, John Baker "Texas Jack" Omohundro, Jr., contributed to the folk image of the plainsman. A Virginian and third of the eight children born to Catherine Salome Baker and farmer John Burwell Omohundro at Pleasure Hill 165 miles from Palmyra on July 26, 1846, he reputedly claimed Irish-Powhatan ancestors named for a tract known as Orme's Hundred. His youth attested to an outdoorsman's enthusiasm and a disdain for the classroom.

Omohundro left home at age thirteen to follow settlers of the Texas Panhandle. At Austin, he immediately joined the Texas Rangers under Captain John Coffee "Jack" Hays, a former Indian agent on the Gila River in Arizona and New Mexico. The nation's oldest law enforcement agency, the unofficial citizen soldiers of Texas received no pay and $1.25 per day for expenses as they battled outlaws, claim jumpers, and warriors of the Comanche, Karankawa, Kickapoo, Lipan Apache, Tawakoni, Tonkawa, Waco, and Wichita. As a cattle drover, for $20 per month, Omohundro spent two years learning wrangling skills by roping and subduing wild longhorns from the saddle.

At age 15, Omohundro attempted to join the Confederate infantry with his older brother Orville. Recruiters accepted Jack as messenger boy and scout. By 1864, he had the age and experience to join the 5th Virginia Cavalry as a courier and spy under General J.E.B. Stuart in Orville Omohundro's regiment. For infiltrating northern forces as a poultry seller, Jack earned the nickname the "Boy Scout of the Confederacy." From May 5–7, 1864, he fought in the Wilderness Campaign in Virginia and incurred a combat wound at the Battle of Trevilian Station, Virginia, fought from June 11–12, 1864.

After the war, Omohundro deserted his devastated home state and boarded a vessel for New Orleans. Later battered by storm on the Gulf of Mexico off western Florida, he settled temporarily to hunt and teach school. At Fort Worth, Texas, he fostered a five-year-old survivor of an Indian attack in Kansas that slaughtered the child's parents. Omohundro named the boy Texas Jack, Jr., later famous for trick riding, lassoing, and sharpshooting in Wild West shows.

Cowboy and Tracker

On a charity drive through Arkansas to a starving community in Tennessee in 1866, Omohundro acquired the nickname "Texas Jack." Near the Taylor ranch outside San Antonio, Texas, he and his rifle foiled seven men trying to break down a door to kidnap Mrs. Sophie Elgin. In the mid–1860s, he drove cattle for three years along the Chisholm Trail,

In the 1870s, Jack and Josephine Omohundro traveled to Denver, Colorado, where pioneer women lived under primitive conditions.

an 800-mile herding and stage route that Jesse Chisholm blazed on the Kansas-Missouri border in summer 1867 from Red River, Texas, northeast to Abilene, Kansas.

From his ranch at Cottonwood Springs, Nebraska, in 1869, Omohundro hunted buffalo and elk. Although he was an ex–Confederate soldier, the army hired him to track and scout on the North Platte River for the 5th U.S. Cavalry at Fort McPherson, Nebraska. He served with William Frederick "Buffalo Bill" Cody as trail agent in range wars, infiltrated a bandit gang preying on U.S. government convoys, and, in April 1872, battled Comanche horse thieves. For disclosing their plot to the high command, Omohundro earned a cash bonus.

On January 14, 1872, Omohundro guided Colonel George Armstrong Custer and Russian duke Alexei Alexandrovich, son of Tsar Alexander II, to stalk buffalo herds with Sioux chief Spotted Tail. That summer, Omohundro received an appointment by General Phil Sheridan to accompany the Pawnee on a buffalo hunt off the reservation to supply their tribe for winter. Armed with a Smith & Wesson revolver and Bowie knife, he also tracked for Irish sportsman Windham Thomas Wyndham-Quin, Earl of Dunraven, at Rush Creek, Colorado, Utah, and Yellowstone, which Congress had declared the world's first national park on March 1, 1872. The earl reprised their adventures in *The Great Divide: Travels in the Upper Yellowstone in the Summer of 1874* (1876).

Actor and Writer

With Cody in Chicago on December 16, 1872, Omohundro dressed in fringed, fur-edge coat and pants for the frontier melodrama *The Scouts of the Prairie,* publicized by showman Ned Buntline, publisher of dime novels. Cody credited his pal Jack with performing the first stage lasso act. At year's end, the actors formed "Cody's Combination" and debuted a revised version, *Scouts of the Plains,* a stage depiction of whites shooting Indians.

Co-starring Cody and James Butler "Wild Bill" Hickok, the production traveled west to Deadwood, South Dakota. To the delight of Eastern newspapers, on September 1, 1873, at St. Mary's Roman Catholic Church in Rochester, New York, Omohundro married a stage star, Italian ballerina Giuseppina (Josephine) Antonia Morlacchi of Milan, who played Dove Eye the Indian maiden. Into 1874, the touring company drew rave reviews in Boston, Richmond, and Norfolk.

When hostilities emerged between the 1,500 Sioux and Cheyenne led by Crazy Horse against the U.S. Army at the Battle of the Rosebud on June 17, 1876, Omohundro returned to scouting. As special columnist for the *New York Herald* and *New York Times* in 1877, Texas Jack published articles on the plains life and launched a theatrical group in St. Louis, Missouri, touring Auburn, Texas, and Sioux City, Iowa, in April 1878 with *Texas Jack in the Black Hills,* another inflated hero play about Indian fighting. In December 1879, he debuted in *The Trapper's Daughter: A Story of the Rocky Mountains,* a melodrama featuring a lynching.

The Omohundros settled on a country estate in Massachusetts, but traveled as a theatrical couple to Denver and Leadville, Colorado, the "Centennial State," which had joined the Union as thirty-eighth state on August 1, 1876. During the region's boom years, when groceries sold for four times their cost in Denver, the couple sought profitable investments and a salubrious climate for Jack's respiratory ills. Josephine opened a dance studio and starred at the Tabor Opera House in the Faustian drama *The Black Crook,* the first example of musical theater.

On June 28, 1880, Omohundro contracted a cold and died of pneumonia at age 33 in Leadville, where he had joined the town volunteer police, Tabor's Light Cavalry Unit. His wife sank into despair and died in July 1886. From the dime novel *Texas Jack, the Lasso King* (1891), retrospects in the *Spirit of the Time* magazine, and the biography *Buckskin and Satin* (1854) by Herschel C. Logan, Omohundro's notoriety increased to the original cowboy-actor and the "Mustang King—Conqueror of Cayuses."

Source

Kassen, Joy S. *Buffalo Bill's Wild West: Celebrity, Memory, and Popular History.* New York: Hill and Wang, 2000.

Parkhurst, Charley (1812–1879)

Concealing her gender, stagecoach driver Charlotte (or Charlene) Darkey "Charley" Parkhurst lived a man's life in California. Legend and conjecture riddle much of her biography, particularly the early years. Born of English ancestry in 1812 in Lebanon, New Hampshire, the second of the three children of Mary Morehouse and Ebenezer Parkhurst, "Lottie" Parkhurst lost her mother and brother, Charles Durkee, before her first birthday. She and her baby sister Maria lived at an orphanage after their father abandoned them and remarried.

Parkhurst developed a taller than average frame and answered to Charles Durkee Parkhurst, her dead brother's name. Dressed in boy's clothes, she ran away to Worcester, Massachusetts, a factory and transportation nexus. With the assistance of liveryman Ebenezer "Eb" Balch, she became a wagoneer controlling six-horse teams, a job requiring the anchoring of sets of traces between the index and middle finger, middle and ring finger, and ring and little finger of each hand. Charley found work as a stagecoach driver at the What Cheer Stables behind the Franklin House Inn in Providence, Rhode Island's prominent immigrant city. In 1849, she drove elegant teams for William Hayden and Charles Henry Childs, owner of a livery stable.

Joining the '49ers

In the guise of a man, in 1851, Parkhurst traveled by the clipper ship U.S.S. *R.B. Forbes* to Panama. After crossing the isthmus, in October 1851, she boarded the S.S. *Golden Gate*, a new vessel launched on January 21 by the Pacific Mail Steamship Company, for San Francisco, California. In addition to jobs in logging camps and on ranches, she covered routes through gold-mining country and over Mount Madonna for the California Stage Company and Pioneer Line. An anecdote declared that she retreated to southern California in 1855 and, at Searsville, gave birth to a stillborn child.

A tight-lipped loner among miners and gamblers, Parkhurst carried her money in a buckskin bag and concealed her slender hands and beardless face by wearing buckskin gloves and a wide-brimmed hat. After an accident while shoeing a horse in 1856 in Redwood City, she added a patch over a damaged left cheek and eye, for which locals called her "One-eyed Charley." She chewed and spit tobacco, smoked cigars, and drank, diced, and gambled with men, but sometimes chose to bed down in the livery rather than share sleeping quarters with other drivers.

Parkhurst earned respect for completing long round trips with a twenty-passenger coach and for surviving a bridge collapse into the Tuolumne River. In an era when miners received $35 per month and sailors earned $20 per month, her contracts reached as high as $125 per month plus room and board. After a robbery in June 1858, she learned to shoot a .44 pistol and shotgun, with which she dispatched a bandit known as Sugarfoot in December 1858 on the Calaveras run. In her mid-forties, she had to avoid flirtatious Mormon women. Impressed with her dedication, in 1859, Wells Fargo dispatched her to Providence, Rhode Island, with a gold shipment.

Keeping the Secret

Details of Parkhurst's life reveal both belligerence and charity in her championing of justice. By registering and voting at Soquel in Santa Cruz County, on November 3, 1868, she may have become the world's first female voter in a presidential election. After she kicked a German immigrant, land developer and road builder Frederick August Hihn, off her farm on July 9, 1864, on December 17, 1869, she pressed a lawsuit against him for claim jumping. The following year, Parkhurst bought foreclosed property and returned it to the widow who had once owned it.

As the railroad cut into the stage business, afflicted with sciatica and arthritis in her hands, Parkhurst retired to Aptos to raise poultry and cattle. On San Vicente Creek a few miles from the lumber mill of her nemesis, F. A. Hihn and sons, she built a stable. In 1870, she operated an Overland Stage Line station between Santa

In 1914, the Yellowstone Trail Association, headed by Joe Parmley, lobbied for the Yellowstone Park Trail.

Cruz and Watsonville. She partnered with wagoneer Frank Woodward on Bean Creek and hauled freight for neighbors until a throat tumor inhibited breathing. Charley declined a tracheotomy and the insertion of a silver tube into the windpipe and treated her ailing throat with horse liniment.

At Parkhurst's death from oral and throat cancer at the Moss Ranch near 7 Mile house in Watsonville, California, on December 18, 1879, preparation for burial disclosed her gender. An autopsy revealed she had previously survived pregnancy and childbirth. She willed $600 to a neighbor, twelve-year-old George Harmon. Contributing to the mystery of her sixty-seven years was a red baby dress and baby shoes in her tin trunk, a will signed "C.D. Parkhurst," and rumors of buried treasure in her stable.

SOURCE
Pryor, Alton. *Fascinating Women in California History.* Roseville, CA: Stagecoach, 2003.

Parmley, J.W. (1861–1940)

A settler of South Dakota and advocate of public works, Joseph William Lincoln "Joe" Parmley foresaw the Yellowstone Trail, the first highway spanning the northern United States from Plymouth Rock, Massachusetts, to Puget Sound, Washington. A first-generation American, he was born on January 12, 1861, at a farm in Mifflin, Wisconsin, to Jane Ashton and Joseph Parmley, a blacksmith from Middleton-in-Teesdale, Durham, England. His family migrated from Middleton, Connecticut, after 1850. The only male in a family of three children, Joe bore the name of four previous generations of Joseph Parmleys, dating to 1734, when the name changed from Parmeley or Parmerley. He studied at a Platteview, Wisconsin, public school and played football and, until his junior year, pursued a science degree at Lawrence College, a coeducational liberal arts institution in Appleton.

Parmley traveled by rail in spring 1883 to south central Dakota Territory and claimed a snowy tract in Aberdeen. He, Sebastian Brainerd Basford of Vermont, and Charles P. Morgan of Chicago raised a 24' × 48" tent they called the Cottonade Hotel, a rest stop for emigrants passing through the Missouri River Valley to the hamlet of Roscoe. By October 2, 1883, the trio platted Roscoe and renamed it Ipswich, county seat of Edmunds County, with Parmley serving as school superintendent, register of deeds, county clerk, and judge.

In his early twenties, Parmley built a reputation for supporting business in Dakota Territory. Throughout concerted activism and letters, he advocated the extension of the Chicago, Milwaukee, and St. Paul rail line through town. Working through the state horticultural society, he proposed the planting of the International Peace Garden, a gesture of goodwill between Dakotans and residents of Manitoba.

Entrepreneur and Booster

Parmley amassed a fortune from the Aberdeen Pressed Brick Company at Mina, where he warehoused 600,000 bricks. After he married on October 13, 1887, to a fellow first-generation American, Eliza Melissa "Lissie" Baker, of Linden, Wisconsin, the couple produced Loren Francis in 1894, Irene Adele in 1898, and Bernice Leone Parmley in 1900. J.W. earned a law license in 1887. He practiced law and raised registered cattle, pigs, and a Shetland pony herd at his farm. Following South Dakota's admission to the Union in 1889, Parmley pioneered the planting of durum wheat, alfalfa, and drought-resistant corn and the use of silos and manure spreaders, which he demonstrated to his neighbors.

In collaboration with English editor Henry Huck, Parmley issued the *Edmunds County Weekly News, Roscoe Herald,* and the weekly *South Dakota Tribune,* forerunners of the *Ipswich Tribune*. With rail passes, he attended press conferences and stirred emigrant interest in Edmunds County. At the Parmley Western Land and Abstract Office on Main Street in Ipswich, he amassed geological and anthropological artifacts, including seashells, calcite crystals, petrified dinosaur bone, meteorite fragments, Amerindian crafts, and quartz from the Homestake Mine, discovered in Lead, South Dakota, in 1876.

Into the 1900s, Parmley served twice in the state house of representatives. As a member of the state Brand and Mark Committee, he rallied economic and political support for South Dakota. With his first car, he investigated remains of pioneer travelers and the rutted roads they traversed. As a trustee of Dakota Wesleyan University, he also promoted education.

In 1907, Parmley advocated an east-west network of scenic roads and bridges linking the former Massachusetts Colony with Washington State, the forerunner of U.S. 12. Local meetings in April 1912 furthered plans to boost plains dirt roads into highways. As a gesture to peace, he foresaw macadamizing stretches with crushed white stone and planting shoulders in white wildflowers, decorations of a "Great White Way."

The Yellowstone Trail

In October 1912 at Minneapolis and March 1913 at Deadwood, South Dakota, Parmley chaired the Yellowstone Trail Association, which lobbied for a highway called the "Twin City-Aberdeen Yellowstone Park Trail." He intended the route to secure national defense and encourage plains tourism across the Dakotas, Montana, and Idaho. As a start on his idea, Parmley adapted a derelict Buick into the "Parmley Patrol," a road grader that scraped the 26 miles from Aberdeen to Ipswich.

As the project progressed, Parmley hired laborers at $3 per day and hand-stenciled arrows as directional markers on road signs pointing the way to Yellowstone. The landmark association collected fees from businesses for trail upkeep, infrastructure, and advertisements. By 1914, the trail reached the Pacific Ocean. The following year, Wisconsin warmed to Parmley's proposal of encouraging vacationers and campers to experience the West.

A visionary booster and president of the state historical society, Parmley supported the Turtle Mountains of North Dakota and, in 1918, the Good Roads Association, an investment in farm transportation. He also proposed a North American north-south thoroughfare from Manitoba to the Panama Canal. To prevent another house fire from destroying his residence, he took time in 1920 to erect a family home in Ipswich on Fourth Street and Fourth Avenue of brick, concrete, and plaster, even the bathtub. The chimneys displayed shells, stones, an iron post from Sitting Bull's grave, and other oddments Parmley amassed during travels across the U.S., Canada, and Mexico.

Parmley's advocacy encompassed populist issues: political compromise, soil and water conservation, prison parole, beautification and forest protection projects, farming institutes, hydroelectric power, and the completion of Gutzon Borglum's sculpting of Mount Rushmore, which began in 1923. Parmley expressed his altruism as president of the South Dakota Peace Association, delegate to the Aberdeen Commercial Club, and secretary of the Old Settlers Association.

After Parmley's death in Sioux Falls, South Dakota, on December 12, 1940, his name on Lake Parmley, the Parmley Highway, and the J.W. Parmley Home Society secured his place in Dakota history. A scion, Richard Parmley, donated property for the Parmley Memorial Park. The Ipswich Memorial Arch and June trail days commemorate Joe Parmley's dream of peace and a coast-to-coast U.S. highway.

SOURCE

Taliaferro, John. *Great White Fathers: The Story of the Obsessive Quest to Create Mount Rushmore.* Cambridge, MA: PublicAffairs, 2002.

Pennington, Elias G. (1809–1869), James Pennington (1833–1868), Larcena Pennington Page (1837–1913)

The first white pioneers in Arizona Territory, the Elias Green Pennington family lived out the nightmare of Southwest Indian attacks and disease. A South Carolinian born of English lineage on April 16, 1809, Elias claimed as progenitor Ephraim Pennington, a colonist of New Haven, Connecticut, in 1644. Elias was the eldest of the eight children of Elijah Pennington, a Continental Army veteran who served at Valley Forge and received a tract in Virginia as compensation. Elijah equipped Elias with horse, saddle, rifle, and dog and a patrimony of $2,100 to begin his adult life.

On September 8, 1831, Elias Pennington married Julia Ann Hood, a sixteen-year-old North Carolinian, and sired twelve children. The couple filled three ox- and mule-drawn wagons and drove their cattle from South Carolina across the Appalachian range. Until 1837, they farmed outside Nashville, Tennessee, the birthplace of James "Jim," Laura Ellen, Larcena Ann "Tid," and Caroline M. "Caz" Pennington.

Crossing the Mississippi River, the family reached Honey Grove east of Bonham in Fannin County, Texas. They packed a bible and school books, which Ellen used to educate Larcena and Caroline. Elias farmed while operating wagon transport from Bonham to Shreveport. Julia gave birth to John Parker "Jack," Ann Reid, Margaret Dennison "Mag," Amanda Jane, Elias "Green," William Henry "Will," Mary Frances, and Sara Josephine Elizabeth "Josie" Pennington. In 1852, Elias left the family to scout more open land at Keechi Creek near the Brazos River in Palo Pinto County, Texas. At age 40, Julia died of malaria in September 1855 at Honey Grove.

From Texas to Arizona

On a subsequent trek with the Sutton convoy toward the California goldfields, the Pennington clan forded the Pecos River and arrived at abundant grassy plains. They passed through Apache country at Tucson, Arizona, feeding themselves on dried fruit, bacon, biscuits, and wild turkey, venison, and bear meat. In June 1857, they made their home near Fort Buchanan along Sonoita Creek, where an army surgeon helped twenty-year-old Larcena Ann Pennington recover from malaria. At the fort, she met her future husband, lumberman and sawyer John Hempstead Page, manager of

In 1858, seventeen-year-old Jack Pennington left home at Sonoita Creek, Arizona, to build relay stations like this one for the Butterfield Overland Mail.

William Hudson "Bill" Kirkland's Madera Canyon timber operation.

More pioneers populated the Sonoita Valley. While raising beans, corn, squash, and pumpkins in their vegetable patch, the Penningtons found work reaping plains hay for the military and sewing uniforms. With cash from the government contracts, they replaced livestock stolen by Apache rustlers. Jack, then age seventeen, departed with a wagon train and worked for the Butterfield Overland Mail building relay stations. On May 12, 1859, Caroline Pennington married Charles M. Burr, a laborer for the Butterfield line at Pinos Altos.

When government employment ended, in September 1859, the Penningtons, including Jack, migrated to Calabasas. At a defunct Arizona cavalry camp, they squatted at the abandoned hacienda of Governor Manuel Gandara. By December, 26-year-old Jim Pennington homesteaded his own Arizona tract on the Santa Cruz River.

On December 24, 1859, Larcena's marriage to John Page became the first wedding performed in Tucson. She tutored Bill Kirkland's Mexican ward, ten-year-old Mercedes Sais Quiroz, in reading English. While cutting pine timber at Kirkland's Canoa Ranch 40 miles from Tucson, John traveled a dangerous route through Chiricahua country to deliver lumber to the U.S. Quartermaster. The pay amounted to 25 cents per board foot.

Captive Women

En route to resettling Larcena and her pupil at the lumber mill in the high country on March 15, 1860, John and his partner, William Randall, camped for the night near Madera Canyon in the Santa Rita Mountains. Five Tonto Apache, disgruntled about the presence of white emigrants on Indian land, grabbed Mercedes and Larcena and falsely reported killing John at the spring. With a stolen pistol and plunder from the tent, the five forced the captives northeast along the San Pedro River some 15 miles. One Apache indicated his ownership of Larcena by carrying her on his shoulder. Both women left fabric strips and broken twigs as trail markers for rescuers to follow.

Meanwhile, John and Randall summoned a posse from the mill to pursue the kidnappers.

Because Larcena weakened at evening, east of present-day Helvetia, an Apache stripped her of skirt and corset and pushed her over a ridge, from which she fell 17 feet. Knocked unconscious by rocks, she appeared lifeless. An Apache stole her boots, wounded her back and arms with sixteen jabs of the lance, and left her in a snow mound, which fortuitously stopped the bleeding.

The posse followed the boot tracks through the Rincon and Catalina mountains. Additional posses from Tucson failed to locate the women. After three days, Larcena, partially clothed and covered in bloody cuts, crawled toward home while surviving on melted snow, seeds, greens, and wild onions. She reached a road on March 26, 1860, and returned to the camp to eat scrapings of coffee and flour from the ground and to sleep. On March 31, the lumberjacks spied her resting place and transported her to a doctor in Tucson. Mercedes Quiroz remained in Apache custody until her ransom in summer 1860.

A year later in March 1861, the 400 warriors of Chiricahua Apache chief Cochise and his father-in-law, negotiator and tactician Mangas Coloradas (Red Sleeves), killed John Page outside Tucson. In the absence of U.S. Army regiments during the Civil War, a surge in abduction, torture, and murder of 150 whites and 600 Mexicans caused the Apache Wars of summer 1861. Retaliation against the Indians by Confederate Colonel John Robert Baylor, the self-proclaimed governor of Arizona, took the form of poisoned flour and the enslavement of Mescalero Apache children. The white settlers' fortunes improved in mid–August, when Jack Pennington rescued a white man targeted by the Chiricahua Apache.

On September 4, 1861, Lorena bore a posthumous child, Mary Ann Page. The Pennington family pressed on to an abandoned adobe with a thatched roof at Tubac, Arizona, and to William Sanders Oury's stone residence with defensive loopholes on the Mexican border near the Santa Cruz River. Elias continued supporting his family with the proceeds of freight transport, lumbering, farming, and cutting hay for officers of Fort Buchanan, who delayed remuneration.

During Elias's absences to deliver goods, his daughters stood guard against Indians. At Sylvester Mowry's silver mine at Patagonia in 1862, Larcena and Mary Ann pulled through a bout of smallpox. Mother and child returned to Tubac in April 1864 to the family farm, an area formerly occupied by Mexicans and Papago. Governor John Noble Goodwin elevated frontier protection by raising five companies of volunteer rangers to scout Apache and Yavapai braves in mountain hideouts and exterminate them. The Barlow-Sanderson Overland Mail Company relieved Larcena's isolation on August 24, 1866, by expanding mail service from the east over the Santa Fe Trail.

The Pennington Fortunes

The Pennington saga worsened on July 3, 1867, with the death of Ann Reid from malaria at the Sópori Wash south of Tucson. Frontier hostilities resumed in 1868 because the U.S. government failed to deliver promised supplies to the Gila Apache. On August 27, 1868, Apaches murdered Jim Pennington on Sonoita Creek near Tucson. On June 10, 1869, Apaches slaughtered Elias and his 21-year-old son Green while they worked their fields in Sonoita Valley, Arizona. The diminished family migrated toward Tucson, stopping when Ellen, then the wife of territorial legislator Underwood C. Barnett, sickened with malaria. A month after Barnett's death from dysentery, on December 3, 1869, Ellen died from pneumonia within days of the demise of her son, James F. Barnett.

Jack returned from Texas in 1870 to retrieve the despairing family. Caroline, Jack, Margaret, Will, Mary Frances, and Josie Pennington clung to Texas as their homeland, with Jack and Will continuing their father's freight business from San Antonio. In June 1873, Jack invested $800 in land along the San Gabriel River. The dispatch of U.S. cavalry in 1875 continued suppressing Lipan Apache raids over traditional Indian land. Caroline suffered postpartum depression and entered an asylum in 1877.

Two remaining siblings, Amanda and Larcena, chose different routes—Amanda to marriage with William Alexander Crumpton on April 23, 1874, and settlement in California and Larcena to permanent residence in Tucson. In August 1870, Larcena wed Scots judge William Fisher Scott, joined the Congregational Church, and bore two more children. In 1902, she chaired the Ladies' Auxiliary of the Society of Arizona Pioneers.

Jack Pennington, the backbone of the dwindling clan began losing his eyesight in 1890 to cataracts. On 1904, he hanged himself from a bed sheet tied to the rafter of his corncrib. Historians continue to study the Pennington family as models of the pioneer commitment to the merciless frontier.

See also Quiroz, Mercedes Sais.

Source
Smith, Victoria. *Captive Arizona, 1851–1900.* Lincoln: University of Nebraska Press, 2009.

Point du Sable, Jean Baptiste (ca. 1745–1818), Antoine Louis Ouilmette (ca. 1760–1841)

The founder of Chicago, farmer Jean Baptiste Point du Sable profited from trade in flour and pork on the southeastern shores of Lake Michigan. A freeborn Afro-Frenchman, he became the source of historical conjecture that his father was a French sailor and his mother a freedwoman living at Vaudreuil outside Montreal. One theory claims that he was born at Saint-Marc, Haiti, around 1745 and converted to Catholicism. He spent his youth working aboard his father's ship. Although illiterate, he may have become a coffee dealer in Louisiana.

In 1771, the Haitian wed a Potowatomi bride, Kittahawa, later called Catherine Point du Sable. He fathered two children, Jean and Susanne, and ascended in rank among the Potowatomi. After departing a home at Bureau Creek, Illinois, by the mid–1770s, he settled his household in a cabin at Chicago. In 1778, the Point du Sables remarried in a Catholic ritual performed at Cahokia, Illinois. While managing farms in Peoria, Jean cultivated a thirty-acre vegetable plot in Chicago, a place name he modified in French from the Indian term for "fetid swamp."

Arrest by British authorities on August 1, 1779, for suspected collusion with Americans involved Point du Sable's imprisonment at Michillimackinac until September and confiscation of his goods. From summer 1780 until May 1784, he oversaw a pine tract north of Detroit, Michigan, for a Scots officer of the British army, Lieutenant Patrick Sinclair. Point Du Sable's family resided in a two-room pine log house.

By the 1780s, Point du Sable, then in his early forties, made his home at an S-shaped portage north of the Chicago River and grew corn, alfalfa, wheat, and hay as well as beef and dairy cattle. In partnership with Pierre Durand of Detroit, the Haitian established a French and Indian trade center encompassing customers across the Great Lakes. He developed his property with two stables, a bakery, hen yard, dairy, smokehouse, icehouse, and horse-powered mill.

By July 1790, the Point du Sables gained neighbors, ferryman Antoine Louis Ouilmette, a French Canadian fur trader and stockman from Montreal, his French-Potowatomi wife, Archange Maria Chevalier, and their eight children. In 1796, Suzanne and husband Jean Baptiste Pelletier lived near the Point du Sable family. Their daughter Eulalie, Jean's first grandchild, made history as the first non-native child born in Chicago.

Perhaps because of Potowatomi losses resulting from the 1795 Treaty of Greenville (Ohio), in 1800, Point du Sable sold his holdings to Jean Laline for $1,200 and, in collaboration with Jean Baptiste, Jr., moved to a farm at St. Charles, Missouri. From June 1813, a friend, Eulalia Barada, cared for Point du Sable during a long illness. Before his death in St. Charles on August 28, 1818, he incurred bankruptcy and lost his son and wife to disease. In 2010, his Chicago homesite at 401 North Michigan Avenue received listing on the National Register of Historic Places.

Source
Davies, Carole Elizabeth Boyce, ed. *Encyclopedia of the African Diaspora.* Santa Barbara: ABC-Clio, 2008.

Rasor, John Henry (1849–1925), Mary Ellen Rasor (1851–1918)

A Baptist pioneer of Plano north of Dallas, Texas, rancher John Henry Rasor promoted hog breeding and cotton growing on the prairie. An Indianan born of Anglo-Scots lineage on November 22, 1849, he was the eldest child of Emily Catherine Liter from Brandenburg, Kentucky, and Civil War veteran of the 3rd Kentucky Cavalry Willis H. Rasor. John Henry was fifteen years old when his father died in mid–February 1865 during a raid on Lancaster, South Carolina, by Union army general William T. Sherman.

John Henry Rasor shared his father's patriotism and faith in family, industry, and integrity. While living in Hardin, Meade County, Kentucky, on December 11, 1872, John Henry married Kentuckian Mary Ellen Rachford. The couple settled in Graham, Iowa, and produced the first five of twelve children. In February 1883, the Rasors rented farmland from Texas Senator James Rowland Gough outside Plano, which they later purchased.

Living Off the Land

In prime grassland, oaklands, and savannas, the Rasor clan became survivalists living on venison, hackberries, wild onion and garlic, black walnuts and pecans and their own hogs, which foraged on acorns. Rasor wisely chose Collin County for its crumbly loam, temperate weather, and humidity. The calcareous soil was fertile to one foot below the surface without the application of fertilizer or manure. By building up smallholdings in the Bethany community, John Rasor acquired wealth from shorthorn cattle, grain for feed, and some 4,000 acres planted in Big Buck large boll cotton.

From wise husbandry of resources, Rasor produced 690 pounds of cotton per acre. His surviving sons—Ernest May "Judge," James Willis, Jesse Begg, John Shrewsberry, Robert Emmit, Chester Dow "C.D.," William H. "Boss," and Carl Hal "Hoss" Rasor—operated barns, feedlots, silos, and a forge and helped pack mule-drawn wagons with cotton for ginning at the McKinney compress near the train depot for export through the port of Galveston. By 1885, cotton dominated county crops at the rate of 54 percent.

Community Investment

A model of the mechanized farm manager and breeder of prize Poland-China boar hogs, Rasor officiated over the Collin County Purebred Livestock Association and showed his animals at the annual county fair. He also flourished as investor in 2,000 acres of county real estate, a county warden, and a trustee of the Allen National Bank at Allen. His daughter Lucy established a reputation as a music teacher; Carl Rasor served Plano as postmaster.

Rasor suffered setbacks in June 1909 after the death of son Frankie Wolford Rasor, on January 23, 1923, following the death of son Tolbert Conley "Con," and on April 3, 1925, after the demise of John's wife, Mary Ellen Rasor. John assisted his sons' families by rearing Con's nine orphaned children and Frank's two daughters.

During several months of illness, John Henry Rasor received nurse care from his daughter Margaret "Debby" Rasor. He died on the farm in the Rowlett Community on November 5, 1925, from influenza complicated by diabetes. His will left to his heirs a block of 2,200 acres of the Blackland Prairie, the richest farmland in Texas. The Rasor name attaches to roads, a park, and an elementary school.

SOURCE
Cline, Janice Craze. *Historic Downtown Plano*. Charleston, SC: Arcadia, 2012.

Reed, James Frazier (1800–1874), Margret Wilson Keyes Reed (1814–1861), Virginia Elizabeth Backenstoe (1833–1921), Martha Jane Reed Lewis (1838–1923), James Frazier Reed, Jr. (1841–1901), Lewis Keseberg (1814–1895)

Two of California's most famous pioneers, James Frazier and Margret Wilson Keyes Reed survived the 1846 Donner Party tragedy, the worst disaster in the history of the Oregon Trail. Born on November 14, 1800, James, an emigrant from Armagh, Ireland, was the son of a Scots-Irish mother, Martha Frazier, and a Polish father named Reednoski. James and

Martha emigrated from home after his father's death and boarded with relatives in Virginia.

From clerking in a store, at age 25, Reed moved on to mining lead in Illinois. He settled in Springfield in 1831. With fellow militia volunteers Abraham Lincoln and Stephen A. Douglass, he fought in the Black Hawk War from May 19 to August 9, 1832. He worked in cabinetry, dry goods, lumber milling, real estate speculation, and factory management before becoming Springfield's U.S. pension agent.

On March 31, 1835, Reed wed Margret Wilson Keyes Backenstoe, a native of Union, West Virginia. A scion of tenth-century Norman-French and of Massachusetts colonists from Lincolnshire and Yorkshire, England, she was born on March 31, 1814, the only girl of the six children of Sarah Handley and Humphrey Keyes. She was widowed at the death of tailor Lloyd Carter Backenstoe from cholera in September 1834. The Reeds reared her two-year-old daughter, Virginia Elizabeth, affectionately known as "Puss." At Springfield, James and Margret produced Martha Jane "Patty," James Frazier, Jr., Thomas "Tommy" Keyes, and Dallas Gershom Francis Reed, who died in 1845 at age eleven months.

Going West

On April 14, 1846, the Reed family and Margret's blind, deaf, and bedfast mother, seventy-year-old Sarah Handley Keyes, accompanied George, Jacob, and Tamsen Donner and their families to Independence, Missouri, in a wagon train of eighty-one settlers. Some sought a new start; Margret hoped for improved health and relief from grief for her baby boy. Other wayfarers expected religious freedom for Catholics in California. For Lewis Christian Keseberg and his party of six Prussians from Westphalia, intentions of prosperity languished because of Keseberg's reputation for violence, petty retaliation, and murder.

Reed provided two servants, an oversized wagon pulled by four yoke of oxen, and two supply wagons driven by hired teamsters. Sarah lay in comfort until her death on May 29 in Alcove Spring, Kansas, from tuberculosis, a loss that further grieved Margret Reed.

The pioneers buried Sarah in a hollow cottonwood tree and inscribed a headstone. Her loss contributed to the total demise of 10 percent of people traversing the Oregon Trail.

The convoy separated on July 20, with Reed and the Donners hurrying on to Fort Bridger. Beginning August 12, the train passed over the Wasatch Mountains. On August 27, they began traversing Great Salt Lake Desert, which extended 82 miles.

The Reeds, like the Donners, drove slower, heavier wagons and fell behind the convoy. At Elko, Nevada, they followed the California Trail, but lost most of their oxen on September 2 during a search for water. The last leg of the trek, begun on September 26, 1846, pressed upward 12,000 feet into the Sierra Nevada, but the emigrants advanced too near snowfall for an unobstructed passage.

On the final 100 miles, at Iron Point, Nevada, on October 5, 1846, Reed shielded Margret from enraged teamster John Snyder by stabbing him to death in the lung with a hunting knife. To avoid hanging from Keseberg's wagon tongue and leaving his family destitute, Reed journeyed ahead the next day to Sutter's Fort to fetch supplies. Along the trail, he scattered the feathers of birds and ducks to mark his campsite and reassure his family that he ate well. In his absence, on October 25, Paiute rustled eighteen oxen and killed twenty-one more.

On October 30, Reed began the return trip with a hindquarter of beef and flour, but he encountered a blizzard that dumped four feet of snow. At Bear Valley, he cached the foodstuffs and shared a meal of stewed dog. Lacking snowshoes, the rescuers returned their pack mules to the fort to await a thaw. While recruiting rescuers, on January 2, 1847, he served as lieutenant to a cavalry regiment at the Battle of Santa Clara. War with the Mexicans reduced the number of men to join another rescue party.

During Reed's absence, Margret had to abandon the oversized wagon, which overhung the mountain passes and weakened the dray animals. She recovered from a life of migraine headaches, and with renewed energy, housed her family in a double cabin and fed them on rug scraps, hide roofing, ox offal, and field mice.

She wept to see eight-year-old Patty still able to play with her wooden doll. To encourage five-year-old Jimmy, the youngest survivor, in struggling through waist-deep snow, Margret promised him a pony. Because the death of the Donners orphaned their girls in March 1847, Margaret adopted six-year-old Frances E. and seven-year-old Mary M. Donner.

Rescue from Starvation

After the immigrants devoured their remaining animals, hunger took its toll in despair and physical collapse. Margret begged other campers for food and bartered with Patrick Dolan for meat by offering James's Mason's medallion and pocket watch. Two of the Reed employees—Baylis Williams, feeble and blind, and teamster James Smith—died in mid–December of malnutrition and exposure. For Christmas dinner 1846, Margret saved dried apples, tripe, and beans. Miraculously, the Reeds' five dogs survived.

On January 4, Margret led an escape party attempting to cross the mountains and, four days later, returned and sought shelter with the Breen family in an abandoned cabin, against which Keseberg had built a lean-to. The Reeds had little recourse but to kill their last dog, Cash. All grew too weak to forage for firewood or chop limbs. On the night of February 9, 1847, a third Reed family teamster, Milford "Milt" Elliot, starved to death. Margret dragged him by the hair to a snow burial.

Reed and a party of rescuers set out to locate the convoy at Donner Lake on February 9, 1847. On the way east on February 21, Reed encountered Margret, Virginia, and James, Jr., and ended their trudging by setting them on mules. He fed them bread he had baked the night before. The search party pressed on to the stranded travelers at the rate of three miles per day and, on February 27, located Patty tending to three-year-old Tommy Reed. A passing Indian shared his food stores by offering the emigrants six fleshy tubers.

Reed heroically searched for survivors and found forty-five starving refugees at Donner Pass. The trekkers survived by killing a bear cub for food and scraping sacks for crumbs and chaff. Forced to return without the emigrants, Reed left the second rescue to another attempt on March 3, when he departed carrying Patty and Tommy. A worse snowstorm lasted from March 5 to 7. Of the original eighty-seven journeyers, only forty-eight arrived alive to California. Among them was the entire Breen family.

Grim stories of cannibalism dogged members of the Donner Party, especially Lewis Keseberg, a sixty-two-year-old Prussian from Westphalia, who clung to life until April 29 by eating corpses. Californians welcomed the survivors with supplies and a purse of $1,500 for their relief. Keseberg found temporary jobs as captain of the schooner *Sacramento,* manager of an inn, and owner of a brewery.

The Reeds successfully distanced themselves from James's banishment from the convoy and the unwise decision to look for a shortcut over the Sierra. In summer 1847, James moved his family to San Jose, where he partnered with son Jimmy in buying property and investing in mining. Margaret gave birth to Charles Cadden Reed on February 6, 1848, and, on December 12, 1850, Willianoski Yount "Willie" Reed, who died of cerebral illness at age nine.

During the California Gold Rush, James Reed enriched himself at Placerville. Margret died in San Jose on November 25, 1861. Reed died on July 24, 1874. Daughter Martha Jane Reed Lewis, widowed in 1876, supported her children by keeping an inn in Santa Cruz and Capitola. In July 1891, the *Century Illustrated Magazine* published "Across the Plains in the Donner Party," Virginia's account of the disastrous ordeal. Virginia Elizabeth Backenstoe, the widow of California pioneer John Marion Murphy in 1892, became the first Pacific Coast female to run a fire insurance business.

Source
Rarick, Ethan. *Desperate Passage: The Donner Party's Perilous Journey West.* New York: Oxford University Press, 2008.

Reed, John Thomas (1805–1843)

Irish sailor and entrepreneur John Thomas "Don Juan" Reed, called the "Father of the Pioneers," diversified his investments in San Francisco. A native of Dublin, he was born to a Catholic family in 1805. He studied navigation with his uncle and set sail for South America. At age fifteen, he emigrated to Acapulco, Mexico, and learned to speak Spanish.

Reed reached California in 1821. While seeking a Spanish land grant for Rancho Sausalito, in 1826, he became the first Anglo and first English speaker to reside in Marin County. Unfortunately, administrators denied his request for a land grant. He built Sausalito's first frame house and initiated a sailboat ferry service across San Francisco Bay from Sausalito to Yerba Buena, carrying freight and passengers. His boat ferried fresh spring water to the 250 residents of Yerba Buena presidio, a protective battery equipped with five cannon.

In 1827, Reed petitioned for acreage from the Cotati, a peaceful band of the Miwok nation in Sonoma County 7 miles south of Santa Rosa. After breaking soil and planting seeds on Crane Creek, he lost his wheat crop to Miwok arsonists, who attempted to rid the bay area of pioneers. He fled to the protection of Juan Amorós, a Franciscan emissary from Spain to the San Rafael Mission who promoted amity among cultures and races.

The Reed Land Grant

A naturalized Mexican citizen, Reed waited until age 26 before occupying and making a *diseño* (stylized map) of his land in Marin County, Alta California. On the stipulation that he provide wood to the presidio, Governor José Figueroa granted him the title of "Don Juan" and the county's first tract—Rancho Corte Madera del Presidio. The one square league (8,878.82 acres) included Strawberry Point, Valentine's Island (present-day Corinthian Island), Belvedere, Larkspur, Ring Mountain, and the salt marshes of Tiburon Peninsula, an area crisscrossed by Miwok tule boats. At Mill Valley near the foot of Mount Tamalpais in 1831, he erected a barn, two corrals, and an adobe house with a pyramidal red roof and hired Rose Rodrigues Da Fonta, an immigrant from the Azores, as housekeeper.

In November 1835, John Reed hired Nereo (or Neri), a Miwok alcalde (magistrate) and interpreter, to survey land boundaries and begin a logging operation. In addition to raising a wood cross on Mount Tamalpais, on Cascade Creek, Reed operated a gristmill and, with a team of Miwok laborers, constructed the region's first sawmill from redwood framing at Cascade Canyon. From Russian hardware dealers at Fort Ross, he transported millstones and a saw blade, for which he bartered 200 cow hides, 300 elk skins, and 20 bear pelts. His workers hewed redwood trunks into 48-foot beams, a 6,000-pound load that oxen moved with block and tackle.

Reed's contributions to the local economy included finished redwood lumber, bricks, quarry stone, pelts, and 26,000 head of hybrid British cattle. He planted almond trees and an orchard, set up a stockyard with 60 horses and 400 cattle, and opened a dairy that sold butter, cream, milk, and cheese in San Francisco. In addition, he ran a rock quarry, salt yard, and brick works and sold salt beef to passing ships.

The Reed Family

After a decade's courtship, on October 12, 1836, at Mission Dolores, Reed married nineteen-year-old Hilaria Sánchez, a wife well connected to two mayors and a commandant. They honeymooned at San Mateo in a colonial Spanish adobe. From late 1836 to April 1837, Reed managed the Mission San Rafael Arcángel, the state's first sanitarium, which treated sick Amerindians. In their adobe residence with encircling veranda, the couple raised son John Joseph and daughters Hilarita and Maria Inez "Matilda." One son, Ricardo, died at age thirteen.

On June 29, 1843, Reed succumbed to the mismanagement of heat stroke complicated by pneumonia. He left incomplete his two-story hacienda at La Goma in Mill Valley that Indians from Sutter's Fort were constructing. His will transferred 2,061.51 acres to John Joseph Reed and smaller tracts to Inez and Hilarita, all of which Hilaria shielded for her minor children against squatters and rustlers. Often challenged in litigation, the Reed property remained in the family until World War II. The surname survives in the Reed Union School District, Reed School, Reed Boulevard, Reed Avenue, and the community of Reed, California.

SOURCES
Fanning, Branwell. *Tiburon and Belvedere*. Charleston, SC: Arcadia, 2010.
Goerke, Betty. *Chief Marin: Leader, Rebel, and Legend*. Berkeley: Heyday, 2007.

Reed, William Whitaker (1816–1891), Emaline Cobb Reed (1825–1890), Michael Reed (1777–1859), Martha Burnett Reed (1786–1855)

One of the first Anglo settlers of east central Texas, William Whitaker Reed staked his family's future on the birth of the Texas Republic. Born the fourth of seven children on January 23, 1816, in Bedford County outside Nashville, Tennessee, he traveled often with his parents, Martha Burnett of Virginia and Michael Reed, a second-generation Irish-American farmer from Pennsylvania and relative of eight veterans of the American Revolution. The Cherokee and Choctaw Cession of October 24, 1816, lured the family to open land in Lincoln County, Tennessee, in 1819.

The restless Reed clan spent 1820 in Limestone County, Alabama, and moved to Tipton County, Tennessee, before their venture farther south toward the Mississippi River. Spirited frontiersmen, they endorsed the pioneer drive for the Texas Republic. From Natchitoches, Louisiana, the family migrated to Bell County, Texas, in 1833.

In the colony of Sterling Clack Robertson, the Reeds sought homesteads in blocs of 177.1 acres for farms and 4,428.2 acres for ranches. With brother Wilson Reed and brother-in-law William Crain Sparks, a colonial ranger, seventeen-year-old William Reed surveyed the area in search of suitable farmland. The region appealed to him for providing good hunting from ducks, geese, and wild turkey as well as alligators, bear, buffalo, antelope, and wild hogs.

Texas Pioneers

South of Little River near present-day Salado, both William and his younger brother, Jefferson "Jeff" Reed, farmed one-fourth league. The homesteaders weathered the territorial clash between colonizers Robertson and Stephen F. Austin, which concluded with Austin's arrest for treason on February 13, 1834. By December 25, 1834, the Reed application for land received approval, but hostilities with Mexican general Santa Anna forced the family to abandon their claim.

Both Jefferson and William Reed fought on the side of the republic in the Texas Revolution, waged from October 2, 1835, to April 21, 1836. After the Mexican slaughter of 344 Texian soldiers at Goliad, William aided the burial party. At war's end, the Reed brothers were hurrying to join General Sam Houston's army when the republicans returned jubilant from a Texian victory over Santa Anna at San Jacinto. The triumph secured Texas independence as well as the Reed homestead.

Indian attacks forced Reed temporarily off his land, to which he returned in 1837 to farm and raise livestock. In a Robertson County wedding on January 15, 1841, he married sixteen-year-old Emaline Cobb, an Anglo-Dutch scion of sixteenth-century residents of Amsterdam, Holland, who had emigrated to the Virginia colonies. Emaline had settled in Robertson's Colony in 1837 with her family, pioneers from Walker County, Alabama.

After pioneers began relocating along the Little River lowlands after 1843, Michael Reed and sons Jake, Jefferson, John Burnett, and William reclaimed acreage in 1845. The formal incorporation of Bell County in 1850 involved fifty-seven white settlers. William Reed helped organize the county's legal structure and, on August 1, 1850, began serving six years as Bell County's first sheriff.

The William Reed Family

To house his six sons and four daughters, Reed constructed a model dogtrot cabin of burr oak logs with limestone chimneys. For safety from possible attacks by Kiowa, Comanche, or Lipan Apache, he pierced the walls

William Stancell Reed profited from the livestock business from 1867 to 1875 by driving cattle over the Chisholm Trail.

with arrow slits rather than windows. His father, Michael Reed, died in 1859, four years after Martha Reed's death in 1855. The Civil War took his brother, twenty-year-old James Michael Reed, who died in Confederate service at the Battle of Glorieta Pass, New Mexico, on May 29, 1862, while supplying the rebel army with cattle. The family lost two of their children—Jefferson at age two in 1863 and one-year-old David in 1867.

During the time that Reed's second son, William Stancell B. "Buddy" Reed, collaborated with his father, they advanced in the livestock business from 1866 to 1885 by directing cattle drives over the Chisholm Trail. Drovers stopped at Salado's Stagecoach Inn, the state's longest operating hotel. Ranchers also profited from the extension of the Gulf, Colorado and Santa Fe Railroad in 1880.

A year after the death of Emaline, William Reed died on August 21, 1891, in Alabama. The Reed siblings—Sarah Atlas "Sally," Martha, Virginia Clinton, Texanna, Wilson Cobb "Wiltz," Harriet, John Burnett, and Jefferson Reed—produced large families and lived out their years in Texas. William Reed's youngest son, Volney Erskine Howard Reed, studied medicine in St. Louis and opened a practice in Cameron, Texas.

Sources

Hodge, Mary Harrison, and Charlene Ochsner Carson. *Salado*. Charleston, SC: Arcadia, 2014.

Sutherland, Anne. *The Robertsons, the Sutherlands, and the Making of Texas*. College Station: Texas A&M University Press, 2006.

Rice, James Stephen (1846–1939), Coralinn Barlow Rice (1849–1919)

An orchardist and civic booster of Orange County, California, James Stephen Rice furthered the growth of Tustin and Santa Ana. A native Ohioan, he was born fourth of five children on October 31, 1846, in Cleveland to Emma Marie Fitch and attorney and Ohio senator Harvey Rice, a descendent of Edmund Rice, a seventeenth-century Anglo-Irish colonist at Massachusetts Bay. Graduated from city schools, James majored in classics at Case Western College in Hudson, Ohio, and completed a B.A. in 1866.

Rather than follow the law career proposed by his father, James Rice partnered in the dinnerware and home furnishing business with his half-brother, Percival Wood Rice, and their brother-in-law, Proctor Rollin Burnett. In Cleveland on October 2, 1872, James wed soprano Coralinn Frances "Cora" Barlow, an Episcopalian native of Rhode Island of Anglo-Welsh lineage who studied at an Ursuline convent. James continued with the Rice & Burnett Company for five more years.

A New Start in the West

To escape cold winters, the Rice family set out for the Pacific coast in winter 1876 to sample California's weather. On January 18, 1877, James and Cora, with preschooler son James Willis and ten-month-old Merrill Barlow, moved to San Joaquin on Newport Bay to reside in a ranch house built by José Antonio Andrew Sepúlveda, a breeder of racehorses. To keep out fleas, James had the house plastered, a first for Orange County.

After collaborating with Irish brother-in-law James Irvine, Rice wearied of isolation at the Irvine Ranch. In 1878, he liquidated investments in cattle, sheep, and hogs to grow muscatel grapes and Valencia oranges at Tustin southeast of Los Angeles. He earned $200 annually just on grapes. During this period, he sired two more sons, Harvey and Percy Fitch. Percy, a budding inventor, rigged a pulley from his bedroom that enabled him to water and feed the hen yard without leaving his bed.

Around 1880, Rice invested $2,500 in fifty acres and expanded his farm, the source of the younger James's interest in citrus culture. The elder James Rice's foal Ricetta, born in 1885, thrived as a racehorse. When property peaked in value in 1886, he profited on the sale of acreage at more than $200,000. The parcel became known as Rice's Addition to Tustin.

The Rice Family in Tustin

On twelve remaining acres, James S. Rice constructed a three-story manse at First and Prospect streets and succeeded at refined entertainments and musicales. He continued raising oranges as well as walnuts, celery, and sugar beets. In winter, he burned brush and tree trimmings in the rows to protect tender crops from frost and snow.

The Rice family established its importance to pioneer history as well as the cultural growth of California. Until her death in November 1919, James's socially prominent wife performed benefit musicals at French's Opera House in Santa Ana. She performed duets informally with James of "Listen to the Mocking Bird," which he accompanied with whistles. She assisted in boosting his centrality to Democratic politics and in his promotion of Laguna Beach.

A noted orator and progressive, James S. Rice advocated an electric rail line to Santa Ana to replace the downtown horse-drawn trolley and aided in raising funds for street signs for Tustin in 1905 by serving as auctioneer at a box social. His son James established his own ranch at Tustin in 1905. A widower for twenty years, the elder James died at home in Tustin in 1939. The family name marked Rice Drive.

Source
Lovret, Juanita. *Tustin As It Once Was*. Charleston, SC: History Press, 2011.

Sakuma, Yonekichi (1839–1927), Kintaro Ozawa (fl. 1840s–1870s), Tomi Ozawa (1849–?)

One of the urban Asiain *gannenmono* (recruits) to Pacific agriculture during the reign of Hawaii's King Kamehameha V, Yonekichi Sakuma recorded eyewitness accounts of migration from Japan to Hawaii. The grandson of a samurai, Sakuma was born on July 11, 1841, in Chiba, Japan, to Mataemon Sakuma and Aki, an illiterate morganatic husband who pre-

In 1868, the first Japanese laborers arrived in Hawaii from Yokohama.

served his father-in-law's noble surname. A farmer at age twenty-eight, Yonekichi joined the first mass transport of Asian carpenters, tailors, printers, potters, cooks, brewers, and soldiers to Hawaii, a location unknown to the recruits.

On May 17, 1868, Yonekichi Sakuma stowed away with one female and 148 male emigrants on the three-masted British ship H.M.S. *Scioto* from Yokohama to Honolulu. On the 33-day voyage, travelers received free passage and board and bore on their clothing one of three stamps: C for California, P for Peru, or S for Sandwich Islands, the original name of the Hawaiian Island cluster. On June 7, Sakuma's friend Kodzu Wakichi died during the crossing. At a Christian service, his companions buried Wakichi at sea.

Reaching Hawaii

The recruits avoided smoking, for which crew handcuffed them, and subsisted on rice, miso, and soy sauce, the first imported into Hawaii. The subsidence of a terrifying storm caused male Japanese passengers to lop off their topknots and throw them overboard in thanksgiving for survival. Sick and weary, they came ashore at Honolulu on June 19, 1868, where the king gave them clothing, hats, and stores of salt fish. In hopes of reviving island profits during the decline of the whaling industry, planters paid $70 each for field workers.

By the first week in July 1868, the recruits were ready for distribution to farms in Kauai, Maui, Lanai, and Oahu. While residing in crowded grass huts floored with tatami mats, they hoped to earn a substantial fortune before returning to Japan. Under contract for 3 to 8 years at the rate of $1 per week, Japanese workers replaced native Hawaiian farm workers whom measles, leprosy, cholera, influenza, whooping cough, gonorrhea, and smallpox epidemics from 1848 to 1854 had reduced by 5,750 deaths or 20 percent of native islanders. Because King Kamehameha III declined to launch an inoculation campaign, the onslaught had reduced life expectancy for pure Hawaiians to 35 years and increased the need for more imported Asian workers.

The Japanese contract laborers sang *hole hole bushi* (labor tunes) as they hoed rows, stripped leaves with knives, and bundled cane for the sugar, molasses, and rum industry. Managing ten-hour days, they faced lost wages and fines of 25¢ for lateness, violating a 9:00 p.m. curfew, losing or damaging tools, injuries, and sickness. By late July 1868, forty recruits broke their contracts because of maltreatment and the sale of contracts to other plantations.

The First Japanese-Hawaiians

Sakuma's fellow emigrants, Kintaro and Tomi Ozawa, in the last month of awaiting their first child, found domestic jobs. Tomi produced Yotaro Ozawa, Hawaii's first *nisei* (second generation) islander and first Japanese-Hawaiian policeman. In spite of King Kalakaua's crusade for native culture and "Hawaii for Hawaiians," Tomi's other children made island history, Itoko Ozawa as a translator for Japanese ambassadors and Arthur Kenzaburo Ozawa as the first Japanese-American attorney and president of the Japanese American Citizenship Association.

Under manager Paul Isenberg, Sakuma lived at the Lihue Plantation, Kauai's second oldest plantation, and became a devout church member. During his residency, as American investors exploited the islands, Lihue Plantation grew by 47,000 acres. He wed Jkatsuna Sakuma. Despite Queen Kapiolani's efforts to increase infant and mother survival rates, Jkatsuna died in 1893 giving birth to daughter Fuyu. At Grove Farm on Kauai, Sakuma married a second wife, Tsuna Omoto, mother of son Yasohachi in 1896.

Because Sakuma cooked until 1875 at Lihue, native Hawaiian planter George Norton Wilcox paid for the education of the two Sakuma children. On monthly pension of $25 at age 63, Sakuma resided with Tsuna at a cottage on Nawiliwili Bay at Papalinahoa. Their son Yasohachi served as a sergeant in the army during World War I. Sakuma died in 1927.

SOURCE
Van Sant, John E. *Pacific Pioneers: Japanese Journeys to America and Hawaii, 1850–80.* Champaign: University of Illinois Press, 2000.

Simmons, Michael T. (1814–1867), Elizabeth Kindred Simmons (1820–1891)

A self-taught millwright on a steady move west, Michael Troutman "Big Mike" Simmons pushed for the equitable settlement of Puget Sound, Washington, by black and white pioneers. A Kentuckian born at Shepherdsville in Bullitt County on August 5, 1814, he was the third of the thirteen children of Jonathan C. Simmons of Maryland and Mary Polly Troutman, a Kentuckian of Anglo-German ancestry. After his father apparently deserted the family, Michael lived with his mother, stepfather James Morton, and nine siblings in Pike County, Illinois, but received no education.

In 1835, Simmons relocated to Clay County, Iowa, and, on January 20, wed fourteen-year-old Elizabeth Kindred of Jackson, Indiana, a great-granddaughter of English emigrants from Cumberland to Virginia who fought in the Revolutionary War. Resettled in Missouri on January 1, 1840, Simmons erected a flourmill at the Nodaway River from an illustrated how-to guide. The drought of 1843–1844 forced him to move on with Elizabeth and their sons—George Washington, David Crockett Kindred, Frances Marion Dekalb, and Macdonald Simmons, all named for historic figures.

The Bush-Simmons Train

Along with 77 families, the couple, accompanied by the Kindred clan, joined a black couple, George Washington Bush and his wife Isabella, on a 2,000-mile trek over the Oregon Trail by ox team. Departing on May 1, 1844, from Clay County, Missouri, under command of Bush and Simmons, the convoy took eight months to reach its destination. Wet weather postponed the arrival at Big Blue River, Nebraska, until June and lengthened the fording of swollen waters to 16 days.

Along the Missouri River, the cavalcade linked up with 800 pioneers led by Cornelius Gilliam, but separated from some of the wagoneers in July, when the train reached Fort Bridger, Wyoming. Along the way, Elizabeth jettisoned a family treasure, her oak chest. Michael Simmons quarreled with Gilliam and resigned his post as second in command. The party pushed on through the Blue Mountains of Oregon in November 1844, trading with the Umatilla for dried meat, and reached The Dalles in Wasco County, Oregon, on December 7, 1844.

At the south of Puget Sound in Thurston County late in winter 1844–1845, the Simmons and Bush clans shared a longhouse lighted by fish oil and made their beds on cedar limbs topped with rush mats. In a sheep pen on April 14, 1845, Elizabeth Simmons gave birth to son Christopher Columbus Simmons, whom Indians nicknamed White Seagull. He was the first American child born north of the Columbia River.

Collaborators in Milling

Simmons partnered with Bush in hunting, fishing, and sowing hops, oats, peas, potatoes, rye, and wheat. For cash, they sold shingles chopped out of cedar. Because of racist laws in Oregon, the two men relocated north into British territory. Guided by a French-Canadian pathfinder, from July to September 1845, the westerers took boats up the Columbia and Cowlitz rivers. At the worst of their struggles, they walked the 58 miles to the Deschutes River Falls, reaching their destination in late October.

At Bush Prairie north of the Willamette River Valley, Simmons and his party built the town of New Market, the beginnings of Tumwater, Washington. To stave off hunger in the first months, they learned from the Chinook how to gather wild greens and shellfish and to seine for salmon. By May 1846, additional American pioneer advances north of the Columbia River forced the British to relinquish claims to present-day Washington State. The Hudson's Bay Company at Fort Nisqually advised the newcomers until 1848, when Simmons wearied of their monarchist attitude. In 1849, the U.S. legitimated claims to Oregon Territory.

In collaboration with Bush, Simmons began logging the Columbia River banks and tributaries. Along the Deschutes River, the frontiersmen erected grist mills and a granary and the first sawmill in the northeast, investment guaranteed to grow as more pioneers arrived. Simmons built the wood business by opening a lumber firm at Budd Inlet north of Olympia. His initiatives earned him the title of "Father of Washington Industry."

In 1850, Simmons sold his claim to sea captain Clanrick Crosby from Massachusetts and moved to Olympia with Elizabeth Simmons and their children. Despite illiteracy, Simmons opened a postal service and shipping line carrying lumber and groceries south to mining camps. The family increased with the births of Benjamin Franklin, Charlotte Elizabeth, Catherine Troutman, Douglass Woodbury, Mary Ellen, Michael Troutman, Jr., and Charles Mason Simmons. In 1852, Douglass died at age nine months.

By 1853, the carving of Washington Territory from Oregon ended some of the pioneer defiance of Oregon racism. From 1854 to 1855, Simmons superintended the Puget Sound Indian agency; as justice of the peace, he negotiated treaties with the Clalam, Chimicum, and Makah. In 1855, following election to the state legislature, he petitioned for the granting of 640 acres to Bush, whom racist property laws denied land ownership. After Simmons died of hepatitis at Drews Prairie on November 15, 1867, his remains received Masonic honors. In 1973, painter Jacob Lawrence commemorated Bush Prairie history with five pioneer scenarios.

See also Bush, George Washington, Isabella James Bush.

SOURCE

Green, Claude A. *What We Dragged Out of Slavery with Us.* West Conshohocken, PA: Infinity, 2006.

Smeathers, William (ca. 1766–1837), Mary Polly Smeathers (1769–1810)

A hunter and Indian fighter, William "Bill" Smeathers (also Smithers, Smothers, Smathers) spent his last 15 years in south central Texas as a colonist in the Brazos River settlement of Stephen F. Austin. Much of Smeathers's biography is conjectural. Born of German-American lineage to Ann Marie Chrisman and hunter Jacob Smeathers in the Holston River region of coastal Virginia (or possibly North Carolina), he may have attended Frederick Finley's school at the home of his uncle, Henry Chrisman, at Willow Shade Plantation along the James River outside Richmond.

In 1778, Smeathers was twelve when his father died of an Indian tomahawk blow to the skull. After his mother's death from trauma nine days later, he reared his sisters, Jane, Elizabeth "Betsey," and Mary "Molly" Smeathers. Sketchy information suggests that William fought in Revolutionary War engagements in his teens at King's Mountain, Guilford Courthouse, and Eutaw Springs, North Carolina, and Camden, South Carolina.

A Youthful Pioneer

Smeathers received historical recognition as an Indian fighter and the first settler of Owensboro, Kentucky. In his mid-teens, he constructed a cabin and Smeathers Station (Fort Hartford), a hunters' lodge, on Rough River, Kentucky. Moving west in the early 1780s, Smeathers assisted in the erection of Fort Vienna in 1782 on the Green River in McLean County at Calhoun, Kentucky. During Chickasaw raids, he and other settlers hid in caves dug in the hills, later replaced by a blockhouse known as Vienna Station.

Around 1788, Smeathers married Mary "Polly" Winters, a nineteen-year-old native of Wythe County, Virginia, of Czech-Hungarian-Prussian lineage. While living in Ohio County, Kentucky, he served in the Tennessee militia and, in 1790, as a constable of Tennessee County. He sired John Bate in 1789, Archibald "Arch" Jacob in 1794, and Mary Smeathers in 1795. Two years later, William Smeathers engaged in homesteading up the Buffalo Trace, a bison migration route to Indiana and Illinois on the Ohio River, and founded a port at Yellow Banks (present-day Owensboro), Kentucky. The family moved to the new quarters in February 1798.

Early in the nineteenth century, Smeathers's responsibilities eased with the marriage of his three sisters. In 1803, he served on the first grand jury and rode with the "Corn Stalk" militia, a trained cadre of spies, scouts, and signalmen who warded off Indians. As land commissioner in 1808, he settled Ohio County property disputes. He exonerated himself in court in April 1809 for slaying his sister Mollie's rapist, a drunken bargee named Andrew Norris.

By 1810, Smeathers was a widower. During the War of 1812, he served along the Wabash River under Toussaint Dubois in the Kentucky Mounted Spies from September 30 until his discharge on October 30, 1812. His son-in-law, gunsmith John Berry, husband of Betsey Smeathers, fought under William Smeathers's command. While residing in Indiana in 1810, Smeathers explored Galveston Island and lived for a year at String Prairie south of Bastrop, Texas, before returning to Kentucky. His daughter Betsey died in Indiana about 1818.

Settling a Colony

In the expedition of Stephen F. Austin to the Texas coast in 1821, Smeathers assisted in choosing a site for the area's first Anglo-American colony, a 200,000-acre settlement of 300 American families. Accompanying him were his son Arch and son-in-law John and second wife, Gracie Treat Berry. On the Brazos at present-day Richmond, Texas, he and four other expeditioners built Fort Bend in 1822 and supplied it with venison to feed forces during Apache and Comanche raids. On July 7, 1824, he petitioned the Mexican government for homesteading rights. A reply on July 16 granted him one league for a ranch on the Brazos above the Coushatta Trace, a crossing that Coushatta Indian traders traversed from Louisiana to Texas.

In the Lavaca River Valley, Smeathers and sons Archibald and John Bate Smeathers made a home for the family at the DeWitt Colony. His married daughter Mary, wife of Henry Jones, remained in Indiana. In 1826, John Berry brought his family to Buffalo Bayou (present-day Houston), Texas, and received a land grant in Robertson County, where he worked the land with sons Joseph, Andrew Jackson, and John Bate Berry. In September 1828, William's son, John Bate Smithers, moved to DeWitt Colony near St. Mary's.

Smeathers continued buying and selling property for a decade. In payment for fighting for the Texians at San Jacinto in April 1836, John Bate Berry received 640 acres in Hamilton County, Texas. When Smeathers died on August 13, 1837, at Columbia, Texas, a will dated August 5 left cash to two grandsons, Andrew Jackson and John Bate Berry. Variations of the Smeathers name identify Smothers Creek and Smithers Lake, Texas.

Source
Meishen, Betty Smith. *From Jamestown to Texas: A History of Some Early Pioneers of Austin County, Texas.* Bloomington: Xlibris, 2010.

Smith, Hiram F. (1829–1893)

A printer, trader, miner, and orchardist, Hiram Francis "Okanogan" Smith fostered the apple industry east of Osooyoos Lake in Washington Territory. A Maine native born in Kennebec County on June 11, 1829, he traveled with his peripatetic family to Iowa in 1837, Illinois in 1842, and Michigan in 1845. He apprenticed as a printer's devil in boyhood, joined the staff of the daily *Detroit Free Press,* and, in 1848, worked as a composer for Horace Greeley's New York *Tribune.*

A '49er at age 20, Smith set out for the California Gold Rush. By autumn 1850, he found work in Sacramento newspaper offices. Upon learning of gold prospecting in Rock Creek north of the Canadian border in British Columbia, he migrated north to The Dalles, Oregon, and over the Cascade Mountains to Washington Territory. While traveling the Indian trail to the Cariboo gold strikes in the northwest, he prospected on the banks of the Fraser River along the British Columbia border with Alberta.

Farming and Orchardry

At present-day Oroville in the early 1850s, Smith delivered mail from the Hudson's Bay outpost at Fort Hope, British Columbia, throughout Washington Territory. After establishing squatter's rights, he bought 1,000 acres from Joseph Tonasket, a chief of the Okanogan nation. In 1856, Smith built a log cabin and farm shed. Traveling by showshoes, skis, or pack train from Fort Hope, British Columbia, he transported pear saplings and 1,200 apple trees—delicious, Blue Pearmain, pippin, Gloria Mondane, and winesap—in fifty shoebox loads at a time and planted them across 24 acres. He brought the total to 35 acres with 3 acres of grape vines and 8 acres of peach trees he propagated from pits.

At Rock Creek in 1860, Smith ran pack trains and a freight transport business in the Okanogan wilderness north of Oroville, the place he called home in summer 1860. He became the first resident stockman. After establishing an amicable relationship with local tribes, in 1861, he married the fourteen-year-old daughter of Manuel, chief of the Colville-Okanogan, Mary Manuel "Old Mary" Smith, whom he taught to read and write English. The couple celebrated their union at a large potlatch and earned a reputation for hospitality and generosity.

In 1863, Smith reared daughter Julia and stepdaughter Lizzie and sent them to a Portland convent school. On the east side of Lake Osooyoos south of the Canadian border, he added 200 fenced acres of farming and stockraising to his business. His farm sold vegetables, pome fruit and berries, and dairy products and added a trading post, the first in the Northwest. He stocked dried fruit and mining equipment, notably, his homemade "rock bottom" sluice box for winnowing out fine particles. His ferry on the Okanogan River charged a profitable toll of $4 per wagon, $1.50 for a mounted rider, 10¢ per pig, sheep, or goat.

A Frontier Life

In 1865, Smith served in the territorial legislature at Olympia and, after the achievement of statehood on November 11, 1889, in the Washington state congress. To reach the state capitol at Olympia, he traveled through Canada and boarded a steamer down the Fraser River.

Because Smith's family outgrew living in the trading post, in 1868, he built a freestanding residence. After 1871, he co-founded Washington's first quartz camp at Mount Chapaka and mined galena ore valued as high as $150 per ton. The addition of a customs house in 1880 increased the importance of the Smith property over a 100-mile radius. By the entrance of Washington as a state in 1889, he enjoyed prominence and respect among pioneers.

In 1893, a year after the death of daughter Julia, wife of ranch foreman John Henry "Jack" Evans, Smith reared his grandchildren, three-year-old Ella and one-year-old Robert Evans. Smith divorced Mary, who lived apart from the home, and married Nancy S. Smith of Seattle. In June, his health declined from respiratory infection and dysentery, which a doctor treated in Seattle. At his death from dysentery and pneumonia in Seattle on September 9, 1893, at the Diller Hotel, Mary Manuel Smith assaulted Nancy Smith and prevented the second wife from claiming Hiram's property.

Neighbors and dignitaries revered Smith as a sitting state legislator and chair of the Mileage and Contingent Expenses Committee. He was respected as the "Father of Okanogan County" and "Father of the Washington State Apple Industry." On November 12, 1975, the National Register of Historic Places listed his orchard.

Sources
Couper, Jim. *The Long and Winding Road: Discovering the Pleasures and Treasures of Highway 97.* Surrey, B.C.: Heritage House, 2006.
Watson, Ben. *Cider, Hard & Sweet: History, Traditions, and Making Your Own.* Woodstock, VT: Countryman Press, 2013.

Snyder, Grace McCance (1882–1982), Charles Henry McCance (1857–1926), Margaret Anna Blaine McCance (1861–1940), Margaret Sarah Garner McCance (1830–1905)

An Irish-American brought up on the central Nebraska plain, Grace Bell McCance Snyder wrote of the trailblazers who led a late wave of settlement into the U.S. Midwest. Born in Cass County, Missouri, on April 23, 1882, she was one of the seven children of pioneers Margaret Anna "Maggie" Blaine of Ohio and Charles Henry "Poppie" McCance of Toulon, Illinois. The family responded to offers of farmland along the Union Pacific Railroad, a route made safe from Indian attack after the removal of Pawnee and Ponca to Oklahoma and the Santee Sioux to South Dakota.

In fall 1884, Charles McCance investigated free homestead plots to the west in the Platte River Valley. The following May 1885, Grace's parents became homesteaders in Custer County in south central Nebraska, where they settled three-year-old Grace, her five-year-old sister Flora Alice "Florry," and six-month-old Stella May in a 12' × 14' buffalo grass sod hut. Charles had preceded them three months earlier, traveling with four mules, the family furnishings, and a sewing machine in a boxcar to a claim northwest of Cozad at the boundary between Custer and Dawson counties, Nebraska.

Charles first dug a "soddie" barn, then plowed a fireguard, a wide soil moat shielding their home from prairie fire. Most of the cabin embellishments made use of simple materials, including a clay wall plaster, plank floor, cigar box shelves, and feed sack curtains embroidered with birds. Until the first harvest of corn, onions, beans, potatoes, cabbage, pumpkins, turnips, and watermelons, the McCances camped out in their canvas-topped wagon.

Working for the Burlington and Missouri River Railroad spur line to Cheyenne, Wyoming, in August 1885, Charles helped extend daily runs of twelve express trains from Nebraska and points east to Chicago, Denver, Lincoln, Omaha, Atchison, Kansas City, St. Joseph, St. Louis, and Peoria. By the time workers completed the spur in December 1887, connections with the Union Pacific to Ogden, Utah, and the Central Pacific to San Francisco formed a cross-continent link. Charles's earnings supplied the family with a milk cow and poultry. With his shotgun, he supplemented their diet with Canadian geese, rabbits, and prairie chickens. He used his gun to slaughter a ball of rattlesnakes, but failed to save Tom, the family cat, from coyote attack.

Plainswoman's Work

Grace summarized the pioneer child's life in a memoir *No Time on My Hands* (1986), which her daughter, historian Nellie Snyder Yost, composed from diary entries dating over five years to 1889. The text honored Grace's mother and paternal grandmother, Margaret Sarah Garner McCance, for their toils, which included hauling buffalo chips from the prairie and water barrels from the pond and delousing rooms with a kerosene-soaked chicken feather. In addition to snakes and vermin, Margaret and Charles McCance survived drought, prairie fire, and blizzards and produced five more children—Maude Elsie, Florence Ethel, Esther Olive, Earl Blaine, and Charles Roy McCance.

Sewing became a necessity and an artistic outlet for the McCance women. Grace's paternal grandma, a sickly woman afflicted with respiratory ills, cut legs from overalls to baste to tattered jacket sleeves and hung embroidered flour sack curtains over the girls' trundle beds. In 1888, Grace completed her first quilt at age six. By 1889, while watching the family's cattle before and after school, she huddled in a straw stack and pieced scraps into complex quilts, adorning them with petit point. One project took as many as 85,800 pieces and 5,400 yards of thread.

Grace emphasized the constant struggle to tend vegetables and livestock, gather chokecherries and wild plums, make jam and cheese, churn butter, cure meat, and dry and grind corn for bread. Detailed chores explained how to search out turkey nests, boil cornmeal and hops, and dry cakes of yeast. For laundry use, she spread potato pulp on canvas to harden into starch. To earn money, she hired out for the winter as a domestic.

Second Generation

While teaching school in Lincoln County at age seventeen, Grace encountered Albert Benton "Bert" Snyder, a cowboy known as Pinnacle Jake at the 101 Ranch in Moorcroft, Wyoming. On October 23, 1903, in Maxwell, Nebraska, Grace married Bert and went to live in another soddie. At their ranch northwest of the North Platte in the Nebraska sand hills, the couple reared Nellie Irene, Flora Alberta "Bertie," Beulah "Billie" Lee, and Miles William "Buzz" Snyder.

Grace used native ingenuity to extend simple materials into home necessities. She topped a wire cot with quilts to pad the frame into a couch and copied dress designs from a Sears catalog onto wrapping paper to make patterns for outfits for her daughters. In 1919, the family moved to a house in Maxwell, Nebraska. Grace continued quilting into her nineties and on December 8, 1982, died at age 100.

Much of the McCance-Snyder frontier experience survives in Nellie Snyder's *Pinnacle Jake* (1951) and a young adult biography, Andrea Warren's *Pioneer Girl: Growing Up on the Prairie* (1988). More significant to pioneer history, Grace's quilts in covered wagon, flower basket, cherries, bird of paradise, and grape patterns captured the handwork involved in turning scraps and thread into household beautification. In 1980, the Quilter's Hall of Fame inducted ninety-eight-year-old Grace, "Nebraska's First Lady of Quilting."

SOURCES

Roberts, Elise Schebler. *The Quilt: A History and Celebration of an American Art Form.* Minneapolis: Voyageur, 2007.

Wishart, David J., ed. *Encyclopedia of the Great Plains.* Lincoln: University of Nebraska Press, 2004.

Sowell, Andrew Jackson (1815–1883), John Newton Sowell, Sr. (1770–1838), Rachel Carpenter Sowell (1785–1860s), John Newton Sowell, Jr. (1811–1856)

Lawman, Indian fighter, scout, and farmer Andrew Jackson "A.J." Sowell defended pioneers at the birth of the Texas Republic. A Tennessean of Anglo-Scots lineage born in Davidson County on June 27, 1815, A.J. lived in sight of Andrew Jackson's Hermitage outside Nashville. A.J. claimed ancestry with Highlander John Sowell and Lewis and William Sowell, casualties of the War of 1812. After 1822, A.J. lived in Boone County, Missouri, with his parents, North Carolina-born gunsmith John Newton Sowell, a veteran of the Indian Wars, and Rachel Carpenter Sowell of Mammoth Cave, Kentucky. Siblings included older sisters Rachel Rebecca and Sarah Carpenter Sowell, and younger brothers William A., Lewis Dean, John Newton, Jr., and Asa Jarmon Lee Sowell.

In 1829, the Sowell clan relocated to Gonzales in Dewitt Colony, Texas, and, except for A.J.'s sister Rebecca, remained residents for life. Blacksmith John Newton Sowell, Sr., built a house on a bluff above the Guadalupe River bend near the confluence with the San Marcos River. He outfitted fellow colonists with farm tools and shaped the first Bowie knife from a pattern drawn by Jim Bowie. A.J. and his brother, blacksmith John Newton Sowell, Jr., kept the family provisioned on fish, turkey, venison, and wild honey and pioneered corn crops outside Walnut Springs in Guadalupe County. Their herd of dairy cows provided milk and butter.

In 1832, A.J. had his first encounter with Comanche raiders, whom Sam Houston, a Texas founder, tried to placate with promises of federal rations. In the rough and tumble gun battle against eighty warriors along the Blanco River, A.J. experienced difficulty with his rifle. He suffered an arrow wound and rolled down a riverbank to safety. In 1834, A.J. weathered the harsh destiny of Texians after he rode in vain after an Indian who stole his horse. On June 8, a dispute in Gonzales preceded the stabbing death of A.J.'s brother, 23-year-old William A. Sowell.

Republican Soldier

At age 20, Andrew Sowell fought in the Texas Revolution at Concepción, Gonzales, the Grass Fight at San Antonio, and, on March 6, 1836, the Alamo. He carried an apron full of scrap chain, horseshoes, and iron slugs from his father's forge to load in a small cannon mounted on wheels. The previous year, Texians had rescued the cannon from Mexican insurgents and transported it to the Alamo's garrison along with cannon balls hammered on John Sowell's anvil. As a messenger, scout, and sharpshooter, Andrew ranged as far as Gonzales to supply the fort with beef. He departed so close to the slaughter at the Alamo, that his name at first appeared on casualty lists, which reported the deaths of frontiersmen Jim Bowie and Davy Crockett.

Following the fall of the Alamo to Santa Anna, Sowell, with the aid of thirteen-year-old Asa, who was fluent in Spanish, escorted their family in an ox-drawn wagon to safety in town from the victorious Mexican army. While the Sowells retreated to the Gulf of Mexico in a small vessel, Andrew caught up with San Houston's troops at San Jacinto. John Sowell, Sr., and his son Lewis died at Gonzales early in 1838. The rest of the clan chartered the town of Seguin in August.

At the platting of Guadalupe County on August 12, 1838, A.J. and his remaining three brothers joined the first purchasers of lots on St. George and Water streets. Over plains menaced by prickly pear and rattlesnakes, he volunteered with his neighbors to scout out horse-thieving Mexicans and Lipan Apache led by Flacco. At Plum Creek on August 7–8, 1840, the rangers battled 500 Comanche raiders of Victoria and Linnville on Lavaca Bay, the largest Indian raid in U.S. history. Led by Chief Buffalo Hump, the warriors rustled 3,000 horses and mules, stole silver bullion, and sacked and burned the towns. The pursuers recovered some of the loot and killed eighty Comanches, including a chief shot by A.J.

Ranger and Confederate Rebel

On July 7, 1842, A.J. Sowell married fifteen-year-old Lucinda Smith Turner of Virginia, who produced Asa Jarman Lee, Mary Mildred, Rachel Elizabeth Virginia Bell, Martha Allen, John William, Lewis Dean, James Andrew, Charles Henry, and Albert Marion Sowell. In the free republic of Texas a month later, A.J. and his surviving brothers joined Captain Mathew "Old Paint" Caldwell and Captain John Coffee "Jack" Hays's Gonzales-Seguin Rangers, thirty-nine volunteers and forerunners of the Texas Rangers. On a salary of $50 per month and state-furnished provisions, carbines, and ammunitions, A.J. and his father-in-law, William Suddarth "Billy" Turner, still had to outfit themselves with clothing, pistols, and horses.

While chasing rebel Vicente Córdova toward Mexico to prevent the burning of Seguin, A.J. and the rest of Hays's Rangers led exhausted horses amid thick mesquite and rattlesnakes on the Prickly Pear Prairie near the Nueces River. At the Battle of Walker's Creek along the Pedernales River eighty miles from San Antonio on June 9, 1844, the company's rapid fire of Colt five-shot revolvers in Nueces Canyon against seventy-five Comanche greatly surprised the War Chief Yellow Wolf's 200 braves. The Colt arms works honored the introduction of the revolver on the 1847 Walker Dragoon.

A.J. Sowell's service as a ranger continued on patrol in Hamilton's Valley on the Colorado River and as a scout for Jack Hays in the Mexican-American War of 1846–1848. After building an agrarian life for his family on the Blanco River in 1852, A.J. joined the Confederates during the Civil War, during which son John William died at age eight. While farming and raising livestock, Andrew Jackson Sowell died on January 4, 1883, at Seguin, Texas. Lucinda died three days later. A.J. and Lucinda's nephew, A.J. Sowell, published two frontier chronicles, *Rangers and Pioneers of Texas* (1884) and *Early Settlers and Indian Fighters of Southwest Texas* (1900), recalling A.J.'s gallantry as a scout and courier for Hays's Rangers.

See also Caldwell, Mathew H.

Sources
Harvey, Bill. *Texas Cemeteries*. Austin: University of Texas Press, 2003.
Moore, Stephen L. *Savage Frontier: 1842–1845*. Denton: University of North Texas Press, 2010.

Speed, Horace (1852–1924)

During the wholesale displacement of Native Americans from traditional lands, attorney Horace Speed used his profession and federal powers to improve law enforcement and justice for Indians and settlers in Oklahoma Territory. A Kentuckian from near Bardstown in Nelson County, he was born on January 25, 1852, the third of the five children of Margaret Hawkins of Crawfordsville, Indiana, and Kentucky farmer Thomas Spencer Speed of Bardstown. The family's English lineage dated to a sixteenth-century geographer and historian in London and Oxford.

At age fourteen, Horace left district schools to work for his father. Speed's introduction to jurisprudence began in Indianapolis, Indiana, in 1867, when he clerked for his uncle, John Parker Hawkins, a veteran organizer of freedmen regiments for the Army of the Potomac. Speed educated himself in a law library. In his mid-twenties, he obtained admission to the bar and practiced law with Benjamin Harrison, Cyrus C. Hines, and William Henry Harrison Miller as well as the U.S. District Court office of John Howland. By 1878, Speed opened his own law firm, which he maintained for twelve years.

Homesteading in Oklahoma

At age thirty-seven, Speed moved to Winfield, Kansas, to ready himself for the Oklahoma Land Run. On April 22, 1889, he joined some 50,000 participants in the property grab, which offered 2,000,000 acres to homesteaders, which the media nicknamed "sooners." He opened an office in Guthrie, Oklahoma, where he aided the Cherokee Commission as secretary in charge of settling Kickapoo allotment disputes. His task required supervising white homesteading on the former reservations of Cherokee, Fox, Iowa, Arapaho, Potowatomi, Sauk, Cheyenne, Wichita, Kickapoo, Tonkawa, Kiowa, Apache, Pawnee, Osage, and Shawnee.

Speed predicated a political career on his legal dealings with Indians. To provide eyewitness reports, he traveled in mule-drawn army wagon and ambulance, rickety ferry, and stagecoach to observe the Cherokee in Fayetteville, Arkansas, and the Creek in Muskogee and Cherokee in Tahlequah, Oklahoma. Because of the weakening of the Cherokee blood lines by mixed races and intermarriage with whites, Speed composed opinion pieces for the *Kansas City Times* and St. Louis *Globe-Democrat* claiming full-blood Cherokee risked extinction. He testified before the House Committee on Territories in Washington, D.C., and lobbied for a fair settlement of native lands.

Seeking Frontier Justice

In August 1889, Speed aided a committee in structuring future laws governing wills, corporations, real estate, roads, education, marriage, peacekeeping, violence, and care for the destitute and mentally ill. At the time, he maintained a law practice at the Commercial Bank Building with William Patrick Hackney, a former Kansas legislator, and Henry E. Asp, a noted criminal litigator. Because of the growth of corruption in the federal land office, in December 1890, Speed's former partner, then U.S. president Benjamin Harrison, named him the first federal attorney for Oklahoma Territory. The

At Winfield, Kansas, on April 22, 1889, attorney Horace Speed prepared to join some 50,000 participants for the Oklahoma Land Run.

job involved stamping out realty fraud and land office graft and prosecuting criminals. Over a four-year period, Speed's integrity raised the expectations in pioneers, western Indians, and cattlemen of equal treatment.

In Louisville, Kentucky, on November 1, 1892, Speed married Jessie St. John Adams, who survived only eighteen months. Because of her illness, he retired from the district attorney's office on April 25, 1894, a month before her death. On August 2, 1895, he wed Matilda Woods McAlester of Mahaska County, Iowa. The couple produced Horace Austin Speed, a West Point graduate who later served as a lieutenant in the U.S. Army.

Speed accepted appointment as a special prosecutor on April 11, 1898, in a sensational case against members of a white mob who tortured two Seminole teenagers—Lincoln McGeisey and Palmer Sampson. The vigilantes chained the pair to a tree and burned them to death for allegedly killing Mary Leard, a Caucasian. As a result of Speed's investigation at Earlsboro, a jury indicted forty-nine arsonists and forty-five kidnappers, whose trials continued into 1899. Historians acclaimed Speed for the first conviction of lynchers in the Southwest.

Because of complaints that Oklahoma's governor, William Miller Jenkins, allowed improper treatment of the mentally ill in state asylums, in 1902, Speed rejected an offer from President Theodore Roosevelt to become the state's sixth governor. In 1905, the attorney investigated charges of guardians mismanaging the care of Indian minors. Speed remained a private attorney with an office in Tulsa from 1913 to 1919, when he partnered with Fred R. Righter and returned to the office of U.S. District Attorney for another four-year term. At his death at home on December 28, 1924, the Masons honored his funeral at the First Presbyterian Church.

Source
Hagan, William T. *Taking Indian Lands: The Cherokee (Jerome) Commission, 1889–1893*. Norman: University of Oklahoma Press, 2003.

Stone, Elizabeth Hickok Robbins (1801–1895), Ezekiel Wright Robbins (1800–1852), Lewis Stone (1799–1866), Elizabeth Parke Keays Stratton (1830–1922)

A pioneer to Minnesota and Colorado, Elizabeth "Betsy" Hickok Robbins Stone shared business ventures with her first and second husbands and, in widowhood, invested in Fort Collins, Colorado. Born in Hartford, Connecticut, on September 21, 1801, the fifth of the twelve children of New Yorkers Adah Baldwin and David Hickok (or Hickox), she claimed kinship with English forebears from Stratford-upon-Avon, Devonshire, and Exeter, England. She grew up in Watertown, New York, and learned basic literacy skills.

On February 22, 1824, Hickok married Ezekiel Wright Robbins, a Watertown physician and Universalist minister. In 1828, they boarded a wagon with three-year-old Lucy Jane and two-year-old Washington Irving Robbins and moved 1,000 miles across the Mississippi River Valley to St. Louis, Missouri. Accompanying them was the rest of the Robbins family—parents Lucy Swift and Robert Robbins and Ezekiel's twenty-four-year-old brother, Solomon Harmon Robbins.

While Ezekiel practiced medicine, Elizabeth bore more children—Theodosia M., Ellen M., Walter Scott, Dewitt Clinton, James Madison, and Chester Robbins, the last of whom died in childhood. After 1838, the family settled at Chester in Randolph County, Illinois, where Ezekiel ran a store, R.H. Robbins and Sons. He organized and taught in public schools at Randolph and advanced a political career as the surveyor of Kaskaskia County and, from 1844 to 1846, a delegate to the Illinois constitutional convention at Springfield. After Ezekiel succumbed to a cholera epidemic at Chester, Illinois, on July 25, 1852, Elizabeth returned with Walter, Dewitt, and James to New York.

Second Journey

In a covered wagon in 1857, Elizabeth braved the Minnesota prairie with her second husband, Judge Lewis Stone, a Canadian widower, and his sons, Lewis, age twenty-four, and fifteen-year-old Wallace. At St. Paul, they settled on the Platte River amid hostile Lakota Sioux and near water of questionable purity. With a brother, George Stone, Lewis established the town of Langola north of St. Cloud, Minnesota, where the family operated the Stone Hotel and Restaurant. Elizabeth and her sister-in-law, Mahalia Stone, ran the inn while Lewis served in the territorial assembly and, in 1858, as a town supervisor.

As a result of discovery of gold at Dry Creek, Colorado, some 100,000 prospectors inundated the state in 1859. In spring 1860, Lewis Stone set up a sluice box at a placer mine at present-day Central City in Clear Creek and Gilpin counties. Two years later, the Stone clan departed from a Sioux uprising in Minnesota. In 1862, they traveled to Denver by covered wagon pulled by dairy cows. Along the way, the swaying of the bed churned their milk into butter.

After the Stones opened an inn at Denver in 1864, the clan split in September. While their son remained at the Denver hotel as manager, at the invitation of a military surgeon, Elizabeth and Lewis Stone settled on the Cache la Poudre River at Camp Collins, Colorado, to manage the Mess House, an officers' dining room. By October 1864, Lewis and "Auntie" Elizabeth Stone occupied the site's first private dwelling, a two-story log building on Jefferson Street that contained their quarters and the officers' refectory. The structure survived as the oldest in Fort Collins, an outpost guarding the Holladay Overland Mail & Express route, carrying freight and passengers from Atchison, Kansas, to Salt Lake City, Utah.

The Widow's Survival

After Lewis's death in January 1866, Elizabeth Stone remained the only white female at Fort Collins and the town's first temperance and suffrage worker and midwife. Her inn boarded eight officers, a source of income. She expanded her family on June 1 by welcoming a niece, teacher and diarist Elizabeth L. Parke Keays, the widow of William Keays, and the couple's ten-year-old son, Wilbur Parke Keays.

Auntie Stone invested in businesses that built the town. In June 1866 in a bedroom of the log cabin, Elizabeth Keays founded the town's first school with fourteen pupils and earned $50 per month. As the enrollment grew, the school spilled over to vacant military barracks. The upstairs of Auntie Stone's house served residential students as a dormitory.

After the decommissioning of Camp Collins in March 1867, Elizabeth Stone purchased 160 acres for commercial purposes. As Larimer County's first female taxpayer, she built new quarters at a three-story flour mill on the river and remodeled the officers' dining room into Pioneer Cabin, a hotel and grocery selling milk, butter, bread, and pastries to soldiers and pioneers traveling the 1,121-mile Overland Trail, a heavily traveled alternate to the Oregon Trail. Elizabeth Keays married Harris Stratton and operated a railroad boarding house. On her first Christmas with Auntie Stone, the two ordered a shipment of apples from Salt Lake City and tomatoes from Denver. They held a dinner and dance for residents at which Auntie's stepson, Lewis Stone, taught steps to celebrants.

In 1870, Elizabeth Stone's entrepreneurial skills extended to a brick kiln at Bent's Old Fort in southeastern Colorado, from which she acquired material for Cottage House, a hotel she opened at Camp Collins on Jefferson Street. At age eighty, she relinquished the operation to her married daughter, Theodosia Robbins Van Brunt. Simultaneously, in 1873, Elizabeth invested in the Metropolitan Hotel, a two-story inn that she sold in 1879 at the approach of tracks for the Union Pacific Railroad.

Residents revered Elizabeth Stone for her energy and refinement. She supported local churches and offered the upper story of her mill for Masonic meetings. By 1890, old age confined her to a wheelchair. At her demise on December 4, 1895, citizens proclaimed her the matriarchal founder of Fort Collins. Her niece, Elizabeth Stratton, died in 1933, leaving unpublished until 1964 her memoir, *The Saga of "Auntie" Stone and Her Cabin*.

SOURCE
Beaton, Gail M. *Colorado Women: A History*. Boulder: University Press of Colorado, 2012.

Street, Joseph M. (1782–1840), Eliza Posey Street (1786–1849)

A settler of Wisconsin and Iowa and Indian agent, for thirteen years, General Joseph Montfort Street intervened for the welfare and civil rights of Indians. Born in Lunenburg County, Virginia, on October 18, 1782, to Mary B. "Molly" Stokes and planter and sheriff Anthony Waddy Street, a veteran of the Revolutionary War, he was the last of eight children. Street claimed Episcopalian grandsires—Captain John Street of Bristol, England, fourteen-century Yorkshire knight Thomas Fitznicholl, and a Gloucester native, Captain Christopher Stokes of Anglo-Norman descent dating to the eleventh century. Street's uncle, Montfort Stokes, governed North Carolina from 1816 to 1823.

Street served as deputy sheriff in his teens and wrote for the *Virginia Gazette* in Richmond. He apprenticed in the law office of U.S. Senator Henry Clay and rode the court circuit in Kentucky and Tennessee. At Frankfort, Kentucky, in July 1806, he formed J.M. Street & Company and joined Scots journalist John Wood in editing *The Western World,* a muckraking Federalist weekly. The Street-Wood broadside issued an exposé on a treasonous plot led by Aaron Burr and furthered by the collusion of District Judge Harry Innis to seize New Orleans. The backlash forced Street to fight his way out of an alley, where thugs shot him in the sternum. He responded with a dirk that lacerated his attacker's jacket.

After recovering, in 1807, Street fled over the western border to Shawneetown, Illinois, where he held the offices of clerk of court, postmaster, and recorder of deeds at Peoria. In Henderson County, Kentucky, on October 9, 1809, he married seventeen-year-old Eliza Maria Posey of Fredericksburg, Virginia, whose ancestry dated to fourteenth-century France and to General Thomas Posey, putative illegitimate son of George Washington. Housed at Westwood Place, the Street family included fourteen children—Thomas Posey, Joseph Hamilton Davisse, Thornton Montford, Mary, Lucy Frances, William B., Alexander, Sarah Ann, Washington Posey, Elizabeth "Eliza" Ann, John Lloyd, Anthony Waddy, Sarah Eleanor, and David Street.

The Wisconsin-Iowa Frontier

In 1812, after the Street family moved to Prairie du Chien on the Mississippi River in

Wisconsin on the Iowa border, they initiated Presbyterianism in the region. Street held prayer meetings at his home, where he delivered Sunday sermons. In 1824, the couple's third daughter, Sarah Ann, died at age nineteen months. In August 1827, Governor Edwards appointed Joseph Street to the rank of brigadier general in the Illinois Militia.

On August 8, 1827, President John Quincy Adams, acting on the advice of Henry Clay, named Street the Indian agent for the Winnebago at Fort Crawford near Prairie du Chien, Wisconsin. Taking office in November with a monthly salary of $100, Street, with the aid of an assistant and an interpreter, protected the interests of the Winnebago and other bands—Ojibwa, Menominee, Yankton Sioux—against the American Fur Company's monopoly over the Great Plains and Rocky Mountains. Challenges to his office were whiskey peddlers, government misdirection, invasive trappers, and misinterpretations of Indian laws. Lobbyists sought Street's removal, but he remained in office via reappointments by presidents Andrew Jackson and Martin Van Buren.

Street moved his family to the Fort Crawford agency in southwestern Wisconsin in January 1828. Because of the rapid settlement of the Iowa-Wisconsin border by white pioneers, squatters, and miners, to prevent war, he lobbied for the removal of Indians from contested lands. He encouraged sobriety and trade school training and complained to the U.S. Congress that white traders targeted Indian women for sexual exploitation. His arrest of French-Canadian timberman Jean Brunett for encroaching on Winnebago land and stealing pine logs resulted in a costly lawsuit and fines for exceeding the agency's legal powers. At Prairie du Chien on August 1829, Street attended the treaty signing to end the Winnebago War of 1827.

The Black Hawk War, fought from May to August 1832, involved both Street and his brother-in-law, physician and militia officer Alexander Posey. To shield the Winnebago, Street urged them to remain neutral. Following the Battle of Bad Ax, on August 27, 1832, Street arrested Chief Black Hawk, his prophet White Cloud, and fifty captives and ordered them transported to Galena, Illinois, without shackles.

For the next year, Street negotiated peace settlements with the Fox and Sauk on a strip of neutral ground. He armed with rifles a volunteer cavalry of Sioux, Winnebago, and Menominee. Integral to the treaty of September 15, 1832, Street began building a farm and school building for the Winnebago. His efforts reduced violence, resulting in zero incidents of white casualties. Contributing to family stress in January 1833 was the death of son Thornton at age eighteen.

Advances for Indians

Unfortunately for the progress Street had made, he could not avoid a bureaucratic transfer to Rock Island, Illinois in November 1836 to establish a new Indian agency. He escorted Chief Black Hawk and thirty-one Indian representatives from Illinois to Washington, D.C., for the signing of a 1,250,000-acre land cession from the Iowa nation on the Des Moines River, site of the Indian agency. Street's defense of native rights placed him at odds with white settlers.

In fall 1837, Street returned to Prairie du Chien, Wisconsin, and hired a Missouri crew to build a residence, agency, council house, barn, and blacksmith shop. He joined Fox chief Wapello and Sauk chief Keokuk on a survey of the north-central plains. By April 1838, peacetime enabled Street to purchase a farm and found Presbyterian missions and schools teaching literacy and agriculture. In April 1839, the Street residence in Agency City, Iowa, stood ready for occupancy on a hill overlooking the Ohio River. During a decline in Street's health in November 1839, his sons maintained the agency. A paralytic stroke took his life on May 5, 1840.

Street's son-in-law, John Beach, husband of Lucy Frances Street, completed Street's last efforts at peacemaking, which concluded in a treaty with the Fox and Sauk on October 11, 1842, and stipend for widow Eliza Street. Tribal members gave property to the Street family. John Beach took Street's post as Indian agent. Upon Wapello's death on March 15, 1842, his tribe interred him at Agency City, in Wapello County, Iowa, next to his friend and colleague, Joseph Street. Eliza Posey Street died on February 2, 1849.

Source
Edmunds, Russell David, ed. *Enduring Nations: Native Americans in the Midwest*. Champaign: University of Illinois Press, 2008.

Stroud, Ethan A. (1788–1846), Beden Stroud (1795–1865)

A trader, stockman, soldier, and Indian agent, Ethan Allen Stroud intervened for Texas natives with settlers and the military. A native of Poss in Morgan County east of Atlanta, Georgia, he was born of Irish-American lineage in 1788 to Sarah "Sallie" Phillips and John Stroud, a North Carolinian and father of four. At age 23, Ethan married Nancy Trammell of Clark County, Georgia, a descendent of English settlers of colonial Virginia. The couple produced six children—Teresa, Logan Almaren "Alma," Sampson Malvery, Appleton Mandred, Napoleon B. "Governor," and Mary L. Stroud.

Ethan and his younger brother, Beden Stroud, lived in Chambers County, Alabama, in 1818 and operated a farm and ranch. The brothers, along with their cousin, Ethan Melton, homesteaded in 1836 in present-day Calvert in Robertson County, Texas, where they each claimed parcels of 640 acres in a region known as Stroud Range. In 1838, Beden won election to the Texas Senate to represent Milam and Robertson counties. He helped to select county seats and contributed to bills determining the citizenship of free blacks in Texas. Ethan's son-in-law, physician Augustine Owen of Lafayette, Alabama, followed the family to Calvert in 1839. With residence in forts and security guards, he shielded his wife Mary and children from Indian raids while he farmed a tract in Navarro County.

Indian Wars

Ethan Stroud defended his fields, which yielded corn supplies crucial to the military. On January 16, 1839, at Morgans Point between Marlin and Waco, he fought seventy Anadarko warriors led by Chief José María in a skirmish known as the Battle of Post Oak Woods. A favorable turn for the Anadarko resulted in ten deaths and three combat wounds for settlers. Ultimately, Texas troops forced the Anadarko into Indian Territory (present-day Oklahoma).

At Springfield, Ethan's son, Logan Stroud, established Pleasant Rest, a 600-acre plantation of corn and cotton employing 100 slaves. Appleton Mandred Stroud built a sizeable estate, as did Sampson Malvery Stroud, who worked seventeen slaves on 2,116 acres. In addition, Appleton traded with the Wichita of Waco Village. In 1840, Logan joined his uncle Beden in volunteering with the three hundred-man Montgomery County militia, which, under leadership of Francis A.B. Wheeler, tracked Cherokee marauders. By 1841, Logan moved to the Brazos Falls to live near his father.

Peacekeeping in Texas

After Texas President Sam Houston initiated a moderate policy intending to assimilate Indians into agrarian communities, in July 1842, both Ethan and Beden accepted appointment to the Indian Commission as intermediaries for the Tawakoni, a tribe related to the Wichita. At Grand Prairie west of Dallas, Ethan arranged a treaty between Texians and the Biloxi and Caddo. Peacekeeping prefaced the removal of the Caddo, Waco, Anadarko, and Tonkawa under U.S. protection to the 40,000-acre Brazos Reservation near Graham. The Comanche occupied a nearby reserve of 18,576 acres.

With Beden, Ethan opened Stroud's Station, a commercial outpost on the upper Brazos River. In 1843, his family located near Waco at Brazos Falls, an area rife with malaria from mosquitoes infesting shallow and surface wells. Both brothers moved farther east to Burr Oak Springs in Limestone County outside Fort Parker the following year, where Beden raised livestock. Ethan remained at Burr Oak Springs until his death on August 6, 1846. Beden died in August 1865.

Sources

Campbell, Randolph B. *The Laws of Slavery in Texas.* Austin: University of Texas Press, 2010.

Moore, Stephen L. *Savage Frontier: 1842–1845.* Denton: University of North Texas Press, 2010.

Tabor, Augusta Louise Pierce (1833–1895), Horace Austin Warner Tabor (1830–1899)

A scorned wife turned Unitarian philanthropist, Augusta Louise Pierce Tabor overcame the scandal of her husband's adultery by donating generously to Denver civic and charitable projects. A debutante from Augusta, Maine, born on March 29, 1833, to Lucy S. Eaton and William Babcock Pierce, a wealthy building contractor, she was third among siblings Lucy Elizabeth, Rebecca Foster, Lucy Malvina, Vesta J., Ruth Elizabeth, William Henry, Nahum Franklin, Mary Frances, Lydia Taylor, and Frederic Marshall "Freddie" Pierce. On January 31, 1857, she wed Horace Austin Warner "Haw" Tabor, a Holland, Vermont, native and descendent of Massachusetts colonists from Cambridge and Kelmington, England. The groom, a quarry laborer and gold and silver prospector, had worked as a stonemason for Augusta's father.

To support the spread of slavery to the frontier, on March 13, 1855, Tabor and other members had departed from the Fitchburg depot in Boston with the first of ten expeditions dispatched weekly by the New England Emigrant Aid Company (NEEAC). On the promise of low-cost transportation and temporary housing, 186 pioneer carpenters, farmers, masons, weavers, cobblers, and machinists journeyed to Niagara Falls and through Ontario to Detroit, Michigan. On the 11-day passage, the convoy continued up the Missouri River to St. Louis, where they purchased ox teams to pull their wagons.

Like some 2,000 members of the NEEAC, Horace Tabor journeyed west to a lonely, treeless prairie. Upon reaching Topeka in Kansas Territory, some sixteen members gave up and returned to New England. Settled in a lean-to west of Topeka at Zeandale in April 1855, Tabor and the others agreed to make $125 worth of improvements to the two lots each claimed. While working at Fort Riley as a stonemason to earn money to marry, he served in the 1856 Topeka Free State Legislature until its dissolution by President Franklin Pierce, Augusta's cousin.

Kansas Homesteaders

Arriving at a dugout in Deep Creek along Tabor Valley, Kansas, on April 19, 1857, after a two-week trek on rutted roads, Augusta and Horace Tabor built a 12' × 16' earth-floored cabin featuring one door, one window, and log and soil roof. Their furnishings consisted of a grass-filled mattress, pole bed, trunk, and cook stove, their source of heat during a brutal winter. While they farmed throughout a drought that depleted the Missouri River, in 1858, they produced a son, Nathaniel Maxcy Tabor. Riley County residents elected Horace to the county commission.

Because of a placer gold strike in Denver, Colorado, in spring 1859, the Tabors and their baby joined two fellow "Fifty-Niners" living in tents while traveling over Kansas and Nebraska along the Republican River. The following spring, the Tabors pressed on along the Arkansas River to Golden and Idaho Springs. A frail woman, Augusta suffered privations and near drowning over the three-month crossing of the Rocky Mountains in a covered wagon.

The Tabors settled at Oro City, Colorado, where Horace sold picks, shovels, food, and whiskey to silver prospectors at California Gulch. Augusta joined the Unitarian church and served local miners as banker, postmistress, grocer, and laundress. She sold homemade pies and served regular meals of bacon and soda biscuits. After a return to Kansas to invest in land in summer 1860, the Tabors wintered in Maine. Augusta saved enough of her earnings to retire the mortgage on the Deep Creek property. In 1861, the couple resumed their provisioning of mining camps around Leadville by opening a mercantile at Buckskin Joe, Colorado, which fetched four times the price of goods in Denver.

By the 1870s, Augusta had saved $40,000

despite Horace's extravagance in bankrolling the Tabor Grand Opera House. In 1877, he prospected in Leadville while Augusta operated another grocery store and post office. A $17 investment in prospecting and one-third ownership of the Matchless Mine made the couple millionaires. Horace became known as "the Bonanza King of Leadville." The Tabors grew apart because of Augusta's frugality and simple public appearance and Horace's longing for prominence as half owner of the Clarendon Hotel.

In the year that Leadville's population rose from 300 to 15,000, Tabor won the election to boom town mayor on February 12, 1878. On the Republican ticket, he served from 1879 to 1893 as Colorado lieutenant governor and a month's term in the U.S. Senate in 1893 by appointment of President William McKinley. In April 1878, the mayor hired Irish gunman and Indian fighter Martin J. "Mart" Duggan to suppress the town's stabbings, lynchings, and mob violence. In May 1880, Tabor activated a management squad known as the Tabor Tigers and employed Duggan to stanch a mining strike for higher wages.

An income of tens of thousands per month from the Little Pittsburg Mine and $2,000 daily from the Matchless Mine further enabled Tabor to purchase a flashy diamond ring, newspapers, a bank, and opera houses in Denver and Leadville. After buying a twenty-room mansion on Broadway in Denver in 1879, he strayed from his wife to an Irish-American divorcee, Elizabeth Nellis "Baby Doe" McCourt. He faked a divorce and scandalized the town by living openly with his mistress on $100,000 a month while failing to support his wife and son. According to revelations in the *Rocky Mountain News,* Augusta divorced Horace in 1883 and retained $300,000 of their fortune.

Changes of Fortune

Horace married McCourt at the Willard Hotel in Washington, D.C., and fathered Elizabeth Bonduel "Lily" and Rose Mary Echo "Silver Dollar" Tabor. A son, Horace Joseph Tabor, died at birth in 1888. By conserving her money and investing in real estate and businesses, Augusta became a prominent Denver millionaire and championed charities and city projects. She established the Pioneer Ladies Aid Society, which promoted the stability and well being of women left penniless after widowhood, divorce, or desertion.

In 1892, Augusta maintained the family home as a boarding house while residing at the Brown Palace Hotel, managed by her son. She continued supporting the Unity Unitarian Church until the collapse of her health in 1894. She lived in southern California until her death in Pasadena on January 30, 1895. The Augusta Pierce Tabor Remembrance Society acknowledges her role in Colorado history.

Horace's hopes of the governorship ended in 1888. He and Elizabeth Tabor's security vanished in the Silver Crash of 1893, which cost them more than $9,000,000. The couple and their two daughters moved to a small hotel room. Although Elizabeth developed area mines, the loss left Horace penniless except for his small salary as Denver postmaster.

Until Horace Tabor's death from appendicitis in Denver's Windsor Hotel on April 10, 1899, he nurtured dreams of gold prospecting in Alaska. On March 5, 1935, Elizabeth, widowed and poor, froze to death in a tool shed at the Matchless Mine in Leadville. In 1956, composer Douglas Stuart Moore reprised the Denver love triangle in the opera *The Ballad of Baby Doe,* a stage vehicle for Beverly Sills.

SOURCES
DeArment, Robert K. *Deadly Dozen: Twelve Forgotten Gunfighters of the Old West.* Norman: University of Oklahoma Press, 2003.
Temple, Judy Nolte. *Baby Doe Tabor.* Norman: University of Oklahoma Press, 2007.

Toponce, Alexander (1839–1923)

An unschooled immigrant, Alexander "Alex" Toponce contributed commerce and transportation to westward settlement. A native of Belfort in east central France born on November 10, 1839, he was the son of farmer Peter Lee and Mary Toponce. Alexander and his siblings—Peter, Chester, Julius J., and

Julia A. Toponce—traveled from Paris to the port of Havre with their parents in late April 1846. Aboard a sailing vessel, Alexander traded chewing tobacco to the crew for potable water.

The seven Toponces entered the United States at Battery Park, New York, on June 22, 1846, and made their home in Buffalo. Three years later, Alex fled his home to chop wood and drive a team for the Carmen family in Jefferson County and, in 1851, work at a sawmill near Antwerp, New York. In 1854, he cut logs in a Missouri lumber camp at Tipton for 75¢ each and sawed the wood into lumber for houses.

A Talented Plainsman

As a wrangler, stagecoach driver, and mail rider in Nebraska, Toponce lived the adventures of the plainsman. In his mid-teens, he drove ox-cart trains to Santa Fe, New Mexico, and Walnut Creek, Kansas, and represented a New Orleans slave and mule dealer as a bilingual agent on passages along the Mississippi River. In 1855, he helped initiate the Butterfield Overland Mail routes by which Concord coaches carried freight and passengers between Tipton, Missouri, and California.

When 3,000 U.S. forces challenged 6,008 of the Mormon Nauvoo Legion during the Utah War early in 1857, Toponce rode for Ben Halliday's Pony Express fifty miles up the Platte River from Fort Kearney, Nebraska. In summer, under General Albert Sidney Johnston, Toponce supervised wagoneers for the army to Fort Bridger, Wyoming. Throughout a bitter winter, he foraged for food and wood outside Fort Bridger.

During the Colorado gold rush of 1860, Toponce suffered frostbitten feet while prospecting for placer mines at Georgia Gulch outside Denver. On February 2, 1863, his attention shifted to Montana gold strikes at Bannack and Alder Gulch. Amid hostilities with Blackfoot and Sioux, Toponce helped construct Virginia City and Nevada City.

Resettled in Ogden, Utah, Toponce profited from mineral wealth through freight and stage service from Salt Lake City to gold miners in Helena, Fort Union, and Fort Benton, Montana. Confederate backers ridiculed and harassed Northerners like Toponce until the victory at Gettysburg on July 4, 1863, when people sided more openly with Yankees and abolitionists. In the last months of the Civil War, the wagoneer lost brothers Peter and Chester Toponce to combat.

Food Routes

On January 2, 1864, Toponce sold his Virginia City freight company and invested in deliveries of sugar, tea, coffee, butter, eggs, pork, and flour to Helena, Montana. Operating one of the largest grocery delivery services of the northwest, he negotiated a contract with the U.S. government in April 1865 to carry buffalo robes to Fort Benton and to supply Plains Indians with food up the Missouri River. Before fulfilling his agreement in September, he fought Sioux.

Toponce's business leanings took him into road building, delivering perishables, and slaughtering and butchering cattle. In 1867, he transported eggs cushioned in newspaper to Helena at two dollars per dozen and, in September, drove 6,000 cattle to Virginia City, the start of a freighting venture to Nevada mining camps. By 1868, he invested in seventy-nine wagons and 500 oxen to ferry meat and rail ties to Union Pacific Railroad workers in Beartown, Wyoming. When the Union Pacific expanded through the Sierra Nevada, Toponce supplied 100,000 crossties.

At Promontory Summit, Utah, on May 10, 1869, Toponce witnessed the inauguration of the transcontinental railroad, marked by the hammering of a gold spike. On September 18, 1870, he married an Irish-American widow, Catherine Ann "Katie" Beach Cullen of Salt Lake City, a member of Daughters of the Utah Pioneers. Alexander adopted her children, John Horace Cullen, Rufus Cullen, and Katie Toponce. Rufus died within the year at age five. After the family made a home at Corinne, Utah, in 1873, his mother and siblings Julius and Julia moved to the area, where Alexander won election to mayor and a contract to build fifty miles of road from Corinne to Malade City.

While continuing his transport business and buying up railroad acreage, Toponce ran a cattle and sheep business on Toponce Creek near Chesterfield, Idaho, until selling out in spring 1879 following the death of daughter Katie. He began carrying the mail from Challis to Bellevue, Idaho. By the 1920s, he operated a boarding house. At his death on May 13, 1923, in Ogden, Utah, he left unpublished his autobiography, *Reminiscences of Alexander Toponce, Written by Himself*, which contains details of frontier gambling, horse racing, and cock fighting as well as vigilantism and lynching.

Source
Essin, Emmett M. *Shavetails and Bell Sharps: The History of the U.S. Army Mule.* Lincoln: University of Nebraska Press, 2000.

Wahl, James M. (1846–1939), Julia Ulberg Wahl (1862–1915)

A Norwegian carpenter, James Magnus Wahl led other Scandinavians to Dakota Territory and Minnesota. Born Jens Magnus Wahl on January 7, 1846, he was a native of Storvahl in the coastal parish of Naerøy along the Norwegian Sea and the first of the nine children of farmer Frederick Andreas Jenssen and Johanna Iversen Wahl. He bore the name of his grandfather, Jens Wahl, born in Fosnes, Norway, in 1790.

Wahl's marriage to Anna Sundvold appears to have ended in their teens. In spring 1867, he led sixty-seven emigrants on a nine-week ocean voyage from Christiana to Quebec and by rail in freight cars southwest to Chicago, Illinois. After boarding passenger cars at LaCrosse, Wisconsin, individuals went their separate ways to Mississippi River sites in Wisconsin and Minnesota.

After graduating in spring 1868 from West Salem Seminary at La Crosse, Wahl traveled aboard the slow, difficult Yankton stage route to Sioux City on the Iowa-South Dakota border. The trip coincided with hostilities of Sioux residents of the sacred Black Hills against gold miners and lumbermen. On a two-day journey to Fort Dakota (present-day Sioux Falls), Wahl followed an army road north. Although his companion refused to buy any of Dakota Territory's flat terrain and returned to Wisconsin, Wahl made his home on the Minnesota-South Dakota border in Sioux Falls.

Recruiting Pioneers

Wahl aided Norwegian pioneers in making the move to Lincoln County. On April 23, 1868, he relocated, traveling on foot from Yankton to southeastern Minnesota through waist-high prairie grass. He gravitated to the tree-lined streams of Sioux Valley, Minnesota, where water power promised abundant milling. In June, a wagon train brought 180 Norwegians in 23 clans from Iowa to the valley. Wahl named the new settlement Canton, which he calculated stood on the opposite side of the globe from Canton, China.

After filing for a homestead, Wahl supported local institutions, co-forming 600 Norwegians into the Bethlehem Lutheran Church congregation in 1872, with services in Norwegian and English. He promoted the opening of Augustana College in Canton, where classes met in the former Naylor Hotel. At age 24, he assumed the offices of justice of the peace and probate judge while building Canton's first public school. In 1872, he accepted appointment as Lincoln County treasurer and represented the area in the territorial legislature, which he served for four years.

In an effort to consolidate a community of northern Europeans, Wahl assumed the task of auditor for the Commissioner of Immigration in 1875 and distributed eighteen thousand five hundred promotional pamphlets issued in English, German, and Norwegian. The following year, the commission increased its advertisement to twenty-two thousand leaflets. With the aid of German saloonkeeper Jacob Brauch of Yankton, Wahl scoured Iowa, Minnesota, and Wisconsin for likely settlers.

To the north, Wahl solicited interested Scandinavians in Montreal and Quebec and offered reduced train fares for prospective settlers of the Great Plains. He led Russian-

German Mennonites from Chicago, New York, and Philadelphia to the south of Dakota Territory. He lived to see the community flourish in 1880 from extension of the Chicago, Milwaukee, St. Paul and Pacific Railroad, which carried freight and mail to pioneer settlements of the far West. In 1881, Wahl selected twenty agents to represent the Allen Steamship Company at the Boston office and escort more Norwegian emigrants from Trondheim to the plains.

Establishing a Family

In 1883, Wahl married 21-year-old Julia Ulberg of Valdres, Norway, the granddaughter of Bishop Peter Lund and daughter of immigrants Rangnild Bakke and Andreas Olsen Ulberg, who arrived in American in August 1868. Over the next decade, the Wahls produced seven children. Albert Fredrik Wahl II and Cora Victoria died in early childhood; five daughters survived—Clara, Hannah Rebecca, Alma Carolina, Pearl Julia, and Cora Wahl. When South Dakota gained statehood in 1889, the family resided at a farm northeast of Lennox. Wahl also claimed pioneer son-in-law, Hans Ramstad, who immigrated from Norway at age 23 in 1900 and wed Hannah Rebecca.

On November 4, 1914, Julia died following a buggy accident caused by a car that startled the horses. In old age, Wahl composed a history of Lincoln County, acquiring for himself the title of "Lincoln County's Grand Old Man." After two years of failing health, he became bedfast in November 1938 under the care of Pearl Julia and died on February 2, 1939, at Sioux Falls, South Dakota.

SOURCE
Odland, Rick D. *Sioux Falls*. Charleston, SC: Arcadia, 2007.

Wilkins, John R. (1835–1904), Laura Smith Wilkins (1835–1921), Katherine Carolina Wilkins (1857–1936)

A restless frontiersman, John R. Wilkins moved his family often in search of investment property, notably, an Idaho horse farm run by his daughter, breeder Kitty Wilkins. A native of Indiana of Gallo-German-Swiss lineage, John was born at Annapolis on November 27, 1835, the last of the ten children of Michael Wilkins, Jr., of Buffalo, Pennsylvania, and Virginian Martha Shirk, whose ancestry included Palatinate Germany and Alsace-Lorraine, France. John claimed as ancestors Margartha Bell and Johann Heinrich Hartman, colonists to Berks County, Pennsylvania; Michael and Margaret Wilkins from Baden Baden, Germany; and Casper Sherch, an emigrant from Bern, Switzerland.

At Fort Madison, Iowa, John wed 21-year-old Laura K. Smith of Bangor, Maine, daughter of pioneers Samuel B. and Elvine Savage Smith. In March 1853, the Wilkins joined a convoy traveling 2,000 miles west over the Oregon Trail, arriving in October. At journey's end in Oregon City on the Willamette River south of Portland, on November 29, 1853, Laura gave birth to Elbert P. "Bert" Wilkins. Within a year, the family moved to the far west to Jacksonville outside Medford, Oregon, the birthplace of John Elville Wilkins on September 22, 1855, and of Katherine Caroline "Kitty" Wilkins on May 15, 1857. Leaving the Rogue River Valley in July 1860, the family pushed on south over the roughest stretch of trail to Placerville east of Sacramento, California.

The Wilkins in Idaho

When the Wilkins arrived in Florence, Idaho, in hopes of riches from an 1862 gold bonanza on the Salmon River, they joined a rush of 10,000 carters, vendors, miners, speculators, and criminals. In a time of rising felonies and general disorder, Laura became the first female resident and, on May 28, 1862, the mother of a third son, Samuel Brannon Wilkins. John continued scrutinizing the frontier and constructed the family's first permanent residence at Pataha City (present-day Pomeroy) northwest of Lewiston, Washington Territory. After trying his luck in Sierra Vista, California, in 1866, he bought a store in Ashby (Silver City) in the gold and silver mining district of southwestern Idaho.

The family migrated to Boise in 1867, a year when the city developed its non-military presence in Idaho. Laura opened her own business in October, when she spent an inheritance from her father on eight dairy cows. Spurred by the advance of the transcontinental railroad, in December 1869, John opened Wilkins's City Market on the main street, where a fire on January 6, 1870, burned twelve businesses, including the grocery store. As the state population swelled to 15,000, John opened a meat market at Samuel F.P. Brigg's Livery Stable. His profits financed Kitty's education by the Sisters of Providence at St. Vincent's Academy in Walla Walla, Washington, and the Sacred Heart Academy in Ogden, Utah, where nuns taught her to play the piano. In 1875, Kitty continued her education at Notre Dame Convent in San Jose, California.

The Wilkins Company

Following a silver strike at the Grand Prize mine in Tuscarora, Nevada, in July 1876, the Wilkins family began building the Wilkins House Hotel, which burned on January 31, 1878. After waiting out the results of the Paiute-Bannock War against the U.S. Army, John departed from earlier occupations to partner with daughter Kitty and son John E. Wilkins in livestock in Bruneau Valley, Idaho. Amid lush grasslands, John R. Wilkins initiated a ranch at Mountain Home in spring 1880, when he invested in cows and horses.

The Wilkins stockyard built up to five thousand horses and a crew of forty wranglers. Kitty amassed a distinguished herd of 800 wild mustangs. By June 1885, the thriving Diamond brand stockyard required a 120-acre ranching station, which John erected on the Jarbridge River at Murphy Hot Springs, an artesian well on the Nevada border in Jarbridge Canyon. The region proved so rich in resources that politicians in Nevada and Washington pressed Congress to divide the land between them. In 1887, President Grover Cleveland settled the matter of sovereignty by preserving Idaho's boundaries.

At the ranch in the decade following Idaho's admission to statehood on July 3, 1890, John E. Wilkins managed cattle. Kitty Wilkins took charge of horseflesh, selling up to 8,000 mounts in 1900 to a Kansas buyer. As both stock dealer and auctioneer, she turned Owyhee County into the nation's equine capital. After John R. Wilkins's death on January 9, 1904, in Los Angeles, California, Kitty became Idaho's horse queen by ousting squatters and rustlers. After the murder of her foreman and fiancé Joseph Pellessier on March 16, 1909, she acquired his 159 acres on the Snake River.

Kitty managed the horse marketing and sales division, shipping thousands of Clydesdales, Normans, Percherons, Hambletonians, and Morgans across the U.S., Alaska, and Canada and auctioning semi-broke animals from Union Pacific rail cars. Wilkins Horse Company stock appeared in rodeos and in corrals on the King Ranch in Texas. They accompanied Buffalo Bill Cody's Wild West riders to European exhibitions, British riders during the Boer War, and U.S. cavalry in World War I.

Dubbed the "Queen of Diamonds" for her brand, Kitty Wilkins faced new challenges in the twentieth century, when a squatter won a lawsuit claiming the hot springs. Because of the rise in automobile travel and steam engines and the diminution of horse ownership, she retired in 1920. While leading a parade, she received accolades at the 1934 Boise Centennial. Three weeks after John R. Wilkins's death at Boise on September 18, 1936, Kitty died of heart disease at her home in Glenns Ferry, Idaho, on October 8, 1936.

Sources

Bragg, Lynn E. *Remarkable Idaho Women*. Guilford, CT: Globe Pequot, 2001.
Turner, Erin H., ed. *Cowgirls: Stories of Trick Riders, Sharp Shooters, and Untamed Women*. Guilford, CT: Globe Pequot, 2009.

Wootton, Richens Lacey (1816–1893)

A plainsman, guide, and freighter, Richens "Uncle Dick" Lacey Wootten explored much of the American Southwest. A native of south central Virginia, he was born on May 6, 1816, at Boydton in Mecklenburg County, the first of the eight children of Frances Virginia "Fannie" Brame and planter David Christopher Wootton. He claimed kinship with English-Scots colonists from Bristol and bore a version of a forebear's Anglo-Saxon name, Virginia colonist Richins Brame, son of a seventeenth-century settler of Warren County, North Carolina.

In 1823, the Wootton family moved to Christian, Kentucky, north of the Tennessee border, where Richens planted tobacco and attended school part time. In his late teens, he lived on his uncle's cotton plantation in Mississippi. He ventured to Independence, Missouri, in 1836, a time when the outfitting of Conestoga wagons brought prosperity.

Wootton found a common job for a young man, driving and guarding a ten-wagon convoy north into Sioux territory. Organized by Charles and William Bent and Ceran St. Vrain, the company headed for Bent's Fort (present-day La Junta) in southeastern Colorado. The train passed through Comanche country at Pawnee Fork on the Arkansas River in Hodgeman County, Kansas. For the first expedition, Wootton secured furs and pelts worth $25,000. The trip introduced him to trapping on the Bayou Salado in Hartsel, Colorado, scouting for John C. Fremont, shooting buffalo, and fighting Pawnee and Comanche.

Businessman and Father

Like many mountain men, Wootten married an Indian. At Pawnee Rock, Kansas, on March 22, 1837, his first wife, Monachee Mollee Sun Bow, bore a daughter, Nucassee Maeeonii Jahan Sun Bow. Wootten committed to the frontier life and, in fall 1838, joined a trapping party that tramped the Rocky Mountains and Yellowstone, Wyoming, north to Idaho. He bartered powder, shot, and butcher knives for beaver pelts and buffalo robes and sold the goods to the Hudson's Bay Company in Washington Territory at Fort Vancouver. The 5,000-mile expedition continued south over California and east into Arizona before returning north to Bent's Fort.

Wootton made his living trapping, guiding soldiers, wagoneering, and trading for hides and ponies with Sioux, Arapaho, Comanche, Cheyenne, Ute, and Paiute. In 1840, he hunted buffalo for the provisioner at Bent's Fort, who supplied meals for explorers, pioneers, and soldiers. As the herds thinned to near extinction, for three years, he raised forty-four buffalo calves amid a herd of cattle on 700 acres near the adobe outpost at El Pueblo, New Mexico,

Pioneers chose St. Louis as the best place to find Conestoga wagons, draft animals, and supplies.

on the Arkansas River and marketed them in Kansas City.

Wearied of ranching, in 1842, Wootton contracted to make weekly freight runs between Bent's Fort and Fort St. Vrain west of Gilcrest, Colorado. During the Mexican War of 1846–1848, he hunted meat and scouted for the U.S. Army. On January 19, 1847, he fought at the storming of La Iglesia de Taos and worked as courier and lookout for the government as far south as Chihuahua, Mexico. After marriage to a Canadian-Hispanic-Norman-French wife, Maria Dolores LeFevre of Taos, New Mexico, on March 6, 1848, he quartered his family at Santa Fe, traded with the Comanche, and promoted peace with the Navajo.

With the help of twenty-two herders, in 1852, Wootton drove 9,000 sheep from Colorado to Salt Lake City over the Old Spanish Trail. Moving west along the Carson River on the California Trail, he reached Sacramento with meat for miners. The 107-day trek lost only nine sheep, some to Ute gunmen and duplicitous employees, and netted a payment of $50,000. On return, in late summer 1853, Wootton co-founded Huerfano Village near Pueblo, Colorado, and constructed a stockade and ferry. He witnessed the results of the Pueblo Massacre on Christmas Eve, 1854, when Apache and Ute traders slaughtered twelve Mexicans and kidnapped two small boys.

Herder and Freighter

By the time of Maria Wootton's death in childbirth on May 6, 1855, the family included Jose Manuel, Elizabeth "Eliza" Ann, Richens Lacy, Jr., Lorretta, Frances Dolores, and George. Wootton supported his family from 1856 by delivering goods and equipment in 36-wagon convoys from Kansas City to Albuquerque and Fort Union, New Mexico. He completed the 100-day journey four times in 1857–1858. Following the founding of Auraria (present-day West Denver) in 1858, Wootton passed through the scruffy settlement on Christmas Eve with a wagonload of "Taos Lightning," a home brew fermented from wheat mash, pepper, tobacco, and gunpowder and settled the squabble over what to name the town.

Wootton decided to stay in Denver and invested his fortune in 160 acres. Opposite Cherry Creek, he opened the town's first dry goods store and log inn, location of the *Rocky Mountain News*. He promoted secession from Kansas and town incorporation and supported Southern sympathizers during the abolitionist era. After marriage at Taos to his fourth wife, Mary Ann Manning, a cousin of Dolores Wootton, in 1858, Mary Ann bore three sons, William, Frank, and Joseph E. Wootton, and died in childbirth on March 25, 1860.

At the onset of the Civil War, Wootton sold his Denver business and, on the Fountaine River, started a farm and ranch that failed. He wed Fannie C. Brown and fathered Frances Virginia "Burt" Wootton, who was born in Pueblo, Colorado, on October 17, 1863. After his wife died in childbirth, on June 24, 1864, he adopted Julian Wootton and sent son Richens Lacy, Jr., to school in Kentucky. The young Richens returned west to serve in the Colorado legislature in 1891 and in law enforcement as sheriff of Las Animas County, Colorado, and chief of police of El Paso, Texas.

The Raton Pass

Near home in Trinidad, Colorado, at age fifty, the elder Wooten observed the struggles of Union army transports through Raton Pass at 8,000 feet in the Sangre de Cristo Mountains. Intending to block the Northern convoys, he partnered with farmer and trader George C. McBride and hired Chief Conniache and his Ute band to construct a 27-mile toll road along the Santa Fe Trail to Willow Springs, New Mexico, an area popularized by travelers for its blacksmiths. At the completion of blasting, clearing, filling, and construction of 57 bridges in April 1865, the route cut several hundred miles off the 1,200-mile journey from Franklin, Missouri, to Santa Fe. The new wagon road, in contrast to the Cimarron Route, took seven days to traverse, but offered greater protection from Indian raids.

Wootton's toll-keeper controlled the chain that allowed Indians, Mexicans, and posses to pass free of charge. He collected from whites 3¢ for sheep, 5¢ for cattle and mules, 25¢ per horse, $1 for wagons with one pair of dray animals, and $1.50 per vehicle drawn by two or more spans. At the family's adobe stage stop, Wootton supplied water and served lunch to passengers on the Denver and Santa Fe Stage and Express line and the Barlow & Sanderson Overland Mail coaches. Young people arrived once a week to hold dances.

In 1867, Wootton married a fifth wife, thirteen-year-old Maria Pauline Lujan, mother of Mary Fidelis, Ida Dillon, Lucy Ann, John Peter, Francis "Frank" Christopher, Gerardus, Mary Fannie, and Jesse Joseph Wootton. Because of dimming eyesight from cataracts, Wootton scratched out a living as forage agent for Fort Union, New Mexico. He parlayed quarterly payments for use of Raton Pass from the U.S. military and a guaranteed railroad pension. Builders of the Atchison, Topeka and Santa Fe Railway purchased the road through the mountains in 1879 as the principle route to New Mexico and reached Santa Fe the following year. Wootton negotiated payment for the pass in a monthly salary, free train tickets, and $25 in groceries for Maria for the remainder of her life.

Surgery improved Wootton's sight. In 1890, historian Howard Louis Conard memorialized the plainsman's adventures in *"Uncle Dick" Wootton: The Pioneer Frontiersman of the Rocky Mountain Region*. After retiring to Trinidad in his mid-seventies, Wootton died on August 21, 1893. His widow survived until March 2, 1935, when she lay interred beside him in the Las Animas County Catholic cemetery. The railroad continued the monthly stipend to Wootton's invalid daughter Fidelis, raised the rate to $75, and honored the pioneer's memory in 1906 by naming a locomotive "Uncle Dick."

SOURCE
Keleher, William A. *The Fabulous Frontier, 1846–1912*. Santa Fe: Sunstone, 2008.

Wysinger, Edmond Edward (1816–1891), Pernesa Wilson Wysinger (1843–1893)

An Afro-Cherokee miner, Baptist clergyman, and member of the last U.S. slave generation, Edmond Edward Wysinger made his way from the enslaved South with the '49ers to a more promising life free of racial bondage. Born Edmond Bush in South Carolina in 1816 to a native mother and a freedman named Bush, both of Mississippi, he became the property of a German owner named Wysinger. Traveling by ox-drawn Conestoga wagon, in October 1849, Edmond traversed Donner Pass, Nevada, before crossing into Grass Valley, location of California's two richest mines.

One of the first pioneer slaves from the plantation South, Wysinger arrived on the Pacific Coast in Miwok territory. In the gold belt at Mokelumne Hill outside Placerville on the American River, he joined some 100 black immigrants panning and digging for surface nuggets. According to the *Sacramento Placer Times,* as of February 9, 1850, the average return amounted to 60 ounces per month for each miner.

An Era of Change

Within months of California's admission to the Union as a free state on September 9, 1850, blacks could work claims, but not obtain deeds to them. From proceeds earned at Diamond Mines, Negro Bar, Mud Springs, and Murphy's Camp, within a year, Wysinger amassed $1,000, which bought his freedom. By 1863, California's black miners had earned $5 million.

On July 24, 1864, Wysinger wed 20-year-old Pernesa "Penecy" C. Wilson, daughter of Susan Hines Wilson, a widowed pioneer who had journeyed with husband Alfred Wilson from Wayne County, Missouri, to Miles Creek, California, from March to December 1853. At a farm in Visalia, the Wysingers welcomed Susan to their household and reared daughters Bertha V., Ethel, and Martha Matilda and sons Jesse Edward, Arthur Eugene, James Walter, Jannie, Reuben Carl, Hervey Monroe, and Marion Andrew. The Wysingers persevered in a community that, in 1861, served as a courier route and stop on the Underground Railroad. In a racially charged atmosphere, conflicting loyalties to the Union and secessionists aroused belligerence that, after June

1862, the 2nd California Cavalry at Fort Babbitt pacified.

Challenge and Opportunity

Edmond Wysinger trusted education to elevate blacks from ignorance and prejudice. In 1875, he petitioned the Visalia School Board to build a school for black students. As the population of Visalia increased to 2,800 by 1888, racism continued to target black families. To secure public education for twelve-year-old Arthur Eugene Wysinger, on October 1, 1888, Edmond Wysinger and his attorneys, Wheaton Andrew Gray and Oregon Sanders, contested segregation in Tulare County by Principal S.A. Crookshank.

On January 29, 1890, the California Supreme Court sided with the Fourteenth Amendment to the U.S. Constitution, which supported integration for blacks as well as Indian, Chinese, and Mexican children. After Edmond's death on February 3, 1891, Arthur Wysinger became the first black graduate of Visalia High School. Pernesa Wysinger lived two more years as the mother of a graduate of Visalia's integrated schools and died on January 29, 1893.

The Wysinger dynasty prospered: Arthur and Walter as porters for the Pullman Palace car Company, Reuben Carl growing peaches and grapes in the San Joaquin Valley, Marion Andrew as a railroad worker, Martha Matilda as wife of a blacksmith, sheriff's wife Bertha V. as a foster mother and civil rights crusader, and Jesse Edward as editor of a populist weekly newspaper, *The Western Outlook*. At his home, Jesse supported Edmond's household on Raymond Street in Oakland, California. Grandchildren succeeded at journalism, modeling, education, military service, and farming. After the 1960s, Edmond Wysinger received acclaim as a forefather of the American civil rights movement.

SOURCES
Faison, Glen. "New Chapter Opens in Historical Figure's Civil Rights 'Journey.'" Porterville (CA) *Recorder* (11 September 2008).
Pilling, George. "The Wysingers of Visalia." *Tulare Valley Voice* (5 October 2005): 1, 5.

Young, Zina Diantha H. (1821–1901), William Huntington (1784–1846), Dimick Baker Huntington (1808–1879), Oliver Boardman Huntington (1823–1909), William Dresser Huntington (1818–1887), Joseph Smith, Jr. (1805–1844), Brigham Young (1801–1877), Eliza Roxcy Snow (1804–1887), Emmeline Blanche Wells (1828–1921)

A women's advocate and one of the most studied practitioners of Mormon polyandry and polygyny, Zina Diantha Huntington Jacobs Smith Young, the wife of a missionary and two prophets, aided some 47,600 Latter Day Saints in building a frontier colony at Salt Lake Valley, Utah. She was born of English Presbyterian stock on January 31, 1821, in Watertown, New York, to home health nurse Zina Baker, a descendent of Connecticut colonizers and fourth-century residents of Essex, England. Zina's father, William Huntington, a farmer and veteran of the Revolutionary War and the War of 1812, claimed as ancestors New England patriots and Samuel Huntington, a signer of the Declaration of Independence.

As the eighth of ten children, Zina acquired basic literacy as well as training in housewifery, fiber work, and cello. The Huntingtons suffered the deaths of one-year-old Nancy Dorcas, eleven-year-old Adaline Elizabeth, and, in 1813, an unnamed baby boy. When Zina reached age fourteen, Mormon proselytizer Hyrum Smith added the family to the rolls of a church organized in 1827 by Joseph Smith, Jr, a religious visionary from Sharon, Vermont. On August 1, 1835, Hyrum baptized Zina in a faith adopted by five of her surviving siblings— Oliver Boardman, Presendia (or Prescendia) Lathrop, William Dresser, John Dickenson, and Dimick Baker Huntington. The oldest boy, Chauncey Dyer, rejected Mormon utopianism, but Zina embraced the faith wholeheartedly, sang in the Mormon Temple Choir, and exhibited glossolalia (speaking in tongues), which she interpreted for others.

The Huntingtons liquidated their assets in October 1836 and traveled by steamer from Buffalo to Rochester via the Erie Canal and overland to the church capital of Kirtland,

Ohio, where they bought a stone house and 230-acre farm for $3,000. Protestant neighbors rejected the new faith and promoted instead secular democracy and capitalism as the ideal philosophies for civilizing the Western wilds. Over two winters, frivolous lawsuits against Mormons reduced William to day labor. The Huntingtons survived on a diet of green beans and corn bread. On May 21, 1838, Zina migrated with the congregation to the scene of the 1838 Mormon War in Far West, Missouri. At Adamondeahman in August, her father operated a mill and advanced to Mormon high priest, provisioner, and almoner for the poor.

On May 14, 1839, orders from Missouri Governor Lilburn Williams Boggs forced the Latter Day Saints northeast across the Mississippi River to Nauvoo, Illinois. To protect Prophet Smith, Dimick Huntington rowed the whole distance until his hands blistered. The elder William Huntington assumed the jobs of sexton, constable, and captain of the Mormon Battalion. During a malaria epidemic, at age eighteen, Zina tended her dying mother, who expired on July 8, 1839.

While recovering from contagion and grief, Zina and brothers William and John lodged with Joseph Smith, his wife Emma Hale, and their three small sons. Throughout this period, Dimick Huntington served the Nauvoo community as constable, coroner, shoemaker, blacksmith, and musician in the Nauvoo Legion Band. After a year's mission through Ohio to western New York, Zina's brother Oliver rejoined the family to apprentice in masonry.

The Rise of Polygyny

Zina Huntington's marital experience set her apart from most frontierswomen. Beginning in 1840, Joseph Smith, Jr., who was, at thirty-five years of age, 16 years older than Zina, wooed her with a secret proposal to become his fifth celestial wife. Upon rejecting him three times, she requested that Smith perform her wedding to Henry Bailey Jacobs, a musician in the Nauvoo Legion Band. Because Smith refused to officiate, on March 7, 1841, John Cook Bennett, the mayor of Nauvoo, conducted the ceremony joining Zina and Henry.

Within one month of the nuptials, Smith united with another married woman, Frances Ward "Fanny" Alger Custer, who served the Smith family in her teens as a domestic before marrying grocer Solomon Custer. Shortly, Smith declared that he lived under a heavenly death threat if he failed to lead Zina to the altar. At the time, he committed himself to celestial mates Fanny Custer, Lucinda Pendleton Morgan Harris, and Louisa Beaman as well as to his first wife, Emma, then grieving the death of their 14-month-old son, Don Carlos Smith. Zina agreed to the offer and married Joseph on October 27, 1841.

Zina began a ministry to the sick, sorrowing, and parturient women. In December 1841, Smith married Zina's 30-year-old sister, Presendia Lathrop Huntington. In June 1841, four months after Emma's unnamed stillborn son died in Nauvoo, Joseph contracted a secret marriage to 37-year-old Eliza Roxcy Snow, a devout teacher and hymnographer. Despite Zina's original misgivings about celestial unions, she formed a sisterly bond with Snow and Joseph's other co-wives, which by then included Cordelia Calista Morley, Desdemona Wadsworth Fullmer, Mary Elizabeth Rollins, Sarah Ann Whitney, Martha McBride, Helen Mar Kimball, Lucy Walker, Sarah Lawrence, Rhoda Richards, Fanny Young, Sylvia Porter Sessions, Nancy Mariah Winchester, Amanda Melissa Barnes, Melissa Snow, Catherine Walker, Sarah Scott, Sarah Stiles, Sophronia Gray Frost, and Malissa Lott.

Following Smith's assassination at a Carthage jail on June 27, 1844, during incarceration for treason against the state of Illinois, Zina underwent eternal sealing to Smith, a ritual preserving their relationship beyond death. Brigham Young, who was 20 years Zina's senior, declared himself proxy husband in place of the murdered prophet and the possessor of Zina and her son Zebulon William Jacobs, then two years old. Still living with Jacobs, a witness to the ritual, on February 21, 1846, Zina wed Young, Smith's theocratic successor.

Young had already taken to wife Miriam Angeline Works (deceased), Mary Ann Angell, Lucy Ann Decker, Augusta Adams, Harriet Elizabeth Cook, Clarissa Caroline Decker, Emily Dow Partridge, Clarissa Ross, Clarissa Blake, Rebecca Holman, Diana Chase, Susanne Snively, Olive Grey Frost (deceased), Mary Ann Clark, Margaret Pierce, Mary Pierce, Emmeline Free, Margaret Alley, Olive Andrews, Emily Haws, Martha Bowker, Ellen Rockwood, Jemima Angel, Abigail Marks, Phebe Morton, Cynthia Porter, and Mary Eliza Nelson. From Smith's multiple marriages, Young also united with Louisa Beaman, Eliza Roxcy Snow, Elizabeth Fairchild, Rhoda Richards, and Mary Elizabeth Rollins.

Within a week of the Jacobs-Young union, protesters forced Mormons out of Nauvoo. During the exodus over the icy Mississippi River, the younger William Huntington coordinated the travels of clusters of refugees. The elder William constructed covered wagons and presided over the new settlement at Mount Pisgah on the plains of south central Iowa. In labor on a cot atop barrels during the move toward the banks of the Chariton River, Zina gave birth to Henry Chariton Jacobs on March 22, 1846. She continued to cohabit with Henry Jacobs.

On May 18, 1846, Brigham Young assigned Henry Jacobs to a church mission in Liverpool, England, beginning June first. In agreement with his superior, Jacobs, ailing and penniless, struggled with his nostalgia for Zina as he departed for the British Isles. Zina's brother Dimick departed in July with the Mormon Battalion to fight in the Mexican-American War of 1846–1848. After their father died of

Incarcerated for treason at Carthage, Illinois, Joseph Smith died in 1844 at the hands of assassins ("Martyrdom of Joseph and Hiram Smith in Carthage Jail, June 27, 1844," lithograph by Charles G. Crehen ca. 1851).

malaria on August 19, 1846, Zina lodged west of Mount Pisgah with siblings Presendia, John, and William Huntington.

The Mormon Exodus

During the pilgrimage of Mormons west to Winter Quarters in Council Bluffs, Iowa, in late September 1846, Zina tended her two boys and herded a milk cow and steers. Upon arrival at the big camp in sight of Omaha, Nebraska, William Huntington built a tavern, store, and houses to accommodate nearly 2,500 pioneers. Other Latter Day Saints upgraded the Mormon Emigrant Trail by shifting boulders, cutting undergrowth, leveling riverbanks, and constructing log ferries and wagon bridges.

By December 27, 1847, Young, the "Mormon Moses" and "Lion of God," took the role of church president and colonizer of Utah, the "Land of the Honey Bee," as well as father of Zebulon and Chariton Jacobs. Zina entered the row of tents occupied by two of Brigham Young's other wives, Louisa Beaman and Emmeline Free. Although no legal divorce separated Zina from Henry, she reverted to her maiden name. Departing for Utah on May 16, 1848, with a column of 1,000 Mormons, Zina crossed the Rocky Mountains in the care of her brother Oliver Huntington, a high priest, school trustee, and bee inspector. Dimick Huntington served the company as a translator during negotiations with Utes.

Zina reached Salt Lake Valley in the provisional state of Deseret on September 20, 1848, where Brigham Young had superintended the counties of Davis, Iron, Salt Lake, Sanpete, Tooele, Utah, and Weber for the previous eight weeks. She resided in a wagon before settling in the first log and adobe house that Young built for his wives. The final rupture of her first marriage caused her to sob by City Creek over yearning for Henry and misgivings about the legality of polygamy. After the death of Clarissa Ross Young on October 17, 1848, Zina reared Clarissa's motherless children—Clarissa Maria, Mary Eliza, Phebe Louisa, and John Willard Young.

On April 3, 1850, Zina and Young produced daughter Zina Presendia Young, a subsequent Mormon matriarch. Elder John Smith conferred a patriarchal blessing on the elder Zina and welcomed her to the priesthood. Mother and daughter grew up among privileged wives and twenty-nine children in the Lion House, a major residence completed one block from Temple Square in 1856. Twelve co-wives occupied the main floor. Children bunked upstairs in twenty bedrooms and studied and performed home chores in the classroom, weaving room, laundry, kitchen, dining room, and cellar.

While the colony expanded, brothers William and Oliver Huntington explored to the southeast and into Arizona and New Mexico in search of a site free of Protestant persecution for a religious community of Maricopa and Pima Indians. Upheaval disrupted Mormon utopianism during the Utah War, a conflict between the Saints and an influx of outsiders that extended from May 1857 to July 1858. In a letter from California on September 2, 1858, Henry wrote Zina of his unhappiness and longing for his sons, even though he had wed three more times and acquired two stepsons.

A Leader of Women

Out of commitment to church principles, "Aunt Zina" cooperated with the unconventional household. At evening, she assembled with family for prayer meetings in the parlor. She taught school with co-wife Harriet Cook Young and studied obstetrics under Brigham Young's cousin, Dr. William Richards. As community midwife, Zina delivered the infants of Young's plural mates.

The erection of Fort Douglas east of Salt Lake City extended military protection of the Butterfield Overland Stage, telegraph lines, and mail delivery. However, the separation of Nevada Territory from Utah Territory on March 2, 1862, placed political control of the anti–Mormon Carson Valley in the hands of Protestants. Passage of the Morrill Anti-Bigamy Act on July 8, 1862, further endangered Latter Day Saints households by imprisoning husbands of multiple wives for five years. Polygamist males faced fines $500 to $900 per charge of lascivious cohabitation or illicit union. With the outbreak of the Black Hawk War on April 9, 1865, Brigham Young's colony faced heightened hostilities intended to prevent white settlement of Utah.

To ensure social welfare, Zina coordinated wellness efforts with Young's co-wife Eliza Roxcy Snow, who established the Latter Day Saints Relief Society in 1866. The following year, Zina blessed son Chariton when he departed on a 3-year mission to England and undertook her own mission to Mormon colonies throughout Utah to form relief societies. By 1868, more than 68,000 Saints had completed the route to Salt Lake City, where Brigham Young maintained dictatorial control via manipulation and intimidation of male elders. The influx imported female Mormons who denounced plural marriage and, led by suffragist Emmeline Blanche Woodward Wells, demanded voting rights, which Utah women obtained in 1870.

In 1872, Zina raised funds for the two-story Deseret Hospital and chaired its board of female directors, which hired primarily women physicians and funded treatment of the poor. She led the school of obstetrics, served the Salt Lake City temple as matron, and championed the relief society's nursing school, which taught first aid, midwifery, hygiene, communicable disease, and invalid care and nutrition. Pioneer women received free tuition in exchange for treating settlers of rural Utah at a reduced charge.

Under Brigham Young's 1876 directive, Zina led the Deseret Silk Association, a women's project associated with abolitionism. By propagating mulberry trees and silkworms, harvesting their output, and spinning silk thread, the women replaced slave-grown cotton in Mormon wardrobes. Another order from Brigham Young appointed Zina and Emmeline Blanche Wells as supervisors of grain storage. In summer 1879, two years after Brigham Young's death from a burst appendix, Zina traveled to Hawaii to recuperate from exhaustion and to assist in the introduction of Mormonism to the Pacific islands.

At age 59, Zina allied with Eliza Snow to reform the Mormon Relief Society and create auxiliaries for children and girls. In 1884, Zina and her daughter labored in the newly dedicated temple at Logan, Utah. As means of consoling and healing troubled people, Zina organized washing, anointing, prayer circles, and rebaptism, a ritual promoting rededication of the spirit, wellness, and confession of sin.

In collaboration with Emmeline Wells, Zina, her daughter, and stepdaughters Maria and Phebe Young promoted temperance as an adjunct of woman's full citizenship and refuted disinformation about Mormon wives. At age seventy, the elder Zina accepted the vice presidency of the International Council of Women, the first global women's human rights agency. In the five years following Utah's admission to the Union in 1896, Zina championed gender equality until her death on August 28, 1901.

Sources

Newton, Honey M. *Zion's Hope: Pioneer Midwives and Women Doctors in Utah.* Springville, UT: Cedar Fort, 2013.

Turner, John G. *Brigham Young: Pioneer Prophet.* Cambridge: Harvard University Press, 2012.

Chronology of Pioneer Achievements

1544   Friar Juan de Padilla, a military chaplain under Francisco de Coronado, establishes a mission to Indians at Quivira, Texas.

1780s   Afro-French fur trader Jean Baptiste Point du Sable builds the first permanent residence at Chicago.

April 19, 1820   At Oahu, Hiram and Sybil Moseley Bingham open the first Christian mission in Hawaii.

November 1, 1825   William Ashley, Robert Campbell, and Jedediah Smith set out to trade at the first Rocky Mountain rendezvous, held at Willow Valley, Wyoming.

September 21, 1832   The U.S. negotiates the Black Hawk purchase of former Winnebago, Fox, and Sauk lands for $640,000.

March 3, 1836   Mathew Caldwell signs the Texas Declaration of Independence.

1838   Pierre Bottineau guides French, Scots, and Swiss pioneers to a Francophone community in the Red River Valley, North Dakota.

1838   Mathew Caldwell co-founds Walnut Branch (present day Seguin), Texas.

1840   Pierre Bottineau co-founds St. Paul Catholic Church in St. Paul, Minnesota.

August 7–8, 1840   At Linnville and Victoria, Texas, 500 Comanche inflict the largest Indian raid in U.S. history.

November 4, 1841   The Bartleson-Bidwell Party becomes the first immigrant train to reach California.

1843   Some 1,000 pioneers cross the frontier on the way to Oregon Territory.

May 2, 1843   Settlers create Oregon's first provisional government.

September 20, 1843   Joseph Ballinger Chiles blazes the California Trail, a turn-off from the Oregon Trail over the Sierra Nevada to California.

June 9, 1844   At the Battle of Walker's Creek, Texas, Captain Jack Hays's Gonzales-Seguin Rangers introduce the Colt five-shot revolver against seventy-five Comanche.

June 27, 1844   An anti–Mormon mob assassinates prophet Joseph Smith in a jail cell in Carthage, Illinois.

1845   At Shasta, explorer Pierson Barton Reading becomes the first white settler of northern California.

summer 1845   Washington State's first black pioneer, George Washington Bush and his party establish a community at Bush Prairie, present-day Tumwater.

May 1846   The foray north of the Columbia River by George Washington Bush and Michael T. Simmons helps to force the British to relinquish claims to present-day Washington.

July 9, 1846   American settlers, led by William Brown Ide, take California from Mexico.

February 27, 1847   The first rescue team reaches the Donner Party at Donner Pass near Truckee, California.

December 27, 1847   Brigham Young takes the role of Mormon president and colonizer of Utah.

January 24, 1848   The discovery of gold nuggets at Sutter's Mill in Coloma, California, starts a gold rush.

June 1848   Joseph Libbey Folsom reserves land for San Francisco's Presidio.

Chronology of Pioneer Achievements

1849   On the Sacramento River, Joseph Ballinger Chiles establishes California's first flourmill.
February 2, 1849   Eliza Wood Farnham recruits single women to establish families in California.
summer 1850   Virulent cholera epidemic, carried up the Mississippi by steamboats, ravages wagon trains.
September 16, 1850   In the canvas and wood storefront of Lewis and Maurice Franklin in San Francisco, Jews attend the first observances of Rosh Hashanah and Yom Kippur in the West.
1851   William Tell Coleman rids San Francisco of criminals by heading local vigilantes.
April 1851   John A.N. Ebbetts explores an alternate route to California over the Sierra Nevada.
July 1, 1852   Pierre Bottineau sets the boundaries of Osseo, Minnesota.
1853   The Emigrant Aid Society begins recruiting pioneers to settle Kansas Territory.
   In one year's time, 27,500 settlers take the Overland Trail west.
1855   The Butterfield Overland Stage line initiates routes from Missouri to California.
1855–1856   During war with the Nisqually, Puyallup, and Duwamish, George Washington Bush builds a fort at Bush Prairie, Washington.
August 5, 1858   Canadian reformer Julia Archibald Holmes becomes the first female to scale Pike's Peak.
September 25, 1858   Pierre Bottineau locates nine salt springs on the Wild River in Minnesota.
fall 1858   The Pike's Peak Gold Rush generates one of the nation's greatest migrations.
1860   Erasmus Darwin French begins operating the Darwin mines in Death Valley near Bodie, California.
   The total emigration to California, Oregon, and Utah reaches 15,000 per year, for a total of 300,000 between 1840 and 1860.
March 16, 1860   In the Santa Rita Mountains, Arizona, Pinal Apache kidnap Larcena Ann Pennington, who escapes after sixteen days on the trail.
December 18, 1860   Jack Cureton's Texas Rangers recover Comanche captive Cynthia Ann Parker.
September 1862   Pierre Bottineau summons help to Fort Abercrombie, North Dakota, which Sisseton Sioux besieged.
November 1, 1862   Pierre Bottineau and son Daniel guide James Liberty Fisk's Northern Overland Expedition over a proposed railroad route to Walla Walla, Washington.
1863   At Oroville, Washington, Hiram F. Smith opens the first trading post in the Northwest.
October 2, 1863   Pierre Bottineau interprets for the Ojibwa during negotiation of the Old Crossing Treaty.
July 12, 1864   Oglala Sioux chief Ottawa kidnaps Fanny Wiggins Kelly and holds her until the following December 12.
May 1866   At Franklin, Peter Lahti founds Minnesota's first Finnish settlement.
June 6, 1866   Charles Goodnight and Oliver Loving blaze the Goodnight-Loving Trail.
summer 1867   Jesse Chisholm initiates the Chisholm Trail from Red River, Texas, through Abilene, to Kansas City.
May 17, 1868   The first pioneering transports of Japanese laborers leaves Yokohama for Honolulu, Hawaii.
1869   Pierre Bottineau leads Jay Cooke's party over the proposed route of the Northern Pacific Railroad, which linked the Twin Cities with the Red River Valley.
May 10, 1869   A golden spike joined the Central Pacific and Union Pacific rail lines at Promontory, Utah.
October 24, 1871   Blacksmith John Goller protests the hanging of seventeen Chinese immigrants from his roof in Los Angeles.
1872–1874   During the slaughter of 4.5 million buffalo, two-thirds were killed for their hides alone.
1874   The Woman's Occidental Board of Foreign Missions begins rescuing enslaved Chinese girls in San Francisco.

Chronology of Pioneer Achievements

1875 James George Bell founds Obed, present-day Bell, California.
1876 Cowboy Frank Henry Maynard pens lyrics to the "The Dying Cowboy," also known as "The Streets of Laredo."
May 1876 Pierre Bottineau recruits 119 French Canadians to Hennepin and Ramsey counties, Minnesota.
August 30, 1876 The Society for the Prevention of Cruelty to Children assists the Presbyterian Chinese Mission Home in rescuing girls from San Francisco brothels.
March 21, 1877 A crisis in farm sustainability precedes formation of the National Farmers' Alliance.
spring 1878 George Algernon Cowles enters the raisin business in San Diego County, California.
September 29, 1879 Utes inflict the Meeker Massacre at Milk Creek, Colorado, killing fourteen cavalrymen.
1880 Albert Anton Booth establishes Edna, North Dakota.
1881 In Death Valley on the California-Nevada boundary, William Tell Coleman pioneers the borax industry.
1884 At Wailuku, Maui, Sister Marianne Cope founds Malulani Hospital, Hawaii's first general hospital.
1887 James George Bell co-founds Occidental College in Boyle Heights, California.
October 1, 1888 Edmond Edward Wysinger presses suit to integrate the white school of Tulare County, California.
1889 William Owen Bush becomes the first black representative to the Washington Territorial Legislature.
April 1889 William Owen Bush co-founds St. Peter Hospital in Olympia, Washington.
1890 William Owen Bush co-founds Washington State College at Pullman.
1891 Mormon pioneer Zina Hutchinson Young accepts the vice presidency of the International Council of Women, the first global women's human rights agency.
summer 1893 Luna Kellie advocates the construction of the Gulf and Inter-State Railway, a north-south transcontinental railroad from Canada to Galveston, Texas.
1897 Ellen Eliza Carter Booth raises funds to erect a church at Rogers, North Dakota.
1899 Historians acclaim investigator Horace Speed for the first conviction of lynchers in the Southwest.
1906 Ezra Meeker memorializes the Oregon Trail by reversing his wagon trip to Washington. Territory and plotting monuments along an 8,000-mile route in Boise, Idaho, and the Continental Divide in Wyoming.
1907 Joseph William Parmley promotes the Yellowstone Trail, a network of scenic roads across the plains states.
spring 1916 Homesteader Nellie Neal becomes the first female contract provisioner for the Alaska Central Railway.

Appendices

A. Ethnicity

Heritage	Occupation	Origin	Destination
African			
Wysinger, Pernesa W. (1843–1893)	housewife	Wayne County, MO (1853)	Visalia, CA (1864–1893)
Afro-Cherokee			
Brown, Clara (1800–1885)	cook, launderer, nurse, recruiter	Gallatin, KY (1856)	Leavenworth, KS (1856–1859) Denver, CO (1859–1885)
Wysinger, Edmond E. (1816–1891)	miner	South Carolina (1849)	Visalia, CA (1849–1891)
Afro-English			
Mitchell, Eliza V. (1809–1881)	merchant	Cape Town, South Africa (1836)	Florence, NE (1852–1881)
Afro-French			
Point du Sable, Jean (ca. 1745–1818)	farmer, trader	Chicago, IL (1800)	St. Charles, MO (1800–1818)
Anglo-Dutch			
Reed, Emaline Cobb (1825–1890)	housewife	Walker County, AL (1837)	Bell County, TX (1837–1890)
Anglo-French			
Street, Eliza Posey (1786–1849)	housewife	Henderson, KY (1809)	Prairie du Chien, WI (1812–1835, 1837–1842)
Anglo-German			
Goodnight, Charles (1836–1929)	Texas Ranger, rancher	Macoupin, IL (1846)	Goodnight, TX (1846–1929)
Goodnight, Elija (1831–1929)	soldier, rancher	Macoupin, IL (1846)	Goodnight, TX (1846–1929)
Lawing, Nellie Trosper (1873–1956)	innkeeper, hunter, postmaster	Buchanan, MO (1901)	Cripple Creek, CO (1903–1914) Seward, AK (1915–1956)
Monk, Hank (1826–1883)	stage driver	Waddington, NY (1852)	Sacramento, CA (1852–1857) Carson City, NV (1857–1883) Deadwood, ND (1881)
Anglo-German-Irish-Anglo-Irish			
Adair, Cornelia W. (1837–1921)	investor, rancher	Philadelphia, PA (1874)	Palo Duro (1874–1921)
Rice, James Stephen (1846–1939)	orchardist	Cleveland, OH (1877)	Tustin, CA (1878–1939)
Simmons, Michael T. (1814–1867)	millwright, Indian agent, postmaster	Nodaway, MO (1844)	Tumwater, WA (1845–1867)
Anglo-Irish-Scots-Polish			
Lewis, Martha Reed (1838–1923)	innkeeper	Springfield, IL (1846)	San Jose, CA (1847–1874)
Reed, James Frazier, Jr. (1841–1901)	land speculator, miner	Springfield, IL (1846)	San Jose, CA (1847–1901)
Anglo-Irish-Scots-Welsh-Norman-French			
Coleman, William Tell (1824–1893)	shipper, borax miner, vigilante	St. Louis, MO (1849)	San Francisco, CA (1849–1893) Columbus Marsh, NV (1871–1888)

Appendix A. Ethnicity

Heritage	Occupation	Origin	Destination
Anglo-Irish-Welsh			
Belshaw, Candace M. (1826–1892)	housewife	Lake County, IN (1853)	Eugene, OR (1853–1892)
McCarty, Jonathan W. (1833–1900)	farmer, merchant, mailman	Lake County, IN (1853)	Pierce County, WA (1853–1870) Seattle, WA (1870–1900)
Anglo-Norman			
Backenstoe, Virginia E. (1833–1921)	insurer	Springfield, IL (1846)	San Jose, CA (1847–1874)
Reed, Margret Keyes (1814–1861)	housewife	Springfield, IL (1846)	San Jose, CA (1847–1861)
Street, Joseph M. (1782–1840)	Indian agent	Shawneetown, IL (1812)	Prairie du Chien, WI (1812–1835, 1837–1842)
Anglo-Scots			
Caldwell, Mathew (1798–1842)	community builder, sheriff, Texas Ranger	Gasconade, MO (1831)	Gonzalez, TX (1831–1842)
Chisum, John Simpson (1824–1884)	rancher	Hardeman, TN (1866)	Paris, TX (1837)
French, Erasmus D. (1822–1902)	physician, explorer, rancher, miner	Albion, MI (1845)	Fort Tejon, CA (1847–1851) San Jose, CA (1848–1860) Darwin, CA (1860–1865) Baja, CA (1894–1902)
Lilly, Benjamin Vernon (1856–1936)	hunter, knife maker, bounty hunter	Jackson, MS (1868)	Mer Rouge, LA (1868–1901) Big Thicket, TX (1904–1908) Gila, NM (1908–1916) Quemado, AZ (1916–1926) Pleasanton, NM (1931–1936)
Sowell, Andrew Jackson (1815–1883)	farmer, Indian fighter, ranger	Boone County, MO (1829)	Gonzales, TX (1829–1883)
Sowell, John Newton, Jr. (1811–1856)	blacksmith, hunter, ranger	Boone County, MO (1829)	Gonzales, TX (1829–1856)
Sowell, John Newton, Sr. (1770–1838)	blacksmith, armorer	Boone County, MO (1829)	Gonzales, TX (1829–1838)
Sowell, Rachel C. (1785–1860s)	housewife	Boone County, MO (1829)	Gonzales, TX (1829–1860s)
Wootton, Richens L. (1816–1893)	guide, freighter, Indian fighter, road builder	Christian, KY (1836)	Independence, MO (1836) Bent's Fort, CO (1836–1847) Taos, NM (1847–1858) Denver, CO (1858–1893)
Anglo-Welsh			
Rice, Coralinn Barlow (1849–1919)	singer	Cleveland, OH (1877)	Tustin, CA (1878–1919)
Assiniboine-Ojibwa			
Bottineau, Pierre (1817–1895)	guide, interpreter, negotiator with Indians	Winnipeg, Manitoba (1832)	St. Paul, MN (1840–1852) Osseo, MN (1852–1877) Red Lake Falls, MN (1877–1895)
Canadian			
Lee, Jason (1803–1845)	missionary, educator, territorial organizer	Stanstead, Quebec (1833)	St. Paul, OR (1833–1844)
Stone, Lewis (1799–1866)	innkeeper, miner, politician	St. Paul, MN (1857)	Denver, CO (1862–1864) Fort Collins, CO (1864–1866)
Cherokee-Scots			
Chisholm, Jesse (1806–1868)	trader, guide, interpreter	Arkansas (1820s)	Hughes County, OK (1820s, 1858–1861, 1868) Tehuacana Creek, TX (1833–1858) Wichita, KS (1861–1868)
Chinese			
Chin, Ah Yane (1869–?)	interpreter	China (1874)	San Francisco, CA (1874–?)
Wu, Tien Fu (1861–ca. 1940s)	interpreter	Canton, China (1876)	San Francisco, CA (1876–ca. 1940s)

Appendix A. Ethnicity

Heritage	Occupation	Origin	Destination
Czech-Hungarian-Prussian			
Smeathers, Mary Polly (1769–1810)	housewife	Wythe County, VA (1788)	Owensboro, KY (1797–1810)
Danish			
Lassen, Peter (1800–1859)	rancher, sawyer, prospector, recruiter, millwright	Farum, Denmark (1830)	San Jose, CA (1840–1843) Rancho Bosquejo, CA (1844–1850) Honey Lake, CA (1855–1859)
Danish-Russo-Norman-Scots-Irish			
Macy, Lucinda Polk (1807–1872)	innkeeper	Washington, IN (1850)	El Monte, CA (1851–1852) Los Angeles, CA (1852–1872)
Dutch-English			
Ebbetts, John A.N. (ca. 1815–1854)	merchant, explorer, diarist	New York, NY (1849)	San Francisco, CA (1849–1854)
Farnham, Eliza Wood (1815–1864)	reformer, writer, rancher	New York, NY (1849)	Santa Cruz, CA (1849–1856) Stockton, CA (1859–1862)
Dutch-Friesian			
Bonnema, Harmen H. (1827–1892)	farmer, merchant	Harlingen, Friesland (1853)	New Amsterdam, WI (1855–1892)
Bonnema, Oepke H. (1825–1895)	lumberman, town builder, barkeep	Harlingen, Friesland (1853)	New Amsterdam, WI (1853–1895)
Haagsma, Broer Baukes (1831–1907)	teacher, accountant, consul	Harlingen, Friesland (1853)	New Amsterdam, WI (1853–1907)
East Indian-Irish			
Bush, George Washington (ca. 1779–1863)	community builder, farmer, stockman	Jackson, MO (1844)	Tumwater, WA (1845–1866)
English			
Belshaw, George, Jr. (1815–1893)	farmer, diarist	Lake County, IN (1853)	Eugene, OR (1853–1893)
Bingham, Hiram (1789–1869)	missionary, lexicographer	Hartford, CT (1819)	Honolulu, HI (1820–1840)
Bingham, Sybil Moseley (1792–1848)	teacher, midwife, seamstress	Hartford, CT (1819)	Honolulu, HI (1820–1840)
Booth, Albert Anson (1850–1914)	farmer, rancher, timberman	Syracuse, NY (1869)	Fond du Lac, WI (1869–1872) Edna, ND (1879–1914)
Bridger, Jim (1803–1881)	trapper, guide, scout	Richmond, VA (1822)	Fort Bridger, WY (1842–1865)
Bunker, Harriet J. (1800–1895)	fund raiser, activist	Massachusetts (1852)	San Francisco, CA (1852–1895)
Carr, Byron Oscar (1835–1913)	railroad manager, banker	Concord, NY (1872)	Truckee, CA (1872–1880s) San Francisco, CA (1880s–1891) Lemoore, CA (1894–1900) Seattle, WA (1900–1913)
Carr, Sarah Pratt (1850–1935)	missionary, writer, activist, librettist	Freeport, ME (1852)	San Francisco, CA (1852–1867, 1913–1935) Carlin, NV (1867–1872) St. Helena, CA (1883–1900) Seattle, WA (1900–1913) Los Angeles, CA (1913–1935)
Cheesman, David W. (1822–1884)	attorney, memoirist, U.S. Mint treasurer	Washington, IN (1850)	El Monte, CA (1851–1852) Los Angeles, CA (1852–1884)
Cheesman, Urania K. (1828–1916)	housewife	Washington, IN (1850)	El Monte, CA (1851–1852) Los Angeles, CA (1852–1884)
Chiles, Joseph B. (1810–1885)	rancher, miller, distiller, ferryman	Jackson County, MO (1841)	Napa Valley, CA (1843–1885)
Cowles, George A. (1836–1887)	raisin grower, financier, horse breeder	Hartford, CT (1878)	Cowlestown, CA (1878–1887)
Dale, Frank (1849–1930)	judge, financier	Somonauk, IL (1871)	Wichita, KS (1871–1889) Guthrie, OK (1889–1930)

Appendix A. Ethnicity

Heritage	Occupation	Origin	Destination
Dale, Martha Wood (1859–1930)	library builder, activist	Oswego, NY (1879)	Wichita, KS (1879–1889) Guthrie, OK (1889–1930)
Dyer, Leigh Richmond (1849–1902)	rancher	Madison, TN (1867)	Belknap, TX (1867) Palo Duro, TX (1876)
Goodnight, Mary Ann D. (1839–1926)	teacher	Hickman, KY (1870)	Pueblo, CO (1870–1871) Palo Duro, TX (1871–1887)
Farnham, Thomas J. (1804–1848)	attorney, writer, freighter	Peoria, IL (1838)	Willamette, OR (1839) Santa Cruz, CA (1839–1848)
Folsom, Joseph L. (1817–1855)	soldier, investor	West Point, NY (1846)	San Francisco, CA (1847–1855)
Goddard, George H. (1817–1906)	cartographer, artist, surveyor, civil engineer	Bristol, England (1850)	San Francisco, CA (1850–1906)
Goodell, Henry Martin (1843–1905)	ferryman, justice of the peace	Vermilion, OH (1853)	Lynden, WA (1884–1905)
Goodell, Jotham W. (1809–1859)	minister	Vermilion, OH (1851)	Portland, OR (1851–1859)
Goodell, Nathan E. (1839–1886)	merchant	Vermilion, OH (1851)	Skagit River, OR (1879)
Goulding, William R. (1805–1865)	surgeon, diarist instrument maker	York, England (1805)	San Francisco (1849–1850)
Holmes, James Henry (1833–1907)	journalist, soldier, territorial secretary	Emporia, KS (1858)	Taos (1858–1863)
Huntington, Dimick B. (1808–1879)	constable, coroner, interpreter	Watertown (1836)	Salt Lake City, UT (1848–1879)
Huntington, Oliver B. (1823–1909)	priest, explorer, missionary	Watertown, NY (1836)	Springville, UT (1852–1909)
Huntington, William (1784–1846)	miller, soldier, sexton, constable	Watertown, NY (1836)	Mount Pisgah, IA (1846)
Huntington, William D. (1818–1887)	explorer, constable, taverner, mailman, miner, musician	Watertown, NY (1836)	Springville, UT (1852–1887)
Ide, William Brown (1796–1852)	recruiter, state president, farmer surveyor, judge, ferryman	Rutland, MA (1845)	Sutter's Fort, CA (1845–1852)
Illingworth, William H. (1844–1893)	photographer	Leeds, England (1845)	Fort Benton, MT (1866)
Isbell, Isaac Chauncy (1800–1886)	prospector, rancher, innkeeper, surgeon	Greenbush, IL (1846)	Santa Clara, CA (1846–1850; 1861–1886) Cancon, TX (1850–1861)
Isbell, Olive Mann (1824–1899)	nurse, seamstress, rancher, teacher	Greenbush, IL (1846)	Santa Clara, CA (1846–1850; 1861–1886) Cancon, TX (1850–1861)
Judson, George (1860–1891)	surveyor, school builder	Vermilion, OH (1853)	Bellingham, WA (1886)
Judson, Holden Allen (1827–1899)	dairier, grocer, postmaster, mayor	Vermilion, OH (1853)	Claquato, WA (1853–1858) Whidbey, WA (1866–1899)
Judson, Phoebe Goodell (1831–1926)	educator, memoirist, foster mother	Vermilion, OH (1853)	Claquato, WA (1853–1858) Whidbey, WA (1866–1926)
Kellie, Luna Sanford (1857–1940)	farmer, editor, songwriter, grocer, activist	Rockford, IL (1871)	Adams County, NE (1877–1884) Hartwell, NE (1884–1901)
Key, Ambrose W. (1829–1908)	orchardist, farmer, tanner, sawyer, freighter	Crawfordsville, IN (1838)	Louisa County, IA (1838–1860)
Key, George (1795–1864)	farmer, trader, blacksmith	Crawfordsville, IN (1836)	Louisa County, IA (1836–1861)
Key, Mary Jones G. (1835–1927)	housewife	Louisa County, IA (1860)	Navasota, TX (1860–1867)

Appendix A. Ethnicity

Heritage	Occupation	Origin	Destination
Key, Rebecca M. (1799-ca. 1860)	housewife	Crawfordsville, IN (1838)	Louisa County, IA (1838–ca. 1860)
Kirby, Georgiana B. (1818–1887)	rancher, suffragist	Staffordshire, England (1831)	Santa Cruz, CA (1850–1887)
Kirby, Richard C. (1817–1904)	whaler, tanner	Staffordshire, England (1842)	Santa Cruz, CA (1850–1904)
Lambert, Rebecca H. (1806–1886)	activist, fund raiser	New York, NY (1852)	San Francisco, CA (1852–1886)
Lawing, William "Billie" (1879–1936)	innkeeper, boat captain	Murfreesboro, TN (1923)	Seward, AK (1923–1936)
Leavitt, Eliza S. Reed (1829–1910s)	innkeeper, depot manager	Boston, MA (1856)	Indian Valley, CA (1860–1880s) Bridgeport, CA (1867–1901)
Leavitt, Hiram Lewis (1824–1901)	innkeeper, judge, depot manager	Boston, MA (1851)	Indian Valley, CA (1860–1880s) Bridgeport, CA (1867–1901)
Loving, Oliver (1812–1867)	rancher	Belknap, TX (1866)	Fort Sumner (1866–1867)
Macy, Obed (1801–1857)	physician, city councilman, innkeeper	Washington, IN (1850)	El Monte, CA (1851–1852) Los Angeles, CA (1852–1857)
Macy, Oscar (1829–1910)	printer, publisher, jailer	Washington, IN (1850)	El Monte, CA (1851–1852) Los Angeles, CA (1852–1910)
Maynard, Frank H. (1853–1926)	memoirist, carpenter, cowboy, song writer	Iowa City, IA (1869)	Towanda, KS (1869–1881) Colorado Springs, CO (1881–1926)
Mead, James R. (1836–1910)	trader, memoirist	Davenport, IA (1859)	Salina, KS (1862–1863) Wichita, KS (1864–1910)
Meeker, Eliza Jane (1834–1909)	farmer, grocer, innkeeper, activist	Eddyville, IA (1852)	McNeil Island, WA (1853–1861) Puyallup, WA (1862–1909)
Meeker, Ezra (1830–1928)	farmer, grocer, innkeeper	Eddyville, IA (1852)	McNeil Island, WA (1853–1861) Puyallup, WA (1862–1894) Cook Inlet, AK (1894–1896) Skagway, AK (1898–1901)
Meeker, Oliver Perry (1828–1861)	farmer, grocer	Eddyville, IA (1852)	McNeil Island, WA (1853–1860)
Merritt, Josiah (1803–1882)	farmer, prospector, musician	Athens, OH (1860)	Snoqualmie, WA (1860–1882)
Miller, Mary Foote (1842–1921)	coal miner, city planner, banker innkeeper	Quesqueton, IA (1863)	Lafayette, CO (1863–1921)
Mitchell, James C. (1810–1860)	merchant, realtor	Council Bluffs, IA (1852)	Florence, NE (1852–1860)
Page, Larcena P. (1837–1913)	teacher	Nashville, TN (1837)	Honey Grove, TX (1837–1857)
Parkhurst, Charley (1812–1879)	stagecoach driver	Providence, RI (1851)	Soquel, CA (1851–1879)
Parmley, J.W. (1861–1940)	brick maker, farmer, publisher	Mifflin, WI (1883)	Ipswich, SD (1883–1940)
Pennington, Elias G. (1809–1869)	farmer, freighter	Nashville, TN (1837)	Honey Grove, TX (1837–1857)
Pennington, James (1833–1868)	farmer, freighter	Nashville, TN (1837)	Honey Grove, TX (1837–1857)
Pratt, Louisa Merrill (1827–1919)	housewife, activist	Freeport, ME (1852)	San Francisco, CA (1852–1867, 1881–1893) Carlin, NV (1852–1872) Salt Lake City, UT (1872–1879) Sacramento, CA (1878–1881) St. Helena, CA (1881–1900) Seattle, WA (1900–1919)
Pratt, Robert Henry (1824–1920)	miner, railroad builder	Freeport, ME (1852)	San Francisco, CA (1849–1867, 1881–1893) Carlin, NV (1867–1869) Salt Lake City, UT (1869–1879)

Appendix A. Ethnicity

Heritage	Occupation	Origin	Destination
			Sacramento, CA (1878–1881)
			St. Helena, CA (1881–1900)
			Seattle, WA (1900–1920)
Rasor, John Henry (1849–1925)	farmer, stockman	Graham, IA (1883)	Plano, TX (1883–1925)
Rasor, Mary Ellen (1851–1918)	housewife	Graham, IA (1883)	Plano, TX (1883–1918)
Reading, Pearson B. (1816–1868)	miner, explorer	Hunterdon, NJ (1844)	Shasta, CA (1843–1868)
Robbins, Ezekiel W. (1800–1852)	physician, minister, merchant, politician	Watertown, NY (1828)	St. Louis, MO (1828–1852)
Santee, Jennie Frances (1838–1931)	school builder	Hartford, CT (1878)	Cowlestown, CA (1878–1931)
Simmons, Elizabeth K. (1820–1891)	housewife	Nodaway, MO (1844)	Tumwater, WA (1845–1867)
Smith, Joseph, Jr. (1805–1844)	prophet, author, translator	Harmony, PA (1827)	Nauvoo, IL (1831–1844)
Snow, Eliza Roxcy (1804–1887)	hymnographer, teacher, social worker	Hiram, OH (1835)	Salt Lake City, UT (1835–1887)
Speed, Horace (1852–1924)	lawyer	Indianapolis, IN (1889)	Guthrie, OK (1889–1913)
Stone, Elizabeth H. (1801–1895)	midwife, hotelier, entrepreneur	Watertown, NY (1828)	St. Paul, MI (1857–1862)
			Denver, CO (1862–1864)
			Fort Collins, CO (1864–1895)
Stratton, Elizabeth P. (1830–1922)	teacher, diarist	Ontario (1864)	Fort Collins, CO (1864–1933)
Stroud, Beden (1795–1865)	farmer, Indian agent, soldier	Chambers County, AL (1836)	Calvert, TX (1836–1865)
Stroud, Ethan A. (1788–1846)	farmer, Indian agent, soldier	Chambers County, AL (1836)	Calvert, TX (1836–1865)
Tabor, Augusta Louise (1833–1895)	grocer, laundress, cook, postmaster, philanthropist	Augusta, ME (1857)	Zeandale, KS (1857–1859)
		Oro City, CO (1859–1861)	Leadville, CO (1861–1879)
			Denver, CO (1879–1894)
			Pasadena, CA (1894–1895)
Tabor, Horace Austin (1830–1899)	stone mason, miner, senator, merchant, mayor, postmaster	Boston, MA (1855)	Zeandale, KS (1855–1859)
			Oro City, CO (1859–1861)
			Leadville, CO (1861–1879)
			Denver, CO (1879–1899)
Wells, Emmeline B. (1828–1921)	teacher, diarist, editor, activist, social worker	Petersham, MA (1844)	Salt Lake City, UT (1846–1921)
Whitman, Marcus (1802–1847)	doctor, missionary	Angelica, NY (1836)	Walla Walla (1836–1847)
Whitman, Narcissa (1808–1847)	doctor, missionary	Angelica, NY (1836)	Walla Walla (1836–1847)
Young, Brigham (1801–1877)	prophet, governor, Indian agent, church builder	Whittingham, VT (1832)	Salt Lake City, UT (1847–1877)
Young, Zina D.H. (1821–1901)	teacher, midwife, missionary, social worker	Watertown, NY (1836)	Salt Lake City, UT (1848–1901)
Finn			
Lahti, Charles (1859–1932)	farmer, investor	Vadsø, Norway (1864)	St. Peter, MN (1864–1932)
Lahti, Johanna Gustava (1840–1919)	farmer	Vadsø, Norway (1864)	St. Peter, MN (1864–1919)
Lahti, Peter J. (1834–1911)	trapper, farmer	Vadsø, Norway (1864)	St. Peter, MN (1864–1911å)
Franco-American			
Sublette, William Lewis (1798–1845)	trapper, trader	Lincoln, KY (1822)	St. Charles, MO (1822–1833)
			Fort William WY (1834–1835)
			St. Louis, MO (1836–1845)

Appendix A. Ethnicity

Heritage	Occupation	Origin	Destination
French			
Docher, Anton (1852–1928)	missionary	Auvergne, France (1887)	Isleta Pueblo, NM (1891–1928)
Toponce, Alexander (1839–1923)	cowboy, stockman, stage driver, road builder, mailman	Belfort, France (1846)	Tipton, MO (1854–1860) Denver, CO (1860–1863) Bannack, MT (1863) Ogden, UT (1863–1879) Chesterfield, ID (1879–1923)
French-Canadian			
Arcouet, Amable (1797–1880)	trapper, trader, farmer, mason	Montreal, Quebec (1833)	St. Paul, MN (1835–1880)
Bottineau, Pierre (1817–1895)	guide, interpreter, negotiator with Indians	Winnipeg, Manitoba (1832)	St. Paul, MN (1840–1852) Osseo, MN (1852–1877) Red Lake Falls, MN (1877–1895)
Liberty, Stephen E. (1843–1911)	scout, translator	Quebec (1862)	Fort Benton, MT (1866)
Mead, Agnes Barcome (1841–1869)	trader	Quebec (1859)	Salina, KS (1862–1863) Wichita, KS (1864–1869)
Robidoux, Antoine (1794–1860)	trapper, guide, interpreter	St. Louis, MO (1832)	Fort Uintah, UT (1833–1844)
French-Canadian-Potowatomi			
Ouilmette, Antoine L. (ca. 1760–1841)	fur trader, ferryman, stockman	Montreal, Quebec (1790)	Chicago, IL (1790–1833)
French-German-Swiss			
Wilkins, John R. (1835–1904)	merchant, hotelier, stockman	Fort Madison, IA (1853)	Oregon City, OR (1854–1860) Ashby, ID (1866–1867) Boise, ID (1867–1876) Tuscarora, NV (1876–1878) Bruneau, ID (1878–1904)
Wilkins, Katherine C. (1857–1936)	horse breeder	Jacksonville, OR (1857)	Bruneau, ID (1880–1936)
German			
Cope, Sister Marianne (1838–1918)	nun, nurse, hospital builder	Heppenheim, Hesse (1839)	Wailiuku, Maui (1884–1887) Kalaupapa, Molokai (1887–1918)
Goller, John (1825–1874)	prospector, wagon maker, blacksmith	Bavaria (1849)	Los Angeles, CA (1850–1874)
Haag, Johann Christoph (1817–1890)	farmer	Württemberg (1851)	Theresa, WI (1851–1859)
Haag, Rosena Christina (1826–1892)	farmer	Württemberg (1851)	Theresa, WI (1851–1859)
Ise, Henry C. (1841–1900)	farmer	Württemberg (1857)	Ross, KS (1871–1900)
German-American			
Bell, Susan Abia (1831–1905)	seamstress, activist	Sedalia, MO (1856)	Obed, CA (1898–1905)
Bush, Isabella James (1801–1866)	community builder, nurse, poultry farmer	Jackson, MO (1844)	Tumwater, WA (1845–1866)
Hollenbeck, John E. (1829–1885)	investor	Nicaragua (1874)	Obed, CA (1874–1885)
Ise, Rosena Haag (1855–1947)	farmer, seamstress	Theresa, WI (1873)	Ross, KS (1873–1947)
Smeathers, William (ca. 1766–1837)	hunter, Indian fighter	Yellow Banks, KY (1821)	Columbia, TX (1824–1837)
German-Scots			
Kinman, Seth (1815–1888)	prospector, hunter, dairier, innkeeper	Pekin, IL (1849)	Shasta, CA (1850–1855) Table Bluff, CA (1855–1888)
Hispanic			
Briones de Miranda, Juana (1802–1889)	rancher, herbalist	Mexico (1802)	Santa Clara, CA (1844–1885)
Padilla, Juan de (?–1544)	missionary, chaplain	Andalusia, Spain (1528)	Quivira, TX (1542–1544)
Indo-Irish			
Gwydir, Rickard Daniel (1844–1925)	soldier, Indian agent	Covington, KY (1887)	Spokane, WA (1887–1925)

Appendix A. Ethnicity

Heritage	Occupation	Origin	Destination
Irish			
Adair, John George (1823–1885)	investor	Queen's County, Ireland (1874)	Palo Duro, TX (1874–1885)
Bush, George W. (ca. 1779–1863)	community builder, farmer, stockman	Jackson, MO (1844)	Tumwater, WA (1845–1866)
Campbell, Robert (1804–1879)	trader, financier, mediator, investor	Plumbridge, Ireland (1822)	St. Louis, MO (1835–1879)
Fisk, Andrew Jackson (1849–1910)	soldier, journalist, farmer, miner, postmaster	Fort Ripley, MN (1866)	Fort Benton, MT (1866)
Fisk, James Liberty (1835–1902)	soldier, guide, journalist, auditor	Fort Ripley, MN (1863) Fort Ripley, MN (1866)	Bannack, MT (1863) Fort Benton, MT (1866)
Fisk, Robert Emmett (1837–1908)	soldier, journalist	Fort Ripley, MN (1866)	Fort Benton, MT (1866)
Fisk, Van Hayden (1840–1890)	soldier, journalist	Fort Ripley, MN (1866)	Fort Benton, MT (1866)
O'Farrell, John A. (1823–1900)	miner, legislator, foster parent	Louisville, KY (1859)	Boise, ID (1863–1900)
O'Farrell, Mary Ann (1840–1900)	foster parent, church builder	Louisville, KY (1859)	Boise, ID (1863–1900)
Reed, John Thomas (1805–1843)	sailor, sawyer, ferryman, rancher	Acapulco, Mexico (1826)	San Francisco, CA (1826–1843)
Irish-American			
Booth, Ellen Eliza C. (1854–1935)	fund raiser	Waupon, WI (1879)	Edna, ND (1879–1914)
Bowman, Sarah A. (1812–1866)	nurse, innkeeper, launderer, madame, cook, foster parent	Clay County, MO (1845)	Corpus Christi (1845–1846) El Paso (1848–1850)
Campbell, Virginia Jane (1822–1882)	fund raiser	Raleigh, NC (1841)	St. Louis, MO (1841–1882)
Kelly, Josiah Shawhan (1824–1867)	farmer	Geneva, KS (1864)	Box Elder Creek, WY (1864)
McCance, Charles H. (1857–1926)	farmer	Toulon, IL (1884)	Cozad, NE (1885–1926)
McCance, Margaret A. (1861–1940)	housewife	Toulon, IL (1884)	Cozad, NE (1885–1940)
McCance, Margaret S. (1830–1905)	housewife	Toulon, IL (1900)	Cozad, NE (1885–1905)
Reed, Martha Burnett (1786–1855)	housewife	Natchitoches, LA (1833)	Bell County, TX (1833–1855)
Reed, Michael (1777–1859)	farmer	Natchitoches, LA (1833)	Bell County, TX (1833–1859)
Reed, William W. (1816–1891)	rancher, sheriff	Natchitoches, LA (1833)	Bell County TX (1833–1891)
Snyder, Grace McCance (1882–1982)	quilter	Cass County (1885)	Cozad, NE (1885–1919)
Irish-Powhatan			
Omohundro, Texas Jack (1846–1880)	cowboy, scout, actor, writer	Pleasure Hill, VA (1859)	Fort Worth, TX (1859–1869) Cottonwood Springs, NE (1869–1872) Leadville, CO (1877–1880)
Irish-Scots			
Culbertson, Margaret (1834–1897)	teacher, missionary	Groveland, NY (1878)	San Francisco, CA (1878–1897)
Bruce, George Whiteley (1851–1927)	rancher, butcher, orchardist, dairier, Indian fighter	Bray, Ireland (1860s)	DeLamar, ID (1860s–1927)
Bruce, Samuel A. (1839–1900)	miner	Bray, Ireland (1860s)	Bannock, ID (1860s)
Heazle, Benjamin Alfred (1880–1936)	postmaster, rancher	Bray, Ireland (1894)	Murphy, ID (1894–?)

Appendix A. Ethnicity

Heritage	Occupation	Origin	Destination
Heazle, George Robert (1876–1924)	postmaster, grocer	Bray, Ireland (1894)	Murphy, ID (1894–?)
Heazle, Jean (1879–1949)	timber cutter, miner, dairier, cattle rancher	Bray, Ireland (1893)	DeLamar, ID (1893–1949)
Monteith, Charles Edgar (1847–1915)	Indian agent	Fulton, NY (1874)	Lapwai, ID (1874–1889)
Sothern, Mary Elizabeth (1856–1935)	housewife	Bray, Ireland (1860s)	DeLamar, ID (1860s–1880s)
Irish-Scots-Canadian			
Holmes, Julia Archibald (1838–1887)	writer, reformer, teacher, explorer	Emporia, KS (1858)	Taos, NM (1858–1863)
Irish-Scots-Polish			
Reed, James Frazier (1800–1874)	land speculator, miner	Springfield, IL (1846)	San Jose, CA (1847–1874)
Italian			
Omohundro, Josephine (1836–1886)	dancer	Milan, Italy (1830s)	Leadville, CO (1877–1886)
Japanese			
Hayashi, Harvey Saburo (1867–1943)	physician, editor, teacher	Tonami, Japan (1885)	San Francisco, CA (1884–1891) Sacramento, CA (1891–1893) Kona, HI (1893–1943)
Hayashi, Matsu K. (1877–1972)	teacher	Honshu, Japan (1896)	Kona, HI (1896–1972)
Imamura, Yemyo (1867–1932)	missionary, labor leader	Fukui, Japan (1899)	Honolulu, HI (1899–1932)
Ozawa, Kintaro (fl. 1840s–1870s)	servant	Yokohama, Japan (1868)	Honolulu, HI (1868–?)
Ozawa, Tomi (1849–?)	servant	Yokohama, Japan (1868)	Honolulu, HI (1868–?)
Sakuma, Yonekichi (1839–1927)	cook	Yokohama, Japan (1868)	Kauai, HI (1868–1927)
New Zealand-Scots			
Cameron, Donaldina (1869–1968)	seamstress, activist	Clydevale, New Zealand (1871)	San Francisco, CA (1895–1968)
Norwegian			
Wahl, James M. (1846–1939)	carpenter, recruiter	Storvahl, Norway (1867)	Sioux Falls (1868–1889) Canton, MN (1883–1889) Lennox, SD (1889–1939)
Wahl, Julia Ulberg (1862–1914)	housewife	Valdres, Norway (1883)	Canton, MN (1883–1889) Lennox, SD (1889–1914)
Polish			
Moczygemba, Leopold (1824–1891)	priest, recruiter	Pluznica, Prussia (1852)	Bandera, TX (1852–1858)
Polish-Jewish			
Franklin, Edward (1809–1873)	merchant	Liverpool, England (1849)	San Francisco, CA (1849–1873)
Franklin, Lewis A. (1820–1879)	attorney, merchant, soldier, judge	Kingston, Jamaica (1849)	San Francisco, CA (1849–1855) San Diego, CA (1855–1860)
Franklin, Lumley (1808–1873)	merchant	Liverpool, England (1849)	San Francisco, CA (1849–1858)
Franklin, Maurice A. (1817–1874)	pharmacist, miner, merchant, teacher, synagogue builder, photographer	Kingston, Jamaica (1849)	San Francisco, CA (1849–1855) San Diego, CA (1855–1859) San Bernardino, CA (1859–1874)
Franklin, Selim (1814–1884)	realtor, auctioneer, merchant	Liverpool, England (1849)	San Francisco, CA (1849–1858, 1866–1884)
Franklin, Victoria J. (1838–1861)	diarist	Manchester, England (1851)	San Diego, CA (1851–1861)
Reich, George Adolph (1846–1896)	pharmacist, doctor	Breslau, Poland (1870)	San Bernardino, CA (1870–1882)

Heritage	Occupation	Origin	Destination
Prussian			
Keseberg, Lewis (1814–1895)	sea captain, brewer, innkeeper	Westphalia, Prussia (1844)	San Jose (1847–1895)
Russian-Jewish			
Meyerowitz, Isadore (ca. 1820–1856)	trader	Russia (1849)	Honey Lake, CA (1849–1856)
Scot			
Bell, James George (1831–1911)	farmer	Sedalia, MO (1856)	Obed, CA (1898–1911)
McBeth, Kate C. (1832–1915)	missionary, teacher	Wellsville, OH (1858)	Lapwai, ID (1879–1915)
McBeth, Susan Law (1830–1893)	missionary, teacher	Wellsville, OH (1858)	Goodwater, OK (1858–1861) St. Louis, MO (1866–1873) Lapwai, ID (1873–1893)
McCoy, John Calvin (1811–1889)	missionary, merchant	Vincennes, IN (1830)	Kansas City, MO (1830–1889)
Morrison, John L. (1819–1899)	carpenter	Independence, MO (1842)	Oregon City, OR (1843–1850)
Scots-Canadian			
Kellie, James Thomson (1850–1918)	farmer, activist, grocer, carpenter, bridge builder, railroad laborer	Toronto, Ontario (1871)	St. Louis, MO (1872–1873) Iowa (1874–1877) Adams County, NE (1877–1884) Hartwell, NE (1884–1901)
Scots-Irish			
Baker, Jim (1818–1898)	rancher, guide, scout, interpreter	Belleville, IL (1839)	Savery, WY (1873–1898)
Swiss			
Bonnema, Luisa S. (1838–after 1910)	housewife	Altnau, Switzerland (1851)	New Amsterdam, WI (1860–?)

B. Departure

Place of Departure	Occupation	Left Original Home	Area of Settlement
Alabama			
Reed, Emaline Cobb (1825–1890)	housewife	Walker County (1837)	Bell County, TX (1837–1890)
Stroud, Beden (1795–1865)	farmer, Indian agent	Chambers County (1836)	Calvert, TX (1836–1865)
Stroud, Ethan A. (1788–1846)	farmer, Indian agent	Chambers County (1836)	Calvert, TX (1836–1846)
Arkansas			
Chisholm, Jesse (1806–1868)	trader, guide, interpreter	Arkansas (1820s)	Hughes County, OK (1820s, 1858–1861, 1868) Tehuacana Creek, TX (1833–1858) Wichita, KS (1861–1868)
China			
Chin, Ah Yane (1869–?)	interpreter	China (1874)	San Francisco, CA (1874–?)
Wu, Tien Fu (1861–ca. 1940s)	interpreter	Sze Yup, Canton (1876)	San Francisco, CA (1876–ca. 1940s)
Connecticut			
Bingham, Hiram (1789–1869)	missionary, lexicographer	Hartford (1819)	Honolulu, HI (1820–1840)
Bingham, Sybil Moseley (1792–1848)	teacher, midwife, seamstress	Hartford (1819)	Honolulu, HI (1820–1840)
Cowles, George Algernon (1836–1887)	rancher, horse breeder, financier	Hartford (1878)	Cowlestown, CA (1878–1887)

Appendix B. Departure

Place of Departure	Occupation	Left Original Home	Area of Settlement
Fisk, Elizabeth Chester (1846–1927)	diarist	Haddam (1866)	Helena, MT (1866–1927)
Santee, Jennie Frances (1838–1931)	school builder	Hartford (1878)	Cowlestown, CA (1878–1931)
Denmark			
Lassen, Peter (1800–1859)	rancher, millwright, prospector, sawyer	Farum (1830)	San Jose, CA (1840–1843) Rancho Bosquejo, CA (1844–1850) Honey Lake, CA (1855–1859)
England			
Kirby, Georgiana Bruce (1818–1887)	rancher, suffragist	Staffordshire (1831)	Santa Cruz, CA (1850–1887)
Kirby, Richard Cornelius (1817–1904)	whaler, tanner	Staffordshire (1842)	Santa Cruz, CA (1850–1904)
Franklin, Edward (1809–1873)	merchant	Liverpool (1849)	San Francisco, CA (1849–1873)
Franklin, Lumley (1808–1873)	merchant	Liverpool (1849)	San Francisco, CA (1849–1858)
Franklin, Selim (1814–1884)	realtor, auctioneer, merchant	Liverpool (1849)	San Francisco, CA (1849–1858, 1866–1884)
Franklin, Victoria Jacobs (1838–1861)	diarist	Manchester (1851)	San Diego, CA (1851–1861)
Goddard, George Henry (1817–1906)	cartographer, surveyor, civil engineer, artist	Bristol (1850)	San Francisco, CA (1850–1906)
Illingworth, William Henry (1844–1893)	photographer	Leeds (1845)	Fort Benton, MT (1866)
France			
Docher, Anton (1852–1928)	missionary	Auvergne, (1887)	Isleta, NM (1891–1928)
Toponce, Alexander (1839–1923)	cowboy, stage driver, stockman, road builder, freighter	Belfort (1846)	Tipton, MO (1854–1860) Denver, CO (1860–1863) Bannack, MT (1863) Ogden, UT (1863–1923)
Germany			
Cope, Sister Marianne (1838–1918)	nun, nurse, hospital builder	Heppenheim, Hesse (1839)	Wailiuku, Maui, HI (1884–1887) Kalaupapa, Molokai, HI (1887–1918)
Goller, John (1825–1874)	prospector, wagon maker, blacksmith	Bavaria (1849)	Los Angeles, CA (1850–1874)
Haag, Johann Christoph (1817–1890)	farmer	Württemberg (1851)	Theresa, WI (1851–1859)
Haag, Rosena Christina (1826–1892)	farmer	Württemberg (1851)	Theresa, WI (1851–1859)
Ise, Henry C. (1841–1900)	farmer	Württemberg (1857)	Ross, KS (1871–1900)
Haiti			
Point du Sable, Jean B. (ca. 1745–1818)	farmer, trader	Chicago, IL (1800)	St. Charles, MO (1800–1818)
Illinois			
Backenstoe, Virginia E. (1833–1921)	insurer	Springfield (1846)	San Jose, CA (1847–1874)
Baker, Jim (1818–1898)	rancher, guide, scout, interpreter	Belleville (1839)	Clear Creek, CO (1859–1873)
Dale, Frank (1849–1930)	financier, judge	Somonauk (1871)	Wichita, KS (1871–1889) Guthrie, OK (1889–1930)
Farnham, Thomas J. (1804–1848)	attorney, writer, freighter	Peoria (1838)	Willamette, OR (1839) Santa Cruz, CA (1839–1848)
Goodnight, Charles (1836–1929)	Texas Ranger, rancher	Macoupin (1846)	Goodnight, TX (1846–1929) Dodge City, KS (1878)
Goodnight, Elija (1831–1929)	soldier, rancher	Macoupin (1846)	Goodnight, TX (1846–1929)

Appendix B. Departure

Place of Departure	Occupation	Left Original Home	Area of Settlement
Hamilton, Ezra (1833–1914)	miner, inventor, manufacturer	Mount Sterling (1853)	Shasta, CA (1856–1861) Los Angeles, CA (1875–1914)
Isbell, Isaac Chauncy (1800–1886)	prospector, rancher, innkeeper, surgeon	Greenbush (1846)	Santa Clara, CA (1846–1850; 1861–1886) Cancon, TX (1850–1861)
Isbell, Olive Mann (1824–1899)	nurse, teacher, rancher, seamstress	Greenbush (1846)	Santa Clara, CA (1846–1850; 1861–1886) Cancon, TX (1850–1861)
Kellie, Luna Sanford (1857–1940)	farmer, editor, grocer, songwriter, activist	Rockford (1871)	Adams County, NE (1877–1884) Hartwell, NE (1884–1901)
Kinman, Seth (1815–1888)	prospector, hunter, dairier, innkeeper	Pekin (1849)	Shasta, CA (1850–1855) Table Bluff, CA (1855–1888)
Lewis, Martha Jane Reed (1838–1923)	innkeeper	Springfield (1846)	San Jose, CA (1847–1874)
McCance, Charles Henry (1857–1926)	farmer	Toulon (1884)	Cozad, NE (1885–1926)
McCance, Margaret Anna (1861–1940)	housewife	Toulon 1884)	Cozad, NE (1885–1940)
McCance, Margaret Sarah (1830–1905)	housewife	Toulon (1900)	Cozad, NE (1885–1905)
Reed, James Frazier (1800–1874)	land speculator, miner	Springfield (1846)	San Jose, CA (1847–1874)
Reed, James Frazier, Jr. (1841–1901)	land speculator, miner	Springfield (1846)	San Jose, CA (1847–1901)
Reed, Margret Keyes (1814–1861)	housewife	Springfield (1846)	San Jose, CA (1847–1861)
Street, Joseph M. (1782–1840)	postmaster, Indian agent, attorney	Shawneetown (1812)	Prairie du Chien, WI (1812–1835, 1837–1842)
Indiana			
Belshaw, Candace McCarty (1826–1892)	housewife	Lake County (1853)	Eugene, OR (1853–1892)
Belshaw, George, Jr. (1815–1893)	farmer, diarist	Lake County (1853)	Eugene, OR (1853–1893)
Cheesman, David Williams (1822–1884)	attorney, memoirist, U.S. Mint treasurer	Washington (1850)	El Monte (1851–1852) Los Angeles, CA (1852–1884)
Cheesman, Urania K. (1828–1916)	housewife	Washington (1850)	El Monte, CA (1851–1852) Los Angeles, CA (1852–1884)
DeVere, Pearl (1859–1897)	madam	Evansville (ca. 1875)	Cripple Creek, CO (ca. 1875–1897)
Key, Ambrose W. (1829–1908)	orchardist, farmer, tanner, sawyer, freighter	Crawfordsville (1838)	Navasota, TX (1860) Houston, TX (1865) Westport, MO (1865–1868) Shawnee, KS (1868–1908)
Key, George (1795–1864)	farmer, trader	Crawfordsville (1836)	Louisa County, IA (1836–1861)
Key, Rebecca Mintun (1799–ca. 1860)	housewife	Crawfordsville (1838)	Louisa County, IA (1838–ca. 1860)
Macy, Lucinda Polk (1807–1872)	innkeeper	Washington (1850)	El Monte, CA (1851–1852) Los Angeles, CA (1852–1872)
Macy, Oscar (1829–1910)	printer, publisher, jailer	Washington (1850)	El Monte, CA (1851–1852) Los Angeles, CA (1852–1910)
McCarty, Jonathan Warren (1833–1900)	farmer, merchant, mailman	Lake County (1853)	Pierce County, WA (1853–1870) Seattle, WA (1870–1900)
McCoy, John Calvin (1811–1889)	missionary, merchant	Vincennes (1830)	Kansas City, MO (1830–1889)
Speed, Horace (1852–1924)	lawyer	Indianapolis (1889)	Guthrie, OK (1889–1913)
Iowa			
Key, Mary Jones Garrett (1835–1927)	housewife	Louisa County (1860)	Navasota, TX (1860–1865)

Appendix B. Departure

Place of Departure	Occupation	Left Original Home	Area of Settlement
Maynard, Frank H. (1853–1926)	cowboy, carpenter, memoirist, song writer	Iowa City (1869)	Towanda, KS (1869–1881) Colorado Springs, CO (1881–1926)
Mead, James R. (1836–1910)	trader, memoirist	Davenport (1859)	Salina, KS (1862–1863) Wichita, KS (1864–1910)
Meeker, Eliza Jane (1834–1909)	farmer, grocer, innkeeper, activist	Eddyville (1852)	McNeil Island, WA (1853–1861) Puyallup, WA (1862–1909)
Meeker, Ezra (1830–1928)	farmer, grocer, innkeeper	Eddyville (1852)	McNeil Island, WA (1853–1861) Puyallup, WA (1862–1894)
Meeker, Oliver Perry (1828–1861)	farmer, grocer	Eddyville (1852)	McNeil Island, WA (1853–1860)
Miller, Lafayette (1840–1878)	innkeeper, farmer, butcher	Quesqueton (1863)	Lafayette, CO (1863–1878)
Miller, Mary Foote (1842–1921)	coal miner, city planner, banker innkeeper	Quesqueton (1863)	Lafayette, CO (1863–1921)
Mitchell, James C. (1810–1860)	merchant, realtor	Council Bluffs (1852)	Florence, NE (1852–1860)
Rasor, John Henry (1849–1925)	farmer, stockman	Graham (1883)	Plano, TX (1883–1925)
Rasor, Mary Ellen (1851–1918)	housewife	Graham (1883)	Plano, TX (1883–1918)
Wilkins, John R. (1835–1904)	merchant, hotelier, stockman	Fort Madison (1853)	Oregon City, OR (1854–1860) Ashby, ID (1866–1867) Boise, ID (1867–1876) Tuscarora, NV (1876–1878) Bruneau, ID (1878–1904)
Wilkins, Laura Smith (1835–1921)	dairier	Fort Madison, IA (1853)	Oregon City (1854–1860) Ashby, ID (1866–1867) Boise, ID (1867–1878) Bruneau, ID (1878–1921)

Ireland

Place of Departure	Occupation	Left Original Home	Area of Settlement
Adair, John George (1823–1885)	investor	Queen's County	Palo Duro, TX (1874–1885)
Bruce, George Whiteley (1851–1927)	rancher, butcher, orchardist, dairier	Bray (1860s)	DeLamar, ID (1860s–1927)
Bruce, Samuel A. (1839–1900)	miner	Bray (1860s)	Bannock, ID (1860s)
Campbell, Robert (1804–1879)	trader, financier, negotiator, investor	Plumbridge (1822)	St. Louis, MO (1835–1879)
Heazle, Benjamin Alfred (1880–1936)	postmaster, rancher	Bray, Ireland (1894)	Murphy, ID (1894–?)
Heazle, George Robert (1876–1924)	postmaster, grocer	Bray, Ireland (1894)	Murphy, ID (1894–?)
Heazle, Jean (1879–1949)	timber cutter, miner, dairier, rancher	Bray, Ireland (1893)	DeLamar, ID (1893–1949)
Sothern, Mary Elizabeth (1856–1935)	housewife	Bray, Ireland (1860s)	DeLamar, ID (1860s–1880s)

Italy

Place of Departure	Occupation	Left Original Home	Area of Settlement
Omohundro, Josephine (1836–1886)	dancer	Milan (1830s)	Leadville, CO (1877–1886)

Jamaica

Place of Departure	Occupation	Left Original Home	Area of Settlement
Franklin, Lewis Abraham (1820–1879)	attorney, merchant, soldier, judge	Kingston, (1849)	San Francisco, CA (1849–1855) San Diego, CA (1855–1860)
Franklin, Maurice Abraham (1817–1874)	pharmacist, miner, merchant, teacher, synagogue builder, photographer	Kingston (1849)	San Francisco, CA (1849–1855) San Diego, CA (1855–1859) San Bernardino (1859–1874)

Japan

Place of Departure	Occupation	Left Original Home	Area of Settlement
Hayashi, Harvey Saburo (1867–1943)	physician, editor, teacher	Tonami (1885)	San Francisco, CA (1884–1891)

Place of Departure	Occupation	Left Original Home	Area of Settlement
Hayashi, Matsu Kawarada (1877–1972)	teacher	Honshu (1896)	Sacramento, CA (1891–1893) Kona, HI (1893–1943) Kona, HI (1896–1972)
Imamura, Yemyo (1867–1932)	missionary, labor leader, writer	Fukui (1899)	Honolulu, HI (1899–1932)
Ozawa, Kintaro (fl. 1840s–1870s)	servant	Yokohama (1868)	Honolulu, HI (1868–?)
Ozawa, Tomi (1849–?)	servant	Yokohama (1868)	Honolulu, HI (1868–?)
Sakuma, Yonekichi (1839–1927)	cook	Yokohama (1868)	Kauai, HI (1868–1927)
Kansas			
Holmes, James Henry (1833–1907)	journalist, soldier, territorial secretary	Emporia (1858)	Taos, NM (1858–1863)
Holmes, Julia Archibald (1838–1887)	writer, reformer, teacher, explorer	Emporia (1858)	Taos, NM (1858–1863)
Kelly, Fanny Wiggins (1845–1904)	memoirist, laundress, innkeeper	Geneva (1864)	Box Elder Creek, WY (1864) Sherman Station, WY (1868–1869)
Kelly, Josiah Shawhan (1824–1867)	farmer, innkeeper	Geneva (1864)	Box Elder Creek, WY (1864)
Larimer, Sarah Luse (1836–1913)	photographer, grocer	Iola (1864)	Sherman Station, WY (1864–1870)
Larimer, William Jackson (1828–1895)	farmer, grocer	Iola (1864)	Sherman Station, WY (1864–1870)
Kentucky			
Brown, Clara (1800–1885)	cook, launderer, nurse, recruiter	Gallatin (1856)	Leavenworth, KS (1856–1859) Denver, CO (1859–1885)
Goodnight, Mary Ann Dyer (1839–1926)	teacher	Hickman (1870)	Pueblo, CO (1870–1871)
Gwydir, Rickard Daniel (1844–1925)	soldier, Indian agent	Covington (1887)	Spokane, WA (1887–1925)
Loving, Oliver (1812–1867)	rancher	Hopkins (1845)	Belknap, TX (1866) Fort Sumner, NM (1866–1867)
O'Farrell, John A. (1823–1900)	miner, legislator, foster parent	Louisville (1859)	Boise, ID (1863–1900)
O'Farrell, Mary Ann (1840–1900)	foster parent, church builder	Louisville (1859)	Boise, ID (1863–1900)
Smeathers, William (ca. 1766–1837)	hunter, Indian fighter	Yellow Banks (1821)	Columbia, TX (1824–1837)
Street, Eliza Posey (1786–1849)	housewife	Henderson (1809)	Prairie du Chien, WI (1812–1835, 1837–1842)
Sublette, William Lewis (1798–1845)	trapper, trader	Lincoln (1822)	St. Charles, MO (1822–1833) Fort William, WY (1833–1835) St. Louis, MO (1836–1845)
Wootton, Richens Lacey (1816–1893)	guide, freighter, Indian fighter, road builder	Christian (1836)	Independence, MO (1836)
Louisiana			
Reed, Martha Burnett (1786–1855)	housewife	Natchitoches (1833)	Bell County, TX (1833–1855)
Reed, Michael (1777–1859)	farmer	Natchitoches (1833)	Bell County, TX (1833–1859)
Reed, William Whitaker (1816–1891)	rancher, sheriff	Natchitoches (1833)	Bell County, TX (1833–1891)
Maine			
Carr, Sarah Pratt (1850–1935)	missionary, writer, activist, librettist	Freeport (1852)	San Francisco, CA (1852–1867, 1913–1935) Carlin, NV (1867–1872) St. Helena, CA (1883–1900) Seattle, WA (1900–1913)
Pratt, Louisa Merrill (1827–1919)	housewife, activist	Freeport (1852)	San Francisco, CA (1852–1867, 1881–1893)

Appendix B. Departure

Place of Departure	Occupation	Left Original Home	Area of Settlement
			Carlin, NV (1852–1872)
			Salt Lake City, UT (1872–1879)
			Sacramento, CA (1878–1881)
			St. Helena, CA (1881–1900)
			Seattle, WA (1900–1919)
Pratt, Robert Henry (1824–1920)	miner, railroad builder	Freeport (1852)	San Francisco, CA (1849–1867, 1881–1893)
			Carlin, NV (1867–1869)
			Salt Lake City (1869–1879)
			Sacramento, CA (1878–1881)
			St. Helena, CA (1881–1900)
			Seattle, WA (1900–1920)
Tabor, Augusta Louise (1833–1895)	grocer, laundress, cook, postmaster, philanthropist	Augusta (1857)	Zeandale, KS (1857–1859)
			Oro City, CO (1859–1861)
			Leadville, CO (1861–1879)
			Denver, CO (1879–1894)
			Pasadena, CA (1894–1895)
Manitoba			
Bottineau, Pierre (1817–1895)	guide, interpreter, negotiator with Indians	Winnipeg (1832)	St. Paul, MN (1840–1852)
			Osseo, MN (1852–1877)
			Red Lake Falls, MN (1877–1895)
Massachusetts			
Bunker, Harriet J. (1800–1895)	fund raiser, activist	Massachusetts (1852)	San Francisco, CA (1852–1895)
Ide, William Brown (1796–1852)	recruiter, state president, judge, farmer, surveyor, ferryman	Rutland (1845)	Sutter's Fort, CA (1845–1852)
Leavitt, Eliza S. Reed (1829–1910s)	innkeeper, depot manager	Boston (1856)	Indian Valley, CA (1860–1880s)
			Bridgeport, CA (1867–1901)
Leavitt, Hiram Lewis (1824–1901)	innkeeper, judge, depot manager	Boston (1851)	Indian Valley, CA (1860–1880s)
			Bridgeport, CA (1867–1901)
Tabor, Horace Austin W. (1830–1899)	stone mason, mayor, senator, postmaster, miner, merchant	Boston (1855)	Zeandale, KS (1855–1859)
			Oro City, CO (1859–1861)
			Leadville, CO (1861–1879)
			Denver, CO (1879–1899)
Wells, Emmeline B. (1828–1921)	teacher, diarist, editor, activist, social worker	Petersham (1844)	Salt Lake City (1846–1921)
Mexico			
Briones de Miranda, Juana (1802–1889)	rancher, herbalist, midwife	Mexico (1802)	Santa Clara, CA (1844–1885)
Reed, John Thomas (1805–1843)	sailor, sawyer, ferryman, rancher	Acapulco (1826)	San Francisco, CA (1826–1843)
Michigan			
Brier, James Welch Brier (1814–1898)	minister	Kalamazoo (1840)	Death Valley, CA (1849)
Brier, Juliet Wells Brier (1813–1819)	memoirist	Kalamazoo (1840)	Death Valley, CA (1849)
French, Erasmus Darwin (1822–1902)	physician, explorer, rancher, miner	Albion (1845)	Fort Tejon, CA (1847–1851)
			San Jose, CA (1848–1860)
			Darwin, CA (1860–1865)
			Baja, CA (1894–1902)
Minnesota			
Fisk, Andrew Jackson (1849–1910)	journalist, postmaster, soldier, farmer, miner	Fort Ripley (1866)	Fort Benton, MT (1866)

Place of Departure	Occupation	Left Original Home	Area of Settlement
Fisk, James Liberty (1835–1902)	soldier, guide, auditor, journalist	Fort Ripley (1863) Fort Ripley (1866)	Bannack, MT (1863) Fort Benton, MT (1866)
Fisk, Robert Emmett (1837–1908)	soldier, journalist	Fort Ripley (1866)	Fort Benton, MT (1866)
Fisk, Van Hayden (1840–1890)	soldier, journalist	Fort Ripley (1866)	Fort Benton, MT (1866)
Stone, Lewis (1799–1866)	innkeeper, miner, politician	St. Paul (1857)	Denver (1862–1864) Fort Collins (1864–1866)
Mississippi			
Lilly, Benjamin Vernon (1856–1936)	hunter, knife maker	Jackson (1868)	Mer Rouge, LA (1868–1901) Big Thicket, TX (1904–1908) Gila, NM (1908–1916) Quemado, AZ (1916–1926) Pleasanton, NM (1931–1936)
Missouri			
Bell, James George (1831–1911)	farmer	Sedalia (1856)	Obed, CA (1898–1911)
Bell, Susan Hollenbeck (1831–1905)	seamstress, activist	Sedalia, MO (1856)	Obed, CA (1898–1905)
Bowman, Sarah A. (1812–1866)	nurse, innkeeper, launderer, madame, cook, foster parent	Clay County (1845)	Corpus Christi, TX (1845–1846) El Paso, TX (1848–1850)
Bush, George W. (ca. 1779–1863)	community builder, farmer, stockman	Jackson (1844)	Tumwater, WA (1845–1866)
Bush, Isabella James (1801–1866)	community builder, nurse, poulterer	Jackson (1844)	Tumwater, WA (1845–1866)
Caldwell, Mathew H. (1798–1842)	community builder, sheriff, Texas Ranger	Gasconade (1831)	Gonzalez, TX (1831–1842)
Chiles, Joseph Ballinger (1810–1885)	rancher, miller, distiller, ferryman	Jackson County (1841)	Napa Valley, CA (1843–1885)
Coleman, William Tell (1824–1893)	shipper, borax miner, vigilante	St. Louis (1849)	San Francisco, CA (1849–1893)
Kellie, James Thomson (1850–1918)	farmer, activist, grocer, carpenter	St. Louis (1871)	Adams County, NE (1877–1884) Hartwell, NE (1884–1901)
Lawing, Nellie Trosper (1873–1956)	innkeeper, hunter, postmaster	Buchanan (1901)	Cripple Creek, CO (1903–1914) Seward, AK (1915–1956)
Morrison, John L. (1819–1899)	carpenter	Independence (1842)	Oregon City, OR (1843–1850)
Robidoux, Antoine (1794–1860)	trapper, guide, interpreter	St. Louis (1832)	Fort Uintah, UT (1833–1844)
Simmons, Elizabeth K. (1820–1891)	housewife	Nodaway (1844)	Tumwater, WA (1845–1867)
Simmons, Michael T. (1814–1867)	millwright, Indian agent, postmaster	Nodaway (1844)	Tumwater, WA (1845–1867)
Snyder, Grace McCance (1882–1892)	quilter	Cass County (1885)	Cozad, NE (1885–1919)
Sowell, Andrew Jackson (1815–1883)	farmer, Indian fighter, ranger	Boone County (1829)	Gonzales, TX (1829–1883)
Sowell, John Newton, Jr. (1811–1856)	blacksmith, hunter, ranger	Boone County (1829)	Gonzales, TX (1829–1856)
Sowell, John Newton, Sr. (1770–1838)	blacksmith, armorer	Boone County (1829)	Gonzales, TX (1829–1838)
Sowell, Rachel Carpenter (1785–1860s)	housewife	Boone County (1829)	Gonzales, TX (1829–1860s)
Wysinger, Pernesa Wilson (1843–1893)	housewife	Wayne County (1853)	Visalia, CA (1864–1893)
Netherlands			
Bonnema, Harmen H. (1827–1892)	farmer, merchant	Harlingen, Friesland (1853)	New Amsterdam, WI (1855–1892)
Bonnema, Oepke H. (1825–1895)	sawyer, recruiter, treasurer, taverner	Harlingen, Friesland (1853)	New Amsterdam, WI (1853–1895)

Appendix B. Departure

Place of Departure	Occupation	Left Original Home	Area of Settlement
Haagsma, Broer Baukes (1831–1907)	teacher, accountant, U.S. consul	Harlingen, Friesland (1853)	New Amsterdam, WI (1853–1907)
New Jersey			
Reading, Pearson B. (1816–1868)	miner, explorer, trapper, soldier	Hunterdon (1844)	Shasta, CA (1845–1868)
New York			
Booth, Albert Anson (1850–1914)	farmer, rancher, timberman	Syracuse (1869)	Fond du Lac, WI (1869–1872) Edna, ND (1879–1914)
Carr, Byron Oscar (1835–1913)	banker, railroad manager	Concord, NY (1872)	Truckee, CA (1872–1880s) San Francisco, CA (1880s–1891) Lemoore, CA (1894–1900) Seattle, WA (1900–1913)
Culbertson, Margaret (1834–1897)	teacher, missionary	Groveland (1878)	San Francisco, CA (1878–1897)
Dale, Martha Wood (1859–1930)	library builder, activist	Oswego, NY (1879)	Wichita (1879–1889) Guthrie, OK (1889–1930)
Ebbetts, John A.N. (ca. 1815–1854)	merchant, explorer, diarist	New York (1849)	San Francisco, CA (1849–1854)
Farnham, Eliza Wood (1815–1864)	reformer, writer, rancher	New York (1849)	Santa Cruz, CA (1849–1856) Stockton, CA (1859–1862)
Folsom, Joseph Libbey (1817–1855)	soldier, investor	West Point (1846)	San Francisco, CA (1847–1855)
Goulding, William R. (1805–1865)	surgeon, diarist, instrument maker	York, England	San Francisco, CA (1849–1850)
Huntington, Dimick B. (1808–1879)	constable, coroner, interpreter	Watertown (1836)	Salt Lake City, UT (1848–1901)
Huntington, Oliver B. (1823–1909)	priest, explorer, missionary	Watertown (1836)	Springville, UT (1852–1901)
Huntington, William (1784–1846)	miller, soldier, sexton, constable	Watertown (1836)	Mount Pisgah, IA (1846)
Huntington, William D. (1818–1887)	explorer, constable, taverner, mailman, miner, musician	Watertown, NY (1836)	Springville, UT (1852–1887)
Lambert, Rebecca H. (1806–1886)	fund raiser	New York (1852)	San Francisco, CA (1852–1886)
Monk, Hank (1826–1883)	stage driver	Waddington (1852)	Sacramento, CA (1852–1857)
Monteith, Charles Edgar (1847–1915)	Indian agent	Fulton (1874)	Lapwai, ID (1874–1889)
Robbins, Ezekiel Wright	physician, minister, merchant, politician	Watertown (1838)	Chester, IL (1838–1852)
Smith, Hiram F. (1829–1893)	trader, miner, mailman, orchardist	New York (1849)	Okanogan, WA (1856–1893)
Stone, Elizabeth H. (1801–1895)	midwife, hotelier, entrepreneur	Watertown (1828)	St. Louis, MO (1828–18520
Whitman, Marcus (1802–1847)	doctor, missionary	Angelica (1836)	Walla Walla, WA (1836–1847)
Whitman, Narcissa (1808–1847)	doctor, missionary	Angelica (1836)	Walla Walla, WA (1836–1847)
Young, Zina D.H. (1821–1901)	teacher, midwife, missionary	Watertown (1836)	Salt Lake City, UT (1848–1901)
New Zealand			
Cameron, Donaldina (1869–1968)	seamstress, activist	Clydevale (1871)	San Francisco, CA (1895–1968)
Nicaragua			
Hollenbeck, John E. (1829–1885)	investor	Nicaragua (1874)	Obed, CA (1874–1885)
North Carolina			
Campbell, Virginia J. (1822–1882)	fund raiser	Raleigh (1841)	St. Louis, MO (1841–1882)
Macy, Obed (1801–1857)	physician, city	New Garden (1850)	El Monte, CA (1851–1852)

Place of Departure	Occupation	Left Original Home	Area of Settlement
	councilman, innkeeper		Los Angeles, CA (1852–1857)
Norway			
Lahti, Charles (1859–1932)	farmer, investor	Vadsø (1864)	St. Peter, MN (1864–1932)
Lahti, Johanna Gustava (1840–1919)	farmer	Vadsø (1864)	St. Peter, MN (1864–1919)
Lahti, Peter J. (1834–1911)	trapper, farmer	Vadsø (1864)	St. Peter, MN (1864–1911)
Wahl, James M. (1846–1939)	carpenter, recruiter	Storvahl (1867)	Sioux Falls, SD (1868–1889) Lennox, SD (1889–1939)
Wahl, Julia Ulberg (1862–1915)	housewife	Valdres (1883)	Sioux Falls, SD (1883–1889) Lennox, SD (1889–1915)
Ohio			
Goodell, Nathan Edward (1839–1886)	merchant	Vermilion (1851)	Skagit River, OR (1879)
Judson, George (1860–1891)	surveyor, school builder	Vermilion (1853)	Bellingham, WA (1886)
Judson, Holden A. (1827–1899)	mayor, grocer, dairier, postmaster	Vermilion (1853)	Claquato, WA (1853–1858) Whidbey, WA (1866–1899)
Judson, Phoebe G. (1831–1926)	educator, memoirist	Vermilion (1853)	Claquato, WA (1853–1858) Whidbey, WA (1866–1926)
McBeth, Kate Christine (1832–1915)	missionary, teacher	Wellsville (1858)	Lapwai, ID (1879–1915)
McBeth, Susan Law (1830–1893)	missionary, teacher	Wellsville (1858)	Goodwater, OK (1858–1861) St. Louis, MO (1866–1873) Lapwai, ID (1873–1893)
Merritt, Josiah (1803–1882)	farmer, prospector, musician	Athens (1860)	Snoqualmie, WA (1860–1882)
Moore, Seymour T. (1827–1876)	soldier, surveyor, explorer	Ohio	Fort Miller, CA (1849–1851) Utah (1853–1854)
Rice, Coralinn Barlow (1849–1919)	singer	Cleveland (1877)	Tustin, CA (1878–1919)
Rice, James Stephen (1846–1939)	orchardist	Cleveland (1877)	Tustin, CA (1878–1939)
Snow, Eliza Roxcy (1804–1887)	hymnographer, social worker, teacher	Hiram (1835)	Salt Lake City, UT (1835–1887)
Ontario			
Kellie, James Thomson (1850–1918)	farmer, activist, grocer, carpenter, bridge builder, railroad laborer	Toronto (1871)	St. Louis, MO (1872–1873) Iowa (1874–1877) Adams County, NE (1877–1884) Hartwell, NE (1884–1901)
Stratton, Elizabeth P. (1830–1922)	teacher, diarist	Ontario (1864)	Fort Collins, CO (1864–1933)
Oregon			
Wilkins, Katherine Carolina (1857–1936)	horse breeder	Jacksonville (1857)	Bruneau, ID (1880–1936)
Pennsylvania			
Adair, Cornelia Wadsworth (1837–1921)	investor, rancher	Philadelphia (1874)	Palo Duro, TX (1874–1921)
Smith, Joseph, Jr. (1805–1844)	prophet, author, translator	Harmony (1827)	Nauvoo, IL (1831–1844)
Poland			
Reich, George Adolph (1846–1896)	pharmacist, doctor	Breslau (1870)	San Bernardino, CA (1870–1882)
Prussia			
Keseberg, Lewis (1814–1895)	sea captain, brewer, innkeeper	Westphalia (1844)	San Jose, CA (1847–1895)
Moczygemba, Leopold (1824–1891)	priest, recruiter	Pluznica (1852)	Bandera, TX (1852–1858)
Quebec			
Arcouet, Amable (1797–1880)	trapper, trader	Montreal (1833)	St. Paul, OR (1835–1880)

Appendix B. Departure

Place of Departure	Occupation	Left Original Home	Area of Settlement
Lee, Jason (1803–1845)	missionary, educator,	Stanstead (1833)	St. Paul, OR (1833–1844)
Liberty, Stephen Edward (1843–1911)	scout, translator	Quebec (1862)	Fort Benton, MT (1866)
Mead, Agnes Barcome (1841–1869)	trader	Quebec (1859)	Salina, KS (1862–1863) Wichita, KS (1864–1869)
Ouilmette, Antoine L. (ca. 1760–1841)	fur trader, ferryman, stockman	Montreal (1790)	Chicago, IL (1790–1833)
Rhode Island			
Parkhurst, Charley (1812–1879)	stagecoach driver	Providence (1851)	Soquel, CA (1851–1879)
Russia			
Meyerowitz, Isadore (ca. 1820–1856)	trader	Russia (1849)	Honey Lake, CA (1849–1856)
South Africa			
Mitchell, Eliza Vandenberg (1809–1881)	merchant	Cape Town (1836)	Florence, NE (1852–1881)
South Carolina			
Wysinger, Edmond E. (1816–1891)	miner	South Carolina (1849)	Tulare County, CA (1849–1891)
Spain			
Padilla, Juan de (?–1544)	missionary, chaplain	Andalusia, Spain (1528)	Quivira, TX (1542–1544)
Switzerland			
Bonnema, Luisa S. (1838–after 1910)	housewife	Altnau (1851)	New Amsterdam, WI (1860–?)
Tennessee			
Chisum, John Simpson (1824–1884)	rancher	Hardeman (1866)	Bosque Redondo, NM (1866)
Dyer, Leigh Richmond (1849–1902)	rancher	Madison (1867)	Belknap, TX (1867) Palo Duro, TX (1876)
Lawing, William "Billie" (1879–1936)	hotelier, boat captain	Murfreesboro (1923)	Seward, AK (1923–1936)
Page, Larcena P. (1837–1913)	teacher	Nashville (1837)	Honey Grove, TX (1837–1857)
Pennington, Elias G. (1809–1869)	farmer, freighter	Nashville (1837)	Honey Grove, TX (1837–1857)
Pennington, James (1833–1868)	farmer, freighter	Nashville (1837)	Honey Grove, TX (1837–1857)
Vermont			
Young, Brigham (1801–1877)	prophet, Indian agent, governor, church builder	Whittingham (1832)	Salt Lake City, UT (1877)
Virginia			
Bridger, Jim (1803–1881)	trapper, guide, scout	Richmond (1822)	Fort Bridger, WY (1842–1865)
Omohundro, Texas Jack (1846–1880)	cowboy, scout, actor, writer	Pleasure Hill (1859)	Fort Worth, TX (1859–1869) Cottonwood Springs, NE (1869–1872) Leadville, CO (1877–1880)
Smeathers, Mary Polly (1769–1810)	housewife	Wythe County (1788)	Owensboro, KY (1797–1810)
Wisconsin			
Booth, Ellen Eliza Carter (1854–1935)	fund raiser	Waupon (1879)	Edna, ND (1879–1914) Tacoma, WA (1914–1935)
Ise, Rosena Haag (1855–1947)	farmer	Theresa, WI (1873)	Ross, KS (1873–1947)
Parmley, J.W. (1861–1940)	brick maker, publisher	Mifflin (1883)	Ipswich, SD (1883–1940)

C. Destination

Destination State/Territory	Occupation	Left Original Home	Area of Settlement
Alaska			
Lawing, Nellie Trosper (1873–1956)	innkeeper, hunter, postmaster	Buchanan, MO (1901)	Seward (1915–1956)
Lawing, William "Billie" (1879–1936)	innkeeper, boat captain	Murfreesboro, TN (1923)	Seward (1923–1936)
Meeker, Ezra (1830–1928)	farmer, grocer	Eddyville, IA (1852)	Cook Inlet (1894–1896) Skagway (1898–1901)
Arizona			
Bowman, Sarah A. (1812–1866)	nurse, innkeeper, launderer, madame, cook, foster parent	Clay County, MO (1845)	Corpus Christi (1845–1846) El Paso (1848–1850)
Lilly, Benjamin Vernon (1856–1936)	hunter, knife maker, bounty hunter	Gila, NM (1908–1916)	Quemado (1916–1926)
Page, Larcena Pennington (1837–1913)	teacher	Nashville, TN (1837)	Tucson (1857–1913)
Pennington, Elias G. (1809–1869)	farmer, freighter	Honey Grove, TX (1837)	Fort Buchanan (1857–1869)
Pennington, James (1833–1868)	farmer, freighter	Nashville, TN (1837)	Fort Buchanan (1857–1868)
British Columbia			
Franklin, Lumley (1808–1873)	merchant	Liverpool, England (1849)	Victoria (1858–1873)
Franklin, Selim (1814–1884)	realtor, auctioneer, merchant	Liverpool, England (1849)	Victoria (1858–1866)
California			
Backenstoe, Virginia E. (1833–1921)	insurer	Springfield, IL (1846)	San Jose (1847–1874)
Bell, James George (1831–1911)	farmer	Sedalia, MO (1856)	Obed (1898–1911)
Bell, Susan Hollenbeck (1831–1905)	seamstress, activist	Sedalia, MO (1856)	Obed (1898–1905)
Brier, James Welch Brier (1814–1898)	minister	Kalamazoo, MI (1840)	Death Valley (1849)
Brier, Juliet Wells Brier (1813–1819)	memoirist	Kalamazoo, MI (1840)	Death Valley (1849)
Briones de Miranda, Juana (1802–1889)	rancher, herbalist, midwife	Mexico (1802)	Santa Clara (1844–1885)
Bunker, Harriet J. (1800–1895)	fund raiser, activist	Massachusetts (1852)	San Francisco (1852–1895)
Cameron, Donaldina (1869–1968)	seamstress, activist	Clydevale, New Zealand (1871)	San Francisco (1895–1968)
Carr, Byron Oscar (1835–1913)	railroad manager, banker	Concord, NY	Truckee (1872–1880s) San Francisco (1880s–1891) Lemoore (1894–1900)
Carr, Sarah Pratt (1850–1935)	missionary, writer, activist, librettist	Freeport, Maine (1852)	San Francisco (1852–1867) Lemoore (1883–1894) St. Helena (1894–1900)
Cheesman, David Williams (1822–1884)	attorney, memoirist, U.S. Mint treasurer	Washington, IN (1850)	El Monte (1851–1852) Los Angeles (1852–1884)
Cheesman, Urania K. (1828–1916)	housewife	Washington, IN (1850)	El Monte (1851–1852) Los Angeles (1852–1884)
Chiles, Joseph Ballinger (1810–1885)	rancher, miller, distiller, ferryman	Jackson County, MO (1841)	Napa Valley (1843–1885)
Chin, Ah Yane (1869–?)	interpreter	China (1874)	San Francisco (1874–?)
Coleman, William Tell (1824–1893)	shipper, borax miner, vigilante	St. Louis, MO (1849)	San Francisco (1849–1893)
Cowles, George Algernon (1836–1887)	raisin grower, financier, horse breeder	Hartford, CT (1878)	Cowlestown (1878–1887)
Culbertson, Margaret (1834–1897)	teacher, missionary	Groveland, NY (1878)	San Francisco (1878–1897)
Ebbetts, John A.N. (ca. 1815–1854)	merchant, explorer, diarist	New York, NY (1849)	San Francisco (1849–1851)

Appendix C. Destination

Destination State/Territory	Occupation	Left Original Home	Area of Settlement
Farnham, Eliza Wood (1815–1864)	reformer, writer, rancher	New York, NY (1849)	Santa Cruz (1849–1856) Stockton (1859–1862)
Farnham, Thomas Jefferson (1804–1848)	attorney, writer, freighter	Peoria, IL (1838)	Santa Cruz (1839)
Folsom, Joseph Libbey (1817–1855)	soldier, investor	West Point, NY (1846)	San Francisco (1847–1855)
Franklin, Edward (1809–1873)	merchant	Liverpool, England (1849)	San Francisco (1849–1873)
Franklin, Lewis Abraham (1820–1879)	attorney, merchant, soldier, judge	Kingston, Jamaica (1849)	San Francisco (1849–1855) San Diego (1855–1860)
Franklin, Lumley (1808–1873)	merchant	Liverpool, England (1849)	San Francisco (1849–1858)
Franklin, Maurice Abraham (1817–1874)	pharmacist, miner, merchant, teacher, synagogue builder, photographer	Kingston, Jamaica (1849)	San Francisco (1849–1855) San Diego (1855–1859) San Bernardino (1859–1874)
Franklin, Selim (1814–1884)	realtor, auctioneer, merchant	Liverpool, England (1849)	San Francisco (1849–1858, 1866–1884)
Franklin, Victoria Jacobs (1838–1861)	diarist	Manchester, England (1851)	San Diego (1851–1861)
French, Erasmus Darwin (1822–1902)	physician, explorer, rancher, miner	Albion, MI (1845)	Fort Tejon (1847–1851) San Jose (1848–1860) Darwin (1860–1865) Baja, (1894–1902)
Goddard, George Henry (1817–1906)	cartographer, artist, surveyor, civil engineer	Bristol, England (1850)	San Francisco (1850–1906)
Goller, John (1825–1874)	prospector, wagon maker, blacksmith	Bavaria	Los Angeles (1850–1874)
Goulding, William Robinson (1805–1865)	surgeon, instrument maker, diarist	York, England	San Francisco (1849–1850)
Hamilton, Ezra (1833–1914)	miner, inventor, manufacturer	Mount Sterling, IL (1853)	Shasta (1856–1861) Los Angeles (1875–1914)
Hayashi, Harvey Saburo (1867–1943)	physician, editor	Tonami, Japan (1885)	San Francisco (1884–1891) Sacramento (1891–1893)
Ide, William Brown (1796–1852)	recruiter, state president, farmer, surveyor, judge, ferryman	Rutland, MA (1845)	Sutter's Fort (1845–1852)
Isbell, Isaac Chauncy (1800–1886)	prospector, rancher, innkeeper, surgeon	Greenbush, IL (1846)	Santa Clara (1846–1850; 1861–1886)
Isbell, Olive Mann (1824–1899)	nurse, seamstress, rancher, teacher	Greenbush, IL (1846)	Santa Clara (1846–1850; 1861–1886)
Keseberg, Lewis (1814–1895)	sea captain, brewer, innkeeper	Westphalia, Prussia (1844)	San Jose (1847–1895)
Kinman, Seth (1815–1888)	prospector, hunter, dairier, innkeeper	Pekin, IL (1849)	Shasta (1850–1855) Table Bluff (1855–1888)
Kirby, Georgiana Bruce (1818–1887)	rancher, suffragist	Staffordshire, England (1831)	Santa Cruz (1850–1887)
Kirby, Richard Cornelius (1817–1904)	whaler, tanner	Staffordshire, England (1842)	Santa Cruz (1850–1904)
Lambert, Rebecca H. (1806–1886)	fund raiser, activist	New York, NY (1852)	San Francisco (1852–1886)
Lassen, Peter (1800–1859)	rancher, sawyer, prospector, recruiter, millwright	Farum, Denmark (1830)	San Jose (1840–1843) Rancho Bosquejo (1844–1850) Honey Lake (1855–1859)
Leavitt, Eliza S. Reed (1829–1910s)	innkeeper, depot manager	Boston, MA (1856)	Indian Valley (1860–1880s) Bridgeport (1867–1901)
Leavitt, Hiram Lewis (1824–1901)	innkeeper, judge, depot manager	Boston, MA (1851)	Indian Valley (1860–1880s) Bridgeport (1867–1901)
Lewis, Martha Jane Reed (1838–1923)	innkeeper	Springfield, IL (1846)	San Jose (1847–1874)
Macy, Lucinda Polk (1807–1872)	innkeeper	Washington, IN (1850)	El Monte (1851–1852) Los Angeles (1852–1872)

Destination State/Territory	Occupation	Left Original Home	Area of Settlement
Macy, Obed (1801–1857)	physician, city councilman, innkeeper	Washington, IN (1850)	El Monte (1851–1852) Los Angeles (1852–1857)
Macy, Oscar (1829–1910)	printer, publisher, jailer	Washington, IN (1850)	El Monte (1851–1852) Los Angeles (1852–1910)
Meyerowitz, Isadore (ca. 1820–1856)	trader	Russia (1849)	Honey Lake, CA (1849–1856)
Monk, Hank (1826–1883)	stage driver	Waddington, NY (1852)	Sacramento (1852–1857)
Moore, Seymour Treadwell (1827–1876)	soldier, surveyor, explorer	Ohio	Fort Miller (1849–1851)
Parkhurst, Charley (1812–1879)	stagecoach driver	Providence, RI (1851)	Soquel (1851–1879)
Pratt, Louisa Merrill (1827–1919)	housewife, activist	Freeport, ME (1852)	San Francisco (1852–1867, 1881–1893) Sacramento (1878–1881) St. Helena (1881–1900)
Pratt, Robert Henry (1824–1920)	miner, railroad builder	Freeport, ME (1852)	San Francisco (1849–1867), 1881–1893) Sacramento (1878–1881) St. Helena (1881–1900)
Reading, Pearson Barton (1816–1868)	miner, explorer trapper, soldier	Hunterdon, NJ (1844)	Shasta (1843–1868)
Reed, James Frazier (1800–1874)	land speculator, miner	Springfield, IL (1846)	San Jose (1847–1874)
Reed, James Frazier, Jr. (1841–1901)	land speculator, miner	Springfield, IL (1846)	San Jose (1847–1901)
Reed, John Thomas (1805–1843)	sailor, sawyer, rancher, ferryman	Acapulco, Mexico (1826)	San Francisco (1826–1843)
Reed, Margret Keyes (1814–1861)	housewife	Springfield, IL (1846)	San Jose (1847–1861)
Reich, George Adolph (1846–1896)	pharmacist, doctor	Breslau, Poland (1870)	San Bernardino (1870–1882)
Rice, Coralinn Barlow (1849–1919)	singer	Cleveland, OH (1877)	Tustin (1878–1919)
Rice, James Stephen (1846–1939)	orchardist	Cleveland, OH (1877)	Tustin (1878–1939)
Santee, Jennie Frances (1838–1931)	school builder	Hartford, CT (1878)	Cowlestown (1878–1931)
Tabor, Augusta Pierce (1833–1895)	grocer, laundress, cook, postmaster, philanthropist	Augusta, ME (1857)	Pasadena (1894–1895)
Wu, Tien Fu (1861–ca. 1940s)	interpreter	Canton, China (1876)	San Francisco (1876–ca. 1940s)
Wysinger, Edmond Edward (1816–1891)	miner	South Carolina (1849)	Visalia (1849–1891)
Wysinger, Pernesa Wilson (1843–1893)	housewife	Wayne County, MO (1853)	Visalia (1864–1893)
Colorado			
Baker, Jim (1818–1898)	rancher, guide, scout, interpreter	Belleville, IL (1839)	Clear Creek (1859–1873)
Brown, Clara (1800–1885)	cook, launderer, nurse, recruiter	Gallatin, KY (1856)	Denver (1859–1885)
DeVere, Pearl (1859–1897)	madam	Evansville, IN (ca. 1875)	Cripple Creek (ca. 1875–1897)
Goodnight, Mary Ann Dyer (1839–1926)	teacher	Hickman, KY (1870)	Pueblo (1870–1871)
Lawing, Nellie Trosper (1873–1956)	innkeeper, hunter, postmaster	Buchanan (1901)	Cripple Creek (1903–1914)
Maynard, Frank H. (1853–1926)	cowboy, carpenter, memoirist	Iowa City, IA (1869)	Granada (1874–1875) Colorado Springs (1881–1926)
Miller, Lafayette (1840–1878)	innkeeper, farmer, butcher	Quesqueton, IA (1863)	Lafayette (1863–1878)
Miller, Mary Foote (1842–1921)	coal miner, city planner, banker innkeeper	Quesqueton, IA (1863)	Lafayette (1863–1921)
Omohundro, Josephine Antonia	dancer	Milan, Italy (1830s)	Leadville (1877–1886)
Omohundro, Texas Jack (1846–1880)	cowboy, scout, actor, writer	Pleasure Hill, VA (1859)	Leadville (1877–1880)

Appendix C. Destination

Destination State/Territory	Occupation	Left Original Home	Area of Settlement
Stone, Elizabeth Hickok (1801–1895)	midwife, hotelier, entrepreneur	Watertown, NY (1828)	Denver (1862–1864) Fort Collins (1864–1895)
Stone, Lewis (1799–1866)	innkeeper, miner, politician	St. Paul, MN (1857)	Denver (1862–1864) Fort Collins (1864–1866)
Stratton, Elizabeth Parke (1830–1922)	teacher, diarist	Ontario (1864)	Fort Collins (1864–1933)
Tabor, Augusta Pierce (1833–1895)	grocer, laundress, cook, postmaster, philanthropist	Augusta, ME (1857)	Oro City (1859–1861) Leadville (1861–1879) Denver (1879–1894)
Tabor, Horace Austin W. (1830–1899)	stone mason, miner, senator, postmaster, mayor, merchant	Boston, MA (1855)	Oro City (1859–1861) Leadville (1861–1879) Denver (1879–1899)
Toponce, Alexander (1839–1923)	cowboy, stockman, drover, road builder, mailman	Tipton, MO (1854–1860)	Denver (1860–1863)
Wootton, Richens Lacey (1816–1893)	guide, freighter, Indian fighter, road builder	Christian, KY (1836)	Bent's Fort (1836–1847) Denver (1858–1893)

Hawaii

Bingham, Hiram (1789–1869)	missionary, lexicographer	Hartford, CT (1819)	Honolulu (1820–1840)
Bingham, Sybil Moseley (1792–1848)	teacher, midwife, seamstress	Hartford, CT (1819)	Honolulu (1820–1840)
Cope, Sister Marianne (1838–1918)	nun, nurse, hospital builder	Heppenheim, Hesse (1839)	Wailiuku, Maui (1884–1887) Kalaupapa, Molokai (1887–1918)
Hayashi, Harvey Saburo (1867–1943)	physician, editor, teacher	Tonami, Japan (1885)	Kona (1893–1943)
Hayashi, Matsu Kawarada (1877–1972)	teacher	Honshu, Japan (1896)	Kona (1896–1972)
Imamura, Yemyo (1867–1932)	missionary, labor leader, writer	Fukui, Japan (1899)	Honolulu (1899–1932)
Ozawa, Kintaro (fl. 1840s–1870s)	servant	Yokohama, Japan (1868)	Honolulu (1868–?)
Ozawa, Tomi (1849–?)	servant	Yokohama, Japan (1868)	Honolulu (1868–?)
Sakuma, Yonekichi (1839–1927)	cook	Yokohama, Japan (1868)	Kauai (1868–1927)

Idaho

Bruce, Samuel A. (1839–1900)	miner	Bray, Ireland (1860s)	Bannock (1860s)
Bruce, George Whiteley (1851–1927)	rancher, butcher, orchardist, dairier, Indian fighter	Bray, Ireland (1860s)	DeLamar (1860s–1927)
Heazle, Benjamin Alfred (1880–1936)	postmaster, rancher	Bray, Ireland (1894)	Murphy (1894–?)
Heazle, George Robert (1876–1924)	postmaster, grocer	Bray, Ireland (1894)	Murphy (1894–?)
Heazle, Jean (1879–1949)	timber cutter, miner, dairier, cattle rancher	Bray, Ireland (1893)	DeLamar (1893–1949)
McBeth, Kate Christine (1832–1915)	missionary, teacher	Wellsville, OH (1858)	Lapwai (1879–1915)
McBeth, Susan Law (1830–1893)	missionary, teacher	Wellsville, OH (1858)	Lapwai (1873–1893)
Monteith, Charles Edgar (1847–1915)	Indian agent	Fulton, NY (1874)	Lapwai (1874–1889)
O'Farrell, John A. (1823–1900)	miner, legislator, foster parent	Louisville, KY (1859)	Boise (1863–1900)
O'Farrell, Mary Ann (1840–1900)	foster parent, church builder	Louisville, KY (1859)	Boise (1863–1900)
Sothern, Mary Elizabeth B. (1856–1935)	housewife	Bray, Ireland (1860s)	DeLamar (1860s–1880s)

Destination State/Territory	Occupation	Left Original Home	Area of Settlement
Toponce, Alexander (1839–1923)	cowboy, stockman, stage driver, road builder, mailman	Tipton, MO (1854–1860)	Chesterfield (1879–1923)
Wilkins, John R. (1835–1904)	merchant	Fort Madison, IA (1853)	Ashby (1866–1867) Boise (1867–1876) Bruneau (1878–1904)
Wilkins, Katherine Carolina (1857–1936)	horse breeder	Jacksonville, OR (1857)	Bruneau (1880–1936)
Wilkins, Laura Smith (1839–1921)	dairier	Fort Madison, IA (1853)	Ashby (1866–1867) Boise (1867–1876) Bruneau (1878–1904)
Illinois			
Ouilmette, Antoine Louis (ca. 1760–1841)	fur trader, ferryman, stockman	Montreal, Quebec (1790)	Chicago (1790–1833)
Robbins, Ezekiel Wright (1800–1852)	physician, minister, merchant, politician	Watertown, NY (1828)	Chester (1838–1852)
Smith, Joseph, Jr. (1805–1844)	prophet, author, translator	Harmony, PA (1827)	Nauvoo (1831–1844)
Stone, Elizabeth Hickok (1801–1895)	midwife, hotelier, entrepreneur	Watertown, NY (1828)	Chester (1828–1852)
Street, Eliza Posey (1786–1849)	housewife	Henderson, KY (1809)	Shawneetown (1809–1812)
Street, Joseph Montfort (1782–1840)	postmaster, Indian agent, attorney	Frankfort, Ky (1807)	Shawneetown (1807–1812)
Iowa			
Huntington, William (1784–1846)	miller, constable, sexton, soldier	Watertown, NY (1836)	Mount Pisgah (1846)
Kellie, James Thomson (1850–1918)	farmer, activist, grocer, carpenter, bridge builder, railroad laborer	Toronto, Ontario (1871)	Iowa (1874–1877)
Key, Ambrose W. (1829–1908)	orchardist, farmer, tanner, sawyer, freighter	Crawfordsville, IN (1838)	Louisa County (1838–1860)
Key, George (1795–1864)	farmer, trader, blacksmith	Crawfordsville, IN (1836)	Louisa County (1836–1861)
Key, Mary Jones Garrett (1835–1927)	housewife	Tipton, MO (1859)	Louisa County (1859–1860)
Key, Rebecca Mintun (1799–ca. 1860)	housewife	Crawfordsville, IN (1838)	Louisa County (1838–1860)
Kansas			
Brown, Clara (1800–1885)	cook, launderer, nurse, recruiter	Gallatin, KY (1856)	Leavenworth (1856–1859)
Chisholm, Jesse (1806–1868)	trader, guide, interpreter	Arkansas (1820s)	Wichita (1861–1868)
Dale, Frank (1849–1930)	judge, financier	Somonauk, IL (1871)	Wichita (1871–1889)
Dale, Martha Wood (1859–1930)	library builder, activist	Oswego, NY (1879)	Wichita (1879–1889)
Goodnight, Charles (1836–1929)	Texas Ranger, rancher	Belknap, TX (1866)	Dodge City (1878)
Haag, Johann Christoph (1817–1890)	farmer	Württemberg, Germany (1851)	Holton (1859–1890)
Haag, Rosena Christina (1826–1892)	farmer	Württemberg, Germany (1851)	Holton (1859–1892)
Ise, Henry C. (1841–1900)	farmer	Württemberg, Germany (1857)	Ross (1871–1900)
Ise, Rosena Haag (1855–1947)	farmer, seamstress	Theresa, WI (1873)	Ross (1873–1947)
Key, Ambrose W. (1829–1908)	orchardist, farmer, tanner, sawyer, freighter	Crawfordsville, IN (1838)	Shawnee (1868–1908)

Appendix C. Destination

Destination State/Territory	Occupation	Left Original Home	Area of Settlement
Key, Mary Jones Garrett (1835–1927)	housewife	Louisa County, IA (1860)	Shawnee (1868–1927)
Maynard, Frank H. (1853–1926)	cowboy, carpenter, memoirist	Iowa City, IA (1869)	Towanda (1869–1881)
Mead, Agnes Barcome (1841–1869)	trader	Quebec (1859)	Salina (1862–1863) Wichita (1864–1869)
Mead, James R. (1836–1910)	trader, memoirist	Davenport, IA (1859)	Salina (1862–1863) Wichita (1864–1910)
Tabor, Augusta Pierce (1833–1895)	grocer, laundress, cook, postmaster, philanthropist	Augusta, ME (1857)	Zeandale (1857–1859)
Tabor, Horace Austin W. (1830–1899)	stone mason, miner, senator, postmaster, mayor, merchant	Boston, MA (1855)	Zeandale (1855–1859)
Kentucky			
Smeathers, Mary Polly (1769–1810)	housewife	Wythe County, VA (1788)	Owensboro (1797–1810)
Louisiana			
Lilly, Benjamin Vernon (1856–1936)	hunter, knife maker	Jackson, MS (1868)	Mer Rouge (1868–1901)
Minnesota			
Bottineau, Pierre (1817–1895)	guide, interpreter, negotiator with Indians	Winnipeg, MB (1832)	St. Paul (1840–1852) Osseo (1852–1877) Red Lake Falls (1877–1895)
Lahti, Charles (1859–1932)	farmer, investor	Vadsø, Norway (1864)	St. Peter (1864–1932)
Lahti, Johanna Gustava (1840–1919)	farmer	Vadsø, Norway (1864)	St. Peter (1864–1919)
Lahti, Peter J. (1834–1911)	trapper, farmer	Vadsø, Norway (1864)	St. Peter (1864–1911)
Stone, Elizabeth Hickock (1801–1895)	midwife, hotelier, entrepreneur	Watertown, NY (1828)	St. Paul (1857–1862)
Wahl, James M. (1846–1939)	carpenter, recruiter	Storvahl, Norway (1867)	Canton (1868–1889)
Wahl, Julia Ulberg (1862–1914)	housewife	Valdres, Norway (1883)	Canton (1883–1889)
Missouri			
Bridger, Jim (1803–1881)	trapper, guide, scout	Richmond, VA (1822)	Indian Creek (1855–1881)
Campbell, Robert (1804–1879)	trader, financier, negotiator, investor	Plumbridge, Ireland (1822)	St. Louis (1835–1879)
Campbell, Virginia Jane K. (1822–1882)	fund raiser	Raleigh, NC (1841)	St. Louis (1841–1882)
Kellie, James Thomson (1850–1918)	farmer, activist, grocer, carpenter, bridge builder, railroad laborer	Toronto, Ontario (1871)	St. Louis, MO (1872–1873) Iowa (1874–1877) Adams County, NE (1877–1884) Hartwell, NE (1884–1901)
Key, Ambrose W. (1829–1908)	orchardist, farmer, tanner, sawyer, freighter	Crawfordsville, IN (1834)	Westport (1865–1868)
McBeth, Susan Law (1830–1893)	missionary, teacher	Wellsville, OH (1858)	St. Louis (1866–1873)
McCoy, John Calvin (1811–1889)	missionary, merch.	Vincennes, IN (1830)	Kansas City, MO (1830–1889)
Point du Sable, Jean B. (ca. 1745–1818)	farmer, trader	Chicago, IL (1800)	St. Charles (1800–1818)
Sublette, William Lewis (1798–1845)	trapper, trader	Lincoln, KY (1822)	St. Charles (1822–1833) St. Louis, MO (1836–1845)
Toponce, Alexander (1839–1923)	cowboy, stage driver, stockman, road builder	Belfort, France (1846)	Tipton (1854–1860)
Montana			
Fisk, Andrew Jackson (1849–1910)	soldier, journalist, farmer, miner, postmaster	Fort Ripley, MN (1866)	Fort Benton (1866)

Appendix C. Destination

Destination State/Territory	Occupation	Left Original Home	Area of Settlement
Fisk, Elizabeth Chester (1846–1927)	diarist	Haddam, CT (1866)	Helena, MT (1866–1927)
Fisk, James Liberty (1835–1902)	soldier, guide, journalist, auditor	Fort Ripley, MN (1863) Fort Ripley, MN (1866)	Bannack (1863) Fort Benton (1866)
Fisk, Robert Emmett (1837–1908)	soldier, journalist	Fort Ripley, MN (1866)	Fort Benton (1866)
Fisk, Van Hayden (1840–1890)	soldier, publisher	Fort Ripley, MN (1866)	Fort Benton (1866)
Illingworth, William Henry (1844–1893)	photographer	Leeds, England (1845)	Fort Benton (1866)
Liberty, Stephen Edward (1843–1911)	scout, translator	Quebec, Canada (1862)	Fort Benton (1866)
Toponce, Alexander (1839–1923)	cowboy, stage driver, stockman, road builder	Denver, CO (1860–1863)	Bannack (1863)
Nebraska			
Kellie, James Thomson (1850–1918)	farmer, activist, grocer, carpenter, bridge builder, railroad laborer	Toronto, Ontario (1871)	Adams County (1877–1884) Hartwell (1884–1901)
Kellie, Luna Sanford (1857–1940)	farmer, editor, songwriter, activist, grocer	Rockford, IL (1871)	Adams County (1877–1884) Hartwell (1884–1901)
McCance, Charles Henry (1857–1926)	farmer	Toulon, IL (1900)	Cozad (1885–1926)
McCance, Margaret Anna (1861–1940)	housewife	Toulon, IL (1900)	Cozad (1885–1940)
McCance, Margaret Sarah (1830–1905)	housewife	Toulon, IL (1900)	Cozad (1885–1905)
Mitchell, Eliza Vandenberg (1809–1881)	merchant	Cape Town, South Africa (1836)	Florence (1852–1881)
Mitchell, James C. (1810–1860)	merchant, realtor	Council Bluffs, IA (1852)	Florence (1852–1860)
Snyder, Grace McCance (1882–1982)	quilter	Cass County, MO (1885)	Cozad (1885–1919)
Nevada			
Carr, Sarah Pratt (1850 1935)	missionary, writer, activist, librettist	Freeport, ME (1852)	Carlin (1867–1872)
Coleman, William Tell (1824–1893)	shipper, borax miner, vigilante	St. Louis, MO (1849)	Columbus Marsh (1871–1888)
Monk, Hank (1826–1883)	stage driver	Waddington, NY (1852)	Carson City (1857–1883)
Pratt, Louisa Merrill (1827–1919)	housewife, activist	Freeport, ME (1852)	Carlin (1852–1872)
Pratt, Robert Henry (1824–1920)	miner, railroad builder	Freeport, ME (1852)	Carlin (1867–1869)
Wilkins, John R. (1835–1904)	merchant	Fort Madison, IA (1853)	Tuscarora (1876–1878)
New Mexico			
Chisum, John Simpson (1824–1884)	rancher	Belknap, TX (1866)	Bosque Redondo (1866) Fort Sumner (1867)
Docher, Anton (1852–1928)	missionary	Auvergne, France (1887)	Isleta Pueblo (1891–1928)
Goodnight, Charles (1836–1929)	Texas Ranger, rancher	Belknap, TX (1866)	Fort Sumner (1866)
Holmes, James Henry (1833–1907)	journalist, soldier, territorial secretary	Emporia, KS (1858)	Taos (1858–1863)
Holmes, Julia Archibald (1838–1887)	writer, reformer, teacher, explorer	Emporia, KS (1858)	Taos (1858–1863)
Lilly, Benjamin Vernon (1856–1936)	hunter, knife maker	Big Thicket, TX	Gila (1908–1916) Pleasanton (1931–1936)
Loving, Oliver (1812–1867)	rancher	Belknap, TX (1866)	Fort Sumner (1866–1867)
Wootton, Richens Lacey (1816–1893)	guide, freighter, Indian fighter, road builder	Christian, KY (1836)	Taos (1847–1858)
Nicaragua			
Hollenbeck, John Edward (1829–1885)	investor	Nicaragua (1874)	Obed, CA (1874–1885)

Appendix C. Destination

Destination State/Territory	Occupation	Left Original Home	Area of Settlement
North Dakota			
Booth, Albert Anson (1850–1914)	farmer, rancher, timberman	Syracuse, NY (1869)	Edna (1879–1914)
Booth, Ellen Eliza Carter (1854–1935)	fund raiser	Waupon, WI (1879)	Edna (1879–1914)
Fisk, James Liberty (1835–1902)	soldier, guide, journalist, auditor	St. Cloud, MN (1864)	Fort Rice (1864)
Monk, Hank (1826–1883)	stage driver	Carson City, NV (1881)	Deadwood (1881)
Oklahoma			
Chisholm, Jesse (1806–1868)	trader, guide, interpreter	Arkansas (1820s)	Hughes County (1820s, 1858–1861, 1868)
Dale, Frank (1849–1930)	judge, financier	Wichita, KS (1889)	Guthrie (1889–1930)
McBeth, Susan Law (1830–1893)	missionary, teacher	Wellsville, OH (1858)	Goodwater (1858–1861)
Speed, Horace (1852–1924)	lawyer	Indianapolis, IN (1889)	Guthrie (1889–1913)
Oregon			
Arcouet, Amable (1797–1880)	trapper, trader, farmer, mason	Montreal, Quebec (1833)	St. Paul (1835–1880)
Belshaw, Candace McCarty (1826–1892)	housewife	Lake County, IN (1853)	Eugene (1853–1892)
Belshaw, George, Jr. (1815–1893)	farmer, diarist	Lake County, IN (1853)	Eugene (1853–1893)
Farnham, Thomas J. (1804–1848)	attorney	Peoria, IL (1838)	Willamette (1839)
Goodell, Jotham Weeks (1809–1859)	minister	Vermilion, OH (1851)	Portland (1851–1859)
Goodell, Nathan Edward (1839–1886)	merchant	Vermilion, OH (1851)	Skagit River (1879)
Lee, Jason (1803–1845)	territorial organizer, missionary, educator	Stanstead, Quebec (1833)	St. Paul (1833–1844)
Morrison, John L. (1819–1899)	carpenter	Independence, MO (1842)	Oregon City (1842–1850)
Wilkins, John R. (1835–1904)	merchant	Fort Madison, IA (1853)	Oregon City (1854–1860)
Wilkins, Laura Smith (1835–1921)	dairier	Fort Madison, IA (1853)	Oregon City (1854–1860)
South Dakota			
Parmley, J.W. (1861–1940)	brick maker, farmer, publisher	Mifflin, WI (1883)	Ipswich (1883–1940)
Wahl, James M. (1846–1939)	carpenter, recruiter	Storvahl, Norway (1867)	Sioux Falls (1868–1889) Lennox (1889–1939)
Wahl, Julia Ulberg (1862–1914)	housewife	Valdres, Norway (1868)	Lennox (1889–1914)
Texas			
Adair, Cornelia Wadsworth (1837–1921)	investor, rancher	Philadelphia, PA (1874)	Palo Duro (1874–1921)
Adair, John George (1823–1885)	investor	Queen's County, Ireland (1874)	Palo Duro (1874–1885)
Bowman, Sarah A. (1812–1866)	nurse, innkeeper, launderer, madame, cook, foster parent	Clay County (1845)	Corpus Christi (1845–1846) El Paso (1848–1850)
Caldwell, Mathew (1798–1842)	community builder, sheriff, Texas Ranger	Gasconade, MO (1831)	Gonzalez (1831–1842)
Chisholm, Jesse (1806–1868)	trader, guide, interpreter	Arkansas (1820s)	Tehuacana Creek (1833–1858)
Chisum, John Simpson (1824–1884)	rancher	Hardeman, TN (1866)	Paris (1837)
Dyer, Leigh Richmond (1849–1902)	rancher	Madison, TN (1867)	Belknap (1867) Palo Duro (1876)
Goodnight, Charles (1836–1929)	Texas Ranger, rancher	Macoupin, IL (1846)	Goodnight (1846–1929)
Goodnight, Elija (1831–1929)	soldier, rancher	Macoupin, IL (1846)	Goodnight (1846–1929)
Goodnight, Mary Ann D. (1839–1926)	teacher	Hickman, KY (1870)	Palo Duro (1871–1887) Fort Worth (1887–1926)

Destination State/Territory	Occupation	Left Original Home	Area of Settlement
Isbell, Isaac Chauncy (1800–1886)	doctor, rancher, innkeeper	Greenbush, IL (1846)	Cancon (1850–1861)
Isbell, Olive Mann (1824–1899)	nurse, seamstress, rancher, teacher	Greenbush, IL (1846)	Cancon (1850–1861)
Key, Ambrose W. (1829–1908)	orchardist, farmer, tanner, sawyer, freighter	Crawfordsville, IN (1838)	Navasota (1860–1865)
Key, Mary Jones Garrett (1835–1927)	housewife	Louisa County, IA (1860)	Navasota (1860–1865)
Lilly, Benjamin Vernon (1856–1936)	hunter, knife maker	Mer Rouge, LA (1868)	Big Thicket (1904–1908)
Moczygemba, Leopold (1824–1891)	priest, recruiter	Pluznica, Prussia (1852)	Bandera (1852–1858)
Omohundro, Texas Jack (1846–1880)	cowboy, scout, actor, writer	Pleasure Hill, VA (1859)	Fort Worth (1859–1869)
Padilla, Juan de (?–1544)	missionary, chaplain	Andalusia, Spain (1528)	Quivira (1542–1544)
Page, Larcena P. (1837–1913)	teacher	Nashville (1837)	Honey Grove (1837–1857)
Pennington, Elias G. (1809–1869)	farmer, freighter	Nashville, TN (1837)	Honey Grove (1837–1857)
Pennington, James (1833–1868)	farmer, freighter	Nashville, TN (1837)	Honey Grove (1837–1857)
Rasor, John Henry (1849–1925)	farmer, stockman	Graham, IA (1883)	Plano (1883–1925)
Rasor, Mary Ellen (1851–1918)	housewife	Graham, IA (1883)	Plano (1883–1918)
Reed, Emaline Cobb (1825–1890)	housewife	Walker County, AL (1837)	Bell County (1837–1890)
Reed, Martha Burnett (1786–1855)	housewife	Natchitoches, LA (1833)	Bell County (1833–1855)
Reed, Michael (1777–1859)	farmer	Natchitoches, LA (1833)	Bell County (1833–1859)
Reed, William Whitaker (1816–1891)	rancher, sheriff	Natchitoches, LA (1833)	Bell County (1833–1891)
Smeathers, William (ca. 1766–1837)	hunter, Indian fighter	Yellow Banks, KY (1821)	Columbia (1824–1837)
Sowell, Andrew Jackson (1815–1883)	farmer, Indian fighter, ranger	Boone County, MO (1829)	Gonzales (1829–1883)
Sowell, John Newton, Jr. (1811–1856)	blacksmith, hunter, ranger	Boone County, MO (1829)	Gonzales (1829–1856)
Sowell, John Newton, Sr. (1770–1838)	blacksmith, armorer	Boone County, MO (1829)	Gonzales (1829–1838)
Sowell, Rachel Carpenter (1785–1860s)	housewife	Boone County, MO (1829)	Gonzales (1829–1860s)
Stroud, Beden (1795–1865)	farmer, Indian agent, soldier	Chambers County, AL (1836)	Calvert (1836–1865)
Stroud, Ethan A. (1788–1846)	farmer, Indian agent, soldier	Chambers County, AL (1836)	Calvert (1836–1865)

Utah

Ebbetts, John A.N. (ca. 1815–1854)	merchant, explorer, diarist	New York, NY (1849)	Utah (1853–1854)
Huntington, Dimick Baker (1808–1879)	constable, coroner, interpreter	Watertown, NY (1836)	Salt Lake City (1848–1879)
Huntington, Oliver B. (1823–1909)	priest, explorer, missionary	Watertown, NY (1836)	Springville (1852–1909)
Huntington, William D. (1818–1887)	explorer, constable, taverner, mailman, miner, musician	Watertown, NY (1836)	Springville (1852–1887)
Moore, Seymour Treadwell (1827–1876)	soldier, surveyor, explorer	Ohio	Utah (1853–1854)
Pratt, Louisa Merrill (1827–1919)	housewife, activist	Freeport, ME (1852)	Salt Lake City (1872–1879)
Pratt, Robert Henry (1824–1920)	miner, railroad builder	Freeport, ME (1852)	Salt Lake City (1869–1879)
Robidoux, Antoine (1794–1860)	trapper, guide, interpreter	St. Louis, MO (1832)	Fort Uintah (1833–1844)
Snow, Eliza Roxcy (1804–1887)	hymnographer, teacher, social worker	Hiram, OH (1835)	Salt Lake City (1835–1887)

Appendix C. Destination

Destination State/Territory	Occupation	Left Original Home	Area of Settlement
Toponce, Alexander (1839–1923)	cowboy, stage driver, stockman, road builder	Denver, CO (1860–1863)	Ogden (1863–1923)
Wells, Emmeline B. (1828–1921)	teacher, diarist, editor, activist, social worker	Petersham, MA (1844)	Salt Lake City (1846–1921)
Young, Brigham (1801–1877)	prophet, governor, Indian agent, church builder	Whittingham, VT (1832)	Salt Lake City (1847–1877)
Young, Zina D.H. (1821–1901)	teacher, midwife, missionary, social worker	Watertown, NY (1836)	Salt Lake City (1848–1901)
Washington			
Booth, Ellen Eliza C. (1854–1935)	fund raiser	Waupon, WI (1879)	Tacoma (1914–1935)
Bush, George W. (ca. 1779–1863)	community builder, farmer, stockman	Jackson, MO (1844)	Tumwater (1845–1863)
Bush, Isabella James (1801–1866)	community builder, nurse, poulterer	Jackson, MO (1844)	Tumwater (1845–1866)
Carr, Byron Oscar (1835–1913)	railroad manager, banker	Concord, NY (1872)	Seattle (1900–1913)
Carr, Sarah Pratt (1850–1935)	missionary, writer, activist, librettist	Freeport, Maine (1852)	Seattle (1900–1913)
Fisk, James Liberty (1835–1902)	soldier, guide, journalist, auditor	St. Paul, MN (1862)	Fort Walla Walla (1862)
Goodell, Henry Martin (1843–1905)	ferryman, justice of the peace	Vermilion, OH (1853)	Lynden (1884–1905)
Gwydir, Rickard Daniel (1844–1925)	soldier, Indian agent	Covington, KY (1887)	Spokane (1887–1925)
Judson, George (1860–1891)	surveyor, school builder	Vermilion, OH (1853)	Bellingham (1886)
Judson, Holden Allen (1827–1899)	mayor, grocer, postmaster, dairier	Vermilion, OH (1853)	Claquato (1853–1858) Whidbey (1866–1899)
Judson, Phoebe Goodell (1831–1926)	educator, memoirist, foster mother	Vermilion, OH (1853)	Claquato (1853–1858) Whidbey (1866–1926)
McCarty, Jonathan W. (1833–1900)	farmer, merchant, mailman	Lake County, IN (1853)	Pierce County (1853–1870) Seattle (1870–1900)
Meeker, Eliza Jane (1834–1909)	farmer, grocer, innkeeper, activist	Eddyville, IA (1852)	McNeil Island (1853–1861) Puyallup (1862–1909)
Meeker, Ezra (1830–1928)	farmer, grocer, innkeeper	Eddyville, IA (1852)	McNeil Island (1853–1861) Puyallup (1862–1894)
Meeker, Oliver Perry (1828–1861)	farmer, grocer	Eddyville, IA (1852)	McNeil Island (1853–1860)
Merritt, Josiah (1803–1882)	farmer, prospector, musician	Athens, OH (1860)	Snoqualmie (1860–1882)
Morrison, John L. (1819–1899)	carpenter	Independence, MO (1842)	Orcas Island, (1859–1899)
Pratt, Louisa Merrill (1827–1919)	housewife, activist	Freeport, ME (1852)	Seattle (1900–1919)
Pratt, Robert Henry (1824–1920)	miner, railroad builder	Freeport, ME (1852)	Seattle (1900–1920)
Simmons, Elizabeth K. (1820–1891)	housewife	Nodaway, MO (1844)	Tumwater (1845–1867)
Simmons, Michael T. (1814–1867)	millwright, Indian agent, postmaster	Nodaway, MO (1844)	Tumwater (1845–1867)
Smith, Hiram F. (1829–1893)	trader, miner, mailman, orchardist	New York, NY (1849)	Okanogan (1856–1893)
Whitman, Marcus (1802–1847)	doctor, missionary	Angelica, NY (1836)	Walla Walla (1836–1847)
Whitman, Narcissa (1808–1847)	doctor, missionary	Angelica, NY (1836)	Walla Walla (1836–1847)
Wisconsin			
Bonnema, Harmen H. (1827–1892)	farmer, merchant	Harlingen, Friesland (1853)	New Amsterdam (1855–1892)
Bonnema, Luisa S. (1838–after 1910)	housewife	Altnau, Switzerland (1851)	New Amsterdam (1860–?)
Bonnema, Oepke H. (1825–1895)	sawyer, recruiter, treasurer, taverner	Harlingen, Friesland (1853)	New Amsterdam (1853–1895)

Destination State/Territory	Occupation	Left Original Home	Area of Settlement
Booth, Albert Anson (1850–1914)	farmer, rancher, timberman	Syracuse, NY (1869)	Fond du Lac (1869–1872)
Haag, Johann Christoph (1817–1890)	farmer	Württemberg, Germany (1851)	Theresa (1851–1859)
Haag, Rosena Christina (1826–1892)	farmer	Württemberg, Germany (1851)	Theresa (1851–1859)
Haagsma, Broer Baukes (1831–1907)	teacher, accountant, U.S. consul	Harlingen, Friesland (1853)	New Amsterdam (1853–1907)
Street, Eliza Posey (1786–1849)	housewife	Henderson, KY (1809)	Prairie du Chien (1812–1835, 1837–1842)
Street, Joseph Montfort (1782–1840)	postmaster, Indian agent, attorney	Shawneetown, IL (1812)	Prairie du Chien (1812–1835, 1837–1842)
Wyoming			
Baker, Jim (1818–1898)	rancher, guide, scout	Belleville, IL (1839)	Savery (1873–1898)
Bridger, Jim (1803–1881)	trapper, guide, scout	Richmond, VA (1822)	Fort Bridger (1842–1855)
Campbell, Robert (1804–1879)	trader, financier, negotiator, investor	Plumbridge, Ireland (1822)	Fort William (1833–1835)
Kelly, Fanny Wiggins (1845–1904)	memoirist, patent clerk, laundress, innkeeper	Geneva, KS (1864)	Box Elder Creek (1864) Sherman Station (1868–1869)
Kelly, Josiah Shawhan (1824–1867)	farmer, innkeeper	Geneva, KS (1864)	Box Elder Creek (1864)
Larimer, Sarah Luse (1836–1913)	photographer, grocer	Iola, KS (1864)	Sherman Station (1864–1870)
Larimer, William Jackson (1828–1895)	farmer, grocer	Iola, KS (1864)	Sherman Station (1864–1870)
Sublette, William Lewis (1798–1845)	trapper, trader	Lincoln, KY (1822)	Fort William (1833–1835)

D. Religion

Beliefs	Occupation	Origin	Destination
Atheist			
Farnham, Eliza Wood (1815–1864)	reformer, writer, rancher	New York, NY (1849)	Santa Cruz, CA (1849–1856) Stockton, CA (1859–1862)
Baptist			
Belshaw, Candace M. (1826–1892)	housewife	Lake County, IN (1853)	Eugene, OR (1853–1892)
Coleman, William Tell (1824–1893)	shipper, borax miner, vigilante	St. Louis, MO (1849)	San Francisco, CA (1849–1893)
Ebbetts, John A.N. (ca. 1815–1854)	merchant, explorer, diarist	New York, NY (1849)	San Francisco, CA (1849–1854)
McCarty, Jonathan Warren (1833–1900)	farmer, merchant, mailman	Lake County, IN (1853)	Pierce County, WA (1853–1870) Seattle, WA (1870–1900)
McCoy, John Calvin (1811–1889)	missionary, merchant	Vincennes, IN (1830)	Kansas City, MO (1830–1889)
Pennington, Elias G. (1809–1869)	farmer, freighter	Nashville, TN (1837)	Honey Grove, TX (1837–1857)
Rasor, John Henry (1849–1925)	farmer, stockman	Graham, IA (1883)	Plano, TX (1883–1925)
Rasor, Mary Ellen (1851–1918)	housewife	Graham, IA (1883)	Plano, TX (1883–1918)
Wysinger, Edmond E. (1849–1891)	miner	South Carolina (1849)	Visalia, CA (1816–1891)

Appendix D. Religion

Beliefs	Occupation	Origin	Destination
Wysinger, Pernesa Wilson (1843–1893)	housewife	Wayne County, MO (1853)	Visalia, CA (1864–1893)
Buddhist			
Imamura, Yemyo (1867–1932)	missionary, labor leader, writer	Fukui, Japan (1899)	Honolulu, HI (1899–1932)
Calvinist			
Bonnema, Luisa S. (1838–after 1910)	housewife	Altnau, Switzerland (1851)	New Amsterdam, WI (1860–?)
Catholic			
Arcouet, Amable (1797–1880)	trapper, trader, farmer, mason	Montreal, Quebec (1833)	St. Paul, OR (1835–1880)
Backenstoe, Virginia E. (1833–1921)	insurer	Springfield, IL (1846)	San Jose, CA (1847–1874)
Bottineau, Pierre (1817–1895)	interpreter, negotiator with Indians, guide	Winnipeg, MB (1832)	St. Paul, MN (1840–1852) Osseo, MN (1852–1877) Red Lake Falls, MN (1877–1895)
Briones de Miranda, Juana (1802–1889)	rancher, herbalist, midwife	Mexico (1802)	Santa Clara, CA (1844–1885)
Cope, Sister Marianne (1838–1918)	nun, nurse, hospital builder	Heppenheim, Hesse (1839)	Wailiuku, Maui (1884–1887) Kalaupapa, Molokai (1887–1918)
Docher, Anton (1852–1928)	missionary	Auvergne, France (1887)	Isleta Pueblo, NM (1891–1928)
Moczygemba, Leopold (1824–1891)	priest, recruiter	Pluznica, Prussia (1852)	Bandera, TX (1852–1858)
O'Farrell, John A. (1823–1900)	miner, legislator, foster parent	Louisville, KY (1859)	Boise, ID (1863–1900)
O'Farrell, Mary Ann (1840–1900)	foster parent, church builder	Louisville, KY (1859)	Boise, ID (1863–1900)
Omohundro, Josephine (1836–1886)	dancer	Milan, Italy (1830s)	Leadville, CO (1877–1886)
Ouilmette, Antoine L. (ca. 1760–1841)	fur trader, ferryman, stockman	Montreal, Quebec (1790)	Chicago, IL (1790–1833)
Padilla, Juan de (?–1544)	missionary, chaplain	Andalusia, Spain (1528)	Quivira, TX (1542–1544)
Point du Sable, Jean (ca. 1745–1818)	farmer, trader	Chicago, IL (1800)	St. Charles, MO (1800–1818)
Reed, John Thomas (1805–1843)	sailor, sawyer, rancher, ferryman	Acapulco, Mexico (1826)	San Francisco, CA (1826–1843)
Sublette, William Lewis (1798–1845)	trapper, trader	Lincoln, KY (1822)	St. Charles, MO (1822–1833) Fort William, WY (1833–1835) St. Louis, MO (1836–1845)
Wilkins, John R. (1835–1904)	merchant, hotelier, stockman	Fort Madison, IA (1853)	Oregon City, OR (1854–1860) Ashby, ID (1866–1867) Boise, ID (1867–1876) Tuscarora, NV (1876–1878) Bruneau, ID (1878–1904)
Wilkins, Katherine C. (1857–1936)	horse breeder	Jacksonville, OR (1857)	Bruneau, ID (1880–1936)
Wilkins, Laura Smith (1835–1921)	dairier	Fort Madison, IA (1853)	Oregon City, OR (1854–1860) Ashby, ID (1866–1867) Boise, ID (1867–1876) Tuscarora, NV (1876–1878) Bruneau, ID (1878–1921)
Wootton, Richens Lacey (1816–1893)	Indian fighter, freighter, road builder, guide	Christian, KY (1836)	Independence, MO (1836) Bent's Fort, CO (1836–1847) Taos, NM (1847–1858) Denver, CO (1858–1893)
Congregationalist			
Belshaw, George, Jr. (1815–1893)	farmer, diarist	Lake County, IN (1853)	Eugene, OR (1853–1893)
Bingham, Hiram (1789–1869)	missry., lexicogrphr.	Hartford, CT (1819)	Honolulu, HI (1820–1840)
Bingham, Sybil Moseley (1792–1848)	teacher, midwife, seamstress	Hartford, CT (1819)	Honolulu, HI (1820–1840)

Appendix D. Religion

Beliefs	Occupation	Origin	Destination
Brier, James Welch Brier (1814–1898)	minister	Kalamazoo, MI (1840)	Death Valley, CA (1849)
Brier, Juliet Wells Brier (1813–1819)	memoirist	Kalamazoo, MI (1840)	Death Valley, CA (1849)
Cowles, George Algernon (1836–1887)	rancher, horse breeder, financier	Hartford, CT (1878)	Cowlestown, CA (1878–1887)
Fisk, Elizabeth Chester (1846–1927)	diarist	Haddam, CT (1867)	Helena, MT (1867–1902)
Hayashi, Harvey Saburo (1867–1943)	physician, editor	Tonami, Japan (1885)	San Francisco, CA (1884–1891) Sacramento, CA (1891–1893) Kona, HI (1893–1943)
Leavitt, Eliza S. Reed (1829–1910s)	innkeeper, depot manager	Boston, MA (1856)	Indian Valley, CA (1860–1880s) Bridgeport, CA (1867–1901)
Leavitt, Hiram Lewis (1824–1901)	innkeeper, judge, depot manager	Boston, MA (1851)	Indian Valley, CA (1860–1880s) Bridgeport, CA (1867–1901)
Page, Larcena P. (1837–1913)	teacher	Nashville, TN (1837)	Tucson, AZ (1857–1913)
Santee, Jennie Frances (1838–1931)	school builder	Hartford, CT (1878)	Cowlestown, CA (1878–1931)

Dutch Reformed

Beliefs	Occupation	Origin	Destination
Bonnema, Harmen H. (1827–1892)	farmer, merchant	Harlingen, Friesland (1853)	New Amsterdam, WI (1855–1892)
Bonnema, Oepke H. (1825–1895)	sawyer, recruiter, treasurer, taverner	Harlingen, Friesland (1853)	New Amsterdam, WI (1853–1895)
Haagsma, Broer Baukes (1831–1907)	teacher, accountant, U.S. consul	Harlingen, Friesland (1853)	New Amsterdam, WI (1853–1907)

Episcopalian

Beliefs	Occupation	Origin	Destination
Bruce, George Whiteley (1851–1927)	rancher, butcher, dairier, orchardist	Bray, Ireland (1860s)	DeLamar, ID (1860s–1927)
Bruce, Samuel A. (1839–1900)	miner	Bray, Ireland (1860s)	Bannock, ID (1860s)
Miller, Lafayette (1840–1878)	hotelier, farmer, butcher	Quesqueton, IA (1863)	Lafayette, CO (1863–1878)
Miller, Mary Foote (1842–1921)	coal miner, banker, city planner, innkeeper	Quesqueton, IA (1863)	Lafayette, CO (1863–1921)
Rice, Coralinn Barlow (1849–1919)	singer	Cleveland, OH (1877)	Tustin, CA (1878–1919)
Sothern, Mary Elizabeth (1856–1935)	housewife	Bray, Ireland (1860s)	DeLamar, ID (1860s–1880s)

Evangelical Unitarian

Beliefs	Occupation	Origin	Destination
Ise, Henry C. (1841–1900)	farmer	Württemberg, Germany (1857)	Ross, KS (1871–1900)
Ise, Rosena Haag (1855–1947)	farmer, seamstress	Theresa, WI (1873)	Ross, KS (1873–1947)

Finnish Apostolic Lutheran

Beliefs	Occupation	Origin	Destination
Lahti, Charles (1859–1932)	farmer, investor	Vadsø, Norway (1864)	St. Peter, MN (1864–1932)
Lahti, Johanna Gustava (1840–1919)	farmer	Vadsø, Norway (1864)	St. Peter, MN (1864–1919)
Lahti, Peter J. (1834–1911)	trapper, farmer	Vadsø, Norway (1864)	St. Peter, MN (1864–1911)

German Baptist

Beliefs	Occupation	Origin	Destination
Bush, Isabella James (1801–1866)	community builder, nurse, poulterer	Jackson, MO (1844)	Tumwater, WA (1845–1866)

German Methodist

Beliefs	Occupation	Origin	Destination
Brown, Clara (1800–1885)	cook, launderer, nurse, recruiter	Gallatin, KY (1856)	Leavenworth, KS (1856–1859) Denver, CO (1859–1885)

Jewish

Beliefs	Occupation	Origin	Destination
Franklin, Edward (1809–1873)	merchant	Liverpool, England (1849)	San Francisco, CA (1849–1873)
Franklin, Lewis Abraham (1820–1879)	attorney, merchant, soldier, judge	Kingston, Jamaica (1849)	San Francisco, CA (1849–1855) San Diego, CA (1855–1860)
Franklin, Lumley (1808–1873)	merchant	Liverpool, England (1849)	San Francisco, CA (1849–1858) Victoria, BC (1858–1873)

Appendix D. Religion

Beliefs	Occupation	Origin	Destination
Franklin, Maurice A. (1817–1874)	pharmacist, teacher, miner, merchant, synagogue builder, photographer	Kingston, Jamaica (1849)	San Francisco, CA (1849–1855) San Diego, CA (1855–1859) San Bernardino, CA (1859–1874)
Franklin, Selim (1814–1884)	realtor, auctioneer, merchant	Liverpool, England (1849)	San Francisco, CA (1849–1858, 1866–1884) Victoria, BC (1858–1866)
Franklin, Victoria Jacobs (1838–1861)	diarist	Manchester, England (1851)	San Diego, CA (1851–1861)
Reich, George Adolph (1846–1896)	pharmacist, doctor	Breslau, Poland (1870)	San Bernardino (1870–1882)
Lutheran			
Haag, Johann Christoph (1817–1890)	farmer	Württemberg, Germany (1851)	Theresa, WI (1851–1859)
Haag, Rosena Christina (1826–1892)	farmer	Württemberg, Germany (1851)	Theresa, WI (1851–1859)
Wahl, James M. (1846–1939)	carpenter, recruiter	Storvahl, Norway (1867)	Sioux Falls, SD (1868–1939) Canton, MN (1883–1889) Lennox, SD (1889–1939)
Wahl, Julia Ulberg (1862–1914)	housewife	Valdres, Norway (1883)	Canton (1883–1889) Lennox, SD (1889–1914)
Methodist			
Goodnight, Mary Ann D. (1839–1926)	teacher	Hickman, KY (1870)	Pueblo, CO (1870–1871)
Maynard, Frank H. (1853–1926)	cowboy, carpenter, songwriter, memoirist	Iowa City, IA (1869)	Towanda, KS (1869–1881) Colorado Springs, CO (1881–1926)
Parmley, J.W. (1861–1940)	brick maker, farmer, publisher	Mifflin, WI (1883)	Ipswich, SD (1883–1940)
Methodist Episcopal			
French, Erasmus Darwin (1822–1902)	physician, explorer, rancher, miner	Albion, MI (1845)	Fort Tejon, CA (1847–1851) San Jose, CA (1848–1860) Darwin, CA (1860–1865) Baja, CA (1894–1902)
Kellie, Luna Sanford (1857–1940)	farmer, editor, activist, songwriter, grocer	Rockford, IL (1871)	Adams County, NE (1877–1884) Hartwell, NE (1884–1901)
Key, George (1795–1864)	farmer, trader, blacksmith	Crawfordsville, IN (1836)	Louisa County, IA (1836–1861)
Key, Rebecca Mintun (1799–ca. 1860)	housewife	Crawfordsville, IN (1838)	Louisa County, IA (1838–ca. 1860)
Lee, Jason (1803–1845)	missionary, educator, territorial organizer	Stanstead, Quebec (1833)	St. Paul, OR (1833–1844)
Mormon			
Huntington, Dimick Baker (1808–1879)	constable, coroner, interpreter	Watertown, NY (1836)	Salt Lake City, UT (1848–1979)
Huntington, Oliver B. (1823–1909)	priest, explorer, missionary	Watertown, NY (1836)	Springville, UT (1852–1901)
Huntington, William (1784–1846)	miller, soldier, sexton, constable	Watertown, NY (1836)	Mount Pisgah, IA (1846)
Huntington, William D. (1818–1887)	explorer, constable, taverner, mailman, musician, miner	Watertown, NY (1836)	Springville, UT (1852–1887)
Smith, Joseph, Jr. (1805–1844)	prophet, writer, translator	Harmony, PA (1827)	Nauvoo, IL (1831–1844)
Snow, Eliza Roxcy (1804–1887)	hymnogrphr, teacher, social worker	Hiram, OH (1835)	Salt Lake City, UT (1835–1887)
Wells, Emmeline B. (1828–1921)	teacher, diarist, activist, editor, social worker	Petersham, MA (1844)	Salt Lake City, UT (1846–1921)

Appendix D. Religion

Beliefs	Occupation	Origin	Destination
Young, Brigham (1801–1877)	prophet, governor, Indian agent, church builder	Whittingham, VT (1832)	Salt Lake City, UT (1847–1877)
Young, Zina D.H. (1821–1901)	teacher, midwife, missionary	Watertown, NY (1836)	Salt Lake City, UT (1848–1901)
nondenominational			
Goodnight, Charles (1836–1929)	Texas Ranger, rancher	Macoupin, IL (1846)	Goodnight, TX (1846–1929)
Presbyterian			
Cameron, Donaldina (1869–1968)	seamstress, activist	Clydedale, New Zealand (1871)	San Francisco, CA (1895–1968)
Chin, Ah Yane (1869–?)	interpreter	China (1874)	San Francisco, CA (1874–?)
Culbertson, Margaret (1834–1897)	teacher, missionary	Groveland, NY (1878)	San Francisco, CA (1878–1897)
Dale, Frank (1849–1930)	judge, financier	Somonauk, IL (1871)	Wichita, KS (1871–1889) Guthrie, OK (1889–1930)
Dale, Martha Wood (1859–1930)	library builder, activist	Oswego, NY (1879)	Wichita, KS (1879–1889) Guthrie, OK (1889–1930)
Goodell, Henry Martin (1843–1905)	ferryman, justice of the peace	Vermilion, OH (1853)	Lynden, WA (1884–1905)
Goodell, Jotham Weeks (1809–1859)	minister	Vermilion, OH (1851)	Portland, OR (1851–1859)
Goodell, Nathan Edward (1839–1886)	merchant	Vermilion, OH (1851)	Skagit River, OR (1879)
Judson, George (1860–1891)	surveyor, school builder	Vermilion, OH (1853)	Bellingham, WA (1886)
Judson, Phoebe Goodell (1831–1926)	educator, memoirist	Vermilion, OH (1853)	Claquato, WA (1853–1858) Whidbey, WA (1866–1926)
Kelly, Fanny Wiggins (1845–1904)	memoirist, laundress, innkeeper	Geneva, KS (1864)	Box Elder Creek, WY (1864)
Lambert, Rebecca H. (1806–1886)	fund raiser	New York (1852)	San Francisco, CA (1852–1886)
Meeker, Eliza Jane (1834–1909)	farmer, grocer, innkeeper, activist	Eddyville, IA (1852)	McNeil Island, WA (1853–1861) Puyallup, WA (1862–1909)
Meeker, Ezra (1830–1928)	farmer, grocer, innkeeper	Eddyville, IA (1852)	McNeil Island, WA (1853–1861) Puyallup, WA (1862–1894)
Meeker, Oliver Perry (1828–1861)	farmer, grocer	Eddyville, IA (1852)	McNeil Island, WA (1853–1860)
Reading, Pearson Barton (1816–1868)	miner, explorer	Hunterdon, NJ (1844)	Shasta, CA (1845–1868)
Speed, Horace (1852–1924)	lawyer	Indianapolis, IN (1889)	Guthrie, OK (1889–1913)
Street, Eliza Posey (1786–1849)	housewife	Henderson, KY (1809)	Prairie du Chien, WI (1812–1835, 1837–1842)
Street, Joseph M. (1782–1840)	postmaster, Indian agent, attorney	Shawneetown, IL (1812)	Prairie du Chien, WI (1812–1835, 1837–1842)
Whitman, Marcus (1802–1847)	doctor, missionary	Angelica, NY (1836)	Walla Walla, WA (1836–1847)
Whitman, Narcissa (1808–1847)	doctor, missionary	Angelica, NY (1836)	Walla Walla, WA (1836–1847)
Wu, Tien Fu (1861–ca. 1940s)	interpreter	Canton, China (1876)	San Francisco, CA (1876–ca. 1940s)
Quaker			
Bush, George W. (ca. 1779–1863)	community builder, farmer, stockman	Jackson, MO (1844)	Tumwater, WA (1845–1863)
Cheesman, David W. (1822–1884)	attorney, memoirist, U.S. Mint treasurer	Washington, IN (1850)	El Monte, CA (1851–1852) Los Angeles, CA (1852–1884)
Cheesman, Urania K. (1828–1916)	housewife	Washington, IN (1850)	El Monte, CA (1851–1852) Los Angeles, CA (1852–1884)
Macy, Obed (1801–1857)	physician, innkeeper, city councilman	Washington, IN (1850)	El Monte, CA (1851–1852) Los Angeles, CA (1852–1857)
Macy, Oscar (1829–1910)	printer, publisher, jailer	Washington, IN (1850)	El Monte, CA (1851–1852) Los Angeles, CA (1852–1910)

Appendix D. Religion

Beliefs	Occupation	Origin	Destination
Merritt, Josiah (1803–1882)	farmer, prospector, musician	Athens, OH (1860)	Snoqualmie, WA (1860–1882)
Scots Presbyterian			
Bell, James George (1831–1911)	farmer	Sedalia, MO (1856)	Obed, CA (1898–1911)
Bell, Susan Hollenbeck (1831–1905)	seamstress, activist	Sedalia, MO (1856)	Obed, CA (1898–1905)
Campbell, Robert (1804–1879)	trader, financier, negotiator, investor	Plumbridge, Ireland (1822)	St. Louis, MO (1835–1879)
Kellie, James Thomson (1850–1918)	farmer, activist, grocer, carpenter, bridge builder, railroad laborer	Toronto, Ontario (1871)	St. Louis, MO (1872–1873) Iowa (1874–1877) Adams County, NE (1877–1884) Hartwell, NE (1884–1901)
McBeth, Kate Christine (1832–1915)	missionary, teacher	Wellsville, OH (1858)	Lapwai, ID (1879–1915)
McBeth, Susan Law (1830–1893)	missionary, teacher	Wellsville, OH (1858)	Goodwater, OK (1858–1861) St. Louis, MO (1866–1873) Lapwai, ID (1873–1893)
Monteith, Charles Edgar (1847–1915)	Indian agent	Fulton, NY (1874)	Lapwai, ID (1874–1889)
Morrison, John L. (1819–1899)	carpenter	Independence, MO (1842)	Oregon City, OR (1843–1850)
Unaffiliated Christian			
Key, Ambrose W. (1829–1908)	tanner, farmer, sawyer, orchardist, freighter	Crawfordsville (1837)	Washington County, TX (1860) Houston, TX (1865) Westport, MO (1865–1868) Shawnee, KS (1868–1908)
Lilly, Benjamin Vernon (1856–1936)	hunter, knife maker	Jackson, MS (1868)	Mer Rouge, LA (1868–1901) Big Thicket, TX (1904–1908) Gila, NM (1908–1916) Quemado, AZ (1916–1926) Pleasanton, NM (1931–1936)
Unitarian			
Carr, Byron Oscar (1835–1913)	banker, railroad manager	Concord, NY (1872)	Truckee, CA (1872–1880s) San Francisco, CA (1880s–1891) Lemoore, CA (1894–1900) Seattle, WA (1900–1913)
Carr, Sarah Pratt (1850–1935)	missionary, writer, activist, librettist	Freeport, ME (1852)	San Francisco, CA (1852–1867, 1913–1935) Carlin, NV (1867–1872) St. Helena, CA (1883–1900) Seattle, WA (1900–1913) Los Angeles, CA (1913–1935)
Kirby, Georgiana Bruce (1818–1887)	rancher, suffragist	Staffordshire, England (1831)	Santa Cruz, CA (1850–1887)
Pratt, Louisa Merrill (1827–1919)	housewife, activist	Freeport, ME (1852)	San Francisco, CA (1852–1867, 1881–1893) Carlin, NV (1852–1872) Salt Lake City, UT (1872–1879) Sacramento, CA (1878–1881) St. Helena, CA (1881–1900) Seattle, WA (1900–1919)
Pratt, Robert Henry (1824–1920)	miner, railroad builder	Freeport, ME (1852)	San Francisco, CA (1849–1867, 1881–1893) Carlin, NV (1867–1869) Salt Lake City (1869–1879) Sacramento, CA (1878–1881) St. Helena, CA (1881–1900) Seattle, WA (1900–1920)

Beliefs	Occupation	Origin	Destination
Tabor, Augusta Louise (1833–1895)	grocer, laundress, cook, postmaster, philanthropist	Augusta, ME (1857)	Zeandale, KS (1857–1859) Oro City, CO (1859–1861) Leadville, CO (1861–1879) Denver, CO (1879–1894) Pasadena, CA (1894–1895)
Tabor, Horace Austin W. (1830–1899)	stone mason, mayor, senator, postmaster, miner, merchant	Boston, MA (1855)	Zeandale, KS (1855–1859) Oro City, CO (1859–1861) Leadville, CO (1861–1879) Denver, CO (1879–1899)
Universalist			
Robbins, Ezekiel Wright (1800–1852)	physician, minister, merchant, politician	Watertown, NY (1828)	Chester, IL (1838–1852)
Wesleyan Methodist			
Heazle, Benjamin Alfred (1880–1936)	postmaster, rancher	Bray, Ireland (1894)	Murphy, ID (1894–?)
Heazle, George Robert (1876–1924)	postmaster, grocer	Bray, Ireland (1894)	Murphy, ID (1894–?)
Heazle, Jean (1879–1949)	timber cutter, rancher, miner, dairier		Bray, Ireland (1893) DeLamar, ID (1893–1949)

E. Occupation

Occupation	Left Original Home	Area of Settlement
accountant		
Haagsma, Broer Baukes (1831–1907)	Harlingen, Friesland (1853)	New Amsterdam, WI (1853–1907)
activist		
Bell, Susan Hollenbeck (1831–1905)	Sedalia, MO (1856)	Obed, CA (1898–1905)
Bunker, Harriet J. (1800–1895)	Massachusetts (1852)	San Francisco, CA (1852–1895)
Cameron, Donaldina (1869–1968)	Clydevale, New Zealand (1871)	San Francisco, CA (1895–1968)
Carr, Sarah Pratt (1850–1935)	Freeport, ME (1852)	San Francisco, CA (1852–1867, 1913–1935) Carlin, NV (1867–1872) St. Helena, CA (1883–1900) Seattle, WA (1900–1913) Los Angeles, CA (1913–1935)
Dale, Martha Wood (1859–1930)	Oswego, NY (1879)	Wichita (1879–1889) Guthrie, OK (1889–1930)
Kellie, James Thomson (1850–1918)	St. Louis, MO (1871)	Adams County, NE (1877–1884) Hartwell, NE (1884–1901)
Kellie, Luna Sanford (1857–1940)	Rockford, IL (1871)	Adams County, NE (1877–1884) Hartwell, NE (1884–)
Lambert, Rebecca H. (1806–1886)	New York, NY (1852)	San Francisco, CA (1852–1886)
Meeker, Eliza Jane (1834–1909)	Eddyville, IA (1852)	McNeil Island, WA (1853–1861) Puyallup, WA (1862–1909)
Parmley, J.W. (1861–1940)	Mifflin, WI (1883)	Ipswich, SD (1883–1940)
Pratt, Louisa Merrill (1827–1919)	Freeport, ME (1852)	San Francisco, CA (1852–1867, 1881–1893) Carlin, NV (1852–1872) Salt Lake City, UT (1872–1879) Sacramento, CA (1878–1881) St. Helena, CA (1881–1900) Seattle, WA (1900–1919)
Wells, Emmeline B. (1828–1921)	Petersham, MA (1844)	Salt Lake City, UT (1846–1921)
actor		
Omohundro, Texas Jack (1846–1880)	Pleasure Hill, VA (1859)	Leadville, CO (1877–1880)
almoner		
Huntington, William (1784–1846)	Watertown, NY (1836)	Mount Pisgah, IA (1846)

Appendix E. Occupation

Occupation	Left Original Home	Area of Settlement
armorer		
Sowell, John Newton, Sr. (1770–1838)	Boone County, MO (1829)	Gonzales, TX (1829–1838)
artist		
Goddard, George Henry (1817–1906)	Bristol, England (1850)	San Francisco, CA (1850–1906)
attorney		
Cheesman, David W. (1822–1884)	Washington, IN (1850)	El Monte, CA (1851–1852)
		Los Angeles, CA (1852–1884)
Dale, Frank (1849–1930)	Somonauk, IL (1871)	Wichita, KS (1871–1889)
		Guthrie, OK (1889–1930)
Farnham, Thomas J. (1804–1848)	Peoria, IL (1838)	Willamette, OR (1839)
		Santa Cruz, CA (1839–1848)
Franklin, Lewis Abraham (1820–1879)	Kingston, Jamaica (1849)	San Francisco, CA (1849–1955)
		San Diego, CA (1855–1860)
Speed, Horace (1852–1924)	Indianapolis, IN (1889)	Guthrie, OK (1889–1913)
Street, Joseph M. (1782–1840)	Shawneetown, IL (1812)	Prairie du Chien, WI (1812–1835, 1837–1842)
auctioneer		
Franklin, Selim (1814–1884)	Liverpool, Eng. (1849)	San Francisco, CA (1849–1858, 1866–1884)
auditor		
Fisk, James Liberty (1835–1902)	Fort Ripley, MN (1863)	Bannack, MT (1863)
		Fort Benton, MT (1866)
banker		
Carr, Byron Oscar (1835–1913)	Concord, NY (1872)	Truckee, CA (1872–1880s)
		San Francisco, CA (1880s–1891)
		Lemoore, CA (1894–1900)
		Seattle, WA (1900–1913)
Miller, Mary Foote (1842–1921)	Quesqueton, IA (1863)	Lafayette, CO (1863–1921)
blacksmith		
Goller, John (1825–1874)	Bavaria, Germany (1849)	Los Angeles, CA (1850–1874)
Key, George (1795–1864)	Crawfordsville, IN (1836)	Louisa County, IA (1836–1861)
Sowell, John Newton, Jr. (1811–1856)	Boone County, MO (1829)	Gonzales, TX (1829–1856)
Sowell, John Newton, Sr. (1770–1838)	Boone County, MO (1829)	Gonzales, TX (1829–1838)
boat captain		
Keseberg, Lewis (1814–1895)	Westphalia, Prussia (1844)	San Jose, CA (1847–1895)
Lawing, William "Billie" (1879–1936)	Murfreesboro, TN (1923)	Seward, AK (1923–1936)
borax miner		
Coleman, William Tell (1824–1893)	St. Louis, MO (1849)	San Francisco, CA (1849–1893)
		Columbus Marsh, NV (1871–1888)
bounty hunter		
Lilly, Benjamin Vernon (1856–1936)	Jackson, MS (1868)	Mer Rouge, LA (1868–1901)
brewer		
Keseberg, Lewis (1814–1895)	Westphalia, Prussia (1844)	San Jose, CA (1847–1895)
brick maker		
Parmley, J.W. (1861–1940)	Mifflin, WI (1883)	Ipswich, SD (1883–1940)
Stone, Elizabeth Hickock (1801–1895)	Watertown, NY (1828)	Fort Collins, CO (1864–1895)
bridge builder		
Kellie, James Thomson (1850–1918)	Toronto, Ontario (1871)	St. Louis, MO (1872–1873)
Sanford, James Manley (1836–1910)	Austin, MN (1871)	St. Louis, MO (1872–1873)
butcher		
Bruce, George Whiteley (1851–1927)	Bray, Ireland (1860s)	DeLamar, ID (1860s–1927)
Miller, Lafayette (1840–1878)	Quesqueton, IA (1863)	Lafayette, CO (1863–1878)
carpenter		
Kellie, James Thomson (1850–1918)	St. Louis, MO (1871)	Adams County, NE (1877–1884)
		Hartwell, NE (1884–1901)
Maynard, Frank H. (1853–1926)	Iowa City, IA (1869)	Colorado Springs, CO (1881–1926)
Morrison, John L. (1819–1899)	Independence, MO (1842)	Oregon City, OR (1843–1850)
		Orcas Island, WA (1859–1899)
Wahl, James M. (1846–1939)	Storvahl, Norway (1867)	Sioux Falls, SD (1868–1939)
cartographer		
Goddard, George Henry (1817–1906)	Bristol, England (1850)	San Francisco, CA (1850–1906)

Appendix E. Occupation

Occupation	Left Original Home	Area of Settlement
chaplain		
Padilla, Juan de (?–1544)	Andalusia, Spain (1528)	Quivira, TX (1542–1544)
church builder		
O'Farrell, John A. (1823–1900)	Louisville, KY (1859)	Boise, ID (1863–1900)
O'Farrell, Mary Ann (1840–1900)	Louisville, KY (1859)	Boise, ID (1863–1900)
Young, Brigham (1801–1877)	Whittingham, VT (1832)	Salt Lake City, UT (1877)
city councilman		
Macy, Obed (1801–1857)	Washington (1850)	El Monte, CA (1851–1852)
		Los Angeles, CA (1852–1857)
civil engineer		
Goddard, George H. (1817–1906)	Bristol, England (1850)	San Francisco, CA (1850–1906)
coal speculator		
Miller, Mary Foote (1842–1921)	Quesqueton, IA (1863)	Lafayette, CO (1863–1921)
community builder		
Bush, George W. (ca. 1779–1863)	Jackson, MO (1844)	Tumwater, WA (1845–1866)
Bush, Isabella James (1801–1866)	Jackson, MO (1844)	Tumwater, WA (1845–1866)
Caldwell, Mathew (1798–1842)	Gasconade, MO (1831)	Gonzalez, TX (1831–1842)
Miller, Mary Foote (1842–1921)	Quesqueton, IA (1863)	Lafayette, CO (1863–1921)
constable		
Huntington, Dimick Baker (1808–1879)	Watertown, NY (1836)	Salt Lake City, UT (1848–1901)
Huntington, William (1784–1846)	Watertown, NY (1836)	Mount Pisgah, IA (1846)
Huntington, William D. (1818–1887)	Watertown, NY (1836)	Springville, UT (1852–1887)
cook		
Bowman, Sarah A. (1812–1866)	Clay County, MO (1845)	Corpus Christi, TX (1845–1846)
		El Paso, TX (1848–1850)
		Yuma, AZ (1850–1866)
Brown, Clara (1800–1885)	Gallatin, KY (1856)	Leavenworth, KS (1856–1859)
		Denver, CO (1859–1885)
Sakuma, Yonekichi (1839–1927)	Yokohama, Japan (1868)	Kauai, HI (1868–1927)
Tabor, Augusta Louise (1833–1895)	Augusta, ME (1857)	Zeandale, KS (1857–1859)
		Oro City, CO (1859–1861)
		Leadville, CO (1861–1879)
		Denver, CO (1879–1894)
		Pasadena, CA (1894–1895)
coroner		
Huntington, Dimick B. (1808–1879)	Watertown, NY (1836)	Salt Lake City, UT (1848–1901)
cowboy		
Maynard, Frank H. (1853–1926)	Iowa City, IA (1869)	Towanda, KS (1869–1881)
Omohundro, Texas Jack (1846–1880)	Pleasure Hill, VA (1859)	Fort Worth, TX (1859–1869)
Toponce, Alexander (1839–1923)	Belfort, France (1846)	Tipton, MO (1854–1860)
		Denver, CO (1860–1863)
		Bannock, MT (1863)
		Ogden, UT (1863–1923)
dairier		
Bruce, George Whiteley (1851–1927)	Bray, Ireland (1860s)	DeLamar, ID (1860s–1927)
Heazle, Jean (1879–1949)	Bray, Ireland (1893)	DeLamar, ID (1893–1949)
Judson, Holden Allen (1827–1899)	Vermilion, OH (1853)	Linden, WA (1871–1899)
Kinman, Seth (1815–1888)	Pekin, IL (1849)	Shasta, CA (1850–1855)
		Table Bluff, CA (1855–1888)
Wilkins, Laura Smith (1835–1921)	Fort Madison, IA (1853)	Oregon City, OR (1854–1860)
dancer		
Omohundro, Josephine (1836–1886)	Milan, Italy (1830s)	Leadville, CO (1877–1886)
depot manager		
Leavitt, Eliza S. Reed (1829–1910s)	Boston, MA (1856)	Indian Valley, CA (1860–1880s)
		Bridgeport, CA (1867–1901)
Leavitt, Hiram Lewis (1824–1901)	Boston, MA (1851)	Indian Valley, CA (1860–1880s)
		Bridgeport, CA (1867–1901)
diarist/memoirist		
Belshaw, George, Jr. (1815–1893)	Lake County, IN (1853)	Eugene, OR (1853–1893)
Brier, Juliet Wells Brier (1813–1819)	Kalamazoo, MI (1840)	Death Valley, CA (1849)

Appendix E. Occupation

Occupation	Left Original Home	Area of Settlement
Cheesman, David W. (1822–1884)	Washington, IN (1850)	El Monte, CA (1851–1852)
		Los Angeles, CA (1852–1884)
Ebbetts, John A.N. (ca. 1815–1854)	New York, NY (1849)	San Francisco, CA (1849–1854)
Fisk, Elizabeth Chester (1846–1927)	Haddam, CT (1866)	Helena, MT (1866–1927)
Franklin, Victoria Jacobs (1838–1861)	Manchester, England (1851)	San Diego, CA (1851–1861)
Goulding, William R. (1805–1865)	York, England	San Francisco, CA (1849–1850)
Gwydir, Rickard Daniel (1844–1925)	Covington, KY (1887)	Spokane, WA (1887–1925)
Judson, Phoebe Goodell (1831–1926)	Vermilion, OH (1853)	Claquato, WA (1853–1858)
		Whidbey, WA (1866–1926)
Kelly, Fanny Wiggins (1845–1904)	Geneva, KS (1864)	Box Elder Creek, WY (1864)
		Sherman Station, WY (1868–1869)
Maynard, Frank H. (1853–1926)	Iowa City, IA (1869)	Colorado Springs, CO (1881–1926)
Mead, James R. (1836–1910)	Davenport, IA (1859)	Salina, KS (1862–1863)
		Wichita, KS (1864–1910)
Stratton, Elizabeth Keays (1830–1922)	Ontario (1864)	Fort Collins, CO (1864–1933
Wells, Emmeline B. (1828–1921)	Petersham, MA (1844)	Salt Lake City, UT (1846–1921)

distiller

Chiles, Joseph Ballinger (1810–1885)	Jackson County, MO	Napa Valley, CA (1843–1885)

editor

Hayashi, Harvey Saburo (1867–1943)	Tonami, Japan (1885)	San Francisco, CA (1884–1891)
		Sacramento, CA (1891–1893)
		Kona, HI (1893–1943)
Kellie, Luna Sanford (1857–1940)	Rockford, IL (1871)	Adams County, NE (1877–1884)
		Hartwell, NE (1884–1901)
Wells, Emmeline B. (1828–1921)	Petersham, MA (1844)	Salt Lake City, UT (1846–1921)

explorer

Ebbetts, John A.N. (ca. 1815–1854)	New York, NY (1849)	San Francisco, CA (1849–1854)
French, Erasmus D. (1822–1902)	Albion, MI (1845)	Darwin, CA (1860–1865)
Holmes, Julia Archibald (1838–1887)	Emporia, KS (1858)	Taos, NM (1858–1863)
Huntington, Oliver B. (1823–1909)	Watertown, NY (1836)	Springville, UT (1852–1909)
Huntington, William D. (1818–1887)	Watertown, NY (1836)	Springville, UT (1852–1887)
Moore, Seymour T. (1827–1876)	Ohio	Fort Miller, CA (1849–1851)
		Utah (1853–1854)
Reading, Pearson B. (1816–1868)	Hunterdon, NJ (1844)	Shasta, CA (1845–1868)

farmer

Arcouet, Amable (1797–1880)	Montreal, Quebec (1833)	St. Paul, OR (1835–1880)
Bell, James George (1831–1911)	Sedalia, MO (1856)	Obed, CA (1898–1911)
Belshaw, George, Jr. (1815–1893)	Lake County, IN (1853)	Eugene, OR (1853–1893)
Booth, Albert Anson (1850–1914)	Syracuse, NY (1869)	Edna, ND (1879–1914)
Bush, George W. (ca. 1779–1863)	Jackson, MO (1844)	Tumwater, WA (1845–1866)
Chiles, Joseph B. (1810–1885)	Jackson County, MO (1841)	Napa Valley, CA (1843–1885)
Cowles, George A. (1836–1887)	Hartford, CT (1878)	Cowlestown, CA (1878–1887)
Fisk, Andrew Jackson (1849–1910)	Fort Ripley, MN (1866)	Fort Benton, MT (1866)
Haag, Johann C. (1817–1890)	Württemberg, Germany (1851)	Theresa, WI (1851–1859)
Haag, Rosena C. (1826–1892)	Württemberg, Germany (1851)	Theresa, WI (1851–1859)
Ide, William Brown (1796–1852)	Rutland, MA (1845)	Sutter's Fort, CA (1845–1852)
Ise, Henry C. Ise (1841–1900)	Württemberg, Germany (1857)	Ross, KS (1871–1900)
Ise, Rosena Haag (1855–1947)	Theresa, WI (1873)	Ross, KS (1873–1947)
Kellie, James T. (1850–1918)	St. Louis, MO (1871)	Adams County, NE (1877–1884)
		Hartwell, NE (1884–1901)
Kellie, Luna Sanford (1857–1940)	Rockford, IL (1871)	Adams County, NE (1877–1884)
		Hartwell, NE (1884–1901)
Kelly, Josiah Shawhan (1824–1867)	Geneva, KS (1864)	Box Elder Creek, WY (1864)
Key, George (1795–1864)	Crawfordsville, IN (1836)	Louisa County, IA (1836–1861)
Lahti, Charles (1859–1932)	Vadsø, Norway (1864)	St. Peter (1864–1932)
Lahti, Johanna Gustava (1840–1919)	Vadsø, Norway (1864)	St. Peter, MN (1864–1919)
Lahti, Peter J. (1834–1911)	Vadsø, Norway (1864)	St. Peter, MN (1864–1911)
Larimer, William J. (1828–1895)	Iola, KS (1864)	Sherman Station, TX (1864–1870)
McCance, Charles H. (1857–1926)	Toulon, IL (1884)	Cozad, NE (1885–1926)
McCarty, Jonathan W. (1833–1900)	Lake County, IN (1853)	Pierce County, WA (1853–1870)

Appendix E. Occupation

Occupation	Left Original Home	Area of Settlement
Meeker, Eliza Jane (1834–1909)	Eddyville, IA (1852)	McNeil Island, WA (1853–1861)
		Puyallup, WA (1862–1909)
Meeker, Ezra (1830–1928)	Eddyville, IA (1852)	McNeil Island, WA (1853–1861)
		Puyallup, WA (1862–1894)
Meeker, Oliver Perry (1828–1861)	Eddyville, IA (1852)	McNeil Island, WA (1853–1860)
Merritt, Josiah (1803–1882)	Athens, OH (1860)	Snoqualmie, WA (1860–1882)
Miller, Lafayette (1840–1878)	Quesqueton, IA (1863)	Lafayette, CO (1863–1878)
Parmley, J.W. (1861–1940)	Mifflin, WI (1883)	Ipswich, SD (1883–1940)
Pennington, Elias G. (1809–1869)	Nashville, TN (1837)	Honey Grove, TX (1837–1857)
Pennington, James (1833–1868)	Nashville, TN (1837)	Honey Grove, TX (1837–1857)
Point du Sable, Jean (ca. 1745–1818)	Chicago, IL (1800)	St. Charles, MO (1800–1818)
Rasor, John Henry (1849–1925)	Graham, IA (1883)	Plano, TX (1883–1925)
Reed, Michael (1777–1859)	Natchitoches, LA (1833)	Bell County, TX (1833–1859)
Santee, Jennie Frances (1838–1931)	Hartford, CT (1878)	Cowlestown, CA (1878–1931)
Sowell, Andrew Jackson (1815–1883)	Boone County, MO (1829)	Gonzales (1829–1883)
Stroud, Beden (1795–1865)	Chambers County, AL (1836)	Calvert, TX (1842–1865)
Stroud, Ethan A. (1788–1846)	Chambers County, AL (1836)	Calvert, TX (1842–1846)
ferry operator		
Baker, Jim (1818–1898)	Belleville, IL (1839)	Savery, WY (1873–1898)
Chiles, Joseph Ballinger (1810–1885)	Jackson County, MO	Napa Valley, CA (1843–1885)
Goodell, Henry Martin (1843–1905)	Vermilion, OH (1853)	Lynden, WA (1884–1905)
Ide, William Brown (1796–1852)	Rutland, MA (1845)	Sutter's Fort, CA (1845–1852)
Ouilmette, Antoine L. (ca. 1760–1841)	Montreal, Quebec (1790)	Chicago, IL (1790–1833)
Reed, John Thomas (1805–1843)	Acapulco, Mexico (1826)	San Francisco, CA (1826–1843)
financier		
Campbell, Robert (1804–1879)	Plumbridge Ireland (1822)	St. Louis, MO (1835–1879)
Cowles, George A. (1836–1887)	Hartford, CT (1878)	Cowlestown, CA (1878–1887)
Dale, Frank (1849–1930)	Somonauk, IL (1871)	Wichita, KS (1871–1889)
		Guthrie, OK (1889–1930)
foster parent		
Bowman, Sarah A. (1812–1866)	Clay County, MO (1845)	Corpus Christi, TX (1845–1846)
		El Paso, TX (1848–1850)
		Yuma, AZ (1850 1866)
Briones de Miranda, Juana (1802–1889)	Mexico (1802)	Santa Clara, CA (1844–1885)
Culbertson, Margaret (1834–1897)	Groveland, NY (1878)	San Francisco, CA (1878–1897)
Judson, Phoebe Goodell (1831–1926)	Vermilion, OH (1853)	Claquato, WA (1853–1858)
		Whidbey, WA (1866–1926)
O'Farrell, John A. (1823–1900)	Louisville, KY (1859)	Boise, ID (1863–1900)
O'Farrell, Mary Ann (1840–1900)	Louisville, KY (1859)	Boise, ID (1863–1900
freighter		
Farnham, Thomas J. (1804–1848)	Peoria, IL (1838)	Willamette, OR (1839)
		Santa Cruz, CA (1839–1848)
Key, Ambrose W. (1829–1908)	Crawfordsville, IN (1838)	Westport, MO (1865–1868)
Maynard, Frank H. (1853–1926)	Iowa City, IA (1869)	Towanda, KS (1869–1870)
Pennington, Elias G. (1809–1869)	Nashville, TN (1837)	Honey Grove, TX (1837–1857)
		Tucson, AZ (1857–1869)
Pennington, James (1833–1868)	Nashville, TN (1837)	Honey Grove, TX (1837–1857)
		Tucson, AZ (1857–1868)
Toponce, Alexander (1839–1923)	Belfort, France (1846)	Ogden, UT (1863–1923)
Wootton, Richens Lacey (1816–1893)	Christian, KY (1836)	Independence, MO (1836)
		Bent's Fort, CO (1836–1847)
		Taos, NM (1847–1858)
		Denver, CO (1858–1893)
fund raiser		
Booth, Ellen Eliza Carter (1854–1935)	Waupon, WI (1879)	Edna, ND (1879–1914)
		Tacoma, WA (1914–1935)
Bunker, Harriet J. (1800–1895)	Massachusetts (1852)	San Francisco, CA (1852–1895)
Campbell, Virginia K. (1822–1882)	Raleigh, NC (1841)	St. Louis, MO (1841–1882)
Lambert, Rebecca H. (1806–1886)	New York, NY (1852)	San Francisco, CA (1852–1886)

Appendix E. Occupation

Occupation	Left Original Home	Area of Settlement
governor		
Young, Brigham (1801–1877)	Whittingham, VT (1832)	Salt Lake City, UT (1877)
grocer		
Heazle, George Robert (1876–1924)	Bray, Ireland (1894)	Murphy, ID (1894–?)
Judson, Holden Allen (1827–1899)	Vermilion, OH (1853)	Claquato, WA (1853–1858)
		Whidbey, WA (1866–1899)
Kellie, James Thomson (1850–1918)	St. Louis, MO (1871)	Adams County, NE (1877–1884)
		Hartwell, NE (1884–1901)
Kellie, Luna Sanford (1857–1940)	Rockford, IL (1871)	Adams County, NE (1877–1884)
		Hartwell, NE (1884–1901)
Larimer, Sarah Luse (1836–1913)	Iola, KS (1864)	Sherman Station, TX (1864–1870)
Larimer, William J. (1828–1895)	Iola, KS (1864)	Sherman Station, TX (1864–1870)
Meeker, Eliza Jane (1834–1909)	Eddyville, IA (1852)	McNeil Island, WA (1853–1861)
		Puyallup, WA (1862–1909)
Meeker, Ezra (1830–1928)	Eddyville, IA (1852)	McNeil Island, WA (1853–1861)
		Puyallup, WA (1862–1894)
		Cook Inlet, AK (1894–1896)
		Skagway, AK (1898–1901)
Meeker, Oliver Perry (1828–1861)	Eddyville, IA (1852)	McNeil Island, WA (1853–1860)
Tabor, Augusta Louise (1833–1895)	Augusta, ME (1857)	Zeandale, KS (1857–1859)
		Oro City, CO (1859–1861)
		Leadville, CO (1861–1879)
		Denver, CO (1879–1894)
		Pasadena, CA (1894–1895)
guide		
Baker, Jim (1818–1898)	Belleville, IL (1839)	Savery, WY (1873–1898)
Bridger, Jim (1803–1881)	Richmond, VA (1822)	Fort Bridger, WY (1842–1865)
Bottineau, Pierre (1817–1895)	Winnipeg, MB (1832)	St. Paul, MN (1840–1852)
		Osseo, Mn (1852–1877)
		Red Lake Falls, MN (1877–1895)
Chisholm, Jesse (1806–1868)	Arkansas (1820s)	Hughes County, OK (1820s, 1858–1861, 1868)
		Tehuacana Creek, TX (1833–1858)
		Wichita, KS (1861–1868)
Fisk, James Liberty (1835–1902)	Fort Ripley, MN (1863)	Bannack, MT (1863)
	Fort Ripley, MN (1866)	Fort Benton, MT (1866)
Robidoux, Antoine (1794–1860)	St. Louis, MO (1832)	Fort Uintah, UT (1833–1844)
Wootton, Richens Lacey (1816–1893)	Christian, KY (1836)	Independence, MO (1836)
		Bent's Fort, CO (1836–1847)
		Taos, NM (1847–1858)
		Denver, CO (1858–1893)
herbalist		
Briones de Miranda, Juana (1802–1889)	Mexico (1802)	Santa Clara, CA (1844–1885)
horse breeder		
Cowles, George Algernon (1836–1887)	Hartford, CT (1878)	Cowlestown, CA (1878–1887)
Heazle, Jean (1879–1949)	Bray, Ireland (1893)	DeLamar, ID (1893–1949)
Wilkins, Katherine C. (1857–1936)	Jacksonville, OR (1857)	Bruneau, ID (1880–1936)
hospital builder		
Cope, Sister Marianne (1838–1918)	Utica, NY (1884)	Wailiuku, Maui (1884–1887)
		Kalaupapa, Molokai (1887–1918)
housewife		
Belshaw, Candace M. (1826–1892)	Lake County, IN (1853)	Eugene, OR (1853–1892)
Bonnema, Luisa S. (1838-after 1910)	Altnau, Switzerland (1851)	New Amsterdam, WI (1860–?)
Cheesman, Urania K. (1828–1916)	Washington, IN (1850)	El Monte, CA (1851–1852)
		Los Angeles, CA (1852–1884)
Key, Mary Jones Garrett (1835–1927)	Louisa County, IA (1860)	Navasota, TX (1860–1867)
Key, Rebecca Mintun (1799–ca. 1860)	Crawfordsville, IN (1838)	Louisa County, IA (1838–ca. 1860)
McCance, Margaret Anna (1861–1940)	Toulon, IL (1900)	Cozad, NE (1885–1940)

Appendix E. Occupation

Occupation	Left Original Home	Area of Settlement
McCance, Margaret Sarah (1830–1905)	Toulon, IL (1900)	Cozad, NE (1885–1905)
Pratt, Louisa Merrill (1827–1919)	Freeport, ME (1852)	San Francisco, CA (1852–1867, 1881–1893)
		Carlin, NV (1852–1872)
		Salt Lake City, UT (1872–1879)
		Sacramento, CA (1878–1881)
		St. Helena, CA (1881–1900)
		Seattle, WA (1900–1919)
Rasor, Mary Ellen (1851–1918)	Graham, IA (1883)	Plano, TX (1883–1918)
Reed, Emaline Cobb (1825–1890)	Walker County, AL (1837)	Bell County, TX (1837–1890)
Reed, Margret Keyes (1814–1861)	Independence, MO (1846)	San Jose, CA (1847–1861)
Reed, Martha Burnett (1786–1855)	Natchitoches, LA (1833)	Bell County, TX (1833–1855)
Simmons, Elizabeth K. (1820–1891)	Nodaway, MO (1844)	Tumwater, WA (1845–1867)
Smeathers, Mary Polly (1769–1810)	Wythe County, VA (1788)	Owensboro, KY (1797–1810)
Sothern, Mary Elizabeth (1856–1935)	Bray, Ireland (1860s)	DeLamar, ID (1860s–1880s)
Sowell, Rachel C. (1785–1860s)	Boone County, MO (1829)	Gonzales, TX (1829–1860s)
Street, Eliza Posey (1786–1849)	Henderson, KY (1809)	Prairie du Chien, WI (1812–1835, 1837–1842)
Wahl, Julia Ulberg (1862–1914)	Valdres, Norway (1868)	Canton, MN (1883–1889)
		Lennox, SD (1889–1914)
Wysinger, Pernesa Wilson (1843–1893)	Wayne County, MO (1853)	Visalia, CA (1864–1893)

hunter

Kinman, Seth (1815–1888)	Pekin, IL (1849)	Shasta, CA (1850–1855)
		Table Bluff, CA (1855–1888)
Lawing, Nellie Trosper (1873–1956)	Buchanan, MO (1901)	Cripple Creek, CO (1903–1914)
		Seward, AK (1915–1956)
Lilly, Benjamin Vernon (1856–1936)	Jackson, MS (1868)	Mer Rouge, LA (1868–1901)
		Big Thicket, TX (1904–1908)
		Gila, NM (1908–1916)
		Quemado, AZ (1916–1926)
		Pleasanton, NM (1931–1936)
Smeathers, William (ca. 1766–1837)	Yellow Banks, KY (1821)	Columbia, TX (1824–1837)
Sowell, John Newton, Jr. (1811–1856)	Boone County, MO (1829)	Gonzales, TX (1829–1856)

hymnographer

Snow, Eliza Roxcy (1804–1887)	Hiram, OH (1835)	Salt Lake City, UT (1835–1887)

Indian agent/commissioner

Gwydir, Rickard Daniel (1844–1925)	Covington, KY (1887)	Spokane, WA (1887–1925)
Monteith, Charles Edgar (1847–1915)	Fulton, NY (1874)	Lapwai, ID (1874–1889)
Simmons, Michael T. (1814–1867)	Nodaway, MO (1844)	Tumwater, WA (1845–1867)
Street, Joseph M. (1782–1840)	Shawneetown, IL (1812)	Prairie du Chien, WI (1812–1835, 1837–1842)
Stroud, Beden (1795–1865)	Chambers County, AL (1836)	Calvert, TX (1842–1865)
Stroud, Ethan A. (1788–1846)	Chambers County, AL (1836)	Calvert, TX (1842–1846)
Young, Brigham (1801–1877)	Whittingham, VT (1832)	Salt Lake City, UT (1877)

Indian fighter

Bruce, George Whiteley (1851–1927)	Bray, Ireland (1860s)	DeLamar, ID (1860s–1927)
Kinman, Seth (1815–1888)	Pekin, IL (1849)	Shasta, CA (1850–1855)
		Table Bluff, CA (1855–1888)
Smeathers, William (ca. 1766–1837)	Yellow Banks, KY (1821)	Columbia, TX (1824–1837)
Sowell, Andrew Jackson (1815–1883)	Boone County, MO (1829)	Gonzales, TX (1829–1883)
Wootton, Richens Lacey (1816–1893)	Christian, KY (1836)	Independence, MO (1836)
		Bent's Fort, CO (1836–1847)
		Taos, NM (1847–1858)
		Denver, CO (1858–1893)

innkeeper

Bowman, Sarah A. (1812–1866)	Clay County, TX (1845)	Corpus Christi, TX (1845–1846)
		El Paso, TX (1848–1850)
		Yuma, AZ (1850–1866)
Isbell, Isaac Chauncy (1800–1886)	Greenbush, IL (1846)	Santa Clara, CA (1846–1850)
Kelly, Fanny Wiggins (1845–1904)	Geneva, KS (1864)	Ellsworth, KS (1866–1867)
Kelly, Josiah Shawhan (1824–1867)	Geneva, KS (1864)	Ellsworth, KS (1866–1867)

Appendix E. Occupation

Occupation	Left Original Home	Area of Settlement
Keseberg, Lewis (1814–1895)	Westphalia, Prussia (1844)	San Jose, CA (1847–1895)
Kinman, Seth (1815–1888)	Pekin, IL (1849)	Shasta, CA (1850–1855)
		Table Bluff, CA (1855–1888)
Lawing, Nellie Trosper (1873–1956)	Buchanan, MO (1901)	Cripple Creek, CO (1903–1914)
		Seward, AK (1915–1956)
Lawing, William "Billie" (1879–1936)	Murfreesboro, TN (1923)	Seward, AK (1923–1936)
Leavitt, Eliza S. Reed (1829–1910s)	Boston, MA (1856)	Indian Valley, CA (1860–1880s)
		Bridgeport, CA (1867–1901)
Leavitt, Hiram Lewis (1824–1901)	Boston, MA (1851)	Indian Valley, CA (1860–1880s)
		Bridgeport, CA (1867–1901)
Lewis, Martha Jane Reed (1838–1923)	Springfield, IL (1846)	San Jose, CA (1847–1874)
Macy, Lucinda Polk (1807–1872)	Washington, IN (1850)	El Monte, CA (1851–1852)
		Los Angeles, CA (1852–1872)
Macy, Obed (1801–1857)	Washington, IN (1850)	Los Angeles, CA (1852–1857)
Meeker, Eliza Jane (1834–1909)	Eddyville, IA (1852)	McNeil Island, WA (1853–1861)
		Puyallup, WA (1862–1909)
Meeker, Ezra (1830–1928)	Eddyville, IA (1852)	McNeil Island, WA (1853–1861)
		Puyallup, WA (1862–1894)
Miller, Lafayette (1840–1878)	Quesqueton, IA (1863)	Lafayette, CO (1863–1878)
Miller, Mary Foote (1842–1921)	Quesqueton, IA (1863)	Lafayette, CO (1863–1921)
Stone, Elizabeth Hickock (1801–1895)	Watertown, NY (1828)	St. Paul, MI (1857–1862)
		Denver, CO (1862–1864)
		Fort Collins, CO (1864–1895)
Stone, Lewis (1799–1866)	St. Paul, MN (1857)	Denver (1862–1864)
		Fort Collins (1864–1866)
Wilkins, John R. (1835–1904)	Fort Madison, IA (1853)	Tuscarora, NV (1876–1878)
instrument maker		
Goulding, William R. (1805–1865)	York, England (1805)	San Francisco, CA (1849–1850)
insurer		
Backenstoe, Virginia E. (1833–1921)	Springfield, IL (1846)	San Jose, CA (1847–1874)
interpreter		
Baker, Jim (1818–1898)	Belleville, IL (1839)	Savery, WY (1873–1898)
Bottineau, Pierre (1817–1895)	Winnipeg, Manitoba (1832)	St. Paul, MN (1840–1852)
		Osseo, MN (1852–1877)
		Red Lake Falls, MN (1877–1895)
Chin, Ah Yane (1869–?)	China (1874)	San Francisco, CA (1874–?)
Chisholm, Jesse (1806–1868)	Arkansas (1820s)	Hughes County, OK (1820s, 1858–1861, 1868)
		Tehuacana Creek, TX (1833–1858)
		Wichita, KS (1861–1868)
Huntington, Dimick Baker (1808–1879)	Watertown, NY (1836)	Salt Lake City, UT (1848–1901)
Robidoux, Antoine (1794–1860)	St. Louis, MO (1832)	Fort Uintah, UT (1833–1844)
Wu, Tien Fu (1861–ca. 1940s)	Canton, China (1876)	San Francisco, CA (1876–ca. 1940s)
inventor		
Hamilton, Ezra (1833–1914)	Mount Sterling, IL (1853)	Shasta, CA (1856–1861)
		Los Angeles, CA (1875–1914)
Kinman, Seth (1815–1888)	Pekin, IL (1849)	Shasta, CA (1850–1855)
		Table Bluff, CA (1855–1888)
investor		
Adair, Cornelia W. (1837–1921)	Philadelphia, PA (1874)	Palo Duro, TX (1874–1921)
Adair, John George (1823–1885)	Queen's County, Ireland (1874)	Palo Duro, TX (1874–1885)
Campbell, Robert (1804–1879)	Plumbridge Ireland (1822)	St. Louis, MO (1835–1879)
Folsom, Joseph Libbey (1817–1855)	West Point, NY (1846)	San Francisco, CA (1847–1855)
Hollenbeck, John E. (1829–1885)	Nicaragua (1874)	Obed, CA (1874–1885)
Lahti, Charles (1859–1932)	Vadsø, Norway (1864)	St. Peter, MN (1864–1932)
O'Farrell, John A. (1823–1900)	Louisville, KY (1859)	Boise, ID (1863–1900)
Stone, Elizabeth Hickock (1801–1895)	Watertown, NY (1828)	Fort Collins, CO (1864–1895)
jailer		
Macy, Oscar (1829–1910)	Washington, IN (1850)	Los Angeles, CA (1852–1910)

Appendix E. Occupation

Occupation	Left Original Home	Area of Settlement
journalist		
Fisk, Andrew Jackson (1849–1910)	Fort Ripley, MN (1866)	Fort Benton, MT (1866)
Fisk, James Liberty (1835–1902)	Fort Ripley, MN (1863)	Bannack, MT (1863)
	Fort Ripley, MN (1866)	Fort Benton, MT (1866)
Fisk, Robert Emmett (1837–1908)	Fort Ripley, MN (1866)	Fort Benton, MT (1866)
Fisk, Van Hayden (1840–1890)	Fort Ripley, MN (1866)	Fort Benton, MT (1866)
Holmes, James Henry (1833–1907)	Emporia, KS (1858)	Taos, NM (1858–1863)
judge		
Dale, Frank (1849–1930)	Somonauk, IL (1871)	Wichita, KS (1871–1889)
		Guthrie, OK (1889–1930)
Franklin, Lewis Abraham (1820–1879)	Kingston, Jamaica (1849)	San Francisco, CA (1849–1855)
		San Diego, CA (1855–1860)
Ide, William Brown (1796–1852)	Rutland, MA (1845)	Sutter's Fort, CA (1845–1852)
Leavitt, Hiram Lewis (1824–1901)	Boston, MA (1851)	Indian Valley, CA (1860–1880s)
		Bridgeport, CA (1867–1901)
justice of the peace		
Goodell, Henry Martin (1843–1905)	Vermilion, OH (1853)	Lynden, WA (1884–1905)
Ise, Henry C. (1841–1900)	Württemberg, Germany (1857)	Ross, KS (1871–1900)
knife maker		
Lilly, Benjamin Vernon (1856–1936)	Jackson, MS (1868)	Mer Rouge, LA (1868–1901)
		Big Thicket, TX (1904–1908)
		Gila, NM (1908–1916)
		Quemado, AZ (1916–1926)
		Pleasanton, NM (1931–1936)
labor leader		
Imamura, Yemyo (1867–1932)	Fukui, Japan (1899)	Honolulu, HI (1899–1932)
laundress		
Bowman, Sarah A. (1812–1866)	Clay County, MO (1845)	Corpus Christi, TX (1845–1846)
		El Paso, TX (1848–1850)
		Yuma, AZ (1850–1866)
Kelly, Fanny Wiggins (1845–1904)	Geneva, KS (1864)	Sherman Station, WY (1868–1869)
Tabor, Augusta Louise (1833–1895)	Augusta, ME (1857)	Zeandale, KS (1857–1859)
		Oro City, CO (1859–1861)
		Leadville, CO (1861–1879)
legislator		
O'Farrell, John A. (1823–1900)	Louisville, KY (1859)	Boise, ID (1863–1900)
Smith, Hiram F. (1829–1893)	New York, NY (1849)	Olympia, WA (1865–1867, 1889)
Stone, Lewis (1799–1866)	St. Paul, MN (1857)	Denver (1862–1864)
		Fort Collins (1864–1866)
lexicographer		
Bingham, Hiram (1789–1869)	Hartford, CT (1819)	Honolulu, HI (1820–1840)
library builder		
Dale, Martha Wood (1859–1930)	Oswego, NY (1879)	Wichita (1879–1889)
		Guthrie, OK (1889–1930)
librettist		
Carr, Sarah Pratt (1850–1935)	Freeport, ME (1852)	San Francisco, CA (1852–1867, 1913–1935)
		Carlin, NV (1867–1872)
		St. Helena, CA (1883–1900)
		Seattle, WA (1900–1913)
		Los Angeles, CA (1913–1935)
lieutenant governor		
Tabor, Horace Austin W. (1830–1899)	Boston, MA (1855)	Oro City, CO (1859–1861)
		Leadville, CO (1861–1879)
		Denver, CO (1879–1899)
madam		
Bowman, Sarah A. (1812–1866)	Clay County, MO (1845)	Corpus Christi, TX (1845–1846)
		El Paso, TX (1848–1850)
		Yuma, AZ (1850–1866)
DeVere, Pearl (1859–1897)	Evansville, IN (ca. 1875)	Cripple Creek, CO (ca. 1875–1897)
mail carrier		
Huntington, William D. (1818–1887)	Watertown, NY (1836)	Springville, UT (1852–1887)

Appendix E. Occupation

Occupation	Left Original Home	Area of Settlement
McCarty, Jonathan W. (1833–1900)	Lake County, IN (1853)	Pierce County, WA (1853–1870)
Smith, Hiram F. (1829–1893)	New York, NY (1849)	Okanogan, WA (1856–1893)
Toponce, Alexander (1839–1923)	Belfort, France (1846)	Chesterfield, ID (1879–1923)
manufacturer		
Hamilton, Ezra (1833–1914)	Mount Sterling, IL (1853)	Shasta, CA (1856–1861)
		Los Angeles, CA (1875–1914)
mason		
Arcouet, Amable (1797–1880)	Montreal, Quebec (1833)	St. Paul, OR (1835–1880)
mayor		
Judson, Holden Allen (1827–1899)	Vermilion, OH (1853)	Claquato, WA (1853–1858)
		Whidbey, WA (1866–1899)
Tabor, Horace Austin W. (1830–1899)	Boston, MA (1855)	Leadville, CO (1861–1879)
merchant		
Ebbetts, John A.N. (ca. 1815–1854)	New York, NY (1849)	San Francisco, CA (1849–1854)
Franklin, Edward (1809–1873)	Liverpool, England (1849)	San Francisco, CA (1849–1873)
Franklin, Lewis Abraham (1820–1879)	Kingston, Jamaica (1849)	San Francisco, CA (1849–1855)
		San Diego, CA (1855–1860)
Franklin, Lumley (1808–1873)	Liverpool, England (1849)	San Francisco, CA (1849–1858)
Franklin, Maurice A. (1817–1874)	Kingston, Jamaica (1849)	San Francisco, CA (1849–1855)
		San Diego, CA (1855–1859)
		San Bernardino, CA (1859–1874)
Franklin, Selim (1814–1884)	Liverpool, England (1849)	San Francisco, CA (1849–1858, 1866–1884)
Goodell, Nathan Edward (1839–1886)	Vermilion, OH (1851)	Skagit River, OR (1879)
McCarty, Jonathan W. (1833–1900)	Lake County, IN (1853)	Seattle, WA (1870–1900)
McCoy, John Calvin (1811–1889)	Vincennes, IN (1830)	Kansas City, MO (1830–1889)
Mitchell, Eliza Vandenberg (1809–1881)	Cape Town, South Africa (1836)	Florence, NE (1852–1881)
Mitchell, James C. (1810–1860)	Council Bluffs, IA (1852)	Florence, NE (1852–1860)
Robbins, Ezekiel W. (1800–1852)	Watertown, NY (1838)	Chester, IL (1838–1852)
Tabor, Horace Austin (1830–1899)	Boston, MA (1855)	Zeandale, KS (1855–1859)
		Oro City, CO (1859–1861)
		Leadville, CO (1861–1879)
		Denver, CO (1879–1899)
Wilkins, John R. (1835–1904)	Fort Madison, IA (1853)	Ashby, ID (1866–1867)
		Boise, ID (1867–1876)
midwife		
Bingham, Sybil Moseley (1792–1848)	Hartford, CT (1819)	Honolulu, HI (1820–1840)
Briones de Miranda, Juana (1802–1889)	Mexico (1802)	Santa Clara, CA (1844–1885)
Brown, Clara (1800–1885)	Gallatin, KY (1856)	Leavenworth, KS (1856–1859)
		Denver, CO (1859–1885)
Stone, Elizabeth Hickock (1801–1895)	Watertown, NY (1828)	Fort Collins, CO (1864–1895)
Young, Zina D.H. (1821–1901)	Watertown, NY (1836)	Salt Lake City, UT (1848–1901)
miller		
Chiles, Joseph B. (1810–1885)	Jackson County, MO (1841)	Napa Valley, CA (1843–1885)
Huntington, William (1784–1846)	Watertown, NY (1836)	Mount Pisgah, IA (1846)
millwright		
Lassen, Peter (1800–1859)	Farum, Denmark (1830)	San Jose, CA (1840–1843)
		Rancho Bosquejo, CA (1844–1850)
		Honey Lake, CA (1855–1859)
Simmons, Michael T. (1814–1867)	Nodaway, MO (1844)	Tumwater, WA (1845–1867)
miner		
Bruce, Samuel A. (1839–1900)	Bray, Ireland (1860s)	Bannock, ID (1860s)
Fisk, Andrew Jackson (1849–1910)	Fort Ripley, MN (1866)	Fort Benton, MT (1866)
Franklin, Maurice A. (1817–1874)	Kingston, Jamaica (1849)	San Francisco, CA (1849–1855)
		San Diego, CA (1855–1859)
		San Bernardino, CA (1859–1874)
French, Erasmus D. (1822–1902)	Albion, MI (1845)	Darwin, CA (1860–1865)
Hamilton, Ezra (1833–1914)	Mount Sterling, IL (1853)	Shasta, CA (1856–1861)
		Los Angeles, CA (1875–1914)

Appendix E. Occupation

Occupation	Left Original Home	Area of Settlement
Heazle, Jean (1879–1949)	Bray, Ireland (1893)	DeLamar, ID (1893–1949)
Huntington, William D. (1818–1887)	Watertown, NY (1836)	Springville, UT (1852–1887)
O'Farrell, John A. (1823–1900)	Louisville, KY (1859)	Boise, ID (1863–1900)
Pratt, Robert Henry (1824–1920)	Freeport, ME (1852)	San Francisco, CA (1849–1867, 1881–1893)
		Carlin, NV (1867–1869)
		Salt Lake City (1869–1879)
		Sacramento, CA (1878–1881)
		St. Helena, CA (1881–1900)
		Seattle, WA (1900–1920)
Reading, Pearson B. (1816–1868)	Hunterdon, NJ (1844)	Shasta, CA (1845–1868)
Reed, James Frazier (1800–1874)	Independence, MO (1846)	San Jose, CA (1847–1874)
Reed, James Frazier, Jr. (1841–1901)	Springfield, IL (1846)	San Jose, CA (1847–1901)
Smith, Hiram F. (1829–1893)	New York, NY (1849)	Okanogan, WA (1856–1893)
Stone, Lewis (1799–1866)	St. Paul, MN (1857)	Denver (1862–1864)
		Fort Collins (1864–1866)
Tabor, Horace Austin W. (1830–1899)	Boston, MA (1855)	Leadville, CO (1861–1879)
Wysinger, Edmond E. (1816–1891)	South Carolina (1849)	Mokelumne, CA (1849–1891)
minister		
Brier, James Welch Brier (1814–1898)	Kalamazoo, MI (1840)	Death Valley, CA (1849)
Carr, Sarah Pratt (1850–1935)	Freeport, ME (1852)	San Francisco, CA (1852–1867, 1913–1935)
		Carlin, NV (1867–1872)
		St. Helena, CA (1883–1900)
		Seattle, WA (1900–1913)
		Los Angeles, CA (1913–1935)
Goodell, Jotham Weeks (1809–1859)	Vermilion, OH (1851)	Portland, OR (1851–1859)
Robbins, Ezekiel Wright (1800–1852)	Watertown, NY (1838)	Chester, IL (1838–1852)
Wysinger, Edmond E. (1816–1891)	South Carolina (1849)	Visalia, CA (1864–1891)
missionary		
Bingham, Hiram (1789–1869)	Hartford, CT (1819)	Honolulu, HI (1820–1840)
Bingham, Sybil Moseley (1792–1848)	Hartford, CT (1819)	Honolulu, HI (1820–1840)
Carr, Sarah Pratt (1850–1935)	Freeport, ME (1852)	San Francisco, CA (1852–1867, 1913–1935)
		Carlin, NV (1867–1872)
		St. Helena, CA (1883–1900)
		Seattle, WA (1900–1913)
		Los Angeles, CA (1913–1935)
Culbertson, Margaret (1834–1897)	Groveland, NY (1878)	San Francisco, CA (1878–1897)
Docher, Anton (1852–1928)	Auvergne, France (1887)	Isleta Pueblo, NM (1891–1928)
Huntington, Oliver B. (1823–1909)	Watertown, NY (1836)	Springville, UT (1852–1901)
Imamura, Yemyo (1867–1932)	Fukui, Japan (1899)	Honolulu, HI (1899–1932)
Lee, Jason (1803–1845)	Stanstead, Quebec (1833)	St. Paul, OR (1833–1844)
McBeth, Kate Christine (1832–1915)	Wellsville, OH (1858)	Lapwai, ID (1879–1915)
McBeth, Susan Law (1830–1893)	Wellsville, OH (1858)	Goodwater, OK (1858–1861)
		St. Louis, MO (1866–1873)
		Lapwai, ID (1873–1893)
McCoy, John Calvin (1811–1889)	Vincennes, IN (1830)	Kansas City, MO (1830–1889)
Padilla, Juan de (?–1544)	Andalusia, Spain (1528)	Quivira, TX (1542–1544)
Whitman, Marcus (1802–1847)	Angelica, NY (1836)	Walla Walla, WA (1836–1847)
Whitman, Narcissa (1808–1847)	Angelica, NY (1836)	Walla Walla, WA (1836–1847)
Young, Zina D.H. (1821–1901)	Watertown, NY (1836)	Salt Lake City, UT (1848–1901)
musician		
Huntington, William D. (1818–1887)	Watertown, NY (1836)	Springville, UT (1852–1887)
Merritt, Josiah (1803–1882)	Athens, OH (1860)	Snoqualmie, WA (1860–1882)
negotiator with Indians		
Bottineau, Pierre (1817–1895)	Winnipeg, Manitoba (1832)	St. Paul, MN (1840–1852)
		Osseo, MN (1852–1877)
		Red Lake Falls, MN (1877–1895)
Campbell, Robert (1804–1879)	Plumbridge Ireland (1822)	St. Louis, MO (1835–1879)
nun		
Cope, Sister Marianne (1838–1918)	Utica, NY (1884)	Wailiuku, Maui (1884–1887)
		Kalaupapa, Molokai (1887–1918)

Appendix E. Occupation

Occupation	Left Original Home	Area of Settlement
nurse		
Bowman, Sarah A. (1812–1866)	Clay County, MO (1845)	Corpus Christi, TX (1845–1846)
		El Paso, TX (1848–1850)
		Yuma, AZ (1850–1866)
Brown, Clara (1800–1885)	Gallatin, KY (1856)	Leavenworth, KS (1856–1859)
		Denver, CO (1859–1885)
Bush, Isabella James (1801–1866)	Jackson, MO (1844)	Tumwater, WA (1845–1866)
Cope, Sister Marianne (1838–1918)	Utica, NY (1884)	Wailiuku, Maui (1884–1887)
		Kalaupapa, Molokai (1887–1918)
Isbell, Olive Mann (1824–1899)	Greenbush, IL (1846)	Santa Clara, CA (1846–1850; 1861–1886)
orchardist		
Bruce, George Whiteley (1851–1927)	Bray, Ireland (1860s)	DeLamar, ID (1860s-1927)
Cowles, George A. (1836–1887)	Hartford, CT (1878)	Cowlestown, CA (1878–1887)
Key, Ambrose W. (1829–1908)	Crawfordsville, IN (1838)	Shawnee, KS (1868–1908)
Rice, James Stephen (1846–1939)	Cleveland, OH (1877)	Tustin, CA (1878–1939)
Santee, Jennie Frances (1838–1931)	Hartford, CT (1878)	Cowlestown, CA 1878–1931)
Smith, Hiram F. (1829–1893)	New York, NY (1849)	Okanogan, WA (1856–1893)
pharmacist		
Franklin, Maurice Abraham (1817–1874)	Kingston, Jamaica (1849)	San Francisco, CA (1849–1855)
		San Diego, CA (1855–1859)
		San Bernardino, CA (1859–1874)
Reich, George Adolph (1846–1896)	Breslau, Poland (1870)	San Bernardino, CA (1870–1882)
philanthropist		
Tabor, Augusta Louise (1833–1895)	Augusta, ME (1857)	Denver, CO (1879–1894)
photographer		
Franklin, Maurice A. (1817–1874)	Kingston, Jamaica (1849)	San Bernardino, CA (1859–1874)
Larimer, Sarah Luse (1836–1913)	Iola, KS (1864)	Sherman Station, WY (1864–1870)
William, Henry I. (1844–1893)	Leeds, England (1845)	Fort Benton, MT (1866)
physician		
French, Erasmus D. (1822–1902)	Albion, MI (1845)	Fort Tejon, CA (1847–1851)
		San Jose, CA (1848–1860)
		Darwin, CA (1860–1865)
		Baja, CA (1894–1902)
Hayashi, Harvey S. (1867–1943)	Tonami, Japan (1885)	San Francisco, CA (1884–1891)
		Sacramento, CA (1891–1893)
		Kona, HI (1893–1943)
Macy, Obed (1801–1857)	Washington, IN (1850)	Los Angeles, CA (1852–1857)
Reich, George Adolph (1846–1896)	Breslau, Poland (1870)	San Bernardino, CA (1870–1882)
Robbins, Ezekiel W. (1800–1852)	Watertown, NY (1838)	Chester, IL (1838–1852)
Whitman, Marcus (1802–1847)	Angelica, NY (1836)	Walla Walla, WA (1836–1847)
Whitman, Narcissa (1808–1847)	Angelica, NY (1836)	Walla Walla, WA (1836–1847)
polemicist		
Kellie, Luna Sanford (1857–1940)	Rockford, IL (1871)	Adams County, NE (1877–1884)
		Hartwell, NE (1884–1901)
politician		
Meeker, Ezra (1830–1928)	Eddyville, IA (1852)	McNeil Island, WA (1853–1861)
		Puyallup, WA (1862–1894)
O'Farrell, John A. (1823–1900)	Louisville, KY (1859)	Boise, ID (1863–1900)
Robbins, Ezekiel W. (1800–1852)	Watertown, NY (1838)	Chester, IL (1838–1852)
Smith, Hiram F. (1829–1893)	New York, NY (1849)	Olympia, WA (1865–1867, 1889)
Stone, Lewis (1799–1866)	St. Paul, MN (1857)	Denver (1862–1864)
		Fort Collins (1864–1866)
Pony Express rider		
Toponce, Alexander (1839–1923)	Belfort, France (1846)	Tipton, MO (1854–1860)
postmaster		
Booth, Albert Anson (1850–1914)	Syracuse, NY (1869)	Edna, ND (1879–1914)
Fisk, Andrew Jackson (1849–1910)	Fort Ripley, MN (1866)	Fort Benton, MT (1866)
Hamilton, Ezra (1833–1914)	Mount Sterling, IL (1853)	Shasta, CA (1856–1861)
		Los Angeles, CA (1875–1914)
Heazle, Benjamin A. (1880–1936)	Bray, Ireland (1894)	Murphy, ID (1894–?)
Heazle, George Robert (1876–1924)	Bray, Ireland (1894)	Murphy, ID (1894–?)

Appendix E. Occupation

Occupation	Left Original Home	Area of Settlement
Ise, Henry C. (1841–1900)	Württemberg, Germany (1857)	Ross, KS (1871–1900)
Judson, Holden Allen (1827–1899)	Vermilion, OH (1853)	Claquato, WA (1853–1858)
		Whidbey, WA (1866–1899)
Lawing, Nellie Trosper (1873–1956)	Buchanan, MO (1901)	Seward, AK (1915–1956)
Simmons, Michael T. (1814–1867)	Nodaway, MO (1844)	Tumwater, WA (1845–1867)
Street, Joseph M. (1782–1840)	Shawneetown, IL (1812)	Prairie du Chien, WI (1812–1835, 1837–1842)
Tabor, Augusta Louise (1833–1895)	Augusta, ME (1857)	Oro City, CO (1859–1861)
		Leadville, CO (1861–1879)
Tabor, Horace Austin (1830–1899)	Boston, MA (1855)	Oro City, CO (1859–1861)
		Leadville, CO (1861–1879)
poulterer		
Bush, Isabella James (1801–1866)	Jackson, MO (1844)	Tumwater, WA (1845–1866)
priest		
Huntington, Oliver B. (1823–1909)	Watertown, NY (1836)	Springville, UT (1852–1901)
Moczygemba, Leopold (1824–1891)	Pluznica, Prussia (1852)	Bandera, TX (1852–1858)
printer		
Macy, Oscar (1829–1910)	Washington, IN (1850)	Los Angeles, CA (1852–1910)
prophet		
Smith, Joseph, Jr. (1805–1844)	Harmony, PA (1827)	Nauvoo, IL (1831–1844)
Young, Brigham (1801–1877)	Whittingham, VT (1832)	Salt Lake City (1847–1877)
prospector		
Goller, John (1825–1874)	Bavaria, Germany (1849)	Los Angeles, CA (1850–1874)
Isbell, Isaac Chauncy (1800–1886)	Greenbush, IL (1846)	Santa Clara, CA (1846–1850)
Kinman, Seth (1815–1888)	Pekin, IL (1849)	Shasta, CA (1850–1855)
		Table Bluff, CA (1855–1888)
Lassen, Peter (1800–1859)	Farum, Denmark (1830)	San Jose, CA (1840–1843)
		Rancho Bosquejo, CA (1844–1850)
		Honey Lake, CA (1855–1859)
Merritt, Josiah (1803–1882)	Athens, OH (1860)	Snoqualmie, WA (1860–1882)
publisher		
Fisk, Van Hayden (1840–1890)	Fort Ripley, MN (1866)	Fort Benton, MT (1866)
Macy, Oscar (1829–1910)	Washington, IN (1850)	Los Angeles, CA (1852–1910)
Parmley, J.W. (1861–1940)	Mifflin, WI (1883)	Ipswich, SD (1883–1940)
quilter		
Snyder, Grace McCance (1882–1982)	Cass County, MO (1885)	Cozad, NE (1885–1919)
railroad builder		
Kellie, James Thomson (1850–1918)	Toronto, Ontario (1871)	St. Louis, MO (1872–1873)
		Iowa (1874–1877)
		Adams County, NE
		Hartwell, NE (1884–1901)
Pratt, Robert Henry (1824–1920)	Freeport, ME (1852)	San Francisco, CA (1849–1867)
		Carlin, NV (1867–1869)
		Salt Lake City (1869–1879)
		Sacramento, CA (1878–1881)
		St. Helena, CA (1881–1900)
		Seattle, WA (1900–1920)
railroad manager		
Carr, Byron Oscar (1835–1913)	Concord, NY (1872)	Truckee, CA (1872–1880s)
		San Francisco, CA (1880s–1891)
		Lemoore, CA (1894–1900)
		Seattle, WA (1900–1913)
raisin grower		
Cowles, George A. (1836–1887)	Hartford, CT (1878)	Cowlestown, CA (1878–1887)
Santee, Jennie F. (1838–1931)	Hartford, CT (1878)	Cowlestown, CA (1878–1931)
rancher		
Adair, Cornelia W. (1837–1921)	Philadelphia, PA (1874)	Palo Duro, TX (1874–1921)
Baker, Jim (1818–1898)	Belleville, IL (1839)	Savery, WY (1873–1898)
Booth, Albert Anson (1850–1914)	Syracuse, NY (1869)	Edna, ND (1879–1914)
Briones de Miranda, Juana (1802–1889)	Mexico (1802)	Santa Clara, CA (1844–1885)

Appendix E. Occupation

Occupation	Left Original Home	Area of Settlement
Bruce, George W. (1851–1927)	Bray, Ireland (1860s)	DeLamar, ID (1860s–1927)
Chiles, Joseph B. (1810–1885)	Jackson County, MO (1843)	Napa Valley, CA (1843–1885)
Chisum, John Simpson (1824–1884)	Hardeman, TN (1866)	Paris, TX (1837–1863)
		Bosque Redondo, NM (1872–1878)
Cowles, George A. (1836–1887)	Hartford, CT (1878)	Cowlestown, CA (1878–1887)
Dyer, Leigh Richmond (1849–1902)	Madison, TN (1867)	Belknap, TX (1867)
		Palo Duro, TX (1876–1887)
Farnham, Eliza Wood (1815–1864)	New York, NY (1849)	Santa Cruz, CA (1849–1856)
		Stockton, CA (1859–1862)
French, Erasmus D. (1822–1902)	Albion, MI (1845)	Fort Tejon, CA (1847–1851)
		San Jose, CA (1848–1860)
Goodnight, Charles (1836–1929)	Macoupin, IL (1846)	Goodnight, TX (1846–1929)
Goodnight, Elija (1831–1929)	Macoupin, IL (1846)	Goodnight, TX (1846–1929)
Heazle, Benjamin Alfred (1880–1936)	Bray, Ireland (1894)	Murphy, ID (1894–?)
Heazle, Jean (1879–1949)	Bray, Ireland (1893)	DeLamar, ID (1893–1949)
Isbell, Isaac Chauncy (1800–1886)	Greenbush, IL (1846)	Santa Clara, CA (1846–1850; 1861–1886)
		Cancon, TX (1850–1861)
Isbell, Olive Mann (1824–1899)	Greenbush, IL (1846)	Santa Clara, CA (1846–1850; 1861–1886)
		Cancon, TX (1850–1861)
Kirby, Georgiana B. (1818–1887)	Staffordshire, England (1831)	Santa Cruz, CA (1850–1887)
Lassen, Peter (1800–1859)	Farum, Denmark (1830)	San Jose, CA (1840–1843)
		Rancho Bosquejo, CA (1844–1850)
		Honey Lake, CA (1855–1859)
Loving, Oliver (1812–1867)	Belknap, TX (1866)	Fort Sumner, NM (1866–1867)
Reed, John Thomas (1805–1843)	Acapulco, Mexico (1826)	San Francisco, CA (1826–1843)
Reed, William W. (1816–1891)	Natchitoches, LA (1833)	Bell County TX (1833–1891)
Santee, Jennie F. (1838–1931)	Hartford, CT (1878)	Cowlestown, CA (1878–1931)

realtor

Franklin, Selim (1814–1884)	Liverpool, England (1849)	San Francisco, CA (1849–1858, 1866–1884)
Mitchell, James C. (1810–1860)	Council Bluffs, IA (1852)	Florence, NE (1852–1860)
Reed, James Frazier (1800–1874)	Springfield, IL (1846)	San Jose, CA (1847–1874)
Reed, James Frazier, Jr. (1841–1901)	Springfield, IL (1846)	San Jose, CA (1847–1901)

recruiter

Brown, Clara (1800–1885)	Gallatin, KY (1856)	Leavenworth, KS (1856–1859)
		Denver, CO (1859–1885)
Ide, William Brown (1796–1852)	Rutland, MA (1845)	Sutter's Fort, CA (1845–1852)
Lassen, Peter (1800–1859)	Farum, Denmark (1830)	San Jose, CA (1840–1843)
		Rancho Bosquejo, CA (1844–1850)
		Honey Lake, CA (1855–1859)
Moczygemba, Leopold (1824–1891)	Pluznica, Prussia (1852)	Bandera, TX (1852–1858)
Wahl, James M. (1846–1939)	Storvahl, Norway (1867)	Sioux Falls, SD (1868–1939)

reformer

Farnham, Eliza Wood (1815–1864)	New York, NY (1849)	Santa Cruz, CA (1849–1856)
		Stockton, CA (1859–1862)
Holmes, Julia Archibald (1838–1887)	Emporia, KS (1858)	Taos, NM (1858–1863)

road builder

Toponce, Alexander (1839–1923)	Belfort, France (1846)	Ogden, UT (1863–1923)
Wootton, Richens Lacey (1816–1893)	Christian, KY (1836)	Independence, MO (1836)
		Bent's Fort, CO (1836–1847)
		Taos, NM (1847–1858)
		Denver, CO (1858–1893)

sailor

Reed, John Thomas (1805–1843)	Acapulco, Mexico (1826)	San Francisco, CA (1826–1843)

sawyer

Lassen, Peter (1800–1859)	Farum, Denmark (1830)	San Jose, CA (1840–1843)
		Rancho Bosquejo, CA (1844–1850)
		Honey Lake, CA (1855–1859)
Reed, John Thomas (1805–1843)	Acapulco, Mexico (1826)	San Francisco, CA (1826–1843)

school builder

Goodnight, Charles (1836–1929)	Macoupin, IL (1846)	Goodnight, TX (1846–1929)

Appendix E. Occupation

Occupation	Left Original Home	Area of Settlement
Goodnight, Mary Ann D. (1839–1926)	Hickman, KY (1870)	Pueblo, CO (1870–1871) Palo Duro, TX (1871–1887)
Judson, George (1860–1891)	Vermilion, OH (1853)	Bellingham, WA (1886) Fort Worth, TX (1887–1926)
Judson, Phoebe Goodell (1831–1926)	Vermilion, OH (1853)	Claquato, WA (1853–1858) Whidbey, WA (1866–1926)
Santee, Jennie Frances (1838–1931)	Hartford, CT (1878)	Cowlestown, CA (1878–1931)
scout		
Baker, Jim (1818–1898)	Belleville, IL (1839)	Savery, WY (1873–1898)
Bridger, Jim (1803–1881)	Richmond, VA (1822)	Fort Bridger, WY (1842–1865)
Bottineau, Pierre (1817–1895)	Winnipeg, Manitoba (1832)	St. Paul, MN (1840–1852) Osseo, MN (1852–1877) Red Lake Falls, MN (1877–1895)
Liberty, Stephen Edward (1843–1911)	Quebec (1862)	Fort Benton, MT (1866)
Omohundro, Texas Jack (1846–1880)	Pleasure Hill, VA (1859)	Cottonwood Springs, NE (1869–1872)
seamstress		
Bell, Susan Hollenbeck (1831–1905)	Sedalia, MO (1856)	Obed, CA (1898–1905)
Bingham, Sybil Moseley (1792–1848)	Hartford, CT (1819)	Honolulu, HI (1820–1840)
Cameron, Donaldina (1869–1968)	Clydevale, New Zealand (1871)	San Francisco, CA (1895–1968)
Isbell, Isaac Chauncey (1800–1886)	Greenbush, IL (1846)	Santa Clara, CA (1846–1850)
Ise, Rosena Haag (1855–1947)	Theresa, WI (1873)	Ross, KS (1873–1947)
servant		
Ozawa, Kintaro (fl. 1840s–1870s)	Yokohama, Japan (1868)	Honolulu, HI (1868–?)
Ozawa, Tomi (1849–?)	Yokohama, Japan (1868)	Honolulu, HI (1868–?)
sexton		
Huntington, William (1784–1846)	Watertown, NY (1836)	Mount Pisgah, IA (1846)
sheriff/deputy		
Caldwell, Mathew (1798–1842)	Gasconade, MO (1831)	Gonzalez, TX (1831–1842)
Gwydir, Rickard Daniel (1844–1925)	Covington, KY (1887)	Spokane, WA (1887–1925)
Reed, William W. (1816–1891)	Natchitoches, LA (1833)	Bell County, TX (1833–1891)
shipper		
Coleman, William Tell (1824–1893)	St. Louis, MO (1849)	San Francisco, CA (1849–1893)
singer		
Rice, Coralinn Barlow (1849–1919)	Cleveland, OH (1877)	Tustin, CA (1878–1919)
social worker		
Snow, Eliza Roxcy (1804–1887)	Hiram, OH (1835)	Salt Lake City, UT (1835–1887)
Wells, Emmeline B. (1828–1921)	Petersham, MA (1844)	Salt Lake City, UT (1846–1921)
Young, Zina D.H. (1821–1901)	Watertown, NY (1836)	Salt Lake City, UT (1848–1901)
soldier		
Bruce, George W. (1851–1927)	Bray, Ireland (1860s)	DeLamar, ID (1860s–1927)
Fisk, Andrew Jackson (1849–1910)	Fort Ripley, MN (1866)	Fort Benton, MT (1866)
Fisk, James Liberty (1835–1902)	Fort Ripley, MN (1863)	Bannack, MT (1863)
Fisk, Robert Emmett (1837–1908)	Fort Ripley, MN (1866)	Fort Benton, MT (1866)
Fisk, Van Hayden (1840–1890)	Fort Ripley, MN (1866)	Fort Benton, MT (1866)
Folsom, Joseph L. (1817–1855)	West Point, NY (1846)	San Francisco (1847–1855)
Franklin, Lewis A. (1820–1879)	Kingston, Jamaica (1849)	San Francisco, CA (1849–1855) San Diego, CA (1855–1860)
Goodnight, Elija (1831–1929)	Macoupin, IL (1846)	Goodnight, TX (1846–1929)
Gwydir, Rickard Daniel (1844–1925)	Covington, KY (1887)	Spokane, WA (1887–1925)
Holmes, James Henry (1833–1907)	Emporia, KS (1858)	Taos, NM (1858–1863)
Huntington, William (1784–1846)	Watertown, NY (1836)	Mount Pisgah, IA (1846)
Moore, Seymour T. (1827–1876)	Ohio	Fort Miller, CA (1849–1851) Utah (1853–1854)
Reading, Pearson Barton (1816–1868)	Hunterdon, NJ (1844)	Shasta, CA (1845–1868)
Smeathers, William (ca. 1766–1837)	Yellow Banks, KY (1821)	Columbia, TX (1824–1837)
Sowell, Andrew Jackson (1815–1883)	Boone County, MO (1829)	Gonzales, TX (1829–1883)
Stroud, Ethan A. (1788–1846)	Chambers County, AL (1836)	Calvert, TX (1842–1846)
songwriter		
Kellie, Luna Sanford (1857–1940)	Rockford, IL (1871)	Adams County, NE (1877–1884) Hartwell, NE (1884–1901)

Appendix E. Occupation

Occupation	Left Original Home	Area of Settlement
Maynard, Frank H. (1853–1926)	Iowa City, IA (1869)	Towanda, KS (1869–1881)
		Colorado Springs, CO (1881–1926)
speculator		
Bottineau, Pierre (1817–1895)	Winnipeg, Manitoba (1832)	St. Paul, MN (1840–1852)
		Osseo, MN (1852–1877)
		Red Lake Falls, MN (1877–1895)
stage driver		
Monk, Hank (1826–1883)	Waddington, NY (1852)	Sacramento, CA (1852–1857)
		Carson City, NV (1857–1883)
		Deadwood, ND (1881)
Parkhurst, Charley (1812–1879)	Providence, RI (1851)	Soquel, CA (1851–1879)
Toponce, Alexander (1839–1923)	Belfort, France (1846)	Tipton, MO (1854–1860)
state president		
Ide, William Brown (1796–1852)	Rutland, MA (1845)	Sutter's Fort, CA (1845–1852)
state senator		
Stroud, Beden (1795–1865)	Chambers County, AL (1836)	Calvert, TX (1842–1865)
stockman		
Bush, George W. (ca. 1779–1863)	Jackson, MO (1844)	Tumwater, WA (1845–1866)
Ouilmette, Antoine L. (ca. 1760–1841)	Montreal, Quebec (1790)	Chicago, IL (1790–1833)
Rasor, John Henry (1849–1925)	Graham, IA (1883)	Plano, TX (1883–1925)
Toponce, Alexander (1839–1923)	Belfort, France (1846)	Ogden, UT (1863–1923)
Wilkins, John R. (1835–1904)	Fort Madison, IA (1853)	Bruneau, ID (1878–1904)
stone mason		
Tabor, Horace Austin W. (1830–1899)	Boston, MA (1855)	Zeandale, KS (1855–1859)
storyteller		
Kinman, Seth (1815–1888)	Pekin, IL (1849)	Shasta, CA (1850–1855)
		Table Bluff, CA (1855–1888)
suffragist		
Kirby, Georgiana Bruce (1818–1887)	Staffordshire, England (1831)	Santa Cruz, CA (1850–1887)
Stone, Elizabeth Hickock (1801–1895)	Watertown, NY (1828)	Fort Collins, CO (1864–1895)
surgeon		
Goulding, William Robinson (1805–1865)	York, England	San Francisco (1849–1850)
Isbell, Isaac Chauncy (1800–1886)	Greenbush, IL (1846)	Santa Clara, CA (1846–1850; 1861–1886)
		Cancon, TX (1850–1861)
surveyor		
Ebbetts, John A.N. (ca. 1815–1854)	New York, NY (1849)	San Francisco, CA (1849–1854)
Goddard, George Henry (1817–1906)	Bristol, England (1850)	San Francisco, CA 1850–1906)
Ide, William Brown (1796–1852)	Rutland, MA (1845)	Sutter's Fort, CA (1845–1852)
Judson, George (1860–1891)	Vermilion, OH (1853)	Bellingham, WA (1886)
Moore, Seymour T. (1827–1876)	Ohio	Fort Miller, CA (1849–1851)
		Utah (1853–1854)
synagogue builder		
Franklin, Maurice A. (1817–1874)	Kingston, Jamaica (1849)	San Francisco, CA (1849–1855)
		San Diego, CA (1855–1859)
		San Bernardino, CA (1859–1874)
tanner		
Key, Ambrose W. (1829–1908)	Crawfordsville, IN (1838)	Houston, TX (1865)
Kirby, Richard Cornelius (1817–1904)	Staffordshire, England (1842)	Santa Cruz, CA (1850–1904)
taverner		
Bowman, Sarah A. (1812–1866)	Clay County, MO (1845)	Matamoros, TX (1845–1846)
Huntington, William D. (1818–1887)	Watertown, NY (1836)	Council Bluffs, IA (1846)
Kinman, Seth (1815–1888)	Pekin, IL (1849)	Table Bluff, CA (1875–1888)
Mitchell, James C. (1810–1860)	Council Bluffs, IA (1852)	Florence, NE (1852–1860)
teacher		
Cameron, Donaldina (1869–1968)	Clydevale, New Zealand (1871)	San Francisco, CA (1895–1968)
Culbertson, Margaret (1834–1897)	Groveland, NY (1878)	San Francisco, CA (1878–1897)
Franklin, Maurice A. (1817–1874)	Kingston, Jamaica (1849)	San Francisco, CA (1849–1855)
		San Diego, CA (1855–1859)
		San Bernardino, CA (1859–1874)

Appendix E. Occupation

Occupation	Left Original Home	Area of Settlement
Goodnight, Mary Ann D. (1839–1926)	Hickman, KY (1870)	Pueblo, CO (1870–1871)
		Palo Duro, TX (1871–1887)
		Fort Worth, TX (1887–1926)
Haagsma, Broer Baukes (1831–1907)	Harlingen, Friesland (1853)	New Amsterdam, WI (1853–1907)
Hayashi, Harvey Saburo (1867–1943)	Tonami, Japan (1885)	San Francisco, CA (1884–1891)
		Sacramento, CA (1891–1893)
		Kona, HI (1893–1943)
Hayashi, Matsu K. (1877–1972)	Honshu, Japan (1896)	Kona, HI (1896–1972)
Holmes, Julia Archibald (1838–1887)	Emporia, KS (1858)	Taos, NM (1858–1863)
Isbell, Olive Mann (1824–1899)	Greenbush, IL (1846)	Santa Clara, CA (1846–1850)
Lee, Jason (1803–1845)	Stanstead, Quebec (1833)	St. Paul, OR (1833–1844)
McBeth, Kate C. (1832–1915)	Wellsville, OH (1858)	Lapwai, ID (1879–1915)
McBeth, Susan Law (1830–1893)	Wellsville, OH (1858)	Goodwater, OK (1858–1861)
		St. Louis, MO (1866–1873)
		Lapwai, ID (1873–1893)
Page, Larcena P. (1837–1913)	Nashville, TN (1837)	Tucson, AZ (1857–1913
Snow, Eliza Roxcy (1804–1887)	Hiram, OH (1835)	Salt Lake City, UT (1835–1887)
Stratton, Elizabeth P. (1830–1922)	Ontario (1864)	Fort Collins, CO (1864–1933
Wells, Emmeline B. (1828–1921)	Petersham, MA (1844)	Salt Lake City, UT (1846–1921)
Young, Zina D.H. (1821–1901)	Watertown, NY (1836)	Salt Lake City, UT (1848–1901)
territorial organizer		
Lee, Jason (1803–1845)	Stanstead, Quebec (1833)	St. Paul, OR (1833–1844)
territorial secretary		
Holmes, James Henry (1833–1907)	Emporia, KS (1858)	Taos, NM (1858–1863)
Texas Ranger		
Caldwell, Mathew (1798–1842)	Gasconade, MO (1831)	Gonzalez, TX (1831–1842)
Goodnight, Charles (1836–1929)	Macoupin, IL (1846)	Goodnight, TX (1846–1929)
Sowell, Andrew J. (1815–1883)	Boone County, MO (1829)	Gonzales, TX (1829–1883)
Sowell, John Newton, Jr. (1811–1856)	Boone County, MO (1829)	Gonzales, TX (1829–1856)
timber cutter		
Booth, Albert Anson (1850–1914)	Syracuse, NY (1869)	Fond du Lac, WI (1869–1872)
Bottineau, Pierre (1817–1895)	Winnipeg, Manitoba (1832)	Orono, MN (1851)
Bush, George W. (ca. 1779–1863)	Jackson, MO (1844)	Washougal, WA (1845)
Heazle, Jean (1879–1949)	Bray, Ireland (1893)	DeLamar, ID (1893–1949)
Simmons, Michael T. (1814–1867)	Nodaway, MO (1844)	Budd Inlet, WA (1845–1867)
trader		
Arcouet, Amable (1797–1880)	Montreal, Quebec (1833)	St. Paul, OR (1835–1880)
Campbell, Robert (1804–1879)	Plumbridge, Ireland (1822)	St. Louis, MO (1835–1879)
Chisholm, Jesse (1806–1868)	Arkansas (1820s)	Hughes County, OK (1820s, 1858–1861, 1868)
		Tehuacana Creek, TX (1833–1858)
		Wichita, KS (1861–1868)
Key, George (1795–1864)	Crawfordsville, IN (1836)	Louisa County, IA (1836–1861)
Mead, Agnes Barcome (1841–1869)	Quebec (1859)	Salina, KS (1862–1863)
		Wichita, KS (1864–1869)
Mead, James R. (1836–1910)	Davenport, IA (1859)	Salina, KS (1862–1863)
		Wichita, KS (1864–1910)
Meyerowitz, Isadore (ca. 1820–1856)	Russia (1849)	Honey Lake, CA (1849–1856)
Ouilmette, Antoine L. (ca. 1760–1841)		Montreal, Quebec (1790)
		Chicago, IL (1790–1833)
Point du Sable, Jean (ca. 1745–1818)	Chicago, IL (1800)	St. Charles, MO (1800–1818)
Smith, Hiram F. (1829–1893)	New York, NY (1849)	Okanogan, WA (1856–1893)
Sublette, William Lewis (1798–1845)	Lincoln, KY (1822)	St. Charles (1822–1833)
		Fort William, WY (1833–1835)
		St. Louis, MO (1836–1845)
translator		
Liberty, Stephen E. (1843–1911)	Quebec (1862)	Fort Benton, MT (1866)
Smith, Joseph, Jr. (1805–1844)	Harmony, PA (1827)	Nauvoo, IL (1831–1844)
trapper		
Arcouet, Amable (1797–1880)	Montreal, Quebec (1833)	St. Paul, OR (1835–1880)
Baker, Jim (1818–1898)	Belleville, IL (1839)	Savery, WY (1873–1898)

Appendix E. Occupation

Occupation	Left Original Home	Area of Settlement
Bridger, Jim (1803–1881)	Richmond, VA (1822)	Fort Bridger, WY (1842–1865)
Lahti, Peter J. (1834–1911)	Vadsø, Norway (1864)	St. Peter, MN (1864–1911)
Reading, Pearson B. (1816–1868)	Hunterdon, NJ (1844)	Shasta, CA (1845–1868)
Robidoux, Antoine (1794–1860)	St. Louis, MO (1832)	Fort Uintah, UT (1833–1844)
Sublette, William Lewis (1798–1845)	Lincoln, KY (1822)	St. Charles (1822–1833)
		Fort William, WY (1833–1835)
		St. Louis, MO (1836–1845)
U.S. Consul		
Haagsma, Broer Baukes (1831–1907)	Harlingen, Friesland (1853)	New Amsterdam, WI (1853–1907)
U.S. Mint Treasurer		
Cheesman, David Williams (1822–1884)	Washington, IN (1850)	El Monte, CA (1851–1852)
		Los Angeles, CA (1852–1884)
U.S. Senator		
Tabor, Horace Austin W. (1830–1899)	Boston, MA (1855)	Denver, CO (1879–1899)
vigilante		
Coleman, William Tell (1824–1893)	St. Louis, MO (1849)	San Francisco, CA (1849–1893)
wagon maker		
Goller, John (1825–1874)	Bavaria, Germany (1849)	Los Angeles, CA (1850–1874)
Huntington, William (1784–1846)	Watertown, NY (1836)	Mount Pisgah, IA (1846)
whaler		
Kirby, Richard Cornelius (1817–1904)	Staffordshire, England (1842)	Santa Cruz, CA (1850–1904)
writer		
Carr, Sarah Pratt (1850–1935)	Freeport, ME (1852)	San Francisco, CA (1852–1867, 1913–1935)
		Carlin, NV (1867–1872)
		St. Helena, CA (1883–1900)
		Seattle, WA (1900–1913)
		Los Angeles, CA (1913–1935)
Farnham, Eliza Wood (1815–1864)	New York, NY (1849)	Santa Cruz, CA (1849–1856)
		Stockton, CA (1859–1862)
Farnham, Thomas J. (1804–1848)	Peoria, IL (1838)	Willamette, OR (1839)
		Santa Cruz, CA (1839–1848)
French, Erasmus Darwin (1822–1902)	Albion, MI (1845)	Darwin, CA (1860–1865)
Holmes, Julia Archibald (1838–1887)	Emporia, KS (1858)	Taos, NM (1858–1863)
Imamura, Yemyo (1867–1932)	Fukui, Japan (1899)	Honolulu, HI (1899–1932)
Kellie, Luna Sanford (1857–1940)	Rockford, IL (1871)	Adams County, NE (1877–1884)
		Hartwell, NE (1884–1901)
Meeker, Ezra (1830–1928)	Eddyville, IA (1852)	Puyallup, WA (1870–1928)
Omohundro, Texas Jack (1846–1880)	Pleasure Hill, VA (1859)	Leadville, CO (1877–1880)
Smith, Joseph, Jr. (1805–1844)	Harmony, PA (1827)	Nauvoo, IL (1831–1844)

Bibliography

Primary Sources

Bancroft, Hubert Howe. *Chronicles of the Builders of the Commonwealth*. San Francisco: History Company, 1891.

Bell, Alphonzo. *The Bel Air Kid: An Autobiography of a Life in California*. Victoria, B.C.: Trafford, 2002.

Campbell, Robert. *A Narrative of Colonel Robert Campbell's Experiences in the Rocky Mountain Fur Trade from 1825 to 1835*. Fairfield, WA: Ye Galleon Press, 1991.

Chiles, Joseph B. *A Visit to California in 1841*. Berkeley: Friends of the Bancroft Library, 1970.

Compendium of History and Biography of North Dakota. Chicago: Geo. A. Ogle, 1900.

Conard, Howard Louis. *"Uncle Dick" Wootton: The Pioneer Frontiersman of the Rocky Mountain Region*. Chicago: W.E. Dibble, 1890.

Earl of Dunraven. *The Great Divide: Travels in the Upper Yellowstone in the Summer of 1874*. London: Chatto and Windus, 1876.

Eldredge, Zoeth Skinner. *The Beginnings of San Francisco*. San Francisco: Z.S. Eldredge, 1912.

Goulding, William R. *California Odyssey: An Overland Journey on the Southern Trails, 1849*. Norman, OK: Arthur H. Clark Company, 2009.

Gunn, Douglas. *Picturesque San Diego*. Chicago: Knight & Leonard, 1887.

Gwydir, Rickard D. *Recollections from the Colville Agency, 1886–1889*. Spokane: Arthur H. Clark, 2001.

History of La Crosse County, Wisconsin. Chicago: Western Historical Society, 1881.

Holmes, Julia Archibald. *A Bloomer Girl on Pike's Peak, 1858*. Denver: Denver Public Library, 1949.

Ise, John C. *Sod & Stubble*. New York: Wilson-Erickson, 1936.

Kellie, Luna. *A Prairie Populist: The Memoirs of Luna Kellie*. Ames: University of Iowa Press, 1992.

Kelly, Fanny. *Narrative of My Captivity among the Sioux Indians*. Hartford, CT: Mutual Publishing, 1871.

Lawyer's Record and Official Record of the United States. New York: A.S. Barnes & Company, 1872.

Mead, James R. *Hunting and Trading on the Great Plains, 1859–1875*, ed. Ignace Mead Jones. Wichita: Rowfant Press, 2008.

Meeker, Ezra. *Washington Territory West of the Cascades*. Olympia: Transcript Office, 1870.

Mumey, Nolie. *The Overland Diary of Elizabeth Parke Keays*. Boulder: Johnson Publishing, 1964.

———. *The Saga of "Auntie" Stone and Her Cabin*. Boulder: Johnson Publishing, 1964.

———, and James Baker. *The Life of Jim Baker, 1818–1898, Trapper, Scout, Guide and Indian Fighter*. Denver: World Press, 1931.

"Murray Bros. & Ward Land Company." *Minneapolis Golden Jubilee, 1865–1917*. Minneapolis: Lakeland Press, 1917, 166.

Ruede, Howard. *Sod-House Days: Letters from a Kansas Homesteader, 1877–78*. Lawrence: University Press of Kansas, 1937.

Sherer, James A.B. *The Lion of the Vigilantes*. Indianapolis: Bobbs-Merrill, 1939.

Snyder, Grace. *No Time on My Hands*. Lincoln: University of Nebraska Press, 1986.

Transactions. New York: American Institute of Mining, Metallurgical, and Petroleum Engineers, 1897.

Van Dyke, Theodore Strong, T.T. Leberthon, and Anthony Taylor. *The City and County of San Diego*. San Diego: Leberthon & Taylor, 1888.

Warner, George E. *History of Hennepin County and the City of Minneapolis*. Minneapolis: North Star Publishing Co., 1881.

Wilson, Warren Hugh. *The Evolution of the Country Community*. Boston: Pilgrim Press, 1912.

Wright, Mary Lindley. *Prairie Legacy*. Self-published, 1981.

Primary Periodicals

Bidwell, John. "Gold Hunters of California: The First Emigrant Train to California." *The Century* 41:1 (November 1890): 106–130.

Bowman, Mary M. "California's First American School and Its Teacher." *Historical Society of Southern California* 10:1–2 (1915–1916): 86–94.

Bradley, Glenn D. "'Uncle Dick' Wootton." *Santa Fe Employes' Magazine* 5:2 (January 1911): 25–36.

Bragg, Lynn E. *Remarkable Idaho Women*. Guilford, CT: Globe Pequot, 2001.

Docher, Anton. "The Quaint Indian Pueblo of Isleta." *The Santa Fé Magazine* 7:7 (1913): 29–32.

"Evidence from Zina D. Huntington Young." *Saints Herald* (11 January 1905): 29.

"Farm and Dairy." Dubuque, Iowa, *Herald* (22 January 1885): 2.

"Indians of Pueblo Mourn Passing of Rev. Anton Docher." *The* (Little Rock, Arkansas) *Guardian* (12 January 1929): 1, 4.

Lewis, William S. "Hiram F. Smith." *Washington Historical Quarterly* 10:3 (July 1919): 168–170.

Mead, James R. "The Chisholm Trail." Wichita *Eagle* (1 March 1890).

"Pioneer Hamilton Left Valuable Estate." *Bakersfield Californian* (25 July 1914).

Poston, Charles D. "The Pennington Family." *Arizona Citizen* (17 January 1896).

Potsch, John. "Hand It to Seward!" *Boys' Life* (November 1932): 16, 23–26.

Restarick, H.B. "Sybil Bingham, As Youthful Bride, Came to Islands in Brig Thaddeus." *Honolulu Star-Bulletin* (15 August 1931).

"Shocking Steamboat Explosion: The Steamer "Secretary" Blown Up." *San Francisco Daily Herald* (16 April 1854).

Stevenson, Victoria Faber. "Yellowstone Trail: Pike's Peak Ocean-to-Ocean Highway." *Sinclair's Magazine* 2 (August 1918): 18–23.

Sylvester, Avery. "Voyages of the Pallas and Chenamus, 1843–45." *Oregon Historical Quarterly* 34:3 (September 1933): 259–272.

Taylor, William H. "Mount Si Trail Dedicated." *Washington Historical Quarterly* 22:3 (July 1931): 213–215.

Young, Zina D. H. "How I Gained My Testimony of the Truth." *Young Woman's Journal* (April 1893): 317–319.

Secondary Sources

Alanan, Arnold Robert. *Finns in Minnesota*. St. Paul: Minnesota Historical Press, 2012.

Anderson, Dale. *Polish Americans*. Milwaukee: Gareth Stevens, 2007.

Anderson, Ruth, and Lori Price. *Puyallup: A Pioneer Paradise*. Charleston, SC: Arcadia, 2002.

Asato, Noriko. *Teaching Mikadoism: The Attack on Japanese Language Schools in Hawaii*. Honolulu: University of Hawaii Press, 2006.

Baker, Roger. *Clara: An Ex-slave in Gold Rush Colorado*. Central City, CO: Black Hawk, 2003.

Ballew, Susan J., and L. Trent Dolan. *Early Carson City*. Charleston, SC: Arcadia, 2010.

Beasley, Edward. *Empire as the Triumph of Theory*. New York: Routledge, 2005.

Beaton, Gail M. *Colorado Women: A History*. Boulder: University Press of Colorado, 2012.

Beckey, Fred. *Columbia River to Stevens Pass*. Seattle: Mountaineers Books, 2000.

Bennemann, William. *Men in Eden: William Drummond Stewart and Same-Sex Desire in the Rocky Mountain Fur Trade*. Lincoln: University of Nebraska Press, 2012.

Burgan, Michael. *Buddhist Faith in America*. New York: Facts on File, 2003.

Campbell, Randolph B. *The Laws of Slavery in Texas*. Austin: University of Texas Press, 2010.

Cherny, Robert W., ed. *California Women and Politics: From the Gold Rush to the Great Depression*. Lincoln: University of Nebraska Press, 2011.

Cline, Janice Craze. *Historic Downtown Plano*. Charleston, SC: Arcadia, 2012.

Cook, Bernard A., ed. *Women and War: A Historical Encyclopedia from Antiquity to the Present*. Santa Barbara: ABC-Clio, 2006.

Couper, Jim. *The Long and Winding Road: Discovering the Pleasures and Treasures of Highway 97*. Surrey, B.C.: Heritage House, 2006.

Davies, Carole Elizabeth Boyce, ed. *Encyclopedia of the African Diaspora*. Santa Barbara: ABC-Clio, 2008.

DeArment, Robert K. *Deadly Dozen: Twelve Forgotten Gunfighters of the Old West*. Norman: University of Oklahoma Press, 2003.

Duncan, Patti. *Tell This Silence: Asian American Women Writers and the Politics of Speech*. Iowa City: University of Iowa Press, 2004.

Edmunds, Russell David, ed. *Enduring Nations: Native Americans in the Midwest*. Champaign: University of Illinois Press, 2008.

Essin, Emmett M. *Shavetails and Bell Sharps: The History of the U.S. Army Mule*. Lincoln: University of Nebraska Press, 2000.

Fanning, Branwell. *Tiburon and Belvedere*. Charleston, SC: Arcadia, 2010.

Farquhar, Francis P. *History of the Sierra Nevada*. Berkeley: University of California Press, 2007.

Fay, Ted. *The Twenty Mule Team of Death Valley*. Charleston, SC: Arcadia, 2012.

Ferndale Museum. *Ferndale*. Charleston, SC: Arcadia, 2004.

Fowler, Ed. *Ed Fowler's Knife Talk II: The High Performance Blade*. Iola, WI: Krause, 2003.

Fuller, Tom. *Oregon's Capitol Buildings*. Charleston, SC: Arcadia, 2013.

Gance, Samuel. *Anton ou La trajectoire d'un père: l'histoire romancée du père Anton Docher*. Paris: l'Harmatton, 2012.

Gibson, Jack. *Mount Tamalpais and the Marin Municipal Water District*. Charleston, SC: Arcadia, 2012.

Gitlin, Jay. *The Bourgeois Frontier: French Towns, French Traders, and American Expansion*. New Haven: Yale University Press, 2010.

Goerke, Betty. *Chief Marin: Leader, Rebel, and Legend*. Berkeley: Heyday, 2007.

Green, Claude A. *What We Dragged Out of Slavery with Us*. West Conshohocken, PA: Infinity, 2006.

Gullett, Gayle. *Becoming Citizens: The Emergence and Development of the California Women's Movement, 1880–1911*. Champaign: University of Illinois Press, 2000.

Hagan, William T. *Charles Goodnight: Father of the Texas Panhandle*. Norman: University of Oklahoma Press, 2007.

_____. *Taking Indian Lands: The Cherokee (Jerome) Commission, 1889–1893*. Norman: University of Oklahoma Press, 2003.

Hagenstein, Edwin C., Sara M. Gregg, and Brian

Donahue, eds. *American Georgics: Writings on Farming, Culture, and the Land.* New Haven: Yale University Press, 2011.

Hallberg, Jane, Barbara Sexton, and Mary Jane Gustafson. *Pierre Bottineau: A Founder of Osseo, Minnesota.* Brooklyn Park, MN: Brooklyn Historical Society, 2000.

Hanshew, Annie. *Border to Border: Historic Quilts and Quiltmakers of Montana.* Helena: Montana Historical Society, 2009.

Harvey, Bill. *Texas Cemeteries.* Austin: University of Texas Press, 2003.

Hedstrom-Page, Deborah. *From Ranch to Railhead with Charles Goodnight.* Nashville: B&H Publishing, 2007.

Hodge, Mary Harrison, and Charlene Ochsner Carson. *Salado.* Charleston, SC: Arcadia, 2014.

Holmio, Armas, Kustaa Ensio. *History of the Finns in Michigan.* Hancock, MI: Finlandia University, 2001.

Hoy, Jim, ed. *Cowboy's Lament: A Life on the Open Range.* Emporia, KS: Emporia State University, 2010.

_____. *Flint Hills Cowboys: Tales from the Tallgrass Prairie.* Lawrence: University Press of Kansas, 2006.

Humphreys, Danda. *On the Street Where You Live: Sailors, Solicitors, and Stargazers of Early Victoria.* Surrey, BC: Heritage House, 2011.

Hunsaker, Joyce Badgley. *Seeing the Elephant: The Many Voices of the Oregon Trail.* Lubbock: Texas Tech University Press, 2003.

Johnson, Yvonne, ed. *Feminist Frontiers: Women Who Shaped the Midwest.* Kirksville, MO: Truman State University Press, 2010.

Jones, Cherry Lyon. *Remarkable Alaska Women.* Guilford, CT: Globe Pequot, 2006.

Kahn, Ava Fran, ed. *Jewish Voices of the California Gold Rush: A Documentary History, 1849–1880.* Detroit: Wayne State University Press, 2002.

Kassen, Joy S. *Buffalo Bill's Wild West: Celebrity, Memory, and Popular History.* New York: Hill and Wang, 2000.

Keleher, Julia, and Elsie Ruth Chant. *The Padre of Isleta.* Santa Fe: Sunstone, 2009.

Keleher, William A. *The Fabulous Frontier, 1846–1912.* Santa Fe: Sunstone, 2008.

Kinro, Gerald. *A Cup of Aloha: The Kona Coffee Epic.* Honolulu: University of Hawaii Press, 2003.

Klinkenberg, Dean. *Driftless Area Travel Guide: Mississippi Valley Traveler.* St. Louis: Travel Passages, 2010.

Kuhns, Elizabeth. *The Habit: A History of the Clothing of Catholic Nuns.* New York: Random House, 2007.

Lal, Brij V., and Kate Fortune. *The Pacific Islands: An Encyclopedia.* Honolulu: University of Hawaii Press, 2000.

Larsen, Dennis M. *Slick as a Mitten: Ezra Meeker's Klondike Enterprise.* Pullman: Washington State University Press, 2009.

Lee, Portia, and Jeffrey Samudio. *Los Angeles, California.* Chicago: Arcadia, 2001.

Levy, JoAnn. *Unsettling the West: Eliza Farnham and Georgiana Bruce Kirby in Frontier California.* Santa Clara: Heyday Books, 2004.

Lindsay, Brendan C. *Murder State: California's Native American Genocide, 1846–1873.* Lincoln: University of Nebraska Press, 2012.

Lovret, Juanita. *Tustin As It Once Was.* Charleston, SC: History Press, 2011.

Lyman, Edward Leo. *Overland Journey from Utah to California: Wagon Travel from the City of Angels.* Reno: University of Nevada Press, 2004.

MacCulloch, Patrick C. *The Campbell Quest: A Saga of Family and Fortune.* St. Louis: Missouri History Museum, 2009.

MacKell, Jan. *Brothels, Bordellos, and Bad Girls: Prostitution in Colorado, 1860–1930.* Albuquerque: University of New Mexico Press, 2004.

Mason, James E. *Wichita's Riverside Parks.* Charleston, SC: Arcadia, 2011.

Massey, Peter, and Jeanne Welburn Wilson. *Backcountry Adventures: Northern California.* Castle Rock, CO: Adler, 2002.

McArthur, Scott. *The Enemy Never Came: The Civil War in the Pacific Northwest.* Lincoln: University of Nebraska Press, 2012.

McDonnell, Jeanne Farr. *Juana Briones of 19th Century California.* Tucson: University of Arizona Press, 2008.

McGinty, Brian. *A Toast to Eclipse: Arpad Haraszthy and the Sparkling Wine of Old San Francisco.* Norman: University of Oklahoma Press, 2012.

McLynn, Frank. *Wagons West: The Epic Story of America's Overland Trails.* New York: Grove, 2002.

Meishen, Betty Smith. *From Jamestown to Texas: A History of Some Early Pioneers of Austin County, Texas.* Bloomington: Xlibris, 2010.

Moore, Stephen L. *Savage Frontier: 1842–1845.* Denton: University of North Texas Press, 2010.

Naparsteck, Martin. *Sex and Manifest Destiny: The Urge That Drove Americans Westward.* Jefferson, NC: McFarland, 2012.

Newton, Honey M. *Zion's Hope: Pioneer Midwives and Women Doctors in Utah.* Springville, UT: Cedar Fort, 2013.

Odland, Rick D. *Sioux Falls.* Charleston, SC: Arcadia, 2007.

O'Malley, Vincent J. *Saints of North America.* Huntington, IN: Our Sunday Visitor, 2004.

Palazzo, Robert P. *Death Valley.* Charleston, SC: Arcadia, 2008.

Peters, Harold J., ed. *Seven Months to Oregon Revisited: As Reflected in the Wyoming County Mirror.* Santa Clara, CA: Harold J. Peters, 2012.

Pryor, Alton. *Fascinating Women in California History.* Roseville, CA: Stagecoach, 2003.

Radzilowski, John. *The Eagle & the Cross: A History of the Polish Roman Catholic Union of America, 1873–2000.* New York: Columbia University Press, 2003.

Rarick, Ethan. *Desperate Passage: The Donner Party's Perilous Journey West.* New York: Oxford University Press, 2008.

Richards, Rand. *Mud, Blood, and Gold: San Francisco in 1849.* San Francisco: Heritage House, 2009.

Ricker, Eli S. *Voices of the American West: The Settler and Soldier.* Lincoln: Board of Regents of the University of Nebraska, 2005.

Roberts, Brian. *American Alchemy: The California Gold Rush and Middle-Class Culture.* Chapel Hill: University of North Carolina Press, 2000.

Roberts, Elise Schebler. *The Quilt: A History and Celebration of an American Art Form.* Minneapolis: Voyageur, 2007.

Robinson, Charles M., ed. *The Diaries of John Gregory Bourke: June 1, 1878–June 22, 1879.* Denton: University of North Texas Press, 2007.

Ruby, Robert H, and John Arthur Brown. *The Spokane Indians: Children of the Sun.* Norman: University of Oklahoma Press, 2006.

Salmon, Maynard Hubbard. *Gila Libre: New Mexico's Last Wild River.* Albuquerque: University of New Mexico Press, 2008.

Seacrest, William B. *California Disasters, 1812–1899.* Sanger, CA: Quill Driver, 2005.

Secord, Paul R. *Albuquerque Deco and Pueblo.* Charleston, SC: Arcadia, 2012.

Shirley, Gayle C. *More Than Petticoats: Remarkable Colorado Women.* Guilford, CT: Globe Pequot, 2002.

Shortridge, James R. *Cities on the Plains: The Evolution of Urban Kansas.* Lawrence: University of Press of Kansas, 2004.

Smith, Robert Barr. *Tough Towns: True Tales from the Gritty Streets of the Old West.* Guilford, CT: Globe Pequot, 2007.

Smith, Victoria. *Captive Arizona, 1851–1900.* Lincoln: University of Nebraska Press, 2009.

Snodgrass, Pat. *Brooklyn Park and Brooklyn Center.* Chicago: Arcadia, 2009.

Southerland, Cindy. *Cemeteries of Carson City and Carson Valley.* Charleston, SC: Arcadia, 2010.

Steele, Edward Eugene. *Ebbets: The History and Genealogy of a New York Family.* St. Louis: E.E. Steele, 2005.

Stone, Ted. *The Legend of Pierre Bottineau and the History of the Red River Trail.* Edmonton: Eschia Books, 2013.

Stull, James B. *Erie.* Charleston, SC: Arcadia, 2011.

Sutherland, Anne. *The Robertsons, the Sutherlands, and the Making of Texas.* College Station: Texas A&M University Press, 2006.

Szasz, Ferenc Morton. *The Protestant Clergy in the Great Plains and Mountain West, 1865–1915.* Lincoln: University of Nebraska Press, 2004.

Taliaferro, John. *Great White Fathers: The Story of the Obsessive Quest to Create Mount Rushmore.* Cambridge, MA: PublicAffairs, 2002.

Taylor, John. *Catholics along the Rio Grande.* Charleston, SC: Arcadia, 2011.

Temple, Judy Nolte. *Baby Doe Tabor.* Norman: University of Oklahoma Press, 2007.

Tonkovich, Nicole. *The Allotment Plot: Alice C. Fletcher, E. Jane Gay, and Nez Percé Survivance.* Lincoln: University of Nebraska Press, 2012.

Turner, Erin H., ed. *Cowgirls: Stories of Trick Riders, Sharp Shooters, and Untamed Women.* Guilford, CT: Globe Pequot, 2009.

Turner, John G. *Brigham Young: Pioneer Prophet.* Cambridge: Harvard University Press, 2012.

Van Sant, John E. *Pacific Pioneers: Japanese Journeys to America and Hawaii, 1850–80.* Champaign: University of Illinois Press, 2000.

Watson, Ben. *Cider, Hard & Sweet: History, Traditions, and Making Your Own.* Woodstock, VT: Countryman Press, 2013.

Watson, Bruce McIntyre. *A Biographical Dictionary of Fur Traders Working West of the Rockies, 1793–1858.* Kelowna, B.C.: Center for Social, Spatial, and Economic Justice, 2010.

Welsh, Robert L. *The Presbytery of Seattle 1858–2005: The "Dream" of a Presbyterian Colony in the West.* Bloomington: Xlibris, 2006.

Wishart, David J., ed. *Encyclopedia of the Great Plains.* Lincoln: University of Nebraska Press, 2004.

Wommack, Linda. *Our Ladies of the Tenderloin: Colorado's Legends in Lace.* Caldwell, ID: Caxton, 2005.

Wright, Cynthia J., and Judy Cox-Finney. *Lemoore.* Charleston, SC: Arcadia, 2010.

Wu, Judy Tzu-Chun. *Doctor Mom Chung of the Fair-haired Bastards: The Life of a Wartime Celebrity.* Berkeley: University of California Press, 2005.

Zesch, Scott. *The Chinatown War: Chinese Los Angeles and the Massacre of 1871.* New York: Oxford University Press, 2012.

Periodicals

Ahmad, Diana L. "'I Fear the Consequences to Our Animals': Emigrants and Their Livestock on the Overland Trails." *Great Plains Quarterly* 32 (Summer 2012): 165–182.

Coté, John, and Suzanne Herel. "160-year-old Home Can Be Demolished." *San Francisco Gate* (9 March 2007).

Faison, Glen. "New Chapter Opens in Historical Figure's Civil Rights 'Journey.'" *Porterville (CA) Recorder* (11 September 2008).

Gilbert, Nina Bachman. "The Jean Heazle Story." *Owyhee Outpost* 41 (2009): 37–52.

Johnson, John, Jr. "How Los Angeles Covered Up the Massacre of 17 Chinese." *LA Weekly* (10 March 2011): 1.

Johnson, Kaylene. "Next Stop, Pristine Wilderness." *Los Angeles Times* (20 February 2005).

Millner, Darrell. "George Bush of Tumwater: Founder of the First American Colony on Puget Sound." *Columbia Magazine* 8:4 (Winter 1994–1995).

Moore, Steve. "Matthew 'Old Paint' Caldwell." *Texas Ranger Dispatch* 11 (Summer 2003).

Pilling, George. "The Wysingers of Visalia." *Tulare Valley Voice* (5 October 2005): 1, 5.

White, Helen McCann. "Captain Fisk Goes to Washington." *Minnesota History* (15 February 2011): 216–230.

Index

Numbers in **bold** indicate pages with major entries. Numbers in *italics* indicate illustrations

abolitionists 57, 74–76, 82, 83, 84, 89, 107, 157, 162, 168; *see also* slavery
accounting 43, 73, 88
"Across the Plains in the Donner Party" 136
activism 42–44; *see also* abolitionists; civil rights; suffrage, woman's
Adair, Cornelia Wadsworth Ritchie **64–67**
Adair, John George **64–67**
Adams, Augusta 166
Adams, John Quincy 153
adobe 5, 15, 24, 37, *48*, 49, 60, 61, 63, 79, 99, 106, 120, 132, 137, 161–163, 167; plaster 140, 146
advertisement 56–57, 59–60, 96, 99, 129; *see also* Farnham, Eliza Burhans Wood; Parmley, Joseph William; recruiters
agnosticism 52
Agua Caliente Indians 62
Alabama 57, 103, 138, 139, 154
Alamo 29, 148
Alaska 3, 4, 5, 8, 49, 100–102, 115, 156, 160, 171; Seward 101
alcohol 8, 15, 24, 31, 37, 40, 53, 60, 70, 87, 89, 97, 99, 101, 107, 108, 115, 121–122; distilling 68; home brew 162; peddling 68, 153; rum 142; smuggling 68; trading 68; *see also* brewing
Aleut 49
Alexandrovich, Alexei 126
Alley, Margaret 166
Alta, California 1, 52, 99
American Board of Commissioners for Foreign Missions 16
American Fur Company 10, 19, 31, 49, 52, 98, 153
American Revolution 5, 36, 57, 66, 91, 113, 130, 138, 142, 144, 152, 164
American Seamen's Friend Society 96–97
Amorós, Juan 137
Anadarko 154
Ancient Order of United Workmen 19
Andrews, Olive 166
Angel, Jemima 166
Angell, Mary Ann 166

annexation 52, 68, 99
Anton ou La trajectoire d'un père 49
Apache 1, 36, 112, 130, 144, 149, 162; Chiricahua 75, 131, 132; Gila 132; Lipan 5, 124, 132, 138–139, 148; Mescalero 66, 132; Pinal 170; Tonto 131–132
Apache Wars 132
aphids 115
appendicitis 156, 168
Aram, Joseph 78
Arapaho 10, 11, 32, 78–79, 92, 107, 112, 117, 131, 149, 161; Southern Arapaho 11
Arcan-Bennett Party 61
Archibalt, Albert William 74–75
Arcouet, Amable 4, **7–10**
Arcouet, Amable, Jr. 9
Arcouet, Charles Leon 9
Arcouet, Jean 9
Arcouet, Marguerite 9
Arcouet, Michel 9
Arikara 10, 32, 52
Arista, Mariano 22–*23*
Arizona Territory 4, 5, 40, 50, 61, 63, 67, 70, 75, 89, 104, 124, 130–133, 161, 167, 170; Gila 62; Tucson 130, 132, 133; Yuma 60
Arkansas 50, 80, 125, 149
arson 39, 57, 67, 85, 148, 150
art 50, 93
Arthur, Mark 109
Ashley, William H. 30–31, 171
Asp, Henry E. 149
assayers 3, 70, 101, *125*
Assiniboine 19, 20, 31–32, 52
Association for Overseas Religious Propagation 76
Association of California Women 53–54
Astor, John Jacob 49
asylums 54, 96, 132, 150
Atchison, Topeka, and Santa Fe Railroad 39, 44
Athapaskan 94
Atkins, John D.C. 68
attorneys 44–45, 53, 59, 60, 74, 82, 103, 105, 118, 119, 123, 129, 142, 149–150, 152–154, 164
Aucotash 11
auction 25, 43, 56, 60, 82, 140, 160; Franklin Real Estate and Auctioneers 59–60

auditors 57, 68, 158
Austin, Stephen F. 138, 143–144

Backenstoe, Virginia Elizabeth 134–136
Bad Ax, Battle of 153
Badlands 11, 39, 56, 90
Baker, Eliza Yanetse 11
Baker, Flying Fawn 11
Baker, James C. 11
Baker, Jim 1, *10–12*
Baker, Linda Upchurch 11
Baker, Marina 11
Balch, Ebenezer 127
Bald Hills War 94
Baldwin, James 63
banking 3, 88, 118, 155; Allen National Bank 134; Bank of Florence 119; Bank of Lamoore 35; bankruptcy 40, 67, 86, 118, 133; Commercial Bank 42; Consolidated National Bank 42; Farmers and Merchants Bank 45; First Bank of Missouri 32; First National Bank of Wichita 113; Guthrie National Bank 45; Merchants National Bank of St. Louis 32; Miller Bank 118; People's Home Savings Bank 34–35; robbery 45; San Diego County Savings Bank 42; Savings Bank of Wichita 113; Stock Growers' Bank of Pueblo 6
Banning shipping line 106
Bannock 8, 11, 109, 124; Bannock Indian War 73
Baptists 25, 27, 38, 49, 105, 109–111, 134, 163–164
Barada, Eulalia 133
Barclay, Forbes 122
barge 19, 96, 144
Barnes, Amanda Melissa 165
Barnett, James F. 132
Barnett, Laura Ellen Pennington 132
barometer, aneroid 51
Bartleson-Bidwell Party 36–38, 169
Basford, Sebastian Brainerd 129
Bautista de Portolá, Gaspar 24
Baylor, John Robert 132
Beach, John 153–154
Beach, Lucy Frances Street 153

229

Index

Beaman, Louisa 165, 166, 167
Bear Flag Revolt 99
Bell, Alphonzo E. 4
Bell, Dorothea A. Reasons 12
Bell, James George **12–13**, 171
Bell, Susan Abia Hollenbeck **12–13**
Belshaw, Ann L. 110
Belshaw, Candace McCarty **109–111**
Belshaw, Frank E. 110
Belshaw, George, Jr. 1, **109–111**
Belshaw, Gertrude Columbia 110
Belshaw, John E. 110
Belshaw, Marshal W. 110
Belshaw, Mary H. 110
Belshaw, Stephen R. 110
Belshaw, William M. 110
Bennett, John Cook 165
Bent, Charles 161
Bent, William 161
Benton, James M. 121
Bent's Fort, Colorado 161–162
Berding, Arnold 94
Berry, Betsey Smeathers 144
Berry, John 144
bicycles 113
Bierer, Andrew Gregg Curtin 45
bigamy 8, 167
Bijlsma, Jan 17
Bill, George 56
Billy the Kid 67
Billy To-Morrow 35
Biloxi Indians 154
Bingham, Hiram, Jr. 16
Bingham, Hiram, Sr. 4–5, **13–16**, 169
Bingham, Sybil Moseley **13–16**, 169
Birch, James E. 121
birds 51, 103, 104, 135; trapping 111
The Black Crook 126
Black Exodus 26
Black Hawk 91, 153, 169
Black Hawk War 26, 135, 153, 168
Black Hills 11, 18
Black Kettle 11, 112, 113
Blackfoot 11, 31, 52, 84; Blackfoot Lakota 90
blacks 3, 24, 27, 58, 63–64, 75, 89, 133, 142–143, 154, 163–164, 169
blacksmiths 17, 37, 52, 62–64, 85, 91, 95, 98, 99, 103, 128, 134, 148, 153, 162, 164, 165
Blake, Clarissa 166
Blanchet, François Norbert 4, 9, 11
blankets 28, 31, 55, 96, 104, 112
blizzard 4, 11, 20, 80–81, 87, 101, 107, 135, 147
bloomers 53, 74
boarding house 60, 64, 90, 101, 114, 152, 156, 158; Grandview Roadhouse 101; Kern Creek Roadhouse 101; railroad 152
Boardman, John 36–37
Boatman, Mary Ann Richardson 111

Boatman, Willis 111
Boer War 160
Boggs, Lilburn Williams 165
Bond, Samuel Robert 55
Bonnema, Harmen H. **16–18**
Bonnema, Luisa Spengler 2, **16–18**
Bonnema, Oepke H. **16–18**
Bonnema, Ytje Steenstra 17
boom towns 4, 113, 122, 126, 156
Booth, Albert Anton **18–19**, 171
Booth, Ellen Eliza Carter **18–19**, 171
Borglum, Gutzon 130
Bosque Redondo Reservation 6
Bottineau, Charles 20
Bottineau, Daniel 19, 21, 55, 170
Bottineau, Genevieve Larance 19
Bottineau, Henry 21
Bottineau, Jean Baptiste 21
Bottineau, Margaret 21
Bottineau, Martha Charlotte 20
Bottineau, Peter 21
Bottineau, Pierre 4, **19–22**, 55, 56, 169, 170, 171
Bottineau, William 21
bounty hunters 2, 4, 58, 104
Bowie, Jim 148
Bowker, Martha 166
Bowman, Alfred J. 22
Bowman, Nancy Skinner 24
Bowman, Sarah A. 4, **22–23**, 24
Boyeau, Mary 90
Bozeman Trail 57, 89
Brady, Matthew 94
Brauch, Jacob 158
Breen family 136
Brewer, Eliza Jane Brown 25–26
brewing 1, 5, 111, 115, 136, 141, 162
brick 8, 9, 21, 46, 63, 69–70, 92, 109, 113, 119, 124, 130, 137, 152; Aberdeen Pressed Brick Company 129
brides 53–54; Indian brides 107, 108; picture brides 77
Bridger, Jim 10–12, 31, 32
bridges 63, 67, 86–87, 129, 167; bascule bridge 123; collapse 127; Missouri Bridge Company 119
Brier, James Welch **62–64**
Brier, Juliet Wells **62–64**
Briones, Pablo 24
Briones de Miranda, Juana 5, **24–25**
British 7–10, 19, 26, 27, 44, 60, 76, 100, 113, 118, 133, 141, 143, 160, 166, 169
British Columbia 85, 115, 116, 145; San Juan Islands 60; Vancouver 8, 9, 27, 60, 61, 93; Victoria 60
Brown, Clara 4, **25–26**
Brown, Frederick 74
Brown, John 74, 76
brown lung 74
Bruce, George Whiteley **73–74**
Bruce, John 73
Bruce, Josiah W. 73

Bruce, Robert 73
Bruce, Samuel A. **73–74**
Brunett, Jean 153
Brunner, Jacob 25
Bryan, William Jennings 88
bubonic plague 76
Buchanan, James 94
Buckskin and Satin 126
Buddhists 5, 76–77
Buena Vista, Battle of 22
buffalo 5, 35, 161–162; beefalo 67; chips 89, 147; depletion 65, 113; hides 32, 44, 106, 112, 170; hunting 90, 111–112, 126, 138, 161; meat 19, 20, 37, 65, 74, 75, 98, 110, 161; migration 80; robes 31, 112, 157, 161; skulls 86; tallow 112
Buffalo Hump 29, 148
Buffalo Soldiers 90, 112
bullboats 31, 32
Bunker, Harriet J. **96–98**
Buntline, Ned 126
Burnett, Peter Hardeman 99
Burns, Hugh 122
Burns, Leopoldina 40–41
Burr, Aaron 152
Burr, Caroline Pennington 131
Burr, Charles M. 131
Bush, Edward 18
Bush, George Washington 4, 11, 26–28, 142, 169, 170
Bush, Henry Sanford 27
Bush, Isabella James 26–28, 142
Bush, Joseph Talbot "Tall" 27, 28
Bush, Rial Bailey 27
Bush, Thomas Jackson January 27
Bush, William E. 18
Bush, William Owen 27, 28, 171
Bush Prairie, Washington 27–28
butchers 3, 66, 68, 73, 75, 117, 157, 160; beef jerky 114, 143; meat 29, 62, 66, 73, 105, 133, 135, 167; meatpacking 66; mutton 73; *Owyhee Meat Company* 73; tripe 136; veal 73
Butterfield Overland Stage 2, 34, 55, 121, *131*, 157, 167, 170
By Ox Team from Salt Lake to Los Angeles, 1850 105

Caddo 154
Caddo Jake 64
Cahuila 60
Caldwell, Hannah Morrison 29
Caldwell, Hugh Curtis 30, 32
Caldwell, Martha A. 28–30
Caldwell, Mathew 5, **28–30**, 148, 169
California 3, 4, 5, 8, 10, 11, 12–13, 36–38, 40–41, 42–44, 49–51, 53–54, 69–70, 85, 94, 98–100, 102–103, 104, 120–122, 123, 127, 130, 139–140, 157, 159, 163, 169, 170, 171; education 77–79; Folsom 59; Monterey 53, 79; Napa Valley 33, 34; republic 99; Sacra-

mento 4, 34, 38, 51, 53, 63, 72, 94, 99, 106, 121, 145, 159, 162; San Bernadino 60; San Diego 41–42, 60, 61; San Diego Bay 60; San Diego Marine Way & Drydock Company 42; San Joaquin Valley 34; Santa Clara 79; Santa Cruz 53; Stanislaus *78*, 79; statehood 163; Yerba Buena 57; *see also* fruit; Los Angeles; San Francisco
California Farmer 53
California, In-doors and Out 54
California Odyssey 50
California Trail *37*, 99, 135, 162, 169
Calispel 68
Calvinism 15
Cameron, Donaldina 3, **42–44**
Camp, Ira Miles 117
Camp, Jeremiah 116–117
Camp, Lucy Ann Merritt 116–117
Campbell, Ann 30
Campbell, Hugh 30, 33
Campbell, Mary Kyle 33
Campbell, Robert **30–33**, *31*, 171
Campbell, Virginia Jane Kyle **30–33**
Campbell, William 32
Canada 7–10, 19, 20, 21, 65, 68–69, 70, 86, 88, 95, 104, 124, 130, 145, 151, 160, 162, 171; Alberta 145; Manitoba 8, 129, 130; Montreal 7, 8, 19, 21, 121, 130, 158; Nova Scotia 74; Ontario 7, 82–86, 89, 121, 155; Quebec 7, 8, 19, 20, 52, 111, 158–159; Winnipeg 19
cancer 81, 82, 93, 128
cane cutters 3
cannibalism 136
canoeing 84, 99, 111, 116
Cape Horn 14, 33, 53, 57, 103, 122, 123
The Capture and Escape; or, Life Among the Sioux 90–91
Caribbean 3, 58, 101, 116, 145; Haiti 133; Jamaica 59
Carleton, James Henry 66
Carlisle Indian School 5, 48
carpentry 17, 69, 85, 106–107, 122–123, 158–159
Carr, Byron Oscar **33–36**
Carr, Sarah Pratt 5, **33–36**
carriages 43, 54, 60, 62, 63, 64, 83, 91
Carrier Indians 8
Carson, Kit 2, 10–11, 21, 32, 61, 99, 113
cartography 4, 8, 20, 36, 50, 55, 62, 137; *Map of the State of California* 51
Castaneda, Francisco 28
Catholics 5, 8, 9, 20, 26, 36, 40, 68, 108, 135; cemetery 163; Franciscans 119–120, 137; French Catholics 15, 47–49, 133, 169; Hispanic Catholics 52; Irish Catholics 123–124, 136–138; Jesuits 53; Sisters of Providence 160; Ursulines 12, 140
cattle 24, 33, 37, 44, 64–67, 73–74, 79, 81, 85, 87, 91, 94, 99, 100, 103, 105, 106, 110, 112, 117, 127, 129, 140, 157, 163; Angus 67, 92; beefalo 66–67; breeding 12, 20, 36, 41, 64–67; bulls 87; calves 84, 89; dairy cattle 79, 84, 89, 96, 133, 146, 151, 160; feral 65; herding 53, 65, 94, 112, 124–125, *138*; herefords 66–67; hides 113, 137; hybrid 137; longhorns 64–67, 124–125; pasturage 61, 107; roundup 107; shorthorns 67, 134; stampedes 62, 107; steers 112; Union Stock Yard and Transit Company 66; *see also* butchers; Chisum, John; Goodnight, Charles; Loving, Oliver; rustling
cavalry, U.S. 5, *10*, 11–12, 22–24, 66, 68, 95, 108, 112, 124, 126, 132, 135, 160, 171; border patrol 68; cavalry physician 61–62; Morgan's Raiders 67–68; rescue 90, 91; security guard 52, 55, 56, 66, 79, 100; volunteer rangers 110, 153
caves 40, 87, 104, 144, 147
Cayuse 8, 35, 114–115
Central Pacific Railroad 1, 34, *35*, 59, 108, 146, 170
Century Illustrated Magazine 136
The Ceremony for Use in Buddhist Temples 76–77
Chamber of Commerce 39
Champoeg meetings 8, 9, 122
Chase, Diana 166
Chavez, Tomás 48
Cheesman, David Williams **104–106**
Cheesman, Urania K. Macy **104–106**
Chehalis 84
Cherokee 25, 50, 89, 112, 149, 154, 163–164; Cherokee and Choctaw Cession 138; Cherokee Commission 149
Chevalier, Archange Maria 133
Cheyenne 5, *10*, 32, 36, 75, 92, 111, 112, 117, 126, 149, 161; Northern 107; Southern 11, 113
Chickasaw 144
Chilcotin 8
child care 25, 41, 43, 53; breastfeeding 87, 91; foster parenting 85–86, 90, 164, 167; nannies 113; *see also* orphans
Children Who Work 76
Chiles, Henry Lee 38
Chiles, Isaac Skinner 38
Chiles, Joseph Ballinger **36–38**, *37*, 169, 170
Chiles, Margaret Jane Garnhart 38
Chiles, William 38
Chilula 94
Chimicum 143
Chin, Ah Yane 1–2, **42–44**
China 8, 43, 72, 77, 158
Chinese immigrants 1, 4, 34, 39, 40, 42–44, 70, *71*, 164, 170; Chinatown 71, 103; inspector 68; laborers 59, 103; victims 63–64; wages 72
Chinook 8, 84, 143; Upper 9; Waponte 9
Chisholm, Jesse 4, 66, **111–113**, 125–126, 170
Chisholm Trail 112, 125–126, *139*, 170
Chisum, John Simpson **64–67**
Chivington, John Milton 1, 11
Choctaw 50, 108, 109, 138
cholera 1, 3, 9, 33, 38, 62, 67, 89, 90, 93, 95, 96, 105, 111, 114, 135, 141, 151, 170
chuckwagon 66
churches 8, 15, 17, 19, 20, 21, 26, 110, 112, 124, 171; Bethlehem Lutheran Church 158; Claquato Chehalis Presbyterian Church 84; Finnish Apostolic Lutheran Church 96; Hilo Japanese Christian Church 72; Immaculate Conception Church 120; Mariners' Church 97; Rose Valley Church 81; St. Paul Catholic Church 169; San Augustín de la Isleta Mission 49; Second Indian Presbyterian Church 109; Trinity Methodist Church 107; Unity Unitarian Church 156; Westminster Presbyterian Church 115; *see also* Baptists; Catholics; Dutch Reformed; French Catholicism; German Methodist; Methodist; Methodist Episcopal; Mormons; Presbyterians; Quakers; Unitarians
Cimarron Route 162
circus 117
civil rights 164, 168
Civil War, American 2, 5, 21, 28, 33, 34, 39, 41, 44, 54, 55, 65, 67, 69, 73, 75, 79, 80, 82, 84–85, 86, 88, 89, 91, 92, 95, 103, 106, 108, 120, 125, 132, 134, 139, 149, 157, 162, 163–164; *see also* Shenandoah, C.S.S
Clacalam, Kilkotah Chamowash 9, 66
Clackamas Indians 122
Clalam 143
Clapper, Edward 100
Claquato Stockade Fort, Washington 84
Clark, Mary Ann 166
Clay, Henry 153
Cleveland, Grover 45, 68, 160
Cochise 75, 132

Index

Cody, Buffalo Bill 107, 113, 126, 160
Coeur d'Alène Indians 68
coffee 22, 23, 28, 38, 73, 75, 79, 89, 101, 112, 124, 132, 133, 157
Coleman, Caroline M. Page Gay 39
Coleman, DeWitt Clinton 38
Coleman, William Tell **38–40**, 170, 171
Colorado Territory 3, 4, 11, 12, 18, 25, 46–47, 101, 106, 107, 113, 117–118, 126, 150–152, 171; Burlington 1, 86, 116, 117, 146; Central City 25, 26, *74*, 151; Denver 4, 25, 26, 46, 47, 87, 117, 118, *125*–126, 146, 151, 152, 154–156, 157; Leadville 126, 155–156; Pueblo 66, 162; statehood 126; *see also* Pike's Peak
Colorado War 117
Colorow, Chief 11
Colt revolvers 2, 30, *65*, 69, 101, 106, 111, 148–149, 169
Colvill, William 95
Colville Indian Reservation 68
Colville-Okanogan 145
Comanche 1, 5, 28, 29, 65–67, 92, 106, 107, 112, 124, 126, 138–139, 144, 148, 154, 161, 162, 169, 170; Noconi 65; *see also* Parker, Quanah
Comancheria 29–30
Comstock, William G. 88
Comstock Lode 1, 51, 121
concrete 2, 69, 130
Conestoga wagon 1, 3, 27, *161*, 163
Congregationalists 13, 41, 57, 62–63, 72, 98, 102, 133
Connecticut 14, 16, 50, 57, 98, 122, 128, 130, 151, 164
Conniache, Chief 162
construction 17, 20, 58, 69, 81, 85–86, 87, 99, 106, 107, 117, 122, 140, 144, 157; William T. Coleman & Company 38; *see also* adobe; carpentry; concrete; dugouts; fort system; log cabins; masons; sod huts; thatching
Continental Divide *114*, 115, 171
Cook, Harriet Elizabeth 166, 167
Cooke, Jay 21, 115, 170
cooking 22–26, *23*, 69, 75, 79, 80, 84, 85, 87, 89, 97, 101, 114, 142; baking 25, 110, 130, 133, 136, 155; bread 152; cornbread 147, 165; meat curing 147; miso 141; pastry 152, 155; soy sauce 141; *see also* inns; vegetables
Coolidge, Calvin 116
Cope, Sister Marianne 4, **40–41**, 171
Córdova, Vicente 148
Corliss, George W. 84, 85
Corliss, Trecia Holden 84, 85
Coronado, Francisco de 1, 47, 169
cotton 26, 41, 64, 99, 103, 104, 134, 154, 161, 168

Coushatta 144
cowboys 3, 4, 65–67, 106–107, 112, 124–126, 147, 157, 160, 171; vaqueros 63
Cowboy's Lament 107
Cowichan 8
Cowles, George Algernon 4, **41–42**, 171
Cox, Jacob Dolson 91
Coxey's Army 88
Crandall, Jared Burdick 121
Crawford, Mary M. 109
Crawford, Medorem 122, 123
Crawford, Ronald C. 122
Crazy Horse 11, 126
Cree 8, 20, 31–32
Creek Indians 57, 149
Creoles 8
crime 38, 39, 44–45, 53, 57, 58, 60, 62, 63–64, 67, 68, 73–74, 80, 81, 85, 97, 100, 107, 124, 126, 132, 159; harbor crime 96–98; swindling 99; *see also* arson; bigamy; domestic abuse; kidnap; law; polygamy; prostitution; rustling; vigilantism
Crockett, Davy 148
Crockett, Samuel 27
Crookshank, S.A. 164
Crosby, Clanrick 143
Crosby, Nathaniel 122
Crow Indians 31, 32, 52, 55
Crowder, Reuben 27
Crumpton, Amanda Pennington 133
Crumpton, William Alexander 133
Cuddeback, Grant Price 64
Culbertson, Margaret 3, **42–44**
Cupeño 60
curandera 24
Cureton, Jack 65, 170
Cureton's Rangers 65
Custer, Frances Ward Alger 165
Custer, George Armstrong 11, 87, 126
customs collection 57–58, 79, 146

Da Fonta, Rose Rodrigues 137
dairying 20, 24, 25, 27, 73–74, 79, 81, 85, 94, 145; butter 2, 20, 25, 27, 79, 81, 87, 114, 117, 137, 147, 148, 151, 152; buttermilk 115; cheese 137, 147; cream 53, 79, 111, 137; milk 137, 151
Dakota Land Company 55
Dakota Territory 4, 18, 19–22, 30, 55, 89, 129, 158–159; statehood 57, 129, 159; *see also* Bozeman Trail; North Dakota; South Dakota
Dale, Arthur H. 44
Dale, David Mark 44
Dale, Frank **44–45**
Dale, John William 44
Dale, Martha Wood **44–45**
Dale, Mary Elvina 44

Dalrymple, Oliver P. 18
Dalton, Bill 45
Dalton Gang 5, 45
dams 5, 20, 37, 59
dance 3, 15, 108, 152, 163; halls 17, 62, 70, 126; Tiwa 49; *see also* saloons
Danes 4, 58, 98–100, 105
Danites 11
Daugherty, Hiram Henry 64
Daugherty, Roy 45
Daughters of the Utah Pioneers 157
Davis, Jerome C. 38
Death Comes for the Archbishop 49
Death Valley 2, 39, 51, 64, 170, 171; discovery 62; naming 61
Decker, Clarissa Caroline 166
Decker, Lucy Ann 166
Declaration of Independence 29, 164, 169
Delaware Indians 29
Demers, Modeste 9
Depression of 1893 70
DeRouge, Etienne 68
Deseret 4, 83, 167
Deseret Silk Association 168
DeSmet, Jean 32, 33, 36
DeVere, pearl **46–47**
DeWitt Colony 28, 30, 144, 147
diabetes 134
diaries/journals 1, 16, 32, 55, 57, 60, 70, 75, 82, 83, 86, 89, 93–95, 104, 105, 106–107, 109, 111, 146–147, 151
Diary of a San Diego Girl, 1856 60
Diegueño 60
Digger Indians 8
dime novels 5, 107, 126
diphtheria 33, 39, 87
divorce 18, 53, 74, 75–76, 104, 123, 156, 167
Docher, Anton **47–49**, *48*
Dodge, William 34
Dogrib 7
dogs 1, 81, 101, 103–104, 130, 135–136
Dolan, Patrick 136
domestic abuse 24, 53, 84, 85
Donation Land Act 27
Donner, Frances E. 136
Donner, George 135
Donner, Jacob 135
Donner, Mary M. 136
Donner, Tamsen 135
Donner Party 1, 4, 78–79, 134–136, 169
Donner Pass 99, 136, 169
Doolin, Bill 45
Douglas, James 60
Douglass, Stephen A. 135
Driskill, John Wylie 107
drought 4, 27, 80–81, 89, 120, 129, 142, 147, 155
drowning 4, 9, 11, 18, 25, 85, 92, 110, 114, 115, 155

drumming 48, 108
Dubois, Toussaint 144
Duggan, Martin J. 156
dugout 66, 80, 81, 84, 86–87, 95, 155
Dunlop, Hannah Jane Meeker 114
Dunlop, Jesse 114
Durand, Pierre 133
Dutch 3, 10, 16, 17, 49, 52, 138
Dutch Reformed 16–18
Duwamish 28, 170
Dyer, Leigh Richmond **64–67**
dysentery 132, 146

Early Settlers and Indian Fighters of Southwest Texas 149
Earp, Wyatt 107
earthquake 5, 24, 25, 40, 51
Easter, John 75
Ebbetts, Amanda Malvina Heath 49–51
Ebbetts, John A.N. **49–51**, *50*, 170
Echallier, Peter 47
ecology 53
Elgin, Sophie 125
Elliot, Milford 136
Emancipation Proclamation 25, 26
engineering 38, 53, 59; *see also* bridges; dams; fort system; railroads; roads
English 1, 14, 16, 17, 33, 50, 52, 54, 59, 60, 61, 64, 66, 67, 69, 73, 77, 78, 92, 100, 102, 103, 106, 109, 118, 121, 123, 128, 134, 135, 140, 142, 144, 147, 151, 152, 155, 161, 166, 168
Enterprise 49
Episcopalians 117–118, 140, 152
Erie Canal 80, 164–165
ethnographer 31, 47–*48*
Evans, John Henry 146
Evans, Julia Smith 146
explorers 3, 5, 11, 20, 24, 36–37, 49–52, 61–62, 93, 144, 160–163, 167, 169, 170; New York Knickerbocker Exploring Company 49–51; Vancouver Island Exploring Expedition 60–61

Fah, Chun 43
Fairchild, Elizabeth 166
Fargo, William George 64
Faribault, David 20
The Farmer's Alliance in Nebraska 88
The Farmer's Wife 88
farming 3, 8, 12–13, 24, 28, 36, 44, 53, 57, 59, 62, 66, 68, 69, 74, 83, 91, 92, 95–96, 98, 100, 101, 103–104, 109–111, 113–117, 130–134, 138–139, 141, 147, 171; equipment 56, 63, 68, 81; manure spreaders 129; silos 129, 134; steam thresher 81; training 85, 112; *see also* cotton; grain; livestock; National Farmers' Alliance; plowman; potatoes; vegetables
Farnham, Eliza Burhans Wood 1, **51–54**, 170
Farnham, Thomas Jefferson **51–54**
feminism 53–54, 87–88; feminist fiction 89; Mormon 164–168
Ferguson, Jesse 27
ferries 11, 17, 36, 38, 81, 85, 93, 99, 110, 118–119, 133, 145, 149, 162, 167; Council Bluffs and Nebraska Ferry 119; Elk Horn and Loup Fork Ferry 119; Hannegan Ferry 85; sailboat 137; steamer 119; Winter Quarter Ferry 119
fever 15, 16–17, 39, 57, 63, 79, 110; chills and fever 32
Figueroa, José 137
Finns 95–96, 170
fire 8, 26, 39, 46, 51, 60, 62, 76, 116, 130, 146, 147, 160; goldfish 70; range fire 106–107, 147; volunteer firemen 63, 117
fish 8, 14, 27, 38, 39, 102, 148; catfish 98; fishpond 15; oil 143; salmon 98, 143; salt fish 141; shellfish 143; sucker 98; trap 85; trout 98, 102
Fisk, Andrew Jackson 56
Fisk, Dell 56
Fisk, Elizabeth Chester **54–57**
Fisk, James Liberty 21, **54–57**, 90, 170
Fisk, John 54
Fisk, Lydia Ann Burson **54–57**
Fisk, Robert Emmett **54–57**
Fisk, Van Hayden **54–57**
Fitzpatrick William Alexander 53
flatboats 25, 55, 91, 111, 116
Flathead 8, 9, 11
fleas 140
flood 1, 25–26, 85, 91, 92, 99, 114, 120, 142
Florida 22, 36, 38, 41, 96, 125
flowers 15, 81, 108–109, 110; roses 42, 75; wildflowers 53, 129
Flynn, C.B. 46
Folsom, Joseph Libbey **57–59**, 169
Foote, James B. 117, 118
Fort Abercrombie, Dakota Territory 21, 170
Fort Babbitt, California 163–164
Fort Belknap, Texas 64–65
Fort Bend, Texas 144
Fort Benton, Montana 55, 56, 157
Fort Boise, Idaho 36–37, 114, 123
Fort Bridger, Wyoming 11, 27, 135, 142, 157
Fort Brown, Texas 22–23, 25
Fort Buchanan, Arizona 24, 130, 132
Fort Clark, Texas 112
Fort Collins, Colorado 151
Fort Colville, Washington 85
Fort Concho, Texas 66
Fort Crawford, Wisconsin 153
Fort Dakota, South Dakota 158
Fort Dalles, Oregon 84
Fort Davis, Texas 112
Fort Douglas, Utah 167
Fort Griffin, Texas 66
Fort Hall, Idaho 36–38, 78–79, 98, 99, 122
Fort Hartford, Kentucky 144
Fort Hays, Kansas 90
Fort Hope, British Columbia 145
Fort Hoskins, Oregon 85
Fort Humboldt, Oregon 94
Fort Kearney, Nebraska 105, 119, 157
Fort Langley, British Columbia 8
Fort Lapwai, Utah 108
Fort Laramie, Wyoming 11, *31*–32, 33, 36, 69, 78–79, 122
Fort Leavenworth, Kansas 61
Fort Madison, Iowa 78, 159
Fort McPherson, Nebraska 119, 126
Fort Mitchell, Kentucky 119
Fort Nisqually, Washington 27, 143
Fort Parker, Texas 154
Fort Reno, Kansas 107
Fort Rice, North Dakota 33, 56
Fort Richardson, Texas 66
Fort Ridgely, Minnesota 54–55, 95
Fort Riley, Kansas 155
Fort Ripley, Minnesota 55, 56
Fort St. Vrain, Colorado 162
Fort Sibley, Missouri 19
Fort Sill, Oklahoma 112
Fort Smith, Arkansas 50
Fort Snelling, Minnesota 19–20
Fort Spokane, Washington 68
Fort Steele, British Columbia 11
Fort Steilacoom, Washington 85, 110
Fort Stockton, Texas 112
Fort Sublette, North Dakota 31, 32
Fort Sully, South Dakota 33, 90, 91
Fort Sumner, New Mexico 66
fort system 56
Fort Tejon, California 61
Fort Union, Montana 11, 31, 32, 55, 56, 157
Fort Union, New Mexico 162, 163
Fort Vancouver, Washington 8, 27, 52, 85, 122, 161
Fort Vienna, Kentucky 144
Fort Walla Walla, Washington 55, 85
Fort William, Montana 56
Fort Worth, Texas 125
Fort Yuma, Arizona 22, 63
'49ers 3, 9, 18, 59, 62–63, 100, 102–103, 123, 127, 145, 163–164; Lost Forty-Niners 61
fossils 113, 129
Foster, F. 64
Fox Indians 91, 111, 112, 149, 153, 169
Fraeb, Henry 10
Francophones 2, 19–22, 57, 171

Index

Franklin, Edward **59–62**
Franklin, Lewis Abraham **59–62**, 170
Franklin, Lumley **59–62**
Franklin, Maurice Abraham 3, **59–62**, 170
Franklin, Selim **59–62**
Franklin, Selim Maurice 61
Franklin, Victoria Jacobs **59–62**
Fred Harvey restaurants 101
Free, Emmeline 166, 167
Free State Party 74
Freedmen's Bureau 39
freight 1, 8, 30, 32, 38–40, 53, 63, 64, 66, 71, 75, 87, 91, 92, 101, 106, 121, 122, 128, 130, 132, 137, 143, 145, 151, 157, 158, 159, 160–163; Cerro Gordon Freight Company 62; cost 88; robbery 73
Frémont, John Charles 10–11, 79, 99, 161
French 8, 47–49, 90, 133, 156–160, 162, 169; French Colonial Wars 47
French, Alfred Channing 62
French, Cornelia Seymour Cowles 61
French, Erasmus Darwin **61–62**, 170
French, Frank 61
French, Joel W. 61
French Canadians 8, 9, 19–22, 56, 78, 111–113, 124, 133, 143, 153, 171
Friesians 16–18
Frost, Olive Grey 166
Frost, Sophronia Gray 165
fruit 38, 72, 73, 84, 113, 115, 117, 145; almonds 137; apples 42, 81, 82, 86, 87, 93, 95, 135, 145–146, 152; apricots 42; black walnuts 134; blackberries 93; cherries 82, 86, 93, 110; chokecherries 147; currants 86, 93; dried 89, 130, 145; gooseberries 80, 93; grapes 42, 140, 145, 164; hackberries 134; jam 147; nuts 42, 84; olives 42, 53; oranges 61, 140; peaches 42, 82, 86, 145, 164; pears 53, 82, 145; pecans 134; persimmons 42; plums 42, 82, 86, 93, 147; raisins 4, 40–41, 42, 105, 109, 171; raspberries 93; strawberries 86, 93; walnuts 140; watermelons 146; wild strawberries 80
Fuller, Desdemona Wadsworth 165
fur/hide trading 7–10, 20, 30–33, 39, 49, 113, 119, 133, 161; bear 94, 104, 137; beaver 31, 32, 112, 161; boar 94; cow 137; coyote 112; elk 137; ermine 101; fox 96, 101; lynx 101; mink 96, 101; muskrat 96; otter 31, 49, 104, 112; rabbit 101; Rocky Mountain Fur Company 30; seal 49; weasel 96; wolf 112; *see also* buffalo; trappers

furniture 12, 14, 42, 60, 81, 84, 140, 143, 146, 147, 155

Gall 56
gambling 4, 5, 15, 53, 57, 68, *71*, 72, 107, 108, 121, 127, 158; cock fighting 158
games 15, 81
Gandara, Manuel 131
gangrene 66
genealogist 105
genocide 1, 5, 94, 132
Geographical Society of the Pacific 61
Georgia 17, 92, 104, 154–155
German Methodists 25
Germans 40–41, 44, 62–64, 64–67, 79–82, 93–95, 100–102, 107, 115, 119–121, 127, 142, 143–145, 158–160
Gervais, Benjamin 20
Gervais, Joseph 9
Gervais, Louis Pierre 19, 20
ghost towns 2, 62, 74, 92, 113
Gilliam, Cornelius 142–143
glass 26, 49, 82, 124
Glorieta Pass, Battle of 139
Goddard, Emily von Essen 51
Goddard, George Henry **49–51**, *50*
gold 58, 62, 127, 159; Bodie Gold Mine 103; Buckeye Gold Mining and Milling Company 107; discovery 64, 70, 151; Ela Helean Gold Mining 46; fields 55, 89, 130; gold rush 11, 18, 25, 33, 37, 50, 58, 60, *78*, 79, 93, 97, 98–100, 102–103, 115, 117, 118, 122, 123, 136, 145, 157, 169, 170; greed 53; Kenai Alaska Gold Mine 101; Lost Goller Mine 63; mining 33, 46, 55, 62, 73, 101, 106; nuggets 55, 63, 64, 68, 123, 169; panning 3, 38, 70, 163; placer mining 2, 25, 46, 64, 68, 93, 99, 123, 151, 155, 163; sluice 100, 145, 151; strike 46, 100, 114, 145; Victor Gold Mining Company 46
Goller, Christina 64
Goller, John 5, **62–64**, 170
Goller, Louisa 64
Goller, Paulena Neidt 63, 64
Gonzales, Battle of 28
Goodell, Henry Martin **82–86**
Goodell, Jotham Weeks **82–86**, *83*
Goodell, Nathan Edward **82–86**
Goodell, William Bird 84
Goodnight, Charles 3, **64–67**, *65*, 170
Goodnight, Corinne Oletta 67
Goodnight, Elija **64–67**
Goodnight, Mary Ann Dyer **64–67**
Goodnight, Mary Charlotte Sheek Collier 67
Goodnight-Loving Trail 66, 170
Goodnight-Thayer Cattle Company 67

Goodwin, John Noble 132
Gookins, Milo 112
Gordon, William F. 91
Gore, St. George 11
Gorgonio, José 24
Gough, James Rowland 134
Goulding, William Robinson **49–51**, *50*
Graff, John 62
Graham, Isaac 98
grain 41, 42, 113, 117, 168; alfalfa 2–13, 18, 69, 70, 129, 133; barley 18; broomcorn 87; clover 18; corn 17, 18, 80, 81, 82, 87, 92, 111, 129, 131, 133, 148, 154; elevators 87; flax 18; flour 87, 89, 99, 114, 132; granaries 27, 81, 143; hay 18, 87, 100, 105, 107, 110, 111, 117, 131, 133; hops 27, 110, 111, 115, 143, 147; millet 18, 82; oats 18, 27, 81, 82, 143; popcorn 105; rice 141; rye 18, 27, 80, 143; sales 92; wheat 8, 17, 18, 27, 80, 81, 99, 110, 129, 133, 137, 143
Grand Review of the Armies 2, 69, 80
Grand Ronde Reservation 9
Grant, Ulysses S. 91, 121
grasshoppers 3, 44, 81, 107, 112, 120
Gray, J.W. 123
Gray, Wheaton Andrew 164
Great Basin 51
Great Depression 47
The Great Divide 126
Great Plains 5
Great Potato Famine 123
Great Sioux Reservation 18
Greeley, Horace 121, 145
Green River rendezvous 98
Grey Bird 95
Griffin, John Smith 98
Griffin, John Strother 61
Grimes, William Bradford 106–107
grocers 3, 17, 73, 84, 87, 90, 99, 115, 143, 152, 155, 157
Gros Ventres 5
guides 3, 10–11, 19, 54–57, 61, 94, 98, 99, 100, 112, 122, 126, 160–163
gunpowder 8, 9, 31, 161, 162
gunsmiths 63, 98, 103, 144, 147
Gwydir, Mary Emma Dobell 68
Gwydir, Rickard Daniel **67–69**

Haag, Anna Maria 81
Haag, Christopher Gottlieb 80
Haag, Henry C. 4
Haag, Johann Christoph **79–82**
Haag, Rosena Christina 4, **79–82**
Haagsma, Broer Baukes **16–18**
Hackney, William Patrick 149
Haida 8, 85
Halliday, Ben 157
Halliday Overland Mail and Express 73

Index

Hamilton, Elsie E. 70
Hamilton, Ezra M. **69–70**
Hamilton, Fred 70
Hamilton, Harriet Ann Moffett 69
Hamilton, Sarah Landson 69
Hanseikai Zasshi 76
Hardin, John Wesley 5, 112
Harding, Florence Kling 101
Harding, Warren G. 101
Harmon, George 128
Harney, William Selby 11
Harris, George S. 86
Harris, Lucinda Pendleton Morgon 165
Harrison, Benjamin 149
Hawaii 3, 5, 8, 13–16, 40–41, 49, 52, 70–73, 140–*141*, 142, 168, 169, 171; *see also* Honolulu; Lanai; Maui; Oahu
Hawaii Buddhist Annual 77
Hawaiian Sugar Planters' Association 77
Hawaiians 8, 13, 40–41, 141
Hawkins, John Parker 149
Haws, Emily 166
Hayashi, Chisato 72–73
Hayashi, Harvey Saburo **70–73**
Hayashi, Matsu Kawarada **70–73**
Hayden, Van 56
Hayes, Rutherford B. 94
Hays, John Coffee "Jack" 124, 148–149, 169
heat stroke 137
Heazle, Benjamin Alfred 73
Heazle, George Robert **73–74**
Heazle, Jean Bruce 4, **73–74**
Heikko, Mikko 95–96
Heintzelman, Samuel Peter 24
hepatitis 143
herbalism 5, 24, 84
Hesperian: A Western Quarterly 53
Hickok, James Butler "Wild Bill" 106, 126
Higbee, Rachael 91
Hihn, Frederick August 127
Hispanics 1, 4, 5, 24–25, 28, 29, 30, 48, 52, 61, 105, 131, 135, 138, 144, 148, 162, 164; bandits 85, 107
historians 1, 2, 3, 5, 12, 13, 29, 33, 35, 38, 54, 57, 70, 77, 88, 102, 104, 105, 109, 111–113, 115, 149, 159, 163
History of Missionary Work in Hawaii 77
Holden, Kenneth 101
Hollenbeck, John Edward **12–13**
Hollister, Ned 104
Holman, Rebecca 165
Holmes, James Henry **74–76**
Holmes, Julia Annie Archibald **74–76**, 170
Home for Young Women 108
homeless 16, 96, 97
Homestead Act 2, 21, 80–81, 83, 95, 117

homesteading 2, 4, 8, 11, 18, 21, 44, 46, 47, 66, 74, 79, 80, 81, 85, 86, 88, 91–93, 96, 102, 107, 110, 111–117, 123–124, 131, 138–139, 144, 146–147, 149, 154–156, 158, 171; claim clubs 87; protests 88
honey 36, 148
Honolulu 5, *13*, 15, 16, 40, 52, 76–77, 140–142, 170; Chinatown 76
Hooks, Ben 104
Hoover, Herbert 101
Hopper, Charles 36
horses 4, 11, 20, 38, 46, 63, 69, 79, 81, 82, 89, 91, 99, 100, 111, 117, 127, 130, 137, 160, 163; Appaloosa 68; breeding 41, 65, 68, 73–74; herding 53, 106–107; military 160; mounts 65; pack horses 61, 79; ponies 82, 109, 116, 129, 136, 161; racing 108, 140, 158; strays 79; theft 67–68, 74, 105, 122, 126, 148; wild mustangs 160
hospitals 28, 40–41, 92; Deseret Hospital 168; Jefferson Barracks 108; Kona Hospital 73; Los Angeles Hospital 61; Malulani Hospital 171; Marine Hospital Mission 97; Mission San Rafael Arcángel 137; Sailor's Home 97; St. Peter Hospital 171; U.S. Marine Hospital 97
hostages 29–30
hotels 17, 30, 85, 103, 109, 115; Barclay House 122; Bella Union Hotel 106; Brown Palace Hotel 156; Clarendon Hotel 156; Cottage House 152; Cottonade Hotel 129; Diller Hotel 146; Eagle Hotel 93; Ellsworth Hotel 93; Exchange Hotel 60; Florence Hotel 42; Florence House Hotel 119; Franklin House 60; Hotel Rafael 39; Hotel Tamalpais 39; Jones House 58; Kenai Lake Lodge 102; La Tienda Barata 60; Leavitt House 103; Mercantile Hotel 97; Metropolitan Hotel 152; Mission San José 58; Ormsby House 121; Pioneer Cabin 152; St. Louis Hotel Company 32; Southern Hotel 33; Stone Hotel and Restaurant 151; Table Bluff Hotel and Pioneer Saloon 94; Warm Springs Hotel 121; Washington House 79; Wilkins House Hotel 160; Windsor Hotel 156
housewives 2, 12, 53, 164
Houston, Sam 28, 138, 148, 154
Hudson's Bay 4, 7–8, 19, 26, 27, 122, 123, 142, 143, 145, 161
Hueston, Tom 45
Huguenots 5, 19, 30
hunger 22, 27, 43, 63, 78, 80, 99, 136, 143; malnutrition 87, 136

Hunt, Ernest 76–77
hunting 9, 19, 21, 27, 32, 93–96, 101, 120, 143, 144; alligators 103, 104, 138; antelope 37, 67, 111, 138; bear 37, 101, 103, 104, 110, 130, 136, 138; cougars (mountain lions) 103, 115; coyotes 103, 104; deer 36, 37, 51, 94, 98, 111, 130, 134, 144, 148; ducks 51, 104, 138; eagles 101; elk 37, 67, 94, 126; geese 138, 146; moose 101; musk ox 101; prairie chickens 146; rabbits 51, 146; razorback hogs 103, 138; wild turkeys 36, 104, 130, 138, 148; wolverines 101; wolves 103, 104; *see also* buffalo
Huntington, Chauncey Dyer 164
Huntington, Collis Potter 34
Huntington, Dimick Baker **164–168**
Huntington, John Dickenson 164, 166–167
Huntington, Oliver Boardman **164–168**
Huntington, Presendia Lathrop 164, 165, 166–167
Huntington, William **164–168**
Huntington, William Dresser **164–168**
Hupa 94
Hurley, Mary 89–90
hygiene 72, 108, 168

Idaho Territory 3, 4, 10, 19, 31, 36–38, 54, 55–56, 73–74, 89, 108, 123–124, 158–160; Boise 115, 123–124, 159–160, 171; gold fields 55, 89; statehood 73, 123, 124, 160
Ide, William Brown 4, **98–100**, 169
idol worship 14, 15, *71*, 72
Ignacio 61
Illingworth, William Henry **54–57**, *56*
Illinois 2, 52, 54, 62, 64, 80, 93, 135, 142, 145, 146, 151, 152, 153, *166*, 169; Chicago 3, 66, 133, 158–159, 169; Nauvoo 2, 38, 78, 165, 166; Peoria 52, 133, 146, 152; Rockford 86
Imamura, Jane Matsuura 77
Imamura, Kanmo 77
Imamura, Kiyoko 77
Imamura, Ryo 77
Imamura, Yemyo 5, **76–77**
immigration 7–10, 15, 16–18, 19, 20, 21, 25, 36, 40–41, 55, 62, 67–69, 76, 97, 98–100, 109–111, 119–120, 122, 123–124, 127, 129, 134–138, 146–147, 158–159, 170; Commissioner of Immigration 158; Emigrant Aid Society 170; illegal immigrants *71*; Women's Protective Emigration Society

Index

54; *see also* Bozeman Trail; California Trail; Old Spanish Trail; Oregon Trail; Overland Trail; recruiters; Santa Fe Trail; wagon trains
In the Land of Alaska Nellie 102
incest 24
Indian agents 11, 67–69, 109, 112, 122, 124, 152–154; Puget Sound Indian Agency 143; Red Cloud Agency 107
Indian Commission 33, 118, 154; Commissioner of Indian Affairs 68
Indian Wars 57, 70, 94, 147
Indiana 16, 25, 54, 67, 68, 91, 105, 106, 109–111, 114, 119, 134, 142, 144, 159; Indianapolis 113, 149
influenza 77, 134, 141
Innis, Harry 152
inns 3, 20, 22, 93–95, 100–102, 112, 117, 136, 162; Magnolia House Inn 59; Stagecoach Inn 139
insanity 96, 104, 116, 132; *see also* asylums
insurance 32, 82, 102; fire 136
International Buddhist Institute 77
International Council of Women 168, 171
International Peace Garden 129
interpreters 3, 8, 11, 43–44, 72, 78, 112, 137, 153, 170; *see also* translators
inventors 2, 3, 5, 42, 69, 70, 94, 102, 124, 140
Iowa Indians 119, 149, 153
Iowa Territory 1, 16, 17, 80, 91, 106, 108, *114*, 117, 118, 126, 134, 145, 152–154, 158, 166; Council Bluffs 90, 118, 167; Davenport 111
Irish 4, 5, 10, 11, 16, 18, 22, 26, 30–33, 38, 53, 54, 67–69, 73–74, 89, 105, 107, 109–111, 121, 123–126, 134–139, 140, 146–147, 154–155, 156, 157
iron 16, 40, 46, 63, 104, 130, 148; *see also* blacksmiths
The Iron Way: A Tale of the Builders of the West 5, 35
Iron Wristband 31
Iroquois/Mohawk 8
irrigation 5, 39, 42, 59, 69, 70
Irvine, James 140
Isbell, Alexander 78
Isbell, Isaac Chauncy 4, **77–79**, *78*
Isbell, James 78
Isbell, Olive Mann 4, **77–79**
Ise, Alma Laura 81, 82
Ise, Billy 82
Ise, Charles 81
Ise, Daniel 82
Ise, Henry Christopher **79–82**
Ise, Herman Thomas 82
Ise, Johann Georg 80

Ise, John Christopher 81, 82
Ise, Luise Katherine Eisenmanger 80
Ise, Minnie 82
Ise, Rosena Haag **79–82**
Ise, Walt 82
Isenberg, Paul 142

Jackson, Andrew 153
Jacobs, Hannah 60
Jacobs, Henry Bailey 1, 3, 165, 167
Jacobs, Henry Chariton 166, 167, 168
Jacobs, Jane 60
Jacobs, Leah 60
Jacobs, Mark 60
Jacobs, Zebulon William 165, 167
Jager, Herman De 17
jail 38, 63, 74, 75, 79, 96, 106, 165, *166*, 169; illegal jailing 96–98; *see also* prison
Japan 70–71, 140–*141*, 142; immigrants *72*, 76–77; laborers 5, 8, 70–73, *71*, *141*, 170; *nisei* 77, 142; Yokohama *141*, 170
Japanese American Citizenship Association 142
Jayhawkers' Party 2, 62, 63
Jean Heazle Horse and Cattle Company 73
Jenkins, William Miller 150
Jews 5, 59–62, 100, 170; Kearny Street Hebrew Congregation 59; Rosh Hashanah 59, 170; Yom Kippur 2, 59, 60, 170
Jingle-Bob spread 66
Johnson, Andrew 94
Johnson, Charles N. 45
Johnston, Albert Sidney 157
Jones, George 27
Jones, Henry 144
Jones, Mary Smeathers 144
José María, Chief 154
Joseph, Chief 68–69, 108
Judah, Theodore Dehone 59
Judson, Anna 83
Judson, Charles 84
Judson, George **82–86**
Judson, Holden Allen **82–86**
Judson, Jack 85
Judson, Louisa 84
Judson, Lucretia R. 84
Judson, Mary 85
Judson, Phoebe Goodell 3, **82–86**
Jumping Bear 90

Ka'ahumanu, Queen 14, 15
Kachinas 3
Kalakaua, David 40, 142
Kalapuya 9
Kamamalu 15
Kamehameha II the Great 13, 15
Kamehameha III 15, 52, 141
Kamehameha V 40, 140
Kansa 119

Kansas State Historical Society 111
Kansas Territory 2, 4, 10,
Kapiolani, Queen 142
Karankawa 124
Karuk 94
Kauai 141
Kaw 111
Kearny, Stephen Watts 61
Keays, Elizabeth L. Parke 151–152
Keays, William 151
Keller, George 20
Kellie, James Thomson 1, **86–89**
Kellie, Luna Sanford **86–89**, 171
Kelly, Fanny Wiggins 56, **89–91**, 170
Kelly, Josiah Shawhan, Jr. 90–91
Kelly, Josiah Shawhan, Sr. **89–91**
Kentucky 12, 25, 27, 28, 30, 34, 36, 64, 66, 67, 80, 123, 134, 142, 144, 147, 149, 150, 152, 161, 162; Louisville 34, 123, 150
Keokuk, Chief 153
Keseberg, Lewis Christian **134–136**
Ketse 8
Key, Ambrose W. **91–93**
Key, Darius 92
Key, George **91–93**
Key, Mary Jones Garrett **91–93**
Key, Rebecca Mintun **91–93**
Keyes, Sarah Handley 135
Kickapoo 124, 149
kidnap 4, 11, 42–44, 56, 65, 85, 89–91, 125, 131–132, 150, 162; impressment 97
Kilborn, Florence Vandenberg 119
Kilborn, Hannah Vandenberg 118
Kilborn, Nathaniel 118
Kill Eagle 90
Killdeer Mountain, Battle of 56, 90
Kimball, Helen Mar 165
Kincaid, Nancy Jane Woolery 110
Kincaid, William 115
Kincaid, William Moore 110
King Ranch 160
Kinman, Carlin 93–94
Kinman, Eleanor Bower 93–94
Kinman, Ellen 93–94
Kinman, Roderick 94
Kinman, Seth 3, **93–95**
Kiowa 25, 28, 29, 65, 92, 112, 113, 138–139, 149
Kirby, Georgiana Bruce **51–54**
Kirby, Richard Cornelius **51–54**
Kirkland, William Hudson 130–131
knives 2, 31, 64, 69, 81, 89, 94, 103–104, 126, 135, 142, 148, 161; lance 132; saw blade 137
Kodiak 49
Kootenay 8
Kuchiba, Giyko 77
Kujo, Takeko 76
Kwantlen 8

labor 1, 5, 34, 39, 40, 59, 72, 76–77, 79, 86–89, 97, 98, 101, 103, 137,

141, 143, 155, 165; Asian 141–143; Bodie Miners' Union 103; press gangs 76; stoop labor 4, 72; United Mine Workers 118
Ladies' Seamen's Friend Society 96–98
Lahti, August 96
Lahti, Charles 4, **95–96**
Lahti, Johanna Gustava Palovainio 1, **95–96**
Lahti, Peter J. **95–96**, 170
Laline, Jean 133
Lamar, Mirabeau Buonaparte 29
Lambert, Rebecca H. Gatchell **96–98**
Lanai 141
Lane, James 75
Langlois, Father Antoine 9
language 1, 3, 5, 48; Caddo 112; Cantonese 43; Chinook 84, 110; English 14, 43, 76, 77, 79, 80, 131, 145, 158; French 157; German 80, 119–120, 158; Hawaiian 14; Japanese 72, 77; Keresan 47–48; Norwegian 158; Sahaptin 108, 109; sign language 11; Spanish 22, 74–75, 79, 137, 148
Langwell, John 22
Lapwei 4, 68
Larimer, Frank 89
Larimer, Sarah Luse **89–91**
Larimer, William Jackson **89–91**
Lassen, Peter 4, **98–100**
Lassen Cutoff 99
Lassik 94
Latter Day Saints Relief Society 168
launderers 14, 22–24, 25–26, 46, 81, 90–91, 110, 155; potato starch 147
law 3, 4, 8, 9, 15, 38, 68, 100, 138, 149–140, 171; anti–Asian laws 72; California Supreme Court 164; circuit rider 152; city council 21, 63, 69, 106; city treasurer 106; clerk of court 152; constable 144, 165; constitutional convention delegate 151; corruption 39, 43, 60, 87; county clerk 129; county commissioner 62, 116, 155; county coroner 122, 165; county supervisor 106; county treasurer 158; court bailiff 68–69; court system 68; governors 8, 15, 20, 26, 37, 44, 60, 94, 99, 100, 131, 132, 137, 150, 153, 165; judges 2, 44–45, 60, 91, 99, 103, 129, 132, 151, 152, 158; justices of the peace 36, 60, 78, 81, 85, 116, 143, 158; Kansas Territorial Supreme Court 45; land commissioner 144; lawsuits 9, 70, 91, 103, 105, 127, 138, 153, 160, 163, 165, 171; lieutenant governor 156; mayors 39, 60, 86, 115, 117, 118, 137, 156, 157–158, 165; North-west Mountain Police 57; notary public 60; police 57, 63, 162; posses 4, 28, 99, 131, 132, 162–163; presidents 99, 154; register of deeds 129, 152; sheriffs 29, 68–69, 74, 106, 109, 112, 138, 152, 162; state representative 109, 112, 129, 143, 155, 162; state senate 112, 134, 154; territorial representative 132, 145, 151, 158; town supervisor 151; trustees 117; U.S. attorney 149; U.S. marshals 45, 84, 106; volunteer police 126; *see also* bounty hunters; crime; lynching, vigilantism
Lawing, Nellie Trosper 4, **100–102**, 171
Lawing, William "Billie" 5, **100–102**
Lawler, Joseph P. 29
Lawrence, Sarah 165
Leard, Mary 150
Leavitt, Alfred 103
Leavitt, Eliza S. Reed **102–103**
Leavitt, Hiram Lewis **102–103**
LeCompte, Antoine 19
Lecouvreur, Frank 63
lecturers 19, 53, 86, 89
Lee, Jason 8, 9, 52
Lee, Patrick 124
legend 3, 21, 22, 47, 64, 89, 100, 104, 109
Leidesdorff, William Alexander 58
Lemhi 8
leprosy 3, 40–41, 72, 141
Leschi, Chief 28, 110, 114–115
letters 1, 16, 25, 31–32, 33, 54, 55, 57, 68, 75, 81–82, 83, 89, 90, 113, 122, 129, 167; *Sod-House Days* 82
Lewis, Martha Jane Reed **134–136**
Lewis and Clark trail 115
Liberty, Stephen Edward **54–57**
libraries 19, 21, 45, 58, 94, 96–97, 115, 116, 149; Buddhist 77
Life in Prairie Land 53
Light House Mission Band 43
lighthouse 85
Lilly, Amazon Lelia Bunckley 104
Lilly, Benjamin Vernon 4, **103–104**
Lilly, Mary Erta Sisson 104
Liluokalani 41
Lincoln, Abraham 5, 17, 21, 25, 55, 75, 77, 80, 94, 112, 135
Lincoln, George 22–23
Little Crow 21, 55, 95
Little Raven 11
livestock 1, 8, 11, 18, 20, 26–28, 36, 60, 62, 64, 81, 114; burros 104; Collin County Purebred Livestock Association 134; dray animals 52, 105, *161*; raids 75; trading 87; *see also* cattle; horses; mules; oxen; pigs; poultry; ranching; sheep
locusts 88
log cabins 3, 8, 11, 27–28, 80–81, 84, 95, 100, 110, 114, 116–117, 123–124, 133, 135, 145, 151, 155, 167; dogtrot cabin 138–139
Logan, Herschel C. 126
loggers 18, 27, 103, 110, 127, 137, 143, 157; camps 127; floating logs 114; log theft 153; logjams 85
London, Jack 107
Lonesome Dove 67
longhouses 27, 143
Loomis, Elisha 15
Los Angeles 11, 12, 35, 36, 39, 51, 60, 62, 64, 69, 70, 94, 102, 104–106, 140, 160, 170; city council 69; Los Angeles County Pioneers 70; Los Angeles Gas Company 63; Los Angeles River 63
Lost Forty-Niners 2
Lott, Malissa 165
Louisa County Iowa Pioneer Society 92
Louisiana 38, 92, 103, 104, 123, 133, 138, 144; New Orleans 17, 26, 123, 125, 152, 157
Lovejoy, Asa 122
Loving, Oliver **64–67**, 170
Luiseño 60
lumber 3, 8, 16–18, 20, 27, 73, 81, 85, 92, 95–96, 123, 127, 130–131, 137, 157; shingles 8, 18, 124, 143
Lummi 4, 85
Lummis, Charles Fletcher 48
Lunalilo 40
Lutherans 54, 996, 158–159
lynching 1, 38–39, 64, 107, 126, 150, 156, 158, 170

Mabry, Seth 107
Macy, Charles 105
Macy, Lucinda Polk **104–106**
Macy, Nancy 105
Macy, Obed **104–106**
Macy, Oscar **104–106**
Madsen, Chris 45
Maidu 100
mail 3, 17, 32, 47, 55, 88, 101, 103, 109–111, 117, 121, 122, 132, 143, 145, 157, 158, 159, 167; Barlow & Sanderson Overland Mail 163; Holladay Overland Mail & Express 151; *see also* post office; Wells Fargo
Maine 33, 50, 69, 96, 102, 106, 122, 145, 155–156, 159
Makah 8, 143
malaria 41–42, 53, 80, 99, 112, 120, 130, 132, 154, 165, 166–167; *see also* fever
Mandan 20, 32, 52
Mangas Coloradas 75, 132
Manifest Destiny 60
Manuel 145
Marcy, Randolph Barnes 11
Maricopa 167
Mariners' Family Industrial Society 96

Index

Marks, Abigail 166
marriage, arranged 42–44
Martin, Jim 61
martyrdom 48
masonry 7–10, 69, 107, 155, 165
Masons (fraternal organization) 19, 99, 100, 117, 136, 143, 150, 152
Massachusetts 14, 16, 74, 82, 97, 98, 102, 104, 117, 126, 128, 129, 135, 140, 143, 155, 159; Boston 14, 22, 53, 97, 98, 102, 122, 126, 155, 159
Masterson, Bat 107
Masterson, Ed 107
Mattole 94
Maui 41, 141, 171
Maynard, Flora V. Longstreth 107
Maynard, Frank Henry 3, **106–107**, 171
McAlister, W.J. 67
McAllister, James 27
McBeth, Kate Christine 4, **107–109**
McBeth, Robert 109
McBeth, Susan Law 3, **107–109**
McBride, George C. 162
McBride, Martha 165
McCance, Charles Henry **146–147**
McCance, Margaret Anna Blaine **146–147**
McCance, Margaret Sarah Garner **146–147**
McCarty, Benjamin Franklin 109
McCarty, Clara 111
McCarty, Frank Truman 111
McCarty, Jonathan Warren **109–111**
McCarty, Ruth Jane Kincaid 110
McCarty, Sara Ann Westbrook 111
McCauley, John F. 54
McClanahan, Nora 86
McCormick, Vincentia 40–41
McCourt, Elizabeth Nellis 156
McCoy, John Calvin 4, **104–106**
McGeisey, Lincoln 150
McKinley, William 57, 156
Mead, Agnes Barcome **111–113**
Mead, Enoch 111
Mead, Fern F. Hoover 113
Mead, James Lucas "Bunnie" 111, 113
Mead, James Richard **111–113**
Mead, Lizzie 111
Mead, Lucy A. Inman 113
measles 9, 15, 28, 68, 80, 111, 141
Meder, John P. 122
medicine 4, 24, 61–62, 70–73, 78–79, 85, 104–106, 119, 132, 139, 151, 154; Chinese 64; female doctors 168; health tourism 70; Hereford, J.H. 47; homeopathy 53, 72; obstetrics 167; optometrist 82; patent drugs 60; surgery 45; *see also* herbalism; hospitals; midwifery; nursing; pharmacists

medicine bundles 108
Meeker, Eliza Jane Sumner 4, **113–116**, *114*
Meeker, Ezra 4, **113–116**, *114*, 171
Meeker, Fred 115
Meeker, Jacob 114
Meeker, John Valentine 115
Meeker, Marion 115
Meeker, Oliver Perry **113–116**
Meeker, Phoebe 114
Meeker, Usual Clark 114
Meeker Massacre *10*, 11–12, 171
Melton, Ethan 154
Mengarini, Gregory 36
Mennonites 158–159
Menominee 153
merchants 15, 17, 30, 32, 38, 41, 49–51, 54, 56, 59–62, 66, 85, 91–93, 95, 101, 109–111, 118, 122, 155–156, 159–160, 162, 167; J.R. Meeker & Sons store 114; Lafayette Supply Company 118; R.H. Robbins and Sons 151; robbery 45; Sears catalog 146; Tienda, California 60
Merritt, Josiah **116–117**
Merritt, Sarah Luckey 116–117
Mesplié, Toussaint 124
messengers 19, 29, 125, 148, 149, 162, 163
Methodist Episcopal 8, 52, 61, 86, 91, 96, 122
Methodist University of Oklahoma 45
Methodists 8, 9, 25–26, 44, 66, 85, 107, 118, 122; Wesleyan Methodist 73, 96
Métis 8, 9, 19–22
Mexican-American War 5, 22–23, 32, 57, 61, 62, 79, 149, 162, 166
Mexico 5, 8, 22, 24–25, 28–29, 30, 37, 67, 79, 132, 135, 148, 269; Acapulco 59, 137; Baja 62; Chihuahua 104, 162; outlaws 85; *see also* Hispanics
Meyerowitz, Isadore **98–100**
Miami Indians 8
Micheltorena, José Manuel 37, 99
Michigan 16, 17, 61, 96, 117, 145; Detroit 120, 133, 155
midwifery 3, 5, 14–15, 24–26, 96, 151, 167; childbirth 84, 105, 117, 127, 162, 166; deaths 142; pregnancy 165; puerperal fever 112
migraine 135
militia 1, 9, 28, 32, 38, 46, 57, 65, 74, 85, 98, 135, 144, 153; California Volunteer Infantry 94; claim clubs 87; colonial ranger 138; Gonzales-Seguin Rangers 5, 28–30, 169; Illinois militia 153; Missouri Militia 32, 74; Montgomery County Militia 154; Mormon militia 11; New Jersey militia 116; Oregon Rangers 122; quartermaster 42, 55, 60, 111; Tennessee

militia 144; volunteer rangers 63, 132
Miller, James 118
Miller, Joaquin 9, 122
Miller, Lafayette **117–118**
Miller, Mary Foote **117–118**
Miller, Thomas Jefferson 118
Millett, Eugene Bartlet 107
milling 93–95, 100, 121, 133, 137, 142–143, 158, 165; corn 17, 92, 114; cotton 41; flour 27, 37–38, 85, 105, 109, 118, 122, 133, 135, 142, 152, 157, 170; grist 27, 92, 137, 143; lumber 17, 122; ore 46; Rock Island Flour Mill 111; stamping 70; wheat 17, 92; wood 91
mining 3, 4, 25, 53, 54, 57, 59, 69, 73–74, 143, 145; accident 96; black miners 163; borax 5, 38, 39, 171; coal 8, 11, 117; copper 60, 62, 70; equipment 56, 59, 155; Eureka Copper Mining Company 60; galena 145–146; gold 33, 46, 62, 73, 101, 106, 156; Hamilton Mining Company 69, 70; Homestake Mine 129; JRM Mining 113; lead 61, 62, 135; Little Pittsburg Mine 156; Lost Goller Mine 63, 64; Lost Gunsight lead-silver mine 61; Matchless Mine 156; Natoma Water and Mining Company 59; quartz 1, 5, 101, 129, 145–146; raids 75; Simpson Mine 118; Stockton Mining 79; strike 46, 156; supplies 85; tellurium 107; timbers 73; Travis Placer Mining Company 113; Vulture Mining Company 63; *see also* gold; silver
Minnesota 1, 4, 5, 19–22, 54–57, 69, 86, 90, 95, 150–152, 158–159, 169, 170, 171; Madison 86; Minneapolis 4, 20, 69, 96, 129; Minnesota Massacre 90; Minnesota Soldiers' Home 57; St. Cloud 56; St. Paul 8, 169; statehood 96; survey 54
Minnetaree 32
Minto, John 27
Miranda, Apolinario 24
miscegenation 27, 107
missionaries 1, 3, 4–5, 8, 9, 10, 13–16, 33, 42–44, 47–49, 52, 53, 72, 76–77, 85, 98, 105, 107–109, 111, 119–120, 122, 137, 169; evangelism 1, 9, 13, 14, 47, 66, 68, 72, 81, 85, 96, 108–109; Goodwater Mission 108; Kamiah Mission Church 109; Ladies' Foreign Mission Society 108; medical missionaries 35–36, 40–41; Mission Dolores 137; Mormon 164–168; ordination 109; Presbyterian mission 153; San Rafael Mission 137; Santa Clara Mission de Asis 79;

Woman's Occidental Board of Foreign Missions 43–44, 170
Mississippi 59, 61, 86, 103, 161, 163, 166
Mississippi River 3, 20, 30, 32, 33, 34, 54, 69, 98, 105, 108, 110, 130, 151, 152–153, 158, 166, 170; Mississippi Delta 17
Missouri 10, 12, 17, 22, 28, 30, 31, 36–38, 83–84, 86, 92, 98, 100–102, 106, 112, 117, 126, 133, 142, 146, 147, 151, 157, 163, 165, 170; Independence 36, 99, 122, 135, 161; Kansas City 105; St. Joseph 78, 90; *see also* St. Louis
Missouri Gazette 30
Missouri Indians 119
Missouri Valley Horticultural Society 93
Mitchell, Eliza Krosnick-Vandenberg 1, **118–119**
Mitchell, J. Ann Floyd 118
Mitchell, James Comly 3, **118–119**
Miwok 24, 49, 103, 137, 163
Moczygemba, Leopold 3, **119–120**
Mojave Desert 34, 39, 61, 62, 63, 70
Molokai leper colony 3, 40–41
Monk, Anna Smith 121
Monk, Hank 4, **120–122**
Montana State Press Association 59
Montana Territory 19, 31, 44, 54, 55–57, 67, 69, 89, 90, 113, 129, 157; Bannock 5, 89, 157; Helena 5, 113, 157
Monteith, Charles Edgar **107–109**
Moore, Mary Carr 35
Moore, Peter 107
Moore, Seymour Treadwell **49–51**, 50
Morgan, Charles P. 129
Morgan's Raiders 67
Morley, Cordelia Calista 165
Mormons 4, 5, 51, *83*, 105, 127, 164–168, 169, 171; glossolalia 164; Mormon Battalion 165, 166; Mormon Relief Society 168; Mormon Trail 38, 167; Mormon War 165; Nauvoo Legion 157; pilgrimage 78; Winter Quarters 118–119, 166–167; *see also* Danites
morphine 32, 47
Morrill Anti-Bigamy Act 167–168
Morrison, John L. **122–123**
Morrison, Robert Wilson 27
Morton, Phebe 166
Moses, Benton 115
Moses, Chief 68
Mount Rushmore 130
Mount Vernon Ladies Association 33
mountain men 1, 10, 131, 36, 51, 93–95, 103–104, 160–163
Mowry, Sylvester 132

Muckleshoot 110
mules 12, 22, 30, 33, 37, 39, 50, 62, 99, 130, 134, 135, 136, 146, 148, 149, 157, 158, 136, 146, 148, 149, 163; dealer 157; mule fiddle 94; mule teams 39–40, 62; theft 11, 29
Munger, Asahel 98
Murphy, John Marion 136
museum 12, 28, 33, 47, 58, 94, 95, 102
musher 101–102, 116
music 1, 3, 106–107, 116–117, 126, 134; cello 164; "Dear Prairie Home" 88; fiddle 36, 94, 116; "The Hank Monk Schottische" 122; *hole hole bushi* 141; hymns 1, 14, 76–77, 108; "The Independent Broom" 88; "Listen to the Mocking Bird" 140; Mormon Temple Choir 164; Nauvoo Legion Band 165; organ 82; piano 160; plainsong 14; singing schools 2, 14; *see also* opera; "The Streets of Laredo"
"My Advice to the Japanese Immigrant Laborers by the Feared, 1893" 72
My Early Years 54

Na Himeni Hawaii 14
Nangatl 94
Narcissa: Or the Cost of Empire 35
Narrative of My Captivity Among the Sioux Indians 91
Nass 8
Nataqua 100
National American Woman Suffrage Association 35
National Farmers' Alliance 1, 87–88, 171
National Woman Suffrage Association 75
Navajo 66, 162
Neal, Wesley 4, 101
Nebraska Farmers' Alliance 86–89
Nebraska Land and Feeding Company 88
Nebraska Territory 1, 3, 86, 105, 107, 110, 114, 118, 126, 143, 146–147, 155; First Territorial Council 119; Florence 119; Grand Island 87; Omaha 88, 146, 167; statehood 34, 119
Nelson, Mary Eliza 166
Nereo 137
neuralgia 87
Nevada Territory 2, 4, 34, 39, 51, 99, 100, 103, 122, 123, 135, 160, 163, 167; Carson City 121; statehood 34, 121
New England Emigrant Aid Company 74, 155
New Hampshire 102, 127
New Jersey 50, 76, 91, 113, 117
New Mexico Territory 3, 4, 5, 11, 33, 47–49, 50, 65, 66, 67, 104, 124, 157, 161–162, 167; Santa Fé 12, 29, 36, 47, 48, 50, 61, 61, 157, 162; territorial secretary 75

New Orleans, Battle of 26
New York 4, 14, 18, 22, 34, 36, 40–42, 44, 49, 50–57, 59, 60, 67, 76, 78, 80, 89, 94, 96, 97, 98, 115, 117, 118, 120, 121, 123, 124, 151, 157, 159, 164, 165
New Zealanders 5, 44
newspapers 2, 3, 35, 43, 70–73; *Alta California* 106; *The Asmonian* 59; *The British Colonist* 60; censorship 75; *Chicago Tribune* 103; *Coso Mining News* 62; *Daily Alta California* 59–60; *Daily Courier* 54; *De Hollander* 17; *Denver Republican* 26; *Detroit Free Press* 145; *Edmunds County Weekly News* 129; *Florence Courier* 119; *Folsom Telegraph* 2, 59; *Frank Leslie's Illustrated Newspaper* 97; *Globe-Democrat* 149; *Harper's Weekly* 39, 71; *Helena Herald* 5, 56–57; *Indianapolis Journal* 113; Japanese-American press 77; *Kansas City Times* 149; *Kona Hankyo* 72; *Los Angeles Star* 63, 106; *Milwaukee Sentinel and Gazette* 55, 99; *National Atlas and Tuesday Morning Mail* 32; *National Era* 74; *New York Herald* 99, 126; *New York Times* 56, 126; *New York Tribune* 121, 145; *Oklahoma War Chief* 91; *Prairie Home* 88; *Rocky Mountain News* 156, 162; *Roscoe Herald* 129; *Sacramento Placer Times* 163; *San Francisco Daily Herald and Mirror* 51; *Sankarin Maine* 96; *Santa Fe Republican* 75; *Semi-Weekly Southern News* 63; *South Dakota Tribune* 129; *Southern Mercury* 88; *Southern Vineyard* 106; *Spokane Falls Review* 68; *Townsend Tranchant* 56; *Virginia Gazette* 152; *The Western Outlook* 164; *The Western World* 152
Nez Percé 1, 4, 8, 35, 68, 84, 108–109
Nez Percé War 108
The Nez Percés Since Lewis and Clark 109
The Nez Percés Since Spalding 109
Niebur, Henry H. 94
Niemi-Johnson, Maria 95–96
Niemi-Johnson, Matti 95
Nisqually 8, 28, 84, 110, 170
Nisqually, Lewis 27
Nix, Evett Dumas 45
Nobles, William Henry 54–55, 100
Nocona, Peta 65
Nooksack 85
Norris, Andrew 144

North Carolina 28, 30, 32, 54, 104, 109, 144, 147, 161
North Dakota 4, 18–19, 21, 55, 56, 130, 169, 170, 171; statehood 57; *see also* Red River Valley
Northern Overland Expedition for the Protection of Emigrants 21, 55, 170
Northwest Territory 35
Norwegians 18, 95–96, 158–159
No Time on My Hands 146–147
nursing 4, 22–25, 26–28, 40–41, 67, 79, 80, 81, 108, 115, 134, 165, 168

Oahu 14, 15–16, 40, 141, 171
Oakes, Daniel Chessman 11
Odd Fellows 19
O'Fallon, John 30
O'Farrell, John Andrew 123–124
O'Farrell, Mary Ann Chapman Lambert 123–124
O'Farrell, Mary Ann Lambert 123
Ohio 12, 35, 50, 56, 67, 68, 78, 80, 82, 88, 92, 106–108, 113, 116, 133, 140, 146, 165; Cincinnati 68, 83, 88; Columbus 94; Kirtland 164–165
Ohlone 24
Ohtani, Kozui 76
Ohtani, Myonyo 76
Ojibwa 17, 19, 20, 21, 89, 153, 170; Pembina Ojibwa 19, 21; Red Lake Ojibwa 21
Okabe, Jiro 72
Okanaga 8, 68
Okanogan 145
Oklahoma 4, 35, 44–45, 113, 146, 149, 150; Indian Territory 57, 65, 92, 106–107, 108, 112, 146, 149–140, 154; land run 1, 4, 45, 149–*150*; McAlester State Prison 45; Oklahoma Humane Society 45; statehood 45
Old Crossing Treaty 2, 21
Old Spanish Trail 36, 162
Omaha Indians 119
Omohundro, Josephine Antonia Morlacchi 3, **124–126**, *125*
Omohundro, Orville 125
Omohundro, Texas Jack 4, **124–126**, *125*
Omohundro, Texas Jack, Jr. 125
open range 2, 67, 88, 107; range war 126
opera 26, 35, 58, 85–86; French's Opera House 140; Goodnight's Opera House 66; Tabor Grand Opera House 126, 156
opium 71, 72
orchards 2, 8, 33, 39, 41, 58, 66, 69, 70, 80, 116–117, 137, 139–140, 145–146; *see also* fruit; vineyards
Oregon Donation Land Act 83
Oregon Indian wars 9
Oregon Territory 4, 8, 10, 33, 36, 51, 55, 79, 84, 93–94, 103, 110, *114*–116, 122–123, 143, 169, 170; The Dalles 4, 9, 27, 143; Eugene 110; Portland 8, 27, 83, 108, 111, 114, 115, 122, 123, 159; provisional government 169; Salem 122–123; statehood 28, 84; U.S. claims 143
Oregon Trail 1, 3, 4, 9, 11, 27, 31, 32, 69, 74, 78–79, 92, 98, 99, 109–111, 113, 115, 123–124, 134–136, 142–143, 152, 159, 169, 171
The Oregon Trail 89
Oregon Trail Memorial Association 115–116
Oregon Treaty 27
orphans 3, 22–24, 26, 30, 41, 48, 86, 127–128, 134, 136, 167
Osage 44, 106, 112, 149
Osborne, Caroline Meeker 115
Otoe 8, 119
Ottawa, Chief 89, 170
Ouilmette, Antoine Louis **133**
Our Lady of Guadalupe 48
Oury, William Sanders 132
Overland Trail 84, 89, 112, 117, 152, 170
Owen, Augustine 154
Owen, Mary 154
oxen 19, 20, 62, 69, 75, 84, 100, 101, 105, 109–110, 114, 115, 117, 130, 135, 137, 142, 148, 155, 157, 163; meat 62
Ozawa, Arthur Kenzaburo 142
Ozawa, Itoko 142
Ozawa, Kintaro **140–142**
Ozawa, Tomi **140–142**
Ozawa, Yotaro 142

Pacific Mail 58, 94, 127
Pacific Northeast 3, 7–10, 49, 54, 57, 84–85
Pacific Wagon Road 100
pacifism 74
Padilla, Juan de 48, 49, 169
The Padre of Isleta 49
Page, John Hempstead 130–131, 132
Page, Larcena Ann Pennington 13, **130–133**, *131*, 170
Page, Mary Ann 132
Paiute 5, 34, 51, 100, 124, 135, 161; Northern Paiute 9, 100
Paiute-Bannock War 160
Palmer, Albert 77
Palmer, Joel 99, 123
Palo Duro–Dodge City Trail 67
Panama 33, 39, 54, 58, 59, 94, 127, 130; Panama Canal 130
Panhandle Stock Association 67
Panic of 1837 32
Panic of 1857 20–21, 25, 32, 119
Panic of 1873 66, 86, 113
Panic of 1893 88, 115, 156
Papago 132
Parker, Cynthia Ann 65, 67
Parker, Quanah 2, 65, 107
Parkhurst, Charley **127**–*128*
Parkman, Francis 89
Parmley, Eliza Melissa Baker 129
Parmley, Joseph William Lincoln **128–130**, 171
Parson, Elsie Clews 49
Partridge, Emily Dow 166
Patterson, Dollie 85
Patterson, James Alexander 85
Patterson, Lizzie 4, 85
Patterson, Nellie 85
Paulina, Chief 9
Pawnee 52, 56, 84, 86, 112, 119, 126, 146, 149, 161
peat 69
Pellessier, Joseph 160
Pelletier, Eulalie 133
Pelletier, Jean Baptiste 133
Pelletier, Suzanne Point du Sable 133
pemmican 19
Pend d'Oreille 8
Pennington, Caroline 132
Pennington, Elias Green 5, **130–133**, *131*
Pennington, Jack 131–133
Pennington, James **130–133**, *131*
Pennington, Jim 131
Pennington, Julia Ann Hood 130
Pennington, Will 132
Pennsylvania 5, 44, 48, 54, 67, 93, 94, 116, 118, 123, 138, 159; Philadelphia 4, 16, 22, 26, 30, 33, 54, 72, 73, 91, 98, 159
Peoria Company 52
Percival, John "Mad Jack" 15
petroglyphs 113
petroleum 4, 45, 70; Bell Petroleum Oil Company 13; Union Oil 4
Pettygrove, Francis William 122
pharmacists 59, 60, 70, 82, 119
Phelps, Benjamin 63
Philadelphian Society 13
photography 2, 3, 48, 56, 60, 89, 90, 94, 102, 117; Franklin Premier Photographic Gallery 60
Pierce, Margaret 166
Pierce, Mary 166
Pierce, Franklin 57, 63, 155
Pierre's Hole, Battle of 31
pigs 14, 20, 37, 81, 91, 95, 96, 99, 117, 129, 134, 140, 145; bacon 116, 130, 155; breeding 134; pork 14, 29, 68, 73, 75, 87, 91, 133, 157; sausage 73; smoked meat 133
Pike's Peak 18, 25, 74, 123, 170
Pima Indians 167
Pinnacle Jake 147
Pioneer Company 14
Pioneer Girl: Growing Up on the Prairie 147
Pioneer Ladies Aid Society 156
A Pioneer's Search for an Ideal Home 86

pirogue 116
Pit River Indians 99
plantations 5, 25, 26, 38, 72, 76–77, 141, 142, 144, 152, 154, 160, 161, 163; Lihue Plantation 142; pineapple *141*; Willow Shade Plantation 143–144
plowing 18, 63, 80, 87, 116, 146
pneumonia 4, 25, 33, 58, 104, 115, 116, 122, 126, 132, 137, 146; typhoid pneumonia 16, 79
poets 1, 34, 35, 62
Point, Nicholas 36
Point du Sable, Jean Baptiste, Jr. 133
Point du Sable, Jean Baptiste, Sr. 3, **133**, 171
Point du Sable, Catherine 133
poison 33, 45, 56, 132
police 1–2, 14, 39, 43, 57, 63, 68, 126, 142, 162
polio 81
Polish 3, 5, 58, 59, 60, 119–120, 134–136
Polish Roman Catholic Union 120
politics 3, 32, 59, 63, 69, 76, 84, 86–89, 108–109, 129, 130, 140, 149, 151, 160, 167; Workingmen's Party 43, 69; *see also* law
polygamy 15, 68, *83*, 90, 108, 164–168
Ponca 119, 146
Pony Express 59, 157
portage 3, 52, 133
Porter, Cynthia 166
Posey, Alexander 153
Post Oak Woods, Battle of 154
post office 3, 12, 17, 18–19, 57, 73, 78, 81, 94, 101, 109, 112, 115, 119, 134, 152, 155, 156; robbery 45; *see also* mail
potlatch 145
Potowatomi 5, 45, 133, 149
Potvin, Joseph 19
Poulin, Andrew Z. 124
poultry 24, 53, 84, 125, 127, 133, 140, 146; Brahma hens 87; chickens 79, 87, 95, 99; eggs 24, 27, 79, 81, 87, 114, 115, 117, 157; prairie fowl 67; turkeys 27
The Power of Destiny 62
Powhatan 124
Pratt, George Lincoln 33
Pratt, Louisa Merrill **33–36**
Pratt, Robert Henry **33–36**
Pratt, Sarah 33–34
Pratt, William Augustus 33
Presbyterian Board of Foreign Missions 108
Presbyterian Chinese Mission Home 1, 43–44, 171
Presbyterians 12, 35–36, 42–44, 82, 84, 86, 107–109, 111, 122–123, 150, 152–153, 164
printers 3, 5, 14, 15, 53, 57, 106, 141, 145–146; printing press 56, 88, 113

prison 30, 43, 45, 52–53, 92, 108, 133, 167–168; Atchafalaya, Louisiana 92; Folsom 59; parole 130; rehabilitation 52; San Quentin 54; *see also* jail
prospecting 4, 9, 11, 18, 22, 25, 51, 55, 55, 61–64, 68, 70, 75, *78*, 79, 83, 84–85, 100, 102, 103, 105, 116, 123, 145, 151, 155–158; *see also* '49ers
prostitution 1, 15, 22–24, 42–44, 46–47, 72, 97, 107, 171
Prussians 63, 119, 120, 135–136, 144
publishing 17, 43, 44, 48, 54, 57, 60, 76, 77, 83, 88, 89, 91, 102, 104–106, 109, 126, 149
Pueblo Massacre 162
pueblos 3, 47–49; Isleta Pueblo *48*
Puget Sound War 84, 110, 114–115
Puritanism 15, 105
Puyallup 28, 170

Quakers 26, 52, 104, 116–117
Quantrill, William Clarke 111
quarrying 59, 81, 137, 155
quicksand 1, 62
quilting 1, 4, 5, 75, 147–148
Quiros, Mercedes Sais 131, 132
Quivera 48

racetrack 32
racism 4, 5, 27–28, 34, 39, 72, 84, 112, 137, 142–144, 163–164, 171; *see also* abolitionists; slavery
Raiche, Peter 19
railroad 5, 11, 20, 21, 33–36, 58, 108, 115, 116, 119, 127, 129, 170; Alaska Central Railway 2, 101, 171; Atchison, Topeka and Santa Fe Railway 101, 163; Atlantic and Pacific Railroad Committee 50–51; Burlington and Missouri Railroad 86, 87, 146; Cairo & St. Louis 86; California Southern Railroad 42; Carson and Colorado Railway 51; Chicago, Milwaukee, and St. Paul rail line 129, 159; Choctaw, Oklahoma and Gulf Railroad 45; Cincinnati Southern Railroad 68; Colorado & Southern Railroad 117; Death Valley Railroad 39; Fort Wayne & Platte River Air Line Railroad 92; Great Northern Railroad 54; Gulf and Inter-State Railway 89, 171; Gulf, Colorado and Santa Fe Railroad 139; Kansas Central Railroad 81; Kansas Pacific Railway 106, 112; Northern Pacific Railroad 21, 86, 170; protests 87–88; Pullman Palace Car Company 164; repair 64; robbery 45; Rock Island Railroad 45; Sacramento Valley Railroad 58, 59; Saint Paul and Pacific Railroad 96; San Diego & Gila Pacific and Atlantic Railroad 60; Sonoma and Marin Railroad 39; Southern Pacific Railroad 12, 34; stockyards 107; strikes 39; Tonopah and Tidewater Railroad 39; Topeka & Southwestern Railroad 113; Virginia & Truckee Railroad 34, 121; Western Pacific Railroad 51; Wichita & Southwestern Railroad 113; *see also* Central Pacific; Transcontinental; Union Pacific

Ramsted, Hannah Rebecca Wahl 159
Ramsted, Hans 159
ranchers 9, 10, 12–13, 18–19, 53, 61–62, 64–67, 79, 98–100, 103–104, 126, 138–139, 160; El Rancho la Libertad 53; Palomares Rancho 105; Rancho Bosquejo 99; Rancho Catacula 37; Rancho Corte Madera del Presidio 137; Rancho la Purísima Concepción 24; Rancho Laguna de Santos Calle 36; Rancho Rio de los Americanos 58–59; Rancho San Antonio 12; Rancho Sausalito 137; San Francisquito Ranch 63; Zayante rancho 98
Randall, William 131
Rangers and Pioneers of Texas 149
Rasor, Carl 134
Rasor, John Henry **134**
Rasor, Lucy 134
Rasor, Mary Ellen Rachford **134**
rats 107; field mice 135
Ravel, Chief 112
Reading, Pearson Barton 5, 93–95, 169
Reading, Piers 5
realty 3, 13, 19, 25, 60, 63, 66, 91, 111, 112–113, 118, 123, 134, 149, 156; claim jumping 127; Florence Land Company 119; Parmley Western Land and Abstract Office 129; realty fraud 150; Wichita Town and Land Company 112
"Reasons for the Necessity of Evangelists in Every Plantation" 72
recruiters 1, 3, 16–18, 26, 28–29, 36, 42–44, 53–54, 55, 75, 108, 115, 122, 140–142, 158, 170, 171
Red Bear, Chief 19
Red Cloud, Chief *31*, 33, 57, 90, 91
Red River trading colony 19
Red River Trail 20
Red River Valley 8, 18, 19–22, 169, 170
Red Wolf 84
Reed, Emaline Cobb 138–139
Reed, Hilaria Sánchez 137–138
Reed, Hilarita 137
Reed, James Frazier, Jr. **134–136**
Reed, James Frazier, Sr. 134–136
Reed, James Michael 139

Index

Reed, Jefferson 138
Reed, John Joseph 137
Reed, John Thomas **136–138**
Reed, Margret Wilson Keyes Backenstoe **134–136**
Reed, Maria Inez "Matilda" 137
Reed, Martha Burnett **138–139**
Reed, Martha Jane "Patty" 136
Reed, Michael **138–139**
Reed, Thomas Keyes 136
Reed, Virginia Elizabeth 136
Reed, Volney Erskine Howard 139
Reed, William Stancell *139*
Reed, William Whitaker **138–139**
Reed, Wilson 138
Reich, George Adolph **59–62**
Reid, Ann 132
Reminiscences of Alexander Toponce 158
A Residence of Twenty-One Years in the Sandwich Islands 16
resorts 32, 39, 70
Rhymes of the Range and Trail 107
Rice, Coralinn Barlow **139–140**
Rice, James Stephen **139–140**
Rice, James Willis 140
Richards, Bartlett 88
Richards, Rhoda 165, 166
Richards, William 167
roads 1, 20, 25, 27, 34, 53, 55, 60, 91–93, 105, 110, 115, 116, 127, 129–130, 132, 134, 149, 155, 157–158; Big Trees toll road 51; commission 92; corduroy roads 112; Fort Ridgely and South Pass wagon road 54–55; legislation 55; Pacific Wagon Road 100; repair 63; Seward Highway 102; Sonora Emigrant Road 51; Sonora Pass Wagon Road 103; toll 162–163
Robbins, Ezekiel Wright **150–152**
Robertson, Sterling Clack 138
Robertson, William 39
Robidoux, Antoine **77–79**
Rockwood, Ellen 166
Rocky Mountain rendezvous 169
Rocky Mountains 11, 30, 35–36, 78, 126, 153, 155, 161, 163, 167
rodeos 107, 125, 160
Rogue River Indian Wars 9, 69
Rollins, Mary Elizabeth 165, 166
Roop, Isaac Newton 100
Roosevelt, Franklin D. 102
Roosevelt, Theodore 104, 150
roping 10, 65, 124–126
Rosebud, Battle of the 126
Ross, Clarissa 166
Rotten Belly, Chief 32
Rottscheff, Alexander 98
Rovainen, Antti 95–96
Rovainen, Maria Matlena Helppi 95–96
Russell, Osborne 122
Russians 8, 49, 76, 98, 100, 126, 137, 158–159

rustling 11, 29, 34, 62, 65, 67, 87, 106, 111, 124, 131, 135, 137–138, 148, 160

Sac 119
The Saga of "Auntie" Stone and Her Cabin 152
sailing 8, 14, 15, 16–17, 30, 33, 40, 53, 57, 58, 60, 73, 79, 95, 96, 97, 98, 100, 123, 127, 133, 136, 137, 157; clipper ships 38, 127; shipwreck 16–17, 51
St. Clair, Arthur 124
St. Louis 1, 10, 17, 25, 30, 32, 33, 38, 55, 62, 83, 86–87, 92, 98, 108, 113, 119, 126, 139, 146, 151, 155, *161*; St. Louis Insurance Company 32; St. Louis University 38
St. Vrain, Ceran 161
Sakuma, Jkatsuna 142
Sakuma, Tsuna Omoto 142
Sakuma, Yonekichi **140–142**
Salado Creek, Battle of 30
Salazar, José 63
saloons 1, 4, 5, 17, 18, 58, 94, 119, 158, 167; Centennial Saloon 62
salt 15, 20, 28, 39, 51, 104, 137, 170; salt beef 14, 137; salt fish 141; salt pork 14; salt salmon 8
Salt Lake City 1, 3, 11, 34, 38, 55, 105, 124, 151, 152, 157, 162, 164–168
Sampson, Lucy 53
Sampson, Palmer 150
Sanchez, Francisco 79
Sanders, Oregon 164
Sanford, Fred **86–89**
Sanford, James Manley **86–89**
Sanford, Jennie Taylor 86, 87
Sanford, Johnny 87
Sanford, Joseph W. 86
San Francisco 1–2, 4, 12, 24, 33, 34–35, 38–40, 42, 43, *50*, 51, 53, 54, 57–59, 60–61, 63, 72, 94, 96–98, 102, 105, 106, 108, 115, 121, 136–138, 146, 170, 171; Alcatraz Island 58; Barbary Coast 97; Black Point 58; Chinatown 3, 42–44, *71*; Clay Street Wharf 59; Industrial Fair 97; Long Wharf 59; Metropolitan Theatre 58; Presidio 5, 24–25, 58, 137, 169; Sailor's Home 97–98; San Francisco Society of Regulators 38; Sepulveda Landing 63; Yerba Buena Cove 57
San Jacinto, Battle of 138, 145
San Pasqual, Battle of 61, 62
Sanpoil 68
Santa Anna 22, 29, 138, 148
Santa Clara, Battle of 135
Santa Fé Magazine 48–49
Santa Fé Trail *74*–75, 132
Santee, Jennie Frances Blodgett Cowles **41–42**

Satanta, Chief 112, 113
Sauk 91, 112, 149, 153, 169, 169
sawmills 17, 18, 27, 32, 56, 68, 85, 92, 98, 99, 124, 137, 143, 157; equipment 99; sawyers 3, 93–95
scarlet fever 53
schools 3, 9, 15, 17, 19, 42, 70, 72–73, 79, 82, 87, 88, 91–92, 96, 112, 115, 116, 118, 151, 153, 162, 164, 168; Augustana College 158; bunkhouse 66; Case Western College 140; Dakota Wesleyan University 129; Fairfield Female Seminary 108; Fairfield University 108; Fort Lapwai Industrial School 109; Goodnight Academy 66; Goodnight College 67; Hebrew Free School 60; homeschooling 33, 80, 105, 106, 111, 130; Iowa College 111; Jackson Military High School 103; Kamiah Valley Day School 108; Kansas Academy of Science 113; Kansas University 82; Lawrence College 129; Lindenwood College for Women 108; literacy 19, 24, 64, 93–95, 140; Mission Bottom 122; Mrs. Adam Bland's Girls' Academy 106; night school 72; North Kona Japanese Language School 72; Northwest Normal School 86; Notre Dame Convent 160; Occidental College 12, 171; Oregon Institute 122; Portland Convent School 145; Rockford Female Seminary 86; Sacred Heart Academy 160; St. Joseph's School 120; St. Vincent's Academy 160; school board 93, 117; segregation 164; singing schools 80; Sisters of Loretto Academy 48; South School 111; Steubenville Female Seminary 108; superintendent 111; temple 76, 129; tutoring 28, 34; University of Arizona 61; University of California at Berkeley 111; University of Colorado 118; University of Washington 111; Ursuline school 123, 140; Vancouver Island Board of Education 61; Wellsville Institute 108; Western College 117, 171; Western Reserve College 78; Western Washington University 82–86; *see also* Carlisle Indian School
Scientific American 111
Scots 5, 8, 10, 18, 19, 28, 30, 33, 38, 42, 44, 54, 61, 66, 73, 86, 103, 105, 108, 112, 133, 134, 147–149, 152, 160–163, 169; Scots Presbyterians 12, 30, 107–109, 122–123
Scott, Sarah 165
Scott, William Fisher 133
scouting 1, 3, 8, 9, 10, 11, 12, 19–22,

27, 30, 42, 51, 54–57, 65, 67, 78, 113, 124–126, 130, 132, 144, 147, 148, 149, 161, 162
The Scouts of the Prairie 126
Scudder, Jehu 122
scurvy 90, 119
sea captain 118, 136, 143
secessionism 5, 108, 162
Seeds Scattered Broadcast 108
Seen, Liang May 43
segregation 3, 27, 171
Seminole 150; Seminole Wars 36; Second Seminole War 2, 57
Sepúlveda, José Antonio Andrew 140
servants 42–44, 72; domestic 35, 80, 89, 101, 108, 135, 142–143, 147; indenturing 17–18; steward 70; *see also* launderers
Sessions, Sylvia Porter 165
sewing 12, 14, 22–24, 43, 54, 79, 108, 120, 147; banner 52; broadcloth 14, 41–42; dressmaking 96–98; knitting 43, 80, 108; linen 14, 30; linsey-woolsey 91–92; machine 146; millinery 107; moccasins 51; tailor 84; training 85; uniforms 131; *see also* quilting
sexual exploitation 3, 153
Shaw, Stephen William 93
Shawnee 149
Sheek, John Wesley 64
sheep 9, 20, 85, 91, 99, 106, 140, 143, 145, 158, 162–163
Shenandoah, C.S.S. 85
Sheridan, Phil 126
Sherman, William Tecumseh 58, 134
shooting 10, 20, 74, 86, 94, 101, 127, 146, 148, 152, 162, 169; cannon 148; gunmen 112, 156; relay firing 28; sharpshooter 55, 106, 125, 148; *see also* Colt revolver; Smith & Wesson revolver; Spencer rifle; Winchester rifle
Shoshone 5, 8, 11, 30, 32, 34, 36, 100, 109; Bannock-Shoshone 124; Eastern Shoshone 31
Sibley, Henry Hastings 19, 20
Sierra Nevada 1, 4, 11, 34, 36, *37*, 50, 51, 57, 62, 100, 103, 105, 121, 135, 136, 157, 169, 170
silkworms 70
Sill, Daniel 99
silver 27, 34, 39, 49, 51, 59, 60, 61, 67, 100, 101, 117, 121, 132, 155, 159, 160; boom 62, 66; Cumberland Mine 73; Darwin silver mines 62; Mineral Fork Mining and Silver Company 61; Ontario Silver Mine 124; silversmith 59; theft 148
Silver Panic of 1893 46
Simmons, Christopher Columbus 143
Simmons, Elizabeth Kindred 27, **142–143**

Simmons, Michael Troutman 27, **142–143**, 169
Sinclair, Patrick 133
Sinkiuse-Columbia 68
Sinkyone 94
Sioux 1, 5, 8, 10, 11, 18–20, *31*, 32, 33, 69, 78–79, 87, 107, 111, 119, 122, 126, 157, 161, 170; Brule 91; Dakota Sioux 95; Hunkpapa 56, 68–69, 90; Lakota 56, 151; Oglala 57, 89–91, 170; Oglala Lakota 11; Santee 90, 146; Sisseton Sioux 21, 55, 170; Yankton 153
Sitting Bull 2, *56*, 90, 130
Skolaskin, Chief 68
Skoqualamooch 84
slavery 2, 5, 25–26, 54, 88, 89, 154, 155, 163–164, 168; dealer 157; freed slaves 32, 133, 149; Indians 132; runaways 24; *see also* abolitionists
Slusher 107
smallpox 4, 11, 24, 28, 52, 100, 109, 110, 111, 132, 141
Smeathers, Archibald Jacob 144
Smeathers, Gracie Treat Berry 144
Smeathers, John Bate 144
Smeathers, Mary "Molly" 144
Smeathers, Mary Polly **143–145**
Smeathers, William **143–145**
smelting 46, 62, 101
Smith, Elvine Savage 159
Smith, Emma Hale 165
Smith, Francis Marion 39
Smith, George 2, 75
Smith, Hiram Francis **145–146**, 164, *166*, 170
Smith, James 136
Smith, Jedediah Strong 30, 171
Smith, John 167
Smith, Joseph, Jr. 1, 4, **164–168**, *166*, 169
Smith, Lot 11
Smith, Mary Manuel 145
Smith, Nancy S. 146
Smith, Samuel B. 159
Smith & Wesson revolver 126
Smithers, John Bate 144
Smithsonian Institution 58, 104, 108, 109
Snake Indians 11, 110
Snake War 9
snakes 60, 146, 147, 148
Snively, Susanne 166
Snow, Eliza Roxcy 4, **164–168**
Snow, Melissa 165
Snyder, Albert Benton 147
Snyder, Grace Bell McCance 4, **146–147**
Snyder, John 135
soap 1, 28, 31, 39, 105
Society for the Prevention of Cruelty to Children 43–44, 171
Society of Arizona Pioneers 133
Society of California Pioneers 2, 38, 39, 58

Society of Colorado Pioneers 26
sod 1, 3, 18, 44, 55, 80–81, 87, 95, 146, 147
Sod & Stubble 82
Sons of the American Revolution 113
sorcery 108
Sothern, Alfred Richard 74
Sothern, Mary Elizabeth **73–74**
Sousa, John Philip 122
South Carolina 134, 144, 163
South Dakota 11, 89, 109, 121, 129–130, 146; Deadwood 126, 129; statehood 129, 159
Southern Emigrant Trail 62
Sowell, Andrew Jackson **147–149**
Sowell, Asa 148
Sowell, John Newton, Jr. **147–148**
Sowell, John Newton, Sr. **147–149**
Sowell, Lucinda Smith Turner 148
Sowell, Rachel Carpenter **147–149**
Sowell, William A. 148
Spanish 42, 49, 52, 53, 62, 137
Spanish land grants 37, 99, 137
Sparks, Anna Maria 58–59
Sparks, William Crain 138
Speed, Horace **149–***150*, 171
Spencer rifle 21
Spengler, Adolph 17
Spirit of the Time 126
Spokane Indians 68
Spotted Tail, Chief 91, 126
spy 67, 125, 144
squatters 58, 76, 85, 100, 131, 137–138, 145, 153, 160
stagecoaches 3, 4, 5, 25, 26, 42, 60, 63, 120–122, 126–*128*, 149, 157–158; Adams & Company 103; California and Atlantic Express 103; California & Oregon Stage Line 34; California Stage Company 121, 127; Carson Valley Express 121; Denver and Santa Fe Stage and Express Line 163; Holladay Overland Mail & Express; James M. Benton Stage Line 121; Leavitt Station 103; Overland Stage 127–128; Pioneer Stage Company 121, 127; robbery 45, 73, 121, 124, 127; Rock Creek station 117; Spearfish-Deadwood stage line 121; stations 17, 45, 70, 103, 106, 163; Wells Fargo 34; *see also* Butterfield Overland Stage; mail
Stanford, Leland 34
Stark, Josephus 55
Stark, Julian Fisk 55
Stark, Mary Jane Abbott 55
steamers 8, 9, 10, 17, 18, 39, 40, 50, 52, 54, 60, 69, 73, 83, 84, 85, 95, 99, 101, 105, 108, 110, 114, 115, 119, 121, 145, 164–165, 170; Allen Steamship Company 159; burial at sea 141; explosion 51; mail 53; North Atlantic & Gulf

Steamship Company 45; Pacific Mail 58, 127; packet 32; paddlewheel 22; racing 51; sidewheeler 8, 32, 33, 94
Steel, George 56
Steenstra, Joannes 17
Stellingwerf, Frouke 17–18
Stiles, Sarah 165
Stockton, Robert Field 99
Stoddard, Thomas Robert 100
Stone, Elizabeth Hickok Robbins **150–152**
Stone, George 151
Stone, Lewis **150–152**
Stone, Mahalia 151
storytelling 3, 93–95, 103–104, 107, 122, 136
Stratton, Elizabeth Parke Keays 4, 15
Stratton, Harris 152
Street, Eliza Posey **152–154**
Street, Joseph Montfort **152–154**
"The Streets of Laredo" 107, 171
stroke 61, 108, 118, 137, 153
Stroud, Appleton Mandred 154
Stroud, Beden **154–155**
Stroud, Ethan Allen 4, **154–155**
Stroud, Logan 154
Stroud, Sampson Malvery 154
Sublette, John C. 118
Sublette, William Lewis 5, **30–33**
suffrage, woman's 3, 34, 35, 51–54, 74, 75, 85, 87, 114, 116, 151, 168
sugar 5, 11, 14, 20, 27, 28, 38, 41, 55, 75, 77, 81, 89, 109, 112, 127, 140, 142, 157; cane 142; maple sugar 20; molasses 142
Sugarfoot 127
suicide 133
Sullivan, Claude 73
Sully, Alfred 90
Sun Bow, Menachee Mollee 161
surveys 3, 8, 19, 20, 24, 29, 38, 48, 49, 51, 54, 58, 59, 64, 82, 86, 99, 100, 111, 114, 115, 137, 138, 151, 153
survivalists 100, 134
Sutter, John 98–99, 123
Sutter's Fort, California 36, 37, 98, 99, 135, 137
Sutter's Mill 58, *78*, 79, 169
Swedes 18
Swift, Gustavus Franklin 66
Swiss 2, 17, 19, 159–160, 169
Sylvester, Charles 90
synagogues 3, 59, 60

Tabor, Augusta Louise pierce 4, **155–156**
Tabor, Horace Austin Warner **155–156**
Taiping Rebellion 43
tanning 53, 91–92, 98, 113
Tate, Charles Montgomery 85
Tauber, Wolfgang 63, 64

Tawakoni 124, 154
tea 38, 49, 157
teaching 1, 4, 19, 42–44, 72–73, 76–77, 77–79, 82–86, 95–96, 101, 107–109, 118, 125, 131, 147, 151, 167; catechism 15, 77, 96; homeschooling 2, 33, 80
Tehachapi 64
telegraph 5, 17, 167
telephone 70, 102
temperance 2, 76, 86, 97, 117, 118, 151, 168
Ten Bears, Chief 112
Tennessee 10, 26, 28, 34, 55, 65, 66, 92, 95, 103, 112, 125, 130, 138, 144, 147, 152, 161
Texas 3, 4, 22–24, 64–67, 79, 104, 107, 108, 112, 119–120, 124–126, 130–133, 134, 138–139, 143–145, 147–149, 154–155, 170; Declaration of Independence 29, 169; Fort Worth 67, 125, *139*; Independence Convention 29; industry 64–67; Palo Duro 66; panhandle 48, 64, 66, 67, 124; republic 138–139, 147; revolution 138, 148
Texas-Indian Wars 29
Texas Jack in the Black Hills 126
Texas Jack, the Lasso King 126
Texas Rangers 4, 28–30, 64–67, 124–126, 148, 170
thatching 15, 81, 117, 120, 132; grass huts 141
theaters 58, 101–102, 115, 126
Thomas, Heck 45
Thomas, W.W. 44–45
Thornburgh, Thomas Tipton 11
tick fever 107, 112
Tilghman, Bill 45, 107
Tillamook 8
Timbisha 62
Timms, Augustus W. 63
Tiwa 47–49
Tjalsma, Sjoerd 17
Tlingit 49
tobacco 15, 19–20, 25, 31, 38, 55, 112, 127, 156–157, 161, 162
Tomlinson, John J. 63
Tonasket, Joseph 145
Tong, Chien Lee 64
Tong, Hip Yee 43
Tonkawa 124
Toponce, Alexander 3, **156–158**
Toponce, Catherine Ann Beach Cullen 157
Toponce, Chester 156, 157
Toponce, Peter 156, 157
tornado 110
tourism 62, 70, 94, 121, 129–130
town halls 17
trackers 9, 10, 28, 45, 64, 65, 126, 132, 154
trading 7–8, 11, 14, 15, 19, 25, 26, 28, 31, 33, 36, 50, 55, 73–75, 78, 79, 85, 87, 91–93, 100, 102, 105, 109–113, 120, 122, 133, 145–146, 154, 161–162, 170; cattle 68, 110; hides 24, 106, 161; horses 68, 161; hostages 30, 90; kidnap victims 90; meat 143, 162; pelts 101; tobacco 157; *see also* fur trading; Hudson's Bay Trading Company; slavery
The Tragedy of Leschi 115
Transcontinental Railroad 1, 33–36, 50, 88, 103, 115, 118, 157, 160, 170, 171
translators 14, 56, 142, 167
trappers 5, 7–10, 19–22, 26, 36, 78, 93, 95–96, 98, 101, 103–104, 123, 153, 161; birds 111; fish trap 85
The Trapper's Daughter 126
Travels in the Great Western Prairies 52
treason 138, 152, 165, *166*
treaties 1, 2, 11, 19, 21, 32, 100, 143, 154, 170; Oregon Treaty 27; Treaty of Greenville 133; Treaty of Guadalupe Hidalgo 37, 58, 75; Treaty of Medicine Lodge 92–93, 112; Treaty of the Little Arkansas 112; Treaty of the Winnebago War 153
Treaty of Greenville 133
Treaty of Guadalupe Hidalgo 37, 58, 75
Treaty of Medicine Lodge 92–93, 112
Treaty of the Little Arkansas 112
Treaty of the Winnebago War 153
tree planting 27, 42, 47, 84, 87, 93, 113, 118, 137, 145, 168
trolley 140
Tsimshian 8
Tsun, Ah 43
tuberculosis 4, 30, 38, 43, 54, 72, 73, 85, 86, 135
Turner, William Suddarth 148
Twain, Mark 87, 122
Twohig, John 120
typhoid fever 79, 80, 85, 92, 108; malarial typhoid 86

Ulberg, Andreas Olsen 159
Ulberg, Rangnild Bakke 159
Umatilla 109, 143
Umpqua 8
"Uncle Dick" Wootton: The Pioneer Frontiersman of the Rocky Mountain Region 163
Underground Railroad 2, 74, 107, 121, 163
Union Pacific Railroad 1, 26, *35*, 66, 87, 88, 112, 146, 152, 157, 160, 170; land fraud 112
Unitarians 33–36, 155–156; Evangelical 81
U.S. Biological survey 104
U.S. Bureau of Indian Affairs 91
U.S. Christian Commission 108
U.S. Department of the Interior 91

U.S. District Attorney 150
U.S. House Committee on Territories 149
U.S. Internal Revenue 68
U.S. Land Office 44–45, 149
U.S. Mint 106, *125*
U.S. Senate 156
U.S. Treasury 68
Universalists 151
urbanism 5
USO 101
Utah Territory 5, 30, 31, 37, 50–51, 61, 62, 82–83, 106, 108, 126, 167–168, 169, 170; Little Salt Lake 62; Ogden 108, 146, 158, 160, 148, 160; Promontory 34–35, 157; statehood 168; territorial legislature 124; *see also* Salt Lake City
Utah War 57, 167
Ute *10*, 105, 161, 162, 167, 169, 171; Grand River 11; Uintah 11; Yumpak 11
utilitarianism 76

Van Brunt, Theodosia Robbins 152
Van Buren, Martin 153
vegetables 24, 81, 87, 100, 102, 108–109, 110, 116, 133, 145, 147; beans 61, 131, 136, 146, 165; cabbage 115, 132, 146; celery 140; garlic 134; greens 105, 132, 143; onions 106, 115, 134, 146; parsnips 115; peas 143; pepper 162; potato digger 94; potatoes 18, 27, 41, 53, 100, 114, 115, 143, 146; pumpkins 114, 131, 146; rhubarb 110; seeds 132; squash 115, 131; sugar beets 140; tomatoes 152; tubers 136; turnips 115, 146; yeast 114, 147
venereal disease 43, 47; gonorrhea 141
Vermont 13, 86, 111, 121, 129, 155, 164
Veuster, Damien de 41
vigilantism 4, 38–39, 53, 57, 63–64, 73, 111, 112, 124, 150, 158, 170; *see also* lynching
vineyards 33, 34, 39, 58, 62, 69, 70, 93, 99
Virginia 10, 64, 91, 107, 109, 124–126, 130, 135, 138, 142, 143–144, 148, 152, 154, 159, 160–161

Waco Indians 124, 154
Wadsworth, Benjamin Franklin 25
wagon trains 10, 18, 25, 27, 36, *37*, 49–51, 54–57, 62–63, 78–79, 83–84, 86, 89–91, 92, 99, 104–106, 109–111, 117, 122, 123–124, 130, 131, 134–136, 142–143, 151, 158–160, 169, 170; abandoned 62, 105; accidents 78, 110; bribes 90; guarding 161; housing 91, 146, 167; Indian attack 56; photographs 56; recycling 99; repair 110; tolls 11, 34, 51, 116, 145, 163; wagon business 63, 83, 87, 120, 127, 148, *161*, 166
Wahl, James Magnus 4, **158–159**
Wahl, Julia Ulberg **158–159**
Wakara, Chief 105
Wakichi, Kodzu 141
Walker, Joseph Reddeford 36
Walker, Katherine 165
Walker, Lucy 165
Walker's Creek, Battle of 148, 169
Walla Walla Indians 114–115
Wapello, Chief 153, 154
War of 1812 36, 49, 57, 144, 147, 164
Ward, Artemus 122
warehouse 9, 32, 39, 63, 73, 91, 95, 129
Washakie, Chief 11
Washington State College 171
Washington State Historical Society 115
Washington State Pioneer's Association 115
Washington State University 28
Washington Territory 4, 27–28, 67–69, 82–86, 101, 109–111, 116–117, 129, 145–146, 159, 169, 170; legislature 84, 115, 145, 171; Olympia 28, 84, 143, 145, 171; Puget Sound 3, 27–28, 84–85, 110, 114, 116, 123, 128, 142–143; Puyallup 113–114; Seattle 35, 60, 86, 101, 102, 110–111, 115–117, 122, 146; Spokane 67–69; statehood 68, 86, 111, 123, 143, 145; Tacoma 19, 28, 84, 110, 111, 114; Walla Walla 21, 25, 52, 55, 84, 85, 116–117, 160, 170; Western Washington University 82–86
"Washington Territory West of the Cascades" 115
Washoe Indians 34, 49, 121
water 4, 12, 30, 37, 51, 59, 62, 63, 105, 123, 135, 137, 147, 151, 156–157, 163; alkaline 69; aqueduct 110; artesian well 160; city 63; conservation 130; contaminated 38, 114; pipes 70; pump 82; tank 102; water power 55, 98, 158; water wheel 106; wells 80–81, 86, 95
Watson, Elmo Scott 107
Weinhard, Henry 115
Wells, Emmeline Blanche Woodward **164–168**
Wells Fargo 34, 117, 121, 127
Welsh 109–111, 140
Wendt, Charles William 35
Whaley, Thomas 60
whaling 3, 8, 15, 24, 53, 141
wharf 12, 57, 58, 59, 85, 93, 105; dock labor 114; drydock 42
Wheeler, Francis A.B. 154
wheelwright 63, 103

Whilkut 94
White, Elijah 122
White, Martin 74
White Cloud 153
Whitman, Marcus 4, **33–36**
Whitman, Narcissa 4, **33–36**
Whitney, Sarah Ann 165
whittling 81
whooping cough 85, 141
Wichita Indians 29, 112, 124, 149, 154
Wiggins, William 98
Wilcox, George Norton 142
Wild West show 122, 160
Wilhardt, Louis 63
Wilkins, John E. 160
Wilkins, John R. **159–160**
Wilkins, Katherine Carolina "Kitty" 4, **159–160**
Wilkins, Laura Smith **159–160**
Wilkins Horse Company 160
Willamette Cattle Company 8
Willamette Valley 2, 8, 9, 52, 84, 98, 122
Williams, Baylis 136
Wilson, Alfred 163
Wilson, Hiram 46
Wilson, Susan Hines 163
Wilson, Woodrow 115–116
Winchester, Nancy Mariah 165
Winchester rifle 67, 104
windmills 82, 87, 102
wine 42, 46, 47, 70, 81
Winnebago 20, *56*, 91, 153, 169
Winnemucca, Rose 124
A Winter with the Mormons 2, *83*
wire, barbed 67, 107
Wisconsin 1, 2, 3, 16–18, 38, 61, 80, 86, 120, 128, 129, 152–154, 158
Wiyot 94
Woll, Adrián 30
Woman and Her Era 54
Wood, John 152
Woodward, Frank 128
wool 27
Wootton, Fannie C. 162
Wootton, Fidelis 163
Wootton, Maria Dolores LeFevre 162
Wootton, Maria Pauline Lujan 163
Wootton, Mary Ann Manning 162
Wootton, Richens Lacy, Jr. 162
Wootton, Richens Lacy, Sr. 5, **160–163**
Works, Miriam Angelina 166
World War I 49, 82, 101, 142, 160
World War II 45, 102, 138
writers 2, 5, 14, 35, 44, 82, 86, 107, 109, 113–116; *see also* diaries/journals; letters
Wu, Tien Fu **42–44**
Wuollet, Jakob 96
Wyatt, Americus 100
Wyndham-Quin, Windham Thomas 126

Wyoming 1, 2, 5, 10–12, 27, 30–31, 32, 56, 66, 69, 79, 84, 86, 87, 89–90, 98, 101, 114, 115, 117, 122, 142, 146, 147, 157, 161, 169, 171
Wysinger, Arthur Eugene 3, 164
Wysinger, Bertha V. 163–164
Wysinger, Edmond Edward **163–164**, 171
Wysinger, Jesse Edward 164
Wysinger, Marion Andrew 164
Wysinger, Martha Matilda 164
Wysinger, Pernesa C. Wilson **163–164**
Wysinger, Reuben Carl 164
Wysinger, Walter 164

Yakima 114–115
Yavapai 132
Yellow Bird 90
yellow fever 21
The Yellow Slave Traffic 44
Yellow Wolf, Chief 148
Yellowknife Indians 7
Yellowstone, Wyoming 56, 87, 161
Yellowstone National Park 21, 67, 87, 126, *128*–130
Yellowstone Trail 2, 128–130, 171
Yellowstone Trail Association *128*, 129
Yost, Nellie Snyder 146–147
Young, Brigham 51, *83*, **164–168**, 169
Young, Clarissa Ross 167
Young, Fanny 165
Young, Zina Diantha Hutchinson 3, **164–168**, 171
Young, Zina Presendia 167
Young-Man-Afraid-of-His-Horses, Chief 90
Yuma Indians 60
Yurok 94

www.ingramcontent.com/pod-product-compliance
Lightning Source LLC
Chambersburg PA
CBHW081550300426
44116CB00015B/2823